THE
ROYAL EXCHANGE
ASSURANCE

BARRY SUPPLE

Professor of Economic and Social History
University of Sussex

THE ROYAL
EXCHANGE
ASSURANCE

A HISTORY OF
BRITISH
INSURANCE
1720–1970

CAMBRIDGE
AT THE UNIVERSITY PRESS
1970

Published by the Syndics of the
Cambridge University Press
Bentley House, 200 Euston Road, London N.W.1
American Branch:
32 East 57th Street, New York, N.Y. 10022

Library of Congress Catalogue Card Number: 72–96101
Standard Book Number 0521 07239 5

Printed in Great Britain
by W & J Mackay & Co Ltd,
Chatham, Kent.

FOREWORD

Since the early eighteenth century the Royal Exchange Assurance has played a proud and honourable role in the development of British Insurance. The formidable task of writing its history in recognition of the two hundred and fiftieth anniversary of the granting of the Corporation's Charter has, in the event, turned out to be a most remarkable example of research into the Insurance Industry in general during that period.

Professor Supple was faced with a lamentable shortage of Archives covering rather more than the first century of the Corporation's history due to the devastating fire of 1838. From that date onwards two World Wars with their accompanying drives for the collection of waste paper, and subsequently the continuous shortage of storage space, both contributed to the paucity of evidence that in retrospect it would have been wise and useful to have collected and guarded for the historian. Sad though this was, it gave an added stimulus to Professor Supple to guide his researches into a wider field and to combine with the Corporation's history that of other contemporary companies and indeed the history of British Insurance generally.

Professor Supple is to be congratulated on producing not only a volume of the greatest interest for all those connected with the Royal Exchange Assurance but also an outstanding work for all students of and parties connected with the Insurance Industry of this country. In writing this Foreword, however, I wish in particular to emphasize that the history of the Royal Exchange Assurance is, in the last resort, the history of the efforts of its members and associates over long generations. This book was envisaged as a permanent record of their achievement. It is, I believe, a worthy one.

KINDERSLEY

CONTENTS

PLATES

FIGURES

TABLES

PREFACE

Among the many problems confronting the business historian one of the most serious is that of relating the development of the enterprise with which he is primarily concerned to the broader themes of industrial and economic history. To what extent can the history of one firm shed light on that of many? How can the particular instance be placed in a general context? In the case of the Royal Exchange Assurance this problem has been eased, if not entirely solved, by its very longevity. 'The history of this ancient Corporation', wrote one reviewer of a brief study of the REA in 1896, 'should be rich in facts elucidating the growth, course of business, and practice of insurance in all its branches in this country.'[1] Almost seventy-five years later, after two and a half centuries of corporate continuity, its historian can only echo these words.

Yet longevity itself, although significant, does not guarantee the representativeness of an institution. Indeed, its very age can be a mark of distinction—perhaps even a handicap—separating it in some important respects from less venerable organizations. Hence, properly to tackle the problem of providing a context for a business history, it is still necessary to go beyond the development of the single business enterprise. This is what this study attempts to do. While concentrating primarily on the history of the Royal Exchange Assurance, it also attempts to provide an analysis of the development of important aspects of British insurance as a whole—and to relate these, by contrast as well as comparison, to that of the Corporation. And in this respect considerable credit is due to the Court of Directors and Officials of the REA itself, for having encouraged the writing of a book which is almost as much a history of other parts of the insurance industry as it is of their own Corporation.

This task would have been easier, albeit much less satisfying, if British insurance had in the past attracted as much scholarly attention as other, and perhaps less important, economic activities. Yet, with the exception of two or three very specialized articles, of a handful of 'serious' histories of individual companies—notable among which is P. G. M. Dickson's impressive treatment of *The Sun Insurance Office, 1710–1960*—and of H. E. Raynes's detailed study, *A History of British Insurance*, there is hardly any systematic work by modern historians.[2]

---

[1] Review of [W. N. Whymper] *The Royal Exchange Assurance: An Historical Sketch* (1896), in *Post Magazine*, LVII, 9 (29 February 1896), 139.

[2] Professor George Clayton's book on *Insurance*, containing a large historical section, and to be published in the summer of 1970, will be a welcome addition to this list.

As a result, much of the industrial, as well as the REA, history in this study had to be derived from contemporary material, including a host of extraordinarily useful articles in trade and professional journals. Necessarily, however, it was not possible to deal with such a vast subject as 250 years of British insurance with any comprehensiveness. Instead, various aspects of that history were selected for special emphasis.

First, it was necessary to concentrate on British insurance *companies*, as distinct from Lloyd's. The latter has been such a special part of the insurance market, and the materials for its history have been of so different a sort, that it was not possible to encompass its history at all adequately with that of the corporate side of the industry. By the same token, the whole field of marine insurance, except in so far as it impinged on the activities of the Royal Exchange Assurance and could be studied through the few surviving records, had to be largely ignored. Second, in light of the significance of the period and the nature of the available material, the nineteenth century, and the first years of the twentieth, have been given a good deal of emphasis. This seemed justified not merely on the grounds of historiographical convenience, but because the decades before the First World War comprised a critical period in the modernization of British insurance; and one in which the pattern of development and structural change are of considerable interest to economic and business historians. Third, in view of the principal objective of the study—the history of the REA as an enterprise—and of my own lack of technical experience, it seemed best to concentrate far more on general business, economic and social issues than on the history of insurance in its technical aspects. As a result, there are bound to be disappointments for those whose primary interests are with the evolution of techniques and institutions. In this sense, and in so far as it is possible to distinguish between them, this history is far more one of the insurance business than of insurance practice.

My approach to the REA has, of course, been shaped by similar factors. In addition, however, as with any business history, there were two further considerations of some significance. The first was the distinctive chronological pattern of record survival. Thus, in 1838 most of the Corporation's then existing business records were destroyed by a disastrous fire which swept through the Royal Exchange—with the result that only fragmentary evidence survives for the Corporation's first century or so of existence. (The main exception is the period of its formation, when public records provide many important details.) And even after 1838 the growing shortage of storage space, the occasional ruthlessness of business spring-cleaning, and the necessities of war-time waste-paper drives, have, alas, wreaked their customary havoc among more modern archives. In spite of all this, however, the history of the Corporation can still be reasonably firmly based on material preserved by dint of its public position, the survival of the most important official series of records, and the devotion of a few of its amateur antiquarians over the last century or so. (Indeed, the activities of the last group have had the understandable yet paradoxical result of preserving more information about the nineteenth than about

some aspects of the twentieth century.) The second consideration which inevitably influenced the chronological balance of the study was the difficulty of
writing in great detail about the recent history of any enterprise. For, on the one
hand, there are various aspects of that history which it would be wrong to
expose to detailed considerations so soon after the event; and, on the other hand,
analytical history is bound to involve or imply judgements on men who are still
living. For these reasons, as well as more technical ones relating to the changing
nature of archives, this history of the REA, as with other business histories, can
only give a relatively superficial consideration to the events of the last generation;
and concentrates only on the highlights of twentieth-century development. Even
so, the co-operation, interest and confidence of the Court and management have
enabled me to deal more fully and frankly with the history of the Corporation
since 1918 than is frequently the case with business histories. Finally, on the
question of coverage, it is appropriate to emphasize here a fact which is obvious
in the main body of the book—namely, that this is far more a history of the
Royal Exchange Assurance than of its associated companies and subsidiaries.
This is partly because the effective forging of the REA Group only came in the
1960s. Before then the links were far more financial than business-based. More
generally, however, the REA itself provides an obvious continuing thread
through 250 years of development: its main subsidiaries were only acquired in
the twentieth century, and the Corporation itself, in its continuity and 'presence',
is a logical, dominating feature of the history of the recent, as well as the remoter,
past.

It is, indeed, this essential 'corporateness' which provides one of the main
themes of this study. The unity and continuity of the REA were the origins of
some of its most considerable strengths and some of its gravest weaknesses. And
their influences—on human beings as well as business endeavours—comprise an
important justification for devoting so much attention to the history of a single
firm. At the same time, however, that history cannot be divorced from the evolution and modernization of the industry as a whole. And the lines which connect
the story of a traditional firm adjusting to unceasing change, and the story of the
development of nation- and world-wide economic and social forces, form a
matrix which is at least some justification for undertaking this particular historical task. Whether the result justifies that effort, is not for me to discuss. But any
study of the conjuncture of enterprise and tradition cannot be without interest
to this country at this moment in its history.

ACKNOWLEDGEMENTS

In a book of this nature the acknowledgements to those whose help and advice have placed the author in their debt consist largely of a list of names. Although various obvious considerations prevent me from departing too far from this tradition, I should like to emphasize how much such a study necessarily owes to the efforts and advice, the wisdom and past labours, of a host of other people.

As far as my work has been concerned, what I subsequently refer to as the 'corporate presence' of the Royal Exchange Assurance has been faithfully and warmly reflected in the unstinting co-operation of its members. To all of them (many unknown to me by name) I must express my appreciation for the frankness and generosity with which they provided me with information, and the tolerance with which they met my gaucheries about the world of insurance and the REA. To the Governor, Lord Kindersley, to Mr H. R. Roberts, former General Manager, and to Mr M. A. Wilkinson, his successor and subsequently Managing Director, I owe a special debt of gratitude for their initiative, encouragement and advice, and for the absolute scrupulousness with which they allowed material to be made available for the writing of a completely independent history. No historian could have had a better or freer atmosphere in which to work. Older members of the REA will understand if I also make special mention of Mr C. D. Baker, former Secretary and a gentle and wise historian of the Corporation, who, alas, died before this study could be completed, but not before he could give me the considerable benefit of his wisdom and knowledge. To his successor, Mr R. M. Eggleston, I am indebted for his unfailing courtesy and help with the manifold problems of a business historian.

Over the past few years I have naturally worked most closely with a limited number of men who acted as guides to the archival and personal intricacies of an ancient Corporation. Without the help and real friendship of Mr D. E. Tyrrell, Comptroller, and Messrs A. E. Dunster, H. R. Jarman and H. R. Witting, of the Secretary's office, I should have been lost. Their genuine feeling for, as well as their extensive knowledge of, the REA contributed considerably to this book. I have also made frequent use of the technical knowledge and historical learning of Mr O. D. Cumming, formerly Actuary and now Assistant General Manager, and Mr A. R. Doublet, formerly Home Fire Manager and now pursuing his scholarly work in retirement. And Mr A. E. Phelps, formerly General Manager, was both kind and forthright in supplying me with a fund of information about the REA since the First World War. In addition to these, however, I have to thank the following past and present members of the REA Group for their work and help: F. P. Balding, R. Brawn, J. W. Burkitt, E. F. Clinton, E. Condé, E. G. Cunnington, P. G. Eastaugh, L. Elias, H. J. Finch, Miss I. Frazer, B. M. S. Gray, W. A. T. Harper, R. N. Hewitt, P. E. Hodge, S. F. Isaac, D. C. Kelly, A. C. King, B. S. Latham, D. W. Parsons, W. Penman, R. E. Phelps, J. W. Roberts, M. Stacey, R. A. Stallard, H. A. Walters, C. F. R. Ward, and the numerous Branch and Area Managers, at home and abroad, who responded to request (and rumour) by sending so much useful information to the Royal Exchange. Finally, among past and present members of the REA who have made a direct contribution to this history, it is right to single out one who was associated with the Corporation a century ago. For John A. Higham crowned his long career as an official of the REA—as clerk (1835–48), Actuary (1848–60), Secretary (1853–61), Cashier (1868–72) and Accountant (1868–90)— by compiling the 'Domesday Book' which contains the Corporation's indispensable financial statistics since its foundation. Without his painstaking care and extraordinary accuracy, my task would have been almost impossible.

In the course of my work I have been fortunate enough to have the help of various research assistants. And although the problems of historical research have meant that my demand for their services has been intermittent, their contribution to the finished product has been enormous. I am therefore especially grateful for the help provided by Miss Ann Greenwood, Mrs Jane Hamilton-Eddy, Mr R. W. Owen, Mr C. Scott and Miss Jane Williams; and should like to add a special word of thanks to Mr G. S. Moore, a former member of the REA staff, whose hopes of a peaceful retirement were shattered by prolonged, but cheerful and effective, service as a research assistant. In addition I must indicate, however imperfectly, my debt to my secretary, Mrs Valerie Hutchinson, whose loyalty and perseverance were only matched by her skill and tolerance.

In measure as this study extends beyond the insular history of the REA, so I am also indebted to those who work in other libraries and archives—to the librarians of the Chartered Insurance Institute and its Secretary, Mr H. A. L. Cockerell; to the staff of the Guildhall Library and its enthusiastic Librarian, Dr A. E. J. Hollaender; to representatives of the British Insurance Association; and to the staffs of the Bank of England's Record Office and the India Office Library. All gave freely of their time and considerable knowledge.

As once before, I also have to thank Professor Asa Briggs for reading the final draft and giving more heart to its author as well as better shape to its matter. It is hardly possible to envisage a wiser, or more pungent, critic. Finally, albeit in ways less directly academic, my fortitude as well as my well-being through a long period of combining research with other duties were sustained by the understanding and co-operation of my wife and children.

BARRY SUPPLE

Lewes, Sussex
April 1969

NOTE

DATES, SPELLING, REFERENCES

Until 1752 the year normally began on 25 March. In this study, however, all dates are given as if the calendar year had begun on 1 January. On the other hand, following contemporary practice, until 1752, the actual references to days and months are based on the Julian calendar which, in England between 1700 and 1752, was eleven days behind the Gregorian calendar. Until 1890, the accounting year used by the Royal Exchange Assurance ended on 30 April. Statistical data referring to the Corporation in the text and footnotes follows this convention: a citation of any year up to 1890 is to be understood as referring to the twelve-month period ending on 30 April of the year cited.

Spelling and punctuation have been modernized throughout. The full titles of books or articles can be found in the *Note on Sources* at the end of the book. The full names of insurance companies are given in the Index.

Footnote references are given to material in archives and libraries outside the Royal Exchange itself. Where facts or quotations have been derived from the archives of the Royal Exchange Assurance, it did not seem worthwhile to reproduce the exact reference in the published work. However, copies of the book, containing fuller references to REA material, have been deposited with the Secretary of the Corporation and in the Libraries of the Universities of Sussex and Cambridge.

ABBREVIATIONS

AM	*Assurance Magazine*
BM	British Museum
Guildhall MSS	Manuscripts in Guildhall Library
HCJ	*House of Commons Journal*
JCII	*Journal of the Chartered Insurance Institute*
JFII	*Journal of the Federation of Insurance Institutes*
JIA	*Journal of the Institute of Actuaries*
JSS	*Journal of the Statistical Society*
PM	*Post Magazine and Insurance Monitor*
PP	*Parliamentary Papers*
PRO	Public Record Office
REAM	*Royal Exchange Assurance Magazine*
SCAA	*Report from the Select Committee on Assurance Associations. Together with the Proceedings of the Committee, Minutes of Evidence, Appendix, and Index. Parliamentary Papers, 1852–53,* XXI
Special Report (1720)	*Special Report from the Committee appointed to inquire into and examine the several subscriptions for fisheries, insurances, annuities for lives, and all other projects carried on by subscription, in and about the Cities of London and Westminster, and to inquire into all undertakings for purchasing joint-stocks, or obsolete charters (1720).* British Museum, 357. b. 3/30.

PART A

Pre-industrial Development: insurance in the eighteenth century

Between the middle of the seventeenth and the middle of the eighteenth centuries the British economy was brought to a level of development which would have been significant even if it had not become the basis for modern industrialization. The evidence for its transformation is to be found at a multitude of points: in the improvement of agricultural techniques and the development of industry; in the modernization of the capital market; in the growth of Empire and the emergence of an international trading network of which Britain was the centre; in the new impetus for innovation; and in the increased sophistication and specialization of business activity, whether in the production and trading of commodities or the provision of commercial and financial services such as banking, insurance, stockbroking, and the like.[1] Given the character of these developments, it was logical (indeed, it was necessary) that the period should also be a watershed in the evolution of British commercial and financial *institutions*—in the ways in which men managed their economic lives. Markets for goods and services became more complex, economic functions more specialized, and the formal organization of economic activity a more marked feature of commercial life.

One of the most striking examples of this institutional change in the period was the increasing importance of joint-stock companies. The beginnings of British joint-stock enterprise had, of course, come in the sixteenth and early seventeenth centuries, when it was associated, in the main, with the beginning of trade with, and colonization of, non-European areas. After 1660, however, there was a marked increase in the number of companies formed—particularly in the 1680s and 1690s.[2] But even more

[1] See Charles Wilson, *England's Apprenticeship, 1603–1763* (1965); P. G. M. Dickson, *The Financial Revolution in England: A Study in the Development of Credit, 1688–1756* (1967).

[2] See W. R. Scott, *The Constitution and Finance of English, Scottish and Irish Joint-Stock Companies to 1720* (1911), III, 461–81; K. G. Davies, 'Joint-Stock Investment in the Later Seventeenth Century', *Economic History Review*, 2nd series, IV (1952).

important than the growing number of companies—most of them, like the Hudson's Bay Company (1670), the Royal African Company (1672), or the Mine-Adventurers of England (1698), established in conventional ways for conventional purposes—was the fact that some few of the new enterprises after 1690 were floated with an unprecedentedly large capital stock, and as the result of extending considerable financial aid to the Government. There were three dominating examples of these new 'monied companies' before 1720: the Bank of England, established in 1694 with a capital of £1·2 million, a commitment to lend that amount to the State, and exclusive banking privileges; the new East India Company formed in 1698 with exclusive privileges in the Indian trade, in return for a loan of £1,662,000 (it was amalgamated with the old company in 1709); and the South Sea Company, floated in 1711, also with monopoly trading rights, and a huge capital of over £9 million, which was used to fund the Government's floating debt. In later years old-line Tory critics of post-1689 finance and politics saw this development as a potentially sinister influence stemming from large-scale borrowing and the growth of the National Debt: 'Thus the method of funding and the trade of stock-jobbing began. Thus were great companies created, the pretended servants, but in many respects the real masters of every administration.'[1]

This was a distorted view of the emergence and rôle of large-scale corporations—partly because it exaggerated their relative ownership of the national debt, and partly because it ignored the fact that in nearly every instance they had real, and important, economic functions to fulfil. Nevertheless, the judgement, stripped of its political overtones, had grasped an important truth: the economic needs of private enterprise and the financial needs of government *had* produced a set of newly powerful institutions. At one extreme, large-scale corporate organizations could not be dissociated from the new and interlocking patterns of finance and commerce which helped shape, even if they did not yet dominate, the economic life of the country. And the Stock Exchange, rooted in the necessities of corporate and public finance, now served as a link (not always a welcome one) between the vicissitudes of the capital market and the course of business in general.

In was in this context of economic growth and financial experiment that the Royal Exchange Assurance, the pioneer marine insurance company, was established by a Royal Charter of 22 June 1720. Together with its sister Corporation, the London Assurance, it was a major innovation designed to meet an important economic need, for, in the words of the

[1] Bolingbroke, quoted in Dickson, *Financial Revolution*, p. 18.

Crown's Law Officers, 'the insuring of ships is of absolute necessity for the carrying on of foreign trade'.[1] Yet it was also a joint-stock 'monied' enterprise whose promotion had been related to the opportunities of speculation implied in the development of the Stock Exchange, and whose privileges rested on the promise of a payment of £300,000 into the Exchequer. Naturally, both Corporations immediately took their places among the other monied companies which loomed so large in the small but robust world of London business.

It is, however, important to remember that the formal establishment of the Royal Exchange Assurance was merely the culminating step in a complicated history of commercial innovation and company promotion. The men most closely concerned with its finance and management had begun their efforts to promote a marine insurance company three years earlier, in the summer of 1717; and they had actually been doing an active and successful marine insurance business since March 1719, with the help of corporate Charters originally issued for quite different purposes. More than this, the chartering of the Royal Exchange Assurance came at the height of, and was crucially related to, the joint-stock boom associated with the name of the South Sea Company. Its promotion had been an important element in the creation of a speculative mood, and the very Act of Parliament which had authorized the issue of the REA Charter in 1720, by declaring illegal all unauthorized companies or corporate procedures, was also to be instrumental in deflating the boom on which the Corporation had been floated into existence.

Clearly, therefore, there are various important strands in the early history of the Royal Exchange Assurance: its creation marks an important stage not only in the development of insurance but in that of the business corporation and of the capital market in Britain. More than this, once it had been firmly established, the new Corporation continued to play an important rôle in the business world of the eighteenth century, and in the modernization of British insurance which coincided with the beginnings of industrialization in this country. The first two chapters consider the origins of the Corporation, and its connection with broader developments in finance and insurance. The next two are concerned with the growth of insurance in the eighteenth century both in general terms and as it was reflected in the structure and activity of the Royal Exchange Assurance.

---

[1] Report on Petition for Incorporation, 12 March 1718, in *Special Report from the Committee appointed to inquire into and examine the several subscriptions for fisheries, insurances, annuities for lives, and all other projects carried on by subscription, in and about the Cities of London and Westminster, and to inquire into all undertakings for purchasing joint-stocks, or obsolete charters* (1720; BM, 357. b.3/30), p. 28.

1

The Origins of a Corporation: insurance and company promotion in the early eighteenth century

INSURANCE AT THE TURN OF THE CENTURY

Marine insurance, which was to be the immediate objective of the Royal Exchange Assurance in 1720, was also the oldest and best-developed branch of insurance—with its remote origins in the maritime loans of classical and early medieval times, and its formal beginnings in the Mediterranean trade of the fourteenth century. While it is almost certain that the Italian merchants who figured so prominently in the medieval trade of northern Europe must have used insurance for their English transactions, the earliest documentary evidence for its practice in England is in the sixteenth century. By the late seventeenth century, therefore, England, although a relative latecomer to the field of sophisticated commercial techniques, nevertheless had a tradition of marine insurance extending back well over a century.[1]

Although a detailed proposal for a marine insurance company was made in 1662, nothing came of the promoters' request for a Charter, and the London marine insurance market, buoyed up by the contemporary expansion in trade (imports and exports rose by about 75 per cent in the last forty years of the century), continued to be managed by individual underwriters and the class of brokers, or 'office keepers', who brought merchant and underwriter together. On the other hand, it is doubtful if there were many specialized, full-time underwriters in the late seventeenth century. Rather, underwriting was carried on in conjunction with other business activities. Even so the underwriting of marine risks called for

---

[1] For the history of marine, and other branches of insurance, see Harold E. Raynes, *A History of British Insurance* (London, 1964); Charles Wright and C. Ernest Fayle, *A History of Lloyd's* (1928).

substantial as well as risky commitments; and when, in 1693, the ships in the Smyrna Fleet were destroyed or captured by the French, 'an incredible number of the best merchants in the kingdom sunk under the load' of insurance losses,[1] and persuaded the Commons to pass a Bill to protect them against their creditors, although the Lords subsequently rejected the measure. The insurance market was, however, sufficiently strong and resilient to absorb even this catastrophe.

By contrast with marine underwriting, fire insurance developed relatively late—in part, perhaps, because it was not then practicable to undertake it on an individual and *ad hoc* basis.[2] Some form of corporate body was needed to provide continuity, a fund and a permanent staff and organization. In England, schemes were proposed in the 1630s, and again at the Restoration, but the first fire insurance office was not established until 1680—fourteen years after the catastrophic Fire of London, an event which, even while it must have made householders and merchants more keenly aware of the advantages of insurance, must also have brought home its problems to potential investors.

Even so, the rebuilding of London on a safer basis after 1666 and the renewal of economic expansion turned men's minds to this novel but obvious form of enterprise. The first company, promoted by Nicholas Barbon, was called the Fire Office; formed in 1680, and confining itself to the insurance of houses in London, it began business in 1681 with a fund vested in trustees as security for the payment of losses. The Fire Office (it was subsequently known as the Phenix) continued in existence into the early eighteenth century—unlike the contemporary and short-lived scheme for a municipal insurance office which the Common Council of the City of London, after deliberations throughout the 1670s, had sponsored in 1681. This only lasted for about a year before the Corporation ceased business in November 1682. A third office, the Friendly Society for Securing Houses from any Considerable Loss by Fire, which survived for about a century, was formed in 1684 on the assessment basis: policyholders paid annual premiums and committed themselves to pay contributions towards losses with upper limits determined by the amount of their insurance; and the undertakers received the annual charge in return for a guarantee of all losses and for meeting the costs of administration. The business of the Friendly Society, like that of the Fire Office, was also restricted to London

---

[1] Daniel Defoe, quoted in Raynes, *British Insurance*, p. 94.

[2] Raynes, *British Insurance*, p. 73. For the origin of fire insurance also see P. G. M. Dickson, *The Sun Insurance Office, 1710–1960* (1960), chapter 1; Cornelius Walford, *The Insurance Cyclopaedia* (1874), III, 438 ff.

houses. In 1696 the fourth and most successful of the pioneer group of offices was formed. Called the Amicable Contributors for Insuring from Loss by Fire, but soon known as the Hand-in-Hand because of its distinctive fire mark, it was a purely mutual association, and its quick success was attributed to the fact that it was 'chiefly carried on and supported by workmen and those concerned in building'.[1] It, too, was only concerned with buildings in the London area.

By the 1690s, therefore, English fire insurance had been reasonably firmly if somewhat narrowly established, even though the three offices which existed in 1700 only did business in London and confined themselves to insuring buildings, as distinct from goods. In 1708–9, however, the Charitable Corporation for the Relief of the Industrious Poor, the main object of which was money-lending, began to insure household goods and stock-in-trade against fire. More significantly, in 1708, Charles Povey, who dabbled in bizarre religious ideas as well as a wide variety of economic projects, established the Exchange House Fire Office, which became the Company of London Insurers in 1709. Since Povey's fire mark was an emblem of the sun, the business came to be known as the Sun Fire Office; and in 1710, when Povey sold out to what was essentially a new company, the Sun began its formal existence. Unlike its predecessors, the Sun insured both houses and goods, and in August 1710 extended its field of activity to Great Britain as a whole—even though, in practice, its business remained both small and confined to London until the 1720s.

Life insurance in its modern form did not appear until the late eighteenth century.[2] Only then were whole-life policies issued at premiums graded by age and based on mortality tables and the assumption that funds would grow by the investment of premiums at compound rates of interest. For at least two hundred years, however, short-term life insurance had been a recognized, if infrequent, practice. In sixteenth- and seventeenth-century England, for example, policies were issued by *ad hoc* groups of underwriters on the same basis, and using similar terminology, as marine insurance. Indeed, once marine insurance was perfected it was logical to extend its principle to other sorts of insurable interest: for example, as in early life insurance, to provide security for a life interest or a loan, or even (as Pepys tells us) to insure against the eventuality of war breaking out within a specified period in 1664.[3] In addition to these developments, by

---

[1] E. Hatton, *A New View of London* (1708), quoted in Raynes, *British Insurance*, p. 84. The Hand-in-Hand remained independent until 1905, when it was acquired by the Commercial Union.

[2] See below, pp. 54–6.

[3] Raynes, *British Insurance*, p. 59.

the late seventeenth and early eighteenth centuries various group schemes were proposed for the payment of annuities to survivors in the case of death. In 1698 the Mercers' Company established a fund guaranteeing annuities of £30 to widows whose husbands had subscribed £100; in 1699 there was a private scheme, the Society of Assurance for Widows and Orphans, by which members (limited to 2,000 under the age of 45) each paid 5s. to any deceased member's nominee; and in 1707 a mutual scheme was established by the 'Workmen of the University Printing House, Oxford'. A more substantial and long-lasting foundation was the Amicable Society for a Perpetual Assurance Office, which received a charter in 1706, and which had a long and venerable history until it was ultimately taken over by the Norwich Union in 1866. The Amicable, also a mutual office, limited its members to 2,000 between the ages of 12 and 45, each of whom paid an entrance fee and a net annual premium of £5. Varying amounts of money (increasing over time) were to be divided among those dying in any one year, although a minimum benefit of £125 was guaranteed in 1757, and raised to £150 in 1770.

The Amicable and the Sun, to take two leading examples, were eminently respectable enterprises. But by about 1710 insurance began to show signs of an unstable adolescence, by responding in a volatile way to changes in the commercial and financial atmosphere.[1] The relative prosperity of the years 1708–10, which was associated with increases in the capitalization and dividends of leading trading companies and the Bank of England, also induced something of an insurance boom—albeit one with strong gambling overtones. In addition to such legitimate ventures as the formal establishment of the Sun Fire Office (1710) and the creation of the short-lived Company of Insurers upon Lives (1709), there was a rash of promotions in 1710 which joined the idea of insurance to the popular habit of wagering on matters of chance. Some of these 'insurance societies' purported to insure against death; but the great majority provided for the payment of a sum on marriage; and a few insured against the contingency of having children or the need to raise capital on the termination of an apprenticeship or a fixed period of domestic service. The element of chance entered because the societies, each associated with a coffee house or inn, were organized on the tontine principle: all premiums, less management costs, were periodically divided among claimants, and the 'benefits' therefore varied according to the number of claimants at a given date. The lack of control, the odd choice of contingencies, and the fact that it was possible to insure a nominee (e.g. insure a third party against marriage),

[1] Scott, *Joint-Stock Companies*, I, 382–5; III, 391–4.

formed very shaky foundations for growth; and, in any case, the boom was sharply curtailed early in 1711 when an Act of Parliament (9 Anne, c. 6, sec. 57) made it illegal 'to erect and set up offices or places for making insurance on marriages, births, christenings or service'.

The mixture of insurance and speculation which was responsible for the brief flurry of promotions in 1710 had only very ephemeral consequences. The speculative offices all disappeared, while those companies (e.g. the Fire Office, the Friendly Society, the Hand-in-Hand, the Amicable and the Sun) with older and deeper roots, survived. In addition, the main trend of development continued: in 1714 a group connected with the original Hand-in-Hand established the Union Fire Office, on a mutual basis, to insure goods and merchandise in London; in 1717 another mutual company, the Westminster Fire Office, was established by a group (among whom members of the building trade were well represented) who seceded from the Hand-in-Hand, which had moved its office to the City. In 1719 the Bristol Crown Office, a partnership, became the first provincial fire insurance enterprise; and in 1720 the Friendly Society was established in Edinburgh on a mutual basis.

As a result of these developments, by the second decade of the eighteenth century marine, fire and life insurance formed an acknowledged part of the London business scene. Although marine underwriting, which was by far the most sophisticated and widely used, continued to be based upon individual enterprise, fire insurance was provided by corporate forms of organization and life insurance was effected partly by societies and partly by individual underwriters. Each had exemplified one of the most important structural consequences of economic growth: a tendency towards differentiation of function. Marine underwriting, which was eminently adapted to individual and part-time activity, and which was intimately linked with the main operation of overseas trade, was only partly dependent on full-time specialists, in that professional brokers were increasingly needed to sustain the complex and sophisticated market for underwriting services which had been developed. However, it is likely that even in the case of marine insurance there was a trend towards more specialized underwriting. Corporate fire and life insurance, on the other hand, demanded continuity and specialization; for they were aspects of a growing economy in which effectiveness was functionally related to a growing complexity of structure and division of labour.

Important as these developments were as an indication of qualitative change in the economy in the period up to 1720, their actual extent should not be exaggerated. Although no quantitative information is available, it is very unlikely that there were more than three or four thousand life policy-holders. By 1719 fire insurance was somewhat more extensive (the Hand-in-Hand was reputed to have 13,000 members in 1708, and the Phenix 10,000 in 1710),[1] although, with the exception of the small Bristol partnership, it was confined to London property; and of the six London offices four insured buildings only, one covered only goods, and the still tiny Sun insured buildings and goods. As a measure of the narrowness of its base it is also relevant to emphasize that three of the fire offices were closely linked: the Union was a friendly offshoot of the Hand-in-Hand, insuring goods in harmony with the latter's insurance of buildings; and the Westminster, formed by a secession from the City-based Hand-in-Hand, provided a parallel service for Westminster. As yet, therefore, only marine insurance, in which the sums, according to one broker, 'amounted to several millions yearly', and for which there were almost 200 regular underwriters,[2] had a large and crucial economic rôle.

In one sense the British economy had already developed sufficiently far to warrant and facilitate a reasonably extensive fire and life insurance industry. Yet the obstacles to such a change, in terms of conventional social habits and lack of institutional and economic specialization, were still strong enough to restrain any decisive growth. It is significant, as the historian of British insurance has pointed out, that only one of the first six London fire offices (the Phenix) gave 'an absolute guarantee in exchange for a fixed premium, and this office proved the most ephemeral'. The rest obliged policyholders to contribute to losses within fixed limits and bound them together by obliging them to take long-term (usually seven-year) policies.[3] This mutual element was also strongly marked in contemporary life schemes. It was only in the 1720s, after the incorporation of the Royal Exchange and London Assurances (each a formal and fully proprietary company and each prepared to insure all sorts of property throughout the country), and the expansion and reorganization of the Sun, that the first stage in the development of modern insurance was completed and the groundwork laid for its ultimate success. Ironically, however, this development was based not merely on the undoubted business prospects for solid

---

[1] Francis Boyer Relton, *An Account of the Fire Insurance Companies, Associations, Institutions, Projects and Schemes Established and Projected in Great Britain and Ireland During the 17th and 18th Centuries, including the Sun Fire Office ; also of Charles Povey, the Projector of that Office, his Writings and Schemes* (1893), pp. 48, 75. The Westminster Fire Office issued almost 3,000 policies in just over four years ending December 1721 (E. A. Davies, *An Account of the Formation and Early Years of the Westminster Fire Office* [1952], p. 56).

[2] *Special Report* (1720), p. 45.

[3] Raynes, *British Insurance*, p. 91.

growth but on an unprecedented fever for speculation and financial manipulation.

THE PROMOTION OF A COMPANY, 1717–1719

The development of insurance enterprise in the late seventeenth and very early eighteenth centuries was characterized by the emergence of new specialized institutions to satisfy, and even help create, new needs. In this sense it was matched by the appearance of specialists and of more sophisticated procedures in the London money and capital markets. Since this was associated with the spread of the habit of impersonal, joint-stock investment and the evolution of more efficient financial institutions, it obviously facilitated the formation of large-scale insurance companies, which might otherwise have found it very difficult to raise a considerable capital stock. Yet the process also worked in reverse. For the flotation of insurance companies was itself an element in, and a potent influence on, the rise of the Stock Exchange and the transformation of financial institutions. Much of this interchange of influence was concentrated in the two years culminating in the South Sea boom of 1720. We have already seen how the financial buoyancy at the end of the first decade of the eighteenth century had been associated with the formation of various ephemeral insurance offices (as well as the more enduring Sun Fire Office). Now, at the end of the second decade, a similar combination of speculative optimism, available capital and a market for insurance produced an even more substantial development. But, as the promoters of the Royal Exchange Assurance were to find in three years of striving after incorporation, raising large amounts of money for the purpose was the easiest of their tasks. The real difficulty lay in persuading the Government to grant them the necessary Charter of incorporation.

The origins of the Royal Exchange Assurance can be traced to 1717, when a subscription 'for raising the sum of one million sterling, as a fund for insuring ships and merchandize at sea' was opened at Mercers Hall on 12 August.[1] The subscribers—there were 286—included the solicitor and company promoter, Case Billingsley, who was to be instrumental in this and later stages of the history of the embryonic Royal Exchange Assurance. More significantly, they also included the three men who were to become the first Governor, Sub-Governor and Deputy-Governor of the Corporation in 1720 (Lord Onslow, Sir John Williams and Sir Randolph Knipe),

---

[1] *Mercers Hall: A List of the Names of Subscribers for Raising the Sum of one Million Sterling, as a Fund for Insuring Ships and Merchandize at Sea; Which subscription was begun the 12th of August 1717 and completed the 16th January 1717/18* (BM, 8225 a. 38). This copy has the phrase 'Royal Exchange Assurance' written across the top of the title-page in a contemporary hand.

and seventeen of its first twenty-four directors. Contrary to later assumptions, this seems to have been the only group concerned in the project which was ultimately to develop into the Royal Exchange Assurance.[1]

The projected size and purpose of the 1717 enterprise meant, almost inescapably, that it could only be carried on by a chartered joint-stock company. For although it was possible to behave in almost every respect like a company, by the various subscribers signing a Deed of Co-Partnership[2] (as in the case of the Sun Fire Office), this had not been done for an enterprise as large, or with as many 'partners', as the proposed marine insurance company. This being so, the most critical need was to ensure that the Crown would grant the requisite Charter to an enterprise, the very size of which would excite a good deal of opposition. And it was no doubt for this reason that so much of the original initiative for the promotion seems to have come from a lawyer, Case Billingsley, who was well versed in such matters. According to his own evidence, Billingsley, together with his partner, James Bradly, held preliminary discussions with the Solicitor-General, Sir William Thompson, even before the subscription was officially opened; took the lead in enticing private underwriters to subscribe; and not only consulted the Solicitor-General again, about the form and content of a petition and a draft Charter, but went so far as to rehearse with him the various arguments in favour of the project before the official hearings.[3] But if all this shows, as it presumably does, that Billingsley was a man of keen, if somewhat cynical, enterprise in relation to some aspects of the project for a new company, the fact is that the main subscribers to the scheme were themselves merchants and financiers of substance and influence, who must have been largely responsible for initiating (as they were ultimately responsible for managing) the innovation of a joint-stock company for marine insurance.

Lord Onslow, who was to become first Governor of the Corporation, was, perhaps, more of a figurehead than an entrepreneur. As with other companies of the time, social rank and political influence could be attained by a connection with a member of the House of Lords (or even the Crown: George I was for a time Governor of the South Sea Company). But it is

[1] Scott (*Joint-Stock Companies*, III, 396) argues that there were two rival groups in 1717— but this is apparently based on a misreading of '14th March 1717' (*Special Report* [1720], p. 44) which leads to the erroneous conclusion that Sir Justus Beck and others were taking subscriptions in March 1717, whereas the source obviously refers to March 1718, N.S., when there was a new subscription for the existing subscribers. (Below, p. 17.)

[2] Below, pp. 59–60.

[3] *Special Report* (1720), p. 32. The main source of information for the Mercers Hall subscription and other developments up to spring 1720 are this *Report*, the *List of Names* referred to above, and *HCJ*, XIX, 287–8, 305–10, 341–51.

symptomatic that, when the REA was finally established, Lord Onslow hardly ever attended Court meetings, and never represented the promoters in the numerous official hearings which proved necessary.

Rather, the lead was taken by men like Sir John Williams, first Sub-Governor, who was a City Alderman and an Assistant (i.e. Director) of the Levant Company; Sir Randolph Knipe, first Deputy-Governor, who was also an Alderman and Assistant of the Levant Company, a Director of the Bank of England (1712–28) and a spokesman for merchants trading to Scandinavia; Sir Justus Beck, the formidable financier, Director of the Bank and East India trader, who was bankrupted by the Stock Exchange crash late in 1720, but apparently stayed on as an REA Director until 1723; and William Dunster, an Assistant- and then Deputy-Governor of the Levant Company (1722–45), who was to be on the Royal Exchange Court for thirty-six years. Even in this short list, of course, the leading rôle of members of the Levant Company stands out. Many lesser subscribers were also Levant traders, while at least eight of the first twenty-seven members of the Court belonged to the Levant Company—including the four men (William Dunster, Richard Lockwood, John Phillips and Henry March) who were to serve on the Court for over thirty years. Unfortunately, there is no indication of any specific reason for this concentration—although the importance of insurance for the long-distance Levant trade and the fact that the Company was just entering a period of depression and decline are two possible, albeit conflicting, explanations.

Whatever their particular business and financial interests, however, the attractions of the Mercers Hall scheme for these men seem, in retrospect, reasonably plain. The market for marine insurance was already very well developed, and merchants and shipowners were accustomed to thinking of it as a necessity—thus ensuring an abundant demand for inexpensive underwriting. On its part a company might hope to persuade insurers that its subscribed capit al and continuity provided a security and a convenience superior, in some respects, to private underwriters who often operated with inadequate capital and in unwieldy partnerships. Further, 1716 and 1717 were years of prosperity in the markets for goods and money.[1] Altogether, therefore, it was a relatively auspicious time to attract subscriptions for a new joint-stock company, even though it was, in prospect, a very large one: the nominal capital of £1 million would have been exceeded by only four other corporations (the Bank of England and the East India, Royal African and South Seas Companies). Yet, presumably because of its size and novelty, it took five months before the subscription

---

[1] Scott, *Joint-Stock Companies*, I, 392–3.

books could be closed. By January 1718, however, the promoters were ready for their next move. On 25 January 1718 they petitioned the King in Council for a Charter of incorporation, the signatories being headed by Beck, with Knipe and Williams coming near the top of the list (Billingsley's name came far down the list, although he also signed as attorney for ten other subscribers). This move naturally produced a reaction from other businessmen, suspicious of large concentrations of wealth, and from individuals who felt that their own established position in the marine insurance market would be threatened by a corporate enterprise. And on 2 February the projectors' petition, together with counter-petitions from London and Bristol merchants and underwriters, were referred to the Crown's Law Officers (Sir Edward Northey and Sir William Thompson) and to the Commissioners for Trade and Plantations, for their opinions.

Since the arguments used on both sides of the resulting controversy remained more or less unchanged until the Royal Exchange Assurance was finally established in 1720, it is worth summarizing them at the outset. On their part, the promoters asserted that a company was needed because it would provide a better, cheaper and more secure service, and because of the losses, inconvenience and failures which, they claimed, were associated with private underwriting: 'the merchants and trade of your Majesty's Dominions do frequently sustain very great losses for want of an incorporated company of insurers, with a joint-stock, to make good all such losses and damages of ships and merchandise at sea, as should be insured by them'. Such a company, it was said, would give greater security to (and would therefore greatly increase) trade, 'and preserve many of your good subjects and their families from that ruin to which they are now exposed, by being assurers in a private capacity'. In the hearings before the Attorney- and Solicitor-Generals, the promoters claimed that a corporation would offer lower rates; more convenient arrangements to the insured with respect to the arranging of policies and the settlement of claims ('for that the Corporation is one, against whom suit may be brought, whereas if twenty or thirty were to join in a partnership to insure, every one must be named in any suit to be brought against them'); and better security because of its capital fund, 'whereas as the present use is, many of the insurers continually fail and there is no deposit whatever to secure their insurances'. Finally, they presented affidavits purporting to show that in the existing circumstances, without a strong marine insurance company in London, it was safer and cheaper to insure in Amsterdam—and that many merchants did so.[1]

[1] *Special Report* (1720), pp. 17, 26–7.

On the other side, the merchants and private underwriters who were quick to oppose the scheme rested their case on three arguments. First, they asserted that existing arrangements were both adequate and efficient, so that 'at this time the premiums given in London, for insuring ships and goods, are much lower than in any other part of Europe, and therefore many orders for insuring in London are sent from foreign parts'. Second, they appealed to the fear of exploitation: 'the granting such Corporation will in consequence end in a monopoly; for . . . having so large a stock, they will in probability insure very low at the beginning to bring people to them, and thereby discourage the present method of insuring . . . and then the Company would put such terms on the insured as they should think fit'. Third, they cast grave doubts on the motives of the syndicate behind the new flotation: 'the subscription is made only for the sake of stock-jobbing; and if a Corporation should be erected, there will be another stock to transact . . . [very many] subscribers . . . being of different trades from the trade of merchandizing'.[1]

In retrospect it is clear that both groups had some right on their side and that, as was often the case in such disputations, both greatly exaggerated some arguments. On the one hand, the private insurance market in London was by no means so unstable, ineffective or unpopular with foreigners as the supporters of the scheme claimed: the balance of evidence suggests that it was already serving an international function. On the other hand, as later events were to show, there *was* room for the services of corporate underwriters, and their incorporation did not produce the disasters of monopoly and exploitation which the private underwriters originally purported to fear. Further, with respect to the charge of stock-jobbing, while the promoters were genuinely committed to setting up business as insurers they were obviously not averse to profiting by the process, and to employing, in Case Billingsley, a man who was far more concerned to float companies than to run them. Billingsley himself knew the value of stock appreciation. 'Those that have a mind to come in', he wrote on 10 March 1718, 'will find it ten times more to their advantage to buy, than to have the capital stock increased.'[2] Moreover, as later investigations were to show, the keenness to get a Charter, the lax *mores* of the age (in which it was usual for the Crown's Law Officers to accept private fees), and the delegation by the subscribers of a 'discretionary commission' to an 'operator' like Billingsley, brought the whole enterprise very near to open

---

[1] The first argument is quoted from the original petition from London merchants; the second and third from the Attorney-General's report: *Special Report* (1720), pp. 21, 26–7.
[2] *Special Report* (1720), p. 30.

bribery. ' The moment we have our Charter', wrote Billingsley to the
Attorney-General on 6 March 1718, 'our fee to you shall be one thousand
guineas, which we will never either directly or indirectly mention to any
soul living.' And four days later, as the Law Officers were completing their
Report, he wrote to him again: 'We have reserved room in the subscription for ten thousand pounds for you, which if you think fit may be subscribed by anyone that you can trust, which we doubt not will be a good
estate to you.'[1]

If the Attorney- and Solicitor-Generals were in practice only a fraction
as co-operative as Billingsley asserted, then the promoters must have been
very optimistic indeed as they awaited the response to their petition in
February and early March 1718. Nor were they put out when their
opponents claimed that the project was suspect because the first subscription was not legally binding on the signatories: after consulting the
Attorney-General as to the wording, a new and more enforceable subscription for £1 million was opened—and completed within fourteen days,
with an initial call of 5s. per cent ('to defray the charges in forming the
said intended Corporation, and obtaining and passing a Charter') to be
followed by a subsequent call to make 10 per cent if a Charter were
obtained.[2] But any optimism about easy success was soon very rudely
shattered. For, two days before the new subscription was completed, the
Law Officers had, in fact, signed a Report (12 March 1718) which was
decidedly cool towards the project, principally on the grounds that its
results were unpredictable and the existing situation satisfactory:

The want of a good method of insuring will be very fatal to trade; and we are
humbly of the opinion, that the making an experiment in a thing of this nature,
if it should prove amiss, would be of the utmost consequence to the trade of this
nation, and that it so highly concerns trade and commerce, that it will be proper
for the consideration of Parliament, and therefore we cannot advise the erecting
of a Corporation, for the insuring ships and goods at sea, against which there are
so many and great objections, especially the method now used being approved
of, both at home and abroad.

Unfortunately, the available records do not make it clear exactly what
happened next. The Law Officers' Report, although it would have to be
taken seriously, was only a recommendation to the King in Council, not

[1] *Special Report* (1720), pp. 28–31. Identical letters were sent to the Solicitor-General. In
1720 Bradly and the main subscribers denied any knowledge of these offers. And in March 1720
Sir John Williams claimed that his associates, having only just discovered the existence of these
letters, wanted to dismiss Billingsley (*Special Report* [1720], p. 11).

[2] *Special Report* (1720), p. 33; *HCJ*, XIX, 344. The latter source gives the date of this subscription as 'on or about the 14th March 1717' (i.e. 1718).

a decision. And some time later in 1718 it seems that the Commissioners for Trade and Plantations produced a Report which, according to the promoters, merely set out the arguments on both sides.[1] There is, however, no record of an official Privy Council response to the original petition, and in March 1720 the Reports from the Law Officers and the Trade Commissioners were said to be 'still depending' before the King.[2] However, from indirect evidence it does seem that at some time in the spring or summer of 1718 it was made clear to the promoters that their initial petition would not secure a Charter—but with the suggestion that they try an 'experiment' in corporate insurance. As a proponent of the scheme later claimed, 'the gentlemen who were then petitioners were told, that they ought to experience the usefulness of the same, and that they would be well entitled to His Majesty's favour when they could make it appear they had so done'.[3]

Yet whatever the official encouragement given to the petitioners it is unlikely that the Government envisaged their ingenious next step. Denied a new Charter, but obviously determined that the time was propitious and profitable for an experiment in corporate marine insurance, the promoters decided on a bold course of action: in the summer of 1718 they bought up the shares of the Mines Royal and Mineral and Battery Works, thus acquiring control of two Charters which, it was felt, could be used to carry on almost *any* corporate business—including the insurance of ships and goods at sea. These two Corporations were Elizabethan in origin, having been originally chartered to mine and manufacture various metals. They were, however, at a low ebb of activity in the early eighteenth century, and had formally united into one enterprise in 1710. After carefully taking legal advice, the insurance projectors acquired the 124 shares of the joint company at a price of £23. 8s. 6d. each; increased the capital of the newly acquired companies by organizing another subscription, for £1,152,000 (10 per cent to be called), dated 27 August 1718; installed Lord Onslow and Sir John Williams as Governors, and Case Billingsley as Secretary; and laid plans to begin insuring under the grandiose title of 'the Governors, Assistants, and Societies of the City of London, of and for the Mines Royal, the Mineral and Battery Works, and for assuring ships and merchandize'.[4]

[1] *Reasons humbly offered by the Societies of the Mines Royal &c. who insure ships and merchandize, with the security of a deposited joint-stock* (n.d. [1720]; BM, 357 b. 3/86), p. 2.

[2] *Special Report* (1720), p. 40.

[3] T.S., *A Letter to a Member of Parliament by a Merchant* (n.d. [1720]; BM, 356, b. 3/62), p. 1. For Sir John Williams's claim that they were 'advised to make this experiment', see *HCJ*, XIX, 344.

[4] *HCJ*, XIX, 344; *Special Report* (1720), pp. 34, 40.

There was some precedent for the use of a Charter to attain business objectives not envisaged when it was originally granted;[1] and once the success of the new venture with the Mines Royal had been shown, the device was used by other groups in 1719–20 to promote insurance enterprise when the speculation associated with the South Sea bubble produced a frenzied search for incorporation. Since the most important example of this—the acquisition in 1719 of the York Buildings Company (a water-supply enterprise) in order to undertake an extensive land development and annuity and life insurance business[2]—was engineered by Case Billingsley, it is likely that he was also the master-mind behind the successful bid to take over the Mines Royal. Admittedly, the marine insurance syndicate itself moved with a good deal of caution, and there is some evidence that it not merely 'consulted . . . several eminent Counsel, that they might insure ships by virtue of the Charters for the Mines Royal, the Mineral and Battery Works', but also secured the general approval of the King 'before they entered on the business of insurance'.[3] In any event, although the new subscription list to the Mines Royal was apparently completed in August 1718, it was another seven months before the syndicate (one should now, more accurately, say the Company) began business. Then, however, on 9 March 1719, after appropriate public advertisement, the Mines Royal began to insure ships and merchandise —'the first that proposed and undertook this method of assurance in England'.[4] The offices of the new enterprise were in the Royal Exchange: a location which was made extremely advantageous by the existing concentration of so much of London's commercial and financial business, and by the fact that Billingsley's own office was there. It began an association between the Royal Exchange Corporation and building which has lasted 250 years.

[1] The Sword Blade Manufacturing Company (1691) became a land company about 1702 and a bank ten years later (Scott, *Joint-Stock Companies*, III, 435–41). It was to play a notorious rôle with the South Sea Company in 1720.

[2] Scott, *Joint-Stock Companies*, III, 420–31; below, pp. 24–5.

[3] *HCJ*, XIX, 344; *Reasons Humbly Offered by the Societies of the Mines Royal &c* (n.d. [1720], BM, 357 b. 3/86), p. 2. The latter source claims that before beginning business the syndicate, 'to avoid doing anything unacceptable to the Crown . . . did . . . petition His Majesty for His Royal favour and protection . . . and were very graciously received'.

[4] *Special Report* (1720), pp. 40, 45, 62. Advertisement in *Daily Courant*, 3 March 1719. The advertisement first announced that the Mines Royal, Mineral and Battery Works were ready to receive proposals for leasing mines and establishing battery works, and also requested the payment of arrears of rent. Next, it announced that 'having received the first payment from the subscribers towards the joint stock for assuring ships and merchandize', the Company would commence marine insurance from 9 March. Details of the provisions for arbitration or speedy legal resolution of disputes about claims were given—presumably to emphasize the advantages of insuring with a company rather than with individual underwriters.

The promoters had adopted a drastic solution to the legal problems posed by their inability to secure official approval for incorporation. For, in spite of the precedents, the use of an existing Charter for a purpose fundamentally different from that envisaged when it had been granted was of doubtful validity. Yet the fact that this device was resorted to reflected both the eagerness with which the investors approached the business prospects of the enterprise and their confidence in their own strength and influence.

In the event, the new marine insurance company almost immediately justified the optimistic determination with which its supporters had worked to launch it. In the next eleven months it underwrote about £1·3 million of marine risks, did business with almost 500 merchants (including not only its own members but a good number who had originally opposed it); and, according to its supporters, enjoyed a ready popularity because of its relatively low premiums, ease of insurance and quick and convenient payments.[1] The novelty of this commercial experiment was considerable, for as the promoters later pointed out, 'the business of insurance, as a distinct employment in private hands, is in itself an innovation, the knowing and wary traders themselves being formerly the only insurers'.[2] But the Mines Royal venture was more than a business novelty. It was a financial success, too. Initially, only 5s. per cent had been paid in on its shares. In February 1719, however, in preparation for commencing business, a further call brought the paid-up capital to £5 per cent. In July this was increased to £10—making a total capital of £115,200. In the summer of 1719, after a period in the spring when it stood at almost 100 per cent above par, the stock settled down to a premium of about 50 per cent. And early in October 1719 the Company paid its first dividend: ½ per cent on par value, but in fact 5 per cent on paid-up capital. By the end of the month its stock had touched 16 on the open market.[3]

Managing a successful and profitable marine insurance business, paying a good dividend and with its stock regularly quoted on the Stock

---

[1] *Special Report* (1720), pp. 42–3, 45; *HCJ*, XIX, 344. According to an affidavit produced by its opponents early in 1720, there were already 'several insurers of good reputation unwilling to underwrite policies, as they used to do before the said company was set up'. And one of its opponents accused it of undercutting the market: 'it was the business of the Company to bring the merchants in to insure with them by insuring cheaper than the private insurers; and by even paying when they had no occasion, in order to beat the private insurers out of their business . . the private insurers insure as cheaply as possible; but the Company insure cheaper, to make themselves acceptable'. All this would seem to indicate the advent of keen, and effective, competition.

[2] *Special Report* (1720), p. 47.

[3] Mines Royal, Dividend Warrants dated 5 October 1719 in REA Archives; J. Castaing, *The Course of the Exchange*.

Exchange since February 1719 and 'bought and sold in Exchange Alley, London, as commonly as other public stocks are',[1] the anomalously named Mines Royal was bound, in the circumstances of the time, to provoke comment and reaction. Given its inevitable impact on private underwriters, it had to meet the challenge of critics. But, much more significantly, given its success at a time of general commercial and financial prosperity, it set a trend, provoking emulation as well as hostility. In the controversy and boom which resulted from the activity of those who wished to destroy and those who wished to emulate the Company, the stage was set not merely for a vital development in the progress of the South Sea bubble but also for a transformation of the syndicate's own position from that of the uneasy resuscitators of all but moribund Charters to the owners and managers of a new and powerful corporation which, starting as a reputed 'bubble', outlived what must have been the most optimistic hopes of its progenitors.

[1] *Special Report* (1720), p. 45.

2

Creating a Corporation: the organization of the Royal Exchange Assurance 1719-1721

SECURING A CHARTER, 1719–1720

The Mines Royal had to confront its critics, at least on paper, within two months of beginning its marine insurance business: on 9 May 1719 the Privy Council referred two petitions to the Attorney-General—one from the Company requesting incorporation, another from London and Bristol merchants requesting the revocation of the Charters then being used by the Company. In the event, the hearings before the Attorney-General did not take place until November and December 1719—and then only after prolonged prompting by counsel for the private underwriters opposed to the Mines Royal.[1] There were, in fact, seven meetings, attended by dozens of lawyers and petitioners; but they were indeterminate. And the whole question of insurance promotions was put in fresh perspective when, in January 1720, at least five new petitions for the incorporation, or legitimization, of different insurance companies were presented to the Privy Council. These petitions, and the much greater groundswell of speculation of which they were merely examples, rapidly transformed the context of the controversy about marine insurance in particular and company promotions in general.

The world of London business and finance in the last months of 1719 and early 1720 was, in fact, increasingly dominated by various developments of a more or less speculative character: by the boom in the Paris stock market associated with the economic and financial schemes of John Law; by the success of the Mines Royal and the promised success of other early promotions; and ultimately, above all, by the grandiose plan, formulated between November 1719 and January 1720, for a take-over of the National Debt by the South Sea Company, which had already

[1] *Special Report* (1720), pp. 8, 34–6; *HCJ*, XIX, 345.

undertaken a partial conversion in July 1719.[1] In this new situation insurance promotions played an important part—embodying, as they did, the prospect of large profits from business enterprise and from the deployment of large sums of capital. Because of their novelty and utility, and their rôle as monied as well as trading companies, insurance companies were therefore in the vanguard of stock market and business development both in England and on the Continent. And even before the impact of the South Sea scheme was strongly felt there was a minor and influential boom in insurance promotion in the last months of 1719 which continued and intensified as it was absorbed into the ebullient events of early 1720. The number and size of these projects, together with the ease with which they attracted investors, reflected not merely a rising tide of financial speculation but also a convergence of more important economic developments: an appreciation of the readiness of the market for an increased supply of insurance services; and the growing availability of risk capital for their provision on a specialized basis.

The most important new project of these months was floated in late August or early September 1719, when efforts began (presumably in direct response to the early success of the Mines Royal), which were ultimately to lead to the incorporation of the London Assurance almost a year later. Largely on the initiative of a goldsmith, Stephen Ram, but with the active help of such leading merchants as Sir William Chapman, a subscription was opened for a marine insurance company. In November, Ram was asked by his merchant backers to take a new subscription, with the object of excluding the large number of 'stock-jobbers and brokers' who had flocked into the first one. The November effort, at Garraway's Coffee House, was a considerable success: £1·2 million was subscribed and a call of 2s. 6d. per cent was paid. At the same time, however, a rival subscription, for £800,000, had been taken at Colebrook's Coffee House. And it was logical that these rivals should think of getting together. A new, joint subscription was therefore opened at the Marine Coffee House on 22 December 1719, and quickly taken up for £2 million with a call of £1 per cent. Within a few days of completing the subscription the new enterprise —variously called the 'New Assurance', 'Ram's Insurance' or 'Chetwynd's Insurance' after Lord Chetwynd, its noble sponsor and first Governor of the London Assurance—entered the lists and challenged the embryonic Royal Exchange Assurance by making a formal application for a Charter. Although some of the opponents of *any* attempt to incorporate an insurance business claimed that this new challenge was specious, merely masking

[1] Dickson, *Financial Revolution*, chapters 5 and 6; John Carswell, *The South Sea Bubble* (1961).

collusion between the two groups, 'to give the appearance and colour of a more general approbation of traders for such an undertaking', the rivalry seems to have been real enough. The promoters led by Stephen Ram claimed that their incorporation would prevent a monopoly arising and that the Mines Royal group were not genuine merchants. (They themselves embodied their claim to be such by proposing that their Company's name should be 'The Merchants' Society for Insuring Ships and Merchandise'.) Their challenge was, in any case, taken seriously by the market: their shares had been quoted at a premium since the middle of December, rising from $1\frac{1}{2}$ on 16 December to an average of 3 in early January.[1]

Although it turned out to be the most long-lasting of the imitators of the 'Old Insurance', as the Mines Royal was sometimes called, 'Ram's Insurance' was not the only one in the last months of 1719. In addition to various fishery and loan and annuity flotations, there was at least one other large subscription for marine business: 'Shale's Insurance', which was opened on 23 December, a day after Ram's combined list, collected signatures for £1 million with £1 paid up, and also petitioned for a Charter in January 1720.[2] Similarly, in the last few months of 1719, and also culminating in petitions for incorporation in January 1720, two large life insurance promotions were floated—one a straightforward subscription for £1·2 million (of which 2s. 6d. per cent was called), and the other an ingenious and complicated attempt to use the landowning powers of the York Buildings water company, together with a new subscription for £1·2 million, to purchase Scottish estates (forfeited after the 1715 Jacobite rising) and to use them as security for granting annuities and insuring lives. In the latter case the similarity to the use of the Mines Royal Charter for marine insurance was more than coincidental: Case Billingsley was behind this manoeuvre, too, and was aided by many of the merchant-financiers who were playing a large rôle in the Mines Royal. (Of the fifty-five men who petitioned on behalf of the York Buildings life insurance venture, twenty-two had subscribed to the original Mercers Hall marine insurance subscription in 1717–18.) And in October 1719, the York Buildings company having been taken over by its new proprietors at a cost of £7,000, the Mines Royal shareholders were given a preferential allotment in the new subscription.[3] Moreover, there were interlocking legal

    [1] For the origins of Ram's Insurance, and the arguments deployed, see *Special Committee* (1720), pp. 51–7, 61–2; *HCJ*, XIX, 346–7; J. Castaing, *The Course of the Exchange*, December 1719–January 1720.

    [2] *HCJ*, XIX, 347. Like Stephen Ram, Charles Shale was a goldsmith. The allotment 'receipts' for 'Shale's Insurance' circulated at a premium of some 50 per cent.

    [3] Scott, *Joint-Stock Companies*, III, 423.

as well as financial interests connecting the York Buildings and the Mines Royal: Sir William Thompson, the Solicitor-General, who had been so close to Billingsley when the Mercers Hall group petitioned for a Charter in 1718, was also Governor of York Buildings on the eve of Billingsley's take-over bid in October 1719.[1]

By January 1720, therefore, the promoters of the future Royal Exchange Assurance, who had submitted their first petition for incorporation as long ago as January 1718, and who had started to underwrite marine risks with the help of the corporate personality of the Mines Royal in March 1719, found themselves now not alone, but at the head of a jostling queue of applicants for authority to form new companies and undertake the profitable business of insurance—and of dealing in insurance shares. On 8 January 1720 the Privy Council referred four petitions to the Attorney-General: first, that of the Mines Royal group, who, in fact, had had to submit a new petition signed by Lord Onslow, Williams, London, Knipe, Beck, Cairnes and thirteen others, because the original one was presented in a 'mistaken form';[2] second, that of Chetwynd's group; third, that of Billingsley's syndicate for taking over York Buildings; and fourth, the rival life insurance promoters.[3] Two weeks later 'Shale's Insurance' petition was similarly referred.

If the legal argument had been complicated and the atmosphere excitable in November and December 1719, when the Mines Royal had been the only serious contender for a Charter, the situation became turbulent and dramatic to an extraordinary extent in January and February 1720. In addition to the five groups which were officially contending for incorporation, other promoters began to jump on the bandwagon, as the prospects for corporate insurance grew even more attractive, as the stock market boomed on the preliminary announcement of the South Sea plan (South Sea stock rose from about 135 in mid-January to over 180 in mid-February) and as the stocks of 'Onslow's Insurance' and 'Chetwynd's Insurance' rose steeply, from 17 and 3 on 8 January to 36 and $5\frac{1}{4}$ on 20 February,

---

[1] For the York Buildings' insurance promotion, see *Special Report* (1720), pp. 66–73; *HCJ*, XIX, 349–50.

[2] It was presented by 'the Governors, Assistants and Societies of and for the Mines Royal, the Mineral and Battery Works, and for insuring Ships and Merchandize'—and its opponents rightly claimed that there was no such Corporation (the last six words having been the promoters' invention). See *HCJ*, XIX, 345–6; *Special Report* (1720), pp. 48–9. The new petitioners (in fact, all members of the Mines Royal) were: Lord Onslow, John Williams, John London, Abraham Cropp, Randolph Knipe, Justus Beck, James Bradly, William Dunster, John Emmett, George Jackson, Thomas Newman, Alexander Cairnes, John Hanbury, Henry March, Thomas Paniwell, John Phillips, John Gould and William Astell.

[3] *Special Report* (1720), pp. 48–9, 51–3, 66–9.

with most of the rise being concentrated in February. In the last two weeks of February ten new subscriptions for insurance companies were opened: seven for fire insurance, one for marine risks, one for burglary, and one for burglary and fire risks, each with proposed capital of either £1 million or £2 million. Of these, however, only two fire insurance promotions need to be noted here: the so-called 'Sadlers' Hall' subscription, organized by Stephen Ram, with a 5s. per cent call on £2 million stock; and 'Overall's Insurance', a subscription of £1 million, with a call of 3s. per cent, of which 6d. went to its promoter, Edmund Overall.[1] Although neither survived for long, the Sadlers' Hall venture was taken over by the Royal Exchange Assurance in the winter of 1720–1,[2] and the London Assurance was to secure Edmund Overall's services first as Fire Clerk (1721–2) and then as Secretary (1722–55).

The atmosphere created by a buoyant stock market, the prospect of profit and a rash of promotions soon became extraordinarily heady. While there were official quotations for Onslow's and Chetwynd's insurances, there was also vast speculation in the others' scrip: the Sadlers' Hall subscription, for example, opening on 16 February, proved so popular, and 'the persons wanting to subscribe crowding very much', that an extra office at the Feather's Coffee House had to be opened, men were reported to be paying 20 and 30 guineas for the right to subscribe, and the receipts were said to be bought and sold at 15s. per cent advance—presumably a premium of 300 per cent on the initial 5s. call. No wonder that their opponents accused Onslow's and Chetwynd's groups of having, as their main aim, stock market speculation, and that one critic claimed 'that all the City run into a method of stock-jobbing . . . and that no trade has been minded since the several subscriptions have been set on foot'.[3]

Meanwhile, the Attorney-General was conducting active and anxious hearings on the various Charter petitions—so anxious that they provoked complaints about the tone and methods used: some weeks later the Solicitor-General, Sir William Thompson, even went so far as to claim that 'there were public biddings for charters, as if at an auction, in the Chambers of the Attorney General'.[4] Admittedly, Thompson himself was not entirely a trustworthy witness; he was embroiled with an apparent offer of a bribe by Billingsley in 1718, had been mixed up in, and bought out of, the York Buildings take-over, and had played a dubious rôle in acting as an intimate legal adviser to Billingsley. Nevertheless, the dangerous custom of the

---

1 *HCJ*, XIX, 347–8; Scott, *Joint-Stock Companies*, III, 446–9.
2 Below, pp. 48–9.
3 *HCJ*, XIX, 347; *Special Report* (1720), p. 55.
4 *Special Report* (1720), p. 5.

Crown's Law Officers receiving private fees from petitioners in such matters led at the very least to a suspicious generosity towards them by the various syndicates then seeking incorporation, even though a committee of inquiry subsequently exonerated the Attorney-General from the charge of bribery.[1]

The flush of enthusiasm and activity which characterized insurance promotions in January and February 1720 did not last. For just as the REA syndicate had been affected by the incursion of other groups of promoters, so the insurance schemes in general were affected by broader events. January and February had also been months of great activity for the promoters of the South Sea scheme. Early in February the plan for the Company to take over the National Debt, issue fresh capital and pay a huge gift to the Government for the profitable privilege, was accepted by Parliament, and work began on a draft Bill of the details. Meanwhile, however, the South Sea Company and its friends in government were beginning to get worried about other speculative company promotions. This was because the South Sea speculation depended, for its success, on the continuous availability of private investment funds—and there was a real danger that alternative promotions would not merely sour the financial atmosphere but would also divert capital from the South Sea Company's own 'money subscriptions'. This factor, together with the genuine concern of some MPs, led the House of Commons to mount an attack on the promotional and speculative activities which were beginning to dominate the London business scene. On 22 February the House appointed a Committee 'to inquire into and examine the several subscriptions for fisheries, insurances, annuities for lives, and all other projects carried on by subscriptions in and about the Cities of London and Westminster, and to inquire into all undertakings for purchasing joint-stocks or obsolete charters'.[2] The proposed investigation sounded innocuous enough. But its implications were obvious to all those directly concerned: Parliament was going to gather evidence which could be used to curb the mushrooming of new companies. The day after the Committee was appointed the price of Mines Royal stock fell from 35 to 29, even though it still retained a generous premium on its £10 call. Significantly, the South Sea Company stock remained more or less steady.

While the House of Commons Committee began its work (on 27 February 1720 the House called for all petitions for insurance Charters

[1] See *Special Report* (1720), pp. 5–13.
[2] For the political influence of the South Sea Company, see Carswell, *South Sea Bubble*, p. 117; Scott, *Joint-Stock Companies*, I, 410–11.

over the previous three years), Sir Nicholas Lechmere, the Attorney-General, was coming to the end of his own labours on the various petitions for incorporation which had been presented in January. And when he reported early in March he was very cautious about issues likely to prove politically and legally sensitive—in particular, the use of Charters issued for other purposes and the size and scope of public companies. On balance, the promoters and petitioners could not have derived much encouragement either from what he said or from the atmosphere in which he said it, even though the content of his reports was a reminder that the substantive questions were really about insurance, and the best means of organizing it.[1] After rehearsing the arguments, and summarizing the voluminous evidence he had taken, Lechmere came out flatly against the use of the Elizabethan Charters for an insurance enterprise:

the transactions which are before stated to have been carried on for the insurance of ships and merchandise, under colour or pretence of the Charters aforesaid, and in the names of the supposed Corporations, are illegal and unwarrantable, and if drawn into precedent, would be of dangerous consequence to the public; those Charters, being granted for the particular ends specified and limited therein, not giving sufficient authority to the Corporations thereby erected, if they are existing, to carry on a business or employment of so public a nature, as that of insurance of ships and merchandise, and which is wholly foreign to the design of those incorporations.

This was unambiguous enough and enshrined a reasonable legal principle which was to be frequently evoked in the troubled year of 1720: that Charters issued for one purpose could not be used for a different one. On the other hand, however, the Attorney-General also went out of his way to emphasize that it was only on legal grounds that the Mines Royal enterprise was open to serious criticisms. Its business achievements had on the whole been commendable:

I do humbly certify your Majesty, that it doth appear that the design of the Petitioners for a Charter, in making use of the said old Charters, was to make the experiment of insuring ships and merchandise as a Corporation; and that they have carried on that undertaking, though in that respect without legal authority, yet without any complaint from the persons with whom they have made insurances, or any objections to the fairness of their proceedings.

Finally, Lechmere turned to the general question of principle raised by the controversy—namely, 'whether it be fit for your Majesty to grant a Charter for erecting a Corporation with a large joint stock, for insuring of ships and merchandise'. On this matter the Attorney-General, while

[1] For the petitions and reports, see *Special Report* (1720), pp. 34–63.

favourably inclined towards the idea of a marine insurance company, as to whose advantages the balance of actual experience and verbal evidence must have been quite persuasive, spoke with considerable circumspection. Established with suitable safeguards, a chartered insurance company might be very beneficial, he argued; but he refused to commit himself on the delicate question of its size:

such a Corporation, not being made in any manner exclusive of others, and being granted under such regulations as are suitable to a matter of so great moment, may be of great advantage to trade; but whether it is advisable to erect such a Corporation with so large a joint stock, as is mentioned in the petition [£1,152,000], may deserve particularly to be considered.[1]

Four days after this Report (on 7 March) Lechmere submitted his Report on the petition from Lord Chetwynd, Sir William Chapman and the other subscribers to 'Chetwynd's Insurance'. In this instance, while repeating and emphasizing the point that a company was to be welcomed, and was welcomed by the generality of traders, he was also much more explicit about the size of the proposed Company: 'the ends of trade will, I think, be sufficiently served by a far less joint stock than is . . . proposed'.[2]

In his Reports upon the petitions from the two groups now formally led by Lord Onslow and Lord Chetwynd, the Attorney-General touched upon all the considerations that he felt to be relevant to insurance matters. On 9 March, in considering the petition from 'Shale's Insurance', he did not add anything to his previous statements; and the next day he dismissed the claim that the York Buildings Company could be used 'for purposes wholly foreign to the ends of [the original] incorporation', arguing that the contract between the Company and the Billingsley syndicate was 'unwarrantable', and simply asserted that it was not advisable to incorporate the second group of life insurance promoters. The Attorney-General's Reports themselves, of course, were not necessarily hostile to the idea of corporate insurance—although their condemnation of the appropriation of old Charters and their suspicions of large-scale companies must have cooled the ardour of many promoters. More important, no doubt, was the fact that the House of Commons Committee on company promotions in general was still sitting in an atmosphere which was patently hostile to new practices. And it is relevant that, after the hectic days of February, no new companies were floated in March or early April. Meanwhile, however, the South Sea Company's plan was gathering steam—helped, no doubt, by the

[1] Quotations from *Special Report* (1720), pp. 47-8.
[2] *Special Report* (1720), p. 57.

absence of rival flotations which might have siphoned off potential investors and capital. Between 1 and 29 March its stock rose from 175 to 320.
Yet the revival of promotional activity in the second half of April showed
that the Company did not have things all its own way. Nor did the hiatus
of promotional activity while the Committee was deliberating place the
Mines Royal at a very great disadvantage: during March its stock, which
had sagged to 25 by the 1st of the month, recovered to 29½—presumably on
the strength of its continued existence and profitability.

The House of Commons Committee finally reported on 27 April. As
was perhaps expected, and certainly must have been anticipated by the
friends of the South Sea Company who were reputed to have initiated it,
the Committee roundly condemned recent developments in the field of
company promotion. In particular, it criticized the raising of very large
subscription with proportionately small amounts paid up and the fact that
various groups were presuming to act as corporate bodies 'without any
legal authority'—all of which, it was held, was prejudicial to the country's
trade and commerce. The House immediately accepted this Report and
ordered the preparation of a Bill 'to restrain the extravagant and unwarrantable practice of raising money by voluntary subscriptions, for
carrying on projects dangerous to the trade and subjects of this Kingdom'.

It might have been expected that this Report, and the prospect of
restrictive legislation, would have dampened the enthusiasm for promotion
and, therefore, the ebullience of the stock market. Yet, curiously, during the
second half of April and in May there was a sustained boom in new subscriptions—rising to an intense and hysterical pitch in June. It is almost as
if the optimism induced, and the financial appetites whetted, by the South
Sea scheme now became reckless of any consideration except their own
new-found self-regenerating impetus. Apparently conventional companies
for manufacturing or fishing or trade competed for subscribers with money-
lending enterprises, a company for buying up the goods of bankrupts, and
one (apparently a hoax—but an illustrative one) for the manufacture of
calicoes and linens, which was proposed by 'several ladies', who were
'resolved as one man to admit no man but will themselves subscribe to a
joint-stock to carry on the said trade'.[1] No doubt many, and perhaps nearly
all, of these subscriptions were opened with little intention of beginning business, but in order that the promoters might profit by 'stock-
jobbing'. This would certainly help explain why they continued under the
threat of legislation, just as the hope of profit on a rising market would
explain the continued influx of funds to the capital market.

[1] Scott, *Joint-Stock Companies*, III, 450. Subscribers had to be women dressed in calico.

What is less explicable, however, is the behaviour of the stock of the Mines Royal, which was already a going concern and which, superficially, was therefore very directly threatened by the promised legislation. For, instead of falling, the stock, listed as 'Assurance of Ships', actually rose: from 30 on the day of the Committee's Report, to $31\frac{1}{2}$ on the next day and $32\frac{1}{4}$ the day after that.

To some extent, of course, even the stock of an established business would have shared in the euphoria surrounding transactions in the securities of new projects. But the most important explanation for the rise was not to be found in public events. For now, after almost three years of trying, the syndicate which had opened the Mercers Hall subscription in August 1717, was near to attaining their objective by means which had only just become possible in their case. As with the other giant companies of the time, they found that the desired privileges could be purchased from an impecunious Government; and that the Government's new and urgent financial needs presented business opportunities which were even more attractive than those which had been originally envisaged. In April 1720 the prospects for incorporation were radically, and abruptly, transformed by a combination of financial pressure and political stratagem.

Some time in April Robert Walpole produced a plan by which he returned to political office and the King and the Prince of Wales were reconciled. As part of this scheme, and in order to make it more attractive to both King and Parliament, it was proposed to pay off the £600,000 of debt which had accumulated on the Civil List (the King's personal income which was used for household, administrative and even political purposes). And the instruments to be used to raise money in order to clear these debts were the two leading groups of promoters of marine insurance companies —whose eagerness for incorporation, it was rightly assumed, would lead them to agree to pay £300,000 each for the award of Charters of incorporation. Furthermore, as an added inducement to the promoters, the Charters of incorporation would not merely provide the organizational legitimacy which they had been working for but would also give them exclusive privileges with respect to corporate underwriting by prohibiting any other company or partnership from undertaking marine insurance.[1]

These matters were, in fact, settled in the last week of April—even though the South Sea Company, hostile, as always, to rival promotions which might attract capital funds, made strenuous efforts to prevent it, including an offer by some of its own Directors to lend the Treasury the

[1] For Walpole's plan, see J. H. Plumb, *Sir Robert Walpole*, I (1956), 285–92.

money 'rather than that those bubbles should take place'.[1] But Walpole would not entertain alternative projects ('By God! Sir, I tell you we will hear no proposals, for these shall do')—and on 26 April, with an easy disregard of political morality, he settled a broker's account for the purchase of £2,550 of stock in the 'Old Insurance' and 'Ram's Insurance' before the plan was widely known. Two weeks later, when news of the scheme had inflated their prices, he sold out at a profit of more than 100 per cent.[2] Meanwhile, the proposal had become public and official: on 4 May, in an Address to the Commons, the King informed them that he was favourably inclined to the two groups of petitioners, and hoped to extend corporate privileges to them in return for their enabling him 'to discharge the debts of his civil government without burdening his people with any new aid or supply'. Delighted at the prospect of paying for government without the need to raise taxes or borrow money, the Commons quickly agreed to the proposal in principle. And the next day, Mines Royal stock, which on 3 May had been just under 34, jumped to 39.

After this, events moved quickly towards the formal incorporation of the Royal Exchange Assurance, which, as a group of men, had tried for so long to achieve this end. Ironically, the Corporation was created not merely at a time when company promotions were coming into increasing disfavour but by enabling clauses tacked on to a piece of legislation, the so-called Bubble Act, which was designed quite precisely to inhibit the development of corporations.[3] With an easy disregard for consistency, the measure (Geo. I, c. 18) was described as 'An Act for better securing certain powers and privileges, intended to be granted by His Majesty by two Charters for assurance of ships and merchandizes at sea, and for lending money upon bottomry; and for restraining several extravagant and unwarrantable practices therein mentioned'.

The Bill passed rapidly through Parliament and received the Royal Assent on 9 June. Between mid-May and mid-June, Mines Royal stock shot up from about 40 to just over 100 (i.e. ten times its paid-up value). On 22 June 1720, pursuant to the Act, Royal Charters were signed incorporating the Royal Exchange Assurance and the London Assurance. No

---

[1] *Mr. Aislabie's Second Speech on his defence in the House of Lords, on Thursday, July 20, 1721* (1721; BM, 517. k. 16/30), p. 14.

[2] Plumb, *Walpole*, I, 291–2.

[3] The relevant, and somewhat ambiguous, clause was 'the acting or presuming to act as a corporate body or bodies, the raising or pretending to raise transferable stock or stocks, the transferring or pretending to transfer or assign any share or shares in such stock or stocks without legal authority, either by Act of Parliament or by any Charter from the Crown to warrant such acting as a body corporate . . . shall for ever be deemed to be illegal and void'.

other companies or partnerships were to be allowed to underwrite marine risks. And in return for these exclusive and therefore valuable privileges the two Corporations were each to pay the very considerable sum of £300,000 into the Exchequer to defray the debts of the Civil List.

Various safeguards against undue concentration of interest and monopolistic behaviour were embodied in the Charters: stockholders or officials in one were forbidden to own stock or hold office in the other; and the Charters could be revoked within thirty-one years on repayment of the gift to the Civil List, or after thirty-one years without any such repayment. But none of this could obscure the fact that two very powerful elements had been added to the business and financial scene, and that after years of striving the Royal Exchange Assurance was incorporated as a potentially wealthier, and certainly more privileged and influential, body than had ever been envisaged by its patient and enterprising promoters.

With the signing of the Charter, and the smooth transition from Mines Royal to Royal Exchange Assurance, those promoters, with one exception, all came into their own. The Charter named Lord Onslow as Governor, Sir John Williams as Sub-Governor, Sir Randolph Knipe as Deputy-Governor, and others of the original group as Directors of the Royal Exchange Assurance. The man whose name was not carried forward was Case Billingsley, even though he had served as Secretary of the Mines Royal as well as an initiator of the original plan. One reason for dropping Billingsley must have been his dubious rôle in the negotiations in 1718: his actions then had bordered so closely on bribery as to be virtually indistinguishable from it, and the adverse effect of the publicity subsequently given to this behaviour early in 1720 could not have been very welcome to the established City merchants who were so closely associated with the Corporation. In March 1720, appearing before the Commons Committee of inquiry, Sir John Williams asserted that the Directors of the Mines Royal had only recently heard about Billingsley's promises to the Law Officers, 'and they are so exasperated at him for it, that he would have been turned out before now, but for that they are under the examination of this Committee'.[1] On this basis, therefore, it seems very likely that Billingsley was indeed 'turned out' of the group—which would also help explain his subsequent bitter and vindictive behaviour, as an ordinary stockholder, when the new Corporation ran into a financial crisis in the autumn of 1720.[2] In addition, however, there is a sense in which Billingsley no longer had a rôle to play. Once a Charter had been granted his main aim had been

[1] *Special Report* (1720), p. 11.
[2] Below, pp. 39–40.

achieved. For Billingsley was essentially a company promoter who looked to stock-jobbing for his profit. And in this respect it is significant that Stephen Ram, who played a similar promotional rôle for Chetwynd's Insurance, also dropped out of the picture, except as an active dealer in its shares, once the London Assurance was established.[1]

Men like Billingsley and Ram had skills which were only very indirectly relevant to insurance companies; and the severance of their links with the REA and the London marked a new style as well as a new phase in the history of those Corporations. Established on a firm legal basis, and anticipating an active and successful extension of its marine underwriting, the Royal Exchange Assurance in June 1720 must have seemed as unshakeable to its members as the Royal Exchange itself—within which the Corporation fitted out its new offices. Within days of receiving its Charter a Court was called and hours of business (11 a.m. to 2 p.m. and 5 p.m. to 7 p.m.) were announced. But the newly assembled Court, meeting at the very peak of the financial boom, could not yet appreciate that the task still remained of ensuring the economic survival of the new Corporation in a business environment which was going to be much less favourable to monied companies than the one during which it had come into existence.

THE VICISSITUDES OF PRIVILEGE, 1720–1721

Although firmly established in the eyes of the law in June 1720, the Corporation could not really settle down to concentrate on the business of insurance until the autumn of 1721. This was due to the unusual circumstances in which it had been founded: chartered at the very peak of the stock market boom (South Sea stock reached its highest point in the third week of June), and committed to raising a very substantial amount of money as the price of its privileges, the REA could not avoid the reality as well as the reputation of being a monied company. The most important context for its first few months was therefore provided not by the market for insurance (although that was real enough) but by the progressive weakening of the stock market. Indeed, subsequently, when the collapse of the South Sea bubble was complete, the ruined Chancellor of the Exchequer claimed that the establishment of the two new insurance companies had added 'unnecessary fuel' to the fire of speculation: 'as the South Sea scheme might give birth to the bubbles, so the bubbles contributed to raise the South Sea to that height which brought us into this condition'.[2]

Admittedly, this claim seems to have been an attempt to shuffle off

[1] Bernard Drew, *The London Assurance: A Second Chronicle* (1949), p. 148.
[2] *Mr. Aislabie's Second Speech on his defence*, p. 14.

responsibility for his own corrupt rôle in the South Sea project. But it had some truth, and certainly exemplified the extent to which the REA found its immediate future inextricably enmeshed in the course of speculation. In the last resort, its basis lay in the business of underwriting; and, as we shall see, it very soon tried to extend that business to fire and life insurance. But in the short run at least its success was to be determined far more by financial than by commercial factors.

From its very beginning the REA had implicitly committed itself to a dependence on the booming stock market. As was also the case with the London Assurance, it had given hostages to fortune by contracting to pay £300,000 for its Charter and by subscribing £156,000 to a Government loan issue (it is likely that this loan was also a condition of the award of a Charter).[1] These were to be spread out over a relatively short period: £100,000 of the 'gift' to the Civil List was to be paid before 22 July 1720, and the remainder in four instalments of £50,000 between July and April 1721; subscriptions to the £156,000 loan were to be made in four equal instalments between 24 June and 1 December 1720. Presumably, therefore, the promoters were confident that they could find a very substantial amount of extra money—by issuing more capital, calling for further payments on the existing stock, or borrowing on bonds (which they were legally entitled to do by using the government loans as securities). But each, or all, of these would depend for success on a continued rising trend in the stock market. As with the South Sea Company, which was absolutely dependent on being able to issue stock at prices very much above par in order to make enormous payments to the Government, the REA itself became a prisoner of the Stock Exchange.

Initially, this was by no means an uncomfortable situation. While the enabling Bill was passing through Parliament, on 18 May 1720, the embryo Corporation (still operating as the Mines Royal) issued a further £60,000 of stock, with £10 per cent paid up, and since the stock market quotation rose from about 60 to 90 in the next few days, it may be assumed that this alone brought in £40,000 or £50,000. This, together with existing capital and the sale of any unissued stock, at prices which were rapidly increasing, must have facilitated the speedy payment of £100,000 towards the Civil List and the advance of £39,000 on the loan, both of which were made

---

[1] Details of the £300,000 payment are in the Charter, and of the £156,000 loan in PRO, T.1/229/11 (10 November 1720). The fact that the London Assurance also lent £156,000 (Guildhall MSS, 8729/1 [22 November 1720]), that both Corporations had to borrow money from the Bank of England in order to lend to the Government, and that the first instalment was paid immediately after the Charter was issued, all seem to indicate that the loan was a more or less formal condition of incorporation.

within days of the issue of the Charter on 22 June. Meanwhile, for a few more weeks, the Corporation's position on the stock market looked extremely promising; its stock doubled in price, from 100 (ten times paid up value) on 22 June to a peak of over 200 on 16 August. Unfortunately, however, the rising trend of stock market prices, on the crest of whose wave the REA had been launched, did not, and presumably could not, continue. From the third week of June leading stocks had begun to weaken —levelling out and slowly turning down for a month or two, and then, by early September, tumbling drastically.

The deflation of the South Sea bubble quickly undermined the financial basis of the Royal Exchange Assurance. But the influence of the South Sea scheme was not confined to the fall in that Company's stock, which accelerated during August. It was also felt through the practical difficulties in the way of the REA issuing more of its own capital. In mid-August, for example, the Royal Exchange and the London both apparently planned huge new issues, but these moves (which would have increased their nominal capital beyond the £1·5 million allowed in their Charters) were strongly opposed by the Government, increasingly anxious about undue speculation, and by the South Sea Company, which, as usual, was hostile to rival promotions which might channel investment capital away from itself. Indeed, the South Sea Directors were subsequently accused of having tried to render 'those two assurances (especially the Royal Exchange) insolvent, and by that means have forced them to forfeit their Charter'.[1] On 22 August the two insurance companies were officially cautioned 'to keep expressly to the limitation of their respective Charters'; and the next day the Corporation announced that transfer books would remain closed. Early in the next month such subscriptions as had been made were returned.[2] More positively, and ultimately more disastrously, on 18 August there came the announcement of a Treasury decision to open proceedings against four companies (the Royal Lustring, the York Buildings, and the English and Welsh Copper Companies) accused of contravening the Bubble Act by misusing their Charters. Designed to impair other 'bubbles' than the South Sea, it helped precipitate a minor collapse on the stock market. In addition, however, in so far as it depressed stocks, the threatened prosecution rebounded on the heads of the South Sea Directors: as general prices fell and the influence of panic sales was augmented by the need to

---

[1] *A New-Year's Gift for the Directors, with some account of their plot against the two assurances* (1721; Guildhall Library), p. 24.

[2] Scott, *Joint-Stock Companies*, III, 404–5; [A. Boyer], *The Political State of Great Britain*, XX, 140; *Daily Courant*, 23 August 1720.

sell stock in order to repay loans incurred in order to purchase it on slender margins, so their own stock tumbled in price. It had been at 850 at the end of July; by 5 September it touched 750; two weeks later it had fallen to 400; and by 4 October it reached 260.

These events were gloomily reflected in the Royal Exchange Assurance's position. The combination of the announcement about the Treasury prosecution and the official challenge to the planned new subscription, provoked a collapse in its stock. In the eight days from 19 to 27 August it declined by roughly one-third, from 195 to 135. By 17 September it had fallen by half, to 65, and by mid-October to 25. (The fall was to continue: the Corporation's stock reached $8\frac{1}{2}$ in mid-December.)

In these circumstances the Corporation found it impossible to raise the money to pay the balance (£200,000) owing to the Government. Certainly the second instalment of the gift (£50,000), which was due on 22 September, must have seemed beyond the Corporation's reach at a time when its stock had fallen to less than half the price at which it had stood in early July, and was still falling. An attempt at a capital issue in August, as already seen, had been blocked. A few weeks later there was a further attempt to raise fresh capital: in mid-September, after the nominal capital had been halved (to £606,000), it was proposed to issue a further £606,000 of capital at a price of 180. But the general slump in stocks and shares made this move a failure.[1] Things were extremely serious: unless some relief were obtained, the Corporation would lose its Charter through non-fulfilment of its side of the bargain.

Now, one possible way of at least slowing the decline in the market value of its stock was for the REA to make its business prospects more attractive by extending its underwriting activities beyond the marine insurance for which it had been chartered. It so happened that this had always been a possibility: within a month of the Charters (i.e. at a time when their financial position seemed strong) both the Royal Exchange and the London Assurance had petitioned for an extension of their powers to include fire and life insurance.[2] But, although there was official approval of the proposal, the whole matter was delayed, and by early October, with heavy arrears in its payments due to the Government, the REA Court concluded that its main hope was to expedite the award of new powers. They informed the Treasury that they would do all they could to comply with the order not to continue the delay in payment of the second instalment, 'but apprehend we shall not be able to do it without the assistance

[1] Below, p. 46.
[2] PRO, T/29/24, part ii (28 July 1720); T.1/228/40 (15 September 1720).

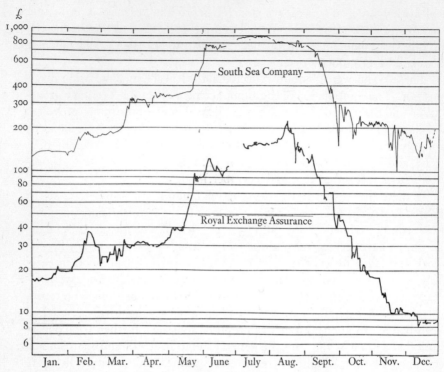

Fig. 2.1: Prices of stock: Royal Exchange Assurance and South Sea Company,
1 January 1720 to 31 December 1720

(Source: J. Castaing, *The Course of the Exchange*.)

of the fire Charter, which they as well as the several proprietors always looked upon as the best part of their agreement . . . That will be the only means to extricate them out of the difficulties which from the necessity of the times and other unexpected disappointments they have met with.'[1]

In spite of this plea, and the fact that the Government was co-operative, the question of the fire and life Charters dragged on—delayed first by objections from existing fire offices and then by difficulties about the specific terms of the grants. Hence, by October 1720 the Royal Exchange and the London Assurance were really dependent on their own resources or on some direct measure of financial relief. Indeed, earlier, in the summer of 1720, both Corporations had already been obliged to borrow extensively from the Bank of England, which was pressing for repayment in October, and even from their own Directors, in order to meet their commitments to the Government. By October, for example, three members of the REA Court (Williams, Knipe and Beck) 'by their own credit . . . had borrowed for the service of the Corporation one hundred and eighty thousand pounds to make up a payment due from the Company to the Government'.[2]

The feeling of desperation which the financial crisis must have induced was already having uncomfortable repercussions within the Royal Exchange Assurance itself. On 6 October a General Court of Proprietors (i.e. stockholders) was called, apparently to confirm arrangements for the new subscription for £606,000 of stock and a call of £10 (i.e. 20 per cent per £50 share, the nominal value of stock having been halved in September) where old or new subscribers had still not paid their calls. But when the Sub-Governor, Sir John Williams, attempted to secure the Court's approval of the minutes of the previous meeting (at which the nominal value of the existing stock had been halved, in order to make way for the new issue) he was initially howled down by chants of 'No, no, no' and 'Let every man have whole stock, whole stock, whole stock'. Williams thereupon warned the Proprietors against intemperate action; the Directors' strategy, he insisted, was the only way to 'secure our present advantages, obtain our fire Charter, and save the Corporation from ruin'. Further, in response to bitter complaints about the fall in the price of stock from the now disaffected Billingsley (whom Williams accused of attending 'only to try to confound them' and of gross insolence), other leading Directors tried to reassure the Proprietors, in the words of Richard Lockwood, the eminent

---

[1] PRO, T.1/229/1 (5 October 1720).
[2] *The Political State*, xx, 305. In February 1721 a Bank loan of £80,000 to the Royal Exchange was still outstanding: Bank of England Court Minutes, 6 October 1720, 7 February 1721.

Levant merchant, that the depreciated stock, which was then participating with all other securities in 'a season of universal calamity . . . would quickly be brought again into a flourishing condition'. Ultimately, helped by these reassurances and by the wildness of Billingsley's behaviour, which alienated other stockholders, the Court's proposals were unanimously accepted.[1]

In the event, however, these plans continued to be frustrated by the state of the capital market. And the General Court had to meet again on 18 October because so much of the subscription had not been taken up. The Court of Directors now came up with a new set of proposals, in a final, and perhaps despairing, attempt at financial reconstruction. The Corporation's capital (nominally £1·5 million) was to be divided into 75,000 shares, of which 24,240 were to be distributed equally to the original proprietors of £606,000 stock and the new subscribers to the extra £606,000 created in September. A further 40,000 were to be retained 'to be hereafter sold for the profit of the . . . Company', and 10,760 were to be immediately sold at £20 each. Finally, the stockholders were not to be called upon for any more payments on their existing stock for at least six months, and (presumably in an attempt to rally sentiment for the stock) a 5 per cent dividend on 'the reduced stock' would be declared—payable in Midsummer 1721 with interest from 29 September 1720. These complicated proposals being immediately agreed to with no opposition, 'a face of perfect unanimity and satisfaction appeared throughout the Court: and a gentleman remarked the happy change among them, from the last time of meeting'.[2]

In spite of the new spirit of amity, the financial climate within which the REA was struggling for its existence was hardly improving. And, in the continuing crisis, it proved virtually impossible to secure subscribers to the new shares. By 22 October (which was, in any case, a month late) the Corporation was only able to scrape together a mere £11,000 of the second instalment of £50,000 due to the Government, and had to deposit security for the future payment of the balance. On 11 November, therefore, the General Court was once more called together to hear the gloomy news 'that notwithstanding all the care and industry of the Directors, in executing the resolutions of the last General Court, the affairs of the Company

---

[1] *The Political State*, xx, 301–7; Scott, *Joint-Stock Companies*, III, 405–6. The London Assurance, which met on the same day, and agreed to further calls on its stock and to the issue of 10,000 new shares, maintained a somewhat better spirit (although the Governor at one point had to check criticism with the plea 'not to pour cold water upon their own affairs'), and one member somewhat smugly referred to their unanimity as 'a happy difference' between them and the Royal Exchange: *The Political State*, xx, 307–10.

[2] *The Political State*, xx, 310–13.

were in an ill posture, through the malicious efforts of the enemies to the Corporation'. Less than 2,000 of the 10,760 shares, which the General Court had decided to issue on 18 October, had been sold. Consequently, the Directors asked for, and secured, full authority to sell shares at whatever price they would fetch—or, in the more dignified wording of the motion, 'at such a price as shall effectually dispose gentlemen to come readily in, to the support of the Company'.[1] Meanwhile, however, the Corporation was negotiating to secure a moderate injection of fresh capital in an indirect way—by the acquisition of the Sadlers' Hall Society, the fire insurance project originally capitalized at £2 million which, by this time, had called £5 per cent (although its real worth had been greatly reduced by an unwise investment in South Sea stock, which had subsequently collapsed). In agreeing to an exchange of shares, in November, although the actual exchange does not appear to have taken place until 1721, the REA Court was presumably more persuaded by the chance of increasing its actual capital without having to sell securities on the open market than by a direct advantage in the way of preparing itself for the business of fire insurance.[2] Yet even this made only a very small difference to its financial problems.

It is clear from all this that, in the context of a complete collapse of confidence on the London stock market, the Corporation's twin strategy of issuing stock for subscription and trying to make that stock more attractive by pushing for the acquisition of a fire insurance Charter was failing badly. As a result, having exhausted both their credit and their ingenuity, the Directors of the REA and the London were obliged to appeal to the Treasury for relief. Negotiations, which had started with urgent pleas for a speedy extension of their power to embrace fire (and life) underwriting, had, in fact, been under way since early autumn 1720. The Lords of the Treasury, who from an early date had agreed in principle to the issue of new Charters, also had to agree, on 10 November, to accept Government securities as tokens of the Corporations' intention to pay £39,000 each to complete the £50,000 instalments due on the gift to the Civil List. And, finally, on 18 November they acknowledged the insurance companies' difficulties by agreeing to extend until the spring and summer of 1721 the

---

[1] *The Political State*, xx, 460-1.

[2] For all these events, see PRO, T.1/229/11; *The Political State*, xx, 460-3. The London Assurance was having comparable problems (in spite of the 'marvellous harmony and perfect concord' which apparently prevailed at its General Court of 6 October): on 22 November its Directors reported that 'the present pressure of money' had prevented any call or issue being made, and had obliged them to appeal to the Treasury for relief: *The Political State*, xx, 307-10, 463-4.

deadlines for the payment of the remaining three instalments (totalling £189,000) of the £300,000 due from each Corporation.[1]

In spite of this gesture, however, the situation of the two insurance companies did not improve. As the stock market depression continued into 1721, they found it impossible to raise the money needed to cover their commitments. After a token payment of £250 each in March,[2] they were left owing the Treasury £188,750, with no apparent means of covering the debt. In July 1721, therefore, they once more appealed to the Treasury, outlining their desperate position and, in effect, throwing themselves on the Government's mercy in the hope of a remission of the bulk of the unpaid monies. The memorial from the REA Court represented that:

the said Corporation have made it their constant study to find out effectual methods for raising sufficient sums of money to discharge the very great engagements which they have unhappily entered into, but the success of their several attempts has not answered their expectations, which may be owing, in great measure, to the calamity of the times and low ebb of public credit, but more especially from a general opinion, that it is impossible for this Corporation, from the uses of their Charter, to support themselves under the weight of so large a sum as £300,000 stipulated to be paid the government, without interest. So that, to their great concern, they find an utter inability to make any further payment, having met with the greatest difficulty imaginable in raising the sum already paid. [In spite of acquiring the Charter to transact fire and life business] it is their misfortune to find the price of their stock much less than the money paid in, and it is to be feared that their credit will daily decrease to the utter ruin of this Corporation—unless timely relieved by His Majesty's graciously remitting the sum [i.e. £150,000] which continues unpaid or unsecured by a deposit already made in His Majesty's Treasury.[3]

This was a cogent appeal. It was also a familiar one, for in the confused aftermath of the South Sea bubble the Government found itself having to deal with similar, although much larger, appeals on behalf of the South Sea Company, and its proprietors. In these instances, in the summer of 1721, there was a remission of a large amount of money owed to the Government by the Company (and the REA Court cited this 'tenderness and indulgence' as a precedent for its own appeal). By the end of July the Government made a comparable response on behalf of the two insurance

---

[1] *Calendar of Treasury Papers, 1720–1728*, p. 22 (13 October and 18 November 1720); PRO, T.1/229/11 (10 November 1720). Initially, the Chancellor of the Exchequer had advised the Corporation to sell its tallies (i.e. its Government securities) on the open market. But the condition of the capital market apparently made this impossible.

[2] Scott, *Joint-Stock Companies*, II, 408.

[3] PRO, T.1/234/49 (14 July 1721). The London Assurance petition is in Guildhall MSS, 8729/1 (18 July 1721).

companies. After the REA and the London Assurance had petitioned Parliament, with the backing of the Chancellor of the Exchequer, it remitted £150,000 of the money each owed—leaving merely £38,750 due. It was, however, a measure of the disturbed state of the capital market, and of their own weak financial position, that three months later the Royal Exchange was *still* £28,750 in arrears, and was obliged to make yet one more appeal, pointing out that it had not been possible to raise money by issuing bonds and that the sale of their Government securities (tallies) was, 'under the present bad state of credit . . . absolutely impracticable'. In these circumstances the Treasury agreed to accept the Government's own tallies in payment of the remaining balance.[1]

Thus, by the end of October 1721, after a long and somewhat sorry tale, the Royal Exchange Assurance was to a large extent clear of the huge financial encumbrance which it had optimistically assumed in the more innocent days of June 1720. In retrospect it is difficult to understand the logic which led the Directors to promise the vast sum of £300,000 even for exclusive insurance privileges—except on the assumption that profits were to be derived from the stock market as well as the insurance market. But this assumption had been rapidly confounded, and it had then become apparent that the Corporation had shouldered much too great a burden; and it was fortunate that the Government saw fit to relent to the extent of half the debt.

Even so, of course, the Corporation had had the very painful task of finding £150,000 in an atmosphere in which it was much more costly to raise money than could ever have been anticipated. Admittedly, the more direct costs of establishing the REA were relatively low: the expenses of securing its marine and fire Charters, legal costs, and the payment for the lease and furnishing of its offices, were all estimated at £7,000. Yet, even after the reduction, the cost of the gift to the Government was very considerable, and the losses for individual subscribers (assuming that they had retained their stock as the market collapsed) very heavy. Moreover, both the Royal Exchange and the London continued to be dependent on loans from the Bank of England.[2] Experience had been purchased at a high price.

In the long run, however, the cost could be absorbed, and the experience turned to good account. For, in spite of the burned fingers and

---

[1] London Assurance Court Minutes, 25 July 1721 (Guildhall MSS, 8729/1); PRO, T.1/235/44 (17 October 1721), T.29/24/part (ii) (26 October 1721).

[2] Bank of England Court Minutes, 14 June and 29 November 1722 (loans of £20,000 to the REA); Guildhall MSS, 8729/1 (27 February 1722, 3 and 9 March 1722).

anxieties which were the inevitable consequence of the flotation of quasi-financial corporations at the height of the agitation and near-hysteria of the South Sea bubble, there was a permanent, important and ultimately prosperous outcome: two chartered insurance companies, operating on a large scale and pursuing not the ends of financial speculation but the business of insurance. To this aspect of the early history of the Royal Exchange Assurance we can now turn.

THE CREATION OF AN INSURANCE COMPANY

In the year or so after June 1720 the Royal Exchange Assurance was deeply involved in the financial problems incidental to its original financial commitments. But there was another range of affairs—the organization of its basic structure, the determination of the scope of its underwriting business, and the development of means to manage that business—which also demanded considerable attention, and which were to have much longer-run consequences for the success of the Corporation.

The basic structure of the REA was, of course, embodied in its Charter (and to that extent was identical with the London Assurance's). In this respect, as far as its formal constitution and terminology were concerned, the Corporation was based on the standard model as exemplified in others of the large-scale and well-established companies of seventeenth- and eighteenth-century England. In particular, while there was strict provision for annual General Courts of the Proprietors, the primary responsibility for policy-making and management lay with a Court of Directors meeting at least once a month, and consisting of a Governor, a Sub-Governor, a Deputy-Governor and twenty-four Directors. The Court was to be elected every three years; with respect to both voting and eligibility for election, there were stipulated minimum stockholdings; and, although votes were to some extent proportionate to ownership of stock, there was an upper limit of four votes for any proprietor.[1] In practice, as with nearly all contemporary joint-stock companies, effective control lay with the Court; that is, not with professional managers, but with merchants and financiers for whom membership of the REA was merely one (albeit for many of them an important one) of their varied economic interests. Initially, the Corporation also adopted a characteristic feature of the other leading companies, by having as Governor a man who was in essence a figurehead: Lord Onslow hardly

[1] A minimum of £500 entitled the proprietor to one vote; £1,000 to two votes; £3,000 to three votes; and £5,000 to four votes. To be elected Governor it was necessary to own at least £2,000 stock; the Sub- and Deputy-Governors needed £1,500; and Directors £1,000. For the structure of eighteenth-century corporations, see A. B. DuBois, *The English Business Company after the Bubble Act, 1720–1800* (1938), Chapter II, especially pp. 287–93.

seems to have attended a meeting and was certainly not active in the Corporation's important negotiations with the Treasury in 1720 and 1721. But when his first term of office ended in 1723 he was not re-elected to the Court, and was replaced as Governor by Sir John Williams, the leading merchant who had helped found the Company—and Williams was in turn followed by William Dunster, who was Governor between 1732 and 1756. Both Williams and Dunster, and all their successors, played a direct and active rôle in the control of the Corporation. Indeed, the Governor was, in effect, a Managing Director, and, together with the Sub- and Deputy-Governors, wielded a great deal of authority. This was the case even though all Governors had other, and often onerous, business commitments. William Dunster, for example, who was a member of the Court from 1720 to 1756 and Governor for almost twenty-five years, was also a leading member of the Levant Company and its Deputy-Governor (in reality, its principal Director) from 1722 to 1745.

However, ordinary members of the Court also played a busy and influential part in the Corporation's affairs. In addition to their attendance at the regular weekly meetings of the Court, the Directors served in rotation each week-day on a Committee in Waiting, which was charged with the oversight of routine underwriting tasks, while other important areas of business decision-making were directly supervised by members of the Court grouped into different functional Committees.[1]

The active rôle of Governors and Directors was inherent in the general situation of a monied company like the Royal Exchange Assurance. Deploying a very large capital, with its financial and commercial influence closely affecting a wide variety of other sorts of business, and even its purely underwriting work involving it directly and continuously in the business of overseas trade, the Corporation could only be effectively managed with an awareness of the larger setting within which its underwriting and its investments played their part. Hence, from the very beginning its structure distinguished more or less sharply between members of the Court on one hand, and officials of the Corporation on the other. This distinction—which was one of task and responsibility as well as status—was to become a permanent feature of the firm's organization.[2]

The capital of the new Corporation underwent some changes in the first few years before it, too, was stabilized. It will be remembered that the

[1] For the management organization of the Royal Exchange Assurance in the eighteenth and nineteenth centuries, see below pp. 68-70 and chapter 14.

[2] Below, pp. 353-4. For the types of businessmen who composed the eighteenth-century Court, see below pp. 75-9.

Mines Royal had £1,212,000 of nominal capital (£60,000 of which had been issued in May 1720) divided into £100 units, on each of which £10 had been paid. On 10 September 1720 the Royal Exchange Assurance agreed that every owner of £100 of Mines Royal stock, should 'be admitted to subscribe' £50 in REA stock.[1] This, of course, had the effect of reducing the nominal capital to £606,000—divided into 12,120 shares of £50 each, on which £10 (20 per cent) had been paid. This move may have been partly designed to circumvent the limit of £1·5 million of nominal capital imposed by the Charter, for by reducing the nominal capital it was now possible to issue more. In any event, within two weeks (on 19 and 20 September) the Corporation offered a new subscription, equal to the existing £606,000 of capital, to registered proprietors at a price of 180 per cent (i.e. £90 for a £50 share) to be paid in £10 instalments. However, this subscription, and a consequent attempt at adjustment, went very badly: only £10 was paid, it took months to secure the money, and the Corporation found itself with many unsold shares still on its hands, in spite of its attempts to sell them to the general public. As we have seen, in the middle of a financial crisis, in October 1720, the Corporation had divided its nominal capital into 75,000 shares of which 24,240 (each with £10 paid up) had gone to existing subscribers. But it had proved impossible to market the remainder, so that by 1721 the Corporation had a nominal capital of £1,212,000—with £242,400 paid up (in £50 shares with £10 called up). In that year a further issue of 3,612 shares, to acquire the Sadlers' Hall insurance venture, increased the paid-up capital by £36,120; and in the next three years it was augmented by an extra £85,664 by comparable issues. In March 1724 the partially paid-up capital was converted into fully paid-up stock and a small deduction in 1725 followed by a very substantial increase (by £150,000) in 1725–6 raised the stock to £508,329—of which the Corporation itself owned £63,235. The capital stock remained at this figure for eighty years —until bonus additions were made in the halcyon days of the Napoleonic wars.[2]

As all this implies, it was not only the need to meet its financial commitments to the Government which led to adjustments of the Royal Exchange Assurance's capital structure. These were also necessary in order to make possible the extension of business activity which soon followed its incorporation.

As far as marine insurance was concerned, of course, the REA could rely

---

[1] *REAM*, I, 5 (February 1904), 82.

[2] For these details see, *REAM*, I, 6 (May 1904), 118–19. Compare Scott, *Joint-Stock Companies*, III, 404–10.

1 The Second Royal Exchange, 1669–1838

on a brief but successful tradition: two days after receiving its Charter, on 24 June 1720, it merely took over the underwriting business of the Mines Royal, which had been insuring marine risks for well over a year, the Mines Royal proprietors remaining liable for any loss or profits incurred by the management up to 24 June. Although there are no data about the REA's premium income, it is likely to have been at least as great as that of the London Assurance, which had an annual average premium income (net of returns) of £28,363 in the period 1721-9.[1] Yet, as this and later evidence shows, no matter how successful we judge the experiment of marine insurance by a joint-stock company to have been, it did not have the dire consequences for private underwriting which its opponents had predicted in the stormy controversy of 1718-20. Instead, Lloyd's and the individual underwriters and brokers continued with relative and increasing prosperity. And the two Corporations settled down into a steady, but not spectacular, participation in the market for marine insurance.

At the same time, however, they were also greatly extending the range of their activities by assuming the power to undertake fire and life insurance. Of these, the former was by far the more important. In fact, even before they received their Charters, it must have been obvious that the prospects of fire insurance were considerable: quite apart from the potential demand in an area where private and commercial habits were rapidly changing, there was the fact that (unlike marine underwriting) fire insurance could in effect only be handled on a corporate, or at least co-partnership, basis. Yet by January 1720 there was only a handful of offices, with a somewhat restricted scope, operating in London: the Phenix (established in 1680), the Friendly Society (1684), the Hand-in-Hand (1696), the Sun Fire Office (1710), the Union Fire Office (1714), and the Westminster (1717). As a result, of the ten subscriptions for insurance companies opened in February 1720, eight were concerned with fire insurance. One of these, the Sadlers' Hall Society, claimed that the existing offices (with the exception of the Sun) restricted their activities to London and the immediate vicinity, that all of them had limits on the amounts they would insure, and that all had insufficient security in the way of a paid-up capital fund. By April 1720 the Sun was sufficiently worried about its situation to appoint an Extraordinary Committee to consider the state of the business, and propose 'such methods as may be for the advancement of it'.[2]

---

[1] Guildhall MSS, 8749A/1. In the period 1720-9 (i.e. 9½ years) the REA had a surplus of premiums over losses of £166,066, compared with the London's £140,051.

[2] *Reasons Humbly Offered by the Sadlers Hall Society for their Establishment to Insure Houses and Goods from Fire throughout England, with the Security of a Deposited Joint Stock* (n.d. [1720]; BM. 357b. 3/101); Guildhall MSS, 11931/2 (9 April 1720).

Against this background, it was logical that as early as July 1720, i.e. within a month of receiving their original Charters, both the REA and the London Assurance petitioned the Treasury for further legal authority to issue fire and life policies, and there were even some suggestions that this had been an expectation since their origin.[1] As already indicated, however, although the Treasury was immediately receptive to these proposals, their realization was delayed for some months. The delay was at first caused by the normal formalities attending the issue of a new Charter, including the opposition of the Sun, the Hand-in-Hand and the Union Fire Office and by the Corporations' belated wish to extend their powers to Ireland. Later, however (when existing offices withdrew their objections and said they would not oppose the grant), some account had to be taken of the objections of the Royal Exchange Assurance itself, which preferred a separate Charter and incorporation to the first proposal by the Government, which was to give new powers to the existing Corporation. For, since the Corporation's original Charter provided for its possible revocation upon repayment of the gift to the Government, 'persons will be discouraged from insuring houses and lives in a Corporation thus precarious, and where they cannot have a certain or permanent interest'.[2] This last difficulty arose in January 1721, and held up the issue of a new Charter until April of that year. Meanwhile, however, there had been a fair amount of activity on the part of the REA looking towards a participation in the fire insurance business. First, and at the same time as a new syndicate assumed control of the Sun Fire Office in August and September 1720, the Royal Exchange acquired seven of the Sun's twenty-four shares, at a price of £1,500 each. However, there is no evidence that this was used by the REA group to participate directly in the Sun's management, and the shares were held in trust until 1725, and sold back to the Sun in 1727.[3] The second move came in November 1720, when the Royal Exchange Assurance agreed to take over the Sadlers' Hall Society (formed to undertake fire insurance, but not yet legally incorporated) by exchanging two of its shares, each of £50 nominal value with £10 paid up, for each £1,000 subscription (with £50 paid up)

---

[1] For details of the applications, and subsequent events, see PRO, T.1/233/13 part (i) 285 (28 July 1720); T.1/228/40 (15 September 1720); T.1/233/13 (12 January 1721); *Calendar of Treasury Papers, 1720–1728*, p. 22 (13 October 1720, 18 November 1720). In October 1720 the Sub- and Deputy-Governors of the REA claimed that they and the proprietors had 'always looked upon [the fire Charter] as the best part of their agreement': PRO, T.1/119/1 (5 October 1720). As early as 29 June 1720 the Sun Fire Office had decided to employ a lawyer to oppose 'any Charter that may be intended to insure houses and goods from loss by fire': Guildhall MSS, 11931/2 (29 June 1720).

[2] PRO, T.1/233/3 (12 January 1721).

[3] Dickson, *Sun Insurance Office*, pp. 41–2.

to the Sadlers' Hall.[1] Since there is no evidence that the Sadlers' Hall Society had begun to insure fire risks, it is likely that the acquisition was seen by the REA Directors primarily as an easier way of acquiring assets, by the issue of shares, than open sale on the demoralized stock market. Nevertheless, there was presumably some anticipation of a new line of business implied in the move, even though it did not lead immediately to the opening of a fire insurance department by the Corporation (that came in May 1721). The actual transfer of shares was not made until some time in 1721.[2]

In any case, by the late summer of 1720 it must have been evident that the REA and the London, representing powerful and determined interests, would sooner or later, but inevitably, invade the field of fire insurance. And in the new atmosphere, the Sun Fire Office looked to its defences: on 2 September its Managers acknowledged that there was discontent among its policyholders at the limit (£500) on the sum which could be insured by any one policy—a discontent which had prevented many from insuring with the office 'and given occasion . . . to other persons to attempt the erecting other societies on pretence at least for the purposes designed by the establishers of this office'. As a result, it was immediately agreed to increase the limits on insurances, and to divide each of its twenty-four shares into 100 parts in order to spread the consequent risks among a greater number of shareholders.[3] Meanwhile, in 1720 and 1721, the Hand-in-Hand, the Union and the Westminster had all extended the limits of their operations, originally confined to the City and Westminster, to an area within ten miles radius. Nevertheless, the fact remains that the Royal Exchange and the London Assurances, with powers to insure both buildings and goods throughout the kingdom, looked like forming powerful new elements in the field of fire insurance. Of their six London rivals only the Sun was willing to insure all main classes of property in Britain; the other five confined themselves to London and either to houses (Phenix, Friendly, Hand-in-Hand, Westminster) or to goods (Union).

While the REA and London did not begin to underwrite fire risks until May 1721, they had been actively preparing for this move since at least the previous August. Thus, in that month the London's Court of

---

[1] *The Weekly Journal or British Gazeteer*, 5 November 1720; *The Political State*, xx, 460 (11 November 1720). In fact, the Sadlers' Hall Society had lost a substantial amount of money in speculating in South Sea stock: Scott, *Joint-Stock Companies*, III, 408.

[2] Since the Sadlers' Hall subscription had been for £2 million, 4,000 REA shares (nominal value £50) were involved. In 1721, however, presumably because not all the subscribers to the Sadlers' Hall Society chose to accept the offer, the transaction was recorded as augmenting the REA capital by only £36,120 (i.e. 3,612 shares).

[3] Guildhall MSS, 11931/2 (2 September 1720).

Directors asked its Committee for the Adjustment of Losses 'to consider of a proper method for this Company to insure houses and goods from fire and to treat with any of the present offices for insuring from fire and that they do from time to time endeavour to get the Charter for insurance from fire perfected as soon as possible'. And in October, when the possibility of the award of the Charter seemed even nearer, there was further intensive consideration of 'a method to proceed in the business of insurance from fire'. Subsequently, the Committee was urged to complete its discussions with all possible speed, and, in addition to these business considerations, regular meetings were held with REA representatives on the matter of the Charter. In December 1720 the London appointed an 'Accountant to the Fire Office' and in February 1721 drew up a proposal form and plans for firemen's badges and fire marks for insured houses.[1]

It was, therefore, after months of preparation that the two marine insurance companies received additional Charters, authorizing them to undertake fire and life insurance. This happened on 29 April 1721. The REA Charter was formally issued to 'The Royal Exchange Assurance of Houses and Goods from Fire', which was also given authority to write life insurance. Strictly speaking, this move incorporated a different institution from the 'original' Royal Exchange Assurance. This, however, was a legal fiction designed to separate the ultimate legal condition and sanctions on which marine insurance on the one hand and fire and life insurance on the other were written. In fact, the Charter stipulated that the membership and structure of the two Corporations should be identical and for all effective purposes the two can be considered as one. The Charter gave authority to insure risks in England, Wales and Ireland (powers to transact insurance business in Scotland and 'in all parts and places whatsoever' were not assumed until 1796).

Obviously, the Royal Exchange Assurance, like the London Assurance, had anticipated the Charter by preparing for the new range of business activity involved in fire insurance. And when the two Charters were issued both companies were very far advanced. Within a week the REA proposal forms were ready, and advertisements in early May invited applications for fire insurance, described the terms of insurance, and indicated that the Corporation had already organized a brigade of several engines and fifty-six uniformed firemen. (The London Assurance seems to have taken slightly longer to begin business: on 20 May the Court was still only deciding to choose its firemen so that fire insurance could be started as soon as possi-

---

[1] Guildhall MSS, 8729/1 (5 August, 28 October, 25 and 28 November, 2, 14 and 24 December 1720; 15 and 17 February 1721).

ble.)[1] On 19 May 'Mr. Spelman' was appointed at a salary of £80 as the first 'Clerk to the Fire Office'—'to give his whole time to the work of the office'.[2] Two days earlier 'At a committee for settling the method for carrying on the fire business' the Surveyor's job was described, and it was further agreed to appoint someone, at an annual wage of £30, to set up fire marks and act as a messenger at the Royal Exchange and an attendant at fires with the ordinary firemen. On 22 May it was agreed to pay a 5 per cent commission to agents, and the first agent, a Mr Palmer of 'Ockingham' (subsequently re-named Wokingham) in Berkshire, was appointed. With the appointment of a Standing 'Committee for the Fire Charter', the Corporation had, at long last, completed the process by which, jointly with its sister foundation, it became the first composite insurance office.

[1] [W. N. Whymper], *The Royal Exchange Assurance: An Historical Sketch* (1896), pp. 17–18, 45–7; Guildhall MSS, 8729/1 (20 May 1721).

[2] It may be that he was related to the Henry Spelman who was one of the original Trustees of the Friendly Society Fire Office in 1684, and who was subsequently credited with its initiation: Raynes, *British Insurance*, pp. 82, 84.

3

Growth and Capital in Eighteenth-century Insurance

The fact that the circumstances surrounding the establishment of the Royal Exchange Assurance had such far-reaching implications means that there is a good deal of public information concerning at least some aspects of its very early history, up to 1721. On the other hand, however, because almost all the Corporation's own records were destroyed in 1838, we know much less about the details of its development over the next hundred years or so. Nevertheless, by relating the small amount of information which has survived to our knowledge of other companies we can piece together the broad outline of its history in the period. The first section of this chapter deals with the framework provided by the eighteenth-century evolution of the insurance industry as a whole. The subsequent sections will deal with the contemporaneous development of the Royal Exchange in terms of its underwriting and its capital.

THE GROWTH OF INSURANCE UNDERWRITING IN BRITAIN

The creation of two new and large-scale insurance companies in 1720, and the extension of their powers to include fire and life insurance in 1721, completed the first stage in the growth of the British insurance industry. Together with the existing offices and Lloyd's, they now formed a basic structure which was to last relatively unchanged until new approaches to, and opportunities for, insurance in the late eighteenth and early nineteenth centuries transformed it into a much more modern pattern of organization and competition.

The industrial structure which had been fashioned in the generation up to 1721 was relatively simple. Underwriting was effectively confined to marine, fire and life insurance. Marine insurance was in the hands of the private underwriters at Lloyd's and the Royal Exchange and London Assurances, to the exclusion of any other company or partnership. Fire insurance was in the hands of a very small number of London offices; and there were no new foundations for almost fifty years after 1720.[1] Moreover, the basic business of fire insurance was in effect dominated by the Sun, the Royal Exchange and (in the last decade or so) the Phoenix (founded in 1782). Finally, life insurance in the period was even more restricted: in addition to the Amicable (1706), the Royal Exchange and the London, only the Society for Equitable Assurances for Lives and Survivorships (1762), the Westminster Life Assurance Society (1792) and the Pelican Life Office (1797) were founded before 1800.

In summary, while marine insurance operated within very tight institutional constraints, fire and life underwriting were, for most of the eighteenth century, more or less set in a mould fashioned before 1722. Only towards the end of the period, and then relatively slowly, did the influence of rapid growth in the economy as a whole find some reflection in the insurance business. The reasons for this limited growth of insurance offices in the eighteenth century lay in a combination of commercial, technical and legal factors.

In the case of the underwriting of marine risks, although the habit of insurance was very widely accepted by merchants and shipowners, the establishment of any new companies was effectively prevented by the Act of 1720, which had granted a corporate monopoly of marine insurance to the Royal Exchange and London Assurances. Ironically, therefore, the chartering of the two Companies, which had been so bitterly opposed by the private underwriters in 1719–20, served, in fact, to protect them from further competition. And the enormous increase in the demand for marine insurance implied in the growth of trade (exports and imports roughly doubled between 1700 and 1780, and trebled between 1780 and 1800)[2] and in the higher premiums induced by the frequent wars of the eighteenth century (especially in 1775–83 and 1793–1815) must have largely benefited Lloyd's underwriters—and thereby strengthened the inherited organization of the marine insurance market. This was particularly so because, as we shall see, the two chartered Corporations approached the expanding demand for insurance with such caution as to retain only a very small proportion. In 1810, for example, it was estimated that, together, they accounted for less than 4 per cent of the total sums insured, which were reckoned to be some £160 million.[3]

In contrast to the situation in marine insurance, the progress of life

---

[1] See Relton, *Fire Insurance Companies*, chapters III–IX; Raynes, *British Insurance*, chapters IV, VI, IX.

[2] B. R. Mitchell, *Abstract of British Historical Statistics* (1962), pp. 179–81.

[3] Report of the Select Committee on Marine Insurance, 1810: *PP*, 1810, IV, 4–5; see below, p. 188.

insurance in the eighteenth century was somewhat inhibited by the relative stability of demand and the failure of entrepreneurs and mathematicians to extend and apply existing knowledge to the technical problems of underwriting. For much of the century, in fact, most policies seem to have been for short (usually one-year) terms, and many of them were designed to protect loans or money advanced in the purchase of life interests rather than to secure the welfare of survivors. Hence, at this period individual underwriting was quite common. Private underwriters also participated extensively in the short-term insurances taken out on the lives of public men as a form of gambling—a practice which was declared illegal by an Act of 1774, forbidding 'all such insurances except in cases where persons insuring shall have an interest in the life or death of the person insured'. And in the late 1760s and early 1770s there was a 'mania' for the establishment of mutual friendly societies (offering death as well as sickness benefits).[1]

None of this was the basis for a significant growth in the practice of life insurance. Nevertheless, as the Equitable demonstrated in the last decades of the century, the apparent low level and fixity of demand was not a situation which had to be accepted passively: changes in methods, and particularly the innovation of level premium insurances with the premiums graded by age of entry and calculated from life tables, soon tapped a large, and rapidly growing, demand for life insurance. But for most of the period, the lack of usable life tables and the inability or reluctance of the few existing life offices and individual underwriters to develop systematic actuarial techniques, kept life insurance at a relatively low and primitive level of development. Thus the Amicable, which was organized on a very restricted mutual basis, limited the number of 'proprietors' to 2,000, between the ages of 12 and 45, each paying the same annual premium, and simply divided the benefits annually available between those dying in the year. The Royal Exchange Assurance and the London Assurance merely issued policies for one-year terms at a standard rate of premium (normally £5 or £5. 5s. per £100 insured) irrespective of age, and in the period 1721–83 the Royal Exchange had an average annual premium income of less than £550. Similarly, it is clear that the moderate amount of life insurance underwritten by individuals was also based upon short-run and unsystematic techniques.

On the other hand, the basis for modern actuarial practice (involving calculations of appropriate premiums based on the probability of death at any given age and the rate of interest at which money could be accumulated)

[1] DuBois, *English Business Company*, pp. 37, 231.

had already been established by the development of probability theory in the mid-seventeenth century and its subsequent application to the chances of death and to actual mortality statistics. Crucial in this respect was the work done in the late seventeenth century by the Dutch Grand Pensionary, Johann de Witt (1625–72) on the principles of the sale of Government life annuities, and by the English astronomer Edmond Halley (1656–1742), who produced the first mortality table derived from statistics (of mortality data from Breslau), and used it to calculate the value of life annuities at different ages. Subsequently, the relevant techniques were perfected and systematized by a Huguenot refugee, Abraham de Moivre (1667–1754), who also applied them to the study of annuities.

As a result, by the early eighteenth century mortality data had been systematically related to the solution of problems involving life contingencies. The link between this work and the practice of scientifically based life insurance came in 1756 when a pupil of de Moivre's, James Dodson (c. 1710–57), proposed the establishment of a life insurance society on the equitable principle 'that the price of insurance on lives might be regulated by the age of the persons on whose life the insurance is made'.[1] Although Dodson did not live to see it, such a society came into existence in 1762 with the formation of the Society for Equitable Assurances on Lives and Survivorships on a mutual basis. And the Equitable's important innovating rôle in these respects was cemented by the work of two pioneers of modern actuarial practice, Richard Price (1723–91) and William Morgan (1750–1833).

New foundations for life insurance were laid with the success of the Equitable—particularly from the early 1780s, when it adopted more adequate premiums and mortality tables, based upon Northampton mortality data, and began to declare reversionary bonuses. In 1783 the REA adopted premiums graded according to age at entry; and the Westminster (founded in 1792) and the Pelican (1797), both proprietary companies, modelled their life insurance practice on that of the Equitable.[2] Thus, actuarial techniques appropriate to an extensive life insurance business were both known and employed well before the end of the eighteenth century, and there had been a marked relative increase in underwriting in the generation before 1800. Nevertheless, considering that almost forty years had passed since the Equitable had been established,

[1] Quoted in Raynes, *British Insurance*, p. 124.
[2] The Pelican was promoted by the Directors of a new fire insurance company, the Phoenix, whose Deed of Settlement prevented the commencement of life insurance by requiring the approval of *all* subscribers before the funds could be used for new purposes: DuBois, *English Business Company*, p. 241.

and almost twenty since it had adopted the much more attractive North-ampton Table, there was, in fact, very little life insurance in force at the end of the century. (The Equitable had about £4 million in sums assured; the Royal Exchange had a premium income of just under £28,000.) The most important set of reasons for this relatively slow development must have been connected with the reluctance of entrepreneurs to adopt a large and somewhat technical innovation, and in the slowness with which the habit of insurance spread among potential policyholders. In addition, such development as did occur was retarded by the desire of life insurance pro-moters to secure the advantages of formal incorporation. In two instances they spent fruitless years in seeking the Charters which, since the Bubble Act, were the only legitimate way of formal incorporation.

The Equitable, for example, petitioned for a Charter in 1757 (and was opposed by the Amicable, the Royal Exchange and the London). Yet the Law Officers did not report until 1761—and then reported adversely. Con-sequently, the promoters formed the Society, in 1762, under a Deed of Settlement, which adapted the concept of private partnership to the needs of a company.[1] Similarly, the Westminster sought incorporation by a Parliamentary Bill in 1789 and only when this was turned down in the Lords did its founders use a Deed of Settlement, in 1792—this time to establish a conventional proprietary company.[2]

In the case of fire insurance the demand from policyholders and the techniques needed to satisfy it already existed in the early eighteenth century. More than this, its potential market—i.e. the stock of private and commercial buildings and commodities—was visibly increasing through-out the period as the economy developed, so that the variety as well as the extent of the demand for insurance expanded. The evidence for the actual amount of insurance is unfortunately very poor until the 1780s. Before then, there is information only about the premium income of three offices —the Sun, Royal Exchange and London—although they must have been moderately representative of main trends. In the case of the Sun, which soon rose to a pre-eminent position, the growth of premium income was very rapid—from £15,000 in 1730 to £106,000 in 1780. In the same period the REA's premiums rose somewhat more slowly, from £6,000 to £25,000, and the London's from £5,000 to £7,000.[3] Thus, between them the three offices increased their premium income almost sixfold in the fifty years

[1] Below, pp. 59–61.
[2] In 1799 the Globe actually secured an Act enabling the King to charter it for life and fire insurance but could not get official approval for its draft Charter.
[3] Dickson, *Sun Insurance Office*, pp. 74, 301–2; Guildhall MSS, 8749A/1. (Figures rounded to nearest £1,000.)

1730–80. Although this no doubt reflects the growth of industry, domestic trade and housing, it is likely that a significant part of the expansion was attributable to the growth of the habit of fire insurance—i.e. a change in attitudes. By the early 1780s, when taxation data (an *ad valorem* duty was payable on fire insurance policies from 1782) first become available, sums

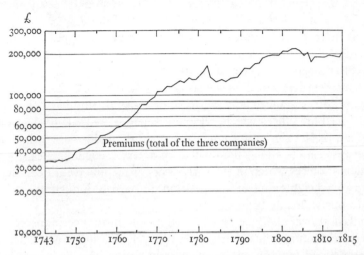

Fig. 3.1: Total fire insurance premiums, 1743–1815: Royal Exchange Assurance, Sun Fire Office, London Assurance

(Sources: REA Archives; P. G. M. Dickson, *The Sun Insurance Office, 1710–1960* (1960), pp. 301–2; Guildhall MSS, 8749A/1.)

insured in England and Wales were just under £150 million. Over the next twenty years, however, the amount of insurance in force rose by only about two-thirds (it was just over £250 million in 1805 in England and Wales)—which was from one viewpoint a relatively small increase considering that the period was one of heightened industrialization and inflation, and that previous twenty-year periods had apparently witnessed more rapid increases. On the other hand, it is likely that the growth of insurance more or less matched the rate of increase of domestic capital, although it was estimated that in 1802 only just over one-third of insurable property in Great Britain and Ireland was actually insured (£223 million out of £613 million[1]).

---

[1] The estimate was made by Sir Frederick Morton Eden, founder of the Globe and published in his *On the Policy and Expediency of Granting Insurance Charters* (1806), pp. 70–83. The data (with arithmetical errors corrected) are reproduced in Cornelius Walford, 'On Fire and Fire Insurance', *JSS*, XL (1877), 403–4.

Quite apart from the fact that the increase in insurance which did take place was far from negligible, the last twenty years or so of the eighteenth century also saw the beginnings of important structural changes in the industry. First, there was a check to the growing dominance of the Sun among established London offices: after much more than doubling in 1760–80, its premium income increased by less than 25 per cent in 1780–1800, while that of the REA trebled, jumping from £25,000 in 1780 to £75,000 in 1800. Second, a powerful new competitor appeared, with the foundation of the Phoenix in 1782—soon to be followed by the British Fire Office in 1799, and by a rash of vigorous rivals in the opening years of the nineteenth century. Third, in the last generation of the eighteenth century the spread of insurance and the nature of demand stimulated the growth of provincial fire offices which, although small in the scale of their operation, comprised a significant new element in the industry.[1] Although the industry was still, in fact, dominated by a very few companies, the proliferation of offices which in the early years of the nineteenth century was to lead to a heightening of competition and a new industrial structure, had obviously already begun.[2]

Looked at over the long run, therefore, the insurance industry in the eighteenth century illustrates a pattern of development which was characteristic of much economic change in the period. To a large extent it was dependent on the evolution of a demand for its 'product'—a demand which went hand-in-hand with growth of output, trade and population. In addition, however, aspects of its development were closely related to changes in social habits—as with the rising tendency to insure houses and goods against fire, and the gradual increase in the demand for life insurance. Moreover, parts of the industry were ultimately transformed by innovation: notably in actuarial techniques, which from the 1760s onwards slowly but surely transformed life insurance into a much more widespread and modern practice. Above all, perhaps, as with industry and trade in general, it is possible to detect a turning-point in the early 1780s. For at that time the Equitable adopted both the more attractive Northampton Table and the modern system of reversionary bonuses;[3] the foundation of the Phoenix introduced the first serious competitor into the field of fire insurance for sixty years; and the REA adapted its Life

---

[1] Relton, *Fire Insurance Companies*, pp. 204–51.

[2] Below, pp. 121 ff.

[3] The historian of the Equitable speaks of 1780 and 1781 as being 'decisive years when the very structure of life assurance was formed'. Maurice Edward Ogborn, *Equitable Assurances: The Story of Life Assurance in the Experience of the Equitable Life Assurance Society, 1762–1962* (1962), p. 111.

Department to the new pattern of demand by issuing whole-life policies at premiums graded by the age at entry. The innovation of bonuses was particularly important: individual policies were now credited with a proportionate share of the surplus (above liabilities) accumulated in the life fund of the Equitable. As a result this form of policy became much more attractive. Stemming partly from these events, the last twenty or thirty years of the century form an important watershed in the history of insurance—as they do in the history of the British economy as a whole. With respect to marine insurance, this was largely a matter of responding to a very rapid acceleration of Britain's growing overseas trade, although the 1720 Act prevented corporations (other than the Royal Exchange and London) from taking advantage of the new opportunities; life insurance, by contrast, was completely changed by new actuarial methods, and placed for the first time on a modern basis; and fire insurance, even though not enjoying an appreciably higher growth rate (the principal spurt in fire insurance occurred after the 1730s), came to be an accepted habit, while the amount of insurance continued to increase and the number and distribution of offices developed right away from the unchanging and small-scale pattern of the mid-eighteenth century.

The increase in the number of insurance companies which accompanied the growth in fire and life insurance may at first sight seem surprising in light of the Bubble Act of 1720. For the Act, apart from establishing the Royal Exchange and London Assurances, had been specifically designed to prevent the flotation of all unauthorized joint-stock companies. By its terms, no group (unless in possession of an enabling Royal Charter or Act of Parliament) could act as a corporate body (i.e. as a body formally endowed with a legal personality) or issue transferable shares.

In fact, however, the Bubble Act was rendered a dead letter through the ingenuity of lawyers and the irresistible pressure of businessmen towards a convenient and flexible means of concentrating and controlling capital—a pressure in which the development and needs of fire and life insurance played a critical rôle.[1] The means to this end was the curious legal device of the unincorporated company: a large partnership which secured most of the advantages of incorporation—ownership of property, perpetual succession, unified action, transferability of shares, even limited liability—by utilizing the concept of the trust and operating within the

[1] For the eighteenth-century development of corporate forms of business organization, and the part played by insurance offices, see DuBois, *English Business Company*, chapters I and III. For this and later developments, also see C. A. Cooke, *Corporation, Trust and Company* (1950), pp. 84–97, 128, 167–8, 187; B. C. Hunt, *The Development of the Business Corporation in England, 1800–1867* (1936), chapters 1 and 2.

jurisdiction of the Law of Equity. The proprietors of such a company merely subscribed to a Deed of Settlement, which established the constitution of the company, committed their capital to a body of trustees and (rarely in the eighteenth, much more frequently in the nineteenth century) limited their individual liabilities to their shares in the capital stock.[1] Although still a partnership in the eyes of the Common Law, such an institution, operated by trustees within Chancery jurisdiction, was in effect a joint-stock company, since it could secure continuity of existence, the right to have property held on its behalf by trustees, and the right to issue transferable shares. Still being common-law partnerships, unincorporated companies might find the process of going to law (for example, to recover debts) an unwieldy one, since all shareholders might have to be joined as plaintiffs or defendants.[2] But even this could be mitigated by arbitration; by ensuring that trustees could bring or defend actions and suits relating to documents signed, or property held, by them; or, in the last resort, as happened in the early nineteenth century, by private Acts of Parliament empowering the group to sue or be sued in the name of one of its officers.

The basic groundwork for this complicated but very effective arrangement had been established in the seventeenth century. In the eighteenth century the needs of business and the skills of lawyers extended and settled the details of internal organization. By the late eighteenth century even the restrictions on free transferability of shares, which had earlier been introduced into Deeds of Settlement in the shadow of the Bubble Act, were omitted. Indeed, so widespread and accepted did the device become that there are instances of the Crown's Law Officers, in spite of the presence of the Bubble Act on the Statute Book, recommending that groups of promoters should make use of it. This happened in 1761, when they responded to the Equitable's petition for a Charter by asserting that if the promoters were confident of success 'there is an easy method of making the experiment, by entering into a voluntary partnership, of which there are several instances now subsisting in this business of insuring'. And the Act introducing the stamp duty on fire insurance in 1782 freely

---

[1] By contrast, the formal liability of stockholders in the Royal Exchange Assurance was limited to the amount of authorized stock (£1·5 million), and there were no procedures by which creditors of such a Corporation could sue its proprietors. Admittedly, it was theoretically possible for the General Court to make unlimited calls on capital to meet debts. But the competitive claim made by the Phoenix (whose proprietors had an unlimited liability) in 1787, that 'the holders of shares in such Corporations stand sheltered from any responsibility beyond the extent of their chartered capital', was strictly true. (DuBois, *English Business Company*, p. 96.)

[2] After the 1777 Annuity Act they were also at a disadvantage if they wished to sell annuities since they would have to register the names of all proprietors each time they transacted an item of such business.

acknowledged that a 'great part of the business of insurance against loss by fire is transacted at offices kept by companies not incorporated', and made provision for the grant of licences to them.[1]

In the course of the eighteenth century, therefore, there were no effective legal limits on the use of a joint-stock organization wherever businessmen felt it was appropriate. Any group of promoters, other than those concerned with marine insurance, could secure virtually all the business advantages which the Royal Exchange Assurance had derived from its formal incorporation by Royal Charter. And, while unincorporated companies sprang up in a wide variety of fields, it is significant that they were particularly popular among fire and life insurance offices—and that their popularity in this field often provided the basis for the perfection of their legal and business utility.

THE DEVELOPMENT OF THE ROYAL EXCHANGE ASSURANCE

The development of the Royal Exchange Assurance in the eighteenth century conformed to the trends described in the previous section. In particular, as is illustrated in Table 3.1, the Corporation's fire and life premium income rose reasonably sharply only towards the end of the period.

Nothing is known about the level of marine premium income until the 1760s, although on the average net premiums seem to have exceeded losses by about £14,000 annually between 1720 and 1760.[2] Thenceforth, premiums generally rose, while fluctuating with the incidence of the American War of Independence and the Napoleonic Wars. By the last thirty years of the century the profitability of marine insurance for the Corporation did not move proportionately to total income, for it seems to have reached its peak in the early years of war (i.e. 1776–80 and 1791–5) before premium incomes, and, apparently, losses reached their heights. Institutionally, there was hardly any change in the Corporation's marine

---

[1] DuBois, *English Business Company*, pp. 30, 74.

[2] In the case of the London Assurance there are annual data on marine insurance premiums in the eighteenth century (Guildhall MSS, 8749A/1). The annual averages of premiums net of returns in particular decades are:

1720–9	£26,500	1770–9	£18,838
1730–9	£20,191	1780–9	£32,230
1740–9	£55,837	1790–9	£52,241
1750–9	£54,690	1800–9	£56,420
1760–9	£33,719	1810–19	£128,454

A. H. John, 'The London Assurance Company and the Marine Insurance Market of the Eighteenth Century', *Economica* (May 1958), p. 130, has a useful graph of that Corporation's marine premium income.

insurance business in the period. Given this, and the shortage of quantitive information, there is relatively little to be said about its underwriting activities for the first century of its existence. Rather, its problems can best be dealt with in the context of marine insurance as a whole in the early nineteenth century.[1]

TABLE 3.1. *REA marine, fire and life premiums and losses, 1721–1810*

(Annual averages, rounded to nearest £100)

	Marine[a]		Fire		Life	
	Gross premiums	Premiums less losses and returns	Gross premiums	Losses and returns	Gross premiums	Losses and returns
1721–4	n.a.	16,600[b]	2,600	1,800	1,100	800
1725–31	n.a.		5,700	2,400	500	700
1732–5	n.a.	13,400[c]	5,400	800	600	500
1736–40	n.a.		4,700	1,000	400	400
1741–5	n.a.		4,800	800	500	200
1746–50	n.a.	12,200[d]	4,500	1,700	200	600
1751–5	n.a.		6,800	3,500	300	[14]
1756–60	n.a.		9,300	7,300	400	200
1761–5	36,600	6,100	10,700	5,300	500	100
1766–70	18,400	5,700	14,700	8,400	500	[27]
1771–5	23,000	8,100	19,200	6,400	500	[10]
1776–80	76,500	29,700	20,300	9,400	600	100
1781–5	116,500	13,300	29,100[e]	12,100[e]	2,900	—
1786–90	73,900	15,800	28,800	19,400	14,500	—
1791–5	155,200	52,600	45,800	32,700	23,000	—
1796–1800	275,100	22,000	64,000	35,100	26,300	—
1801–5	165,000	(–4,700)	79,800	50,900	41,000	—
1806–10	220,200	17,300	72,900	48,200	66,400	—

[a] Marine premiums include returns, which in the period 1796–1815 averaged just over 25 per cent of gross premiums.
[b] 1720–9.   [c] 1730–9.   [d] 1740–58.   [e] Average for 1780–3.

In the case of its fire insurance business, the Charter for which had seemed of such critical importance in 1720-1, the REA was apparently content with a relatively low level of operations for thirty years. Indeed, the trend of its fire insurance business closely approximated to the conventional view of the industrial revolution as a sharp discontinuity occurring in the late eighteenth century. After beginning on a very small scale, its annual premium income averaged only about £5,000 between 1725 and 1750—and even displayed a slightly falling tendency, touching

[1] See below, pp. 199–206.

an average of £4,487 in 1746–50. There was some increase in the 1750s, but, even so, fire premiums averaged only £10,713 in 1761–5, compared with over £50,000 for the Sun. Thenceforth, however, and in contrast to the latter office, the Royal Exchange maintained the growth rate of premium income, which increased by about 50 per cent in most decades,

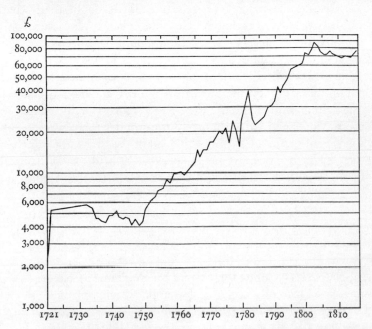

Fig. 3.2: REA fire insurance premiums, 1721–1815[1]

(Source: REA Archives.)

and more than doubled in the 1790s, when the combination of continuing industrialization and war-time inflation seems to have led to a substantial increase in business. By the end of the century its annual premium income averaged some £64,000—and in 1803 attained a peak of £87,993, which was not to be exceeded for another thirty-six years. (The business and competitive details of this expansion will be dealt with in the next chapter.)

The Corporation's life insurance business in the eighteenth century illustrated in an even more marked way the trends of long-run stability, even stagnation, followed by an abrupt increase in the last decades. Admittedly, there was a reasonably promising start: gross premiums (i.e.

[1] The accounting year ended in April of the year indicated. Data for 1721–32 represent annual averages.

including returns) averaged some £1,100 for the first three years (May 1721 to April 1724).[1] After that, however, there was a decline, and for the next fifty years annual gross premiums exceeded £1,000 in only two years (1765 and 1771), and fell below £200 in six of them. Altogether, in the years 1721–69 the average life income was merely £479. (There was a very slight increase in the 1770s.) There can be little doubt that, whatever other causes were at work, the fact that life policies were issued only on an annual basis, and at a £5 per cent premium irrespective of age (an upper limit of 60 was imposed in 1752), seriously limited the development of the Department. And, conforming to this unscientific procedure, the Corporation did not credit the account with interest, and subtracted from each year's premium income the losses and returns for the same period. With these results and attitudes, it is little wonder that, in opposing the Equitable's petition for a Charter at the end of the 1750s, the REA should bring forward its own disheartening experience as evidence of the market's lack of potential. In the thirty-eight years between 1721 and 1759 its *total* gross life premium income had been only £18,446—and out of this it had had to pay £15,944 in losses and returns of premium, quite apart from the costs of management. In any case, returns are likely to have reduced the premiums to less than £11,000, or an annual average of just under £300.

In the course of the controversy about the Equitable's Charter, the Royal Exchange was apparently accused of charging 'unreasonable' premiums. Certainly, the flat rate of £5 per cent had little defensible basis, and when it became clear that the Equitable's new system of life insurance, based on mortality tables and whole-life premiums, was a success, the Corporation had to look to its own position. The premium table originally proposed for the Equitable in 1756 had, in fact, produced rates *below* £5 for all ages up to 43;[2] and its premiums were even further reduced in 1781, with the adoption of the Northampton Table. This Table indicated premiums very much below what the Corporation was charging in 1782: for a one-year policy the premium was less than £2. 10s. od. per cent for all ages up to 47 and for a whole-life policy less than £5 for all ages up to 53. Thus, even bearing in mind the fact that the Equitable, with a commendable, but quite excessive caution, charged an extra 15 per cent for safety until 1786, the

---

[1] Relatively little is known about early policy conditions. In 1727 the Court resolved that life policies should normally include a clause excluding death from 'suicide or execution by law' —although the Committee in Waiting was given authority to dispense with this requirement in particular cases, as happened in 1781, when it was agreed that a policy for £6,000 on the life of the King of Poland should include the risk of dying from 'the hands of Justice'.

[2] Ogborn, *Equitable Assurances*, p. 32.

Royal Exchange Assurance's business was seriously threatened. And, presumably as a direct result of this move by the Equitable, the REA itself took the plunge towards more scientific life insurance in December 1783, adopting 'a table of calculated premiums assuring for the whole of life and requiring accumulation at interest'. In future, insurances were to be issued on an annual basis, or for periods up to seven years or for the whole of life.[1]

In agreeing to adopt this innovation, however, the Treasury Committee tempered its enterprise with extreme circumspection. First, some basic conditions were confirmed or amended. Policies were normally to be confined to lives between 10 and 60 years old, and no proposal for £1,000 was to be accepted by the Committee in Waiting without the consent of the whole Court. Lives proposed for insurance were to appear before the Court or the relevant agent; and if they could not do so, the policy was to be issued only after other proof of the state of their health and the payment of an extra premium. For whole-life policies the additional once-for-all charge for non-appearance was £1 per cent on the sum insured, paid with the first premium. And duelling was added to suicide and execution at the hands of the Law as an exception from cover.

But the most striking indication of the Treasury Committee's extraordinary caution was the stipulation that Royal Exchange Assurance premium rates should be at least 20 per cent higher than those of the Equitable! Hence, although the Corporation's newly introduced premium table gave rates of less than £5 (the former flat rate irrespective of age) for all ages up to 42, they were too high for a continuing and long-run increase in life business. The relative youth of the Equitable may have shielded the REA for a while, but sooner or later some reduction was inevitable, and may have come within a few years. For in December 1799, when the Royal Exchange finally brought its rates down to a level directly based on the Northampton Table, the announcement that 'the Company has made a further reduction on their life rates' implied that there had also been an earlier reduction. These new rates, which brought the Corporation into line with the Equitable, came into effect on 1 January 1800. They coincided with those used by *all* offices by the end of the first decade of the century.[2]

[1] The London Assurance's life business had an even less impressive record in the eighteenth century: not only was its premium income low, but there were several years (1785, 1793–5, 1805–7) when it received no premiums at all! It finally adopted an actuarial basis for its business in 1809: Drew, *London Assurance*, p. 285.

[2] In 1810, Francis Baily (*An Account of the Several Life-Assurance Companies Established in London*, see the second edition [1811], pp. 30–1) pointed out that all life offices had virtually the

It so happened, however, that the new system had had an immediate and beneficial effect on the life business of the Royal Exchange in the early 1780s (i.e. even at a time when its premiums were about 20 per cent higher than those of the Equitable). By the year ending April 1785 its premiums had leaped to £6,519—more than the total premiums in the entire decade of the 1770s. Premiums continued to rise until the end of the century, when, in 1800, they stood at £27,616. There had been a slight decrease in 1798, which might well have explained the decision, in 1799, to introduce lower premiums from the next January. Thenceforth, for some years, as in the previous two decades, the REA life business continued to grow at a reasonably healthy rate. This was the case even though it only issued non-profit policies, in contrast to the Equitable which, as a mutual office, offered bonus participation in its profits to its members. The continued strength of the REA Life Department (even in the 1780s and 1790s, when its non-profit policies were issued at higher premiums than the Equitable's with-profit policies) was presumably due to the fact that, in this early period of life insurance, policyholders were frequently as much concerned with the providential aspect of insurance and with the age, wealth and security of the office with which they dealt, as with the possibility of earning profits on an investment.[1]

One other eighteenth-century development related to life insurance should be mentioned here. In 1793 the Corporation secured an Act of Parliament empowering it 'to grant, purchase and sell annuities upon or for lives'. Up to that time the granting of annuities had been effectively confined either to the Government itself or to individuals. The justification for this step, embodied in the preamble, was that annuity business was too much 'in the hands of improper persons, who make an exorbitant gain thereby' and that it would be advantageous 'if a known office, long established, were empowered to do so'. There was, apparently, some opposition to the proposal, but the day was carried by the Corporation's

---

same premium rates, varying only by 'a trifling difference of penny or two-pence per cent'. Examples of the premium rates per £100 for a whole-life policy were:

Age	REA 1783			REA 1800			Equitable 1786		
	£	s.	d.	£	s.	d.	£	s.	d.
20	3	0	0	2	3	6	2	3	7
30	3	13	6	2	13	3	2	13	5
40	4	14	0	3	8	0	3	7	11
50	6	5	0	4	10	9	4	10	8

In 1800 the Corporation also charged ¼ per cent (i.e. 5s. per £100 insured) as 'admission money'.

[1] For the ultimate significance of with-profits policies see below, pp. 133–4.

arguments that it had a secure capital; that, being already established, it could 'carry on business at less expense than any new society'; and that 'there is yet no public society possessed of known funds who are engaged in this business, which is now carried on generally by private contracts, when frequently the contractor on one part makes exorbitant advantages of the necessity of the other party'.[1]

The fear that those granting annuities might be exploiting their creditor position, which was an important reason for empowering the Royal Exchange to undertake the business as a possible counterweight to private capitalists, was also reflected in the conditions imposed upon the Corporation. The table of rates had to be displayed in a conspicuous place in the office; monies received had to be invested in Government securities, and could not be touched until the death of the annuitant; and certification of the death and burial of each annuitant had to be advertised in the *London Gazette* and available for inspection at the office.

By 1800 the Corporation's income from annuities was some £15,000 (of which £7,450 was received in the year ending April 1795), and it was paying £1,174 in life annuities. By 1816 (by which time the other leading life offices had secured similar powers) annuity payments had risen to £4,591, although they then levelled off until the mid-1820s. In 1810, however, an informed commentator criticized the REA's annuity rates (and those of all the other leading offices—which had the same rates), since they were not based upon published observations: 'neither do they agree with any probable rate of human mortality; but seem to have been formed at random, without any regard to the true principles of the science'. The values for lives under 50 were said to be 'much too low', and those above too high—while, compared with the Government rates set in 1808, all values were said to be too high, thus acting as an effective disincentive to purchase an annuity at the Royal Exchange.[2]

At the turn of the century, therefore, the Corporation still undertook only a moderate life insurance, and a quite small annuity, business. It had nevertheless adjusted its life-underwriting procedures to the demands of scientific insurance; and, in adopting premium rates based on the Northampton Table, it began its nineteenth-century career on the same

[1] *Considerations on, and answers to, the reasons presented to the Honourable the House of Commons against the passing of a Bill brought in by the Royal Exchange Company for the granting, purchasing, or selling annuities upon, or for lives* (1793). The Act established the Royal Exchange Assurance Annuity Company, which was in practice identical with the original Royal Exchange Assurance.

[2] Baily, *Life Assurance Companies*, pp. 7–8. For the difference between the offices' annuity rates and the Government's, see below, p. 134 n..

basis as other proprietary offices. Only after another generation would it begin to feel the need for an even greater adjustment of procedures.

A MONIED COMPANY: CAPITAL AND CONTROL IN THE EIGHTEENTH CENTURY

When it was established in 1720 the Royal Exchange Assurance was immediately, and rightly, classed among the great monied companies which excited such criticism and admiration in the economic world of the early eighteenth century. Together with its sister Corporation, the London Assurance, the REA was, in fact, the last to join the ranks which included at their very apex the Bank of England, the East India Company and the South Sea Company, and, somewhat lower down, the Hudson's Bay Company, and the Royal African Company. Each, of course, carried on a different type of business and to that extent played a different type of rôle in the contemporary world of finance and commerce. Nevertheless, each embodied a large concentration of capital in an economy where such concentrations were rare and remarkable; and, together with the huge amount of Government securities, their stocks and shares dominated the Stock Exchange until well into the nineteenth century.

The fact that the REA was a large-scale institution as well as an important insurance office naturally influenced the composition of its Court of Directors, in the same way that it had influenced the composition of the group that had originally promoted the Corporation. Throughout the eighteenth century (and beyond), the Court represented some of the most influential commercial and financial elements in the City of London.[1] Leading merchants and bankers served as Governors and Directors not merely because of the intrinsic rewards and attractions of helping to direct the fortunes of a leading City company, but because the activities of the Corporation—the underwriting of large marine risks, the insurance of warehouses and goods against fire, the extensive dealings in securities— naturally impinged directly upon the business of merchants and trading companies, banks and warehouse firms.

In fact, all important aspects of underwriting, as well as the funds of the Corporation, were directly supervised by the Governors and Directors. Thus, the responsibility for accepting or rejecting even routine proposals for insurance lay with the Committee in Waiting, on which all Directors served in rotation, and which sat daily (at the end of the century it met from 11.45 a.m. to 4 p.m., except on Saturday, when it finished at 2 p.m.).

[1] Below, pp. 75–9.

And, in May 1721, at the outset of the fire business, Mr Spelman, who as 'Clerk to the Fire Office' was the official responsible for fire insurance, was ordered to secure the approval of the Committee in Waiting before making out any policy. He was also expected to keep the Committee fully informed, in writing, about all matters relating to the fire business. Nor was this general situation confined to fire insurance: with respect to the marine and life business as well, the Governors and Directors, whether in the Committee in Waiting, in the specialist marine or fire Committees, or in the Treasury Committee, fulfilled the rôle of underwriting managers. (A special Life Committee was only appointed when life insurance grew large enough to warrant it, in the nineteenth century.) Not until the nineteenth century introduced new elements of scale and technical complexity was this task assumed by salaried officials. On the other hand, it was not always easy for Directors to act as underwriters collectively. Hence, at the London Assurance, which was organized along similar lines to the REA, a member of the Court was appointed to act as 'Extraordinary Attendant' on a full-time basis at a stipend of £350 (in addition to his Director's fee). This was in 1741, and the arrangement lasted until 1831, when the post was superseded by various departmental managers.[1] In the case of the Royal Exchange Assurance, the absence of surviving records makes it impossible to know how far it, too, concentrated some of the Court's authority in an individual at an early date—although certainly by 1783 a secretarial official was regularly elected to the Court and nominated as 'Sitting Director' with explicit responsibility for marine underwriting, together with some responsibility for the clerical establishment and (at least in the early nineteenth century) for negotiating on behalf of the Corporation on such matters as fire insurance tariffs.

In general terms, however, the real authority for underwriting continued to lie with the Court and its substructure of Committees—including the Treasury Committee, which controlled funds and investments, the Committee of Averages, which looked after marine business, the 'Committee for the Fire Business', and the Committee of Accounts. As was the case with the other Companies, the REA also instituted an elaborate system of fines for non-attendance or late arrival at Court and Committees.[2] Clearly the Governors' and Directors' 'allowances'—£250 and £150 respectively—although by no means trivial sums in the context of

[1] Drew, *London Assurance*, pp. 114, 158.
[2] For the detailed workings of this Committee structure in the early nineteenth century, see below, 354–9.

eighteenth-century prices, were not paid to the holders of sinecures. The Court consisted of working Directors.

The staff controlled by the Court was very small, and stayed small well into the nineteenth century.[1] Indeed, as late as 1838, the first date for which exact information survives, there were less than fifty officials, clerks and messengers employed at the Royal Exchange. And for much, if not all, of the eighteenth century, it is likely that the number of clerks was less than the number of men on the Court (twenty-seven). The London Assurance was able to start business with a Secretary, an Accountant, three clerks, a doorkeeper and a messenger, although it apparently added a few more clerks by November 1720;[2] and presumably at that time the REA operated on the same scale. A Court Minute of 1737 implies that there were only two clerks in the Fire Office—which is not surprising in view of the small premium income. By the 1770s, however, there were at least five fire clerks, and, one assumes, more than that in each at least of the marine insurance and accounts departments. It is perhaps relevant to note that in 1793 the Sun, with a much larger fire (but no life or marine) business, employed twenty-five clerks,[3] and this was probably near to the Royal Exchange's establishment at the time. Certainly by the early 1790s the great expansion of fire business had obliged the Corporation to employ more clerks, and in the summer of 1792 the 'Fire Office' was reorganized into Town and Country Departments: their first clerks sharing the penny in the pound formerly allowed to the first clerk in the single office.

As was still the case in the nineteenth century, the clerk's position in an eighteenth-century monied company like the Royal Exchange was one of high prestige and relative security—even though it was not adequately formalized, nor were the conditions and expectations acknowledged, until the later period.

There seems to have been neither fixed salary scales nor automatic increases in the eighteenth century. On the other hand, there were frequent payments for overtime and, apparently, generous 'gratuities' (i.e. bonuses). Further, clerks were for much of the time apparently allowed to carry on another trade or employment—although this was forbidden, without permission, in 1792. (In that year three clerks were given permission to engage

---

[1] Since the basic departmental and clerical structure of the REA changed very little throughout much of the eighteenth and nineteenth centuries, the organization of the office establishment will be considered in the framework of the nineteenth century, for which more detailed information is available: below, pp. 359 ff., 375–6. For a useful and detailed eighteenth-century comparison, see Dickson, *Sun Insurance Office*, chapter 3.

[2] Guildhall MSS, 8729/1 (8 July and 23 November 1720).

[3] Dickson, *Sun Insurance Office*, p. 58.

in the business of a coal merchant, a shopkeeper and a corn chandler, respectively.)

As with all other leading joint-stock companies, the attractiveness and scarcity of these clerical positions were in part indicated by the fact that appointments to a clerkship were in the gift of the Governors and Directors in rotation. Hours of work were not very demanding by contemporary standards, although, with a two- or three-hour break in the day, they were somewhat bizarre. In 1786, for example, the Court ordered that the normal 'day' for clerks should be from 10 a.m. to 2.45 p.m. and 5 p.m. to 7.30 p.m. Arrangements were made for individual clerks to be in the office all the time by staggering the $2\frac{1}{4}$-hour dinner break and in 1788 it was also arranged that two clerks should be in attendance from 9 a.m. until 4 p.m. Ultimately, in 1794, the somewhat old-fashioned and certainly inconvenient practice of a 'split' day was abandoned, and the Court set the hours of attendance at from 9 a.m. until 4.15 p.m. At the same time, however, it rescinded an order of 1768, which had granted the request of officers and clerks to keep, 'one in each office', the same holidays as the staff of the Bank of England, when business permitted.[1]

The long-run capital structure of the enterprise within which these clerks worked, and which the Court controlled, was stabilized within a very few years of its incorporation. As we have seen, from July 1726 the Corporation's stock stood at £508,329 throughout the eighteenth century (bonus issues in 1807, 1809 and 1811 raised the stock to £768,264). However, although its stock represented a capital of over half a million pounds, this was by no means the amount of money which the REA could deploy in support of its business activities. For one thing, £150,000 had been paid away to the Crown as the price of the Charter (it appeared as an asset until April 1796, when it was written off, quite appropriately if belatedly, under the heading of 'bad debts'); secondly, the Corporation itself owned some of its own stock valued at £63,062; and thirdly, in spite of initial low estimates there had been considerable expense involved in the formation of the Corporation. As late as 1734 (the first year for which a balance sheet is available) this last item stood at £39,000 in the books, having been written down at an unknown rate since the early 1720s. Hence, in 1734, the actual available capital was only £256,267—which had been augmented to £341,892 by accumulated assets in the underwriting accounts.

The ownership of the Corporation's stock fluctuated in size: in 1732, for example, there were 239 owners of stockholdings of £500 or more (the

[1] The Bank was closed on about forty 'holydays' in the year: John Giuseppi, *The Bank of England: A History from its Foundation in 1694* (1966), pp. 35, 100-1.

lower limit for voting rights); by 1762 this had risen to 321; but by 1790 it had fallen to 194. There was, of course, a reasonably large number of stockholders with relatively small holdings: in 1790, for example, there were seventy-three owners of less than £500 each (the equivalent numbers for 1732 and 1762 are not known), forty of between £500 and £999, and ninety-four (about a third of the total) of between £1,000 and £1,499. On the other hand, just under 13 per cent of all stockholders in 1790 each owned over £3,000 of stock; and since the average holding of these twenty-one individuals must have been at least £4,000 and most likely more, it is safe to assume that they controlled about a fifth of the Corporation's publicly owned capital.[1]

From one viewpoint, the REA was not, initially, a profitable venture. For, as is shown by the figures of capital and assets already given, over £500,000 had been invested in it in the 1720s, and assets in 1734, even including accumulated profits, were less than £350,000, after allowance for the costs of securing the Charter and commencing business. Indeed, it was not until the late 1770s that assets net of the £150,000 paid to the Government exceeded the original amount of paid-up capital. On the other hand, if we ignore the amount paid for the Charter, the Corporation made a profit on the capital retained in the business, and paid a steady if unspectacular dividend: 5 per cent annually in 1726–8, over 4 per cent for most of the 1730s, 3 or 3½ per cent in the 1750s and 1760s (a period of very low interest rates generally), 4 per cent in the 1770s, and 5 per cent rising to 7½ per cent in the 1790s. By 1806–15, the last and very profitable years of the Napoleonic Wars, it regularly paid 10 per cent, quite apart from substantial stock bonuses of 20 per cent in 1807 and 1809 and 10 per cent in 1811.

In terms of its underwriting business, the basis for the Corporation's profits in the eighteenth century lay in marine, and to a somewhat smaller

---

[1] These data are calculated from printed lists of stockholders entitled to vote and stand for election. A more detailed breakdown of numbers gives the following:

REA: number of stockholders, 1732–1801

Stockholding	1752	1762	1790	1801
£5,000 and over	17	13	10	10
£3,000–£4,999	14	17	11	13
£2,000–£2,999	32	28	24	28
£1,500–£1,999	11	24	15	11
£1,000–£1,499	90	130	94	84
£500–£999	75	109	40	43
Total £500 and over:	239	321	194	189
Under £500	n.a.	n.a.	73	84

extent in fire, insurance. In the case of marine underwriting, between 1720 and 1758 premiums exceeded losses by about £13,000 annually; and, since about £5,400 was annually charged for expenses, this left a net gain of some £7,000. Marine profits then fell somewhat in the 1760s and 1770s, and subsequently rose during the War of Independence. With the Napoleonic Wars there was an intensified spurt: the marine underwriting surplus (allowing for expenses) averaged almost £30,000 annually in the 1790s. Fire profits in the 1730s and 1740s were between about £3,000 and £4,000, fell in the 1750s, rose to their former level in the 1760s, and averaged about £10,000 in the 1770s. They rose again, to over £15,000 annually, in 1780–3, dropped drastically in the later 1780s and then rose very rapidly in the late 1790s, when they averaged over £20,000. Thus, for much of the first half of the century the Corporation's total underwriting profits averaged just over £10,000 annually, and after falling somewhat in the 1760s, and rising again in the 1770s, shot up to about £50,000 in the boom years of the late 1790s.

From one viewpoint, of course, these figures hardly represented a dramatic return on an original investment of over £500,000—even when scaled down to take account of the payment of £150,000 to the Crown. Nevertheless, it is misleading to treat the capital of an insurance company as one might treat that of, say, a manufacturing enterprise. For an insurance company is more than an underwriting business. Its capital is not locked up in the production of the underwriting service which it sells; rather, it is available for *independent* investment which generates income to augment underwriting profits. Thus, in the case of the Royal Exchange Assurance in the eighteenth century, the annual average interest earned increased from about £10,000 in the 1730s to some £40,000 in the 1790s. The Corporation was, in essence, an institution with a twin function, and two sorts of income. As a financial enterprise it invested its proprietors', and ultimately its life policyholders', money; as an insurance office it sold underwriting services. And there was little difference in the relative importance to the proprietors of the two income streams which resulted from this dual rôle.

As an investing institution, and in contrast to its subsequent rôle in the nineteenth century, the REA in the eighteenth century tended to place its capital in a relatively limited and unchanging range of outlets. The overwhelming preponderance of its invested assets between 1734 and 1784 (when balance sheets are available) were, in fact, in the securities of the Government, the East India Company and the Bank of England:

TABLE 3.2. *REA main categories of invested assets, 1734–1784*[a]

Total	October 1734 £365,238	April 1759 £413,149	April 1784 £666,340
	£	£	£
REA Stock	63,062	63,062	63,062
Loan to Government	68,500	—	—
Government Securities	81,430	136,727	356,953
East India Company Bonds	102,938	5,213	—
East India Company Annuities	—	65,748	57,853
Bank Stock	15,000	20,855	132,423
South Sea Stock	2,929	4,726	—
Loans at interest	17,900	—	11,500

[a] Excluding £150,000 paid to the Crown, £40,000 'Fire Office Stock' paid for the Sadlers' Hall enterprise (written off in the 1780s) and a declining amount derived from the costs of establishing the Corporation.

In contrast to some other insurance companies in the eighteenth century, the Corporation obviously placed a very small part of its investments in direct loans and, apparently, none at all in mortgages.[1] There is, admittedly, evidence for a loan of £12,000 to one of its promoters, Sir Justus Beck, in 1720 and of an offer to lend £20,000 to the Bank of Scotland for nineteen years in return for an agreement to share some of the Bank's profits.[2] But even taking these into account, together with the other loans to individuals which appear on the balance sheets, all this is small beer compared with the activities of other offices—notably those of the London Assurance, whose advances (mostly on the security of stocks) rose steadily from 1720 and reached very considerable proportions in the 1750s before declining to a negligible amount in the last thirty years of the century. As far as mortgages were concerned, the REA did not receive statutory authority to make this form of investment until 1826, although the right to hold land to the annual value of £1,000, mentioned in each of the marine and fire Charters, could apparently be used to justify mortgage loans to the annual value of £2,000 by placing the securities in the names of trustees.[3] This was presumably the basis for the London Assurance's making some relatively small mortgage loans (never exceeding a total of £11,000) before the 1770s; and for the REA lending equally small amounts

[1] For a detailed analysis of the investments of insurance companies in general, see A. H. John, 'Insurance Investment and the London Money Market of the 18th Century', *Economica* (May 1953), pp. 137–58. Compare Dickson, *Sun Insurance Office*, chapter 12.

[2] John, 'Insurance Investment', *Economica* (1953), p. 148.

[3] See the legal opinion obtained by the London Assurance (which was similarly placed) in 1731: DuBois, *English Business Company*, p. 134.

in the early nineteenth century. It may therefore be assumed that it was choice as much as legal difficulty which restrained the Corporation from placing its capital in this form of security. Certainly, the Sun at first and then the Equitable chose otherwise: the former had invested £98,000 by 1750 and £345,000 by 1780;[1] and the latter £115,600 by 1788 and £405,481 by 1798.

The striking feature of the Royal Exchange Assurance's investment pattern was, therefore, its reliance on the then limited range of Stock Exchange securities. To this extent, however, it participated in the important rôle of insurance companies in making an institutional contribution to the development and improvement of the capital market. And, whatever their other drawbacks, Government, Bank and East India Company securities did at least have the advantage of being easily saleable —an important consideration for an insurance company liable to pay unpredictably varying claims for marine and fire losses. In the early part of the century East India Company Bonds were particularly important in this regard. Later on, however, as the attractiveness of Government investment was increased, especially after the great consolidation of debts in 1752–4, so the REA increased the amount of its capital in public securities. By 1784 they accounted for over half of its total investments. By that date, too, Bank of England stock, which in the early part of the century fluctuated too much for comfort, was more attractive: in 1784 it accounted for some £132,000 (roughly 25 per cent) of the Corporation's investments.

Clearly, therefore, both as an insurance business and as a financial institution, the Royal Exchange played a large rôle in the eighteenth-century economy. Yet that rôle was not played in isolation. Although too little biographical information has survived to construct an accurate 'profile' of the eighteenth-century Court of Directors, such data as are available exemplify the strong links between the Royal Exchange Assurance and the City's general economic and social life.

Of the 120 Governors and Directors (out of an eighteenth-century total of 158) for whom *some* occupational information is available, over 100 were 'merchants' of one sort or another—with investments in and commitments to overseas trade. The exact areas of their commitment are in most cases unknown, but even on the basis of fragmentary information it is clear that the Levant trade, which had been so heavily represented among the original promoters, continued to supply a significant number

---

[1] Dickson, *Sun Insurance Office*, pp. 245–6. The Sun's long-term investments in the eighteenth century were divided between mortgages and Government stock roughly in the ratio of 60:40, with wide fluctuations over time.

of members of the Court: perhaps as many as 20 per cent of the Directors had some connection with trade to the eastern Mediterranean. In addition, among the 120 men for whom information is available, there were at least eight West India merchants (including William Tryon [Director 1720–6], who in 1742 was referred to as 'the oldest and most considerable West India merchant in London'),[1] six Hamburg merchants, and five Russia merchants. The strong representation of overseas traders on the Court was, of course, a reflection of the Corporation's orientation towards marine insurance—as was the fact that at least fourteen Directors were listed as 'Captains',[2] sometimes in the service of the East India Company, or of Trinity House (the REA established a convention, which still exists, of always having at least one representative of Trinity House on the Court). Further, at least fifteen members of the Court were bankers, including some who were also listed as 'merchants' in contemporary directories.

Perhaps as important as the large number of overseas traders who sat on the Court of the Royal Exchange Assurance was the smaller but still significant number of Directors who were also at some time Directors of the other leading City companies: twelve, including two Governors, in the case of the Bank of England; six, including one Governor, in the East India Company (including Sir Francis Baring, who founded the House of Baring Brothers and was reputed to be 'the first merchant in Europe'); six, including one Sub-Governor, in the South Sea Company; four, including two Sub-Governors, in the Royal African Company; and three, including two Governors, in the Russia Company.[3] Given this sort of interlocking with London's commercial and financial 'establishment', it was natural, too, that a fairly large number of REA Directors were also Members of Parliament: at least fifteen in the eighteenth century. Finally, the fact that at least twenty Directors were naturalized immigrants or the sons of immigrants—Huguenot families were particularly strongly represented[4]—may be taken as indirect evidence of the connection of the Corporation with London's cosmopolitan business life.

[1] *London Magazine* (1742), p. 257.

[2] In 1810 the Corporation's Chief Clerk to the marine insurance department told a House of Commons Committee that 'our direction is composed generally of merchants and captains of vessels in the East and West Indies Trade'. Evidence of John Holland to Select Committee on Marine Insurance: *PP* (1810), IV, 116.

[3] These are minimum numbers. In some instances, of course, the same man was a member of more than one company.

[4] Among the Huguenot families who were represented on the eighteenth-century Court were the Agassiz, André, Beck, Blaquière, Bosanquet, Cazenove, Chalié, Debarfré, Fannereau, Fremeauz, Lindigren, Lucadou, Newman, Simond, Tonnies, and de Visme. The Huguenot influence was equally strongly marked on the Court of the London Assurance: its historian lists sixteen names from its first fifty years (Drew, *London Assurance*, p. 217).

Like the other great City institutions, the Royal Exchange Assurance was, in fact, part of a close-meshed network, held together not merely by individuals' multiple membership of companies and trades but by personal and familial ties between men and companies, and by the tendency for business commitments to be handed down between the generations. Perhaps the best, but by no means the only, example of this almost dynastic element in the eighteenth-century history of the REA was afforded by a great Levant trading dynasty, the Bosanquet family.[1]

The first of the Bosanquets to serve as Director of the Royal Exchange Assurance was Samuel, who was a member of the Court between 1744 and 1764. It was his father, a Huguenot refugee in 1685 after the Revocation of the Edict of Nantes, who had established the family fortunes by developing an abundant and prosperous Levant trade. Samuel's elder brother, David, besides extending the family's Mediterranean trade, had served as a Director of the London Assurance from 1729 until his early death in 1741. And Samuel's change of allegiance was presumably occasioned and facilitated by his marriage in 1733—for his wife's father was the powerful William Dunster, a leading Levant merchant who, after helping to establish the REA, went on to become both Deputy-Governor of the Levant Company (1722–45)[2] and Governor of the Royal Exchange Assurance (1732–56). Now, Samuel Bosanquet's nephew Richard (who was also connected with the Corporation on his mother's side of the family, for his aunt had married into the Fannereau family, and Martin Fannereau was a Director from 1765 to 1770) had set up in business for himself as a Hamburg and West India merchant; and in 1759 he, too, became a Director of the REA. He, however, was aptly known as 'Richard the Rake', and resigned from the Court in 1767. Ten years later, after a chequered social as well as economic career, including service as a Director of the Bank of England (1768–72), he went bankrupt and had to flee to France. Meanwhile, however, Samuel's second son, William, had become a Royal Exchange Director, in 1768, some four years after his father's death. William Bosanquet, in fact, achieved considerable success both inside and outside the Corporation. A member of the Court from 1768, he became Deputy-Governor in 1791 and Sub-Governor in 1810. He was also an active trader to the Mediterranean and, like his grandfather,

---

[1] For the family history see Grace Lawless Lee, *The Story of the Bosanquets* (Canterbury, 1966). The surviving Bosanquet Mercantile papers are at Dingestow Court in Monmouthshire, and I am much indebted to the kindness and warm hospitality of Lady Bosanquet in allowing me to examine them.

[2] The Governor was a figurehead, and the Deputy-Governor therefore effective head of the Levant Company.

William Dunster, a Director and the Deputy-Governor of the Levant Company.

The links between the Bosanquets and the REA did not stop with these three individuals: Samuel's eldest son, Samuel II, who was a substantial figure in the City, being both Governor of the Bank of England and Deputy-Governor of the Levant Company, was connected with two Governors of the Corporation through his partnership, in the early 1780s, in a private banking house, Forster, Lubbock, Bosanquet & Co. The firm's principal partner, Edward Forster, was an enormously successful City businessman: besides becoming Governor of the REA (1785–1812), he was also Governor of the Russia Company for almost thirty years and Master of the Mercers' Company. Further, Samuel Bosanquet and Edward Forster were also associated with the banking family of the Lubbocks— and Sir John W. Lubbock became a Director of the Royal Exchange Assurance in 1798, going on to become Governor (1838–40) and to found a new dynasty of influential members of the Corporation's Court.[1]

The Bosanquets are an outstanding example of a general situation. For, given the nature of eighteenth-century commercial conditions, with their dependence on personal relations and trust between individuals, family continuity was an important element in business organization—at least until a particular family became wealthy enough to retire from the press of daily enterprise to the splendours of life as landed gentry. And the dynastic principle was particularly strong among minorities—whether Quakers, Huguenots or Jews—who were not easily and automatically absorbed into the ordinary social life of the country. Thus, in the case of the Royal Exchange Assurance, the Bosanquets were far from being the only example of the influence of a Huguenot family on the Court: John Peter Blaquière (1750–8) was followed by his two sons Jacob (1759–76) and John (1768–70); and later in the century the Agassiz, also Huguenot and also Levant traders, produced two members of the Court: Lewis (1771–97) and A. D. L. Agassiz (1798–1824). But it was not only Huguenots whose family influence was strongly felt: William Tryon, the City's leading West India merchant, was a Director from 1720 to 1726 and was immediately succeeded by his son Thomas, who carried on the same trade, and served on the Court from 1726 to 1750; Benjamin Mee, Hamburg merchant and Bank Director, was a Director from 1750 to 1770, and was followed for another six years by his son Benjamin Mee, Jr, India merchant and also Bank Director: the Raikes family provided another father and son combination in William (1768–85) and William M. (1786–1823); and the

[1] Below, pp. 352–3.

Pelly family, a race of sea captains closely connected with the East India Company and with Trinity House, were represented on the REA Court by three generations: Captain John Pelly (1741–61), Captain Henry Hinde Pelly (1780–1815), and Captain Sir John H. Pelly (1816–24), who went on to become Governor of the Hudson's Bay Company, Governor of the Bank of England, and Deputy Master of Trinity House.[1] A striking feature about virtually all of these examples is their continuity. Particular families (i.e. particular commercial or financial businesses) replaced one member of the family with another, on the Court of Directors, immediately the former's death or resignation created a vacancy. It was almost as if a hereditary place was made available for particular families; and the explanation can only be that the relevant family firm stood in some special business relationship with the Royal Exchange Assurance. It was, no doubt, this factor which helps explain the important and continuing rôle which Levant merchants (with their need for large-scale marine insurance) or bankers played on the Corporation's Court.

In terms of the Charter, the men who managed the Corporation's affairs had to have a sizeable share in its capital, for the minimum qualifications for Governor, Sub- and Deputy-Governor, and Director, were £2,000, £1,500 and £1,000 respectively. Nevertheless, to judge from a list of stockholders compiled in 1802, the contribution that they made to its affairs was far more of a personal or business than direct financial character. For example, in 1802 almost half of the Directors had no more than the required minimum of £1,000 of stock—although, given the current price of about 187, this reflected a larger commitment of capital than was superficially apparent. Admittedly, the Corporation's largest single stockholder, Captain Henry Hinde Pelly, who owned just over £12,000 of stock, was a member of the Court; but apart from him there were only two other Directors (Henry Hendley Norris, with £6,000 of stock, and Pascoe Grenfell with £5,000) whose holdings exceeded £4,000, as against at least eight proprietors who were not on the Court—four of them owning more than £8,000 each. The Governor himself, Edward Forster, who was presumably a very rich man, owned the legal minimum of £2,000 stock. In any case, of course, with a Corporation like the REA,

[1] Many of the REA Directors must also have been related by marriage, although less information is available about these alliances. One interesting example starts with Thomas Cooke, a Levant merchant who was a Director 1720–3, going on to become Governor of the Bank. Cooke's niece married another Levant merchant, James Fremeaux, who was a Director of the Corporation from 1762 to 1767; and Fremeaux's daughter married T. L. Boddington, a West India merchant who was also a Director of the Bank, who served on the REA Court from 1777 to 1782.

expertise, influence and authority were far more important than wealth alone. And in these respects the Court of Directors in 1802 was a very powerful body. Besides the men already mentioned (Edward Forster, Sir John W. Lubbock, A. D. L. Agassiz, Henry H. Pelly and William M. Raikes) it contained Sir J. W. Anderson (Governor of the Eastland Company, M.P., and an industrial promoter in Cornwall and Anglesey), Stephen Thornton (son of a Governor, and himself a Director, of the Bank of England) and William Vaughan (who was elected Governor of the REA in 1816, and was also Governor of the New England Corporation besides being an amateur scientist and engineer, an expert on canals and docks, and a promoter of wet docks in London). Indeed, the Court at the end of the eighteenth century was, if anything, more experienced and influential—and it certainly represented more varied economic interests—than the by no means negligible group which had assembled in the first Court of 1720. In the intervening eighty years the REA had lost nothing of the stature with which it had commenced business—or, rather, the only thing it had lost had been the speculative overtones of a 'bubble' creation. It had become firmly ensconced in the top ranks of the City's institutional establishment: preserving and enlarging its capital, extending its under-writing activities, an eminently sound and respectable Corporation. In-deed, if anything, it was too 'sound' to be well equipped for some of the more volatile and demanding aspects of nineteenth-century insurance. And in the course of the next century or so the worth and solidity which had been built up in its first eighty or ninety years, and which had in some respects hardened into conservatism, had to confront the searching test of novel conditions and radical problems.

4

Competition and Harmony in Eighteenth-century Fire Insurance

As we have seen, the fire insurance business of the Royal Exchange Assurance remained at a relatively low level for a generation or so after 1721. Only in the last thirty or forty years of the eighteenth century was there any significant growth; and then the Corporation's annual premium income rose from just over £10,000 in the early 1760s to about £64,000 at the end of the century. Partly by accident, but principally because of its organizational needs and the types of management problems to which it gave rise, far more is known about the fire business than either of the other two branches of the Corporation's underwriting. This chapter is concerned, first, with the nature and competitive problems of eighteenth-century fire business; and, second, with the fire brigades and agencies which were the products of competitive expansion.

PATTERNS AND PROBLEMS OF FIRE INSURANCE

Even on the basis of the very fragmentary information that survives it is clear that, in the eighteenth century, fire insurance in the country as a whole developed in terms not merely of amount but of complexity. Thus, an analysis of the Sun Fire Office's policies in 1716 and 1790 shows the extent to which the structure of insured risks grew more complicated, while the growing predominance of trading and commercial classes (with 'an important top-dressing of aristocratic and institutional clients') meant that by the end of the century the business function of the London offices 'had changed from merely providing security for individual householders to providing services essential for the development of domestic industry and foreign trade'.[1] Indeed, the sustained spurt in fire insurance in the last decades of the century must have been critically dependent on the contemporaneous spurt in industry and trade, and its associated proliferation of economic activity.

[1] Dickson, *Sun Insurance Office*, p. 78.

Unfortunately, the surviving Royal Exchange Assurance policy registers do not lend themselves to a comparable analysis of the changing pattern of the Corporation's insurance in the course of the eighteenth century. However, a sampling of the policy registers for 1755 does yield an interesting cross-sectional view of the structure of new (as distinct from routine renewal) policies in the middle years of the period.[1] These policies, in aggregate, accounted for £1,164,562 sums insured, and if the ratio between this figure and sums insured by renewals was the same as that between the respective figures for premiums, the then *total* sums insured (new and renewal) by the Corporation in 1755 was some £3·2 million—for a premium income of £7,609.

New insurances in 1755 were very heavily concentrated around London: the Capital, together with Middlesex, Essex, Surrey and Kent, accounted for almost 80 per cent of sums insured and just over 70 per cent of premiums paid. London alone accounted for 68 per cent of sums insured and 49 per cent of premiums (the discrepancy being accounted for by the preponderance of low-rated goods as distinct from higher-rated buildings insured in London). This was comparable to the figures for the Sun, which derived 37 per cent of its premium income from London in 1716 and 58 per cent in 1790.[2]

This concentration in London should not be interpreted as a concentration on private dwellings. For although there were some large domestic insurances, and private houses and their contents accounted for just under 40 per cent of total sums insured (houses alone accounted for 28 per cent), the stocks of merchants and manufacturers represented 47 per cent, and their premises a further 14 per cent, of all new insurances. On the other hand, because premises tended to be insured at higher rates than commodities, the pattern of the Corporation's premium income was somewhat different: private houses accounted for 40 per cent, stocks for 32 per cent, commercial premises for 19 per cent, and furniture for 9 per cent. The average premiums per £100 insured varied from 6s. 2½d. for houses and 6s. for commercial premises, to 4s. for furniture, 3s. for stocks and 2s. 5d. for clothes.

Turning to the occupation of policyholders, a very high proportion of

---

[1] The Corporation's surviving registers are in the Guildhall Library. Those for 1755 are classified M.7252/2 and 3. They contain details of policies issued in respect of new insurances (including changes in existing insurances), and account for one-third of that year's premium income. The registers were sampled by taking every fourth entry out of a total of 1,173 (there were originally 1,179, but six have not survived). Because of duplicate and triplicate policies, the total number of policies in the sample turned out to be 399.

[2] Dickson, *Sun Insurance Office*, pp. 77–8.

premiums was derived from merchants, middlemen and shopkeepers (35 per cent) as distinct from craftsmen and manufacturers (6 per cent) —reflecting the balance of a pre-industrial economy dependent, apart from agriculture, on the supply and processing of goods. In addition, and emphasizing this point, ships accounted for 10 per cent of premiums.

By the late eighteenth century much of this picture must have been altered, as industrial development both changed Britain's economic structure and penetrated into areas remote from London. The great extension of the REA's agency network in the second half of the century is itself powerful evidence of new geographical trends in its fire insurance business within Britain.[1] In addition, the increasing preoccupation with cotton and other textile factories, with steam-engine risks, and with the problems of a new industrial technology, exemplified a substantial diversification of interest—even though it was also associated with a concern with dock insurances and with such conventional types of policy as that issued to Charlotte, the Queen Consort, in 1799, which covered £4,000 on Frogmore House and £6,000 on its luxurious contents.

The critical problems confronting a fire insurance business in the eighteenth, as in the twentieth, century involved the classification of risks and the setting of appropriate premium rates and conditions. And in the eighteenth century the fact that the number and complexity of risks were very much less than in more recent times was more than outweighed by the fact that the fire offices were still only feeling their way in a new, technical and changing field—and, for much of the time, on an unco-ordinated basis. In this process, we shall see, there evolved many of the general procedures which were to be characteristic of fire insurance in modern times.

By contrast, the development of the basic principles of modern insurance are shrouded in greater historical obscurity. Only occasionally is there indirect evidence about specific technical practices. Thus, the first recorded reference to the use of the average clause in British fire insurance came in January 1723, when the REA Fire Committee ordered the addition of the following note to all policies for £500 and upwards: 'if in case of loss or damage it appears that there was a greater value than the sum hereby insured and part thereof saved, then this loss or damage shall be

---

[1] Throughout this period the Royal Exchange Assurance effectively confined itself to British and Irish risks—although it had 'a Committee for the fire business in foreign parts' in the 1750s, and occasionally issued policies on property in foreign or colonial areas (e.g. the West Indies) in the third quarter of the century. For overseas insurance in the nineteenth century, see below pp. 155–7, 241–3.

taken and borne in an average'.[1] However, matters did not run smoothly. Within two months it was decided to confine this note to policies relating to goods in trade; a week later it was restricted to sums insured of £1,000 or more, although it was also resolved that 'nothing of the clause of average be printed in the Proposals', and in June 1723 it was ordered that the note should apply to all houses in the country insured for £1,000 or more. In October 1725 the Fire Committee decided to replace the previous addition of a note to fire policies with a regular clause; and early in 1726 they re-emphasized that the average clause should be omitted from policies relating to London houses, but apply to houses in the country (as well as to all goods). In February 1727 it was ordered that the clause be used in policies for all buildings insured at £3,000 or more. Ten years later, however, it was decided to omit the average clause from all policies. Clearly, there was a good deal of uncertainty, in these early years, about the competitive impact of the use of average. It is not known when the average clause was generally revived, although in 1756 the Corporation ordered its use for all insurances of risks in 'foreign parts' and it is clear that it was reasonably widely used towards the end of the century.[2]

From the viewpoint of the fire offices as business enterprises, however, the technical development of their policies, although relevant, was less important than the determination of premium rates and classes of risk.

In the late seventeenth century the only operational distinction seems to have been between brick and timber buildings, in which the hazards of fire were obviously quite different, and the tendency was to charge twice as much for timber as for brick. In 1714, however, the newly established Union Fire Office apparently used a threefold classification of risks, which partially anticipated the basic classification into 'common', 'hazardous' and 'doubly hazardous' risks which was to prevail from the 1720s for well over a century.[3]

When it first began fire business in 1721 the REA restricted its insurances to sums of £250 or more, and imposed a charge of 7s. 6d. (5s. for the policy, 2s. 6d. for the fire mark) for any new insurance. With regard to the actual premiums, the Corporation established four basic rates: one for brick or stone buildings and ordinary goods in them; another for timber,

---

[1] The average clause was intended to guard against under-insurance by specifying that if the sum insured was less than the value of the property, then the claim actually paid would be scaled down proportionately (as compared with the actual loss). For example, if the sum insured was only half the actual value of the contents of a warehouse, and a fire caused £1,000 of damage, then only £500 would be paid.

[2] See Insurance Institute of London, Historic Records Committee, *Development of Mercantile Fire Insurance in the City of London* (1962), pp. 18–19.

[3] Walford, *Insurance Cyclopaedia*, III, 398.

plaster and thatched buildings, or ordinary goods in them; and two rates for property belonging to 'more hazardous' occupations depending on whether they were housed in brick and stone or timber and thatched buildings.[1] These premiums were quoted in terms of rates for £250 insurance, and were 5s., 8s., 7s. 6d., and 12s. In addition, insurances in excess of £1,500 had to pay higher rates with respect to the entire sum, i.e. not merely on the excess—which were, in the case of non-hazardous goods, 7s. 6d. and 12s. respectively for the two types of building.

This system of classification was similar to that adopted at the same time by the London Assurance—which, however, proposed a more elaborate scheme, dividing insurance into 'common' (brick buildings and ordinary goods), 'hazardous' (timber buildings, ordinary goods in timber buildings, or hazardous trades and goods in brick buildings) and 'doubly hazardous' (hazardous trades in timber buildings). Within each category the premiums, which were slightly higher than those of the REA, varied according to the amount insured.[2] In the event, the London Assurance's type of classification came to be preferred: in 1727 the Sun adopted the same system, while the Royal Exchange had done so before that date, possibly in 1722, when it was ordered that new proposals should be 'dispersed about the Town and pasted up in the Office'. This basic classification remained the standard procedure throughout the industry (with inevitable changes in detail) for almost 150 years.

Limits on individual policies were also matters of considerable importance, and were also adjusted by competitive pressures. Both the REA and the London were willing to insure quite large sums of money (and thereby forced the Sun to dispense with its former limit of £500 on one policy), although they did impose some upper limits. In the case of the Royal Exchange, for example, a temporary limit of £5,000 was imposed in 1723; but this did not last, and it was in any case perhaps more common to consider the question on an *ad hoc* basis. In 1724 it was ordered that all proposals exceeding £6,000 on goods in any one building should be referred to the Court, and in the previous year when considering the question of renewing the £30,000 insurance on the Earl of Sunderland's library, the Court restricted the insurance to £10,000 at 5s. per cent. Later in the century, as the practice of (and competition for) fire insurance extended, so general limits were raised. In 1791, for example, the REA extended its

---

[1] The 'more hazardous' occupations were those of apothecaries, bakers, brewers, chemists, colourmen, distillers, dyers, oilmen, powder men, soap boilers, sugar bakers and tallow chandlers. Glass and china were also considered 'more hazardous goods'.

[2] Walford, *Insurance Cyclopaedia*, III, 477.

limits to £10,000 for 'capital mansion houses' and goods in provincial warehouses, and to £20,000 on non-hazardous goods in well-built public warehouses.

As the habit of fire insurance grew, so, too, competition led to the adjustment (and convergence) of premium rates and the extension of the limits within which rates applied. In 1734, for example, the Corporation appointed a Committee 'to consider of the fire premiums and to make such reductions as they should see fit'. As a result, a new standard table of rates was adopted:

TABLE 4.1.   *REA premium rates per £100 insured against fire, 1734*

Sum assured	Brick		Timber		Hazardous goods	
	s.	d.	s.	d.	s.	d.
Up to £200	4	0	6	0	10	0
Above £200 and up to £1,000	2	0	3	0	5	0
Above £1,000 and up to £2,000	2	6	4	0	7	6
Above £2,000 and up to £3,000	4	0	6	0	—	

But this was only the beginning. In the 1740s and 1750s the premiums for larger risks were progressively reduced so as to extend the limits within which the lower rates applied. Further, in 1784, in order to encourage insurances among large-scale merchants, the premium on goods between £5,000 and £10,000 in brick buildings was reduced to 3s. Other reductions followed. And in the first decade of the nineteenth century, when new offices were greatly intensifying the pressure for business, the Corporation was obliged to extend limits even further: by June 1808 all common insurances up to £5,000 were rated at 2s., and those above £5,000 and up to £10,000 at 2s. 6d. (By that time, too, the rates for insurances in Ireland, which had previously exceeded the English premiums by about a shilling, were brought into line.) These rates, which were similar to those of other offices, remained more or less the same until a fresh bout of competition in the 1820s forced them down again.

Looked at from the viewpoint of the standard categories of risks, therefore, the development of eighteenth-century fire insurance tended towards both simplicity of classification and the extension of limits. From the viewpoint of day-to-day insurance business, however, this is a misleading picture. In fact, standardization in this respect went hand-in-hand with a growing complexity in the offices' approach to many types of insurance. This arose because of the need to pay particular attention to distinctive categories of risk, and as increasingly sophisticated attempts were made to adjust the structure of premiums and conditions to the different levels of risk of the different types of insurance.

Almost from the outset of its fire business the Royal Exchange Assurance was obliged to take note of particularly hazardous risks—such as stacked hay, distilleries, chemists' shops, thatched buildings, and the like —and to prohibit their insurance or set special rates for them. Theatres and theatrical performances, given eighteenth-century conditions and lighting, were considered hazardous risks: in August 1747, for example, the Corporation insured Covent Garden Play House for £4,000 at a premium of £8, and renewed the £3,000 policy on the Lincoln's Inn Play House at the old premium of £6. And in 1789 it was ordered that ordinary policies should not cover loss or damage from fire during or because of 'any play or dramatic or scenic exhibition . . . or . . . the holding of any masquerade or . . . public entertainment'. Insurances on theatres, scenic exhibitions and the like were to incur special rates of 5s. up to £2,000 insured, 7s. 6d. up to £4,000, and 10s. up to £10,000. There were, however, three main types of risk which were both important and destined to present perennial problems to the leading fire offices. They were: sugar manufacturing, in which the heating devices used could be particularly dangerous; Thames waterside risks, involving the insurance of ever-larger concentrations of various inflammable goods and materials; and, at the end of the century, cotton factories, where the novelty and variety of the industrial processes involved, together with the primitive methods of drying, lighting and heating, presented particularly knotty problems.

The problems of insuring 'sugar houses', while they were confronted almost immediately after the REA began fire insurance, were never satisfactorily solved, and continued to plague the Corporation, and other offices, for over a century.[1] In 1723 insurances for sugar bakers had been limited to half the value of the risk, and premiums were set at the very high rates of 10s. per cent up to £1,000 insured value, 15s. up to £2,000 and £1 up to £5,000. But these obviously proved insufficient: in 1747, even first-class risks (where the sugar houses were equipped with 'arched stoves' with iron doors) were rated at 18s. per cent—and even this was judged to be 'inadequate to the risk' in 1761, when it was raised to 22s. for the first £2,000 insured, with higher premiums for larger amounts. The significance of the problem of sugar house insurance—the need to secure a sufficient return yet retain a reasonable share of a volatile market—was brought home in 1782 when the disaffection of the sugar refiners led them to establish a rival insurance company, the 'New Fire Office', which shortly

[1] For the Sun's experience, see Dickson, *Sun Insurance Office*, pp. 85–6.

after was re-christened the Phoenix[1]—even though there is no evidence that the Phoenix, any more than the REA or the Sun, was able to provide cover at uneconomic rates for the extreme risks of the sugar industry. In the 1790s and into the early nineteenth century the Royal Exchange pursued a necessarily erratic policy with regard to sugar house rates—lowering them in the face of competition (e.g. in 1793-4 and 1818), only to encounter the need to raise them to prevent excessive loss (e.g. in 1800 and 1821).

In contrast with this situation, the problems of insuring commercial risks along the Thames, although not satisfactorily resolved until well into the nineteenth century, were tackled with less volatility, and more co-operation, by the leading fire offices. This was, perhaps, because they were in any case of much more importance to the London companies. The various offices began to experience difficulties with the insurance of water-side risks along the Thames south of London Bridge in the second half of the eighteenth century, as London's trade boomed and crowded its docks with wooden ships and its quaysides and poorly constructed warehouses with inflammable goods.[2] It was, in fact, in relation to London dockside insurances that the Royal Exchange Assurance and the Sun (and later the Phoenix) began the informal co-operation that was to be a marked feature of fire insurance business by the end of the century. In June 1775 the two offices increased their rates (by 1s. per cent) on risks below London Bridge on both sides of the river, because (in the words of the Sun's Committee of Management) 'the very great fires that have lately happened by the riverside below London Bridge' meant that 'the premiums now paid for the same area are by no means adequate to the risk'.[3] Six years later the REA Fire Committee followed suit when the Sun once more increased its rates, following 'many alarming fires' in Wapping and Rotherhithe.[4]

These new premium rates for Thames waterside risks soon received a challenge, for in September 1782 the recently established Phoenix decided that the rates for Wapping, Rotherhithe and contiguous areas were excessive. Earlier, in August, the Phoenix had promulgated a simple table of rates for Wapping, St Catherines, Shadwell and Limehouse, which had been significantly below the Royal Exchange and Sun rates of 1781. In

---

[1] DuBois, *English Business Company*, pp. 236–42.
[2] For the Sun's experience, see Dickson, *Sun Insurance Office*, pp. 86–90.
[3] Dickson, *Sun Insurance Office*, p. 87.
[4] The new rates were:

	Up to £1,000		£1,000–£2,000		£2,000–£3,000	
	s.	d.	s.	d.	s.	d.
Common (brick warehouses)	5	6	6	0	7	6
Hazardous (timber warehouses)	7	6	9	0	10	0
Doubly hazardous	10	0	12	0	15	0

September the Phoenix's Committee of Trustees and Directors, judging that business could be widely written at cheaper rates, provided that strict control was maintained, ordered a survey of the banks of the Thames, which was divided into fifty-two divisions, on each of which a limit of £6,000 was imposed. On this basis, a new systematic and relatively low table of rates was propounded.[1]

There is no indication of how the new Phoenix rates affected the Royal Exchange and the Sun in 1782, or whether competition at this level continued for long. But this seems unlikely, since as early as 1787 the REA and the Phoenix, and presumably the Sun, were standardizing their rates for short-term insurances on goods in warehouses and quays and on ships and cargoes in harbour. In 1790, and possibly earlier, the leading offices were also co-operating in surveys of the public warehouses throughout London, and in the next year, after detailed discussion between their representatives, the Royal Exchange, the Sun and the Phoenix substantially reduced the rates for Thames-side insurance.[2]

The difficulties of waterside insurance, like those of other special categories of risk with which the insurance companies had to deal in the eighteenth century, reflected the intensification of reasonably familiar problems. However, with the acceleration of industrial growth at the end of the period a quite different situation emerged: the offices were called upon to insure property involved in new manufacturing processes and exposed to risks for the assessment of which there was little historical basis. Thus, at a general level, the introduction of the steam engine (formerly sparsely used in mining) into various industries involved a new range of insurance considerations. And their importance was brought home in March 1791, when the Albion Flour Mill (just south of Blackfriars Bridge), a seven-floor showpiece of the application of steam-power technology, was burned down. The amount insured was £41,000, and of the five offices involved, the REA, with £15,000 on stock and £5,000 on the building, had by far the heaviest commitment.[3] This experience was no doubt instrumental in its decision, ten months later, to increase the premium rates on trades using steam engines to 5s. up to £1,000, 6s. up to £2,000 and 7s. 6d. above £2,000.

However, the most spectacular and important example of the implications of industrial innovation for fire insurance came from the 1780s onwards with the very rapid growth of the cotton industry—the mills and

1 Insurance Institute of London, *Mercantile Fire Insurance*, p. 14.
2 Insurance Institute of London, *Mercantile Fire Insurance*, pp. 15–16.
3 Raynes, *British Insurance*, pp. 196–200.

factories of which were at first powered by water, and subsequently by steam. The Royal Exchange Assurance was involved in this field of insurance at least as early as the 1780s; and in 1785 issued a policy on Richard Arkwright's steam-powered mill, valuing the mill and engine-house at £4,000. The problem with cotton mills was that the rapidity of their growth and the variety as well as complexity of their construction and technology, made it difficult to propound clear guidelines for premiums and conditions. This difficulty was further compounded by the fact that the cotton industry soon displayed an alarming tendency to an erratic experience. The result was that rates needed frequent adjustment and that the three leading fire offices were driven into yet another area of co-operation in order to establish the best technical basis for their cotton mill business, and to present a united front when premiums had to be raised or conditions tightened.

Discussions between the three offices started at least as early as 1788–9 (the Royal Exchange had already raised its basic cotton mill rate to 5s.), and in 1790 the REA, Sun and Phoenix organized a joint expedition to six Midland and Northern counties. But the resulting scale of rates also proved insufficient and over the next few years the three offices were in almost constant communication, making regular increases in the premiums for cotton risks. In December 1791, for example, the REA announced higher rates (which ranged from 5s. to 20s. for three types of mill) 'in consequence of the frequent claims upon the London offices, for losses sustained by fire, in the cotton manufactories of different descriptions'. In 1793 the Phoenix Directors empowered their 'Friday's Committee' 'to acquiesce with the Sun and the Royal Exchange Companies in any rates that may be thought suitable for the future insurance of cotton factories'; and in 1794 the rates were once more adjusted. In spite of this, however, losses continued to be very heavy, and reached something of a record in 1796, when the three main offices, pooling their information about their losses on all types of mill and factories over the previous seven years, found that they aggregated £255,000—of which cotton mill losses alone amounted to £135,000.

This dismal experience was bound to be taken very seriously by the offices concerned. Inevitably, the London companies were bound to reconsider the premium rates involved, as the Phoenix pointed out in a circular to its agents in December 1796:

Although the losses in every year . . . far exceeded the amount of the premiums . . . the Managers were willing to hope that further experience and additional precautions, which they had a reliance would have been supplied, might have enabled them to measure out insurance at the low rates of their last proposals.

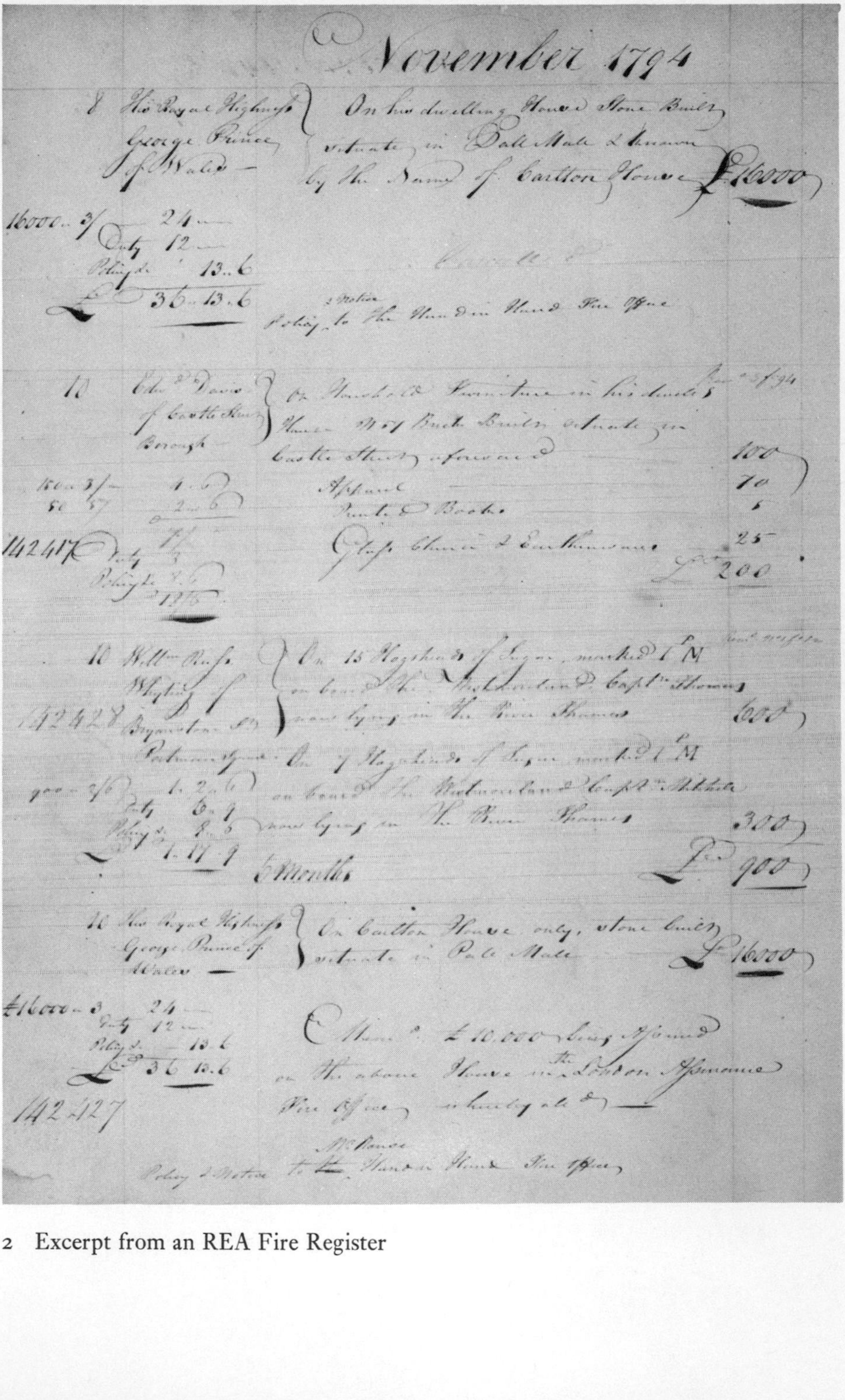

2 Excerpt from an REA Fire Register

3   An early fire mark

4 Interior of the Second Royal Exchange, 1746 *Canaletto*

They have not, however, been so fortunate as to find their expectations answered in this respect.

Against this background the three offices agreed to an immediate suspension of the existing table of rates (dated November 1794). The Sun and the REA adopted temporary rates of between 21s. and 25s., while the Phoenix refused any renewals after Christmas 1796, pending an upward revision of premiums. The Sun and the Phoenix also agreed to ban the insurance of cotton mills containing drying stoves for cotton wool, and to establish a firm limit of £3,000 (the REA limit was £5,000) on insurances of cotton, worsted, flax and water-drive corn mills or on any factory 'worked by mills or steam engines'. Early in 1797 the Royal Exchange, presumably in line with the other offices, extended the temporary rates and conditions for mills and factories which had been established the previous December. And in the spring of 1797 it increased the premium rates on cotton mills which were rented out in multiple occupancy (the new rates were 25s. for first-class and 31s. 6d. for second-class mills) because of 'several heavy losses the Company have sustained in cotton factories let out in a variety of different tenures'.[1] Clearly, a drastic problem had called for drastic, if short-term, remedies. In the process the offices, by appealing to the self-interest and possible co-operative spirit of factory-owners, and urging them to prevent heavy losses, anticipated an important line of insurance policy in the nineteenth century, when classification and rating were increasingly used as explicit incentives to induce improvements in construction and fire prevention.

These various aspects of the eighteenth-century problem of rating and classification make clear the extent to which many of the difficulties, and some of the solutions, which were to characterize the fire insurance industry throughout the nineteenth century were anticipated within a few decades of the 1720s. On the one hand, the simplification of the approach to large areas of risk was accompanied by an appreciation that there were many important and special types of insurance, particularly in a developing economy, which needed meticulous, systematic and technical rating. On the other hand, there was a constant tension between competition and co-operation—the one forcing companies into line with economic reality, the other increasingly and inevitably used to rationalize the classification

---

[1] These aspects of cotton mill insurance in the 1790s are dealt with in the REA records, and in Dickson, *Sun Insurance Office*, pp. 91–2. Data on the Phoenix, including the circular letter to agents (17 December 1796), were kindly made available by Mr L. M. Wulcko of the Working Party on Mercantile Fire Insurance of the Insurance Institute of London's Historical Records Committee.

of special risks and to adjust premium rates to the actual risk experience of the various offices. Moreover, a significant feature of this last tendency was the exchange and pooling of information about losses, which was to be continued in the next century.

The driving force behind the expansion of fire insurance in the eighteenth century was undoubtedly market competition. Sometimes this took a rather crude form as when the Royal Exchange agent in Norwich published an advertisement in 1725 which drew attention to possible drawbacks and inconveniences of the Sun's procedures for its policyholders.[1] But as far as the main fire offices were concerned this was largely a symptom of their adolescence. In later years public disputes about the attractiveness of rival offices were in the main associated with the appearance of young and aggressive companies. More general and continuous indications of market pressures were the lowering of premiums and the extension of limits for both ordinary and special risks, which have already been mentioned and which were particularly important in the second half of the century. In addition, there were periods in which there was a systematic effort to develop business, or to provide the basis for its development, quite apart from the lowering of premiums and the relaxation of limits. In 1736, for example, the REA ordered its Surveyor to 'make observation where any new buildings are and shall be erected and finished in and near London and enquire out the owners thereof and deliver to them the Company's proposals of assurance from fire and use such other methods as shall be most effectual to induce them to insure with this Company'. And when, in 1785, the pressure of increasing business obliged the Corporation to appoint one or more extra surveyors in each of the east, west, north and south 'quarters' of London, they were offered a 10 per cent commission on the first premium of all insurances recommended by them.

But the cutting edge of competition was obviously keenest when new fire offices were formed, and disturbed the conventional practices of the old. For example, the advent of the Phoenix in 1782 led directly to the REA and the Sun abolishing the traditional practice of making losses subject to a 3 per cent deduction: thenceforth, following the Phoenix's precedent, they paid all agreed losses in full. A second important example of the

---

[1] The *Norwich Weekly Mercury*, September 1725. The advertisement, by John Fransham, warned that 'all persons in this country concerned in the Sun-Fire-Office would do well to consider the difficulty of paying their money in London, and also the meaning of their 9th and 11th Articles'. In Articles 9 and 11 the Sun's policies required that notice of claims should be given at their London Head Office, implied that policyholders might have to wait three weeks for settlement of claims, and required proof of loss before a Judge or Master in Chancery. These Articles were substantially modified in 1727.

impact of aggressive newcomers to fire insurance concerned the issue of so-called 'free policies'. During most of the eighteenth century the REA, in company with other leading offices, imposed a charge for issuing a policy and fire mark—in its case, the charge in 1720 was 5s. for the policy and 2s. 6d. for the mark, although by 1783 at least the total charge was 8s. 6d. This, however, might obviously operate as a handicap in the search for new business—especially where a potential policyholder was insured with a rival company and could expect to renew his policy without the charge. As a result, as early as 1738 the Royal Exchange Court empowered the Committee in Waiting to issue a policy and fire mark free to anyone transferring an insurance of £1,000 or more from another office—although a sampling of the 1755 fire policy register gives no sign that free policies were then being issued.

The problem of free policies became more acute with the formation of new fire insurance companies in the second half of the century, simply because their issue was obviously a powerful device with which new and unknown offices might quickly secure business. This happened in the case of the Bath Fire Office (1767), which offered free policies to policyholders transferring from established companies. And in 1784, at a time when competition in fire insurance must have received a fillip from the formation of the Phoenix (1782), the Royal Exchange decided to allow policies free of the expense of policy and mark not merely to policyholders transferring from other companies but also to persons already insured with the Corporation and wishing to amend their policies.

Later in the 1780s the REA, Sun and Phoenix agreed not to issue 'free policies' in London: but this move only had a limited success. And the most decisive inroad came in 1799, with the establishment of the British Fire Office, which publicly advertised its intention 'to grant policies free of expense to any person removing assurances from other offices'. The Royal Exchange Assurance made an immediate but restrained riposte to this threat and informed its agents:

that however unpleasant it is to this Company to adopt a similar measure, yet it authorizes you where the party requires a policy *gratis* upon any alteration of assurance, to allow the same accordingly; but you are expressly directed not to interfere, if it can possibly be avoided, with the other London offices, or with such of the provincial offices as are not in the habit of giving policies.

But this attempt to hold the line on free policies by issuing them under pressure without affecting the business of other offices was obviously unrealistic. In May 1799, less than a month after warning its agents about the British Fire Office, the REA exhorted them 'to lose no assurance through the want of giving the policy where the annual premium is equal to the charge of the policy'. And by June of the same year there was no restricting the impetus of competition: the Corporation announced that it would allow free policies on all insurances of £300 or more and that an increased commission (in fact, a flat payment of 2s. 6d. for each new policy of £300 or more) would be paid to agents—a move which, it was expected, might 'greatly tend to the increase of the Company's business'.

As has been seen, in spite of—or, more precisely, in the very process of adjusting to—this level of competition in the late eighteenth century, the three leading offices developed a close working relationship by consultation and co-operation. This process had begun at least as early as the mid-1770s (before the Phoenix was established), when the REA and the Sun both raised their premium rates for London waterside risks. But it was in the 1780s and the 1790s that the links between all three were forged and strengthened. Their co-operation took many forms which anticipated the more formal, effective and widespread devices of the mid-nineteenth century: their surveyors joined forces to investigate particular risks; they pooled information about losses and premium rates; they agreed on common procedures towards such matters as the issue of free policies and office hours (when the Royal Exchange altered its hours in 1794, the Phoenix and the Sun immediately followed its example); in 1781 they established, with the agreement of the City of London, a co-operative night watch based on their respective engine houses;[1] and, most significantly, they frequently came to amicable agreements about the most appropriate premiums for particular types of risk.

All this was very well in a period of relatively restrained competition. Yet the situation was much more precarious than it looked precisely because there were so few large offices established before the end of the century. More than this, the co-operation which the three main offices achieved was used in a restrictive and even jealous manner. As the historian of the Sun has put it, 'the three "Great Offices" at first behaved towards their new competitors like the members of an exclusive club who find that they have unexpectedly to put up with unwelcome company in their smoking-room'.[2] Admittedly, their preponderance in the market must have provided some encouragement to this attitude. Yet, as the first decade of the nineteenth century was to show, neither the attitude nor the competitive stability on which it was based could long survive any substantial growth in

[1] Dickson, *Sun Insurance Office*, pp. 60, 65. The Sun provided twelve men, the REA and the Phoenix nine each.
[2] Dickson, *Sun Insurance Office*, p. 96.

the fire insurance industry. It would be another generation or more before the leading offices—and this time many more of them—could reconstitute the co-operative procedures which were to serve as the future basis of organization and action in fire insurance.[1]

FIRE-FIGHTING AND BUSINESS-GATHERING

The most colourful of the employees of any eighteenth-century fire office had only an indirect, but nevertheless important, connection with the actual business of fire insurance. These were the members of the company's fire brigade. In the years before there was any effective public fire-fighitng service, when fire offices had a direct and measurable financial interest in minimizing fire damage, and when the existence of these uniformed and stalwart bravoes was itself a potent advertisement, no important office could afford to be without its own brigade in London, and other, smaller, units in the more important provincial centres. Little is known about the Royal Exchange brigade in the eighteenth century, although this is one respect in which its facilities must have been almost identical with those of other leading offices. We know from the early decisions about the design of the Corporation's fire mark, and from the appointment of James Furness at an annual salary of £30 'to set up marks, to be at all fires, and in his vacant hours to attend the office as a messenger', that the REA was conforming to the universal system of fire offices being concerned with fires as well as insurance. And in May 1721, in its first fire insurance advertisement, the Corporation could already boast of having 'several engines, and 56 firemen —viz., 14 watermen to work the engines, 21 other watermen provided with proper instruments to extinguish fires, and also 21 porters having proper materials for removing goods, all clothed in yellow, and have every one badges on which is impressed the Royal Exchange and Crown to distinguish them from servants belonging to others'. (At some unknown later date the Corporation's official colour must have been changed from yellow to green.) Presumably in order to help the REA fire brigade, in 1726 Spelman, the Chief Clerk of the Fire Department, was ordered to report on the water supply of all areas of the City. And in the same year a list of large insurances was given to Mr Heming (presumably the foreman of the brigade) and Mr Furness, and they were 'desired to take particular care at those places if any fire should happen'.

In fact, parishes were under a legal obligation to maintain public fire-fighting services, but these were rarely effective at the best of times, and as the insurance companies entered the field, so the parish engines fell into

[1] Below, pp. 127–30.

greater disrepair and disrepute. When the REA founded its London brigade, there was already a reasonably long tradition, going back to the Fire
Office of 1680, of having a private fire-fighting force decked out in uniforms and badges—and in 1697 Defoe referred to the brigades of the Fire
Office and the Friendly Society as 'a set of lusty fellows, generally watermen', who acted as fire-fighters on a part-time basis.[1] The practice of using
the services of Thames watermen—a pre-selected group of strong and
reckless men—continued throughout the eighteenth century.

The attractions to serve in the brigades were considerable, and included not merely generous pay (normally, in the eighteenth century, a shilling for the first, and sixpence for each succeeding, hour) and the attractive
uniform, but also the immunity from the naval press-gang granted to
registered members of the brigades by an Act of 1707.[2] There were long
waiting lists for vacancies—which were filled by ballot among the Court of
Directors.[3] The life was not soft: the men were a rough and brawny lot,
and the competitive spirit of fire-fighting on a private-enterprise basis
could provoke brawls and drunkenness as well as speed and bravery. This
atmosphere was, perhaps inevitably, aggravated by the fact that, to encourage both their own firemen and the willing bystanders who were needed
to man the engines' pumps, the insurance companies provided a liberal
supply of free beer at London and provincial fires—although sometimes, as
at a fire in Bolton in 1798, this seemed too liberal to Alexander Watson, the
Secretary of the Royal Exchange: 'Pray what number of persons do you
imagine were really useful in extinguishing the late fire?' he wrote to the
local agent, 'By the very high charge made on the Company for liquors
we should imagine if yourself had not been present that the same had been
indiscriminately distributed to the idle spectators as well as the active
assistants.'[4]

According to popular myth, the fire brigades only dealt with conflagrations in property insured by their respective companies. In fact, however,
and inevitably, once in existence, they were drawn into action to fight all

[1] Relton, *Fire Insurance Companies*, p. 433. Also see G. V. Blackstone, *A History of the British Fire Service* (1957), p. 66.

[2] Blackstone, *British Fire Service*, pp. 67–8. The men were expected to carry an Exemption Certificate at all times.

[3] This is a detail from the London Assurance (Drew, *London Assurance*, p. 50), but is almost certainly an accurate description of most leading offices.

[4] This problem was obviously a common one. In 1808, for example, the Essex and Suffolk Secretary wrote to that Office's Chelmsford agent: 'The Directors certainly will not pay the bill for repairing the pump at the Blue Boar; the charge is absolutely infamous. The guzzling bill at the same place is almost as bad. I must trouble you for the particulars of the amount of £16 2s for men working the engine and for beer': Bernard Drew, '*The Fire Office*', *being the history of the Essex and Suffolk Equitable Insurance Society Limited, 1802–1952* (1952), p. 46.

fires—whether the building was insured by their companies or not insured at all.[1] Quite apart from the fact that the fire offices could and did compensate each other for the action of their respective brigades, it was not always convenient to check whether property was actually insured (the fire marks might be kept on exterior walls long after the policies had lapsed), nor safe to assume that a fire in an uninsured property would not spread to neighbouring buildings which *were* insured. In any case, there was a very powerful, and effective, element of advertising in the system of company fire brigades—an element which was made manifest by the magnificent uniforms of the firemen and emphasized by the regular parade ('The Day of Marchings', as it was called by the London Assurance)[2] with music and refreshments which was organized from the early eighteenth century. (The REA arranged such a march within three months of starting fire business.) It was this spirit which made large fires into occasions of publicity and competition—with keen rivalry, intensified by financial incentives, to get to the fire (and to the most effective source of water) first.[3]

The most important centre of all these activities was, of course, London, where there was the greatest concentration of insured property and potential business. Nevertheless, as the practice of fire insurance spread into the provinces the companies came to play a fire-fighting rôle there—either supporting their own brigades in the larger towns, such as Manchester, Liverpool and Bristol, or, where there was a smaller amount of business, providing pieces of equipment or financial subsidies for municipalities and parishes.[4]

All this naturally placed the insurance companies in an ambiguous

---

[1] Blackstone, *British Fire Service*, p. 70.

[2] Drew, *London Assurance*, p. 51.

[3] The atmosphere at such a fire was described in a poem by Horace Smith celebrating the opening of the Drury Lane Theatre after its third destruction by fire (quoted in Blackstone, *British Fire Service*, p. 71):

> The summon'd firemen woke at call
> And hied them to their stations all
>
> *   *   *   *
>
> The engines thund'red through the street
> Fire-hook, pipe, bucket, all complete;
> And torches glared, and clattering feet
> Along the pavement paced.
>
> *   *   *   *
>
> The *Hand-in-Hand* the race begun
> Then came the *Phoenix* and the *Sun*,
> The *Exchange*, where old insurers run,
> The *Eagle*, where the new.

[4] For the REA's help to provincial fire-fighting in the early nineteenth century, see below, pp. 163–4.

position: having started by undertaking a private task, they ended by being expected to maintain a public, and expensive, obligation. In 1798, for example, the Corporation's Secretary informed the Bolton agent that if the 'charge for assistance' in a recent fire were 'fair and moderate', the Corporation would allow it:

And if so it is an additional reason why the town itself should as hitherto repair the engines . . . it should be remembered also that the Company keep their own engines which are exercised for the service of the town . . . and they give equal assistance if the parties are assured or not. I really can see no just reason for throwing every expense on the shoulders of the insurance offices when perhaps not a quarter of the property in a place is insured.

Less colourful, but in the last resort far more important, than the firemen of the insurance company were its agents. For if the provision of fire brigades in provincial towns was a possible consequence of the geographical extension of a London company's fire business, the creation of an agency network was an unavoidable prerequisite. In the case of the Royal Exchange Assurance, as we have seen, this was acknowledged from the very outset: on 22 May 1721 Mr Palmer of 'Ockingham' (later Wokingham) was appointed as agent 'in Berkshire and several other places there-abouts', and it was agreed that country agents should be paid a 5 per cent commission for procuring business. At the end of May the Fire Committee agreed to approach as many country postmasters as possible, to see if they would serve as 'correspondents'; and in the next year, 1722, the REA opened an office and appointed an agent (Luke Gaven) in Dublin, thus in effect being the first company with a branch office in Ireland. Further, in June 1722, the Corporation appointed an agent, Thomas Myatt, near Charing Cross, 'for those who live in the City and Liberty of Westminster'. The Westminster Agency, which like the one in Dublin, ultimately became more like a small branch office, represented a move westwards, to tap fashionable business, which was common to other City-based fire offices (the London Assurance opened an agency, and the Sun an office, in Charing Cross in 1722 and 1726 respectively). In 1766 the REA's agency was in Conduit Street and in 1794 the office in Pall Mall was opened: it remained there, with a growing business, until the twentieth century.

In spite of this early start, there is no evidence that the REA built up an extensive agency connection until near the end of the eighteenth century. Indeed, the contemporary balance sheets which have survived indicate that there were outstanding agency accounts with only four provincial towns in 1734, eight in 1750, fifteen in 1758, twenty-six in 1766 and forty-four in 1775. It may well be that there were others, conducting a cash business, who might not have been listed, and it was apparently common practice for agents to appoint their own sub-agents in the locality. But the very small size of the agency network is hardly surprising in view of the relatively limited extent of the Corporation's business for most of the century. In any case a large proportion of the few thousand pounds of fire premiums must have come from London property, or from substantial insurances (e.g. country houses) effected through Head Office or the West End agency. In 1755, for example, London and the Home Counties accounted for some 75 per cent of new, as distinct from renewal, premiums. Only in the last twenty years of the century, with an increase in premium income, was there a significant growth in country agencies: the number listed in the balance sheet jumped from about sixty in April 1780 to 195 in October 1788. (In 1805 there were to be 316 British and three Irish agents.) The Sun, by contrast, which did not appoint its own first agent until 1721, had made about fifty more appointments by 1740—although in 1786 there seem to have been only 123, compared with the REA's 195 two years later.[1]

In October 1734, according to the balance sheets, the Corporation's four agencies were located in Dublin, Liverpool, Norwich and Portsmouth —even though in 1729 there must have been a vigorous representative at Newcastle, where, according to a report by the Sun, 'the agent for the Royal Exchange Office seems to have the advantage of Mr. Ogle', the Sun's representative.[2] By 1758 the accounts show further agencies at Newcastle, Alresford, Bury St Edmunds, Devizes, Hull, Plymouth, Manchester, Newbury, Lancaster, Dover, Blandford and Wistanwick. If, as is most likely, the Royal Exchange agents were drawn from the same sort of social and economic groups as those of the Sun, then they tended to be shopkeepers, well-to-do artisans, merchants and professional men. Typical, perhaps, was John Fransham, a dealer in linens, who was appointed agent to the REA in Norwich in 1725, and advertised the fact together with a warning about the presumed difficulty of doing business with the Sun, and a notice that he had in stock 'all sorts of linens, from three pence a yard to fifteen shillings'. Most of the business of such agents was, of course, concerned with fire insurance, for which the normal commission seems to have been 5 per cent. They did, however, handle life business, too—even though it presented much more difficult problems for a group of agents who had no training in technical matters and were still unsupervised. This was especially so in the days before medical examinations became routine. For,

1 For Sun's agents, see Dickson, *Sun Insurance Office*, pp. 67–72.
2 Dickson, *Sun Insurance Office*, p. 69.

even though all proposed lives in London were expected to appear before the Court, in the provinces the agent bore a heavy responsibility for detecting unusual risks. 'Be pleased to inform me', wrote the 'Life Accomptant' (i.e. the Actuary) to one agent in 1799, 'whether Mr. Thomas Wardle is known to be a temperate man: if he is corpulent or inactive mention it: when a life to be assured is an innkeeper these matters are worth particular consideration'. Surprisingly the 'Life Accomptant' also had to explain, twenty-five years after the relevant legislation, that it was illegal to insure someone unless the proposer had a financial interest in the life insured. Clearly, on the very eve of the nineteenth century, some aspects of the Corporation's organization had not yet been adjusted to its new rôle in an industrializing society.

PART B

British Insurance
in a Period of
Economic Growth
1780-1870

In describing the eighteenth-century development of insurance under-writing, it was impossible to ignore the quickening of pace, and the change of character, which began in the 1780s.[1] Yet, although these developments had roots in the past, they are far more significant as indications of what was to come. For it was in the late eighteenth and early nineteenth centuries, and with a heightened impetus derived from the combination of industria-lization and war in the years around 1800, that fire, life and marine insur-ance underwent some of their most important changes. These reflected, and were also components of, the transformation of the British economy and British society in a period of sustained growth. They were part, as well as a product, of the Industrial Revolution. Quantitatively, the amount of underwriting was greatly extended as Britain's domestic capital and over-seas trade expanded, and as economic development brought a multiplica-tion of national income, major shifts in its distribution and in savings habits, and new patterns of demand for insurance. Qualitatively, the growth of underwriting was affected by a dramatic and continued increase in the number of insurance offices, a consequent intensification of competition, and crucial changes in the service offered to policyholders (e.g. lower pre-miums in the case of fire insurance, and with-profits policies in the case of life). Finally, the nature and risks of competition led, on the one hand, to a distinctive form of public regulation of life insurance, relying far more on publicity and far less on direct control than that of any other modern country; and, on the other, to new attitudes towards co-operation and industrial self-discipline in almost all branches of underwriting.

The evolution of the conventional lines of insurance towards maturity was based on both specific and general factors. At one level, each branch of underwriting was heavily influenced by economic and social trends specific

[1] Above, pp. 58-9.

to itself, which provided a distinctive 'shape' for its history. More generally, however, there were also overriding influences at work: for example, the interconnected growth of industry, income and trade, which increased the demand for *all* sorts of insurance; and business, financial and legal factors, which made it convenient to combine different branches of insurance in one company. For this reason, although the development of each branch of insurance can most conveniently be traced more or less in isolation (as is done in the following chapters), it is as well to remember that long-run economic growth had a general impact on the various types of underwriting. Indeed, the determining rôle of general factors was also well illustrated in relatively short-run developments.

For example, a need and opportunity combined during the Napoleonic Wars to increase the demand for all three branches of insurance, and yet, at the same time, to put their inherited structure under great pressure. This led to an abrupt proliferation of offices and an intensification of competition in fire and life business, and to a strong campaign to broaden the basis of marine insurance by abrogating the exclusive privileges of the two chartered Corporations. All these developments came to a head in the first decade of the nineteenth century, when the number of fire and life offices was doubled, fire competition was drastically intensified, life insurance was greatly extended, and the pressure of capital produced a very critical investigation of the limits on corporate competition in marine business.

A similar, and in some ways much more significant, concentration of pressures with multiple but related consequences, came in the mid-1820s at the peak of the trade cycle and in the midst of a general boom in company promotions which, while based on general financial influences, greatly increased the number of insurance companies.[1] In the years 1824–5 the older fire offices finally grouped their ranks in the face of the new competition, and drastically lowered premium rates; in life insurance the victory of the bonus system, with all its consequences, was finally assured; and a renewed assault upon the marine insurance privileges of the Royal Exchange Assurance and London Assurance was finally successful. These developments, in their turn, set the scene for industrial change in the middle years of the century: for the growth of co-operation between fire offices, whose regular meeting culminated in the formal creation of the Fire Offices' Committee in 1868; for the unrestrained growth of life offices to the point

---

[1] Insurance share prices rose by almost 20 per cent between October 1823 and October 1824: A. D. Gayer, W. W. Rostow and A. J. Schwartz, *The Growth and Fluctuation of the British Economy, 1790–1850* (1953), I, 373.

at which fears of instability led to the enactment of the Life Assurance Companies Act of 1870; and for the creation of marine insurance companies, accelerating in the 1860s until, by the early 1870s, the pre-eminence of Lloyd's was seriously challenged for the first time since 1720. By the 1870s, therefore, by which time specialist railway accident companies were also well established, the insurance industry as a whole had completed a prolonged process of growth and structural adjustment to an industrial society. The next stage—the attainment of maturity in a recognizably modern context—was then concentrated into the forty years before the First World War. This will be dealt with in Part C.

This long evolution towards modernity presented severe problems as well as striking opportunities to the Royal Exchange Assurance. For, although its traditions and experience provided skills and resources which facilitated some changes, they also served as obstacles to flexibility and adaptation. And a large part of the interest of the period between the beginning of the Napoleonic and the First World Wars lies precisely in observing the process by which inherited corporate structures, policies and attitudes were adapted to new needs, new threats and new prospects.

The relatively superficial aspect of this story is reflected in formal changes in corporate powers and structures. Thus, the original powers of the Corporation were extended by Act of Parliament to include the purchase and sale of annuities (1793), fire and life insurance overseas (1796), the insurance of vessels and cargoes on inland waterways in the United Kingdom (1801), and the loan of money or stock on the security of mortgages (1826). In the later nineteenth century, by contrast, it proved possible to begin accident, liability and related forms of insurance without special legislation.

On the other hand, the powerful stresses of change, and the long and sometimes hesitating process of corporate adaptation, should not be confused with a series of relatively isolated legal events—important as these may have been as symptoms of some aspects of that process. Rather, the development of the Royal Exchange Assurance, as of any company, is to be seen in terms of the details of business procedures, organization and decisions. But these can only be effectively appraised in the context of the industry as a whole: the resilience and rigidity of the Corporation were, after all, relative matters. Hence a large part of the story of the nineteenth century is concerned with the changing environment as well as the Corporation's response to it; with the patterns and problems of industrial change as well as corporate modernization.

5

The Growth of
Fire and Life Insurance
to 1870

The basis of the growth of insurance during the Industrial Revolution lay in the provision of familiar, rather than relatively new, services. Even the apparent innovation of with-profits life insurance policies was, in fact, an extension of the practice of the Equitable Society—an eighteenth-century mutual office. Hence, although the industry was radically transformed by its new size, by far-reaching changes in structure, and by basic innovations in its business practice, it was transformed within the traditional frame-work of fire, life and marine underwriting. The risks were essentially those against which eighteenth-century policyholders had insured themselves.

The evolution of marine underwriting will not be considered here, since for most of the period it was dominated by a quite distinctive institutional structure (Lloyd's).[1] This chapter will deal with the general development of fire and life insurance, leaving until the next the problems of competition and control which were raised by the rapidity of that development.

THE GROWTH OF FIRE UNDERWRITING

The measurement of the growth of fire insurance during the Industrial Revolution is made relatively easy by the survival of taxation data relating to the *ad valorem* duty on fire policies. These provide a reasonably accurate indication of the extent and rhythm of expansion. As is illustrated in Table 5.1 and Figure 5.1, the well-established habit of insurance combined with the growth of domestic housing, industrial capital and commercial build-ings and stocks to produce a substantial rise in insured values. Between the late 1780s and the late 1860s there was a ninefold increase in sums insured; while in the twenty years after 1786–90, which coincided with the outbreak of war, the value of insurances more than doubled.

In money terms, therefore, the period as a whole witnessed a most im-pressive increase in insured values. But in order to appraise the true economic significance of these figures it would be necessary to take into

---

[1] For the evolution of corporate marine insurance, see chapter 9.

TABLE 5.1. *Fire insurance in the UK: average annual sums insured, 1786–1868*[a]

| (£ million) | England and Wales | | | |
Period	London offices	Country offices	Total	United Kingdom
1786–90	132	(6)[b]	138	n.a.
1796–1800	183	(8)[b]	191	n.a.
1806–10	273	33	307	n.a.
1816–20	312	76	388	n.a.
1826–30	345	124	469	n.a.
1836–40	437	170	607	673
1846–50	535	200	735	820
1856–60	n.a.	n.a.	910	1,019
1861–5	693	389	1,082	1,233
1866–8	784	481	1,265	1,403

[a] The data for 1826–30, 1836–40, 1861–5 and 1866–8 have been calculated from the original returns of the fire insurance duty which were regularly printed in the Parliamentary Papers. Those for 1856–60 were derived from Mitchell, *British Historical Statistics*, p. 461; and those for 1786–90, 1796–1800, 1806–10 and 1816–20 from S. Brown, 'On the Progress of Fire Insurance in Great Britain, as compared with other Countries', *AM*, VII (April 1858), 267–8. For a comprehensive series, see *PP* (1870), XX. The annual data are unreliable until the early 1850s because of the erratic timing of the payment of the duty by fire insurance companies. The difference between the figures in Mitchell and in *PP*, (1870), XX, is explained by the fact that whereas Mitchell took as the relevant year the calendar year in which the twelve-month accounting period ended (1 August until 1798 and 5 January until 1854), the official series took the year in which the period commenced. The latter seems preferable in the years 1800–53, when, for example, '1827' would refer to the twelve months from 6 January 1827 to 5 January 1828.

[b] Deduced from balance of 'London' and 'Total' which, for these years, are based on separate estimates.

account changes in the price level, for price movements could obviously affect the value of property insured without a commensurate change in the physical amount insured. For example, part of the boom in fire insurance at the time of the Napoleonic Wars (1793–1815) can be explained in terms of the inflation of those years (which merely increased the monetary value of insured property), rather than by any spectacular growth in either the habit of insurance or the actual amount of insurable property. It is possible to take some account of price changes, although by no means in a very accurate way, by using price indices for commodities in general as substitutes for a measure of price changes in the property and goods actually insured.[1] These indicate that prices rose by about 50 per cent between 1786–90 and 1806–10; that in the next forty years they fell by about 40 per cent, with most of the decline concentrated in the period 1806–10 to 1826–30; and that they increased by about 15 per cent in the

[1] See the various price indices in Mitchell, *British Historical Statistics*, pp. 469–74.

1850s. If we make allowance for these sorts of price trends, in order to approximate to a measure of changes in the 'real' value of sums insured in England and Wales, the spurt of business during the Napoleonic Wars is somewhat less impressive: an increase of merely about 50 per cent between 1786–90 and 1806–10. On the other hand, in the two decades after 1806–10 (when general prices were falling, although sums insured kept rising) the 'real' amount of fire insurance more than doubled; and this rate of increase, just over 3·5 per cent annually, was almost maintained in later years.[1]

These procedures are necessarily imperfect and the measures very rough. But it is perhaps significant that, in allowing for price changes in this way, the most rapid period of growth in fire insurance is displaced from the Napoleonic Wars to the decades after the War—thus coinciding with what seems to have been the period of most intensive growth in capital accumulation in general.[2]

Looking at the period as a whole, it is not possible to say precisely how much of the development of fire insurance was due to an increase in the amount of property, and how much to a change in attitudes and habits, since there is little reliable information about the accumulation of capital in the early nineteenth century. Nevertheless, it is obvious that an increase in the *practice* of insurance was very significant, since it is unlikely that the

[1]

	Price indices (1816–20 = 100)				Indices of growth of fire insurance in England and Wales (1816–20 = 100)				
					Current values	Values deflated by price indices (1)—(4)			
	(1)[a]	(2)[b]	(3)[c]	(4)[d]	(5)[e]	(1)	(2)	(3)	(4)
1786–90	68	—	—	—	36	53	—	—	—
1796–1800	89	94	96	—	48	54	51	50	—
1806–10	102	111	114	123	77	75	69	68	63
1816–20	100	100	100	100	100	100	100	100	100
1826–30	—	82	77	76	121	—	148	157	159
1836–40	—	84	79	83	156	—	186	192	188
1846–50	—	73	65	69	190	—	260	292	275
1856–60	—	—	—	80	233	—	—	—	290
1866–8	—	—	—	79	323	—	—	—	409

[a] 'Consumers' goods other than cereals', compiled by Elizabeth B. Schumpeter for 1660–1822; reprinted in Mitchell, *British Historical Statistics*, p. 469.

[b] 'Domestic commodities', compiled by A. D. Gayer and others for 1790–1850; reprinted in Mitchell, *British Historical Statistics*, p. 470.

[c] 'Domestic and imported commodities', compiled by A. D. Gayer and others for 1790–1850; reprinted in Mitchell, *British Historical Statistics*, p. 470.

[d] 'Overall index', compiled by P. Rousseaux for 1800–1913; reprinted in Mitchell, *British Historical Statistics*, pp. 471–2.

[e] Calculated from values of sums insured given in Table 5.1 in text.

[2] Phyllis Deane and W. A. Cole, *British Economic Growth, 1688–1959* (1962), p. 263.

amount of capital was being doubled every twenty years. This impression is corroborated by contemporary estimates which imply that between 1802 and 1855, while insurable property increased about threefold, the proportion of it actually insured rose from roughly one-third to about one-half.

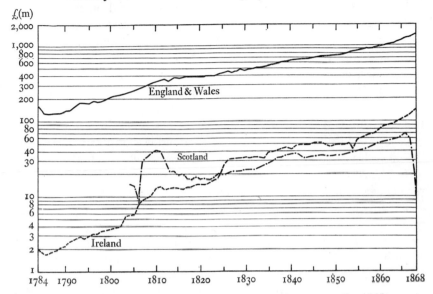

Fig. 5.1: Fire insurance: value of property insured, 1784–1868[1]
(Source: B. R. Mitchell, *Abstract of British Historical Statistics* [1962], p. 461.)

By the 1860s it was estimated that as much as two-thirds of the nation's insurable property was covered by fire insurance policies.[2] Yet quite apart from the evolution of new habits (and new anxieties), there would have been a substantial increase in demand for insurance cover. For the general and sustained economic growth which characterized the period was associated with a very rapid multiplication of precisely those forms of property (houses, warehouses, stocks of goods, factories) which were more or less automatically insured against fire.

It would, of course, be extremely useful to know more about the

[1] Between 1801 and 1868 the figures in the source have been displaced by one year in order to take account of the fact that the 'year' ended on 5 January (1801–54) or 31 March (1854–69) of the year mentioned in the source. I.e. in the above figure '1827' is the twelve-month period ending on 5 January 1828, whereas in the source this twelve-month period is referred to as '1828'. Until 1800 the 'year' ended on 1 August of the year actually cited.

Owing to the erratic way in which insurance companies paid in the fire insurance duties (the official returns of which form the basis of the statistical information) the annual figures are not absolutely reliable before the early 1850s. However, the trend implied *is* reasonably accurate.

[2] Walford, 'On Fires and Fire Insurance', *JSS* (1877), 403–5.

pattern of fire insurance with regard to the different types of risks insured. But the national figures only indicate the relative significance of one sort— farm insurances (produce, livestock and implements), which amounted to just over 7 per cent of all sums insured in the 1830s and 1840s. Other than this, there is only occasional evidence from individual offices. Thus, in 1840 the Sun drew a third of its premium income from warehouse risks, 25 per cent from dwelling-houses, 9 per cent from cotton mills, 6 per cent from farms and 3 per cent from shops.[1] And in the 1820s, of the premium income derived by the Royal Exchange Assurance from risks of £5,000 and more (roughly one-fifth of its total fire business), private houses accounted for some 26 per cent, mercantile warehouse risks for just over 20 per cent, and cotton factories for about 11 per cent. But each company obviously had its individual characteristics, and it is impossible to generalize on such a narrow basis. What is certain, nevertheless, is that the growth of fire insurance was a national phenomenon. Not only did it affect all sectors of a rapidly developing economy, but as the industrialization of the country pulled resources into formerly 'underdeveloped' regions, so the provinces became a more important factor in the insurance industry. Property outside London accounted for about two-thirds of all sums insured in 1831. Thirty years later its share (as reflected in official returns) had risen to three-quarters. It is not fanciful to see this as further evidence of the growing importance of industry and industrial capital—an importance which was to be matched by the spectacular development of provincial insurance companies in the second half of the century.[2]

THE GROWTH OF LIFE UNDERWRITING

Compared with fire insurance data, reliable statistics about the progress of life insurance are not available until relatively late in the nineteenth century. As a result, for any useful indication of its growth up to the middle of the century, we have to rely on estimates concerning the number of offices rather than sums assured or premiums paid. These figures, however, corroborate the impression of a quite dramatic increase in insurance which was reported by contemporary observers.

As was seen earlier, life underwriting was very restricted indeed throughout the eighteenth century, and even in the last two decades, when the success of the new system effectively pioneered by the Equitable in the 1780s brought imitation and some expansion, its extent was still limited. By 1800 there were only six life offices: the Amicable (1706), Royal Exchange

---

[1] Dickson, *Sun Insurance Office*, p. 140.
[2] Below, pp. 124, 214–15.

Assurance (1720), London Assurance (1720), Equitable (1762), West-minster (1792), and Pelican (1797). But in life as in fire insurance a turning-point came in the first decade of the nineteenth century, in the middle of a war-induced prosperity for many sectors of the economy. Between 1803 and 1808, for example, at least eight new London companies (including the Globe, the Rock, the London Life and the Atlas) were formed—five of them also undertaking fire insurance. Altogether during the Wars about fifteen life offices were promoted. There was a continued rapid increase in the post-war period, with twenty-nine offices firmly established in the period 1815–30—and a large number unsuccessfully promoted (in the company speculation of the boom years 1824–6 there were over twenty flota-tions, which almost doubled the number of life offices). Thenceforth, to the anxiety of many observers, the rate of growth continued: fifty-six offices were successfully established in the fifteen years between 1830 and 1844; while in the subsequent eight years (1845–52) about eighty seem to have been sufficiently firmly established to survive until 1852, although given the hectic joint-stock boom many more were actually floated, some of which rapidly sank. Although the estimates vary, it is certain that by the early 1850s the number of life offices was at least 150 (some observers said 180)—a striking contrast with the six of 1800. The promotional boom continued until the mid-1850s, when there were about 190 offices in existence, and then subsided: by 1871 the number had fallen to 114.[1]

Although continuous figures of sums insured have not survived, the amount of life insurance in force by the middle of the nineteenth century (when the first authoritative estimates were made) also indicates a very sharp contrast indeed with the situation fifty years earlier. Around 1800, for example, it is doubtful if the *total* insurance in force could have been much more than £10 or £12 million. (The Equitable—a giant among a tiny handful—insured just under £5 million.) When Victoria came to the

[1] Figures in the text are taken from tables presented by Samuel Brown to the Select Com-mittee on Assurance Associations in 1853 (*PP*, [1852–3], XXI, Q.1683), and David Deuchar, 'The Progress of Life Assurance Business in the United Kingdom during the last Fifty Years', *JIA*, XXVIII (1890), 443. For 1824–6, see Anon., 'History and Principles of Life Assurance', *Edinburgh Review*, XLV (1826–7), 496. A full version of Deuchar's article together with year-by-year statistics is in *Transactions of the Actuarial Society of Edinburgh*, II, 5. In fact, there are discrepan-cies between Brown's figures and Deuchar's; and, while Brown seems to have given information only about offices which survived to 1852, Deuchar provided statistics of the number of offices discontinued as well as established. It should be emphasized that no such data can be authorita-tive: offices were often registered without being successfully established, or established only to be absorbed, or active but not widely known. However, all contemporary estimates agree with the orders of magnitude indicated in the text. Other lists and statistics are in H. W. Andras (ed.), *Historical Review of Life Assurance in Great Britain and Ireland: A Supplement to the Insurance Guide and Hand Book* (Fifth Edition, 1912), Appendices A and B; Cornelius Walford, 'History of Life Assurance in the United Kingdom', *AM*, XXVI (1886–7).

throne in 1837 it is likely that annual life premiums were just over £3 million, sums assured about £100 million, and life funds about £27 million. 'A very loose guess' in 1843 held that about 100 offices insured sums of £100 million in 100,000 policies. In 1852 it was more firmly estimated that British offices accounted for £150 million of life insurance, with a premium income of £5 million and invested funds of £50 million. And by 1870, after two more decades of mid-Victorian prosperity, sums assured had risen to over £290 million, premiums to £9·7 million and funds to £88 million. In the first half of the century, alone, therefore, there must have been at least a tenfold increase in the value of life insurance— and at least a fivefold increase in insurance per head of the population. No wonder that contemporaries felt that they were witnessing the flowering of a new and distinctive economic and social institution. Moreover, in the early nineteenth century that institution was best developed in Britain—a fact which contemporaries attributed not merely to the country's economic development, but also to its superior economic and social security. Life insurance companies, they felt, could only be successful 'in a country where public credit has been long established on the basis of good faith, and property of all kinds secured by just and equal laws'.[1] By 1852 the sum assured was well over £5 per head of the population—compared with a mere two shillings for Germany and less than a shilling in France. By 1870 it was an impressive £9 per head. Life insurance was compared with other marvels of the Industrial Revolution at mid-century, and a member of the Government could claim in 1853 that 'he knew of nothing in the history of modern inventions, or in the progress of modern ingenuity, which, in a social point of view, was of greater importance than the establishment of these offices'.[2] Greatly outstripping the expansion of

---

[1] [John Barrow], 'Babbage on Life Assurance Societies', *Quarterly Review*, XXXV (1827), 1–2. Compare Anon., 'History and Principles of Life Assurance', *Edinburgh Review*, XLV (1826–7), 487: 'The practice of life assurance is as yet, in a great degree, confined to England. The fact however, is not to be traced to an ignorance of the principles among the Continental nations, but to the comparative instability of their institutions, and to a consequent want of that security, which is the first and last requisite in life assurance operations;– to the comparative poverty of some nations and the prevalence of a light-hearted inconsiderateness in others.'

[2] On Equitable: Ogborn, *Equitable Assurances*, p. 117, and *SCAA*, Q.3386; 1837 data: Deuchar, 'Life Assurance Business', *JIA* (1890), 445; 1843 guess: Select Committee on Joint Stock Companies, *PP* (1844), VII, Q.1856–8; 1852 estimates: *JIA*, XXVI (1888), 315, 442, *PM*, XIII, 36 (4 September 1852) and 39 (25 September 1852); 1870 data: official returns published by the Board of Trade. National data for insurance: F. Hendricks in *AM*, IV (1854), 342. (It should be noted that the separate figures for England and Wales [£116 million] and Scotland [£34 million] in 1852 indicate that proportionate to the population, there was twice as much life assurance north of the border.) For James Wilson's comment as Secretary to the Treasury, see his speech in *Hansard's Parliamentary Debates*, 3rd Series, CXXIV, columns 1320–8 (8 March 1853).

either population or incomes, the boom in life insurance amounted to a minor social revolution—involving far-reaching changes in the use and distribution, as well as in the amount, of personal incomes.

In this respect, the first point to be made is that life insurance was predominantly a middle-class habit: the product of a keen sense of individual thrift, a providential care for one's family, and an ability to purchase long-run security after having provided for everyday necessities. As early as the 1820s Charles Babbage made the significant point that the assured population had a lower than average mortality precisely because they were 'selected from the middle and higher ranks of society, and are consequently exempt from many sources of unhealthiness to which the poor are liable'. A generation later the *Post Magazine* still had cause to regret that many members of the working class thought of ordinary life insurance as 'an institution, like the club-houses at the West End of London, for the exclusive association of the wealthier orders'. And although by the 1850s there were already signs of a new trend towards so-called industrial assurance among the poorer members of society, this was very much a future development. While in the first half of the century large numbers of the working class supported their own forms of savings and insurance institutions (building and friendly societies, burial and sickness clubs and the like), the poverty of most people, the cost of insurance, and the need to pay premiums quarterly or half-yearly, largely confined regular life insurance to men of at least moderate means. In 1849, of an estimated £14·5 million of new sums assured, about £10·5 million was accounted for by policies of more than £500. 'A new power has silently sprung up among the people', wrote one observer in 1848. 'It has quietly sunk its roots deep amongst the middle classes.'[1]

The relevance of this point to the multiplication of life insurance in the early nineteenth century is explained by the apparent trend of income distribution. For, as the economy developed and national income grew, there seems to have been an increased relative flow of income to people with middling incomes—neither too poor to think of insuring their lives, nor so wealthy that their accumulated capital made insurance seem less

[1] Charles Babbage, *A Comparative View of the Various Institutions for the Assurance of Lives* (1826), p. 7; *PM*, No. 469 (30 June 1849); 1849 data in Walford, 'Life Assurance', *AM* (1886–7), 442; 1848 quotation: *Tait's Edinburgh Magazine*, xv (1848), 192. See also P. H. J. H. Gosden, *The Friendly Societies in England, 1815–1875* (1961), and E. J. Cleary, *The Building Society Movement* (1965). The Trustee Savings Bank movement started in 1817, and by the 1850s there were almost 600 banks, over 1,250,000 accounts and over £33 million deposits—but much of this was accounted for by domestic servants, the lower middle class, and middle-class children, rather than by the industrial working class (see Albert Fishlow, 'The Trustee Savings Banks, 1817–1861', *Journal of Economic History*, xxi [1961], 27–40).

urgent. Rather, some of the principal beneficiaries of redistribution were those with an increasing surplus of income for expenditure beyond conventional necessities—and an urgent need to fill the income gap which would be created by their death. Life assurance was bound to appeal to 'every man engaged in either of the three *professions*, whose emoluments arise from his own personal abilities and exertions,—every one pursuing a *naval* or *military* life, whose income will cease at his death,—every person engaged in *manufactures*, *commerce*, or any other employment, whose own immediate exertions are the support of the concern in which he is engaged'.[1] Unfortunately, there are few adequate statistics on income distribution—although a contemporary statistician like G. R. Porter could produce evidence in 1852 of a much greater increase in the number of incomes between £150 and £500 than in the number of larger incomes. And the *Assurance Magazine* published a significant gloss on Porter's statistics, claiming that 'instead of growing poorer every day, and the wealthy growing richer . . . the middle class is as great, as powerful, and as flourishing as ever'.[2] Of course, such generalization depends on how 'middle class' is defined; but setting aside the distinction between the middle class and the very wealthy, it would seem that industrialization increased the relative as well as the absolute amount of the national income going to the wealthy. By the 1860s about 50 per cent of the national income went to some 630,000 families (10 per cent of the total)—of whom just over 500,000 had an income between £100 and £300 and 120,000 had an income in excess of £300. The average income of the whole group was £500.[3] The increased use of life insurance presumably played a prominent part in that enrichment and diversification of the middle-class standard of living which characterized the two or three decades before 1870.[4]

As part of this general trend, there was also a rapid expansion of the number of professional and semi-professional people needed to provide the services and skills relevant to industrial and social modernization.[5]

---

[1] Baily, *Life-Assurance Companies*, pp. iii–iv. See also [John Barrow], 'Babbage on Life Assurance Societies', *Quarterly Review*, xxxv (1827), 1: 'Among the various institutions in which Great Britain may justly pride herself, as being instrumental to public as well as private benefit, there are none of more importance, or of more general utility, than those associations that have been formed with the view of securing a competency to the widows and children of such persons, chiefly in the middle ranks of society, as have only a life-interest in their incomes.'

[2] *AM*, ii (1852), 300.

[3] Harold Perkin, *The Origins of Modern English Society, 1780–1880* (1969), pp. 419–20.

[4] See J. A. Banks, *Prosperity and Parenthood, A Study of Family Planning among the Victorian Middle Classes* (London, 1954), chapters iv, v, and vi. Also see pp. 109–12 for a discussion of the substantial increase in the number and amount of middle-class incomes in the 1850s and 1860s.

[5] See W. J. Reader, *Professional Men* (1966).

And this growth of a salary-earning class is directly relevant to the history of life insurance—for it was precisely this sort of person, receiving a steady income but with his principal capital embodied in individual skills which would die with him, who stood in the greatest need of life insurance. The entrepreneurs who established the host of life offices with names like the Clergy Mutual (1829), the Provident Clerks (1840), the Architects and Builders (1847), and the Schoolmasters and General (1851), were presumably well aware of this implication of social change.

If the rising class of people earning moderate incomes increased the potential demand for life insurance, that insurance was also made much more attractive by the fact of its becoming effectively cheaper. On the one hand, the improvement of actuarial knowledge and practice, the compilation of more adequate life tables and the growth of competition led to a reduction of premiums. On the other hand, competition and innovation increased the benefits offered for a standard premium by enforcing the universal adoption of participating (or bonus) policies.[1] In 1853 a further incentive was added: as if to emphasize the nature and social composition of its market, life insurance premiums were made valid deductions against income tax, whatever the income of the policyholder. (In 1806 the allowance —first introduced in 1799—had been restricted to persons earning less than £150 annually.)[2]

To a great extent, therefore, the growth of life insurance reflected the drive for middle-class family security and individual thrift and prudence. But it was also related to the growing sophistication of the economic system. Although there is no way of measuring the amount involved, a good deal of life insurance was effected as an element in other commercial transactions: as security for a personal or business loan; as a means of protecting one partner's interest in a firm against the hazard of another partner's death (when the latter's investment might be withdrawn by the heirs); as a provision against premature death where the inheritance of private fortunes depended on survivorships; as a safeguard against the early death of a wife where a marriage settlement was contingent upon her survival. Even such investments as the purchase of an Army Commission were regularly safeguarded by the purchase of a life policy.[3]

In fact, by the 1840s, there were some life offices which used life insurance as a means to a loan business: lending money on condition that

[1] Below, pp. 132–4.
[2] There was no income tax between 1816 and 1842. From 1842 to 1853 premiums were not deductible.
[3] Reader, *Professional Men*, p. 77.

a life policy (usually to about twice the value of the loan) was effected and assigned as partial security. As one witness before the Select Committee on Joint-Stock Companies put it in 1841:

A few years ago, 20 or 30 years ago, insurance was the act of a provident man: now if only provident people were to insure their lives, half the companies might shut their offices; insurance has become an adjunct to money-lending, and the most advantageous ally an insurance office can have is a good money-lending attorney; loans are granted, and the policy is assigned as collateral security, which is perfectly legitimate.[1]

Even though, among some of the older offices, the practice of inducing men to insure their lives in order to be able to borrow money was considered a somewhat shady practice,[2] the connection between life insurance and a variety of financial transactions was now indissoluble and permanent —yet one more indication of the intimate connection between insurance and economic change.

Finally, in explaining the early Victorian upsurge in life insurance, we have to take account of the fact that, quite apart from a fall in the effective price and an increase in the number of potential purchasers, there seems to have been a genuine transformation of social attitudes and behaviour. While the trade Press tried to excite guilt feelings about people's tendency 'to spend their money on pic-nics instead of premiums—and to feel more pride in having a cabinet piano-forte than a policy in their cabinet', its interests coincided with a new enthusiasm for what was called 'the most serviceable invention of modern times for defeating contingency, disarming fate, and depriving casualty of its terrors'.[3] Life insurance was seen, and appropriately seen, as one product of an age of social improvement—a product which both reflected the importance of individualism and independence, and buttressed the institution of the family and the habit of prudence. To this extent, life insurance was bound to benefit from and exemplify the extension and strengthening of middle-class virtues in Victorian Britain. 'To make provision for a wife or family out of the savings of a salary, or wages, or small income,' urged the Select Committee on Friendly Societies in 1852, 'is an object which ought unquestionably to be fostered and encouraged.' And in 1853 *The Economist* argued that the problem of insurance was more than ever important because 'providence, so long recommended, has grown into a strong and

---

[1] *PP* (1844), VII, Q.250.

[2] See evidence of C. J. Bunyon to Select Committee on Friendly Societies, *PP* (1852), V, Q.1191–1200.

[3] *PM*, XI, 15 (13 April 1850); *Edinburgh Review*, CXCIV (April 1852), 415.

almost general passion'.[1] In 1858 in the course of a correspondence in *The Times* on the cost of middle-class living, insurance (fire as well as life) figured as a prominent essential. For example, a clergyman's wife reported that in 1856 her family had spent £35. 10s. (5 per cent of total outlay) on insurance.[2]

The practice of insurance was explicitly related to the habit of thrift which dominated so much of the contemporary economic ethos. Quite apart from the element of savings involved in the 'pure' life insurance component of any policy, the rapid rise of with-profits policies, which meant that policyholders shared in the accumulation of surplus funds, quickly guaranteed that life insurance took its place with other important outlets for investment funds, and benefited from the contemporary tide of capital accumulation in private hands. It was, in fact, this combination of individual forethought for a hazardous future and the careful husbanding of private funds for profitable saving and investment which made the insurance company, as it harnessed the virtues of the individual to the good of society, into a characteristic Victorian institution.

There were, of course, other institutional developments which embodied the ethos of self-help and individualism. But the special character and the long-term nature of the life insurance interest gave it an important rôle in the contemporary debate about social change in an industrializing society. In the words of the *Daily News* in 1852, 'the providence of individuals is the conservative spirit of society'. And to a Scottish newspaper it seemed that 'the only practical socialism which can ever exist is an insurance company'. The poor, it was felt, were already beginning to exercise prudence and thrift; and their support of savings banks, building societies and freehold land associations provided evidence 'that the people have money to invest, and will most assuredly apply it to insurance as our moral progress continues'. Meanwhile, moral progress seemed to contemporaries to be producing public good as well as private welfare; and in Parliament the Secretary to the Treasury could assert, with no contradiction, that those who paid the £5 million of annual life insurance premiums were 'the best and most deserving class of society—a class who, from the provident habits which they exhibited, the self-denial they exercised, and the enormous amount of their annual savings, were, he thought, justly and properly entitled to all the protection which the House could give them'.[3]

---

[1] XI, 223 (26 February 1853).

[2] Banks, *Prosperity and Parenthood*, p. 62.

[3] *Daily News* and *Scottish Press* quoted in *PM*, XIII, 40 (2 October 1852), and XIV, 3 (15 January 1853); letter on working class quoted in *PM*, XIV, 2 (8 January 1853); *Hansard's Parliamentary Debates*, 3rd Series, CXXIV, column 1328 (8 March 1853).

THE LEGAL BASIS OF ORGANIZATION

Whatever the economic and social implications of the remarkable growth in the number of fire and life insurance companies (those in London increased from eight in 1790 to over 200 in the 1850s), they were absorbed with relative ease into the contemporary framework of corporate law and practice. That the existing law was perfectly adequate for such a radical change in fire and life insurance was almost entirely due to eighteenth-century developments, which had legitimized the unincorporated joint-stock company, possessing all the necessary attributes of formal corporations.[1] The Globe, having already been established by Deed of Settlement in 1803, and guided by Sir Frederick Morton Eden's 'large views and undaunted energy',[2] made a second, unsuccessful attempt to secure a Charter in 1806. But, apart from this, the rash of companies which appeared in the first decade of the century all comfortably and confidently established themselves with the by now time-honoured device of a Deed of Settlement. And the old slight anxiety about the complications of a common-law partnership going to law was now resolved almost as a matter of routine by old and new companies securing private legislation enabling them to sue and be sued in the names of their chief officials. Five such Acts were passed in 1807 alone;[3] and about 100 in the first forty-four years of the century. By this time, too, proprietors could approach the question of limited liability with greater confidence: the offices now went out of their way, in both Deeds of Settlement and the wording of their policies, to limit the liability of proprietors to the extent of their nominal capital. Altogether, therefore, as had, in fact, been the case for most of the eighteenth century, 'the mysterious terrors of the unintelligible Bubble Act were a feeble obstacle to the establishment of joint-stock companies';[4] and in 1825 the Act itself was repealed.

The easy growth of unincorporated insurance companies continued to play an important part in the evolution of the business corporation in the

---

[1] Above, pp. 59–61. For the nineteenth-century situation, see C. A. Cooke, *Corporation, Trust and Company* (1950), and B. C. Hunt, *The Development of the Business Corporation in England, 1800–1867* (1936).

[2] Walford, *Insurance Cyclopaedia*, v and vi, 423, 'Globe'. In 1806 Eden wrote a cogent pamphlet *On the Policy and Expediency of Granting Insurance Charters*—much of it a plea for new corporations in the field of marine insurance.

[3] About this time those life offices which wished to participate in the annuity business also secured private Acts exempting them from the Annuity Act of 1777 which would otherwise have necessitated the constant registration of the names of all their proprietors.

[4] John Austin in *Parliamentary History and Review* (1825), p. 711, quoted in Hunt, *Business Corporation*, p. 28.

first half of the nineteenth century—helping pave the way for the modern joint-stock company by institutionalizing corporate structures, transferable shares, limited liability and articles of association. By 1844 some 170 out of 950 companies were life and/or fire offices. In that year, following a period of speculative promotion in which some insecurely based insurance companies had created an unsavoury scandal, joint-stock legislation established a new procedure for the formation of companies.[1] Designed to protect the public by ensuring the provision of information on the basis of which investors could, hopefully, make better judgements, the Joint-Stock Companies Act of 1844 stipulated that all new 'partnerships' with more than twenty-five subscribers and transferable shares had first to register with the Registrar of Joint-Stock Companies. Only then could they be publicly promoted. Subsequently, they had to provide details of their accounts and constitution, before they were allowed to complete their registration, call up capital and begin transacting business.

Although the main rationale of this legislation had been to protect the investor rather than help company promoters (e.g. it did not provide for limited liability), it was a device for registration rather than regulation, and was therefore a convenient and popular means of forming new companies. Indeed, its critics claimed that it frustrated its original objectives by not preventing considerable abuses and by facilitating the formation of weak companies which could make the specious claim that they had been 'established' or even 'empowered' by Act of Parliament.[2] Its period of operation, until the mid-1850s, also happened to coincide with a sustained boom in insurance—and particularly life insurance: of the 910 joint-stock companies provisionally registered under the Act between 1844 and 1856 no less than 219 were insurance offices, although many, and perhaps most, failed to begin business.[3] In 1856, however, insurance companies and banks were excluded from the operation of the Joint-Stock Companies Act which was passed in that year, and which greatly facilitated the formation of limited liability joint-stock companies. Six years later this situation was remedied when insurance offices were included in the Companies Act of 1862, which established the procedures for company formation and operation on a firm basis and which made the grant of either limited or unlimited liability automatic.

On the whole, therefore, there were few effective obstacles to the formation of insurance companies in the nineteenth century. Yet, whatever the

[1] Earlier, in 1837, legislation had made it possible for the Crown to establish a company by the issue of letters patent, but this procedure was only rarely used.

[2] *SCAA*, Q.2820, 2974-6, 3397-400.

[3] Hunt, *Business Corporation*, p. 88.

facility with which insurance offices could secure a legal and corporate personality, the resulting intensity of their development at certain times was bound to have significant repercussions for the competitive environment and business structure of the industry as a whole. These will be dealt with in the next chapter.

6

The Transformation of British Fire and Life Insurance: competition and control in the nineteenth century

The nineteenth-century growth of fire and life insurance, in terms of the number of companies and amount of business, gave rise to new problems of competition. The reaction to these problems, the changes in attitude and industrial structure, varied between the two branches of underwriting. At the same time, however, there were strong common elements in the situation which each had to face and in the way in which their problems were tackled. In the last resort, the companies were concerned to control the impact of 'excessive' competition. In the case of fire insurance this was achieved through a new institution: the Fire Offices' Committee. In the case of life insurance, market forces and a modicum of legislation in 1870 left all offices much freer. But for all insurance companies the perennial thrust of expansion and ambition was likely to disturb formal or informal arrangements.

FIRE INSURANCE: THE SEARCH FOR COLLECTIVE SECURITY

Between the 1780s and the 1860s the growth in the number of fire offices, and the intensification of competition in underwriting, took place in two more or less distinct stages. The first, largely influenced by economic developments during the Napoleonic Wars, lasted until the early 1820s and was characterized by a new scramble for business and the disruption of the relatively harmonious relationships between the very small number of leading offices. In the second stage, which commenced with a boom in company promotions in the mid-1820s, a new co-operation between the now greatly enlarged number of leading companies gradually led the way to fundamental changes in the structure and competitive environment of fire insurance.

In the late eighteenth century British insurance was still dominated by London offices—and London offices by the Royal Exchange, the Sun and the Phoenix. In 1805 there were eleven London companies insuring some £235 million of British property, as against the £31 million insured by sixteen country offices. Even so, contemporaneous developments posed a serious threat to the hegemony of the older offices. In the years 1801–10 nineteen new offices were founded, including such important and heavily capitalized London companies as the Globe (1803), Imperial (1803), County (1807), and the Atlas (1808). By 1810 there were thirty-six London and provincial fire offices, compared with twelve in 1790—and it had become obvious that the pattern of competition could no longer be controlled more or less on their own terms by the traditional giants of fire insurance. As competition became at once more ruthless and less controlled, the procedures of the three main offices began to diverge.[1] More significantly, premiums began to fall sharply: in 1806 Sir Frederick Morton Eden estimated that the impact of the Globe and the Imperial had reduced the premium rates for the newly opened West India Docks from 5s. to 3s. per £100, and that over the previous twenty years average fire premiums had fallen by at least 25 per cent under the influence of competition.[2] Four years later Jenkins Jones, Secretary of the Phoenix, complained that 'at the present moment, the competition of companies for fire insurance has brought the price in most branches below what will absolutely pay for the risk'.[3]

Meanwhile the competition of provincial offices was being seriously felt for the first time. The rather unyielding position of London companies had provoked a more aggressive attitude, and a new wave of promotion, in country areas. The new offices in particular naturally appealed to local suspicions of unfair treatment by remote London businessmen. Thus, the meeting called to found the Essex (later the Essex and Suffolk) Equitable Society in 1802 was informed that 'As it is a well-known fact that the losses that happen by fire in the country bear a very small proportion to those that take place in London, it follows that these large profits [of the established offices] arise from too high a premium being paid by the country insurers—or in other words, that a considerable sum is annually paid by persons residing in the country to insure London property against losses by fire'.[4]

[1] Dickson, *Sun Insurance Office*, pp. 95–7.
[2] *Insurance Charters*, pp. 89–90.
[3] Evidence to Select Committee on Marine Insurance, *PP* (1810), IV, 38.
[4] Drew, *Essex and Suffolk*, p. 10.

After the end of war (1815) the strain of competition got worse, rather than better. An increase in the duty on fire insurance in 1815 was met by a fruitless protest from fifteen offices arguing that competition 'has now reached its limit'.[1] Offices began to turn their attention to such defensive schemes as with-profits fire policies—which the Atlas adopted in 1816 in light of the need 'to make every effort to increase the fire business', and of the success of the Norwich Union and the County in raising their premium incomes by a similar move to return profits to policyholders. Meanwhile, by 1820 the vigorous young provincial offices were insuring one-fifth of the national total, thus doubling the proportion of fire insurance they had handled in 1806. More generally, however, the situation was aggravated by the post-war deflation and economic problems, for these were reflected in a slackening of the increase in fire insurance (at least, reckoned in current values): between 1815 and 1823 sums insured in the country as a whole rose by the negligible amount of 5 per cent.[2]

The retardation of growth in the decade 1810–20 was reflected in a stagnation of industrial structure, for only two new offices, both in the provinces, were established. In the next decade, however, more particularly from about 1824, there was a marked resurgence of activity and fire insurance entered a new phase of rapid growth and heightened competition, followed by a restoration of some of the elements of co-operation which had been disturbed by the pressures of the earlier rivalry for business.

In the 1820s as a whole sums insured rose by more than 20 per cent, while twenty-nine new offices were established and fourteen went out of business. Nearly all of this growth in the number of firms and amount of business was concentrated in the years after 1824. To contemporaries, the most important cause of the insurance boom in the 1820s was the joint-stock 'mania' which characterized the capital market in 1824–5: in those two years alone, twenty fire offices were floated, although only fourteen of them survived until 1827. But the development of the 1820s cannot be attributed to a mere superabundance of speculative capital. The low cost of establishing an insurance office, and the promise of good profits at a time of growing demand, undoubtedly played their part. (The returns of fire insurance duty show a 10 per cent increase in business between 1824 and 1826.)

---

[1] Dickson, *Sun Insurance Office*, p. 99.

[2] Since prices were falling in the period, the 'real' amount of insurance was increasing at a faster rate. But money premium incomes were probably the crucial indicators of prosperity for individual companies.

The fact that fire insurance was entering a period of sustained, and competitive, expansion reinforced some existing trends in the structure of the industry. Admittedly, the London companies remained supreme: in 1806–10 they had underwritten almost 90 per cent of all fire risks, and although they had slipped back to about 75 per cent by the late 1820s, they retained this position for the next thirty years. Only in the early 1860s—with the rise of such powerful provincial offices as the Norwich Union, the West of England, the Royal, the Manchester, and the Liverpool & London—did offices outside London account for as much as a third of British fire insurance. Nevertheless, within the London group the traditional leaders lost some of the supremacy which they had enjoyed in the first decade of the century: the Sun, the REA and the Phoenix, for example, which had handled 60 per cent of all English insurances in 1806, were responsible for just under a third by the late 1820s, and in the next few decades. Even this, however, was an impressive performance. And as late as 1853, when there were over sixty companies transacting fire business in the country, ten London offices, all established before 1810, accounted for more than half of that business.[1]

Clearly, age and size, experience and organization, continued to count for much in fire insurance. Nor was this surprising. For the growth of insurance brought with it increasing complexity and risk, in which care in selection and caution in expansion were essential prerequisites of success. Old-established firms had the necessary agency network and technical expertise, as well as financial reserves, which were often needed to weather hard, competitive times. In addition, their very size enabled them to secure some benefit from the otherwise inconvenient duty on fire policies, which, at 3s. per £100 insured (the rate set in 1815), was a relatively heavy burden on policyholders. There were two incidental advantages to the companies. First, the Government allowed a rebate of 4 per cent on London and 5 per cent on provincial policies, in return for the collection of the duties by the offices. In 1851, for example, the Sun retained £7,750, the Pheonix £6,500, the Royal Exchange £3,300 of the duty. Since the cost of collection was probably not proportionate to the amount collected, larger firms presumably benefited more than smaller ones. The second advantage of the duty was that the offices, being obliged to make their return only four times a year, had, in effect, an interest free loan of the total duty collected. More than this, until 1850 large arrears were allowed to accumulate, so extending the period of the 'loan'.

---

[1] The data on industrial structure in the text were calculated from the official returns of the stamp duty.

In general, therefore, with fire insurance as with manufacturing industry, large-scale producers were in a strong position. But they maintained their dominance at a price—albeit one which was less than that paid by smaller, and younger, competitors. Looking back in 1853, the *Leeds Mercury* argued that the supposed profitability of fire underwriting had proved an illusion over the previous twenty-five years. In that time over sixty offices had been forced to discontinue business; and of the thirty-five who were making profits in 1853 (out of an industry total of sixty-two), all but three were old offices. If losses were set against profits, the journal argued, 'it would, no doubt, be found that fire insurance business, on the whole, is far from yielding a high average profit'.[1]

The decisive impact of the new period of competition had occurred in 1824–5. Initially, to judge from the comments of the Atlas Directors, the situation had been viewed calmly: in July 1824 they reported to their proprietors that the increase in new offices 'certainly presents a formidable competition . . . but the Directors anticipate no defalcation of their business from this powerful rivalry'. But by 1825 it became clear that more drastic steps were needed. Early in that year the Sun appointed a special committee to consider whether its premium rates should be altered in light of the new promotions. Subsequently, discussions between the older offices led, as usual, by the Sun, the Royal Exchange and the Phoenix, produced a fruitless petition to the Treasury to reduce the fire insurance duty.[2] In the summer the inevitable finally took place: normal premiums on the three standard classes of risk (common, hazardous, doubly hazardous) were each reduced by 6d. to 1s. 6d., 2s. 6d. and 4s. 6d. per cent respectively. By September 1825 a Special Court of the Atlas had to be convened to approve a similar reduction in light of the action of the REA and the Phoenix (the Directors' reluctance being overcome by the fear of the alternative: 'any lengthened resistance on the part of the Atlas would have been attended with the loss of the greatest part of its fire business'). And at the Royal Exchange Assurance in February 1826 a recently established Special Fire Committee grappled with 'the necessity of reducing premiums' to meet the competition of offices giving a return to policyholders. These reductions reflected the desire, and the need, of the older offices to present a united front to their new competitors.

Writing some years later, Frederick Smith, Secretary of the Scottish Union Insurance Company, claimed that the premium reductions of 1825 had been designed to check the system of profit return to policyholders

---

[1] Quoted in Walford, *Insurance Cyclopaedia*, III, 500.
[2] Dickson, *Sun Insurance Office*, p. 146.

and to force minor fire offices out of business.[1] Certainly, it was successful in the latter aim. Altogether, at least twenty offices ceased fire underwriting between 1824 and 1832, while the continued high mortality among young companies meant that the number of offices hardly grew at all between 1831 and 1845—by which time it was about forty-four. Indeed, the competitive *riposte* by the principal fire offices soon undercut the position of substantial as well as small-scale companies. In 1827, for example, the Hope and the Eagle (both founded in 1807) had given up their fire business, while the Beacon (1821), the Aegis (1825) and two provincial offices had withdrawn altogether. On the other hand, the leading offices also suffered from the direct effects of their premium reductions. Thus, the Atlas had a premium income of £24,000 in 1824, which dropped to £22,700 in 1826, before sharply recovering on the basis of an expansion of country business (its London premiums did not regain their 1824 level until 1836); the Sun's income also fell; and the REA, whose premiums had been undergoing an intermittent decline since their peak of £88,000 in 1803, found that the rate-cutting of 1825 accelerated the fall. In the year ending April 1826 its income of £50,400 contrasted sadly with the £60,300 of two years earlier. In March 1828 the Special Fire Committee estimated that the rate reduction accounted for a fall of £5,500 in premiums in the year ending April 1827—even though the sum assured rose by £1·2 million to a total of £35·1 million.

Over the longer run, however, this general check to incomes, and the measures adopted to meet competition, seem to have had an invigorating effect. At the Royal Exchange, for example, there was a moderate recovery in the late 1820s, followed by a sharp revival in the early 1830s. By 1839 its premium income stood at £89,000 (it reached a temporary peak of £112,400 in 1845). Other offices also revived reasonably soon. Indeed, given their superior ability to withstand losses and the rising trend of insurances in general, it was not surprising that the competition of the 1820s should only impose a brief check on the trends of premium income at the large offices. By 1832 the Atlas Directors reported that as a result of the reduction of rates the Company 'has not suffered as much as might have been expected'. Nevertheless, the leading offices had to adjust their attitudes and practices to a more stringent atmosphere than they had formerly known. Close attention had to be paid to the extension and control of agency networks, to the careful selection of risks, and to the systematic oversight of organization and expenses.

[1] Frederick G. Smith, *Practical Remarks on the Present State of Fire Insurance Business: The Evils of Competition Pointed Out, with Hints for Improvement* (1832).

If one important result of the 'distressing confusion arising from the contagious spirit of rivalry between the men belonging to the different offices'[1] was an overhaul of the business outlook and policies of the individual major companies, another was a re-appraisal of the potentialities of co-operation. In his bitter comments on the extremes of competition, Frederick Smith had also hoped to induce the offices 'to at least consider the propriety and possibility of concurring in establishing some uniformity in the rates of premium'.[2] In fact, the trend towards closer co-operation was already strong. After the 1820s the offices moved towards more continuous and far-reaching co-ordination of their activities and procedures —a move which culminated with the formal organization of a nation-wide tariff organization in the 1860s.

The business co-operation which, in the 1790s, had been a feature of the operations of the REA, the Sun and Phoenix included a measure of association in their fire-fighting activities. But the combined night watch which had begun in 1791 only lasted for fifteen years.[3] And the extent to which even this form of united action had become more difficult was illustrated in 1808 by the lack of response to a pioneering proposal by Sir Frederick Morton Eden for 'an associated Engine Establishment, of which the expenditure should be defrayed upon equitable principles with reference to the interest of the different offices concerned'. In fact, the newly established Atlas (as yet without its own brigade) was the only office to show any enthusiasm, and even when the plan was limited to a proposal for each of three offices to provide twenty men it came to nothing. Within twenty years, however, the Sun, the Royal Exchange and the Phoenix once again came together on the matter of fire protection; and in 1832 ten leading London offices agreed to take the next and logical step, of uniting the various establishments within a single organization—the London Fire Engine Establishment, 'which would be much more economical and at the same time render the exertions of the firemen more united and effective'.[4]

The logic of combining in order to combat fires was clear. But extensive and continuing co-operation on such matters as premium rates and the classification of risks was more difficult to achieve, even though the demand for it became insistent at every period of competition and poor loss experience. After unsuccessful attempts to unite in order to increase rates, it was, in fact, the crisis of the mid-1820s which once more brought

---

1 Smith, *Practical Remarks*, p. 56.
2 Smith, *Practical Remarks*, p. vii.
3 Dickson, *Sun Insurance Office*, p. 65.
4 For these developments, see below, pp. 164–6.

the main offices together—first, to agree on a united and drastic lowering of standard premiums in 1825, and then to secure an increase in the tariff for Liverpool mercantile risks in 1826. The Liverpool mercantile tariff, which was the principal achievement of these years, seems to have been initiated at discussions between representatives of the Sun, the Royal Exchange Assurance, the Phoenix and the Imperial—driven together by their unprofitable experience on Merseyside. In the ten years ending 1825 their aggregate premiums had been £36,811, but their losses had amounted to £76,113, and their expenses to £7,958. On their initiative, and provided with this information, eighteen other offices joined the original four in coming to an agreement on a common tariff.[1]

Another stimulus to united action soon came from north of the Border, where the Scottish offices formed an Association of Managers in 1829. Discussion between this body and representatives of English offices, led by Jenkins Jones of the Phoenix, soon produced agreements on tariffs for cotton and flax mills, distilleries and textile mills with drying stoves. As Jones argued in 1830: 'We are generally losing money and adversity is a great teacher.'[2] But all was not plain sailing. In 1829 an agreement among representatives of major London offices (the Royal Exchange, the Sun, the Phoenix, the Globe, the Imperial, the Guardian and the Alliance) to maintain a rate of 3s. at St Katharine Docks collapsed in the face of a reduction to 2s. by the London Assurance and 1s. 6d. by the Phoenix, the Sun and the Alliance—even though, in spite of repeated efforts, the Royal Exchange Court of Directors refused to allow its Fire Committee to follow suit until 1832. And there were other examples of disharmony. Nevertheless, by 1842 the atmosphere and the inter-office links of fire insurance were well on the way to their final transformation. From early in that year there began regular and systematic meetings of the leading London fire offices, under the Chairmanship of Charles Ford of the Sun. By 1846 almost fifty offices adhered to the various tariffs, and as early as 1849 Bird, the Fire Manager of the REA, reported to his Committee that the meeting of offices were 'parties to . . . tariff rates' for cotton and woollen mills,

---

[1] The beneficial effects for the REA were to be seen in lower sums assured, lower losses and higher premiums:

REA Liverpool mercantile risks

Year	Sum assured £	Premium £	Losses £
1825	1,542,559	1,576	6,833
1826	1,164,091	2,389	1,760
1827	1,161,287	2,696	881
1828	1,142,194	2,737	*nil*

[2] Raynes, *British Insurance*, pp. 331–3.

London piece-good warehouses, Manchester, Glasgow and Paisley ware-houses, besides the old-established tariffs for Liverpool and London dock-side risks.

There is no need here to follow the history of the 'meetings of offices' for the eighteen years in which they were essentially preparing the ground for the establishment of a nation-wide Fire Offices' Committee in 1860, and the adoption of a written constitution and rules (as well as an official name) in 1868–9.[1] As well as raising rates, the conference was frequently forced to lower them, as with mercantile warehouses in 1849, 'to check the competition which has of late arisen'. Some of its well-established members were restless at the restriction on their competitive powers and the effect of high rates in 'calling into existence many new offices'; the powerful Manchester Fire Office left the tariff system between 1852 and 1858 on the issue of its discounts and bonuses to policyholders; and the offices were frequently reminded (in the words of the London Assurance Fire Committee) that the danger of competition from the establishment of new offices was 'a result which more than once followed agreement amongst the offices affecting particular interests'.[2] Yet in spite of all this, and more, the principal characteristic of the period was a steady drive to co-operation, tariff organization, and a much more harmonious set of relationships between the main fire insurance offices.

To the outside world—and frequently to themselves—the principal object of the offices was, of course, the maintenance and increase of fire-insurance premiums. Yet the harsher criticisms made against the offices were not always justified. For one thing, violent competition, if it produced rates less than the risk warranted, could well lead to the sort of insecurity and failures which would do harm to the public as well as the industry. More generally, however, the functions of even these early tariff discussions and agreements were very broad: they enabled the offices to pool experience and knowledge; they helped produce a much more systematic classification of related risks; they facilitated co-operative arrangements in surveying and salvage; and, at a time of rapid economic and technical change and increased complexity, they facilitated orderly expansion by diffusing knowledge and by shedding light on new risks. Finally, and among the most important of their tasks, by co-operative action and advice, as well as by the more direct incentive of differential premium rates, the

[1] This is admirably summarized in Dickson, *Sun Insurance Office*, pp. 149–56.

[2] Quoted in 'Minutes of the Meetings of Offices', vol. I, under 23 April 1842 (preserved by the Sun Insurance Office Ltd, to whom I am grateful for the opportunity of consulting these records).

tariff offices could substantially lessen fire risks and improve fire-fighting facilities. This was, indeed, one of the first consequences of the agreement and organization of 1842 with respect to safety in the Liverpool Dock area.

As far as fire insurance was concerned, a good deal of industrial and organizational history had been compressed into the first half of the nineteenth century. Confronted with an enormous increase in the demand for insurance, the handful of fire offices was rapidly augmented. This pro-liferation of companies naturally brought in its train a competitive violence which forced the offices into a reassessment of their business practices and organization and, ultimately, of the respective roles of competition and combination. By the 1840s, it was a truism among the leading offices that control, rather than individual competition, was the best framework for industrial development. To its proponents the rationale of the association of offices was clear. Apart from matters of technique and communication, they argued that fire insurance was different from the production of most other goods and services. In those cases, as economic theory readily taught, competition forced down costs as well as prices. But in the case of insurance the largest cost—that involved in fire losses—was beyond anyone's control, while the costs of management *increased* with competition. Hence, it was argued, too much competition led inevitably to bankruptcy and general insecurity; insurance was merely a sharing of risks in which all stood to gain by ensuring that the sharing was equitable.

LIFE INSURANCE: THE SEARCH FOR RESTRAINT

Although the problems of fire and life insurance were in many important respects different, the vast expansion of life insurance in the early nine-teenth century was characterized by trends comparable to those associated with the history of fire insurance. Thus, the opportunities which led to expansion, the extremes of competition which flowed from the prolifera-tion of the offices, and the resulting pressures for control and restraint were familiar aspects of both stories, even though they manifested them-selves in different ways and led to different institutional results.

Compared with most other forms of business, life assurance needed very little capital investment. Indeed, given the predictability of mortality among large numbers of people, as long as as the actuarial approach was sound and the number of policyholders sufficient, the risks of the life insurance business were relatively small. This factor obviously facilitated the rise of mutual offices. But the low cost of entry also led to a rapid influx of new capital and businessmen into proprietary life insurance by the middle of the century. In the boom period between 1845 and 1852, for example, in the twenty new proprietary life offices for which data were available, a mere £713,000 (of a nominal £5,980,000) capital was paid up —contrasting with the £4·7 million paid-up capital for twenty-four companies established before 1834.[1]

In the last resort, however, the growth of offices, although enormously facilitated by the relatively low cost of entry, was also stimulated by the promise of ample profits—either securely based on scientific actuarial practice or to be snatched by short-run schemes or by the creation of sinecures. The profits or surplus of life offices in the early nineteenth century were due to two main factors. First, their premiums were based on mortality tables implying higher death rates than actually occurred among assured lives, and on assumed rates of interest which were much lower than the rates actually earned. Second, they enjoyed the temporary and fortuitous advantage of having invested in very low-priced Government securities during the Napoleonic Wars. As a correspondent of the *Post Magazine* observed in 1852:

The public are not aware of the cause of the old life assurance institutions becoming so wealthy—they are these—the mortality has been less than estimated, the premiums have accumulated at a higher rate of interest than calculated in the Tables; the expenditure has been but a *small percentage* of the receipts, and last, though not least, the capital has been enormously increased. They have purchased largely in the public funds when very low, and sold out above par; and invested that increased capital upon first-class mortgages and other securities at a higher rate of interest, realizing above 5% and 6%.[2]

For many years the most commonly used mortality table for determining life insurance premiums was that derived from the death records of All Saints parish in Northampton for 1735–80, which had been compiled by Dr Richard Price for the Equitable in 1781. Although the use of the Northampton Table led to a reduction of premiums in the 1780s, it produced premium scales which, by the early nineteenth century, were much too high—not only because of changes in actual mortality, but also because at best it reflected the mortality of the general population, which was appreciably higher than that which obtained among the carefully selected groups of mostly middle- and upper-class people who actually insured their lives. It is significant that the mortality experiences of offices like the

[1] *SCAA*, Q.1683. In the industry as a whole there were 141 proprietary (besides forty-two mutual) offices with a paid-up capital of only some £13 million—and many of these undertook an extensive fire business as well as life underwriting.

[2] *PM*, XIII, 52 (25 December 1852).

Economic and the Atlas were only about 60 per cent of that indicated by the Northampton Table. Rates based on the Northampton experience bore particularly heavily on younger people. Thus the Equitable premiums for £100 (which became the model for those of other offices) were £2. 3s. 7d. per cent at age 20 and £2. 13s. 5d. at age 30. Yet if the premiums had been based upon the Equitable's own experience, and raised as much as 30 per cent to cover expenses and other contingencies, these rates would still only have been £1. 18s. 4d. and £2. 10s. 1d. respectively. As early as 1810 it had been pointed out that rates based on the Northampton Table were as much as one-third more than they need have been. And in 1826 Babbage claimed that the surpluses resulting from their use were 'immense', for the number of deaths among the assured was bound to be 'less than those occurring amongst an equal number of persons of all classes, indiscriminately taken in a large town'.[1]

Although many offices continued to use the Northampton Table well into the nineteenth century (the Atlas, for example, did not change until the 1850s), a superior Table, based upon mortality data for Carlisle in the period 1779–87, had been constructed in 1815. This showed a much lower mortality at younger ages, and the resulting differences in premiums could therefore be considerable. In general, however, actuaries were cautious about the use of new mortality data: in 1843, when at least fifteen offices still based their premiums on the Northampton Table, it was claimed that life office experience with lower rates than those based on Northampton was still too brief to be useful, while 'a vast number of those adopting lower rates had in fact gone out of business'.[2]

In almost any other industry—or, indeed, in fire or marine insurance—the high profits and inflated surpluses which were associated with the continuing use of the Northampton Table would have led to the influx of new capital and enterprises, and a substantial fall in prices. In the distinctive case of life insurance, however, although there *was* a spectacular increase in new offices established to share in 'the immense profit that is made by this species of daily traffic',[3] competition had a slightly different outcome.

[1] Economic experience: *AM*, VII (July 1857), 78–80. Atlas experience: Atlas Court of Directors, 8 December 1835. Equitable rates: Babbage, *Comparative View*, Appendix. 1810 estimate: Baily, *Life-Assurance Companies*, p. 34. Babbage's comments: *Comparative View*, pp. 4, 65.

[2] P. R. Cox and R. H. Storr-Best, *Surplus in British Life Assurance* (1962), p. 29; evidence to Select Committee on Joint-Stock Companies, *PP* (1844), VII, Q .1840. Almost a generation earlier Edwin Chadwick had attacked those actuaries who still defended the Northampton Table, as 'practical men' (a term he meant to be derogatory): 'To their indifference to the reception of any new facts, and the consequent incompleteness of their information for any practical purpose, may be added their incompetency to weigh evidence, free from bias, in most cases of direct monied interest'. See 'Life Assurances', *Westminster Review*, IX (1828), 391.

[3] Baily, *Life-Assurance Companies*, p. 34.

In addition to some reductions in price (premium) there was an increase in the benefit: the profits on life funds were distributed to policyholders. The rise of with-profits policies in the early nineteenth century reflected the increasing tendency to think of life insurance as an investment opportunity. At the same time the offices were safeguarded, in that they were not committed to a specific bonus (as they would have been committed to a specific premium-reduction) until it had been justified by earnings. As Charles Ansell, the Atlas Actuary, put it, by giving bonuses life offices effectively reduced premium rates, 'but by accomplishing it in this way they have in hand the value of the reduction before they venture to make it'.[1] Put another way, the conservatism of actuarial practice with respect to premium tables built up a substantial competitive pressure with respect to bonuses—and reduced shareholders' profits indirectly rather than by a fall in prices.

The rise of 'mixed' offices (proprietary companies distributing bonuses to policyholders as well as dividends to shareholders) dates from the early years of the nineteenth century, when the Equitable's enormous advantage as a mutual office became clear. Thus, the Rock Life and the Provident Institution, both established in 1806, shared profits between proprietors and policyholders. And in 1816, when the Atlas decided to adopt the bonus system, it was obvious to the Directors that a company doing a non-profit business 'would not be able to bear up against the successful rivalry' of mixed offices; the Atlas, they presciently argued, should anticipate the time when all life insurance would 'be universally conducted upon such or similar principles'. The Atlas had chosen a good moment for the innovation, since the Equitable (fearing 'an improper increase in members') had just decided to limit its bonus distribution to the oldest 5,000 policies on its books. Helped by this, and by its own new system, the Atlas premium income underwent a rapid increase: from £19,900 in 1816 to £80,500 in 1826.

By 1826 two out of every three proprietary offices were paying, or planning to pay, bonuses. From one viewpoint, of course, even this was a surprisingly small number. In 1810 Francis Baily had pointed out that offices issuing non-participating policies at the same rates as the Equitable, with its huge bonuses, must have been securing policyholders only by 'ignorance, persuasion, or necessity'. But the caution, as well as ignorance, of the public, and the significance of financial security, help explain the fact that, rapid as the growth of with-profits insurance was, it still left pockets of tradition: as late as 1826 there were six offices, all founded

[1] Evidence to Select Committee on Joint-Stock Companies, *PP* (1844), VII, Q.1853.

before 1810, which not only issued non-profit policies, but did so at the high premiums indicated by the Northampton Table—although Babbage rightly warned that this degree of extra security was 'dearly purchased'.[1] Thenceforth, however, the insuring public learned the lesson: by the early 1840s only a tiny handful of offices were still loyal to the non-participating system.

But it was not only the treatment of profits which was transformed by competition. For commercial competition of the sort which created bonus-paying companies led inevitably to keener rivalry at the point of sale. And this, in its turn, led to the increased use of advertising and the development of agency networks. These last could only be sustained by the payment of commission: by the early years of the century rates of 10 per cent on the first, and 5 per cent on renewal, premiums had become common. This development, admittedly, led to alarm and despondency among traditionalists, since 'agents' were often solicitors or brokers on whose advice and integrity potential policyholders relied, and who nevertheless accepted a payment (or, as its critics preferred to call it, a bribe) from the seller of the service being purchased.[2] Nevertheless, although a letter to the *Morning Chronicle* in September 1852 could still castigate 'the roguish system of commission', the use, and therefore the payment, of agents was an unavoidable concomitant of the spread of life insurance. Indeed, by the mid-1850s most English and all but one Scottish office gave a double commission (10 per cent) on the first premium, although a minority of companies in 'the first rank of respectability' stuck doggedly to 5 per cent. In fact, it was the new offices of the 1840s and the early 1850s which were particularly active. As the *Daily News* claimed in 1852: 'They employ agents, they enter into correspondence, they write and run to excite the public to be provident.' They were even said to retain agents on fixed

[1] Cox and Storr-Best, *Surplus*, pp. 19–21; Baily, *Life-Assurance Companies*, p. 23; Babbage, *Comparative View*, p. 25. The six offices were: the Royal Exchange Assurance, London Assurance, Westminster, Pelican, Globe, Albion and Eagle. The use of the Northampton Table was an even more serious, and less remediable, matter in the determination of annuity rates—as the Government found after 1808, when its annuity sceheme was based upon the excessive mortality of that Table. The consequent low cost of annuities to purchasers resulted in a loss of some £2 million before the situation was remedied in 1828. And insurance companies, although they found it unprofitable to sell annuities at anything like the same price, earned large profits, by purchasing Government annuities at very favourable rates. See H. W. Andras (ed.), *The Insurance Guide and Hand Book* (Fifth Edition, 1912), I, 36; Walford, *Insurance Cyclopaedia*, I, 55; Baily, *Life-Assurance Companies*, pp. 42–3; *PP*, 1890–1, XLVIII, 205–20. There is a sustained assault on the excessive conservatism which meant that 'public money was expended at an enormous loss in granting annuities', in an article by Edwin Chatwick on 'Life Assurances' in the *Westminster Review*, XIX (April 1828), 384–421.

[2] Baily, *Life-Assurance Companies*, p. 29; Babbage, *Comparative View*, p. 132; Walford, *Insurance Cyclopaedia*, I, 39.

salaries 'for the purpose, in the first place, of forcing business'. Much as some men might find this sort of activity reprehensible (although it should not be forgotten that the older offices also advertised keenly and employed agents), it is difficult to see how life insurance in the period could have become so popular without the publicity and the pressure brought by commercialism and agencies. Francis G. P. Neison, Actuary to the Medical and Invalid Life Office, put the extreme case in 1853: 'It seems to me, looking at it as a simple matter of mercantile enterprise, that business is to be acquired only by a ramified system of agencies; you must saturate the country with a number of agents who are active in making the institution known, and the advantage which it is capable of conferring.'[1]

Thus it was that life offices, if they wished to be successful, could not ignore their potential rôle as nation-wide institutions actively selling a service. And, in order to sell it, they had to provide incentives to their salesmen. Successful life offices had to have salesmen scattered throughout the country; and once they appreciated this they also began to appreciate the need to educate and energize their agents. As early as the 1820s, for example, an office like the Atlas was anticipating the future evolution of inspectors by dispatching an auditor, Mr Ward, on frequent visits to 'corresponding solicitors' and agents 'with a view to stimulate their exertions in increasing the orders for assurance'. And in 1853 Neison continued his arguments about agency systems by emphasizing that the agents needed to be not merely appointed but also 'for some time instructed until the whole are indoctrinated with the principles of the institution, and are capable of representing its advantages fairly'.

Agencies were, of course, held by many different sorts of people as part-time occupation: by merchants and retailers, by teachers and general brokers, by bankers and estate agents. But in this respect the rise of life insurance was crucially dependent on the rôle of the legal profession. Lawyers were not only trusted business and personal advisers, but were intimately concerned with the very affairs—the making of wills and family settlements, the oversight of loans and partnership arrangements, the disposition of capital and income—which were likely to generate a demand for life insurance. As a consequence, the life offices made extensive use of lawyers as agents. The Atlas, for example, based its strategy on 'corresponding solicitors', and the power of its life department was, in retrospect, attributed to the resulting 'most respectable and influential

[1] Letter to *Morning Chronicle*: quoted in *PM*, XIII, 37 (11 September 1852). Commissions in 1856: REA Rough Treasury Minutes, 20 February 1856. *Daily News*: quoted in *PM*, XIII, 40 (2 October 1852). Salaried agents: *SCAA*, Q.1029. Neison: *SCAA*, Q.2324.

connection'. In this case, however, although the practice continued until the 1840s, its very success proved self-defeating: in 1823 the Law Life Office was established, partly on the initiative of George Kirkpatrick, the Atlas's first and accomplished Actuary. Kirkpatrick, according to a report to the Atlas Directors in 1864, 'was well acquainted with the plan adopted here. Having a proprietary body consisting exclusively of the legal profession, it [the Law Life] exercised great influence over the connection which the Atlas had formed with much labour . . . and the current of business which heretofore had flowed to this company was diverted to another channel'. The success of the Law Life led to the establishment of other legal assurance companies, and 'respectable' offices like the Royal Exchange Assurance and the Atlas were particularly hard hit, since leading solicitors handled large, good-quality risks. In subsequent years the decline in the REA premium income after 1824 was explicitly attributed to the establishment of the Law Life.

Although the Royal Exchange managed to arrest the decline in its life premium income by adopting bonus policies in the early 1840s, it and other offices like it were then entering a new phase of competitive difficulty. Whereas some forty offices had been successfully established between 1833 and 1842, in the next ten years no less than ninety-one were formed. The premium income of the Atlas, which had quadrupled between 1816 and 1826, grew by just under 50 per cent in the next ten years, by less than 10 per cent in the decade 1836–46, and then not at all for twenty years. In order to increase their attractiveness to policyholders, offices like the Guardian (in 1835) and the Atlas (in 1846) had to reduce or dispense with the practice of deducting interest on capital from life surpluses as a compensation for management. In 1850 the Guardian, which had paid 50 per cent of its surplus to its with-profits policyholders since its foundation in 1821, had to raise the proportion to 80 per cent.[1] The new offices were vigorous, thrusting and unconventional—transforming not merely the agency and bonus systems but also relationships with the medical profession by paying substantial medical fees.[2]

As the pace of competition intensified, so the dismay of the old-established offices deepened. Already obliged to issue with-profits policies, they now had to confront a host of other, and more theatening, competitive devices. By the 1840s, and even more in the early 1850s, the extraordinary growth rate of new offices ushered in a period of doubt and debate: one

[1] A. W. Tarn and C. E. Byles, *A Record of the Guardian Assurance Company Limited, 1821–1921* (1921), pp. 23, 47–8.
[2] *SCAA*, Q.3134.

in which the gloomy fears of the older offices were reflected in the anxieties of journalists, politicians and the public at large. Had competition gone too far? Should the insurance business be controlled? Was the ideology of free competition and individualism inappropriate to the social needs and economic character of life assurance? In one way or another the ensuing public controversy was associated with an attempt to restrain the formation of new offices—an attempt which, precisely because it was undertaken in the context of a *laissez-faire* orthodoxy, proved almost impossibly difficult.

The mid-century boom in life assurance offices—springing up 'like mushrooms' in the words of a contemporary journalist—was, of course, directly related to the growing popularity and profitability of insurance. To many observers it seemed that 'there is now no better investment for capital than a life assurance company'.[1] In addition, however, it was also part of a general boom in joint-stock flotations, which was reflected in the railway 'mania' of the 1840s, and in the establishment of hundreds of new companies under the easier procedures afforded by the Joint-Stock Companies Act of 1844: as we have seen between 1844 and 1856 over 900 companies of all sorts were registered.

Whatever the relationship with the state of the capital market, however, the influx of new capital, and the growth of competition, gave rise to special anxieties. For one thing, it was feared that the potential market for life insurance was near saturation. The opponents of expansion argued that life assurance was different from other trades: that it consisted of 'a redistribution of the capital of the public—a deduction of the portion which one man may save out of his profits in the course of a long life, for the benefit of a family of another who does not live to save it'. To this extent, therefore, while competition in an ordinary business would reduce prices, extend the market, and lower costs, 'the assurance of life depends upon laws of population and of interest of money, quite beyond the control of those who guarantee the fulfilment of the contracts. The conclusion, in fact, is singularly opposed to the doctrines of trade; for the more capital the adventurers employ, the less profit they obtain.'[2] In effect, it was argued, the basic cost of insurance was determined by mortality tables and interest rates, and 'as no office can frame a new law of mortality', it could not reduce its basic costs. Moreover, 'if its premiums be not consistent

[1] First quotation: *PM*, XIII, 40 (2 October 1852); second: *The Economist*, X, 1007 (11 September 1852). In fact seventy-three of the ninety-one offices established in 1843–52 were proprietary.
[2] Samuel Brown, 'On the Sufficiency of the Existing Companies for the Business of Life Assurance', *AM*, IV (1854), 16–21.

with that which exists—that is, if they be too small for the risk incurred—destruction and ruin will soon overwhelm it'.[1]

Naturally enough, it was the danger of 'destruction and ruin' which was most stressed in public arguments about the insurance boom. But anxiety about competition was aggravated by the fear of corruption. 'There is a great danger looming at present in the path of society', wrote the *Daily News*: the state of insurance is a strong temptation 'to avarice and fraud'. And, it was asserted, the pitfalls were peculiar to life assurance, for the unwary or uninformed might never notice them until too late; they might not need the service which they purchased for years, or even decades: 'Let it never be forgotten that, of all public institutions, a life assurance company is that which may be the longest carried on under false colours, and which, in the end, may terminate the most disastrously for those who have relied on its obligations.'[2]

What was particularly, and understandably, emphasized by the cautious and the conservative was the danger of sharp practice. Nor did they have to point to merely theoretical dangers: the notorious West Middlesex General Annuity Assurance Company (established 1836, although its prospectus boasted 1796) and its associated Independent West Middlesex Fire and Life Insurance Company, with fictitious shareholders owning a non-existent capital of £1 million, had already mulcted the public of £200,000 by the sale of annuities at ridiculously low rates. The West Middlesex—established by 'the greatest swindlers that ever existed in London', according to an official of the Bank of England—was exposed by a Select Committee in 1841, lampooned by Thackeray as 'The West Diddlesex Fire and Life Insurance Company', and apparently gave Charles Dickens the idea of the 'Anglo-Bengalee Disinterested Loan and Life Assurance Company' which 'started into existence one morning not as an Infant Institution but as a Grown-up Company running along at a great pace and doing business right and left', and boasted a capital of 'a figure of two and as many oughts after it as the printer could get into the same line'.[3] No wonder that in 1851 the *Post Magazine* warned that unless something were done to prevent additions 'to the many rotten schemes which already exist', within twenty years life offices 'will be as plentiful as

---

[1] Letter from Thomas Carr to *Morning Herald*, reprinted in *PM*, XIII, 40 (2 October 1852). Compare *PM*, XIII, 45 (6 November 1852).

[2] Articles reprinted in *PM*, XIII, 40 (2 October 1852), 46 (13 November 1852).

[3] David Jones, *On the Value of Annuities and Reversionary Payments* (1843), II, 190–1; Select Committee on Joint-Stock Companies, *PP* (1844), VII (evidence of Sir Peter Laurie); W. M. Thackeray, *The History of Samuel Tidmarsh and the Great Hoggarty Diamond* (1841); Charles Dickens, *The Life and Adventures of Martin Chuzzlewit* (1843).

gin shops'. And four years later, in a mock-humorous vein, it classified insurance managers into two groups: 'one composed of intelligent, quick-sighted persons, acting for and with Boards of Directors as shrewd and as far-seeing as themselves, the other of keen fellows, sharp as needles, who would get the teeth out of your head if you were to open your mouth in their presence'.[1]

In the last resort, however, warnings about conscious fraud were less important than complaints about unrestrained competition leading to speculation, excessive cost-ratios and fundamentally unsound practices. As the publisher of the *Post Magazine* put it in 1852, 'the facility with which new assurance offices are set on foot, the tempting promises with which each new scheme is baited . . . have . . . converted a scheme of infinite utility and philanthropy into one of the greatest speculative projects of the present day'. And the greatest danger was not immediate and outright failure but the 'undetected poverty of a necessitous institution'.[2] These complaints came stridently to a head in 1852 when the *Post Magazine*'s long campaign against unstable offices was capped by the publication of a widely read pamphlet by Robert Christie (the Manager of the Scottish Equitable Assurance) and a series of articles in the *Morning Chronicle*, which took up Christie's complaints and claimed that speculative competition had been 'carried to a desperate and dangerous pitch, which can only tend to ruin and demoralize a great branch of public enterprise'.[3] Christie himself, in an open letter to the President of the Board of Trade, wrote in an alarming and sensationalist way about the large number of new offices and the high ratio of expenses to premiums. He called for an immediate Government inquiry into the solvency of all new offices. Although many would come out of the ordeal with credit, he claimed, 'my impression,—nay, my entire conviction, as to others,—notwithstanding the

---

[1] *PM*, XII, 10 (8 March 1851); XVI, 25 (23 June 1855). Also see Anon., 'History and Principles of Life Assurance', *Edinburgh Review*, XLV (1826–7), 506: 'In most other descriptions of business, when things are going wrong, the evil, for the most part, soon appears. But here [in life assurance] the business may be proceeding on principles which insure its absolute ruin, but for many years there will be every appearance of full prosperity.'

[2] W. D. S. Pateman, quoted in Ogborn, *Equitable Assurances*, p. 236.

[3] Robert Christie, *A Letter to the Right Honourable Joseph W. Henley Esq., M.P., President of the Board of Trade, Regarding Life Assurance Institutions, with Abstracts of all the Accounts Registered by London Life Assurance Companies* (Edinburgh, 1852). Three basic articles from the *Morning Chronicle* were reprinted in two consecutive numbers of the *PM*: XIII, 36 (4 September 1852), 37 (11 September 1852). W. D. S. Pateman published another attack on the new companies in the same year (*Life Assurance: its schemes, its difficulties and its abuses*), and besides yet other criticisms, there was a vigorous counter-attack by defenders of the new practices. See the anonymous pamphlet (*Hints to Agents*) and other pamphlets by Alexander Colvin, James H. James, Francis G. Neison, B. A. Strousberg, William Swiney, and W. T. Thomson in section 4 of the *Note on Sources*.

flaming accounts of their prosperity contained in Reports and Speeches at Annual Meetings,—is, that they are rotten; and are in effect, though perhaps not in design, fraudulent'.

As presented to the public, these and similar arguments (which, with the new popularity of life insurance, were very widely disseminated) had all the appearance of reasonably objective statements. On the other hand, of course, the new and young offices were not lacking in their supporters. To them it seemed that the new offices were neither extravagant nor insolvent, that the criticism and publicity of the early 1850s emanated from the lethargy and spite of well-established offices, 'terrified by the danger of competition from more spirited companies'. The older companies were accused of having for long attempted to secure legislation restricting the growth of the industry; of having 'formed themselves into a league to crush the young ones'; and of having been instrumental in drawing up the Joint-Stock Companies Act of 1844 so as to exclude old companies from its requirements, and therefore concentrate adverse publicity on the new, while they (the older offices) 'have nearly all of them scrupulously concealed the state of their affairs'.[1] Nor were the newer companies lacking in a technical defence. Christie soon found himself embroiled in a public controversy about life assurance accounts with Francis G. Neison, Consulting Actuary to the Law Property Assurance & Trust Society—one of the companies attacked. Neison categorically denied that expenses were excessive in light of prospective new business, and argued that old and sound offices had themselves been accustomed to spend their first year's premium to keep up business. To Neison, the criticisms merely reflected the fact that men like Christie were 'evidently jealous of the increasing influence, growing importance, and superior tact, judgement, and intelligence of young assurance companies'. The affairs of the older companies were themselves 'involved in much obscurity'. Compared with the new, 'all the obscurity and doubt devolves on the state and condition of the older'.[2]

In spite of the vehemence of this sort of defence, the doubts which had been sown, the widespread insecurity generated, and the consequent emergence of a new scepticism and timidity about insurance, demanded an authoritative and official attempt at resolution. In any case, some

[1] For all these arguments see a letter by J. Baxter Langley to the *Manchester Courier*, reprinted in *PM*, XIV, 2 (January 1853); and B. H. Strousberg, *Conspiracy Detected; in a letter to the Right Honourable Joseph W. Henley Esq., M.P., President of the Board of Trade, in Refutation of Certain Statements published by Robert Christie, Esq., and others on the Subject of Life Assurance* (1852). Strousberg also wrote *Judgement Before Trial* (1853). The new companies were obviously behind the publication of a new journal, *The Register: A Family and Economic Journal*, which, from March 1853, provided them with a vigorous and virulent defence.

[2] Letter to *Morning Chronicle*, quoted in *PM*, XIII, 38 (18 September 1852).

members of the Earl of Aberdeen's newly formed administration now wished to see the matter taken up for political reasons.[1] In March 1853, therefore, James Wilson, Secretary to the Treasury, moved for the establishment of a Select Committee on Assurance Associations. Emphasizing the importance of the issues and interests involved, 'where the operations were so great and the effects so distant', he argued that Parliament was morally obliged to prevent fraud and abuse. Since 1844, he said, 335 offices had been projected and 149 founded—of which only fifty-nine had survived. Although 'anxious to avoid creating any unnecessary alarm in the public mind', Wilson claimed that many new companies were 'of a mushroom description', deserving the name of 'swindling establishments'; and that, since 'hundreds of associations were springing into existence one day, and falling like an autumn leaf the next', the House could not let things continue without making an effort to call public attention to the abuses 'and by means of a Parliamentary inquiry to try and discover some mode by which associations of so much importance could be placed on a safer footing'.[2]

The Select Committee, which met in 1853, was the climax of the insurance controversy not merely because it focused discussion by many expert and experienced witnesses, but also because its *Report* reflected the dilemma produced by this new and critically important development in British economic and social life. On the one hand, it acknowledged the argument that life insurance might be so different from ordinary business as to be an exception to the 'rule' about 'the general wisdom of noninterference on the part of Government in matters of trade'. On the other hand, however, it had to recognize that regulation might well hamper 'the free development of private enterprise' and induce a 'lulling' of 'private prudence and vigilance'.[3] The harshest critics of the new competition were, in fact, conscious of the difficulty of abating the mischief without 'interfering with that perfect freedom of industry and employment of capital, upon which the whole of our modern commercial legislation widely proceeds'.[4]

In the event, the Select Committee confined its recommendations to proposals that life offices be obliged to invest £10,000 of their paid-up capital in public funds, and that there be a uniform and distinctive joint-stock law, with a single system of registration for all companies. The compulsory paid-up capital coincided with a proposal of the Institute of Actuaries, and was designed as 'caution money', to ensure (in the words of

1 James H. James, *Modern Assurance Companies Vindicated* (n.d., 1853?), p. 4.
2 *Hansard's Parliamentary Debates*, Third Series, CXXIV, columns 1320–32 (8 March 1853).
3 *SCAA, Report.*
4 *Morning Chronicle*, quoted in *PM*, XIII, 37 (11 September 1852).

John A. Higham, the REA Actuary) that every office gave 'a guarantee for the honesty of its intentions, and its ability to pay out what it professes'.[1] In fact, the Committee was forced to confess that the situation was not so bad after all—that the general condition of life offices 'is more satisfactory than they had been led to believe before they entered upon their enquiry', and that the undoubted abuses which existed were swindles which it would be difficult to prevent 'so long as private persons exercise so little precaution in the conduct of their own affairs'.

With the relatively mild Report of the Select Committee, the insurance controversy which had raged furiously for a few months abruptly subsided. As the Committee made clear, it was far easier to express anxiety about the competitive situation than to formulate an acceptable solution. Indeed, there were times when it seemed that the principal origin of the debate was the jealousy and competitive fears of established and conservative offices—and its main objective the dissemination of adverse publicity about new and young offices. And although the spokesmen of the older companies were obviously justified in pointing to the instability and unsound practices which characterized the insurance boom, the tone and sweeping generalization of their complaints, and the one-sided nature of the 1844 law in regard to the publication of accounts, all give the impression of a conscious and co-ordinated programme of detraction, the object of which was 'to see the younger companies over-ridden or bullied out of the market'.[2]

Quite apart from the fact that the strident controversy about life insurance produced no authoritative proposals for sweeping changes in the law, even the mild recommendations of the Select Committee were not enacted immediately. In the 1850s there were only half-hearted attempts at new legislation. It was not until 1870, after a specific and quite spectacular scandal (the failure of the Albert Life Assurance Society, dragging down with it some twenty-six other offices which it had absorbed), that a Life Assurance Companies Act was passed.[3] This Act, which introduced the idea of 'regulating' insurance by a combination of freedom and publicity, obliged new life offices to deposit £20,000; stipulated that the life fund be separately accounted for; provided for a standard form of accounts and regular publication of valuations; and established procedures to regulate the amalgamation or winding-up of offices. In fact, this legislation still allowed life offices a great deal of freedom—for life insurance was too

[1] *SCAA*, Q.2381–2.
[2] *Tait's Edinburgh Magazine*, xx (1853), 462.
[3] Raynes, *British Insurance*, p. 349.

complicated and subtle a matter for there to be any easy agreement on a single technique of valuation or direct comparability of accounts. Hence practicality as well as ideology precluded positive and systematic regulation.

In any case, even in the 1850s, some of the objects of the exercise had been achieved by market forces and publicity. In the mid-1850s the combination of adverse publicity, the unsettled state of the law, and bad commercial conditions led to a temporary falling-off of business and a significant decline in the number of offices through amalgamation. And in 1856 the Government inquiry of 1853 was said to have improved the practice of life offices. The insurance boom and controversy had, after all, proved partially self-adjusting.[1]

In the last resort, however, the controversy was significant not because it had a direct or indirect effect on the course of events, but because it was a symptom of a new and more modern epoch in the history of life assurance. The critics of the young companies were no doubt justified in some of their anxieties about fraud and unsound practices. But, in more general terms, their criteria of soundness and respectability were derived from a period when life assurance was at a quite different level of development. By the mid-nineteenth century it had ceased to be exclusively used by a narrow range of the middle class; more and more different social groups were involved, industrial assurance for the working and lower middle classes was beginning its sustained rise,[2] and the commercial element was well to the fore. This tapping of new markets for life assurance was, of course, bound up with the growing prosperity of Great Britain in the 1850s. But, in addition, it was inevitably associated with a new vigour and purposefulness in insurance competition: the business-seeking, risk-taking characteristics of the new offices were the products not of any exceptional sinfulness on the part of their promoters, but of the demands and opportunities of a new commercial situation. As one proponent of the younger offices argued, new levels of business might best be tapped by new companies 'for those who promote them set new springs in motion which operate upon circles hitherto unexplored'. Further, this increase in business had been necessarily associated with disturbance, since the innovators 'found it indispensable to infuse into their operations that energy which is the characteristic of all those who have their fortunes to make, in order to compete successfully with old-established companies, who were favoured

---

[1] Walford, 'Life Assurance', *AM* (1887), pp. 447–8; Raynes, *British Insurance*, p. 250. The number of life offices declined from a peak of 193 at the end of 1855 to 117 seven years later (Deuchar, 'Life Assurance Business', *Transactions of the Actuarial Society of Edinburgh*, II, 5, Appendix).
[2] Below, pp. 218–19.

by the prestige of past success and great accumulated capital'.[1] In this new environment it was inevitable that competitive practices should become more spectacular, and that expense ratios should rise.

The initial conservatism of the older companies, while it brought security and honour, also made it very difficult for them to respond to the new situation in any except an apprehensive way. They laid themselves open to the charge of having 'remained fast asleep, whilst the world around them was advancing . . . [and] endeavouring to crush . . . competition . . . by a course of declamatory assertion and invective'.[2] For a moment they took fright at such an abrupt and painful disturbance of their inherited and hitherto unquestioned ideas and practices. In this sense competition *could* be beneficial and even inevitable, as Francis G. P. Neison, a proponent of the new practices, somewhat cruelly pointed out in 1852:

The exclusive system on which the old, dignified and plethoric corporations were accustomed to transact their business, forced into the field active competitors who were willing to concede to the public such privileges and facilities in their transactions as were soon appreciated and approved. The whole history of life assurance most emphatically shows this to be the case and produces the strange anomaly that the wealthy and powerful companies, as they are generally esteemed to be, are lagging behind, mere copyists of the methods, peculiar features and privileges from time to time introduced by younger societies.[3]

Neison was perhaps exaggerating the passivity of the old-established companies. Many of them gained a fresh resilience from the newly invigorating atmosphere of competition in the second half of the century. But there can be little doubt that he was right in the first instance. The old offices had to learn from the new. By the early 1860s, for example, H. M. Tyndall, the Assistant Actuary of the Atlas, in a report to his Directors, emphasized the intensity of competition and the liberal terms (for foreign residence, renewals, assignments, etc.) of the younger offices: 'They have advertised more, canvassed more, offered higher rates of commission and promised more largely: and thus the old-established assurance companies have, to a great extent, been driven into obscurity: relying too much perhaps, upon their known respectability, actual wealth, sound condition.' To Tyndall, life assurance was now a 'struggle' for business. And, although it was still vital to avoid unnecessary risks and wasteful expenses, only a new competitive vigour could answer modern needs.[4]

---

[1] Strousberg, *Conspiracy Detected*, pp. 4, 13.

[2] William Swiney, *Letter to the Right Hon. B. Disraeli, M.P., Chancellor of the Exchequer* (1852), p. 3.

[3] Letter to *Morning Chronicle*, reprinted in *PM*, XIII, 38 (18 September 1852).

[4] For a response to the same situation by the Actuary of the Royal Exchange in 1863, see below, pp. 182–4.

As if to corroborate this view, in the same year that Tyndall wrote this Report (1864), the Government put forward an ill-fated scheme to sell life assurance and annuities through the Post Office. The idea of insurance backed by the State had been anticipated in a proposal for 'The Poor's Assurance Office' at least as early as 1807, and in 1864 was welcomed by *The Economist* as 'the greatest of undeveloped economic forces'. Nevertheless, after ten years' activity the Post Office had sold a mere 4,478 policies, insuring a derisory £343,797. Clearly, the public had to be *sold* life assurance in the context of economic enterprise; and as a commentator put it in 1876: 'All the life assurance that would result from voluntary action in the United Kingdom would easily be transacted by some half a dozen offices.' The complete failure of the Government scheme, even though it dragged on until 1928, reflected, accurately and decisively, the weakness of any view of life insurance which denied its competitive character.[1]

INSURANCE AT MID-CENTURY

By the 1850s an insurance company was no longer a rare and novel institution. Like textile manufacturing or banking, shipping or coal-mining, insurance had become an established part of the British economy and British society. It had also passed through periods of intense competition which had produced widespread debate and important changes in its structure and the relationships between different offices. Competition had the most obvious effect in the case of fire insurance. Its influence, together with that of the ever-changing technicality of risk assessment and fire underwriting, produced not merely a traditional trade association, but a powerful and reasonably effective tariff organization by mid-century. Fire insurance became a major industry relatively late; but it was a pioneer of the practice of formal industrial co-operation.

Life insurance, although it had its own problems of instability and competition, did not, of course, attain this degree of institutional harmony and co-operation. This was because life underwriting was based upon a fundamentally different order of risk-sharing than fire insurance. On the one hand, the 'cost price' was much more accurately (or safely) determined—on the basis of mortality tables and interest rates. On the other, competition produced not so much a pressure on premium rates (which might have driven them below levels of safety), but a sharing of residual

[1] For the Government scheme, see Walford, 'Life Assurance', *AM* (1886–7), 122, 450–1; Dermot Morrah, *A History of Industrial Life Assurance* (1955), pp. 29–33. Between 1865 and 1918 only 29,415 policies (insuring well under £2 million) had been sold. Among the many defects of the scheme was the decision not to use canvassers and collectors.

profits by bonus payments which did not have to be declared until the profits were known. Precisely because the economics, or more accurately the mathematics, of life insurance could be 'routinized', market forces obliged a sharing of material benefits with policyholders.

This last was a special and noteworthy feature of the life insurance 'industry'. For its operations depended pre-eminently on the application of technical, systematic and rare skills—those of the actuary. More than this, the weight of moral and social responsibility which rested on the management of a life office controlling funds in trust for the future, was also unavoidably focused upon the actuary, on whose professional expertise as well as ethics depended the safety and welfare of the policyholders. The consequent demand for continuous and intensive technical training and the presence of moral obligations which transcended medium-run profit-making, in fact produced a new profession in Victorian Britain.[1]

Insurance at mid-century had compressed a good deal of experience and evolution into the two or three generations of its popularization. It had become not merely accepted but inextricably integrated with the operation of a complex economy and a sophisticated society. It had grown spectacularly, and market forces and pressures had enforced a significant degree of competitive restraint and business co-operation. The industry had grown to the point at which its indirect rôle as a set of financial institutions assumed an independent significance in the country's capital markets;[2] and the nature of its task, particularly as regards life insurance, had produced a new profession—one more contribution to the changes in social habits and institutions which were provoked by the modernization of insurance.

[1] For the evolution of the Institute of Actuaries, see R. C. Simmonds, *The Institute of Actuaries, 1848–1948* (1948). In 1856 Scottish members seceded to form the Faculty of Actuaries in Scotland. See A. R. Davidson, *The History of the Faculty of Actuaries in Scotland, 1856–1956* (1956).

[2] See chapter 13.

7

The Royal Exchange Assurance in the Early Nineteenth Century: fire underwriting

The Royal Exchange Assurance continued to play an important rôle in British fire insurance in the early nineteenth century, even though its position, together with that of the other traditional offices, was somewhat weakened in the first two decades. In 1805 it had been responsible for 13 per cent of all sums insured by English offices in Britain. This percentage had fallen to less than 8 by 1824, and fell, somewhat more slowly, to 5·6 in the early 1860s. (Sums insured in Britain by the REA fell from £35·3 million to £31·9 million, and then rose to £58·3 million, at these three dates.) Broadly speaking, the Corporation's belated response to the competitive inroads of new offices in the 1820s arrested the sharp decline in its business, and it managed to hold this line for another generation by an adaptation of its outlook and management policies. By the 1860s, however, it was becoming clear that events were once again outstripping the Corporation's ability to adapt to them.

The long-term situation is shown in the graph on page 148, which indicates the fluctuations in fire premiums between 1780 and 1870, and compares them with those of the Corporation's contemporary, the Sun. The Royal Exchange obviously took excellent advantage of the underwriting opportunities inherent in inflation and industrialization at the turn of the century, and it clearly benefited more than the Sun from the initial thrust of expansion in the Wars. Between 1790 and 1803 its premium income rose from £34,000 to £88,000.[1] But the dominant position which it attained in the opening years of the century was rapidly eroded by the onset of new competition. The steady fall in premiums in the last years of the Wars continued into peace-time, and reached its nadir in 1826, with an income of merely £50,407. After 1826, however, even taking into account

---

[1] Until 1891 the Corporation's financial year ended in April. Consequently, '1790' refers to the twelve-month period ending April 1790, and so on.

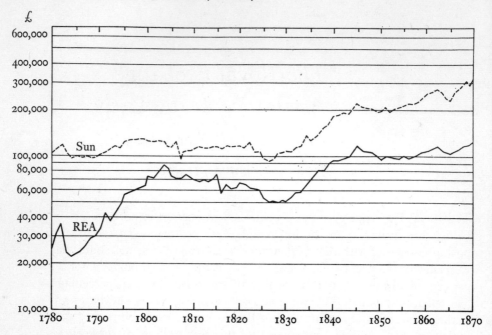

Fig. 7.1: Fire insurance premiums, 1780–1870: Royal Exchange Assurance[1]
and Sun Fire Office

(Sources: REA Archives; Dickson, *Sun Insurance Office*, pp. 302–4.)

[1] The accounting year ended in April of the year indicated.

the lower premium rates introduced in that year, there was a solid recovery of business into the 1840s. By the late 1840s annual premiums regularly exceeded £100,000. Stable in the 1850s, they rose slightly in the 1860s, to an average of some £113,000. At the latter date, with the Sun and Phoenix, the REA was still one of the three largest offices in the country. Table 7.1 provides more precise measures of these trends and indicates the main pattern of losses and costs:

TABLE 7.1. *REA fire insurance premiums, losses and expenses, 1780–1870*

(Annual averages rounded to nearest £100)

Period	Premiums (£)	Losses, returns and commission (%)	Expenses (%)	Surplus (£)
1780–3	29,100	41·5	8·0	14,715
1786–90	28,800	67·5	17·5	4,298
1791–5	45,800	71·5	14·8	6,262
1796–1800	64,000	54·8	11·6	21,475
1801–5	79,800	63·8	13·5	18,143
1806–10	72,900	66·1	13·6	14,845
1811–15	71,300	64·6	13·1	15,913
1816–20	64,000	58·7	17·3	15,362
1821–5	61,000	60·6	19·3	12,239
1826–30	51,300	60·8	20·9	9,368
1831–5	61,700	58·1	14·0	17,189
1836–40	84,500	75·7	9·5	12,168
1841–5	101,600	89·2	12·4	(−1,642)
1846–50	104,000	62·4	14·4	24,421
1851–5	99,100	67·2	15·5	17,139
1856–60	102,900	68·1	16·5	16,131
1861–5	110,100	77·4	16·8	6,329
1866–70	116,300	63·4	16·4	23,535

In the early nineteenth century, as Table 7.1 indicates, the trend of underwriting profits roughly matched that of premium income. Thus in the first twenty-five years losses more or less fell as premiums declined. On the other hand, proportionate expenses rose quite steeply—as was only to be expected at a time of diminishing income, when so much of total expenses was accounted for by overhead costs at Head Office. In this period the underwriting profit fell below £10,000 only four times, while there were five years (ending April 1803, 1804, 1807, 1813 and 1814) when it exceeded £20,000. The prosperous years around 1800 were very rewarding indeed: between 1796 and 1815 the annual average underwriting surplus (£17,600) was just over 24 per cent of premium income. Of course, intensifying competition depressed profits as well as premiums after 1815; but even at their low point in the late 1820s they were still running at the healthy level of almost 20 per cent of premium income. Nevertheless, after 1825 the Corporation's experience *was* somewhat more erratic, and even when levels of profit reached their former heights, a greatly increased amount of underwriting had to be done in order to earn it. In addition, there were spectacularly exceptional losses: one very near home, when the Royal Exchange itself was burnt down in January 1838, with the result that the Corporation had to pay £45,000 to the Mercers' Company and the City; an enormous one at Hamburg in 1842 which cost the Corporation well over £90,000; and a substantial one at Liverpool in September of the same year in which the Corporation lost some £30,000. But these were exceptions. Between 1827 and 1840 the annual average underwriting surplus exceeded £14,000. Similarly between 1841 and 1870 the surplus averaged some £14,300, or 13 per cent of premiums. (The rebate on the fire duty brought in a further £2,300 annually.)

The REA was, of course, pre-eminently a 'solid' fire office—priding itself, and in many ways relying, on its financial strength rather than its competitive vigour. Even so, the Court had to exercise constant oversight of the reserves. In the very early years of the century the Corporation had an extremely large 'Fire Fund': £509,065, as against £71,573 premiums in 1814. This was, however, very much reduced in 1825 and 1830, when it was drawn upon to the extent of £263,974 and £187,322 to help pay the 100 per cent bonuses distributed to stockholders in these years. Finally, in August 1831 a new Profit and Loss Account was opened, and received £114,781 from the Fire Fund. Thenceforth, the Corporation's main reserves were kept in the Balance of Profit and Loss (known as the 'Rest')—which, in 1832, was £178,488.

By October 1841 the 'Rest' was down to £98,426. Earlier in the year the Court had, in fact, been warned that 'considering the large amounts which it is necessary for this Corporation to insure in single risks, it becomes obviously expedient to allow a large fund to be accumulated for meeting liabilities'. Within a year, the huge loss at Hamburg provided them with a 'very painful confirmation of the correctness of the view then taken'. By 1856 the Court was advised by the Treasury Committee that the 'Surplus Capital Account' (i.e. the Balance of Profit and Loss) should be 'considerably augmented' in view of 'the enormously increased extent of the Company's operations in every Department'. In fact, the middle years of the century did see a substantial accumulation of reserve funds.

In the first quarter of the century the REA, together with other traditional firms, found it difficult to keep up with the vigour, and even riskiness, with which the new offices pursued business. In particular, it seems that it was an initial unwillingness to meet competition by reducing ordinary premium rates, or even an inability to combine against a common threat, which was the crucial factor. For the Corporation, as for the other leading offices, the decisive break with the competitive caution of the early years of the century came in 1825. In addition to lowering premiums, in October 1825 the Court of Directors emphasized the continuing nature of the problem by appointing a special Committee of eight Directors for 'the general superintendence of the fire business of the Company'. (The Sun also appointed a similar group in 1826, to investigate ways of meeting competition.)[1] This Committee embodied a new and systematic vigour in the oversight of fire underwriting. It initiated surveys of the Corporation's experience with cotton mills, with London mercantile risks, and with Ireland, and began a rigorous classification of all losses over the previous ten years. It sought information on the cost of the Corporation's fire engine establishment in various provincial towns, and asked for a regular flow of detailed statistical information on the fire business. In the course of 1826 further data were collected on the loss experience over ten years in at least seven provincial towns and overseas. Clearly a new wind was blowing.

In February 1826 the Committee confidently reported that the lower premium rates should 'lead to a considerable extension of this branch of the Company's business'. In contrast, premiums on poorer risks had been raised, and some insurances refused. Two years later it informed the Court that economies had been effected by cuts in advertising, by reducing fire-engine establishments in the provinces and London, and by arranging a competitive contract for the firemen's clothes. In addition, the return of the duty on fire insurance was now confined to the amount actually collected in the accounting period, rather than including business done between the end of that period and the date of the return, thus increasing income by the interest earned on an average sum of £8,000. (Serendipity as well as forethought was coming to the aid of the REA: the Committee confessed that the possibility of this economy had been brought to its attention by the accident of the Commissioner of Stamps calling for additional particulars about the quarterly returns of duty!) Altogether, the Committee was happy to report an annual saving of some £3,700 from these measures. Since fire expenses were running at about £12,000 annually in the mid-1820s, this was obviously a significant reduction. The ratio of expenses to premiums, which had averaged over 23 per cent in 1825–8, had been reduced to 15·6 per cent by 1830. But economies of this sort, although important, were only part of the story. It was also vital to increase

[1] Dickson, *Sun Insurance Office*, pp. 132–3.

income. After 1830 the more positive aspects of the new attitudes began to take hold and there was a rapid recovery of premium income in the 1830s: from £50,900 in 1830 to £93,000 in 1840. In the 1840s, however, there was a levelling-off. Between 1843 and the end of the 1850s premiums ranged between £98,000 and £105,000. As premiums rose so, of course, did the amount of property insured, although it is possibly indicative both of the elimination of extreme competition and of the new situation of loss- and risk-consciousness, that the value of sums assured (i.e. property actually at risk) rose significantly less than premium income after 1829. (The average premium per £100 insured was 2s. 10d. in 1830 and 3s. 6d. in 1845.)

Oddly enough, the drive for increased premiums did not, in the first instance, lead the Special Fire Committee to look favourably on advertising. On the contrary, as already indicated, their economy drive led to a reduction of expenditure under this head. In 1826 it was decided to cease all advertising in England and Scotland on the grounds that its advantage 'was by no means equal to the expenses'. And in February 1827 the new policy and its necessary implications were explained to the Corporation's agents by the Secretary: 'a personal application of the Company's agents, and a judicious distribution of their Proposals for fire insurance, will tend more to an increase of business, than publishing their terms in a newspaper which is only partially read'.

In spite of this confidence, however, the cuts in advertising were, in fact, a backward-looking economy: they exemplified the attitudes of the past not the future. Marketing was becoming one of the most important elements in insurance. It is not surprising, therefore, that in June 1827 the usual advertisement in each of eight London papers was reinstated, since 'it might be detrimental to the Company's interest' to discontinue them entirely; and that by September 1830 the Committee had retraced its steps by allowing advertisements in each of twenty-one provincial towns. By the early 1850s the Corporation was inserting regular advertisements in over fifty provincial and twelve London journals.

Whatever was happening to advertising, however, the basic strength or weakness of any insurance company's competitive position lay in its 'field' staff: in the extent and strength of its agency organization. Thus, in the aftermath of the combined reduction in premium rates in 1825, the Special Fire Committee took care to keep the Corporation's agents informed of the opportunities which arose as competitors were forced to withdraw from the fire business. This happened, for example, in February 1827, when agents were told that the withdrawal of such offices as the Hope, the Eagle, the Aegis, and the Beacon, as well as smaller provincial companies, led it to hope 'that you will obtain an accession of business for this Company, by applying for, and procuring some of the insurance hitherto effected with those Companies, for which no policy charge will be made'. And two months later the agents in nine widely scattered towns were informed that the official tax returns indicated that many offices had a 'share of assurances . . . on so small a scale, barely if sufficient to pay their expenses', and that several more were likely to go under. The representatives were therefore exhorted to send 'a line in confidence' about any rumours of possible bankruptcy, and to 'keep yourself alive to this probability as well as to any other means which may present itself of increasing the Company's business in your agency'.

Even though branch offices did not really appear until the second half of the century, it was possible—and even competitively necessary—to move towards a more flexible and a closer system of agency control. As far as the REA was concerned, a more purposeful attitude to agencies began to influence its organization and policy in the summer of 1828. In July the Court of Directors empowered the Fire Committee to vary the security demanded from representatives according to special circumstances, and to be the official arbiter of applications for agencies. More significantly the Committee was authorized to depute a person or persons;

to call upon the Company's agents in the several districts and report on the state of regularity in which the business is conducted; to obtain such local information as the state of mills, manufactories, or other special risks, and of the circumstances which may affect the Company's interest in the several districts, also to procure agents at places where it may be considered eligible to make appointments, and for such other purposes as they shall deem to be for the Company's benefit.

This proposal obviously anticipated the appointment of what were later to be known as inspectors—acknowledging the need of a greater degree of committed effort. In fact, immediately after this the Special Fire Committee dispatched Matthew Ward, the Fire Superintendent, on a tour of forty-nine towns where the Corporation was not represented, to gauge the fitness of agents and appoint new ones—and in the weeks which followed he sent back a heartening number of applications. On the other hand, however, this function continued to be undertaken by the ordinary officers of the Corporation; and the appointment of specialists was, perhaps unduly, postponed.[1]

Under these sorts of pressures, and in recognition of the untapped market for life as well as fire insurance, the number of agents naturally increased in the first half of the nineteenth century: from 320 in 1816 to

[1] Below, pp. 288–9.

430 in 1830, and 574 in 1853. (No doubt the growth would have been greater had the Corporation put more effort into the development of provincial business.)[1] As with other companies, the REA used agents from a very broad spectrum of occupations. In 1848, for example, the Corporation had 555 agents, of whom 271 were professional men, officials, agents and 'gentlemen'; 112 were merchants, manufacturers and businessmen of various sorts; and 172 were shopkeepers. The biggest individual groups, apart from the ambiguous category of 'gentlemen', were: solicitors (95), grocers (39), drapers and mercers (34), booksellers (27), auctioneers (27), bankers (25), and builders (20).

The relative significance of an agency system was of course intimately connected with the relative significance of 'country' (as against London, or 'town') business. And in this respect, from at least the late 1820s, the broad geographical pattern of the Corporation's fire underwriting remained relatively unchanged. In the early 1830s, for example, out of a total premium income of almost £61,000 annually, the London area accounted for just over £16,000 (26 per cent), the rest of Britain for £38,000 (62 per cent), Ireland for £5,000 (8 per cent), and foreign and Channel Island risks equally for the balance of less than £1,500. Twenty years later, when total annual premiums had risen to £98,000, there was little alteration. The London area still generated 29 per cent of all premiums; the rest of Britain 61 per cent; Ireland 6 per cent; foreign risks (mainly Germany) 4 per cent; and the Channel Islands a negligible amount. There is little information about the main concentrations of insurance activity outside London. Obviously, a few provincial centres, like Liverpool, Manchester and Dublin, were reasonably substantial. In Liverpool, for example, sums assured on mercantile risks alone were over £1 million in the 1820s, and mercantile premiums averaged almost £9,000 in the next decade. The Manchester agency, heavily committed to the cotton textile industry, produced an average of £2,660 in the period 1820–9 and £7,057 in the period 1838–50. And Dublin's two agencies exceeded £3,000 premium in the 1850s. In cities such as these the Corporation was obviously willing to subsidize the expenses of maintaining the agents' offices. But there were numerous agencies like those at Leeds and Halifax, which in the 1820s had annual premium incomes of about £510 and £740 respectively—and even more like Bristol, which in the depth of the competitive slump, in 1825, enjoyed a premium income of merely £83. 12s. 10d.—but was still running a fire engine at an annual cost of some £60!

The fact that the REA maintained a relatively constant pattern of

[1] Below, p. 155.

5   Destruction of the Second Royal Exchange, 10 January 1838   *William Heath*

One Hundred Pounds Reward.

London, *June* 24, 1802

AS there is Reaſon to fuſpect that many Fires have been occaſioned by the wilful Attempts of evil-minded Perſons, the *Governor* and *Company* of the *Royal-Exchange Aſſurance*, the *Managers* of the *Sun Fire-Office*, and the *Directors* of the *Phœnix Fire-Office*, do hereby offer a REWARD of

One Hundred Pounds,

To be paid on the Conviction of any Perſon, who ſhall, within the Term of One Year from the Date hereof, have wilfully and maliciouſly been the Occaſion of any Fire, which ſhall have happened in any Part of *GREAT BRITAIN.*

This Reward will be paid by either of the ſaid Offices, over and above all Parliamentary, Parochial, or any other, Rewards whatever.

By the ACT *of the* 9th *of* GEORGE I. *Chap.* 22, *it is enacted,*

That, if any Perſon or Perſons ſhall wilfully and maliciouſly ſet Fire to any HOUSE, BARN, or OUT-HOUSE, or to any HOVEL, COCK, MOW, or STACK of CORN, STRAW, HAY or WOOD, they ſhall be adjudged guilty of FELONY, and ſhall ſuffer DEATH without Benefit of Clergy.

LONDON, PRINTED BY J. DIGGENS, ST. ANN'S LANE.

6   Offer of reward for information about arson, 1802

geographical interest for most of the early nineteenth century meant, of course, that as its premium income grew, the main areas benefited in roughly the same proportions. The economic significance of this fact is, however, somewhat ambiguous. On the one hand, the Corporation thereby seemed to be taking less advantage of the very considerable expansion of the provincial market for fire insurance in general, which was significantly greater than the growth of London's potential: between the early 1830s and the early 1860s all London fire offices increased their metropolitan insurance by 45 per cent and their English provincial business by 114 per cent, whereas the comparable rates of increase for the REA were 50 per cent and 41 per cent.[1] On the other hand, the Corporation had *started* from a position of considerable provincial strength, for in the early 1830s roughly two-thirds of its business was derived from country areas—compared with about 50 per cent for the other London offices.

In terms of the distribution of its business within Britain, the principal rationale of the Corporation's fire underwriting therefore seems to have been a reliance on its traditional patterns. This relative caution was also exemplified in the division of its insurances between Britain and other areas. Thus its Irish business grew by merely one-third at a time (1830–60) when total Irish fire insurance grew three-fold. More significantly, in light of the world-wide nature of the Corporation's organization in the twentieth century, the foreign field was treated with the utmost circumspection. As we have seen, foreign insurances accounted for less than £4,000 out of an average annual premium income of £98,000 in the early 1850s. Ten years later they represented even less: at a time when younger fire offices like the Royal or the Liverpool & London & Globe were greatly extending their overseas business, the Corporation's foreign premiums amounted to less than £3,000 out of total premiums of about £110,000.

As far as foreign business was concerned, it was obviously the risks implied in the lack of communication and control which most worried the Corporation. In June 1826 the newly appointed Special Fire Committee reported that its investigations of foreign insurances were encouraging as

---

[1] These data were calculated from the detailed returns of stamp duty collected (the returns distinguish between policies issued in London and those issued in the provinces) and assume that all policies issued in London were for metropolitan risks, and that all farm risks were covered by country agents. The basic figures are:

Annual average sums assured in England (£ million)

	LONDON			PROVINCES		
	1831–5	1851–5	1861–3	1831–5	1851–5	1861–3
All London offices	181	224	262	195	363	418
Royal Exchange	14	20	21	27	35	38
Sun	42	51	53	46	78	93

far as business transacted directly at Head Office was concerned; but that the business done by (overseas) agents 'does not afford sufficient encouragement for attempting to extend the same by the establishment of agents general on the Continent'. In fact, small agencies had been set up in a few towns in Belgium, Holland and Germany at the end of the Napoleonic Wars; but, with the exception of the Hamburg agency (although even that was limited to the acceptance of risks in specified north-German towns), these remained relatively unimportant.

In spite of the relatively high level of premiums received from and through Hamburg (almost £8,000 annually by the early 1840s), the loss experience was not at all good (between April 1836 and Christmas 1841 losses, commission and expenses exceeded premiums by some £9,000). Reluctantly, therefore, in February 1842 the Special Fire Committee, after considering 'the difficulties which there is reason to fear will always operate against such a control of the selection of risks by a Continental Agent, and more especially by his Sub-Agents, as may secure a favourable result . . . unanimously arrived at the conviction that the interests of the Company would be best promoted by closing the fire business of the Hamburg Agency'. The Court of Directors confirmed this resolution and steps were therefore taken to ensure that the agent, R. V. Swaine, should decline all new insurances and renewals. Within three months, however, Hamburg, and the Corporation, were struck by a disaster greater than any premonition which might have led to the decision to cease doing business there. On 6 May Swaine informed Head Office of the occurrence on the previous day 'of a most disastrous conflagration by which one-fourth of that City had been destroyed and which was still raging'. In light of the Corporation's extensive commitments, this was very serious news, and two Directors and the Fire Manager were immediately sent to Hamburg to appraise the situation.

In the event, the Corporation was, indeed, very severely hit: its losses in the fire were about £95,000 (total damage was later estimated at £7 million). Curiously enough, however, within a week of receiving Swaine's first letter the Special Fire Committee had decided to recommend a *renewal* of the Hamburg Agency, at least as far as local risks were concerned. The 'altered state of circumstances' which had led to this *volte-face* provide an interesting commentary on the competitive situation and business attitudes towards it. For, as was to happen with even more destructive fires in later decades, it was found that heavy damage overseas, by enabling premium rates to be increased and by demonstrating the soundness and integrity of the large British offices, was not always so disadvantageous as it first appeared. In May 1842 the Special Fire Committee recommended the continuation of business:

being of opinion that the apprehended instability of the Hamburg companies when contrasted with the promptitude of the English companies to meet their liabilities, cannot fail to secure to the latter a higher confidence and corresponding preference; considering, also, the very great destruction of property and the probability that the loss of public confidence may lead some of the local companies to discontinue business, thereby narrowing competition and insuring a material advance in the rates of premium—and finally anticipating that the danger of extended conflagration, as well as the degree of loss from future fires in Hamburg will be diminished by improved and more systematic means of extinguishing them and of saving property.

The Committee's optimism was justified: the British offices agreed to a doubling of premiums at Hamburg, and between 1844 and 1852, although annual premiums did decline from almost £8,000 to just over £3,000, the Corporation's loss ratio only once exceeded 50 per cent, and six times fell below 40 per cent. By June 1852 the REA was ready to agree to a reduction of rates charged by British offices doing business at Hamburg, in response to a decrease in the rates of German companies and in the light of improvements in building and fire-fighting since 1842.

Yet, although there were occasional periods of enthusiasm or anxiety about overseas business, the United Kingdom was the overwhelming preoccupation of the Corporation's Fire Department. However, that preoccupation was not only seen in terms of competition. As has already been mentioned, for example, one of the main tasks assumed by the Special Fire Committee immediately on its appointment in October 1825 was a detailed survey of the Corporation's long-run experience with different types and geographical locations of fire risks and losses. Behind these painstaking and sustained efforts lay a perennial problem of fire insurance: the accumulation of knowledge about (and the consequent careful selection of) both individual and distinct classes of risks. In the early nineteenth, as in the eighteenth, century this problem was compounded by the limited experience which any company might have of certain types of risk, and by the difficulty of securing systematic co-ordination of the expertise of different offices. Many of the concomitant problems arose in relation to unusual or hazardous types of insurance. Sugar refineries, for example, continued to be the same cause for anxiety which they had been in the eighteenth century: in 1818 premiums for the best class of refinery were reduced from 21s. to 16s. per cent to meet competition, although three years later the original rate was reinstated, and further increased in 1827;

and in June 1830, after studying details of all fires in London 'sugar houses', the Special Fire Committee concluded that the risk was so high 'that a remunerative rate of premium could not be obtained', and therefore agreed to decline such insurances in future. Similar special categories were saltpetre and pawnbroker risks. The premium rates for the former were reduced in January 1827 after both experiments and representatives of the Corporation's Fire Brigade had assured the Committee that saltpetre was not exceptionally dangerous. Pawnbrokers came under consideration in 1828, when the experience of the previous thirty-nine years was examined and the fact that those insuring with the REA were 'of a respectable class and in good situations' was noted. In the event however, it was decided not to reduce premiums, even though the lower rates charged by competitors had reduced premium income to about £150.

On a different level of significance, woollen and cotton mills received rather special consideration. Occasionally, for example, industrial strife might carry the danger of incendiarism—as happened in 1805, when the Corporation was warned by dissident cloth workers not to insure Yorkshire woollen mills containing advanced machinery, since they might take the law into their own hands.[1] But, in the main, the new industrial risks were hazardous enough without resort to malice and arson. Thus, premiums on woollen mills were increased in April 1828 after a study of seventeen years' experience had showed a net loss (after the payment of agents' commissions) of over £3,000 on gross premiums of almost £13,000. Nevertheless, by this time, premiums on woollen mills were less than £600 annually, so that it can hardly be said that this particular industrial risk was very important. By contrast, cotton mill insurance did play a moderately significant rôle in the Corporation's fire business—rising from an annual average of £3,202 premium income in 1826–35 to £8,080 in 1846–55. By the mid-1840s sums insured were about £1 million. In 1809, after the uncertainties of the late eighteenth century, the better construction of mills led to a reduction of premium rates. Yet when, in the summer of

---

[1] An anonymous letter to the REA is quoted in E. P. Thompson, *The Making of the English Working Class* (1965), p. 529. It ran:

Gent. Directors,

   At a general but private meeting of the Chairmen of all the Committees of cloth workers in this country (viz. York) it was ordered to desire you (for your own profit) not to insure any factory where any machinery was in belonging the cloth workers. For it was ordered again to petition parliament for our rights; and, if they will not grant us them, by stopping the machinery belong us, we are determined to grant them ourselves, but does not wish you to be any loser thereby.

                    By order of the
                    Cloth Workers.

1828, a rash of fires in cotton factories led to an exchange of information between the REA, the Sun and the Phoenix, the Corporation's survey for the period 1818–28 showed a decline in *annual* premiums from over £4,000 to less than £3,000, and a loss of £38,235 on a total premium income of £41,062. In 1814–29 the Sun lost £22,531 on a premium income of £30,048.[1] These figures must have been of some help in the agreements about minimum cotton mill rates between London and Edinburgh offices in 1829 and 1830.[2] The REA certainly had an incentive for action: its share of this substantial market had fallen from almost £600,000 sums insured in 1819 to about £330,000 in 1828. By December 1841, however, the Corporation's cotton mill insurances had tripled. By that time, too, the leading offices were in a stronger and more co-operative position, and their informal association and agreements were extended to the formulation of a tariff. The cotton mill tariff, which was published early in the next year, was one of the first, and provides an excellent example of detailed rating and careful surveying—with strong financial incentives to mill-owners to achieve improved standards of construction and thereby improve the risks.[3] In the short run, however, according to the REA's Special Fire Committee in 1841, there was to be an increase in premium rates 'in consequence of the very numerous and destructive fires in cotton mills, particularly in Scotland, during some years past, greatly surpassing in amount the premiums received by insurance companies in that branch of their business'.

Further, as with some other forms of property, the 'moral hazard' in mill insurance was a factor to be reckoned with, for the vicissitudes of the cotton trade meant that the attitude of mill-owners towards a fire might be ambiguous. Mrs Gaskell illustrated this in her novel *Mary Barton* (1848) with a cynical comment by a workman on a mill fire:

Carsons' mill! Aye, there is a mill on fire somewhere sure enough by the light, and it will be a rare blaze, for there's not a drop o' water to be got. And much Carsons will care, for they're well insured, and the machines are a' th'oud-fashioned kind. See if they don't think it a fine thing for themselves. They'll not thank them as tries to put it out.

At the other economic extreme, risks in agricultural districts gave the Royal Exchange some cause for anxiety in these years. For example, insurances on the thatched areas of Devon, Dorset and Somerset were found to have involved the Corporation in an underwriting loss of almost £2,500

[1] Dickson, *Sun Insurance Office*, p. 145.
[2] Raynes, *British Insurance*, pp. 332–3.
[3] Raynes, *British Insurance*, pp. 335–6.

in the seven years ending Christmas 1826. And, as a result, in October 1827 a limit of £1,000 per risk was placed upon policies issued without the express consideration of the Special Fire Committee. One of the principal fears about the insurance of thatched buildings was, of course, of arson. And there were times when arson was a quite widespread danger in rural areas. Thus, during the agricultural distress and disturbances of 1830, the outbreak of rick-burnings, particularly in the South-East, presented the REA with severe problems. The trouble (stemming from poverty, unemployment and the introduction of threshing machines), began in the summer in Kent, with machine-breaking and incendiarism. By November it had spread to the Sussex Weald, and at the Royal Exchange it was ruled that because of 'the late incendiary proceedings' in parts of Kent all proposals for farm insurances in that county had to be submitted first to the Fire Committee—which soon had to arrange an extra two meetings weekly to consider all such proposals from Kent, Sussex and Surrey. Other companies also experienced difficulties. For example, the Essex & Suffolk, which was particularly badly hit because of the localized character of its business, subsidized the employment of 'Bow Street Officers' to guard against arson, refused all farm risks in 1829, and in 1830 relaxed this embargo only with respect to farms which did not use the provocative threshing machines.[1] This particular bout of incendiarism died down after December 1830 and, in retribution for the outbreaks, nineteen men were hanged (sixteen for arson), 644 jailed and 481 transported.[2] In September 1831 after a survey of the Corporation's experience, it was resolved to go ahead with all renewals of farm insurances. Incendiary fires did not continue to characterize farm insurances. By the 1840s and 1850s the latter had become one more matter of negotiation between the leading offices: an agreement on rates for farm buildings seems to have been reached in 1844, and another for farm stock in May 1850.

As the consideration of cotton mill and agricultural insurances indicates, the period after 1825, and particularly from the early 1840s, saw both a greater desire for the fire offices to pool their individual experiences in determining premiums and a more successful pressure towards their acting in unison. These forces naturally led to the establishment first of an informal and then of a formal tariff association. And the REA, as a leading company, played an important part in this process. Indeed, by the 1840s

[1] Drew, *Essex and Suffolk*, pp. 33–4. Compare Aubrey Noakes, *The County Fire Office, 1807–1957* (1957), p. 47; Dickson, *Sun Insurance Office*, p. 142; Eric Hobsbawm and George Rudé, *Captain Swing* (1969), pp. 225–6.

[2] See George Rudé, 'English Rural and Urban Disturbances on the Eve of the First Reform Bill, 1830–1831', *Past and Present*, 37 (July 1967), 87–102.

the minutes of its own Special Fire Committee provide ample evidence that some of the main functions which the Committee had been expected to fulfil in the 1820s were now comfortably, and more appropriately, being carried out by the meetings between the representatives of the different fire offices. In effect, the tasks of assessing categories of risk, classifying and rating them, and arriving at appropriate changes in premiums was now undertaken collectively, and the results reported to the Committee by the Fire Manager for approval. A crucial area in which this process of enforced co-operation came to operate, and one which also illustrates the Corporation's own problems, is that of docks and mercantile insurances.

We have already seen how the pooling of information about Liverpool dock risks in 1826 led to an agreement to increase premiums and an improvement in results for the Corporation.[1] In spite of this, however, another severe fire in the Liverpool docks in 1833, in which total losses were about £150,000, led the REA to reconsider the extremely suspect state of fire prevention and protection in Liverpool. As a result of another inter-office conference, the basic rates for buildings was increased from 4s. to 8s. and for floating policies from 7s. to 12s. per cent. In promulgating these new rates, the offices expressed their keen disappointment that property-owners and civic authorities in Liverpool had failed to carry out their promises, made in 1826, to improve fire protection and establish a fire police. After repeated fires for over thirty years, the higher rates were therefore designed as a joint effort to induce property-owners to take better precautions 'and to bring them more within the range of those calculations which govern the operations of fire offices'. The offices promised to reduce them when appropriate steps had been taken to ensure an effective supply of water and to provide an effective fire brigade at public expense. But although the Liverpool Police Fire Brigade was authorized in 1834 and established in 1836, and there was a 2s. reduction of premium rates in that year, apparently followed by other reductions, there was another very severe fire in September 1842, in which the total loss was some £366,000, of which £30,000 was borne by the REA. This was immediately followed by a substantial increase in rates, a new and very careful classification of risks and districts, and quite explicit incentives to introduce improvements in the construction and protection of warehouses. By March 1845 the Corporation's Fire Committee heard that measures to provide water 'were in a great state of forwardness', so that rates were somewhat reduced. And two years later the Fire Manager reported that London and pro-vincial offices had agreed to reduce premium rates 'in consequence of the

[1] Above, p. 128.

extensive improved construction of warehouses, as also the supply of water in the warehouse districts'.

In the case of London dockside risks it was some time before the co-operation achieved before 1800 could be re-established in the newly competitive environment of the early nineteenth century. Thus, after the opening of the new St Katharine Docks in 1828, the REA failed to hold the line at a 3s. rate for insurances there—even though it had originally secured the agreement of other offices. By the end of August the Phoenix, the Sun and the Alliance were all charging 1s. 6d., although it was not until September 1832 that the REA followed suit.[1]

Ten years later, the Royal Exchange Assurance, together with the other principal offices, was still wrestling with the knotty problems of dock and floating insurances. It was, indeed, the latter question which gave rise to a meeting of the representatives of seven companies (the Alliance, Globe, Imperial, London, Phoenix, REA and Sun), in February 1842, which is generally regarded as a turning-point in the association of offices, leading directly to the formal establishment of the Fire Offices' Committee. Yet, as we have seen, there had already been a good deal of co-operation for seventeen years, and this meeting itself did not, in fact, produce agreement. By August 1842 the REA Court was sufficiently worried to urge the Special Fire Committee to look carefully into the question of the Corporation's commitments in docks and waterside warehouses, and on floating policies, in London. The Committee found that in addition to insurances of £247,000 on buildings, merchandise insurances were £1,167,700 with respect to goods in warehouses and £267,100 on floating policies. The Committee felt that the current rate of 1s. 6d. was 'inadequate to the insurance of merchandise, a portion of which is of a hazardous nature'. More significantly, unable to get others to agree, the Committee wanted the Corporation to strike out on its own:

The attention of the Committee has been for some time past applied in conjunction with the other principal London offices, with a view to an improvement in the mode of granting dock insurances, but without having been able to succeed in coming to a general understanding with them. The Committee are therefore disposed to try independently of other offices the experiment of a moderate advance of premium on merchandise in docks and uptown warehouses, which they deem preferable to a direct reduction on the sum insured.

Following this line, in August 1842 the Corporation increased its basic mercantile rate to 2s., and communicated to the Sun, the Phoenix and the Globe, 'the readiness of this Corporation to unite with them in a *further*

[1] Above, p. 128.

advance of 6d. per cent, should they so determine'. The REA succeeded: what could not be achieved spontaneously was attained by example. In September 1842 the Fire Manager reported having attended a meeting of the Sun, the Phoenix, the Globe, the Atlas, and other offices, at which they had agreed to follow the Corporation's lead in an upward revision of the London mercantile tariff. At a meeting on 21 October 1842, extending the area of formal association, the offices also agreed to increase premium rates for Liverpool and Manchester mercantile risks, and for cotton mills throughout England.

As in the eighteenth century, co-operation about rates and conditions was associated with, and sometimes anticipated by, co-operation about the vital and expensive area of fire-fighting. Indeed, to a company like the Royal Exchange, the organization, conditions and cost of fire protection continued to be an important matter—in provincial towns as well as London.

The Corporation was concerned with fire-prevention and fire-fighting at various levels. In 1819, for example, it made gifts of ten guineas to a Mr Gregory of Poplar to help him perfect 'a machine for preserving life and property at fires', five guineas to Thomas Moreton 'towards the improvement of a fire escape' and two guineas to Isaac Bickmore 'as an encouragement of a plan to extinguish fire'. But the principal form of this sort of help lay in the support or maintenance of fire brigades. The Corporation had its own fire engines in some provincial centres—for example, Liverpool, Manchester, Dublin, Newcastle, and Andover—where the extent of its fire insurance business warranted the outlay. In 1826, however, the Special Fire Committee recommended the abolition of the fire-engine establishment at Bristol and one of the two engine establishments at Dublin. In July 1826 the establishment at Birmingham was also disbanded, and by March 1831 it was decided to abandon the engine establishments at Newcastle and Manchester because their cost was not justified. In some towns the existence of engines owned by other offices was a further safeguard: the recent growth of other fire offices and establishments in Dublin was an argument in favour of reducing the provision of REA engines. In June 1857, however, it was decided to replace the Corporation's forty-year-old engine in Dublin with a new and more powerful one in light of the premium income of over £3,000.

In general, of course, the proliferation of individual engines and brigades was undesirable; and severe local problems might arise (such as the high cost of contracting for a horse always to be available in Dublin—which led to the apparently curious decision to hire one only when a fire actually happened!). In any case the early nineteenth century witnessed a substantial improvement in the public provision of fire brigades. Concomitantly, therefore, a fire office like the Royal Exchange Assurance, while reducing its commitments in terms of engines and establishments, offered help of various sorts to local authorities—ranging from the frequent gift of buckets and other equipment to regular subscriptions towards the cost of brigades, such as 10s. to the parish of Wolverhampton, in 1826, or the £10 which the Aberdeen agent was authorized to subscribe to the Commissioners re-forming the local fire-engine establishment in the same year.

Although only about one-third of the Corporation's fire risks were in the London area in the early nineteenth century, these were, of course, very highly concentrated. It is not surprising, therefore, that the Fire Brigade in London should have occupied so much attention—quite apart from its traditional rôle as a prestigious and public representative of the REA in the City. The various offices' brigades were an important part of the London scene—participating not only in their own regular parades, but also civic ceremonies.[1] For a Corporation like the REA, therefore, its brigade was an object of investment—and when, for example, the annual parade was held in 1813, the thirty-two firemen, eight porters and four carmen were each given £1. 10s. 'for making up their clothes', 2s. 6d. 'as a compensation for the loss of time the day they walk at the West End of the Town', and 7s. for dinner. From as early as 1801 the firemen were also obliged to insure their lives for £100—the premiums being paid by the Corporation, with some deductions from the men's monthly pay.

Important as its rôle was, however, the Fire Brigade was also a costly part of the Corporation's organization. And, in pursuing its initial economy drive in 1826 and 1827, the Special Fire Committee naturally turned its attention to the London Brigade as well as to the costs of provincial fire-fighting. Apart from a small saving on the clothing contract, the Corporation dispensed with the customary payment of 2s. to the foreman and 1s. to each fireman for every alarm for a chimney fire, and disposed of its two Thames engine boats, since 'the advantage derived therefrom was very inadequate to the expenses' (£429 annually). But the most substantial economy measure derived from the realization, shared by the other principal companies, that efforts and therefore costs were being duplicated by the existence of individual brigades. As a result, the 1820s were a decisive turning-point in the history of London fire-fighting as well as of competition in fire underwriting.

---

[1] In 1809 and 1810 for example, the Atlas firemen were sworn in as special constables for special occasions, including Lord Mayor's Day—and paid by the Atlas for their attendance.

7   REA hand fire engine, 1825

8 REA fireman

In December 1826 the REA Court accepted a report from the Sitting Director, Browne, concerning an agreement negotiated with the Sun and the Phoenix 'relative to combining their respective firemen and engines under one Superintendent'. The point of this scheme, which came into operation on 1 January 1827, was that the companies would maintain their separate establishments (e.g. the Royal Exchange and the Phoenix were each to have two engines, each with an engineer, and eighteen men, and the Sun was to have three engines and engineers, one floating engine, and twenty-two men), but that these would be under the ultimate control of one Superintendent—S. M. Hubert of the Sun, 'applying the men of each office preferably to protect the interests of the office to which they belong, but with power to combine their services as circumstances may require'. As a result of this agreement between the three companies, the REA was able to reduce the number of its engines from four to three: the Wapping engine-house was closed, leaving engines in King Street and Jeffries Square in the City, and Stoney Lane in Southwark. This, together with the more general economies, meant that the expenses of its engine establishment were reduced from £3,276 in 1825 to £1,741 in 1827—a saving which was further augmented by £50 by the signing of a five-year contract for the supplying of the firemen's clothing. (Under the new contract hats cost 21s., boots 28s., firemen's suits £5. 1s. 0d., and carmen's and porters' suits £4. 12s. 6d.) The 'brigading' of the separate fire-fighting forces obviously worked well from the beginning. And it was presumably a model for a similar proposal for a joint engine establishment by J. A. Beaumont of the County Fire Office—which was declined by the Atlas Court of Directors on 24 September 1830. Instead, in January 1831, in response to overtures by the three offices concerned, the Atlas agreed to place its own brigade under the single Superintendent.

In the spring of 1832, however, Ford, the Secretary of the Sun, was mustering support for the idea of a 'General Fire Engine Establishment', which would more effectively and completely combine the separate brigades. Presumably in anticipation of this step, when Hubert retired in the summer of 1832 the REA was asked to approve his replacement at the Sun and as Superintendent of the brigades by the formidable James Braidwood, perhaps the most famous fireman of the nineteenth century, and formerly the youthful commander of the Edinburgh Fire Police. Braidwood's appointment was merely the inevitable prelude to a much more substantial change in organization. In September a Director from the Royal Exchange went to the Sun's offices where, under the chairmanship of the Sun's Secretary, the representatives of these two and seven other offices (the

Alliance, Atlas, Globe, Imperial, London, Protector and Westminster) met to discuss the establishment of a centralized London Fire Engine Establishment. By November the plan was sufficiently far advanced to be formally accepted by the Corporation. The new Establishment, under Braidwood's disciplined superintendence, had eighty professional firemen and nineteen fire stations. Its firemen were an independent force and had their own uniform. The Royal Exchange Assurance Brigade, after a century, was disbanded, and most of its men absorbed in the London force. The six who were not were given pensions ranging from £5 to £60. All London offices contributed to the Brigade's costs in proportion to the value of their insurances in London. Some ten years after the start the total income was £11, 906 and the normal cost (excluding new equipment) to the Royal Exchange alone just over £1,000. The Engine Establishment enjoyed a successful career until it was replaced by the Metropolitan Fire Brigade in the early 1860s.

The first half of the nineteenth century was clearly a period of considerable change for an eighteenth-century office like the REA. On the one hand, it was no longer one of a handful of companies dominating a small fire insurance industry; on the other, growth and competition shattered the inherited structure of premium rates, produced a new institutional framework for co-operation between offices, greatly improved methods of risk investigation and rating, and helped towards a more rational organization of the fire-fighting services. The Corporation played a leading part in these trends. But unfortunately, apart from the general information already summarized, there is relatively little surviving information about the more technical aspects and terms of fire insurance by and with the Corporation in the period. As we have already seen, competitive forces obliged it to extend limits on ordinary insurance in the Napoleonic Wars; and in 1826 it abandoned the traditional practice of charging higher premiums on larger risks as a matter of course. In some senses, however, there was relatively little change. The basis of rating depended throughout the first half of the century on the traditional classes of common, hazardous and doubly hazardous assurances—with a fourth class to embrace the new sorts of risks involved in an industrializing economy. And although in 1844 it was decided to omit from policies the old condition that certificates for fire losses had to be signed by Ministers of Parishes, this was merely a formal ratification of existing practice, for, according to the Fire Committee, the certificate 'has not for some years been called for'.

Thus, many of the Corporation's traditional procedures were abandoned under the pressures of changing times. Among them, it may be noted, was the practice of issuing fire marks—a practice which was the less necessary with the improvement of fire-fighting and its co-operative control. In addition, according to the Secretary almost thirty years later, the REA stopped issuing marks in the late 1830s, since 'by publishing the fact that the buildings on which they appear are insured, they may attract the notice of some evilly disposed persons and thus lead to an incendiary fire'.[1] On the other hand, there were some conventions which survived into an era of intensified competition, and which no doubt strengthened the Corporation as a result. This was particularly so with regard to its tradition of liberality towards clients. In June 1838, for example, the Court ordered the payment of £100 towards a loss of £120 to Mathias Calaghan of Middleton, who had forgotten to renew one of his many insurances; and in March 1856 an *ex gratia* payment of £50 was awarded to Mrs Anne Watts of Hullingbury in Essex, who had insured her property with the Corporation for almost thirty years, but allowed the policy to lapse because of 'reduced circumstances', and had then been 'plunged into deep distress' by the loss of her house and most of her furniture, valued at £74. 10s., in a fire.

In many ways, however, the strengths of the REA fire insurance business were traditional in character. These had been of considerable use in the decades after the early 1820s, when the industry's leaders combined to resist the instability of uncontrolled competition. Yet competitive expansion and adventurousness were still called for even within the framework of the Fire Offices' Committee—and these were elements which the Corporation still lacked. By the 1870s and 1880s, therefore, it seemed excessively cautious, and its premium income stagnated accordingly. It had to wait for new men and a new outlook before its growth could be resumed.[2]

---

[1] In fact, the logic could work the other way: farmers who feared arson in the years around 1830 tended to display fire marks in order to indicate to potential arsonists that they might escape the cost of a fire by being insured.

[2] Below, pp. 241–6.

8

The Royal Exchange
Assurance in the Early
Nineteenth Century:
life underwriting

In its life insurance business in the early nineteenth century, the Royal Exchange Assurance found it necessary to depart very radically from traditional attitudes and practices. As we have already seen, the enormous growth of life insurance in the period, accompanied as it was by a proliferation of offices and a heightening of competition, led to a much more active search for business and to the emergence and victory of the new system of bonus policies.[1] Correspondingly, therefore, the contemporary history of the REA Life Department was shaped by the timing, and problems, of the Corporation's inescapable decision to share its profits with its policyholders. In contrast to its position in relation to fire insurance, however, the Corporation was in this respect for long out of line even with other old and traditional offices. It was, in fact, almost the last company to give way under market pressure. And when it finally decided to take the plunge in 1841, the Actuary, Bartholemew Parkin Bidder, noted wryly that new offices invariably offered participating policies and that all the other older offices except the Albion (1805) and the Globe (1806) 'found it expedient to follow the stream'. This is one indication, as subsequent developments provided others, that it was far more difficult to secure concerted action in the case of life than in that of fire insurance. Competitively speaking, the Corporation was much more on its own in this period—even taking into account the united fervour with which the old life offices attacked the new in the early 1850s.

In so far as it is possible to trace the statistical history of a Life Department by changes in premium income alone (no other quantitative data have survived from the period before 1841), the turning-point for the Corporation came in 1824. Up to that date life premiums had increased steadily from the mid-1780s. They had averaged some £19,000 around 1790,

---

[1] Above, pp. 132–5.

£41,000 in the years 1801–5, and £158,000 in 1821–5. After 1824, however, premium income fell to a low point of £129,237 in 1842, and then, under the influence of the issue of the Corporation's own with-profits policies, recovered to £158,000 in 1851–5.[1] Subsequently, premium income sagged, as the momentum gained from the introduction of bonuses faltered. And the Corporation entered the last quarter of the century with a depressingly stable life income. (In 1793 the Corporation had also taken powers to deal in annuities, although this was not to be an important part of its business in the period: the payment of 'common' annuities rose from just over £1,000 annually in the late 1780s to more than £6,500 in the late 1820s, and then declined to less than £2,000 in the early 1850s.)

TABLE 8.1 *REA life insurance premiums, 1788–1870 (annual averages)*

1788–92:	£18,900	1836–40:	£138,200
1801–5:	£41,000	1838–42:	£133,000
1806–10:	£66,400	1841–5:	£132,900
1811–15:	£95,800	1846–50:	£146,400
1816–20:	£130,400	1851–5:	£157,700
1821–5:	£157,600	1856–60:	£159,700
1826–30:	£155,500	1861–5:	£156,800
1831–5:	£151,000	1866–70:	£150,000

The break in the trend of premium income which came after 1824 coincided with a sharp intensification of competition as measured by the number of companies founded, even though not all of them survived for long. Thus, while the number of offices established between 1801 and 1819 had averaged less than one annually, eight were founded in 1820–2, seven in 1823, and twenty-eight in 1824–5. Like the Atlas, the REA was also very hard hit by the successful foundation of the Law Life (1823), which tended to cream off some of the best business through its contacts with solicitors.[2] But, unlike the Atlas, which had issued participating policies since 1816, the Corporation gave no public sign of any change in its outlook. In fact, its premium rates, for non-profit policies, were still based on the Northampton Table at 3 per cent, and were therefore the same as those offices which *did* offer bonus policies. In these circumstances, it was inevitable that its life business should begin to suffer. Up to the 1820s, conceivably, traditional strength and security had still meant

[1] All data in the text relate to twelve-month periods ending in April of the 'years' indicated. Hence '1842' appears as a low point even though the rejuvenating bonus system was introduced on 1 January, because in the accounts it represents the period 1 May 1841–30 April 1842.
[2] Above, pp. 135–6.

enough to potential policyholders to warrant their paying relatively high rates for them. (The Corporation's premium income quadrupled in the first quarter-century.) But this could not last indefinitely. In 1839 the Dublin and Cork agents were confident that the Corporation was missing a 'great increase of good business' by not holding out 'the inducement of

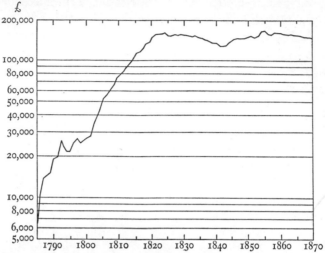

Fig. 8.1: REA life insurance premiums, 1785–1870[1]

(Source: REA Archives.)

a small participation in the profits'. And in 1840 the Falmouth agents must have been one example among many in finding 'that for a long time past they have been unable to prevail upon their own clients [the agents were solicitors] to effect life assurances with a company like this charging high rates and giving no bonus'. There was, in fact, no ignorance of the cause of the trouble; and in April 1840 the Court had prevailed upon the Governor, Sir John William Lubbock, not to resign, 'in the particularly arduous circumstances in which the affairs of the Company are placed by the expectations of the proprietors on the one hand, and by the rivalry of surrounding new offices on the other'.

Already in 1840, under pressure from the example of offices like the Atlas, the Guardian, the Pelican and the Sun, the Corporation had greatly extended the 'free limits' for foreign risks in times of peace. But by 1841 the Actuary and Directors knew that, unless a massive innovation in terms

---

[1] The accounting year ended in April of the year indicated.

of participating policies was introduced, then the REA would face a severe crisis. And at the invitation of the Fire and Life Committee the Actuary drew up a detailed report on the situation in November 1841. Before analysing the technical points involved, Bidder drew attention to the fact that whereas the annual fall in life premiums between 1824 and 1833 had been £937, between 1833 and 1841 it reached £3,356. This great decrease in the Company's business, he argued, was entirely due to 'the preference which the public naturally gives to offices which hold out to the insured the principle of participation'. On these grounds, Bidder went on, the cause of the decrease in the Corporation's life business 'is permanent, and must, if unchecked, operate in an accelerated ratio to exhaustion. The only alternative which presents itself is accordingly that of being passive under the all but certain prospect of entire exhaustion, or of adopting the principle of participation.'

In November and December the Treasury Committee and then the Fire and Life Committee each considered this sobering document, and the latter concluded that 'a change of the system is imperatively called for'. Participation in profits was the only alternative that could be adopted 'with a view to the preservation of a fair share of the business of life insurance'. As for the amount of the bonus, two-thirds of the surplus was suggested, on the grounds that anything less would not be a sufficiently great inducement to policyholders, while anything more 'would lead to too small a margin for the profits which the proprietors of the stock of this Corporation would be entitled to expect'. The profit-sharing was to be either by an addition of a bonus to the sum assured or by a reduction in the premium—although, unlike some other life offices (e.g. the Sun), the relevant option had to be chosen when the policy was first issued.

On 15 December 1841 the Court of Directors accepted the Report and resolved to recommend the new system to a General Court of Proprietors on 22 December, 'in order to avert a continuance of the decrease [in life business] which has been experienced and found to be progressive; and which if unchecked, cannot fail to operate in an accelerated ratio, to the entire exhaustion of that Branch of the Company's business'. The Proprietors approved, and on 1 January 1842 there began a new era in the Corporation's life business.

The general outcome of the radically new approach to life underwriting has already been touched on: in spite of intensifying competition, in ten years premium incomes regained the ground lost in the previous twenty. But these figures mask the true course of events, because they conflate the 'Old Series' (non-profit) with the 'New Series'. Their separation provides a better indication of the accession of business produced by the offer of bonus policies. By the end of the 1840s the participating had overtaken the traditional business:

TABLE 8.2. *REA life insurance sums assured and premiums under bonus and old systems, 1842–50*

Year ending 30 April	Sums assured (£000)	Premiums (£000)
1842: Bonus system	124	5
Old system	3,996	124
1845: Bonus system	1,048	41
Old system	2,646	99
1849: Bonus system	1,919	74
Old system	2,026	73
1850: Bonus system	2,119	82
Old system	1,889	68

Initially, the REA valuations were at seven-year intervals; and at the first valuation the surplus for the seven years to December 1848 was found to be £47,234 on the British Account and £32,233 on the Irish: a total of £79,467. Ironically the first policy to receive a bonus, according to one source,[1] was that of the innovating Actuary, Bidder himself, for he had retired in the midst of a severe illness in 1848, and died on 4 January 1849 —a mere fortnight before his successor, John Adams Higham, completed the first valuation report.

When Higham came to report on the second valuation, for 1849–55, he found a substantial surplus of £222,583—of which the Corporation's one-third share amounted to £74,194, and the policyholders' was £148,389. As a result, the policyholder derived 'a bonus such as very few Companies have been able to give during the same period'. The object of altering the system in 1841–2 had 'been more than attained', for the decrease in premium income had been changed into a 'material increase' and the Corporation's one-third of the new profit was considerably more than twice as great as the falling-off of profit on the old account. Profit as well as turnover had been revived by the belated decision 'to follow the stream'— which by this time was much more like a torrent.

To this extent, therefore, the move to a participation scheme had clearly been a success—even though the transition to participating policies had also occasioned a problem of public relations. The 'old assured' (i.e. those insuring their lives before 1842, by traditional non-bonus policies) were in many cases aggrieved that they were not to share in any future profits—

[1] Walford, *Insurance Cyclopaedia*, I, 275.

a situation which led to widespread dissatisfaction, and obliged the Actuary to explain repeatedly and at length to some agents, 'the reasons with which it was expedient that the remonstrances of the old assured at their exclusion from the bonus system should be met'. Clearly some business was lost as a consequence: in a report on Devon and Cornwall in 1842 Bidder reported that the Company's agents felt that they needed the Company's help in publicity and advertising, 'and they thought it the more incumbent on this Company to do so as in consequence of the prejudices existing against them in the minds of the old assured it is necessary to open new channels of business'.

In spite of these problems, the REA was committed to business expansion in life insurance from the early 1840s onwards. New prospectuses and advertisements were issued stressing the advantages of bonus policies and of the strength and stability of an ancient corporation. And in the early 1850s, presumably based in part on the successful experience of the first septennial period and in part on the intensified pressure of brash young competitors, further innovations were introduced. In January 1850, for example, after lengthy discussion, it was decided to grant endowment assurances and to revise premium rates. The next year, following another suggestion by the Actuary, it was agreed to re-introduce non-profit policies at lower rates than bonus policies. More than this, the Directors also agreed to an adjustment of premium rates for with-profits insurance—reducing them at younger, and increasing them at older, ages—which 'by approximating the practice and tables of the Corporation to those of other Companies would be calculated to promote its interests'. Finally, in July 1853, Higham proposed that the valuation period be reduced from seven to five years. Under the septennial system, since bonus payments were limited to policies on which three or more premiums had been paid, some policyholders, commencing two years before a valuation, would otherwise have to wait nine years for any profits. Given the fact that 'the young companies all divide at short intervals, and among the old ones there is a disposition to lessen the periods', the Court accepted the recommendation.

The introduction of with-profits policies in 1842, and the various other changes in premium rates and assurance practices ten years later, served, however belatedly, to bring the Royal Exchange Assurance into the category of 'modern' insurance companies. In this process the Corporation was obviously indebted to its Actuaries, Bidder (who assumed the office in 1838) and Higham (who was merely 27 when he became Actuary in 1848). Indeed, it is perhaps significant and certainly symbolic that Bidder was the first head of the 'Life Branch' to assume the modern title of 'Actuary'—his predecessor John Diggles Bayley being known by the traditional title of 'Life Accomptant'. But, whatever the influence of individuals, the rôle of adversity cannot be doubted: reform was a direct response to the pressures of competition. Anxiety as well as ambition was a motive. And in this context it was no coincidence that so many improvements came in the early 1850s when the competitive assault of the new offices was reaching a crescendo.

The atmosphere of hectic competition and keen anxiety in the early 1850s inevitably coloured the outlook of the REA. No wonder that in its contemporary advertisements the Corporation claimed that its experience and reputation, acquired during more than 125 years, 'afford a guarantee that [the] bonus has been legitimately declared out of realised surplus and not by the new system of anticipating profits', and that it offered the advantages 'of a safely constituted and thoroughly tested office, combining all the real improvements of modern practice'. And in its Prospectuses (e.g. that of 1853) the Royal Exchange dealt in some detail with the presumed risks of mutual assurance and the heavy responsibilities of life offices. Above all, it warned potential policyholders of the dangers inherent in bad insurance practices with regard to rating and valuation; 'neither large dividends nor declarations of large bonuses can safely be taken as indications of prosperity, or even of solvency'. These dangers arose not only with companies 'without capital or integrity', but also with 'companies honestly conducted, but founded on erroneous principles'. Indeed, the latter were even more hazardous, since they might go longer without discovery. 'Even large capitals, combined with the highest integrity in the managers, will not sustain companies under the weight of liabilities improvidently incurred, without sufficient care in the selection of lives, and at inadequate premiums.'

These awful warnings were characteristic not only of the atmosphere of contemporary life assurance but also of the image which the Royal Exchange Assurance had of its own probity, integrity and meticulous trustworthiness. Absolute respectability was clearly the banner underneath which the Corporation marched into the commercial battle of the mid-nineteenth century—and it is symptomatic of its actual and designed appeal to specific social groups that as late as 1853, when life insurance had become a very widespread social habit, its Prospectus was still emphasizing the appropriateness of life insurance for clergymen, pensioners and annuitants. In this context, too, it was only to be expected that the Corporation should feel itself bound by moral obligations. Thus, in 1830 the Court ordered the payment of a £75 annuity to Mrs E. Hart, 'whose husband committed suicide which vitiated an assurance of an annuity of £100 in case she survived him'. It is also, perhaps, significant that in 1850 the Directors should refuse to renew a policy for £10,500 on the life of Benjamin Disraeli on the grounds that 'the circumstances in which he is placed politically, render his life ineligible for assurance',[1] although it is only fair to add that in the early years of the century the Corporation had issued a policy for £2,500 on the life of the wealthy socialist, Robert Owen.[2]

The Corporation tended to work closely with other traditional offices —as in 1846 when it agreed to accept two proposals for £10,000 each on the lives of two noblemen only on condition that half the risk was taken by the Pelican 'or some other eligible company'. (It was the Pelican's Actuary, Tucker, who about this time was reputed to have reacted to the rise of 'pushing' offices by claiming that 'in ten years time, Sir, this will be no fit occupation for a gentleman'.)[3] And the REA also had its share of the bizarre types of insurance which inevitably arise when complicated property rights and dealings are involved—as in 1852, when the Corporation took £5,000 of a total of £50,000 insurance on the life of the Reverend Sir John Barker Hill, Bart., aged 49 and childless although married, payable only if he died leaving issue; or in 1878 when, for a single premium of £2. 2s. per cent, the Corporation accepted an assurance of £6,000 against the contingency of Sir James Hay Langham, then aged 75, marrying and leaving lawful issue.

The Corporation's undoubted position in the social and economic world of life insurance was in large measure attributable to its age, its experience, and the care which typified its business activity. In addition, given the long-term nature of insurance and the need for trustworthiness, the abilities and character of the men associated with the REA were naturally of considerable significance. At one level the Court of Directors represented the sort of financial respectability, commercial integrity and established reputation which instilled confidence in those who needed it. At another, the technical competence and obvious caution of the Life Department guaranteed an appropriate, and genuine, air of sheer professional scrupulousness.

[1] J. A. Higham to Manager of West End Branch, 9 March 1850. The policy (annual premium £225. 15s. od.) had been originally effected for seven years, in 1843, by Edward, Viscount Exmouth of Canonteign. In 1850 Disraeli unsuccessfully approached the Norwich Union for a loan of £4,000 on personal security. He was ultimately lent some money by Samuel Bignold, the Secretary of the Norwich: Robert Blake, *Esto Perpetua: The Norwich Union Life Insurance Society* (1958), p. 46.
[2] R. G. Garnett, *A Century of Co-operative Insurance* (1968), p. 14n.
[3] C. D. Higham, *Notes on the Actuaries' Club* (1929), p. 15.

The Corporation's Actuaries tended to be members of the aristocracy of the actuarial world. In the 1830s, Bayley, for example, used to meet regularly, if informally, with the Actuaries of the Atlas, Guardian, Law Life, Economic, Imperial and Universal to discuss matters of mutual interest. Bidder was almost equally well known, and his successor, Higham, who was chief Life Officer at the Royal Exchange between 1848 and 1860, was one of the outstanding actuaries of the mid-nineteenth century. He was obviously much respected, and his strict and unwavering ideas on the correct method of valuing assets and liabilities were argued at length in the columns of the contemporary Press and presented forcibly to the Select Committee on Assurance Associations in 1853. As the REA Treasury Committee later pointed out, the table for ascertaining minimum reserves, which he then proposed, and 'which cost a large amount of time and labour', was printed in the Evidence of the Committee and was subsequently 'regarded by many of the principal offices as a safe test and is used by them'.[1] In his extensive evidence to the Committee, Higham was also reluctantly brought to advocate some legislative interference with life insurance 'both on account of the long period over which the contracts extend, and especially for this reason, that life assurance offices are now taking to make up their accounts on principles that would be scouted from any other department of commercial enterprise'.[2]

Higham was obviously in the vanguard of his profession. But in later years the staff magazine claimed that the prestige of the Corporation's Life Department as a whole was sufficient for it to be 'regarded as the training school for actuaries'. And although not many examples of this sort of migration have come to light, there was probably a good deal of truth in the claim. In 1836, for example, David Jones left the Life Department to become Actuary to the Universal Life Assurance Society; in 1839 William Tarray became Actuary and Secretary to the Victoria Life Insurance Society; and in 1845 Percy M. Dove left to become the first Manager and Actuary of the newly established Royal of Liverpool—and to rise, with his new Company, to the pinnacle of the insurance world.

Paucity of surviving records makes it difficult to appraise the structure and extent of the life business overseen by Bidder and Higham—let alone their more obscure predecessors, Bayley and Fairman. It is reasonably

---

[1] Higham's powerful arguments against counting all the future premium (including the 'loading' for expenses) as assets was subsequently strongly urged by the two officials of the Board of Trade who reported on the working of the Life Assurance Companies Act of 1870 (see *Report* by Mr Malcolm and Mr Hamilton, 10 July 1874, reprinted with Board of Trade Returns, 1874).

[2] *SCAA*, Q.2394.

certain, however, that the practice of life insurance was relatively unchanging. It was, for example, very much a personal and central activity
for the Corporation. The Court still considered major proposals and it was
still the practice 'to take the appearance': a proposed life was seen by the
Directors or the relevant country agent—although it was not until 1838
that a medical certificate was required, and not until 1842 (after it had been
decided that the adoption of the bonus system necessitated the examination of all applicants by a doctor) that the Corporation appointed its own
medical adviser.

Information about the geographical distribution of the Royal Exchange
Assurance's life business becomes available for the 1840s, illustrating some
important trends. Thus, in the last year of the old, non-participating
system (1841), 4,796 life policies were in force. Of these, almost 60 per
cent (2,715) were issued in Ireland—a fact relevant to the opinion of the
Actuary in 1876 that 'at one time the Company had almost a monopoly of
the life business effected in Ireland'. Of those issued in Britain, over 80
per cent were handled by provincial agents rather than the Head Office.
This disparity was somewhat less marked when the *size* of life policies is
taken into account. The average policy was for £706—but the average
Irish policy was for £741, the average provincial British policy was £521,
and the average Head Office policy was £1,445. Clearly, the life business
transacted at the Head Office was of a quite substantial kind, presumably
because the Corporation's prestige business tended to accumulate there.
The result was that of the total premium income of £129,911, some 13
per cent (as against a mere 7 per cent of the number of policies) was
derived from Head Office.

Nine years later, in 1850, the character of the Corporation's life business
was beginning to change. Considering only the policies in the new bonus
system, the average sum insured had increased to £844 (presumably reflecting the tendency of the Corporation to deal with reasonably wealthy
people who were already in the habit of insuring their lives, rather than
participating in the growth of the habit of insurance among lower-income
groups). Ireland's share of the total number of policies had shrunk to
barely 40 per cent, and Irish sums assured had now fallen below the
Corporation's average, so that their share of the total was less than 39 per
cent. By contrast, and again illustrating the prestige element which
dominated the Life Branch in the cut-and-thrust competition of the
1840s, policies issued at Head Office now accounted for some 17 per cent
of all policies (18 per cent of British) and no less than 31 per cent of all
premium income (52 per cent of British premium income).

In spite of its relative decline, the Irish life business was obviously a very important element in the Corporation's activities throughout the early nineteenth century. Yet it gave the management continuing cause for anxiety. In particular, to judge from a communication to Irish agents dated 23 April 1839, speculation in life policies was 'extensively and systematic-ally' carried on there in contravention of the Act (1774) against wagering policies, which forbade the effecting of life policies on the life of another when the person insuring had no financial interest. The Corporation's agents were therefore warned against the acceptance of proposals by people who were 'totally incompetent' to pay the premiums and who immediately assigned the policy 'to those speculators by whose contrivances the assurances are made'. The agents were reminded of a lawsuit at Cork in 1837 which related to a £1,000 policy on the life of someone who had just left a workhouse and 'was "dressed up" for the purpose of making a respectable appearance by the speculator to whom the policy was im-mediately conveyed'; and told that it was the indispensable duty of every agent to make 'the most rigid inquiries into the collateral circumstances of character and respectability' of the referees and life proposed. The hope was expressed that the agents' vigilance would increase 'with their sense of the dangers with which life assurance is fraught in Ireland'. The pre-eminence of the REA in Ireland was subsequently attributed by Higham to the fact that 'other Companies had become shy of Ireland on account of speculative traffic in bad lives'; and this situation led the Corporation to maintain separate Life Accounts for Ireland and Britain when its bonus policies were introduced—for fear that higher mortality in Ireland would produce lower bonuses. As a consequence, according to Higham, 'Irish-men took advantage of visits to London to make their proposals here and secure the anticipated larger bonus'. (In fact, these anticipations were disappointed: the Irish bonus came out very near the British—hence 'the distinction made us unpopular in Ireland without doing us any good in England'.)

But the Corporation's mid-century problems were not confined to Ireland. The annual average number of new British policies rose from 209 in 1842–8 to 261 in 1849–55, and then fell back to 219 in 1861–5 before rising to 227 in 1865–70. Hence, after the first decade and a half of success with the new system of participating policies, the growth of the Corpora-tion's life business began to decelerate.

The main point to be made in this regard is that, in adopting with-profits policies in 1842 the REA had only taken one step—albeit a very large step—into the new era of life insurance. That era, as we have already seen, was characterized by a new competitive vigour, an increased reliance on advertising, a much more energetic use and oversight of agents, variety in services offered and a restlessness in the search for business. That the Corporation appreciated some of this is indicated by the efforts it made to adjust its premiums and to introduce new policies in the early 1850s. But, in general, and in company with other old-established and reputable offices, it was inhibited from too drastic a participation in all the risky, and sometimes disreputable, novelties of the age.

The relative handicaps of the Corporation's own inheritance became obvious immediately after the introduction of bonus policies, when in 1842 and 1843 the Actuary undertook a survey of the Company's agencies—quite clearly as a concomitant of the 'new look' in the Company's life business. Again and again he was struck by the lack of knowledge on the part of the Company's representatives, to whom he had to explain both the implications of a bonus system and the fact that if the Corporation's premiums were higher than some of its competitors' this might be more than compensated for by its more generous terms for the policyholders' participation in profits. But this need was only a particular case of a general problem: the lack of what Bidder called 'activity and zeal' on the part of many agents. A constant refrain in the Actuary's reports is the quiescence and even resigned ineptitude of many agents in the face of competition. Many represented other companies as well as the REA and Bidder was more than once shocked to discover not only an absence of any signboard for the Company but a prominent notice or placard advertising a rival in the agent's office! Many more did a pitiable amount of business and neglected their agency: 'there is nothing on the door to notify the agency to the public and here as elsewhere I often found it impossible to find out the agent by enquiring for him as such'.

Now, some of this was simply a survival of the days when the Corporation charged high rates and gave no bonus—and hence lost business which no agent could have retained. But it was also due to failings on the part of agents and a lack of purposeful activity on the part of the Corporation. Indeed, the main lesson which Bidder derived, and which was emphasized by the Fire and Life Committee, was the need for care and constant *personal* vigilance in the choice and supervision of agents:

There are few agents whom I have seen who do not themselves require information upon most points on which they are supposed to be competent to inform the public. The numerous complaints they make that the Company's rates of premiums are not so low as those of other offices show that similar objections when made by a person contemplating assurance are more likely to be concurred in than to be removed by them. From this prevailing delusion with respect to low premiums I believe that many assurances are lost to the Company.[1]

And yet, implicitly and explicitly, the Actuary acknowledged that the responsibility for this state of affairs was not all on the side of the agents. Many of them were eager to learn and to do business, but had been frustrated by the lack of advertising and publicity by the Company. Wherever he went in the South-West Bidder found a readiness to receive 'posting bills' from Head Office and an eagerness for supporting advertisements. Thus, Mr Hunt of Plymouth (who seemed 'both in address and intelligence . . . to be exceedingly well qualified to be a very efficient agent') was 'anxious to be supplied with posting bills and urged greater frequency in advertising as other offices were very active in the employment of similar means for obtaining business'. And the Bristol agent 'remarked that whilst the agents of other offices were actively advertising and adopting every means of obtaining notoriety, he had, until within these two years, been interdicted by the Company from advertising at all'.

As far as life business was concerned, therefore, the restriction on advertising, which was the vestigial survival of the economy drive of the late 1820s, was having a very detrimental effect. As with the fire business, it had proved a retrogressive step; and its relaxation was therefore hastened.[2] Even so there had clearly been a good deal of negligence in not counteracting the influence of more 'pushing' rivals and in not publicizing more widely and effectively the fact of the Corporation's new bonus policies. In some towns there was even general ignorance of the fact that the REA had gone over to a participation scheme. Equally serious, however, was the fact that most agents seemed to have felt in some measure isolated from and even ignored by Head Office—with results that were both predictable and inevitable. On his tours in 1842–3, Bidder (who had become Actuary in 1838) was meeting for the first time agents who had been merely signatures to him; and he was quick to appreciate the crippling drawback entailed in the Head Office's remoteness from and ignorance of local affairs and agencies. In Falmouth, for example, he discovered that the nominal agent had, in fact, for some years left the insurance business to his partner, who carried on the correspondence with Head Office, and that the

---

[1] Compare the arguments before the Select Committee on Assurance Association in 1853 that a successful life insurance enterprise needed to ensure not merely the appointment of many agents but that they should be 'for some time instructed until the whole are indoctrinated with the principles of the institution, and are capable of representing its advantages fairly' (*SCAA*, Q.2324).

[2] Above, p. 152.

fact that the Corporation never addressed its letters to him, but rather to the nominal agent, was attributed 'to *hauteur* and to an indifference respecting the agency'.

In general terms, therefore, an area of considerable weakness had been exposed. The REA had apparently neglected its agency system at a time when others were sharpening, tightening and energizing theirs. Bidder recognized that the answer lay in much more direct and personal contact; and he foresaw, albeit somewhat hazily, that this would be most effective not merely through the selecting, supervising and advising of agents (important though these undoubtedly were) but through extending the Corporation's *direct* activities into the field—becoming, in a more explicit way, a nation-wide business unit. To secure a good agent, he argued,

a personal selection is not of more value than a personal inspection of the neighbourhood in which the agency is situated, for the latter would enable the Company to judge of the aptitudes of the place for business and to inform the agent of the best mode of competing with the particular offices that may chance to possess the greatest influence. In this way a few hours of personal communication with the agent would inform him much more of the nature of assurance and of the duties that he has undertaken, than could possibly be accomplished by correspondence.

Bidder's reports undoubtedly had some effect—with respect to both decisions about particular agencies and a new awareness of the importance of publicity and improved communications between London and the provinces. But they did not mark any significant turning-point in outlook or policy. The 1840s were a time of expansion on the crest of the wave of the Corporation's principal innovation: the bonus policy. As we have seen, too, the second valuation period (1849–55) saw even more growth in new life policies than the first. In the late 1850s, however, there was a significant fall below the level of the mid-1840s. But when the consequent problems and anxieties came to be discussed, it soon emerged that there had been no fundamental change in the weaknesses of the agency network and of the Corporation's publicity since the early 1840s.

In January 1861, reviewing the outcome of the previous quinquennium, when new British business began to suffer, the new Actuary, Thomas B. Winser, touched on three themes which were to be reiterated in the following years: the extremes of competition, the need for improving the agency system, and the long-run advantages of the Corporation's soundness and strength. He emphasized the need to keep the public fully informed as to the advantage of insuring with the REA in the face of 'a vast amount of unscrupulous competition'. The best means of doing this was by the appointment of agents, since 'it is only by the personal exertion of men of intelligence, position, and local influence, aided by such information as will always be readily supplied from this Office, that the specious arguments put forth for the sole purpose of deluding the public can be exposed and combated'. If, by these means, the Corporation could secure a fair share of new business, then it was obvious that 'the safe and equitable principles upon which their business is conducted must ultimately bear a most advantageous comparison with those Societies who, having anticipated the profits of future years, must be left with inadequate reserves to meet inevitable claims'.

Two years after these comments, in June 1863, Winser was sufficiently worried by the unsatisfactory level of new business to analyse the situation in a special memorandum—and to lose just a little of his complacency.

First he indicated the decline in the Corporation's new business since 1855, at a time when other 'offices of far inferior standing' were steadily increasing theirs. He listed eight such offices (including the notorious Albert, which was to crash in 1869, but also such powerful competitors as the Scottish Widows' and the Royal), the average of whose new sums assured in 1862 and been over £650,000—contrasting with the REA's £223,000. Yet although the Corporation 'cannot pretend to compete with these offices', some having accumulated business by amalgamation and others by 'reckless trading', the disparity between their record and that of the Corporation was obviously excessive, since much of their business was perfectly legitimate, 'and if so we ought to have a larger share'. It was on these grounds that Winser was also obliged to confess that the increase in competition was not alone a sufficient explanation of the Corporation's poor position—for in spite of competition other offices had doubled or trebled their business while 'we have been falling off'.

Advertising, Winser argued, had been a powerful weapon in the search for new business, and he cited the Royal, of Liverpool, as 'a remarkable instance of the extent to which this system can be carried'. The Royal, he claimed, spent £20,000 or £30,000 annually (more than its first-year premiums): 'Almost every Review, Magazine, Almanac or other similar publication contains a prospectus of that Company printed in all the colours of the rainbow', apart from their advertisements in all the railway stations 'and places of public resort in the kingdom'. Yet, although this device was undoubtedly a help to an office like the Royal, Winser argued that it was not recommended for the REA: 'as it would be inconsistent with the position of a Company like ours, and also of doubtful policy at this period of our existence'. Characteristically, dignity and the concept of the Corporation's 'image' were considered to be directly relevant to its commercial position.

For these reasons, the Actuary came back to the old question of the Corporation's agencies: 'Really influential and *intelligent* agents appear to be of the most essential service in promoting life business.' Technical knowledge and commercial conscientiousness were of vital importance; and the REA was in many areas relatively poorly represented as far as life business was concerned. It can be safely assumed that little had changed since 1848—when only half the Corporation's 555 British agents brought in any life business, and fifty-six solicitors and eighteen bankers accounted for more than a third of all sums assured by British agents. In 1863, therefore, Winser proposed that more effort be put into the choice of representatives and that someone be sent out occasionally to stimulate old and recruit new agents. He also urged that the Corporation increase its agency commission rates, which appear to have lagged behind other old and first-class offices, which were generally paying 10 per cent in the first year (a procedure which enabled the agent to pay a 5 per cent bonus to sub-agents). In point of fact a similar proposal had been considered and rejected by the Treasury Committee in February 1856. By July 1863, however, the situation had fundamentally altered, and the Treasury Committee agreed to increase the commission on the first premium to 10 per cent—'most of the leading life offices having adopted the system of doing so'.

In the last resort, therefore, the Actuary's prescription for the recovery of the life business after the troubles of the late 1850s was an exhortation to more active agency representation. As an example, he cited the Godalming agent, Richard Whitbourn, 'a pushing and active man', who had done business which would not have shamed Liverpool or Manchester or Birmingham or Bristol. Admittedly, Winser also touched on the very important question of the policy conditions with which other offices attracted policyholders;[1] on the possibility of encouraging the West End Branch at Pall Mall by allowing the manager 'to take the appearance' instead of having to send proposed lives to the City; and on the possibility of ameliorating the Life Department's position by reducing its proportion of general expenses from one-third to one-quarter. But his basic argument

---

[1] For example, allowing whole world limits after five years. Winser rejected this sort of approach as being unjust to the rest of an office's policyholders. In a similar analysis of the Atlas's problems in 1864, H. M. Tyndall listed the following complaints against the older offices: non-acknowledgement of notices of assignment; insecurity of assignees of policies in the event of suicide; hard terms or troublesome conditions for the revival of accidentally lapsed policies; and other matters 'trivial in themselves, but impediments in the struggle for business that was being carried on with younger offices, which had rid themselves of these obstacles'.

remained unchanged. On the one hand, it was extremely difficult to make the public aware of the advantages of insuring with a first-class office, since they were easily 'misled by specious promises and an array of figures which are made to represent prosperity that does not exist in fact'. On the other hand, the process of education and of salesmanship could only be achieved in the field and by intelligent, knowledgeable and keen agents who were well chosen and carefully supervised. In his quinquennium report almost three years later (February 1866), Winser made the pertinent point that agents who were useful in fire business might know very little about life insurance. And he gave some hair-raising examples of technical incompetence, to conclude that 'it is clear that these agents are ignorant of the very first principles upon which life assurance depends, and consequently unable to cope with shrewder men who represent very inferior offices'.

Clearly, there was a good deal in what the Actuary had to say. Nevertheless, it seems doubtful if his prescription for increasing new business ('the competition of the times must be met by a corresponding increase of exertion on the part of all concerned in the welfare of the Corporation') was alone sufficient for success. It placed too much responsibility on the psychology and energy of the agents, and too little on the policies they had to sell, the rewards which they were offered, and the institutional framework and incentives provided by the REA itself. The agents of successful competitors were effective not because they were, by chance, superior salesmen, but because they offered the public policies which were more attractive in terms of costs and conditions, could be less demanding (and take more risks) in selecting lives, were given greater incentives, and were more tightly integrated into a nation-wide network and therefore more effectively supervised and activated.

The result was frequently a pattern of behaviour and a degree of risk which the REA would have found unacceptable. But, as the Actuary himself acknowledged, the Corporation was missing a vast amount of quite legitimate and acceptable business. When all things were considered, its relative lack of success could not be explained by its superior dignity and reputation. Rather, it still had to learn that modernization involved a continuing series of innovations—in organization, in agency systems, in policies and rates, in attitudes—rather than a once-for-all change from non-profit to bonus policies. Nor was there much comfort in the frequently expressed view that the Corporation's superior financial strength would ultimately turn the tide: many of the rapidly growing and adventurous offices were equally secure. The main lesson, in the words of the Atlas

Actuary in 1864, was that 'the phases of society . . . change; and it is needful that the management of commercial undertakings, should so far as possible coincide with those changes. Systems which in time past may have answered their purposes well, get antiquated, and must give place to others more suited to the requirements of the passing time.' The acceptance of this lesson, and the benefits which flowed from it, had not yet been attained by the REA. Rather they were to form the history of the Life Department in the generation before the First World War.[1]

[1] Below, pp. 251–8.

9

Privilege and Competition: marine insurance and the Royal Exchange Assurance to 1870

In the case of fire and life insurance, crucial changes in both growth rates and industrial structure coincided with the beginnings of modern industrialization in Britain. Marine insurance, however, offers a contrast with this historical pattern: although it, too, underwent a rapid expansion from the 1780s, the main factor influencing its organization—the legal rights of the Royal Exchange and London Assurances—did not change until 1824. For this reason the late eighteenth- and early nineteenth-century history of marine underwriting is best considered as a whole. On the other hand, the structural change which occurred with the repeal of the two Corporations' exclusive privileges in 1824 is comparable with the impact of structural change which was felt in both fire and life insurance at the same time. However, in the case of marine insurance by companies it happened that the transition to open competition was absolute and abrupt. Indeed, privilege and counter-pressure to privilege provided the context for the history of corporate marine insurance for a century after the REA was established.

THE USES OF PRIVILEGE

To contemporaries, the chartering of the Royal Exchange and London Assurances in 1720 must have seemed a major turning-point in the development of English marine underwriting. It was expected that the two Companies would quickly dominate the London market. In fact, however, although the consequences of their foundation were indeed far-reaching and long-lasting, they hardly conformed to either the hopes or the fears which had accompanied their prolonged birth-pangs. For, on the one hand, the two new Corporations rapidly invaded the fields of fire and life underwriting, thus diversifying their investments and efforts away from a close dependence on marine business; and, on the other, their legal standing in marine insurance, while not leading to any very great participation by the Companies in the business which was done, paradoxically served to stimulate the growth of underwriting by private individuals and to strengthen the position of Lloyd's as the institutional focus of their activities.

The monopoly of corporate marine insurance enjoyed by the two Corporations strengthened the position of private underwriters and of Lloyd's in various ways. First, the enabling Act effectively prevented the appearance of any more companies[1] which might have competed with individual underwriters. Second, the Act also prohibited underwriting by partnerships, so that whereas, before 1720, underwriting on a partnership account had meant that the failure of an underwriter merely placed the policyholder in the weak position of any other creditor, after that date underwriting accounts were entirely separate from the partnership's accounts, and policyholders, in the event of the bankruptcy of partnerships to which their underwriter belonged, had prior access to the private resources (including the premiums owing) of the underwriter.[2] Finally, by introducing a modicum of competition, the two companies accelerated the emergence of specialized underwriters and gave added impetus to the formal organization of Lloyd's as the strong, central, institutional framework for underwriting business. As the Select Committee on Marine Insurance reported in 1810, the 'effect [of the Act of 1720] in the City of London has been to compel individuals to assemble together, in order to underwrite separately, while it has prevented them from associating to make insurances jointly. Hence the establishment of Lloyd's Coffee-House, where every person meaning to underwrite must attend during the time necessary for that purpose . . . This exclusive privilege, therefore, operates as a monopoly not merely to the Companies, but to Lloyd's Coffee-House.'[3] Facilitated by factors such as these, although in the last resort underpinned by its intrinsic strength and flexibility, there was a rapid development of Lloyd's in the course of the eighteenth century.

By the early nineteenth century the fact that the existence of the two Corporations was a safeguard against other and possibly more uncomfortable forms of competition was obviously appreciated: when their rights were threatened in 1810 and 1824 the private underwriters rightly

---

[1] Except for a few rather special mutual associations which were active in the early nineteenth century (below, p. 192).

[2] See Charles Wright and C. Ernest Fayle, *A History of Lloyd's* (1928), pp. 64–5; Joseph Marryatt, 'Copy of a Report proposed as an amendment to the Report adopted by the Committee on Marine Insurance', in *The Substance of a Speech Delivered in the House of Commons on the 20th February, 1810, upon . . . Marine Insurances*, (1824), p. 91.

[3] *PP* (1810), IV, 6.

interpreted the attack as an assault upon themselves, and organized a joint defence accordingly. To the Lloyd's Subscribers, as their historians have said, the privileges formed the 'paradoxical ark of their covenant'.[1]

In the last resort, the two Companies posed no great problems to other underwriters, because their marine business was relatively small. With the possible exception of the period immediately after their foundation in 1720, it seems likely that at no time in the eighteenth century did they do as much as 10 per cent of London's underwriting: and in 1810, at the height of the war-time boom in underwriting, a careful estimate concluded 'that the two chartered Companies insured less than four parts out of one hundred of the whole insurances effected in Great Britain'. In 1809 the REA and the London were responsible for £3·91 million and £2·25 million, respectively, out of a total of £162·5 million of insurances.[2] From their own viewpoint, no doubt, the business done by the two Companies was reasonably extensive: thus, the gross premiums of the REA averaged about £27,000 in the 1760s, almost £50,000 in the 1770s, some £95,000 in the 1780s, and £215,000 in the 1790s; while the annual excess of premiums over losses and returns, which averaged just over £13,000 between 1720 and 1758, and fell to less than £7,000 in 1761–75, was almost £30,000 in 1776–80, some £14,500 in the 1780s and £37,000 in the 1790s.[3] But there can be little doubt about their minimal impact on the marine insurance market in general: the 1810 Select Committee went so far as to conclude that 'the amount insured by the London Company would be hardly more than a single mercantile house might require, and both added together would not exceed what two of the most considerable individual underwriters would write in one year'.[4]

The fact that the two chartered companies did less marine insurance business than they might have done can be attributed partly to the institutional strength of the Lloyd's underwriting market, and partly to their own lack of vigour in pursuing a large amount of business.

Lloyd's itself, in spite of complaints about the problems of underwriting big risks, the difficulties in securing marine insurance, and the possible insolvency of individual underwriters, seems to have provided a flexible, adequate and fairly efficient service. Its communication network, the concentration of brokers and underwriters, and the degree of co-

---

[1] Wright and Fayle, *Lloyd's*, p. 307; below, pp. 194–7.
[2] *PP* (1810), IV, 4–5.
[3] See Table 3.1, above, p. 62. For the London Assurance, see A. H. John, 'The London Assurance Company and the Marine Insurance Market of the Eighteenth Century', *Economica* (May 1958), p. 130; and statistics in Guildhall MSS, 8749A/1.
[4] *PP* (1810), IV.

operation which it facilitated—all produced a reasonably well-adjusted market mechanism; while the presence of a fairly large number of underwriters provided a strong element of competition as well as a wide variety of expertise. More than this, the mere existence of Lloyd's as a popular centre of marine underwriting served to reinforce its dominance: the fact that underwriters were frequently also merchants who themselves might wish to insure commodities led to a good deal of mutual support. As one proponent of the Lloyd's system put it, 'the practice so prevalent amongst merchants who are also underwriters, of interchanging their risks with each other for their reciprocal benefit, is assigned as a great cause of the limited proportion, which the business done by those companies bears to the whole insurance business of the country'. In addition, the argument was put forward that the possibility of insuring 'risks of an inferior description' at Lloyd's (the two Companies avoided such risks) also attracted most of the better risks, for brokers knew that the former were only acceptable in conjunction with the latter.[1]

But, however powerful the pull of Lloyd's in terms of its intrinsic advantages as a centre of marine insurance, the REA and London Assurances were themselves responsible for at least some of the handicaps under which they laboured. In particular, by the time of the Napoleonic Wars (and presumably earlier) their caution about many aspects of marine underwriting was seen by many merchants, underwriters and brokers as an important reason for their relative lack of popularity.

In various trades, for example, their premium rates were said to be higher than those of private underwriters, and many witnesses before the Select Committee cited examples of rates which were 20 or 30 per cent above those of Lloyd's. While some witnesses argued that the Companies' prompter payment of claims and other advantages outweighed their higher cost, the balance of evidence decisively indicated that it was somewhat more expensive to insure with them.[2] More important, perhaps, than the actual cost of securing cover from the REA and London were the restrictions which they imposed on business dealings—and, in particular, the effective limit of about £10,000, which they normally imposed on any one merchant ship. Indeed, there was some evidence that merchants would prefer to do business with the Companies, often in spite of their higher premiums, but were prevented from doing so by the restriction on the sum insured. Thus, Alexander Glennie, a general merchant, claimed that:

[1] Marryatt, 'Copy of a Report', p. 72; *PP* (1810), IV, 89, 94.
[2] *PP* (1810), IV, 17, 21, 24, 61, 72, 73, 103, 111–12. For other examples of higher premium rates charged by the Corporations at earlier dates, see Eden, *Insurance Charters*, pp. 31–2.

If I could do all my business at the public offices I should undoubtedly prefer doing it with them . . . In all risks that they will take, they in my opinion are preferable to Lloyd's Coffee house; in the first place, I feel myself perfectly insured, I feel that my property is safely insured; I know also that if a loss takes place I shall receive my loss in bank notes, deducting the premium, the Thursday after the loss is notified . . . I do not think that I can state properly that they are of little service on account of the difference of premiums; I think it is in the amount that they take; they limit themselves in so small an amount that it is impossible to do risks where property is so much enhanced in value; instead of having a sum that they will do on one risk, it is three, four or five times as much as they will take.[1]

In addition to the obstacles to the growth of corporate marine insurance implied in high premiums and low limits, there were other restrictions which were disincentives for merchants and brokers seeking insurance cover. Chief among these was the unwillingness of the two Companies to accept 'cross risks'—that is, risks involved in trade between two overseas ports, as distinct from between British and overseas ports—in contrast to Lloyd's, where the enormous variety of underwriting skill and knowledge meant that there was always *some* group of underwriters willing and able to accept risks which (to a single company) might appear hazardous because their context and details were unknown. This was, presumably, a recent, or at least a war-time, development, since it is known that the London Assurance did write cross risks in the eighteenth century—albeit to a declining extent (they fell from just under 30 per cent of sums insured in 1728–9 to about 17 per cent in 1769–70).[2] But it became particularly critical, in the midst of the Napoleonic struggle. As one defender of Lloyd's put it, 'in what are called cross risks, in those new and perilous modes of carrying on commerce to which the state of Europe has lately obliged us to resort, the public offices come into no competition with Lloyd's; for they refuse to write them at any premium'.[3] Further, beyond the limits on cross risks, it was also the case that the two Companies were reluctant to insure against capture in enemy ports (Lloyd's underwriters normally gave this cover in insuring neutral ships in war-time), and that they had 'particular clauses of average and other conditions in their policies' which for many merchants were less favourable than the provisions of ordinary Lloyd's policies.[4]

Of course, the relative advantages of insuring with Lloyd's or the two Companies did not run all one way: the security offered by companies,

[1] *PP* (1810), IV, 52–3.
[2] John, 'Marine Insurance Market' *Economica* (1958), pp. 132–3.
[3] Marryatt, *The Substance of a Speech*, p. 14. Compare *PP* (1810), IV, 60.
[4] *PP* (1810), IV, 19, 23, 47, 52.

their promptness in payment, and the general convenience and facility of dealing with them, were adduced by various merchants as reasons for insuring with them when possible. And one of their severest critics, after rehearsing the various disadvantages inherent in their high premiums, restrictive clauses and conditions, and narrow limits, admitted that 'the effects . . . are in some degree counterbalanced, by the confidence placed in their solidity, by their mode of payment when losses happen, and by their allowing greater advantages in the shape of discount, to those who transact business with them, than are allowed by individual underwriters'.[1] Nevertheless, in general it seems clear that, by their ultra-cautious and relatively rigid approach to marine insurance, they denied themselves a good deal of business. 'It appears probable', as the 1810 Select Committee argued, 'that the Companies, by relaxing in some degree the rigour of their terms, might command much additional business'.[2] Yet they did not do so, and accordingly retained a reputation for caution and only a limited amount of business.

THE ASSAULT ON PRIVILEGE, 1806–1824

Even granting the relatively small share of the eighteenth-century marine insurance market controlled by the REA and London Assurance, their premium incomes, as we have seen, grew rapidly, if erratically. This was an apt reflection of the two main forces making for an increase in marine underwriting in general: the expansion of Britain's trade and the irregular incidence of war which, when it did come, boosted both the need for and the price of insurance. By the end of the eighteenth century these twin elements of growth were operating at their most powerful as war, and war-time inflation, were superimposed upon Britain's commercial expansion. And from the resulting spurt in the demand for marine underwriting services there arose a demand that the exclusive privileges of the companies should be taken away, in order to open the field of marine insurance to rival companies and to partnerships.

The growing need for insurance facilities in the late eighteenth century, in so far as it was reflected at Lloyd's and in the two Companies, can be relatively easily measured: the annual gross premiums of the Royal Exchange, which had averaged some £23,000 in 1771–5, touched £275,000 in 1796–1800; and at Lloyd's the number of Subscribers rose very rapidly (Joseph Marryatt, who was Chairman of Lloyd's 1811–24, estimated an

---

[1] Marryatt, 'Copy of a Report', pp. 71–2. Compare *PP* (1810), IV, 110–13; Eden, *Insurance Charters*, p. 35.
[2] *PP* (1810), IV, 5.

increase from seventy-nine in 1771 to almost 1,500 in 1810—although that included many who did relatively little business).[1] It was in this period, too, under the influence of demand associated with the effect of the Napoleonic Wars, that the increaed flow of capital into underwriting was associated with the emergence of professional, large-scale underwriters, providing a now indispensable service based upon full-time commitment and specialist expertise.[2]

These, however, were not the only indications of a heightened demand for marine insurance. Increasing numbers of merchants, and even underwriters and brokers, began to feel that the institutional facilities for underwriting were inadequate for the needs of commerce—or, at least, could be profitably supplemented, if only the law would allow it. In fact, by the first decade of the nineteenth century this situation had already produced rival facilities in the shape of underwriters in provincial ports and some twenty-nine 'associations' of shipowners (mostly of colliers) in particular trades or ports which insured marine risks on a mutual basis—and were, strictly speaking, illegal within the terms of the 1720 Act.[3] But these were judged insufficient, and there eventually arose a powerful demand for a repeal of the Act which had confined the privilege of corporate marine insurance to the REA and the London Assurance—although it is not easy to determine how far this move to establish new companies reflected a genuine complaint that Lloyd's services were inadequate and inconvenient, and how far it was a symptom of the desire of investors to participate in the business of a newly profitable field.

The first organized assault came in 1806. It was mounted by Sir Frederick Morton Eden and the Globe Insurance Company, who petitioned the Treasury for the grant of a Charter of incorporation for fire, life and marine business—and sweetened their request with a promise reminiscent of the events of 1720: that on the passing of an Act of incorporation they would pay £100,000 to the Government.[4] This request obviously appealed to the Government, for the Treasury asked for a draft Bill without delay, and in the subsequent debate in the House of Commons the Chancellor of the Exchequer spoke in the Bill's favour and it was given a second reading. However, it was then referred to a Committee—which got no further

---

[1] Marryatt, *The Substance of a Speech*, p. 22. Compare the somewhat different figures in Wright and Fayle, *Lloyd's*, p. 174.

[2] Wright and Fayle, *Lloyd's*, pp. 194–8. These specialists were, however, still in a minority: a large amount of business continued to be done by merchant-underwriters.

[3] *PP* (1810), IV, 9.

[4] For the Globe, see Raynes, *British Insurance*, pp. 212–13; Walford, *Insurance Cyclopaedia*, V and VI, 423–7; Eden, *Insurance Charters*.

than to hear objections from the Royal Exchange Assurance, and then discontinued proceedings.[1]

Within a few months of the failure of this effort to incorporate a rival to the REA and London, Sir Frederick Morton Eden returned to the attack on a broader, and more public, front by writing a cogent and persuasive pamphlet: *On the Policy and Expediency of Granting Insurance Charters*. Dismissing the opposition of the two Corporations (they claimed to have purchased their rights for a 'valuable consideration') 'as, not only unjust, but as . . . unnecessary and impolitic', Eden went on to emphasize the need 'to correct the impediments which the defective codes of ancient times may now present to the various complex operations of increasing wealth and extended commerce', by facilitating the formation of joint-stock companies.

In publishing his pamphlet, Eden had, in fact, opened a new line of public debate about the privileges of the two marine insurance companies. On the one hand, he pressed for the creation of additional incorporated companies because existing insurance facilities and modes of organization were held to be inadequate. On the other, he touched more general, ideological chords by appealing to the virtues of free competition. This latter set of arguments was obviously a powerful weapon to use against the Royal Exchange and London Assurances. For the monopoly which they enjoyed was now almost 100 years old, and was being used (or, as their critics said, insufficiently used) in an age which was on the whole much more suspicious of exclusive rights, and much more attracted by the economic arguments in favour of free competition. Hence Eden argued that the Corporation's privileges, by restraining competition, necessarily kept the market for marine insurance understocked and raised insurance 'above its natural price'. The remedy seemed to him quite plain: the law should permit all sorts of insurance, and particularly marine insurance, to be transacted by joint-stock companies 'with no other privilege than a right to offer . . . capital and . . . protection to the discriminating judgement of the mercantile world'. In this way, he felt, 'competition, the essence of trade, would be attained, prices would be reduced, and business increased'.[2]

This combination of private interest (the prospect of investing in profitable new marine insurance companies) and public principle (the growing commitment to freer competition) was obviously a powerful element in the discussion of marine insurance in the first decade of the nineteenth century,

---

[1] Eden, *Insurance Charters*, p. 59.

[2] For the various quotations in the above two paragraphs, see Eden, *Insurance Charters*, pp. 1, 4, 36, 45–6.

when the demand for underwriting services was expanding so rapidly. And in 1810 there came a much more serious attack on the privileges of the REA and London. At the end of a decade which had already seen an unprecedented influx of new companies into fire and life insurance, many merchants and financiers in the City gave their support to a project for a huge new marine insurance company to be capitalized at £5 million, which would secure a large amount of business from its powerful shareholders. A subscription list was opened late in 1809, and it soon became obvious that the project was a genuine and serious threat to the established basis of marine insurance: not merely did many merchants subscribe (the promoters estimated that it was supported by 90 per cent of London's mercantile firms), but a substantial number of Lloyd's underwriters and brokers reluctantly applied for shares because, in spite of their forebodings about its effects on Lloyd's, 'if the company obtained a Charter they considered that it would be a profitable concern, and on that account they wished to have a share in it'.[1]

The Phoenix Fire Office, which had already promoted a life company (the Pelican) in 1797, was also a strong influence in the new scheme: its Secretary, Jenkin Jones, who had recently been to North America and the West Indies in order to make 'very particular enquiries' about marine insurance companies, claimed that the new company 'was set on foot by myself with a view to additional benefit to the Phoenix Office'.[2] But, once publicized, the scheme assumed a much more general importance: first, because of the degree of support which it gathered; second, because the proposal for a new company was based not so much on the presumed drawbacks of the REA and the London as on the presumed need to enlarge and improve insurance facilities in general. In the last resort, therefore, the new promotion was an attack on Lloyd's—in which the criticism of the two Corporations was an important but incidental skirmish. The underwriters and brokers of Lloyd's knew this very well, and in January 1810, before the new company had made any official move, they met to form a defence committee and to pass a unanimous resolution that it would be 'highly detrimental to the Subscribers of this House in general and ruinous to numerous individuals who have made insurance their sole business, if any new company should be legally authorized by charter or otherwise to effect marine insurances'.[3]

[1] *PP* (1810), IV, 80. Compare pp. 49–50, 79, 93, 98.
[2] *PP* (1810), IV, 38.
[3] Wright and Fayle, *Lloyd's*, p. 243. It was, of course, particularly worrying to Lloyd's underwriters that so many leading merchants, who generated a vast amount of insurance business, were subscribers to the proposed company.

The promoters of the new company petitioned Parliament on 8 February, arguing that the two chartered companies were no longer important underwriters, that several companies had been established abroad 'to the great loss of revenue and the inconvenience of the merchants in this country', and that London merchants, 'having insurances to make . . . [but] finding additional means wanting', wished to form a new large-scale company for the purpose. They therefore requested either that the exclusive privileges of the two existing companies should be repealed or that the new company be empowered to undertake marine insurance in spite of the 1720 Act. At the same time, recognizing that this was a new opportunity of achieving the objective which they had been the first to seek, the Directors of the Globe also petitioned for the right to undertake corporate marine insurance, emphasizing the enormous increase in trade and the need to extend insurance facilities for it.[1]

Within a week of the petitions the Commons had referred them to a Select Committee 'to consider of the state and means of effecting marine insurance in Great Britain'. The actual proceedings of the Committee (which included Pascoe Grenfell, a Director of the REA) need not concern us here. There was relatively little criticism of the two chartered companies, whose small share of the market was attributed to factors already mentioned. Rather, the hearings were primarily concerned with the merits or drawbacks of Lloyd's—principally with such questions as the security and solvency of Lloyd's underwriters, the difficulties of securing the payment of losses, the problems of insuring large amounts or winter risks, and the general convenience of transacting business at the Coffee House.

The Report, which was made in April, came out quite decisively in favour of abolishing the privileges of the two companies as anomalous and harmful impediments to necessary changes in marine insurance. By implication, too, the facilities at Lloyd's were found to be inadequate, and the Committee welcomed the possibility of a new and more freely competitive situation.

In the course of a systematic and closely reasoned Report the Committee argued that the privileges of the two chartered companies could now be shown, in the words of the original Act, to be 'hurtful or inconvenient to the public'. This was said to be so less because of any positive abuse of their monopoly position than because their business remained comparatively insignificant and they had not attained the scale or type of insurance envisaged on their behalf in 1720: 'there can be little doubt of the absurdity of suffering a monopoly to exist, more effectual in its hindrance than its

[1] Wright and Fayle, *Lloyd's*, p. 242; Raynes, *British Insurance*, pp. 213–16.

performance, where such a monopoly can, as in the present instance, be repealed without violation of public faith'.[1]

Turning to the system of marine insurance in use at Lloyd's, the Committee endorsed many of the criticisms levelled at the Coffee House, and argued 'that there can be little doubt that partnerships and associations will be formed, if the law should permit it; and at all events, merchants and underwriters, being left to manage their concerns unfettered by any restrictions, will soon fall into that system best suited to their general convenience'. This last point was, in fact, the most important of those made in the Report—which was presented far more as an advocacy of *laissez-faire* than as an attack on, or defence of, any particular mode of organizing a marine insurance market: 'it is not the intention of your Committee to recommend the enforcement of any particular system by Law; but, on the contrary, to release this branch of business from the restraints now existing, and to leave it to shape itself as it then infallibly would do, in conformity with the true interest of the public'.[2]

All these were powerful and persuasive words. They held out the promise of greater opportunities for investors wishing to form insurance companies and for merchants seeking improved insurance facilities; and they also appealed to the growing number of those who believed in the general economic advantages and social virtues of freedom of competition. Indeed, the opponents of the petitions for incorporation, led by Joseph Marryatt (a future Chairman of Lloyd's) and Pascoe Grenfell in the House of Commons, apart from asserting that Lloyd's *did* provide a secure, flexible and inexpensive service, were obliged to appeal to a related ideological sentiment—namely the fear of the monopolizing tendencies of all corporations: 'The principle of this company is not competition, but combination; it even precludes the possibility of competition; for the proprietors tell you that they possess nine-tenths of the commercial interest of the City of London, and that they wish to form themselves into a company, for the purpose of effecting their own insurances. Who then can wrest them out of their hands?' Even if other companies were established, Marryatt argued, they would effectively eliminate all individual underwriting and broking, and 'we should have a system of close and secret combination. The Secretaries of the different offices, by a good understanding with each other, might regulate the premiums as they pleased'.[3]

In the last resort, however, the defenders of the *status quo* were obliged

[1] *PP* (1810), IV, 2, 6.
[2] *PP* (1810), IV, 7, 9.
[3] Marryatt, *The Substance of Speech*, pp. 29, 32–3; *Hansard's Parliamentary Debates*, 14 February 1810, cols. 416, 418.

to take up an essentially conservative position. Naturally enough, the Royal Exchange Assurance objected to the proposal to repeal its privileges —as it had done in response to the Globe's attempt in 1806. But it rested its case merely on the existence of its Charter and the large number of wealthy Lloyd's underwriters whose presence meant that there was no difficulty 'in effecting insurances of undoubted security, to any amount which the exigencies of the increased trade of the country requires'.[1] The Corporation's sense of outrage was registered by their counsel at the bar of the House of Commons: 'they could not conceive on what ground this company of adventurers could call upon Parliament to deprive them of their privileges, and of these rights for which they had paid a considerable sum to the public'.[2] Marryatt himself, in a pamphlet criticizing the Select Committee's Report, bitterly opposed the *laissez-faire* view: 'This is reviving the Epicurean doctrine of the fortuitous concourse of atoms: on the same principle, the Report might recommend the destruction of this world . . . in order to take the chance of a better world being formed by a fresh jumble. Common sense dictates, that before we destroy existing establishments, we should be sure that we can replace them with better.'[3]

Although these arguments were not, on the surface, very persuasive, and in spite of the strength and apparent reasonableness of the Select Committee's Report, in fact the Royal Exchange and the London managed to retain their privileges in the face of the onslaught. This was, perhaps, far more because those privileges were seen as a bastion of Lloyd's position than because of a deep respect for chartered rights—although even this factor should not be ignored. In any event, they co-operated very closely with Lloyd's in the campaign against the new proposals; and, no doubt with the help of some judicious lobbying, the attempt at a new promotion came to nothing: a Bill to repeal the exclusive privileges of the two chartered Corporations received a first reading in May 1810, but was then dropped: and in February 1811, after it had again been introduced, and counter-petitions heard, it was very narrowly defeated on a second reading, in a small House, by 26 votes to 25.

Thus, in large part because of the fortuitous identification of interest between the Corporations and Lloyd's, the legal position of the REA, and the structure of marine insurance within which it operated, remained untouched in the early nineteenth century—at a time when both fire and life

---

[1] These quotations come from a printed memorial of 1810.

[2] See Report of proceedings in Appendix to Marryatt, *The Substance of a Speech*, pp. 11–12.

[3] Marryatt, 'Observations upon the Report of the Committee', in *The Substance of a Speech*, pp. 54–5.

insurance were being almost completely transformed by structural change and the intensification of competition.[1] Nevertheless, the slimness of the victory in 1810–11, the forces which stood to gain from the breaking-down of the monopoly, and the anomalous character of that monopoly at a time of commercial expansion and economic liberalization, all meant that it was really only a matter of time before the assault on the exclusive privileges would be successfully renewed.[2]

The inevitable repeal of the Corporations' monopoly position came in 1824. Once more, as in 1806 and 1810, the prime movers of the attack were a rival group of insurance promoters—although this time they were, if anything, more powerful. In the spring of 1824, largely under the influence of Nathan Rothschild and Sir Moses Montefiore, but with the active participation of Samuel Gurney, Francis Baring and John Irving, a very powerful group of City men—'the whole united money interest of the Empire', according to one critic[3]—formed the Alliance British & Foreign Fire & Life Insurance Company (capitalized at £5 million with £500,000 paid up). Although the original prospectus did not mention marine underwriting, it was the intention of the promoters to invade that field, too, if they could; and they therefore began to muster their forces—including the co-operation of Huskisson, the President of the Board of Trade —to secure an Act to repeal that part of the 1720 Act which prohibited marine insurance by any company or partnership other than the Royal Exchange or London Assurances. With formidable support in Parliament, including favourable interventions by the Prime Minister, the Chancellor of the Exchequer, and the President of the Board of Trade, the Bill had a relatively easy passage (it secured 51 votes, as against 33, on the committal after the second reading in the Commons, and 559 as against 159 on the third).

In fact, by the mid-1820s general sentiment was even more inclined towards freeing trade than it had been in 1810. Huskisson reflected this in the first debate on the Bill for repeal: 'It was said that that arrangement would destroy Lloyd's Coffee-House. Unquestionably, the public would go wherever they could get their business done in the best and cheapest manner. And why, he begged to ask, ought they not to be permitted to do so? All that he said was—let the parties interested suit their own convenience and wishes.'[4] Indeed, the move for repeal came at a time of general

---

[1] Above, chapter 6.
[2] There was, apparently, an unsuccessful attempt to get the Privy Council to revoke the Corporations' privileges in 1813: *Hansard's Parliamentary Debates*, 17 May 1824, col. 773.
[3] *Hansard's Parliamentary Debates*, 28 May 1824, col. 932.
[4] *Hansard's Parliamentary Debates*, 17 May 1824, col. 772.

'liberalizing' reform in the field of economic regulation. Largely under Huskisson's influence, in 1824 and 1825 alone there were sweeping reductions in import tariffs; an easing of the application of the Navigation Laws and the repeal of various laws regulating industrial methods. In the same years the Combination Laws, in effect prohibiting trade-union activity, were repealed; the restrictions on the emigration of skilled artisans were abolished; and the Bubble Act, with its resounding but somewhat illusory ban on unauthorized companies, was finally laid to rest. In addition to this element, however, the commercial and financial forces working for a liberalization of marine insurance were formidable in the extreme: one of their opponents referred to 'that mass of wealth which has been put in motion on this occasion', and Pascoe Grenfell, still an MP and by now Sub-Governor of the Royal Exchange, admitted that 'nothing could be more respectable or substantial than the security [of the promoters]; the Bank of England could not be better'.[1] Finally, simply in pragmatic terms, it was difficult to counter the arguments in favour of repeal, or to provide any except lame answers to rhetorical questions of the sort put by the Bill's sponsor, Fowell Buxton: 'while every other species of trade was conducted by firms, what reason . . . could be advanced for crippling marine insurances by this restriction?' Indeed, in retrospect, it is impossible not to agree with Buxton's claim (made without any disrespect towards the Corporations as they then stood) that their 'chartering . . . had commenced in a job, and their powers had continued longer than they had a right to hope for'.[2] Backed by arguments like these, the success of this final assault on the Corporations' privileges was never in serious doubt—although Lloyd's took its defeat badly: until 1840 the new Companies were repeatedly refused the right (enjoyed by the REA and the London since 1814) to purchase regular 'intelligence' of ships and commercial matters.[3]

MARINE INSURANCE BUSINESS, 1790–1870

Marine underwriting seems to have generated only a few business records in the ordinary course of events; and the fact that the REA archives were destroyed in 1838 makes it impossible to say very much about the

---

[1] *Hansard's Parliamentary Debates*, 28 May 1824, cols. 924, 933. Grenfell went on to doubt the permanency of the Alliance's security if the founders sold their shares.

[2] For the Commons debates see *Hansard's Parliamentary Debates*, 17 and 28 May 1824, cols. 766–75, 920–33.

[3] Wright and Fayle, *Lloyd's*, pp. 316–17, 340–1. Further, a bye-law was passed in 1824 forbidding Lloyd's Subscribers to underwrite in partnership—continuing the tradition of 'each for himself and not one for another', and in 1834 Subscribers were prohibited from underwriting directly or indirectly on behalf of a public company.

characteristics of its marine business before that date. Indeed, one of the few things that is known about the activities of the Marine Department helps explain why so few records survived in any case. For, even within a Corporation, marine underwriting was very much an individual and personal activity (just as it was, pre-eminently, at Lloyd's). In contrast to fire and life business, which involved a complicated departmental structure and continuous written communication and record-keeping, marine business depended upon a series of knowledgeable decisions by an underwriter when confronted with a series of individual proposals. Hence, in one sense, the two Corporations in the eighteenth century had shared at least one important characteristic with Lloyd's: they each entrusted a very large responsibility to a single underwriter—known as the Sitting Director in the case of the REA. It was he who made the decisions about marine underwriting, although 'when any difficult matter or any risk has been offered which has not been usual, the Committee or the Governors have been applied to generally by the Sitting Director for their advice and opinion',[1] and it is likely that restrictions on his freedom of action were in part responsible for the excessive restraint which characterized the Corporation's underwriting in the late eighteenth century.

The rôle of Sitting Director was a constant element in the eighteenth and early nineteenth century organization of the REA. He provided an exception to the general rule that officials of the Corporation were not members of the Court; for the Sitting Director was not merely a member of the Court with the specific responsibilities of Marine Underwriter, but from at least 1783 onwards[2] the three Sitting Directors—William Kekewich (1783–92), Samuel Fenning (1792–1825), and Edward Browne (1825–37)—had been either Secretary, as with the first two, or First Clerk in the Secretary's Office, as with Browne. The post of Sitting Director then lapsed with Browne's death in 1837. His successor, Alexander Green, who had been employed in the Sea Office, was known simply as the Underwriter and did not have a seat on the Court. In 1841, however, the Court found itself having to appoint an Underwriter from outside the Corporation and this man—Henry Warre—stipulated that he should also be elected to the Court. In fact, this Directorship was strictly independent of his function as Underwriter, and in the event Warre remained on the Court for only three years (1843–6), although he served as Underwriter from 1841 to 1864—and transformed the Corporation's marine business.

---

[1] Evidence of John Holland, Chief Clerk in the REA marine insurance department, to Select Committee on Marine Insurance: *PP* (1810), IV, 116.
[2] Information about personnel for the earlier period is not available.

The background to these developments was provided by the Corporation's disappointing results for marine insurance after the buoyant years of the Napoleonic Wars (net premiums in 1814 were £545,290—a level which was not reached again for 100 years). Altogether, in the twenty-one years 1793–1813, helped by such spectacular underwriting profits as £102,722 for 1795 and £145,157 for 1811, the Corporation secured an aggregate marine underwriting surplus of some £684,000—an average of about £32,500 annually. Thenceforth, however, there was a quite different experience: in the next twenty-one years (1814–34), while net premiums fell steeply, reaching a nadir of £14,562 in 1824, profits disappeared entirely: fourteen years were unprofitable, and aggregate losses were £434,000 (an average underwriting deficit of just over £20,000 annually).

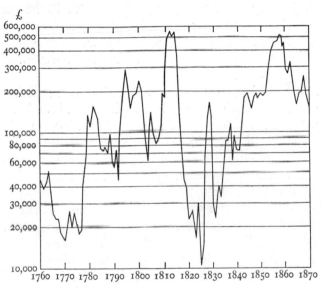

Fig. 9.1: REA marine premiums, 1760–1870[1]

(Source: REA Archives.)

As far as can be discerned, these trends were independent of legal and institutional change. Indeed, far from declining after the marine insurance market was thrown open to other companies in 1824, the REA's net premium income spurted forward in the late 1820s to a significantly higher level than it had been before the repeal, rising from some £20,000 annually in 1821–5 to £85,000 in 1836–40.

[1] The accounting year ended in April of the year indicated. Premiums are given gross until 1795 and net of discount, returns and reinsurances from 1795.

Lloyd's, too, found that the threat from newly established marine insurance companies after their legalization in 1824 was more a product of horrible imagining than any reality. In fact, Lloyd's proved to be both much stronger and much more firmly entrenched in the marine markets than either its enemies or its friends had thought, and few successful companies were established.[1]

Lloyd's relative competitive position *vis-à-vis* potential newcomers to marine insurance immediately after 1824 was made the stronger by the fact that for about ten years the market for insurance was depressed by falling trade values.[2] Yet these trends, even while they must have hampered the growth of rival concerns, were equally uncomfortable for many established underwriters. As we have seen, for two decades after the Napoleonic Wars the REA had a very unsatisfactory experience in marine insurance. And, even though the account showed a welcome surplus in 1832–7 (average about £10,000), persistent losses between 1838 and 1840 must have given the Directors, as well as Alexander Green (who had been appointed Underwriter in 1837), much cause for alarm.

As was only logical, any anxiety about the marine business had to concentrate on the question of the Underwriter and his duties. In spite of being given greater freedom of action than his predecessors, Green continued the long tradition by which the Secretary's and the Marine Departments were closely interlocked—a tradition which was made even more manifest when on becoming Secretary in 1840 he also continued as Underwriter. This conjoining of the Secretary's and Marine Departments perpetuated, in the words of a Committee of Directors in 1843, 'many of those inconveniences which usually result from distracted attention and the want of systematic allotment of duties to all'. Second, as Secretary, he was not able to devote sufficient attention to the continuous and demanding tasks of marine underwriting. Finally, his own business experience and skills were not really relevant to the complex and highly specialized needs of underwriting. By the early 1840s the Court was obliged to take all these points very seriously.

The first important reform of the position of the Underwriter came in the summer of 1841, when the Governors and the Sea Committee, having studied the depressing condition of the marine business 'and anxiously deliberated with a view to devising means for its improvement', came to two far-reaching conclusions: first, that the efficient management of the

---

[1] See F. Martin, *History of Lloyd's and Marine Insurance in Great Britain* (1876), pp. 303–10; Raynes, *British Insurance*, pp. 312–13.

[2] Wright and Fayle, *Lloyd's*, chapter XVI.

Marine Department, far from being able to be combined with any Secretarial functions, 'required the individual as well as the unremitting attention of the person entrusted with it'; second, and an unprecedented assumption for the REA, 'the person entrusted with the management of it should possess that peculiar description of experience and information, which in the opinion of the Committee can best, if not exclusively, be acquired by extensive practice in underwriting at Lloyd's'. These two conclusions pointed to radical departures in the Corporation's procedures. And in accepting them the Court of Directors also accepted the proposal that Henry Warre be appointed to the post. In addition, it had to accept the corollary of such an appointment—which was that an eminent and successful Lloyd's underwriter could only be tempted to join the Corporation in return for the prospect of considerable financial rewards. Thus, Warre was promised the first vacancy on the Court, a salary of £2,000 annually, and a tempting profit commission of 10 per cent on the first £15,000, 7½ per cent on the next £10,000, 5 per cent on the next £10,000, and 2½ per cent on any further profits over £35,000. Finally, he was to receive a lifetime pension of £1,000 if the agreement were ever terminated for any other reason than his misconduct.

Warre's appointment was marked by the opening of an office nearer Lloyd's, at 71 Broad Street, at his request, and by a sharp increase in premiums (net premiums rose from £72,807 in the year ending April 1841 to £196,529 in the year ending April 1844). Yet the actual outcome of this increased business was disappointing: between 1 October 1841 and 31 December 1844 the Corporation lost £2,566 on its marine underwriting account, quite apart from expenses, incurred in the sea business, of £28,851. However, in spite of 'considerable anxiety' and a keen sense of disappointment, a special Committee of Directors accepted Warre's reasoning that the very unsatisfactory outcome was due to transitory factors—notably, the exceptionally bad underwriting year of 1842 and the time which a new Underwriter inevitably needed to weed out 'objectionable accounts' and build up an extensive and good 'connection'. Although, therefore, the Underwriter gave up his Directorship and his formal rights to participate in profits (it was, however, understood that, if the account proved profitable, 'the Court will liberally consider my services'), in 1845 the Court agreed to extend his appointment for a further three years, to give him the requisite time to carry out his improvements and 'for testing the merits of the new system that he had adopted'.

When another Committee came to examine the results of this further period of trial in 1849 they concluded their investigations with mixed feelings. For, although the three years 1846–8 showed an estimated profit of £14,381, the Committee could not escape 'the mortifying fact' of an overall loss of £33,074 on the first seven years of Warre's management. And this record excited similar emotions to those of 1845:

It is impossible to contemplate the result of the experience of so long a period, without a feeling of very great disappointment when it is considered with what sanguine expectations of profit the arrangements for that management were entered into: results so different from those which were then confidently anticipated must naturally lead to some distrust of the future.

Nevertheless, the Committee did not conclude that Warre's appointment should be terminated. Instead, they pinned their hopes on the possibility that the 1847–8 results marked a turning-point, which 'ought in fairness to be considered as affording a presumption of improvement in the management, and to give Mr. Warre a claim to be allowed a further trial, for the chance of his being able to retrieve the hitherto disastrous character of the Marine Branch of the Company's business'.

It was just as well that the Court continued to have some faith in the potential abilities of the Underwriter, even after almost ten years of generally 'disastrous' results. For 1848 did, indeed, mark a decisive turning-point in the history of the Corporation's marine business: that year itself proved more profitable than had been originally estimated, and the surplus in 1849 surged forward even further (in June 1850, although not all risks had 'run-off', it was estimated to be £48,941). In fact, in June 1850 a Committee was able to report with considerable satisfaction that whereas Warre's underwriting account had lost £66,374 between 1841 and 1846, in the next three years (i.e. 1847–9) this had been more than recouped by a profit of £91,310. Thenceforth, with the help of the mid-Victorian trade boom, Warre's underwriting was spectacularly successful: in the decade 1850–9 the aggregate underwriting surplus was £932,200—i.e. an annual average of over £93,000 (even deducting expenses this still left an average of £79,968). As the Directors were reminded by the Treasury Committee when Warre was contemplating retiring in December 1863, his exertions, 'principally . . . in obtaining a superior connection', had made him 'eminently successful'. In fact, the gross profit earned by his Department in the eleven years ending 1860 far exceeded the total capital of the Corporation. Although he had relinquished his absolute right to a profit commission in 1845, he received substantial gratuities almost every time a large underwriting profit was realized (including £6,000 in each of 1859, 1860 and 1861). Between 1850 and 1867, in addition to his annual salary of £2,000,

Warre was presented with more than £62,500 in recognition of his services—including £10,000 on his retirement in 1864 and further amounts in
later years as the accounts of the early 1860s were closed. Munificent as this
may seem, it was no more than common practice at a time when (as the
REA Court appreciated in 1864) an 'enormous remuneration' might be
needed to induce an underwriter 'to give up a good private business in
order to take charge of that of a public company'. Indeed, by others'
standards, Warre was not exceptionally well paid.[1]

The splendid performance of the Corporation's Marine Department in
the 1850s and early 1860s obviously came as a great relief after the disappointments of the first half of the century. It was, moreover, carried on
by Warre's successor, John Leatherdale (1864–75), under whose management the Marine Department was able to transfer an annual average surplus
of £41,000 to the Profit and Loss Account. Altogether, even including the
grim years of the 1840s, the total profits of the period 1841–75, subsequently referred to as 'a veritable golden age for the Marine Department',
were £1,380,684.[2]

The 1850s and 1860s were also prosperous years for marine underwriting in general. The growth of international trade and the long-run rise in
prices greatly increased insurable values. In addition, in the 1860s London
was deriving considerable advantages as an underwriting centre, as the
American Civil War (1861–5) attracted a large amount of American insurance, and helped boost the prospects of the three new companies which
had been founded in 1860. They were followed by further promotions in
1863, and by yet more later in the prosperous 1860s. By the early 1870s
there were about twenty solid companies competing for business—a
situation which led one commentator to make the somewhat exaggerated
claim that underwriting had 'passed, for the most part, from the hands of
private underwriters into those of joint-stock companies'.[3]

In the 1870s, however, the tide turned. Premium rates slumped and
premium incomes fell rapidly. For the REA, too, the later part of the century was to be of a time of severe competitive difficulty.[4] In this sense,
therefore, the golden age of the 1850s and 1860s seemed merely an inter-
lude—albeit a long-lasting and prosperous one. Yet it had been a clear
indication that the Corporation *could* manage—and manage very well—

---

[1] In the late 1850s and early 1860s the Underwriters of the Indemnity Marine and the Marine
Insurance Companies received (in addition to regular salaries of £2,000) annual gratuities of
£10,000 and £8,500 respectively.

[2] *REAM*, II, 3 (November 1905), 62–3.

[3] Quoted in Raynes, *British Insurance*, p. 315.

[4] Below, pp. 258–60.

without the protection of exclusive privileges, which in any case had not been reflected in a great measure of profit in the 104 years in which they had been 'enjoyed'. Henry Warre demonstrated a lesson which was to be deduced from fire and life underwriting at other times—namely, that vigour, confidence and flexibility were of greater importance than an unyielding reliance on tradition and inherited prestige in adjusting the Corporation's business to the needs and opportunities of modern insurance.

PART C

The Drive to
Industrial Maturity
1870-1914

The growth and structural change which had characterized insurance in the early nineteenth century had been largely confined to its traditional branches in fire, life and marine underwriting. They were, in effect, the counterparts of the 'classic' Industrial Revolution which transformed conventional industries—textiles, coal, iron—at the same time. By the 1870s, as also happened with the initial process of industrialization, the first phase of modern growth in insurance underwriting, and its institutional and legal framework, had been completed. Clearly, however, in the words of an earlier commentator, it was 'difficult to set a limit to the application of the principle of assurance to the various operations and accidents of society'.[1] And in the later nineteenth and early twentieth centuries, just as general industrial development proliferated into the expansion of new sectors of the economy—steel, chemicals, electricity—so the complexities and risks of modern society were to stimulate new types of insurance: against railway and industrial accidents, theft, legal liability, and the hazards of travel by motor car and airplane.

Looked at on an even broader basis, the four or five decades before the First World War were a quite distinctive period in Britain's economic and social history. In general terms they were marked not only by the beginning of a shift away from the original bases of industrialization, but also by the growth of new service occupations, by a more highly developed international economy and the export of huge amounts of British capital, by a new concern with social reform, and by new forms of economic and social organization. Much of this general trend was also reflected in British insurance. At one level traditional as well as new modes of underwriting (in particular fire and life) both grew and penetrated new levels of society and economic activity, until, in terms of their popularity and the means used to

[1] *PM*, XI, 37 (14 September 1850).

sell them, they became items of mass consumption. Even more significantly however, the pressure of competition and expansion led to the emergence of large-scale, amalgamated offices; and the opportunities of world-wide economic development led to the rapid growth of overseas business. In terms of the scope and new variety of their business, the scale of their operations and its organizational problems, and the techniques needed to maintain the momentum of growth, insurance offices paralleled, in microcosm, the larger developments which were shaping the twentieth-century economy. As in the period of the classic Industrial Revolution, their drive to maturity was both a response to and a precondition of broader economic and social change.

The general pattern of growth in fire, life and accident underwriting will be considered in chapter 10.[1] In chapter 11 the experience of the Royal Exchange Assurance will be examined. And the implications of growth for the Corporation in particular and the industry in general—in terms of new competitive techniques and the articulation of new structures for control and organization—will be dealt with in chapter 12.

---

[1] Marine underwriting does not lend itself to similar treatment, because of its special characteristics. It will only be dealt with incidentally, in the analysis of the Royal Exchange Assurance's marine business in chapter 11.

10

The Growth of
Insurance Underwriting
1870-1914

FIRE INSURANCE: THE DRIVE TO UNIVERSALITY

Although new types of insurance radically changed some of the basic characteristics of the industry in the decades before the First World War, in one important respect at least it was unchanged: fire underwriting remained the backbone of its organization and profitability. In the words of the *Post Magazine* in 1914:

Although the many departments of insurance which have sprung up in recent years rather tend to divert attention from fire insurance, it is still to this branch that the companies look for the bulk of the profit which is to provide dividends for shareholders. If this department is not flourishing, there is little consolation elsewhere, for the combined resources of all the others are by no means sufficient as yet to make up for the deficiency.[1]

In light of this, it is perhaps appropriate that after the 1860s the basis of our knowledge about the growth of fire insurance changes from statistics of the sums insured, which concentrate attention on the extent of the insurance habit, to data about the course of premium *incomes*, which emphasize the size and profitability of the industry itself.[2] On the other hand, interesting as it would be to have a quantitative picture of the extent and pattern of fire insurance, by the late nineteenth century the effective victory of the habit of fire insurance presumably meant that its growth was largely a function of the increase in buildings and other capital and insurable assets—although the halving of the fire insurance duty in 1866, and its abolition in 1869, gave a fillip to the habit.

This view is to some extent corroborated by the data for London (that is, the area served by the Metropolitan Board of Works), where the fact that the fire offices paid a levy towards the Metropolitan Fire Brigade

---

[1] *PM*, LXXV, 15 (3 January 1914).

[2] Information about the value of sums insured in the United Kingdom is no longer available after 1869 because of the repeal of the fire insurance duty—bringing to an end the series of official returns. In the last part of the century, however, the spread of joint-stock organization and improvements in communication and publicity make available what is missing for the earlier part—namely, reliable statistics of premium incomes.

in proportion to their sums insured enables us to measure the amount of insurance in force. There, the insured value of property rose from just over £400 million in the late 1860s to more than £1,100 million on the eve of the First World War. The biggest proportionate as well as absolute increase came in the 1870s. But throughout the period 1870–1913 the insured value of London property grew at a remarkably similar rate to that of the official assessments of metropolitan property—as is indicated by the negligible variation in the ratio of sums insured to those assessments.[1] Temporarily at least (they were to change after 1914) habits had become fixed, and the extension of insurance followed the growth of property.

There are no comparable measures of the growth in the value of sums insured for the country as a whole after 1869. Up to that date there had been a slowing down of the rate of increase (although a growth rate of, for example, over 40 per cent in the decade 1859–69 was still perfectly respectable). Subsequently, there is no reason to imagine that the course of events in London in the late nineteenth century was unrepresentative of the country as a whole. The British market for fire insurance was increasingly dependent on the growth of property rather than on any change in the habits of potential policyholders. By 1862 it was estimated that in England and Wales some £1,000 million of property was insured at any one time, leaving about £450 or £500 million of property uncovered, although much of this last category was in too small quantities to be easily insurable.

In spite of this situation, the total premium income of British fire offices increased by very large amounts after the mid-nineteenth century. In 1856, it was estimated, premiums had been about £2 million. By 1870 these were estimated at some £3·7 million, and by 1872 at £5·3 million.[2] Thenceforth, they rose to some £20 million at the end of the century, and almost £30 million in 1913. Thus, between the early 1870s and the First World War fire premiums increased sixfold (the rise was not steady: premiums doubled in the 1880s, but grew by only about 25 and 30 per cent in the next two decades). This impressive growth rate was not inconsistent with the apparently slower growth of the national capital and of sums insured in Britain.[3] For the approaching saturation of the British fire

[1] K. Maywald, 'Fire Insurance and the Capital Coefficient in Great Britain, 1866–1952', *Economic History Review*, 2nd series, IX, 1 (August 1956), 91.

[2] Walford, *Insurance Cyclopaedia*, 154; Walford, 'On Fires and Fire Insurance', *JSS* (1877), pp. 412, 417.

[3] Between 1875 and 1913 total reproducible capital in the country did not quite double (Deane and Cole, *British Economic Growth*, p. 274) compared with perhaps a fivefold increase in premiums. Between 1878 and 1902 sums insured in London increased by 60 per cent, but total premiums rose by 130 per cent.

TABLE 10.1. *British offices' fire insurance business, 1881–1913*[a]

Year	Number of companies reporting	Premium incomes (£000)	Ratio to premiums of			Fire funds (£000)
			losses	expenses	surplus commissions	
1881	50	9,535	66·2	30·5	3·3	12,660
1891	59	17,596	61·4	32·7	5·8	26,629
1901	52	20,270	63·5	34·2	2·3	27,636
1911	132	27,986	54·7	36·8	8·5	25,248
1913	131	29,242	52·0	36·6	11·5	27,846

[a] Annual data for 1881, 1891 and 1901 are taken from the table in the *Finance Chronicle*, 15 October and 16 November 1903. The figures are not absolutely comprehensive, but they refer to all the important companies and leave only a tiny amount of insurance out of account. After the Assurance Companies Act of 1909, fire offices had to make annual returns. The data for 1911 and 1913 are therefore taken from the Board of Trade Returns for 1912 and 1914. They include *all* insurance companies (hence the apparent increase in the number of offices) but in 1911, for example, this includes sixty-nine with premiums of less than £5,000, of which forty-one had less than £1,000.

insurance market had already forced British companies (and especially the younger and more adventurous of them) to turn their attention overseas. It was there that the sources of the great rise in premiums lay. The distinctive feature of the fire insurance industry in the second half of the century was, therefore, the invasion of foreign and colonial markets by British fire offices, and the consequent transformation of the structure of fire premiums and business.

The most important market for British fire insurance services was the United States, which accounted for at least 40 per cent of total premium incomes by the end of the century. Indeed, by 1905 the nine leading British companies, which between them accounted for about two-thirds of all fire premiums, earned half their £15·6 million premium income in the United States.[1]

But the United States, although dominant, was not alone. The world-wide extension of British fire insurance was a function of the world-wide scope of economic development, and the rôle of the British capital and services in that development. In South America and Australasia, in South Africa and the Far East, the extension and sophistication of economic activity, the growth of industry and agriculture and the spread of cities and trading networks, demanded multitudinous commercial and financial services. Insurance was among the most crucial of these, and it was natural that, in this most complex and delicate of matters, merchants, manufacturers and householders should turn to companies which combined the skills, the experience, the stability and the reserves appropriate to their

[1] Calculated from data in *The Times Financial and Commercial Supplement*, 27 August 1906.

needs. The characteristic British fire office now had branches or large agencies in Melbourne and Sydney, Cape Town and Johannesburg, Bombay and Calcutta, New York, Chicago and San Francisco, Manila and Yokohama, Buenos Aires and Santiago—and scores of other places in every continent.

Unfortunately, it is not possible to measure the relative significance of the different overseas sources of premium income, since the companies tended merely to report their aggregate fire premiums. And it is even very difficult to appraise the overall importance of all overseas as against home insurance. By the opening years of this century, however, at a time when the United States accounted for about 40 per cent of all premiums, it is likely that other overseas areas generated a further 20 per cent or even, conceivably, more. In 1891, for example, the Sun earned some £405,500 in home premiums, £361,300 in US premiums, and £190,600 from all other areas. At the turn of the century the giant Commercial Union seems to have derived three-quarters of its total premiums from overseas (and three-quarters of *those* from the United States). While even the REA, which came relatively late into the foreign field, earned £476,000 of its total premium income of £749,500 from overseas areas (£250,600 from the United States).[1]

The far-reaching changes in the pattern of fire insurance (as with the substantial changes in British life insurance a generation earlier) had been largely induced by young and thrustful offices. In the case of fire insurance the newcomers had been keen to take advantage of the enormous leverage exerted by overseas, and particularly American, markets. By 1901 the five leading offices were the Royal of Liverpool (premiums: £2·51 million), the Commercial Union (£1·97 million), the Liverpool & London & Globe (£1·79 million), the North British & Mercantile (£1·62 million), and the London & Lancashire (£1·17 million).[2] Of these, three originated in Lancashire (and were obviously helped by the intimate connections between Merseyside and the American economy), and four had been established since 1844. The 'older generation', although still lively, had slipped back (or, as with the Globe, was joining the new). This was particularly marked in the new and expanding markets. Thus in 1897 the Sun, the REA and the Phoenix still accounted for 23·5 per cent of insured values in

---

[1] Dickson, *Sun Insurance Office*, p. 305; Edward Liveing, *A Century of Insurance* (1961), p. 54, mentions that by 1899 the Commercial Union's foreign fire premium income 'more than trebled that obtained in the United Kingdom'. If these proportions still applied in 1905, when the Commercial Union had total premiums of £2,075,000 and US premiums of £1,016,000 (*The Times Financial and Commercial Supplement*, 27 August 1906), then its total overseas premiums (of which the US accounted for some 75 per cent) were £1,556,000.

[2] *Insurance News*, 15 December 1902.

London, as against 14·0 per cent for the Royal, the London & Lancashire and the Liverpool & London & Globe.[1] But when it came to total premium incomes (i.e. overseas and home) the story was spectacularly different: in 1899 the older three earned £2·7 million fire premiums, as against £7·9 million for the younger, northern, three—and this out of total British premiums of just over £20·2 million.

The growth of a world-wide system of fire insurance in the two generations before the First World War was not, of course, uneventful. Between 1877 and 1902, for example, the aggregate underwriting surplus of the industry varied between a loss of just over 1 per cent of premium income in 1893 and a gain of 17·8 per cent in 1878–9, with an overall average gain of just under 7 per cent. These fluctuations were more violent than those of the ratio of fire losses to premiums—which in all but six of these twenty-five years varied only between 56 and 66 per cent, although this itself might not have been entirely reassuring to the very cautious General Manager of the North British & Mercantile, who asserted in 1867 that 'we generally consider that the losses ought not to exceed between 50 and 55 per cent with the view of making anything like a profit'.[2]

To some extent these problems, and certainly the upward movement of the expense ratio, can be attributed to the implication of heightened competition and international expansion. However, the most important vicissitudes came from these events which fell outside the 'normal' expectations of fire underwriters—for it was sometimes a particular 'crisis' in the business of fire insurance which was responsible for a shift in the nature and direction of the industry's development.

In this context, within Britain itself, one of the most momentous events of the century came in London in June 1861 with the great fire (the greatest since 1666) at Tooley Street, Southwark. The fire, apparently started by spontaneous combustion in stored hemp, fed furiously on warehouses crammed with foodstuffs, tea, sulphur, tallow, coffee, jute, oil and paint. It was not brought under control for two days nor fully extinguished for a fortnight. At one point the Thames itself seemed to be in flames, as molten and burning tallow poured out of the warehouses on to the waters. The fire offices sustained what was, by contemporary standards, an enormous loss of between £1 and £2 million.[3] More important than the short-run loss, however, was the fact that the Tooley Street fire was responsible for a

---

[1] *The Finance Chronicle*, 16 January 1899.
[2] Select Committee on Fire Protection, *PP* (1867), X, Q.1616.
[3] In 1861 the REA losses (£136,442) for the year ending April 1862 exceeded premiums (£116,168) for the first time since the Hamburg fire of 1842. The Sun lost £270,680 as against home premiums of £239,891.

fundamental reorganization of London's fire-fighting service, for the creation of powerful new offices, and for far-reaching changes in the character of the co-operation between the different fire insurance companies.

Since 1833 the defence of London against fire had rested with the Fire Engine Establishment—directly financed by the combined offices.[1] The Tooley Street fire brought home to the companies the scope of the job of fire protection which a modern city demanded—and which, it seemed to them, was far more a public than a private obligation. Yet they were then spending some £25,000 annually to provide the only effective fire-fighting force in London—a force which ('asking no questions and asking for no payment'[2]) benefited many more people than those who were prudent enough to insure their property, and which was both increasing in cost and diminishing in relevance to the problems of a greatly expanding metropolis. Immediately after the fire, therefore, the offices advised the Home Secretary that they could no longer remain solely responsible for the safety of London (they pointed out that in no large city abroad and in few provincial towns at home was the fire-fighting service not in the hands of a public authority and maintained out of rates and taxes), and that they were going to disband the Establishment and offer its stations and equipment to whatever new authority was appointed by the Government.[3] After an official inquiry and some vacillation, the Government agreed to the establishment of the Metropolitan Brigade on 1 January 1866. And although the various offices gratuitously transferred some £30,000 of equipment to the new Brigade and continued to contribute part of the cost, their expenditure was considerably less than it had been.

Besides bringing home to the companies the problems of fire protection, the Tooley Street fire also induced a state of general alarm about London mercantile risks. In fact, this alarm—based on a decade of net loss and shock at the extent and uncontrollability of fire in warehouses thought to be reasonably safe—led to an immediate panic, which the companies were to regret. Within a few days of the fire the established fire offices had agreed on an extraordinary increase of between three- and fivefold in the rates for waterside warehouses.[4]

[1] Above, pp. 165–6.

[2] William Newmarch, Secretary of the Globe, quoted in Blackstone, *British Fire Service*, p. 170.

[3] As the offices readily acknowledged, the Establishment did not (and could not possibly hope to) cover large parts of London. Broadly speaking, its stations were confined to ten square miles in central London—centered on the Royal Exchange—where the bulk of insurance risks were.

[4] For the effects of the Tooley Street fire on fire insurance competition and practice, see Raynes, *British Insurance*, pp. 340–3; Insurance Institute of London, *Mercantile Fire Insurance*, pp. 52–60; P. E. Ridley, 'The Tooley Street Fire', *JCII*, xxxv (1932), 25–58.

But this was an instance when extreme action produced an extreme, and very powerful, reaction. The enormous increase in rates provoked 'a storm of fury in the City'.[1] Hundreds of merchants, brokers, bankers and warehousemen petitioned the Lord Mayor to call a public meeting, complaining bitterly against the increase in rates and what they took to be the unfair exercise of the power of combination. The meeting was a stormy affair, and the spokesman for the offices (William Newmarch, Secretary of the Globe) went so far as to promise concessions on the new rates in return for new classifications of merchandise and limits on the size of warehouses.

But these concessions failed to satisfy the protestors, and the fact that they were put into practice in August did not abate the feelings and emotions generated at the meeting of 25 July. As a direct result of Tooley Street and its aftermath, therefore, two new companies were formed by commercial interests, no doubt seeking high profits as well as cheaper insurance. The new companies—the Mercantile Fire Insurance Company and the Commercial Union—were quickly to play a powerful rôle in fire insurance. Within months of its establishment the Mercantile had agreed to amalgamate, on equal terms, with the North British Insurance Company (established in Edinburgh in 1809), which had only a negligible fire business in London. The Commercial Union and the North British & Mercantile were responsible for a substantial revision of the London Mercantile Tariff, for each refused to use the Tariff Offices' rates for London mercantile risks—and in 1863 negotiations with the associated companies resulted in a definitive agreement, which in general terms produced lower rates. They also very rapidly increased their business: by 1904, with almost £2 million premium income each, they were the third and fourth British fire offices in point of size.[2] In later years it could be acknowledged that the leading fire offices had exemplified a tendency 'towards panic legislation' after Tooley Street, but that they had learned a lesson as a result so that the Fire Offices' Committee 'has been less ready to raise rates, and has never, or hardly ever, gone beyond what the future outlook very amply warranted'.[3] In an important sense, the consequences of the Tooley Street fire lasted well into the twentieth century.

The other really spectacular fires of the period occurred not in Britain, but overseas—and principally in the United States. But it is important to note the difference in the consequences of disastrous fires such as those at Chicago (1871), Boston (1872), and above all San Francisco (1906),

---

[1] Liveing, *A Century of Insurance*, p. 5.
[2] *Finance Chronicle*, 2 October 1904.
[3] D. Deuchar, 'The Necessity for a Tariff Organization', *JFII*, VI (1903), lix.

compared with Tooley Street.[1] For in the United States the operations and reputation of the British companies contrasted very favourably with those of other offices. Besides their greater experience and more systematic control, the British offices had much greater reserves (accumulated at home and elsewhere in the world) on which to draw in emergencies. As a result, although their losses were very heavy (in 1871 and 1872 the loss ratio of all British offices jumped to over 70 per cent compared with 58·3 per cent in 1870),[2] their ability to pay claims and the promptness with which they did so provided powerful evidence of their soundness to American policy-holders. Hence, even though these fires, like that in Tooley Street, led to an increase in premiums, they also resulted in a consolidation and streng-thening of the position of the established British offices—confirming and emphasizing their world-wide supremacy in the great age of international economic expansion.

LIFE INSURANCE: FROM PRUDENCE TO INVESTMENT

By the middle decades of the nineteenth century life insurance had become an established social habit and an important economic institution. Widely accepted among men of moderate means, based on motives of thrift as well as providence, it was becoming a crucial and representative feature of Victorian middle-class society. And its popularity continued to grow. In the late nineteenth century this continued growth was characterized by two main features. First, in what amounted almost to a social revolution, the habit of insurance spread decisively to other social and economic classes. The argument of its earlier advocates that, far from being merely 'the luxury of the rich' life insurance was 'far more the necessity of the working man',[3] was now virtually realized in practice. Second, while the factors which had combined to initiate modern 'ordinary' life insurance in the early part of the century—the growth of middle-class wealth, changes in habits, the increased complexity of the economic system—continued to influence its expansion, the rôle of endowment, as distinct from whole-life, insurance grew dramatically in importance: the investment element in insurance came to dominate its practice for the policyholder as well as the life office.

There is no need here to consider in any detail the rise of industrial assurance[4]—i.e. life insurance based upon the regular weekly or monthly

---

[1] For the San Francisco Fire, see below, pp. 246–51.

[2] Walford, *Insurance Cyclopaedia*, III, 510; IV, 154.

[3] *PM*, No. 483 (6 October 1849).

[4] For a brief history, see Morrah, *Industrial Life Assurance*. Also Chapter 10 ('The Rise and Progress of Industrial Assurance') in Andras, *Historical Review*; and Bentley B. Gilbert, *The Evolution of National Insurance in Great Britain* (1966), pp. 318–25.

collection of premiums,[1] and therefore particularly suited to the needs of the relatively poor, who could only envisage insuring their lives if the individual premium payments were small. As early as 1849 and 1852 offices like the Industrial & General Life Assurance & Deposit Company and the British Industry Life Assurance Company were floated with the explicit aim of adapting the objectives and regulations of traditional life companies 'to the wants and wishes of the "Industrial Classes"' by collecting premiums frequently and in small amounts.[2] To their publicists in the 1850s it seemed as if the young industrial offices 'could be raised into one of the great improvements of the age'.[3] In a general sense these hopes were realized. From the 1850s premium income amounted to £1·5 million; a generation later, in 1905, it had reached almost half that of ordinary insurance (£11·5 million as against £24 million), insuring sums about one-third as large: and by 1912 industrial premiums were being paid at the rate of £16 million annually. Between the early 1890s and 1912 the sums assured rose from some £125 million to £350 million.

In one respect, therefore, industrial assurance underwent an even more significant change than ordinary life insurance. It was also dominated by a single giant: in 1905 the Prudential was responsible for over half of all premiums.[4] By the early twentieth century, in 1905, with over 25 million policies issued to a population of 43 million, it had become virtually a universal habit: the number of policies apparently exceeded the number of family units. In spite of this, however, and much as industrial assurance bridged the gap in habits of prudence and thrift between the poor and the middle class, it seems fundamentally to have fulfilled a different social and economic function. In 1905, for example, the average ordinary policy insured £345, whereas the average industrial policy represented a sum assured of just under £10: an amount, in the words of a contemporary, 'little more than sufficient to pay funeral expenses'.[5] To a large extent industrial assurance was not being used to provide for surviving dependants. Rather, it served to guarantee payment of the costs of burial and to channel tiny

---

1 The Collecting Societies and Industrial Assurance Companies Act of 1896 defines an Industrial Assurance Company as one providing life insurance for sums less than £20, receiving premiums through collections at greater distances than ten miles from the registered office, and at less intervals than two months.

2 *PM*, XI, 11 (16 March 1850).

3 *PM*, XV, 16 (22 April 1854).

4 Five years later, at a time when competition for ordinary life insurance was producing ever-increasing amalgamations of life and composite offices, the Royal Exchange Actuary drew attention to 'the giant industrial companies headed by the Prudential, whose connections are so vast and whose organization is so perfect, that they threaten to overshadow in the long run all other separate life companies'.

5 *The Economist*, LXV, 546 (30 March 1907).

savings into endowment policies. (Both aspects were exemplified in the practice of insuring children's lives: in England and Wales in 1906 about 5 million out of a total 7·2 million children under 10 years were so insured.)[1] These factors, combined with the obvious fact that different types of policy-holders and basically very different modes of organization were involved, naturally drew a sharp distinction between the contemporary history of industrial and ordinary insurance.

TABLE 10.2. *UK offices ordinary life insurance business,*[2] *1870–1914*[3]

Year	Number of offices	Premiums (£000)	Sums assured (£000)	Life funds (£000)	Sums assured per capita UK population £ s. d.
1870	101	9,750	292,557	87,767	9 7 2
1880	99	11,658	382,680	123,675	10 19 0
1890	89	14,833	478,972	165,920	12 15 11
1900	85	21,796	675,960	246,130	16 8 5
1914	94	28,999	869,739	390,054	18 17 10

The development of ordinary life insurance in the period is reflected in the growth of premiums, sums assured and life funds. As Table 10.2 indicates, between 1870 and 1914 the ordinary life business of UK offices trebled—with a particularly rapid increase in the 1890s. Even taking into account the increase in population, the amount of ordinary insurance in force doubled—increasing by a third in the last decade of the century. Between 1883 and 1913 the amount of life premiums (ordinary and industrial) per head of the population grew from 8s. to just over £1.[4] Once again, as in the early years of the period, the growth of life insurance out-

[1] Andras, *Historical Review*, p. 81. Of the estimated 5 million policies, the Prudential issued half.

[2] The ordinary business of industrial offices is included in the above totals. (By 1914 the ordinary life funds of the Prudential were about £46 million).

[3] Although the Board of Trade published the returns of individual companies annually from 1872, its summary totals only begin in the early 1880s. Even then, the totals are not absolutely accurate. In the case of premiums and funds this was because the accounting year was not precisely the same for all companies. In the case of sums assured, the individual offices provided information only when they had conducted formal valuations of life assets and liabilities—i.e. normally every five years. These quinquennia did not coincide for all companies, so that the totals in any one Board of Trade publication refer to the accounts of companies published over the previous five (or more) years. Hence, the totals for 'sums assured' in fact, and unavoidably, refer to different years depending on the valuation period and date of the various individual offices. In the Table, data for 1870 were derived from Deuchar, 'Progress of Life Assurance Business', and those for 1880, 1900 and 1914 from the Board of Trade Returns published in 1882, 1892, 1902 and 1915 respectively. For 1880, for which there is no official summary of valuation data, sums assured had to be calculated from returns published between 1879 and 1883.

[4] *Statist*, LXXVIII, 1865 (22 November 1913), 430.

stripped not only the increase of population but also the growth of national income: the population continued to spend an increasing proportion of its growing income on life insurance. Between 1881 and 1914 the proportion of net national income represented by ordinary life premiums rose from 1·2 per cent to 1·6 per cent—with most of the increase concentrated in the 1890s.[1]

These aggregate figures, however, conceal a fundamental shift in the structure and even purpose of life insurance. For much of the increase was associated with the new-found popularity of endowment policies, which provided for the payment of the amount insured either at the end of a stipulated period or at death if that occurred earlier. In contrast with conventional whole-life policies, on which the amount is payable only at death, endowment policies involved a quite explicit savings and investment element. For most of the century this type of policy had been of negligible importance, and as late as 1870 nearly all insurance policies had been whole-life. By the late 1880s, however, about 19 per cent of all policies and about 9 per cent of all sums assured were endowment in character. In the next decade there was a spectacular increase in endowment insurances—which, by 1900, had grown to some 47 per cent of policies in force and 24 per cent of all sums assured.[2] By the eve of the First World War almost

TABLE 10.3. *UK life offices ordinary endowment business, 1890–1913*[3]

Year	Number of policies	Sums assured (£000)	Endowments as % of total policies	Endowments as % of total sums assured
'1890'	192,187	44,743	19·3	9·3
'1900'	929,353	164,991	47·3	24·4
'1910'	1,798,282	307,468	60·6	37·2
'1913'	2,017,052	339,447	62·4	39·0

[1] Calculated from national income data in Mitchell, *British Historical Statistics*, pp. 367–8, and premium data in G. W. Murphy and J. Johnston, 'The Growth of Life Assurance in the United Kingdom since 1800', *Transactions of the Manchester Statistical Society*, 1956–7, pp. 74–5.

[2] At this relatively early date these figures underestimate the significance of endowment policies: in the 1880s and 1890s the total sums assured included large amounts on policies taken out years before. Hence the endowment percentage on *new* insurances must have been considerably greater than 9 per cent in 1890 and 24 per cent in 1900.

[3] Sources: Board of Trade Returns, 1892, 1902, 1912 and 1915. The Board of Trade Returns were based upon individual companies' returns of their own valuation accounts. As noted above (p. 220 n. 3) this means that the summary figures are not (and cannot be) exact indications of the sums assured or policies in force in any given year. In contrast to Table 10.2 (where premiums and funds were derived from annual accounts mostly published in 1914), Table 10.3 is based solely on valuations. It therefore seems more appropriate to list the data derived from the Board of Trade's 1915 Return as referring to '1913' (valuation dates actually varied from 1910 to 1914), even though it refers to the same total of sums assured as is listed under 1914 in Table 10.2.

two-thirds of all policies, and over one-third of all sums assured, were endowment contracts. Between 1890 and 1913 whole-life insurance (sums assured) had increased by barely 25 per cent—whereas endowment insurance had multiplied sevenfold.

The rise to prominence of the endowment policy was in some respects comparable to the development of with-profits policies early in the nineteenth century. On the one hand, it was a response to public needs 'under the quickening impulse of a keen competition'.[1] On the other, it reflected an increased emphasis on the use of life insurance as a device for productive savings—employing the skills of life offices to accumulate funds for the future, whether for 'school expenses, the support of sons at college, the dowry of daughters, the entry of sons into professions or business',[2] or for ordinary adult purposes, retirement and old age (endowment policies were sometimes referred to as 'old-age policies').[3] Nor was all this dependent on individual initiative alone: by the end of the century professional organizations were extending their care for their members' interests to embrace the field of life insurance. Thus in 1890 the REA, along with other offices, was circularized by both the Teacher's Guild of Great Britain and the *Lancet*. The former had appointed a Thrift Committee (with the object of impressing upon teachers of all classes the importance of making provision for old age, and for their families in the event of death, and of assisting them to do so) and was gathering data in order 'to circulate a succinct statement in tabular form'. The *Lancet* also wanted information in order to publish a 'Special Life Assurance Supplement' for the benefit of its readers.[4] These were merely small symptoms of a massive shift in savings habits.

Clearly, although it is not possible to assess the relative significance of the different factors which led to the growth of life insurance in the late nineteenth century, the great increase in endowment insurance was an unambiguous indication of the increased emphasis on personal thrift. And in this respect, the 1890s were obviously a crucial decade—reflecting, perhaps, not merely a general pressure of middle-class savings, but also the falling rate of return on traditional investments which must have made an insurance policy an even more attractive outlet for savings.[5] Only in the

---

[1] S. G. Warner, 'Twenty Years' Changes in Life Assurance', *JFII*, XII (1909), 74–5.

[2] Prospectus of the National Life (1873) quoted in Walford, *Insurance Cyclopaedia*, II, 498.

[3] *Statist*, LXXVIII, No. 1865 (22 November 1913), 431.

[4] The *Lancet* had already conducted a survey of its readers, which showed that 43 per cent preferred endowment and 28 per cent with-profits whole-life insurance—a further indication of the element of thrift involved.

[5] Below, pp. 331–5.

early twentieth century was there some deceleration of the growth of endowment and with-profits policies in general—a response, it was said, to the increased death duties in Lloyd George's 1909 Budget, which led to a 'substantial extension' of whole-life without-profits insurance to provide for their payment.[1] Even so, they continued to grow at an impressive rate. By this time, too, the ordinary life offices had begun to appreciate the extent of the market for insurance which, owing to the continued development of the habits of thrift and prudence, existed among lower social classes than they had been accustomed to deal with. This lesson was in any case forcibly brought home by the striking example of the growth of industrial insurance and the invasion of the field of ordinary policies by the giants of the new industry, the Prudential and the Refuge: between 1890 and 1913 there had been a threefold increase in industrial business; and by 1914 the Prudential's premium income from ordinary business exceeded £5 million, and the Refuge's was £1·3 million. (The REA's premium income was then only some £420,000.) The ordinary offices followed suit by abandoning their sole reliance on reasonably wealthy professional and middle classes. They began to emphasize 'thrift policies' for small amounts, embodying a savings element and directed at lower middle or upper working classes; payment was made more convenient; and medical examinations were dispensed with. Social change was changing life business. 'Insurance companies', said the REA's Irish Branch Manager in 1910, 'are becoming more and more the poor man's banker.'[2] These forces found reflection in a decline in the average size of life policies: between the later 1880s and 1913 the average sum insured by endowment policies fell from £215 to £170, and by whole-life policies from £535 to £452. The 'striving working classes' were beginning to appreciate the attractions of ordinary life business.[3] And by 1913 the *Statist* commented that 'no recent development of life assurance is more remarkable and encouraging than the success which has attended systematic efforts to cater for the small policy-holder, who was formerly considered almost beneath attention'.[4]

As we shall see, competition, sales pressure and the 'education' of the public played important rôles in the contemporary expansion of life insurance.[5] So did improved actuarial practice, which combined with

[1] Andras, *Historical Review*, p. 74. In 1900 without-profits policies accounted for about £121 million sums insured, as against £555 million in with-profits policies. By 1920 they accounted for £326 million as against £818 million.
[2] W. S. Kinnear, 'Insurance in the Twentieth Century', *REAM*, III (3 January 1910), 108.
[3] *PM*, LXXV (1914), 876 (14 November 1914).
[4] *Statist*, LXXVIII, 1865 (22 November 1913), 441.
[5] Below, pp. 273–93.

market forces to extend the range of attractive offerings while standardizing and cheapening the most popular types of policy.[1] In its maturity, life insurance had assumed some of the characteristics of a mass-production industry, particularly with respect to its drive for large turnover and its use of intensive marketing arrangements. At the same time, however, its total bundle of 'products' was becoming less standardized precisely because, in order to expand, it had to cater for an increasing variety of needs. In the last resort it was this element of demand which did most to shape life insurance as a whole. And the appropriate context in which to consider the development of life insurance is, precisely, that of social change. For from the cheapening of postal and transport services (which enormously facilitated the control of agency and branch systems) to fundamental developments in income distribution and middle-class attitudes, life insurance could not escape its environment. It was, indeed, itself a powerful expression of social development, and could be seen as a measure of that apparent durability of economic and social progress which so impressed contemporaries: 'a great and many sided industry moving forward under the stress of great social forces—a keen competition, an expanding population, a busy and prosperous people'.[2]

THE RISE OF ACCIDENT INSURANCE: THE SEARCH FOR COMPREHENSIVE SECURITY

The continued growth of fire and life insurance in the late nineteenth century was in one sense a logical extension of earlier developments. In the second half of the century, however, the insurance industry was quite radically changed by the extension of underwriting to cover risks which had not previously existed, or which had hardly before been the object of insurance. This development entailed a proliferation into a multitude of separate fields of insurance practice, each with its own specific characteristics—into insurance against personal accident and disease, employers' liability, fidelity guarantee, burglary, plate glass damage, public liability and loss of liquor licences, culminating in that most characteristic of twentieth-century ventures, motor insurance. In spite of this apparent fragmentation, however, there are good reasons for considering all these branches together, quite apart from the historical convention by which they were grouped under the collective name of 'accident insurance'. The first is that in organizational terms (precisely because they appeared after

---

[1] Andras, *Insurance Guide and Hand Book*, I, 10–11.
[2] Warner, 'Twenty Years' Changes in Life Assurance', *JFII* (1909), p. 85.

fire, life and marine insurance had settled into an established structural framework) offices tended to group them into a single department for underwriting and administrative purposes. Secondly, the coincidence of their development suggests that they were all influenced by a common set of economic and social factors at work in late nineteenth-century Britain.

Of course, when the various types of accident insurance are studied individually, the specific reasons for their growth seem to be related to different aspects of economic, social and technological development. Nevertheless, it is possible to see how each was in some important way related to the general character of economic and social development in Britain in the decades before 1914. As the nation matured, so its maturity demanded new sorts of services.

As capital grew more abundant and technology more sophisticated, so quite new types of costly hazards—railway and motor car accidents, plate glass breakage, boiler explosion and other engineering risks[1]—became increasingly frequent to the point at which systematized insurance was both feasibly and mutually profitable. The continued expansion of professional and middle-class incomes, together with the cultural influences of insurance, naturally turned men's minds to the need to protect their incomes against the consequence not merely of their deaths, but also of injury, sickness and disablement—and against the possibility of theft, of damage to their or other people's property, and of claims by injured third parties. The complexity and impersonality of a growing commercial system placed more men in positions of trust with a consequent need to ensure their fidelity. Finally, continuing change in the technical, economic and social systems, also raised questions of social and legal responsibility with regard to the injury of industrial and other sorts of employees: and these, as much the outcome of economic maturity as was the evolution of a substantial class of professional and businessmen, were resolved by a series of laws which, creating an explicit liability, led immediately to the creation of a new type of insurance. Whether we see the march of insurance as a symbol of the beneficent spirit of co-operation in which policyholders joined together to offer each other mutual indemnities against loss, or as a symptom of a property-orientated society, eager to monetize the consequence of accident and disaster, it must figure prominently in any

---

[1] Boiler, engine and lift and crane insurance, because of the substantial and continuing technical problems involved, tended to be a more or less specialist branch of the industry, largely confined to a few firms, which provided a regular inspection and engineering service as well as insurance.

account of socio-economic change in Victorian and Edwardian Britain.[1] As examples of the pattern of development we may take the three most important sections: personal accident, employers' liability and motor vehicle.

Personal accident insurance was the product of the enormous spurt in railway travel in the 1840s; between 1843 and 1849, for example, the number of passengers rose from 24 million to some 64 million.[2] Well within a single generation, and therefore with a particularly strong social and cultural impact, the railway had become an integral part of everyday life—completely different in sheer physical presence from anything the generality of the public had seen before. It was therefore not so much their statistical significance as their novelty and the spectacular nature of railway accidents—which could beat a man down and whirl him away 'upon a jagged mill, that spun him round and round, and struck him limb from limb, and licked his stream of life up with its fiery heat, and cast his mutilated fragments in the air'[3]—which focused public attention on them. Yet even the bare statistics were impressive: in the first six months of 1849, for example, railway accidents caused ninety-six deaths and seventy-five injuries—substantial enough figures considering a mileage of less than 5,500, and no doubt justifying the opinion of *The Times* that 'railway accidents are of almost daily occurrence, generally ending in the loss of limb—often of life'.[4]

The concentrating of public attention on the new risks of accidental death and injury implied in the spread of railway travel coincided, after 1844, with the adaptation of joint-stock law which immensely facilitated the formation of insurance companies. As a consequence, between 1845 and 1850 some thirteen companies were provisionally registered for insurance against railway accidents. In the event, only two came to fruition. And of these, the real pioneer was the Railway Passengers Assurance Company, which began business in 1849. The Railway Passengers issued tickets (identical in size and style to ordinary travel tickets) through railway booking-clerks, to cover risks on particular

---

[1] The historian of accident insurance gives the following 'commencing dates' (i.e. first specialized policies) of accident insurance in the United Kingdom: fidelity guarantee and hailstorm: 1840; livestock: 1844; personal accident: 1848; plate glass: 1852; engineering: 1858; public liability: 1875; employers' liability: 1880; burglary: 1887; liquor licences: 1890; credit: 1893; motor vehicle: 1896; contract guarantee: 1901 (W. A. Dinsdale, *History of Accident Insurance in Great Britain* [1954], pp. 44–5).

[2] Dinsdale, *Accident Insurance*, p. 51.

[3] Charles Dickens, *Dombey and Son*, chapter LV. The novel was published in 1846–8.

[4] *The Times*, 19 January 1849. Total deaths from 'accidental violence' in 1849 were 12,255 (Walford, *Insurance Cyclopaedia*, I, 4).

journeys or for specified periods. In the case of the single journey, premiums (irrespective of the length of the journey) were 1d., 2d., and 3d., for third-class, second-class and first-class passengers, and death benefits were £200, £500 and £1,000. (The reputed reason for the discrimination in benefits was that third- and second-class carriages, being roofless, were more hazardous.) The Company secured a private Act which, among other provisions, exempted its insurance compensation from being taken into account for the reduction of damages recoverable at common law or under statute.[1] In its first year of operation the Railway Passengers operated on thirty-two railways, sold 2,808 periodical tickets and 110,074 single-journey tickets, and paid claims to thirty-seven people. In 1855 the somewhat cautious Company extended its operations to all types of personal accident, and by 1858 its premium income was £22,435 —as against compensation paid of £8,368.

Railway accident insurance was only one, albeit a vitally important, aspect of this branch in the mid-nineteenth century. In 1850, for example, the Accidental Death Insurance Company began business, issuing policies against fatal and non-fatal accidents in *any* field (thus effectively beginning general personal accident insurance).[2] In 1852 it absorbed the two-year-old Railway Assurance Company, and by 1858 its premiums (which had been merely £1,228 in its first year) reached £33,200. After a series of crippling frauds by policyholders its business was transferred to the Traveller and Marine Insurance Company in 1857, and in 1859 the latter changed its own name to the Accidental Death Insurance Company (No. 2). Between 1857 and 1859 this company absorbed various others, including the Maritime Passengers, and in 1866 it was amalgamated into the Accidental Insurance Company. Soon after, that Company provided a further innovation in the form of a 'specific compensation' policy, which

[1] As a consequence of Court interpretation of the Fatal Accidents Act of 1846 (Lord Campbell's Act) any insurance payments, other than those derived from a Railway Passengers Company policy, owing to the estate of a deceased victim of an accident, were set off in reduction of damages, since the payments were held to reduce the pecuniary loss. This special situation seems to have been overlooked until early in the twentieth century, when payment under a £1,000 policy with the Ocean Accident was deducted from damages of £2,100. The Ocean immediately secured a private Act (1907) giving it the same privileges as the Railway Passengers. The other accident offices were therefore alerted to the position, and systematic pressure by the Accident Offices' Association (formed in 1906) secured the passing of the Fatal Accidents (Damage) Act of 1908, by which damages had to be paid *in full* irrespective of any insurance money.

[2] For people not exposed to any special occupational risks annual premiums were £1 for £1,000 death benefit; and £3. 10s. for the same death benefit plus £5 per week during total disablement and up to £10 for medical treatment. The medical benefit was soon dropped when it was found that doctors and patients abused it.

included £100 for the loss of an eye or a limb, £50 for a hand, £25 for one or more fingers, etc. In 1880 the Lancashire & Yorkshire introduced a bonus (10 per cent) to total abstainers—an example soon followed by others.

Personal accident insurance largely grew up in the 1850s; in the 1860s only eight (most negligible) companies were formed; and in the 1870s eleven, somewhat more substantial, offices came into existence. But the really dramatic period of growth in general accident business came in the last twenty years of the century. Between 1881 and 1897 some 100 new accident insurance companies were formed—and a further 125 were registered between 1897 and 1910. Total accident premiums which were a mere £520,354 in 1884 rose to £1,753,657 in 1895 and £5,180,942 in 1905.[1] However, the main cause of this development had hardly anything to do with personal accident insurance as it had been known before 1880. Rather, it was primarily concerned with the abrupt rise of employers' liability (workmen's compensation) insurance.

This form of insurance was unique in that the risks involved were almost entirely created by statute: the Employers' Liability Act of 1880, and the two Workmen's Compensation Acts of 1897 and 1906. Basically, such insurance was designed to indemnify employers against claims by their employees alleging injury as a result of negligence. Before 1880 this whole area was regulated by the common law, as modified by court decision and by such statutes as the Fatal Accidents Act (Lord Campbell's Act) of 1846, which gave the right of action against the negligent person to specified relations of a deceased victim of an accident. (Until 1846 the common law held that the right of action died with the injured person.) In reality, however, the common law afforded very little protection indeed to an injured workman, since it also embodied doctrines such as that of common employment (by which it was held that a workman could not sue his employer for injuries sustained as a result of the action of his fellow workmen) and of *volenti non fit injuria* (which held that an employee willingly and contractually assumes the normal risks incidental to his employment). Against this background, the disabilities of workmen with respect to their legal position became more and more painfully apparent. And in 1880 the more severe of these were removed by the Employers' Liability Act—which made the employer liable for injuries caused by the negligence of his servants, and placed manual workers (other than those who had entered into a contract of service) in the position of ordinary members of the public in so far as concerned the right to sue employers.

[1] Calculated from *Post Magazine Almanacks*.

Even before this Act came into force, but in anticipation of it, a new and pioneer office was floated: the Employers' Liability Assurance Corporation. This office secured over £30,000 premiums in its first nine months of operation. The Employers' Liability was undoubtedly the most successful office in the field: by 1889 its total premiums, for all types of accident insurance (no separate data for liability insurance are available), reached some £254,000. Its only effective competitor in the general accident business was the older Railway Passengers—which was empowered to undertake employers' liability insurance in 1881, and whose total premiums were £243,000 by 1891. Apart from these two, however, the field was relatively undeveloped. In 1895, for example, when total accident premiums were some £1,750,000, four companies (Employers' Liability, Railway Passengers, Ocean Accident and London Guarantee) accounted for about half of the national business. None of the older fire or life offices did a significant amount of accident insurance—that was not to happen until the early twentieth century.

The 1880 Act proved to be deficient in practice—both because negligence was difficult to prove and because a subsequent court decision made it legal for an employee to contract away his rights to sue his employer for negligence. (In 1893 it was estimated that, in spite of a vast amount of litigation, annual damages secured through the courts were less than £8,000.) As a result, in 1897, the Conservative Government passed the Workmen's Compensation Act. Admittedly, the Act only applied to specified occupations of a hazardous nature (e.g. railways, mines, quarries, factories, engineering work, buildings over 30 feet high). But in principle and practice it was a fundamental departure. Not only did it prevent contracting-out but it enacted the entirely new principle that compensation should be paid to an injured worker for all accidents, whether or not caused by the negligence of his employer or fellow workers, unless the accident was caused, in Joseph Chamberlain's words 'by his own gross and wilful default'. Asquith, in opposition, emphasized the significant factor from the viewpoint of social development: 'What is the principle upon which the Bill rests? It is that it is to the interest of the community, as a matter of public policy, that the workman who sustains an injury in the course of his employment should, as far as money can do it, have the right to be indemnified. It is a new right you are creating for the workman, and a new obligation you are imposing on the employer.'[1]

From the viewpoint of the development of insurance, however, the passing of the 1897 Act marked a decisive step towards the establishment

[1] Quoted in Raynes, *British Insurance*, p. 294.

of a mature employers' liability branch—even though its immediate result was an uprush of competition and instability. The Act came into force on 1 July 1898 and well before then various accident companies had formed a 'Committee of Representative Offices' to draw up a tariff. But as *The Economist* subsequently pointed out, no sooner did the Act come into force 'than the tariff had to go by the board'. As new companies were hastily floated, as some fire and life offices rushed in, and as powerful accident companies like the Ocean Accident & Guarantee Corporation, the General Accident and the Scottish Employers', refused to have anything to do with the tariff, rates were cut all round in what the Royal Exchange Accident Manager later referred to as 'a reckless scramble for business'. Some of the more venerable accident offices (e.g. the Railway Passengers, and the Employers' Liability) refused to participate at such rates—although this course was a difficult one according to *The Economist*, since companies 'are pressed on all hands by agents and others to compete'.[1]

In spite of this atmosphere of instability, accident (i.e. liability) business expanded rapidly. Between 1895 and 1905, for example, total accident premiums trebled. In this development the specialists continued to lead the field: of total premiums of £5,180,942 in 1905, the Ocean Accident accounted for over £1 million, the Employers' Liability for £342,000 and the Railway Passengers for £308,000.[2] After the 1897 Act, however, older companies could no longer ignore the field of liability insurance, and even though most of them waited a few years before beginning accident underwriting, a handful began accident business on a small scale at the end of the nineteenth century. Among these was the Royal Exchange Assurance. As fire and life offices found it necessary to enter the accident business to extend—and sometimes merely to preserve —their existing premium income, so they illustrated a new trend in the insurance industry. Ten years later the trend proved a dominating one. As early as 1903 the REA found that its annual accident premiums had shot up to £112,876 (from £24,000 in 1900)—of which virtually all was for employers' liability policies—even though, as the Actuary put it in 1904, the Corporation 'steadily held aloof' from the tactics by which 'many highly responsible companies have shown themselves determined to secure the business at any price, in order to build up what they believe will ultimately prove a very profitable connection'.

[1] *The Economist*, LX, 331–2 (1 March 1902).

[2] *Post Magazine Almanack* (1900). Competition did, however, eat into profit margins. The Ocean Accident for example, had a favourable underwriting balance of £203,834 on premiums of £717,924 in 1898; but this had fallen to a loss of £8,122 on premiums of £1,090,502 in 1901 (*The Economist*, LX, 331–2 [1 March 1902]).

The next phase in the development of accident, and particularly employers' liability, business came in 1906 and 1907, and the years immediately afterwards. In 1906 a new Workmen's Compensation Act extended (as from July 1907) the provisions of the 1897 Act to virtually all occupations and workers and to specified industrial diseases as well as injuries. The only important exceptions were persons employed on non-manual labour earning more than £250 annually. Most critically for some offices, the terms of the Act now became applicable to domestic servants. The result was predictable: on the one hand, a redoubled influx of new and old-established offices into the business and an intensification of the business of existing accident departments;[1] on the other hand, a closer-than-ever link between employers' liability and fire insurance. For the markets for both, whether industrial or commercial establishments or middle- and upper-class homes, were now co-extensive—a point quickly appreciated by both policyholders and agents.[2] 'Connections' in each sphere could best be protected by undertaking business in both. And while this (together with the vicissitudes of the accident business alone) meant that accident companies increasingly invaded the field of fire insurance, it also marked the decisive entry into the accident field of some substantial offices which had hitherto held aloof.

The effect of the Act was noticeable immediately: in 1907 (i.e. including only six months' operation of the Act), while the net accident premiums of five large specialist accident companies were just over £4 million, those of eleven predominantly fire and life offices, mostly new to the business, exceeded £1 million—demonstrating 'the great possibilities of this form of insurance'.[3] In the first full year of operation, 1908, total national premium income from employers' liability insurance was £2,602,260—which, however, was slightly exceeded by claims (63·4 per cent), commission (13·7 per cent) and expenses (23·3 per cent).[4]

As we shall see, the growth of accident insurance in the first decade of this century led not merely to a rivalry between accident and fire offices but to a series of amalgamations which fundamentally altered the structure

[1] See below, pp. 296–9.

[2] As an indication of the new potential market for employers' liability insurance, in 1901 there were some 2,350,000 men and women employed in 'domestic offices and personal services' —some 15 per cent of the total labour force.

[3] *The Economist*, LXVI, 1037 (16 May 1908). Of the composite companies, the most important accident department was that of the London & Lancashire (£432,766 premiums—including, however, a very substantial income from the recently acquired Law Accident); next came the REA (£164,753).

[4] *PM*, LXXI, 28 (9 July 1910), 561.

of the whole industry.[1] As a consequence it came to be dominated by large-scale composite offices, combining fire, life and accident departments, and embracing in the last of these personal accident, plate glass, burglary and fidelity guarantee as well as employers' liability insurance. This position had been reached by a long route which was in many ways characteristic of much insurance history. The original needs and opportunities of new fields for insurance were first recognized by new offices, which were quick to take advantage of novel situations. These firms—the Railway Passengers, Accidental Death, Employers' Liability, for example—grew very rapidly and built up a formidable agency connection and a powerful body of skill and knowledge. Older offices were relatively cautious—in part with good reason in light of the variations of the market's profitability and the vicissitudes of premium rates. In the last resort, however, the really decisive expansion of accident business as a whole depended on the growth of composite offices—that is, on the economies and interlocking connections which only a single organization, a single network of agents, and an over-lapping set of markets, could bring to fire and accident, and to some extent life, insurance. And, given the continued pre-eminence of fire insurance, that expansion had to wait for a more flexible attitude towards accident business by existing fire offices. Some, like the REA, made a large commit-ment to the new field when workmen's compensation insurance was opened by the legislative advance of 1897–8. This trend became dominant with the passing of the 1906 Workmen's Compensation Act, when the vast extension of the market pulled accident and fire companies together. In particular, the logic of the situation demanded that large, existing fire offices expand their interests by amalgamation and absorption with specialist firms, which already had the agencies and the skills which they needed in abundance. Thus, broadly speaking, when the pioneers had demonstrated the potentiality of the new field, they were absorbed by their more cautious but more wealthy elders; and, it is fair to add, received a generous return for their efforts.[2]

The evolutionary pattern just described was dramatically exemplified in the case of personal accident and employers' liability insurance. Some-what later, it was also illustrated in that child of the modern age, motor vehicle insurance. As with employers' liability, motor business was made possible only by developments outside the insurance field. In the fertile and lively atmosphere of late nineteenth-century insurance, however, any

[1] Below, pp. 296–9.
[2] For example, in 1910 the Ocean Accident and Guarantee shareholders received twelve times the value of paid-up capital from the Commercial Union: £7 in cash and £5 in redeemable debenture stock for each £1 share (Liveing, *A Century of Insurance*, p. 82).

change in social habits was bound to stimulate business experiment. When, in the 1880s and 1890s, 'safety' bicycling developed from a sport to a craze, attempts (this time unsuccessful) were made to provide specialized policies—e.g. by the short-lived Cyclists' Accident Assurance Corporation (1883). In the case of motor vehicles, however, the technical innovation was both more hazardous and more obviously destined for very widespread use. Consequently, the appropriate insurance cover began to be developed more or less at the same time as the risk appeared.

This happened in the late 1890s. In October 1895 a Horseless Carriage Exhibition was held at Tunbridge Wells; and before the end of the year two voluntary associations (the Motor Car Club and the Self-Propelled Traffic Association) had begun to press for a reform of the Locomotives Act of 1865, as amended 1878, which had imposed discouragingly slow speed limits and the need for one man to walk ahead of a locomotive or car.[1] These restrictions were removed by the Locomotives on Highways Act of 1896. (The speed limit was to be 14 m.p.h., but under powers granted to the Local Government Board this was reduced to 12 m.p.h.) And, in celebration, the first run between London and Brighton was arranged for 14 November.

The implications of all this for the insurance industry were quickly appreciated. Thus the Scottish Employers' Liability & Accident Company offered insurance cover for the day of the Brighton trial at £5 per cent on the car and £1 per cent on passengers, as well as on an annual basis; and even before the emancipation run steps had been taken to form the short-lived National Cycle & Motor Car Insurance Company—which earned £4,000 premiums in its first twelve months, before succumbing to mismanagement and excessive claims. But the first regular motor insurance of a modern type was undertaken by the Law Accident Insurance Society, soon after the 1896 Act. And, after a period of rapid development, the Law Accident issued a so-called 'blanket' policy, which was a precise forerunner of the modern comprehensive policy, covering in the words of Frederick Thoresby, its inventor, 'all insurable risks arising in this connection'.[2] Thoresby was, in fact, that rare creature in insurance history—an identifiable innovator with respect to a far-reaching aspect of

---

[1] The requirement that he carry a red flag (imposed by the 1865 Act) was dispensed with by the 1878 Amending Act. His function was to warn people and to assist in case horses were frightened.

[2] Thoresby was born in 1870 and had previously worked for the Scottish Employers' Liability, the Rock Life Office, and the Ocean Accident. His policy covered personal accident for the owner and driver; accidental damage to the car through collision with any object; fire, explosion or self-ignition; third-party indemnity; loss by burglary, larceny or theft.

insurance practice. And he is particularly significant in the history of motor insurance, and indirectly of the REA, in that in 1903, after some years of devising attractive schemes for the Law Accident, he struck out on his own to form the Car & General Insurance Corporation Ltd, which was the first specialized motor insurance company,[1] and which in 1917 was to be amalgamated (although it did not lose its separate identity) with the Royal Exchange Assurance.

In its first years of existence the Car & General epitomized and in a sense dominated the early history of motor insurance. After the extension of the speed limit to 20 m.p.h. in 1903, the potential market expanded enormously: between 1904 and 1914 the number of private cars in Britain rose from about 8,500 to 132,000—and the number of all motor vehicles from just under 18,000 to 275,000.[2] Here was certainly a new situation. And the Car & General, under the vigorous and expert leadership of Frederick Thoresby, took full advantage of it. Its net premiums, of which two-thirds were for motor insurance, bounded from £17,886 in 1904 to £345,684 in 1914, while by 1912 it had opened thirty-three British branch offices (the company was very reluctant to undertake overseas business) and appointed 15,000 agents. To the public at large the Car & General were 'the capital pioneers of motor-car insurance'.[3] To George Bernard Shaw it was a vital necessity of modern life. As he wrote to Mrs Patrick Campbell in 1913: 'Something really important. Attend . . . Stella: is that car insured? If not, insure it *instantly*. Send up at once to the Car & General Insurance Corporation, 1 Albemarle Street, Piccadilly, and say you want "cover" at once. It will be anything up to £18 or so for a whole year.'[4]

[1] In fact, the Car & General did sickness, accident, plate glass, employers' liability, fire and burglary insurance in its first years. But it was best known as a motor company—and in 1910 about two-thirds of its premium income came from motor business.

[2]
Motor vehicles in use in Great Britain

	Cars	Hackneys	Goods	Total	Motor cycles, etc.
1904	8,465	5,345	4,000	17,810	—
1914	132,015	51,167	82,000	265,182	123,678
1916	141,621	51,293	82,100	275,014	152,960

(Source: The Society of Motor Manufacturers and Traders, Ltd.)

[3] Typescript of prospectus of Armstrong-Whitworth scheme to include insurance by the Car & General in the price of its cars, 1910 (REA Archives.)

[4] Shaw went on: 'What is urgent—what you must have above all is insurance against "third party claims". If you get killed you are dead. If the car is smashed, *it* is dead. But if it runs into a motor bus or a beanfeast, everybody in it can take action against you, and even keep on taking actions against you until the end of their lives every time they have a fresh nervous symptom, and get enormous damages. You may have to support them and their children for ever. And you will have to buy a new bus for the company. Your salary will be attached; you will be reduced to beg on the streets. This always happens in the first 5 minutes with an uninsured car. And you must insure your driver. Otherwise he will sprain his thumb or knock out his eye,

The early success of the Car & General was obviously due to various factors and it is not easy to identify all of them so many years after the event. Thoresby himself, writing almost fifty years later, attributed it to extraordinary caution, simplicity of procedures and policies, and the meticulous technical expertise of 'a staff of full-time salaried fully-trained engineers'.[1] In addition, however, as we know from evidence at the time, the Car & General was characterized by a systematic and very detailed form of statistical control which must have rationalized the problems of management to a very rare degree. Thus, in 1910, when negotiating with Armstrong-Whitworth for a contract to insure all their new cars as sold to customers, Thoresby took some pains to reassure the motor manufacturers of his office's financial stability:

Ever since the Corporation's inception I have never hesitated to spend a considerable sum of money in maintaining an efficient Statistical Department, and which consists of ten officials, including an A.I.A. [Associate of the Institute of Actuaries] whose duties are to keep the results of every department of business and to make me monthly returns, so that even during the first years of the history of the Corporation I have never been working in the dark or trusting to luck, but have always known exactly how we stood at any moment, and I attribute our weathering some of the most difficult insurance conditions which have ever beset a company in its endeavour to establish itself, to the fact that I have been able to steer this Company through such conditions with absolute knowledge as to our strength and capacity, and at the same time I have been enabled, by such knowledge, to gradually and deliberately get rid of all top hamper.[2]

Finally, the Car & General was extremely careful not to underwrite foreign risks, not to tie its hands to contracts of longer duration than twelve months, not to accept reinsurance and treaty obligation, and to effect substantial reinsurance arrangements with others.

The fact that the Car & General's success in the competitive and unstable market for motor insurance which developed from about 1906 was founded on caution and painstaking effort does not mean that it was

---

and live on you for the rest of his life.' (Quoted, with kind permission of the Publishers, from *Bernard Shaw and Mrs. Patrick Campbell: Their Correspondence*, edited by Alan Dent [Victor Gollancz Ltd, 1952], pp. 132–3.)

[1] Quoted in Dinsdale, *Accident Insurance*, p. 205.

[2] REA Archives, folder on negotiations with Sir W. G. Armstrong and Whitworth Ltd. The simplicity which typified its internal arrangements also characterized its public accounts. On 25 January 1905, for example, in commenting on the Car & General's first annual report, the *Policy Holder* congratulated Thoresby: 'We are particularly pleased with the straightforward simplicity of the accounts. There is no mysterious subtlety in the arrangements of the figures— no jumbling of claims and commission, no conglomeration of reinsurance and claims, and, in fact, no effort at devious and obfuscating concealment.'

conservative or unenterprising. Its management was energetic in propounding new schemes. For example, virtually from the beginning it devised a 'motor factors' policy to meet the particular needs of motor traders.[1] And between 1904 and 1906 it was the official and exclusive insurance office for members of the Motor Union, a federation of motor clubs, which had over 7,000 members in 1905. However, this scheme ultimately broke down because of strong objections by leading Car & General agents, who saw no justification in giving preferential terms to motorists merely because they were members of the Motor Union. As a result, the voluntary association of motorists, then numbering 13,000, formed the Motor Union Insurance Company in 1906. When, in 1910, the Motor Union amalgamated with the Automobile Association, the joint body (known as the Automobile Association/Motor Union until 1923) established special relationships with the Motor Union Insurance Company.[2] The latter's premium rose from less than £50,000 in 1907 to £115,000 in 1911.

Of course, the Car & General was by no means alone either as a leading motor insurance office or as a pioneer—although Thoresby acknowledged that until early 1906 there was hardly any effective competition.[3] Older accident companies, like the General Accident and the Law Accident, continued to participate extensively; after 1906, when fire offices extended their underwriting into the general accident field, they also began to underwrite motor risks to a significant extent; and new offices were formed, including the Red Cross Insurance Company (1907), backed by Lloyd's underwriters, which was the brain child of another innovator in the field, W. C. Bersey, former engineer to the Law Accident.[4] As a result of all this, premium rates were severely depressed, with rate-cutting for both motor and workmen's compensation business in 1908; and in that year the Car & General declined more than three-quarters of the new business offered, because of inadequate rates, and passed its dividend (however, premium income shot up in 1909). Nor was the Car & General's welfare improved by the appearance in 1906 of a new office calling itself the Law Car & General Insurance Corporation, which set about 'writing for premiums' with a suicidal recklessness, attaining an income of £192,000 for 1908 and £344,000 in the first nine months of

[1] Dinsdale, *Accident Insurance*, p. 207.

[2] As Dinsdale emphasizes, motor clubs played a prominent part in the evolution of motor insurance as well as motoring. The most notable pioneers were the Self-Propelled Traffic Association and the Motor Car Club (1895–6), the Automobile Club of Great Britain (1897, became RAC in 1907), the Motor Union (1901) and the Automobile Association (1905).

[3] Andras, *The Insurance Guide and Hand Book*, II, 162.

[4] In 1912 the Red Cross company's name was changed to the 'White Cross' as a result of the Geneva Convention Act, 1911. See Dinsdale, *Accident Insurance*, p. 206.

1910 (with claims of £442,000 and expenses of £128,000). In the inevitable collapse, some of the disrepute naturally rubbed off on the Car & General because of the similarity in names—and could only be dispelled by an expensive advertising campaign and the dispatch of tens of thousands of postcards to policyholders and agents.

By the First World War, therefore, after less than twenty years of any sort of underwriting experience, and merely a decade of mature development, motor insurance had gone through stages which, in earlier periods of insurance history, had taken decades or even generations for other types of underwriting. Pioneer policies had given way to innovating and specialist companies; other offices had extended their underwriting into the new field when its extent and relationship with other sorts of accident insurance became obvious; mushroom companies had sprung up and collapsed; competition had ruthlessly cut premium rates. And on the very eve of the War the inevitable happened: the companies, through the Accident Offices' Association, adopted a private motor tariff in 1913–14— although the Car & General (while maintaining friendly relations) did not join, relying rather on its leading position and long experience in the field of motor insurance. There only wanted one more step to match the evolutionary trend of personal accident and employers' liability insurance —namely, that the independent pioneers should become associated or amalgamated with older and more extensive offices. As we shall see, this further step in the process of industrial maturity came during and after the First World War with such events as the acquisition of the Car & General and the Motor Union by the REA in 1917 and 1928 respectively, and of the White Cross by the Northern in 1925.

Unfortunately, data on UK motor premiums do not become available until 1931 (they were then £32,530,000 as against £22,750,000 for other accident and miscellaneous income). But, given the fact that in 1914 the Car & General's total premium income was £345,684 (implying a motor premium income of about £215,000) and the Motor Union's motor income was £113,182, it is most likely the national figures approximated to at least £1 million, and perhaps considerably more. By 1914, too, personal accident premiums were £2,087,003 and employers' liability premiums £3,793,643. Of course, even the total of these, together with the smaller amounts attributable to other branches of the accident business, fell short of the £29 million of fire insurance premiums of that year. Nevertheless, accident business had an important niche even in the prewar insurance industry. And its influences on competition and organization, as well as its potential for future growth, were formidable in the extreme.

11

The Development of the Royal Exchange Assurance
1870-1914

In the first decades of the nineteenth century the Royal Exchange Assurance, after an initial period of stagnation and even decline, successfully began the adaptation of its traditional business to the pressures of a new and competitive environment. Later on, however, while the industry as a whole continued to develop throughout the mid-Victorian era, the Corporation's various underwriting departments experienced a marked levelling-off in their activities. It was almost as if the effort of adaption before the 1850s had drained the Corporation of energy and even enthusiasm for any substantial development afterwards. By the 1880s the REA was remarkable, in the words of the *Post Magazine*, for 'its "rest and be thankful" policy in not seeking to extend its borders'. Fortunately, however, a generation later, its former 'retirement and unconcern' had given way to a more vigorous outlook.[1] By the 1890s fire and life underwriting income had begun an abrupt but sustained recovery and marine insurance was more active, if not more profitable. This revival, together with the dramatic growth of a new source of premiums in accident business, carried the Corporation into the twentieth century as one of the leading composite insurance offices.

The relative stagnation, followed by substantial growth, which characterized the Corporation's underwriting after the mid-century can be most simply, albeit somewhat crudely, represented by data on premium income, as in Table 11.1 and Figure 11.1. In the case of fire and life insurance, the trends, including the discontinuity around 1890, are quite clear. After 1850 annual fire premiums were reasonably steady at about £100,000 or slightly more until they grew to some £140,000 in the 1870s and 1880s. Within ten more years, however, they had increased almost threefold, and by 1910 had exceeded £800,000 (gross premiums were then over £1 million). Life income exemplified the same trend, hovering between £140,000 and £160,000 for most years between 1845 and 1890,

[1] *PM*, XLVI, 27 (4 July 1885); LXVI, 29 (22 July 1905), 561-2.

TABLE 11.1. *REA fire, life and marine premiums, 1866–1915*

(Annual averages, rounded to nearest £100)

| Period | Fire | | Life | Marine | |
	Gross	Net		Gross	Net[a]
	£	£	£	£	£
1866–70	116,300	n.a.	150,000	242,700	199,900
1871–5	142,100	138,200	141,100	186,500	145,200
1876–80	149,600	142,800	139,700	159,200	119,200
1881–5	145,300	137,200	132,700	212,400	170,800
1886–90	153,800	144,700	136,400	150,000	103,300
1891–5	274,500	241,200	160,300	217,700	101,600
1896–1900	465,300	389,800	225,400	226,700	116,800
1901–5	712,600	612,600	272,300	287,300	168,200
1906–10	894,600	750,600	319,600	421,400	199,300
1911–15	1,052,500	859,900	404,200	883,900	426,100

[a] Net of returns and discounts until 1891, and of returns, reinsurances and discounts from 1891.

before spurting to almost £250,000 in 1900 and £350,000 in 1910. Marine premiums behaved altogether more erratically, but even they suggest something like the same pattern. By the late 1850s, Henry Warre had raised annual net premiums to more than £500,000. They then fell to a low point of some £100,000 in 1879, rose and fell back in the 1880s, and then began a long, unsteady, upward trend, which by 1910 took them to the levels of fifty years before, and by 1914 attained £350,000 (gross premiums exceeded £800,000).

To contemporary observers, inside as well as outside the Corporation, this general pattern of long-run stability followed by sustained expansion was explicable largely in terms of management attitudes and business policies. Certainly, the late nineteenth-century environment, with its ramifying if novel opportunities and the growing market for insurance, was not hostile to expansion—as was shown by the development of the industry as a whole and the appearance of giant new offices. And the relative abruptness of the recovery in the 1890s was widely associated with new management blood and new business ambitions in the Corporation. The nature of this process and its causes can be documented for each of fire, life and marine insurance in turn, considering last of all the innovations which changed the character of the Corporation in the early twentieth century.

FIRE INSURANCE, 1870–1914

At the very turning-point of its modern history, in April 1890, when the retirement of O. E. Fooks left a vacancy in the Fire Managership, the *Post*

Magazine was able to epitomize the Royal Exchange Assurance as follows: 'Unconscious of its strength, or unambitious to exert it, caution and timidity have been the ruling principles of its action.' The caution seemed all the more surprising in view of the Corporation's resources and business prestige. And the tiny growth of fire income in the 1880s (a mere £1,000)

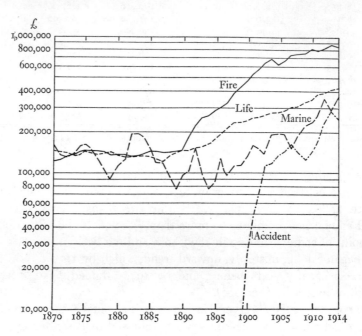

Fig. 11.1: REA net premium income, 1870–1914[1]

(Source: REA Archives.)

was said to be 'amazingly little for a giant who controls some of the most valuable connections and lines of business that any company can boast'. On the other hand, it was also possible (as the same journal had argued five years earlier) to see in the Corporation's 'valuable connection' the justification for, as well as an explanation of, its 'conservative management and disinclination to extend its business'. For the low losses, the good underwriting profits and the huge funds (over £4 million in 1882) of the Corporation deterred the management from attempting any marked expansion in fire income precisely because, as the *Post Magazine* argued

[1] The accounting year ended in April of the year indicated until 1890. Thenceforth it ended on 31 December.

in 1890, it would or might have entailed a concomitant relaxation of 'the conservative strictness which has always characterised the Corporation'.[1] Some years later readers of *The Citizen* were reminded that even in this unadventurous period the Royal Exchange was in one sense in an enviable position: 'Any insurance man who has a lengthened touch with the business will remember that their portfolio of risks were of a class which enabled the fire manager to sit serenely on an income of about one hundred thousand pounds and rule up his account with losses well set in the region of the thirty per cents.'[2]

If the general hallmark of the management outlook of the REA Fire Department before 1890 was its caution and avoidance of undue risk, the most important expressions of these attitudes lay in the careful central control of underwriting, the reluctance to establish home branches, and (perhaps most telling of all) the avoidance of any real commitment to overseas business. As the Corporation itself acknowledged in later years, although UK branches had been organized from 1886, 'they had not been worked with any energy, and the foreign business was left at the almost negligible quantity which characterized it'. Thus, until the late 1880s, while the Royal Exchange relied at home on a traditional agency network invigorated (or, perhaps, overlooked) by occasional visits from Head Office officials, abroad it neglected a market of vast potential: in the year ending 30 April 1885, out of total fire premiums of £143,600, foreign business accounted for a mere £3,000—at a time when the relatively young but enormously vigorous Commercial Union was earning almost £600,000 in foreign premiums, out of a total premium income of £867,600; and even the venerable Sun Fire Office enjoyed a foreign income of about £360,000.

All this was changed, and changed quite dramatically, after 1889, as is made clear by Table 11.2, which shows the structure as well as the progress of fire premiums. By 1900 premiums had more than trebled, and overseas premiums exceeded those earned at home. This drastic change in the performance of the Fire Department was associated quite explicitly with a change in personnel and also in outlook.

In April 1890, when the vacancy at the head of the Department was 'creating a good deal of excitement' in the insurance world,[3] the Directors of the Corporation confounded strong rumours that they had a marked

---

[1] *PM*, XLVI, 27 (4 July 1885); LI, 17 (26 April 1890); LI, 33 (16 August 1890).

[2] *The Citizen*, 11 July 1903 (quoted in the *REAM*, I, 3 [August 1903], 5). Loss ratios were, in fact, somewhat higher than 30 per cent. Nevertheless the average fire underwriting surplus, after deducting expenses as well as losses, in the 1870s and 1880s was just over 25 per cent compared with less than 10 per cent for the industry as a whole.

[3] *PM*, LI, 17 (26 April 1890).

TABLE 11.2. *REA fire insurance premiums (by geographical area), 1880–1914*

(Premiums: net of reinsurance and returns, rounded to nearest £100)

Year Ending	Total	UK	All Overseas	USA
	£	£	£	£
April 1880	137,800	133,600	4,200	nil
April 1890	147,600	145,200	2,400	nil
December 1891	187,700	163,200	24,500	16,900
December 1900	478,500	219,000	259,500	151,700
December 1910	809,400	290,000	519,400	295,200
December 1914	856,000	266,600	589,400	319,000

aversion to overseas expansion by filling it with a man whose experience and attitudes fitted him for precisely such a policy. John Heron Duncan had been with the London office of the Royal Insurance Company—the most formidable of the relatively young fire companies, and one with a very highly developed overseas connection.[1] (It was an interesting quirk of history that, while the Royal Exchange had provided the Manager, Percy M. Dove, who helped create the Royal, forty-five years later the Royal supplied the Manager who was to help transform the Corporation.) Duncan, who must himself have had an extensive knowledge of the overseas insurance market, also brought E. B. Hiles into the Fire Department, as the Corporation's first 'Foreign Clerk', with specific responsibility for overseas business. Even before the end of the year premium figures began to move sharply upwards as the new Manager moved into action, while the REA had already agreed to establish a joint agency with the Royal and the Norwich Union in San Francisco, and in America the insurance Press was anticipating a visit from Duncan, who was reputed to have 'a favourable impression of American business'.[2] In 1891 the Corporation began underwriting in the United States—earning premiums of almost £17,000 in the first year. As early as 1892 the *Post Magazine* was commenting on the 'infusion of new blood' which had brought 'a very large accession of vitality'; the increase in fire premiums, especially from overseas, marked 'a new era in the Company's history and a new departure in its policy'.[3]

Under Duncan's guidance the 1890s was a hectic decade of quite unprecedented expansion. In the United States agencies were opened first

[1] In 1891, for example, the Royal (established in 1845) was the largest British fire office, with premiums of £1,607,030 (*Insurance News*, 15 December 1902). As early as 1873–5 it earned an annual average of £372,579 in the United States (Walford, *Insurance Cyclopaedia*, III, 163).

[2] Quoted in *PM*, LI, 51 (20 December 1890).

[3] *PM*, LIII, 30 (23 July 1892).

in California (1891) and then, in rapid succession, in Massachusetts and New York (1891), Illinois and Philadelphia (1895), Michigan and Minnesota (1896), Kentucky and Louisiana (1897). In 1897 Robert Dickson, who had been the Corporation's first General Manager at San Francisco, was moved to a new office in New York for the control of the Corporation's fire business in the United States—a sub-office for the western States being opened in Chicago at the same time. Meanwhile, agencies were established throughout continental Europe, in the Middle and Far East, in Australia and South Africa, and in Central and South America.[1] Just before Duncan assumed office in 1890 fire premiums, in round figures, had been £157,000 gross (£148,000 net); when he retired in 1902 they had grown enormously to £670,000 (£579,000)—of which £352,000 (£323,000) were derived from overseas. In this last year the United States alone accounted for £198,000 —more than the *entire* fire income in 1890.

When Duncan retired in 1902, E. B. Hiles and E. H. Britton were appointed as joint Fire Managers. But the records make it reasonably clear that the former, with special responsibilities for and experience in foreign business, was the dominant partner. And in the event Hiles, 'an underwriter of wide experience and magnetic personality',[2] maintained much of the momentum of the 1890s up to the First World War. By 1909 northern Italy was said to be the only part of the Continent not served by a Royal Exchange agency; and in the next year the Corporation's interests in the New World were rounded out by the commencement of business in Canada, then undergoing sustained economic development, after an extensive trip by Hiles had produced a detailed and enthusiastic report. By 1913, compared with 1902, the Fire Department had almost doubled its overseas business. Net foreign premiums stood at £621,373 (out of a total of £883,989), and included over £300,000 from the United States, almost £100,000 from western Europe, and about £50,000 each from Canada and Russia. The Corporation had become a world-wide fire office. Barely 30 per cent of its premium income came from the United Kingdom—less, in fact, than was earned in the United States.[3]

The spectacular growth of non-British business should not be allowed completely to overshadow events at home. Admittedly, the Corporation keenly felt the impact of competition in the early years of this century:

---

[1] For example, *in 1890*: Egypt, Belgium and Denmark; *in 1891*: Holland, Germany, Ceylon, Turkey, South Africa, France, the Philippines, Trinidad and Burma; *in 1892*: Australia, Java, Peru, Jamaica, and Russia; *in 1895*: Japan, Argentina, Mexico; *in 1896*: Spain and Singapore.

[2] *Insurance Index*, XXIII, 2 (July 1908), 31. On Britton's retirement in 1905 Hiles remained sole Fire Manager until 1912, when he was joined by F. A. Daniell.

[3] For the Corporation's overseas business, see below, chapter 20.

in his address to the Branch Managers in 1911 the Governor regretted the lack of resilience in home fire premiums and affirmed that 'we must have the fire business promoted rather more strongly than it has been in the past. I wish all of you to feel that you must devote your time more to that business than you have done in the past.' Even so, however, compared with the stagnation of 1870–90, the doubling of home premium income between 1890 and 1910 had been a significant achievement. It was aided by the same sort of vigour and systematic attention to operations remote from Head Office as had helped develop foreign business. There was, in fact, a much more positive attitude towards branches and provincial business. By 1890 the two district offices of 1889 (Birmingham and Manchester) had become fully fledged branches, and been joined as such by Bristol (1887), Glasgow (1889), Leeds (1889), Liverpool (1887) and Newcastle (1888). Between then and 1914 other provincial branches were established at Brighton (1905), Dublin (where a modern branch replaced the original office in 1890), Dundee (1907), Edinburgh (1907), Hull (1908), Lincoln (1897), Nottingham (1906), Plymouth (1907), Sheffield (1908) and Southampton (1910). District offices were also established at Belfast (1895), Bedford (1913) and Tunbridge Wells (1912).

But the very considerable achievements of the period after 1890 had not been gained by new ambition and enterprise alone—although 'the determination of the Directors to take their place in the ranks of the pushing offices' had naturally been of vital importance. J. H. Duncan was also noted for his overhaul of the Corporation's statistical reporting, and throughout this period the Fire Department was acknowledged to have introduced new and much more systematic methods of organization and control. The office was 'modernised and brought into line with the most advanced working in the business'.[1] Instead of relying, as once it had done, 'upon its dignity and status for a moderate share of public favour', the REA had 'adopted the business methods of the day [and] its progress became swift and substantial'.[2]

In the context of its own history, therefore, the years 1890–1914 were critical and eventful ones for the REA Fire Department. Their keynote was modernization—of methods, of organization and of type of business. Within a decade a radical revision had transformed the Corporation from 'competitive smallness . . . to a position of considerable prominence',[3]

---

[1] Both quotations from *The Citizen*, 11 July 1903 (quoted in *REAM*, 1, 3 [August 1903], 4–7).
[2] *PM*, LXV, 32 (6 August 1904), 577.
[3] *PM*, LXIII, 30 (26 July 1902), 541.

and from a national to a world-wide business. But in the context of the industry as a whole these trends were little more than a somewhat belated making up of lost ground. For in terms of both size (the Corporation ranked twelfth among fire offices on the eve of the First World War) and the importance of foreign business, the way had earlier been shown by other, and relatively younger, offices, like the Royal, the Commercial Union, the Liverpool & London & Globe, and the North British & Mercantile. Admittedly, the REA had made its new mark from its own resources, whereas the others had accumulated much of their business by extensive amalgamations. Nevertheless, by comparison with other leading companies, its attainments could seem like a 'quiet prosperity'. It was this new prosperity, rather than any drama, which impressed outside observers. In the words of one journalist, 'there was sufficient of romance in the inception and youth of this now ancient establishment; and in its matured age it is preferable that the effect of exciting visitations should be neutralised by the making of money rather than of history'.[1]

For the Royal Exchange, as for other companies, however, the making of money was a somewhat more difficult exercise by the end of the nineteenth century—in spite of the remarkable growth in its business. Ironically, the most profitable decade of the century had been the 1870s—when, in fact, the Corporation was earning a reputation for excessive caution and even stagnation. In the 1870s the annual surplus exceeded £40,000, and amounted to some 29 per cent of net premiums. However, the 1870s were the last golden years of more or less 'easy' profits. In the 1880s the fire surplus dropped below £25,000 annually, and when, after 1890, the Corporation launched into very rapid growth it found that the growth of profits did not match the increase in premiums. By 1896–1900 the underwriting surplus (which averaged £36,953) was less than 10 per cent of net premiums.

In the long run, therefore, the Corporation, like other fire insurance companies, found that it had to work harder for proportionately (although not absolutely) less return. Intensified competition and the running costs of necessary extensions of business, meant that premium incomes grew faster than profits. If we compare the opening years of the nineteenth and twentieth centuries, and ignore the catastrophe of San Francisco in 1906, which cost the REA over £600,000, fire premiums had grown tenfold, but profits only fourfold.

On the other hand, however, it is one of the distinctive features of fire insurance that very substantial increases in turnover can be secured

1 *PM*, LXX, 23 (5 June 1909), 459.

without commensurate increases in actual investment—so that, while the profits might be declining as a proportion of income, they could be increasing as a proportion of capital investment, simply because the increased cost of doing a larger business is borne by income, not capital. There was, nevertheless, a possible disadvantage of rapid growth: if the pace at which the Corporation's business was extended exceeded its ability to control and select risks, then the chances of very large losses would be high.

FIRE INSURANCE AND CATASTROPHE: SAN FRANCISCO, 1906

The extent and pattern of the growth in the Corporation's business had almost inevitably given rise to new, and more spectacular, risks. Of course, the nineteenth-century history of fire insurance had always been punctuated by conflagrations so extensive as to swamp any normal effort to limit individual or geographical risks: apart from the Corporation's loss of £45,000 in the fire which destroyed the Royal Exchange in 1838, it paid £94,488 in claims following the great Hamburg fire of 1842, £29,748 for a Liverpool fire in the same year, and £80,000 after the Tooley Street fire of June 1861. By the first decade of the twentieth century, however, the fact that the Royal Exchange Assurance was undertaking a very extensive overseas business (in 1899 foreign fire premiums exceeded home premiums for the first time) significantly increased the risk of substantial loss—partly because of the spectacular nature of fires in the fast-growing towns, often containing many wooden buildings, of young countries; and partly because the pace of the Corporation's expansion overseas had in some areas outstripped its ability to control the types and location of risks accepted.

The dangers inherent in this situation were brought home in 1906, when, within a year of the replacement of an incompetent REA Manager in America, and before his successor could reduce the Corporation's commitments, San Francisco was largely destroyed by one of the most extensive, and certainly the most expensive, natural disasters of modern times.

The great San Francisco earthquake struck the city just before 5.15 a.m. on Wednesday, 18 April 1906.[1] The extremely violent shocks (the first one lasting fifty seconds) naturally caused very extensive damage.

---

[1] Contemporary accounts from the insurance viewpoint are to be found in: Robert Kirkwood Mackenzie, 'San Francisco: The Earthquake and Conflagaration of the 18th April 1906', *JFII*, x(1907),251–79; S. Albert Reed, *The San Francisco Conflagration of April 1906: Special Report to the National Board of Fire Underwriters' Committee of Twenty* (New York, May 1906).

In addition, however, the tremors had two further disastrous results—on the one hand, starting fires among the wrecked and damaged buildings, and on the other, crippling the city's main water supply to such an extent that the Fire Brigade, already handicapped by the death of the Chief Officer, could not effectively function. The resulting fire lasted three days and two nights. Together with the earthquake, it destroyed more than 25,000 buildings spread over four square miles of the city, including most of the business and much of the residential sections. Estimates of the cost varied. Actual real estate destroyed seems to have represented about 80 per cent of San Francisco's property values; while the more conservative estimates of total losses (i.e. including the contents of buildings) put them at about $350 million, or £70 million at the current rate of exchange.

Of the property destroyed, some £225 million was claimed on insurance policies issued by over 200 companies. And of this total British offices accounted for about $50 million (£10 million) after reinsurance.[1] To the European and American companies involved the San Francisco catastrophe obviously came as a very severe blow: wiping out in three days the entire underwriting profit on American fire business over the previous thirty-five years.[2] The blow must have seemed all the greater in that fire business in San Francisco had a very good reputation among British offices: many of them, including the REA, started their American business there; it was reputedly a very safe city: and it had been characterized by exceptionally low loss ratios (that of the REA for 1898–1905 was 21·6 per cent). But the disaster struck home with considerable force. The Royal Exchange alone lost £619,396, and there were four companies which lost more, out of the total claims of £10 million paid by British offices.[3] But the importance of San Francisco to the insurance business in general, and the REA in particular, was not confined to the unprecedented size of the losses involved. The settlement of the claims itself involved significant considerations.

The main point here involved the actual validity of insurance claims. For nearly every insurance company involved in the disaster could have denied liability for much of its loss: a few had issued policies with a specific 'Earthquake Clause' excluding liability for losses caused directly or indirectly by an earthquake; and most used the 'New York Standard' policy, which contained a 'Fall Clause' automatically terminating the insurance cover if a building or any large part of it collapsed, except as the

---

[1] Alfred M. Best Company, *Best's Special Report upon the San Francisco Losses and Settlements* (New York, 1907); *The Economist*, LXIV, 1342 (11 August 1906).

[2] Mackenzie, 'San Francisco', *JFII* (1907), 256.

[3] The London Assurance paid out over £900,000, as did the Royal. The Liverpool & London & Globe lost some £800,000, and the London & Lancashire £700,000.

result of a fire. Quite apart from the legal ambiguity of this clause in cases of partial damage, it was in practice of doubtful use to the companies. This was partly because of the problems of obtaining evidence that the damage had, indeed, preceded the fire, but mainly because of the hostile atmosphere which any such move soon aroused in the distraught population of San Francisco. W. N. Whymper, the Corporation's Secretary, who was sent to San Francisco from London immediately news of the disaster was received, summed up the situation in his Report. In the event of a lawsuit, he wrote,

Every man on the jury would be policyholders [*sic*]; the building in question is a heap of bricks which affords no evidence whether the earthquake had damaged it or not before it was burned; witnesses, if obtainable, would be those who at the time they were called on to give evidence of what they saw were in a state of panic and distress, not unnatural during such a time, and eye witnesses will certainly be scarce, since their evidence would be directed against their friends and neighbours.

In fact, there was extensive evidence that what Whymper euphemistically called 'local conditions' were a very effective obstacle to the insurance offices. In his report, the Corporation's American Manager, Uberto C. Crosby, claimed that about two weeks after the disaster property-owners and local officials and lawyers began to minimize the damage done by the earthquake and to refer pointedly to the 'Great San Francisco Conflagration'. 'In fact', he wrote, 'it was a rare incident later to find an individual who would admit that there had really been an earthquake in San Francisco.' The confusion and 'utter lack of co-operation' between all the companies involved (partly based on loss of records) also served to excite suspicions, and the local Press, said by Crosby to have been 'constant in their abuse' over four months, exacerbated them in passages like this: 'If in a mining camp a group of gamblers who had been busy raking in willing bets should suddenly go into solemn council to decide just what portion of their first loss they should not pay, a situation would be created which exactly parallels the insurance situation in San Francisco today.'

It was in this atmosphere, therefore, that the insurance companies had to respond to the largest total of claims ever made upon them. In the rare instances where earthquake destruction could be demonstrated, they managed to deny liability. In most cases, however, they worked for compromise settlements (only three offices paid 100 per cent value on the claims). In fact, compromise agreements had been recommended by the REA Secretary as 'the wisest course' after he had surveyed the situation in May. Some companies confined this to securing a discount of 1 to 5 per cent for immediate cash payments of claims, while others (including the Corporation), when the circumstances were doubtful, obtained compromises of 10 per cent and more discount from the face value of the policy. Considering that over $200 million were paid, as the Corporation's Manager put it, for a hazard 'not included in the rate and premium paid, not considered when fixing our liability, and not contemplated in our policy contracts', the insurance companies came out of the crisis reasonably well. 'The whole system of joint-stock fire insurance has been put to a searching test', wrote a contemporary, 'and it must be admitted to have justified itself.'[1]

On the other hand, not all the companies concerned passed the test equally well. For the very scale of the losses inevitably meant that some ran out of resources before they could meet their obligations. What is significant in this respect is that the British companies involved distinguished themselves in comparison with their competitors. All were able to pay their losses in a liberal spirit and from ample reserves—whereas, for example, more than half of the ninety American, and many of the Continental, companies defaulted. The words of the REA representative obviously applied to other British offices, too: 'We have made friends in San Francisco, and I am confident that it is generally admitted that our position has been honourable, and our settlements on a correct basis and fair to the assured.'

In the last resort, therefore, as *The Economist* argued, the San Francisco losses could be regarded 'as a splendid advertisement for the British fire offices', and likely to lead to increased business and profits in the United States.[2] In the case of the REA, that advertisement consisted in the relative case with which it was able to meet the enormous loss of £619,396. Yet, because of the policy with respect to reserves, the money had to come out of the Balance of Profit and Loss (rather than the relatively small Special Fire Reserves), which was thereby reduced from over £725,000 to little more than £150,000. Between May and November 1906 there were extensive sales of investments, and over £600,000 was remitted from England. Almost a year after the disaster Crosby reported that, with respect to the payment of losses, 'the Royal Exchange Assurance stands in the front rank; it has held to the high standard maintained for nearly two hundred years, and proved its ability to meet a great disaster ... I believe the American people understand this and will show their appreciation in the future.' In fact, within a month of the fire Crosby had indicated

1 Mackenzie 'San Francisco', *JFII* (1907), 273.
2 *The Economist*, LXV, 935 (1 June 1907).

a dramatic improvement in American business, with 'a general advance in rates' and 'a more frequent demand for policies in English companies'. And on the very aftermath of the disaster, writing from California, the REA Secretary informed the Governor that the enhanced reputation of British offices, together with the 'disappearance' (i.e. bankruptcy) of small, local companies, meant that 'an opportunity arises for securing the best class of business, such as residential property, situated outside the congested areas and more or less isolated'. The Governor, speaking at the Annual Court in June 1906, claimed that the prospects of American business had 'vastly improved'. And British companies did indeed prove very popular in the months which followed, diverting business from foreign companies not merely in the United States but on the Continent as well.

Nevertheless, when all was said and done, the San Francisco fire had dealt a very hard blow to the insurance industry, and its consequences, in terms of depleted reserves and new attitudes and procedures, were felt for many years afterwards. The REA, for example, intensified the care with which it used limits on sums insured in particular areas of large cities—fixing them with respect not only to city blocks but also to large districts. By 1907 the Fire and Life Committee had taken 'drastic measures . . . to lessen the possibility of another catastrophe in consequence of holding an undue amount of insurance in congested areas'. In general, American business was better spread, of a higher quality, and underwritten at higher premium rates and lower costs, than before April 1906. Even so, however, the Corporation exercised the utmost caution immediately after the fire—particularly in California. On the one hand, the expansion of general accident business in 1906–7 was restrained as a consequence of the fall in reserves;[1] on the other, it refused to write Californian business without an Earthquake Clause in the policies, and this led to its withdrawal from that State in 1908. In general, the Corporation obviously limited the growth of its American business. Dollar premiums which had exceeded $1·5 million in 1904 and were some $1·2 million in 1905, averaged just under $1·5 million in 1907–11 and just over that figure in 1911–14. Finally, as the Secretary, Whymper, pointed out in a talk given in 1907, San Francisco reminded the fire insurance companies of the need to keep a large part of their reserves in readily realizable investments. In the event, he pointed out, Stock Exchange fluctuations softened the blow; and it may be well to give him and Kipling the last word on the most eventful fire in the history of insurance:

[1] Below, p. 266.

9   San Francisco after the earthquake and fire, April 1906

It is but poor consolation to know that we are now buying back many of the securities sold to meet last year's disaster, at considerably lower prices than those at which they were sold—but it is an ill wind that blows no one any good, and for the moment it is perhaps well to be satisfied. We may, as regards San Francisco, quote Rudyard Kipling and say 'let us admit it fairly as a business people should, we have had no end of a lesson, it will do us no end of good.'

LIFE INSURANCE, 1860–1914

If the growth of its fire business was one of the most spectacular aspects of the pre-war history of the Royal Exchange Assurance, it is significant that in many ways the main trend was paralleled, at least in aggregate terms and in timing, by its life underwriting. As early as the 1870s the trade Press, commenting on the Life Department, wondered how long the shareholders would 'remain content to see opportunities wasted through lack of that commercial enterprise which each in his own business, in all probability, prides himself on showing', and damned with faint praise a small increase in premiums by referring to it as 'a satisfactory improvement, taking into account how slight are the efforts made by the executive to attract business'. By 1881 it was said that the Life Department 'seems to be in a state of equilibrium, easy to be disturbed in the direction of progress by a little enterprise and outlay, if thought desirable, which, apparently, it is not'.[1]

The statistical evidence for this situation is best provided by data on new life assurances, which stagnated well into the 1880s, before rising sharply in the 1890s (total premiums are given in Table 11.1). Indeed, the

TABLE 11.3. *REA new life insurance business, 1851–1915*

(Rounded to nearest £100) Quinquennium	Sums assured	Premiums	Quinquennium	Sums assured	Premiums
	£	£		£	£
1851–5	1,432,800	55,900	1881–5	1,059,000	35,600
1856–60	1,284,400	45,500	1886–90	1,280,400	55,600
1861–5	1,030,300	37,000	1891–5	2,075,500	82,200
1866–70	932,000	33,400	1896–1900	3,325,500	148,800
1871–5	1,011,700	n.a.	1901–5	3,066,900	117,500
1876–80	994,200	n.a.	1906–10	3,936,800	153,700
			1911–15	4,286,700	173,200

achievements of the early 1850s, when new premiums averaged over £11,000, were not to be exceeded for forty years. Meanwhile, there was little variation from the level of about £1 million new sums assured (£33,000 to £37,000 premiums) in each quinquennium between 1861 and 1885. The Life Department was particularly badly hit in Ireland, where

[1] *PM*, xxxv, 27 (4 July 1874), 265; xxxvi, 28 (10 July 1875), 264; 32 (6 August 1881).

new sums assured dwindled from some £82,000 annually in the early 1850s to a mere £21,000 in the early 1880s. In 1885 the British and Irish accounts were amalgamated, partly because of the 'comparatively small proportion' of the latter.

Thomas B. Winser was Actuary throughout this period (he held office between 1860 and 1888), and the tone of his Quinquennium Reports indicates that he was fully aware of the general nature of the problem, although for long at a loss for an adequate and specific remedy.[1] Indeed, his dilemma must have been painful to observe. On the one hand, the Corporation was suffering keenly from a rising tide of competition—often ruthless and hazardous in its techniques, always carried on by methods and with public gestures antipathetical to the Corporation's traditions.[2] On the other hand, given that the REA bonus to policyholders (two-thirds of profits) was comparatively small, to meet the competition in a 'respectable' way by increasing the bonus on a sound basis, would have entailed a reduction in the proprietors' share of life profits. The situation was cogently described in 1909, when a report on the life business emphasized that by the late 1880s 'the Life Department was on the down grade and a difficult problem presented itself. The premium income was growing smaller; the proprietors, taking a larger share of the surplus than was common, were in the habit of receiving £20,000 per annum as profit from the Department. It was clear that if a radical change were not made there would soon be no business and no profit.'

But Winser was at first obviously reluctant to press for any radical change. Instead, his early Reports constantly emphasized the pressure of 'unscrupulous' and 'reckless' competitors and the need to extend, exhort and support the Corporation's agency network. Admittedly, his analysis and prescription grew more complex and subtle after his first Report (1861). By the 1880s he was aware that the countering of competition involved adjustments in agents' commissions, the appointment of skilled life inspectors, the granting of procedural concessions to policyholders, the reduction of premium rates, and the pushing of endowment insurance. And in each of these respects he had positive recommendations to make. In 1886, presumably on his direct initiative, premium rates were revised and a new scale of commissions and allowances was adopted 'to infuse greater energy' into the agents. Nevertheless, even in 1886 it was clear that the Actuary was reluctant to be too extreme in experiment or too ruthless in the pursuit of business—not least, it would seem, because he was tem-

[1] Above, pp. 181–5.
[2] Below, pp. 274–5.

peramentally unhappy in the new setting: 'Offices who are determined to do a certain amount of business, regardless of the future, are constantly on the alert and ready to outbid others. Indeed there seems to be such a great want of *principle* shown by many concerns in the conduct of their business that I find myself at times utterly at a loss to discover how we ought to compete,—where to stand, and where to yield.'

Winser was unduly pessimistic, since the measures he recommended in 1886 were along the right lines. Nevertheless for the Actuary to express such gloomy sentiments was hardly calculated to produce either confidence among the Directors or vigorous action in the Life Department. In fact, the turning-point in the Corporation's life business came at the end of the 1880s; and, as happened with fire insurance, it was associated with a change in management. In 1888 Winser retired (he was 65), and was replaced not, as has happened with earlier Actuaries, by an existing member of the Corporation's Life Department, but by an 'outsider'—Gerald H. Ryan, aged 29, until then Actuary to the Marine & General Life Office. Ryan's influence was immediately felt, with a reduction of premiums 'in accordance with the most recent experience of assured lives (the Institute of Actuaries' Tables)' and the issue of a new and improved Prospectus: endowment policies were made eligible for bonus payments; the Corporation was to fall into line with the growing practice of declaring interim bonuses; residence limits were extended and 'whole-world policies' issued at no extra cost; lapsed policies could be revived; surrender values were guaranteed; and the payment of claims was to be expedited. In general, too, the Prospectus was said to be improved 'in its literary aspect', and it was warmly welcomed as 'a good first step towards a great development of the new business'.[1] In addition, Ryan's vigour was deployed in organization: in 1888 he secured the appointment of district inspectors for London ('which seems to claim first attention in any measures to be taken for increasing the business of the Corporation') and pushed ahead with the development of branches in the provinces. These new and improved practices, together with fresh confidence and vigour at the top, were immediately reflected in the life statistics. Thus, new sums assured in the year ending 30 April 1888 had been £173,332; but in the next year, Ryan's first as Actuary, they jumped to £303,558—at only a slight cost in terms of an increased expense ratio (from 12·35 per cent to 13·33 per cent).

---

[1] *PM*, XLIX, 37 (15 September 1888). It should, in fairness, be noted that Winser, in his last Report (in 1886) had advocated just such a systematic revision of the Prospectus—the only exceptions being that he did not mention interim bonuses and that he was still unduly cautious about with-profits endowment policies.

This, together with the fact that the Directors undertook the further in-novation of publishing the accounts, was warmly welcomed by the trade Press. By 1890 new business, which had averaged merely £212,000 in the early 1880s, stood at £417,806 and, symptomatically, the Directors changed the terminal date of the financial year from 30 April to 31 December, thus offering 'one more indication they have shown of late years of a determina-tion to bring the Corporation into line of action with other of the solid and . . . progressive life offices'.[1] In the five years 1891–5 new business averaged over £400,000 annually (compared with £256,000 in the previ-ous five years), and in the late 1890s grew to £665,000. By 1911–15 it was to exceed £850,000.

In the late 1880s, therefore, the REA came into line with many of the changes which were transforming the industry as a whole—particularly those involving more attractive commissions for agents and conditions for policyholders. These, associated with revised premiums and more modern valuation methods,[2] completely changed the competitive position of the Corporation by 1890, at the end of a decade which was a turning-point for the industry as a whole. As Ryan, the new Actuary and architect of the change, wrote in 1891:

The quinquennium just closed has been an important one in the history of the Corporation. It has been marked by the establishment of Branch Offices in several large commercial centres, by a complete revision of the terms and con-ditions of assurance and of the rates of premiums, and by an alteration in the methods and basis of valuation. These changes have enabled the Corporation to maintain its high position among the large and flourishing companies which are actively seeking the support of the insuring classes.

In fact, Ryan was with the Royal Exchange for only a relatively brief time: he resigned in 1893, going to the General Managership of the Brit-ish Empire Mutual and then the Pelican office (both associated with the Phoenix), before completing a most distinguished career as the first General Manager of the Phoenix (1908–20) and the Chairman of its Board (1920–31). But Ryan's successor, Harry E. Nightingale, who had been with the REA since starting work and was to remain as Actuary until 1922, obviously pursued the same policies and completed the transforma-

---

[1] *PM*, L, 28 (13 July 1889); LII, 42 (17 October 1891).

[2] As a result of Ryan's arguments, the Royal Exchange valuation for 1886–90 was based upon the Institute of Actuaries' Tables (H^m and H^{m5}) at 3 per cent, and only net premiums were brought into the account—the entire loading being left as a provision for future expenses and profits. This basis, the Actuary claimed, 'is the strongest in use among life assurance companies, except in the case of two Companies which employ a lower rate of interest'. Prior to this the REA had used an old-fashioned reinsurance method of valuation, clinging in the words of the *Post Magazine* (XLVII, 29 [17 July 1886]) 'to its old systems with staunch conservatism'.

tion of the Life Department. That transformation was in the last resort based on a realistic confrontation of the issues which had led to indecision in the period before the late 1880s. Modernization depended on a drive for new business which would have to be paid for. Ultimately, too, it could only be successful if the bonus were maintained at a reasonably competitive level. In 1901, therefore, bonus arrangements were altered to give policy-holders six-sevenths rather than two-thirds of profits. It was in this way hoped to increase business and, ultimately, aggregate profits. This doctrine was, of course, precisely the same lesson then being learned in manu-facturing and retailing: high volume and low margins might yield greater profits than a small business with high profit margins. It was, in essence, a doctrine based upon the economics of mass production.

If the extension of the Corporation's life business in the late nineteenth and early twentieth century was, therefore, rooted in a relatively new appreciation of the demands of modern insurance 'marketing', the frame-work for this was provided by a modernization of its distributive structure —by the extension of its branch organization and the appointment of life inspectors.[1] By 1906–10 branches and inspectors in London and the provinces accounted for over 70 per cent of all new sums assured (in the late 1870s they had procured barely 40 per cent). In addition, its policies were made more appealing (as we have seen with the new Prospectus of 1888) and it began to produce new sorts of policies with an eye to the selling power of novelties—as with a child endowment policy in 1891 and a marriage settlement endowment policy in 1893.[2]

When we turn to examine the general pattern of the Royal Exchange Assurance's growing life business after 1890, two features stand out—both of which characterized the development of the industry as a whole. They were: the rise to prominence of endowment assurances, and the extension of policyholding in terms of the types of social groups which insured with the Corporation.

We have already seen the extent to which endowment insurance became increasingly important on the national scene in this period.[3] At the Royal Exchange the same sort of trend was exemplified. Thus, whereas in 1890 there had been a mere 663 endowment, as against 5,356 whole-life, policies in force, by 1910 endowment assurances numbered 10,034, compared with 8,190 whole-life. Meanwhile, net sums assured under endowment policies had surged from less than 6 per cent to some 34·5 per cent of all the

---

1 Below, pp. 288–91.
2 *PM*, LII, 42 (17 October 1891); LIV, 49 (9 December 1893).
3 Above, pp. 221–2.

Corporation's assurances. The significance of this in terms of the business orientation of life offices is, in fact, somewhat masked by a concentration on sums assured, since endowment assurances were for smaller sums and at higher premium rates than whole-life policies. Thus in 1910, endowment assurances accounted for just over 50 per cent of all policies in force with British companies, compared with just under 37 per cent in 1900. These figures refer to policies in existence (i.e. including old policies). If we use the more sensitive measure of *new* business, it is significant that as early as 1900 more than half (54·3 per cent) of all newly issued policies were for endowment assurance. By 1905 they had reached 60 per cent.

In concentrating so heavily on endowment assurances, the Corporation's Life Department was, of course, going with the mainstream of insurance development. The savings motive had become almost as important as the precautionary motive in life insurance. As the Actuary pointed out in his Report on 1901–5, endowment assurances had an 'extraordinary popularity . . . Every year shows an increasing demand for this class of benefit.' But since the premium rate per cent was greater for endowment than whole-life assurances, and since individual policyholders were not able to pay higher premiums merely because they demanded different benefits, the result was a striking decrease in the average sum assured— from £765 in 1885 to £467 in 1910 and £444 in 1915.

On the other hand, this decline was not explained by the rise of endowment assurances alone. For, at the same time, there was a second important (although somewhat slower) change in the character of the Corporation's life business. It will be remembered that even in the 1840s and 1850s, when the Corporation's life business began its modern growth, there had been little change in what might be called its 'social appeal'. As far as can be gathered from indirect evidence, policyholders still tended to be drawn from reasonably wealthy landed, professional and commercial classes. The Corporation's social prestige continued to be reflected in that of its customers. But by the opening of this century it became clear that this situation could not be maintained at a time of rapid and sustained growth, if only because such growth critically depended on tapping new layers and sources of life insurance. 'In the process of expansion', wrote the Actuary in the 1905 Report, 'the Department has been forced by competition to extend its area of cultivation, and to include a somewhat lower social grade in the sphere of its operations.' Nightingale explained this at greater length in a special report on new business in 1908, when he indicated that intense competition together with the decisively better bonuses paid by rival offices made it very difficult 'to maintain the business derived from the better social classes who carefully study the merits of the various offices'. Steps were being taken to remedy this situation, but 'meanwhile the Actuary is organising for business among the lower middle classes and first-class artisans, for here competition has not yet rendered the position untenable'. The far-reaching economic and social changes on which the rise of the great industrial assurance offices was based was thus beginning to influence even an ancient Corporation like the REA. By the Report of 1910 the Actuary could claim that the special effort to push 'Thrift Assurances' in association with the waiving of the medical examination in select cases had been very successful. New premiums and sums assured, which had stood at £25,027 and £660,932 in 1908, had by 1910 jumped to £40,440 and £1,049,509.

It is obvious, therefore, that the Royal Exchange Life Department had compressed very important changes into the twenty or thirty years after the mid-1880s. Admittedly, as happened with the transformation of fire insurance in the same period, these changes were more impressive when compared with the Corporation's immediate past history than when compared with the growth of other leading insurance offices. On the other hand, however, set against the contemporary history of life insurance as a whole, the REA, always remembering its belated start, successfully held its own. This was true in terms of both the structure of its life business (i.e. the growing percentage of endowment assurances) and the overall rate of growth of policies and sums assured, which was comparable to national developments, even if it lagged behind some competitors. Between 1885 and 1910 the Corporation's life funds increased from £2,046,000 to £3,230,000 and its sums assured from £4,668,000 to £9,527,000.[1]

Closely associated with the life insurance operations of the Royal Exchange was, of course, its annuity business. As with life business, however, annuity dealings only rose to a position of any significance after 1890. Thus, whereas annuity purchase money averaged a mere £3,046 in the 1870s and £12,678 in the 1880s, by the 1890s it was £46,580. In these dealings the Corporation soon found itself in difficulties, however, owing to the 'exceptionally light mortality' among its annuitants—and as a result rates were increased at the beginning of the century 'in order to discourage the business', and somewhat later the Actuary tried to attract 'lives in poor health with the offer of special terms'. This was successful, within limits,

---

[1] During the same period the funds of all British life offices (doing ordinary business) rose from £142 million to £356 million and their sums assured rose from £427 million to £827 million. The North British & Mercantile, by contrast, which was already a large office in 1885, trebled its life business and funds in the same period.

but most annuity business continued to be of a very select character, involving annuitants with high expectations of life, so that the Corporation had to continue to exercise the utmost caution in the management of the account and the investment of its funds.

MARINE INSURANCE, 1870–1914

The third branch of the Royal Exchange's traditional underwriting was marine insurance. And, unfortunately, as has been pointed out before, the distinctive character of sea business and the individualistic nature of its organization mean that the details of its history are somewhat elusive. In spite of this, however, its main features in this period are reasonably clear.

Fluctuations in marine underwriting were much more marked than in either fire or life insurance. But the vicissitudes of marine insurance were also in some measure associated with changes of personnel at the top— although the market in general experienced nothing comparable to the development of overseas insurance in fire or the emergence of new patterns of policies in life underwriting, to impose a demand for sweeping management innovation. In the middle of the century, under the guidance of the Corporation's eminently successful Marine Underwriter, Henry Warre, net marine premiums increased from an annual average of about £100,000 in 1836–40 to £528,533 in 1856–60. However, they fell back to £268,713 in 1861–5 (Warre having retired in 1864), apparently as a result of the sharp increase in competition from newly established marine insurance companies. These had sprung up even before the American Civil War (the Ocean, for example, was established in 1859 and earned average premium income of £182,000 in its first three years) and during the War itself, and the associated transfer of more underwriting business to the English market led to an even greater, and more speculative, inrush of new companies. As early as June 1860 the REA General Court of Proprietors was warned by the Court of Directors that 'the numerous and powerful marine assurance offices which have been recently formed' would provoke 'a serious additional competition'—although the next year the Court's report to the Proprietors was confident that the connections formed by the Corporation would prove loyal albeit 'a large reduction in the rates of premium' had already been experienced. As we have seen, by the end of the 1860s the new companies were powerful enough to threaten the age-old dominance of Lloyd's.[1]

Warre had produced profits of well over £1 million in twenty-three years. And profits were well maintained under his immediate successor,

[1] Above, p. 205.

John Leatherdale (Underwriter 1864–75), although with both Leatherdale and Edward Gedge (Underwriter 1875–88) the trend of premiums was (with some short-term recoveries) firmly downward. Profits fell in the late 1870s, and by the early 1880s the Corporation was losing money on the marine account (£32,066 in 1882, for example). By 1886–90 average net premiums had fallen to £114,058, after an unsuccessful attempt in the early 1880s to increase profits by taking 'rougher business at comparatively high rates' had increased losses more than income. Competition, always fierce in marine underwriting, was particularly fierce in these years both from Lloyd's underwriters and other companies, both at home and abroad. During the late 1870s, when premiums and profits were decreasing, 'considerable feeling was . . . expressed by many of the Directors that endeavours should be made to increase the business and maintain the leading position of the Company'. As a result the Chief Sea Clerk, R. V. Pol, was sent to the Far East to see if the business captured by local mutual companies, and others, could be recovered. But his report was distinctly gloomy, arguing 'that the time had passed when any good could be done, owing to the ground being so fully occupied by mutual and other companies'. By December 1887 it was obvious that the Underwriter's policies were not going to succeed. As a result, Gedge resigned as from March 1888.

The new Underwriter was Francis Stockdale Toulmin, brought in from Lloyd's on generous terms: an annual salary of £3,000 and a 5 per cent share in net annual profits (rising to $7\frac{1}{2}$ per cent on profits in excess of £20,000). Toulmin, on his own appraisal, had enjoyed 'an uninterrupted success as an Underwriter for myself, and others at Lloyd's for over 20 years'. During his regime, from the late 1880s, gross premiums began to climb, although the fact that he also began to pay away a large part (about 50 per cent) in reinsurances, meant that net premiums actually fell slightly between the late 1880s and the early 1890s. However, between 1886–90 and 1901–5 annual net premiums rose from £103,271 (£149,951 gross) to £168,178 (£287,265 gross). On the other hand, the generalized programme of expansion in the 1890s included the acquisition of part or all of other and smaller companies—with whom much of this reinsurance was effected, thus indirectly retaining the Corporation's interest. This indirect extension of the Corporation's marine underwriting included two acquisitions in 1890: the Home & Colonial Marine Insurance Company (for £15,000 plus £5,000 compensation to its management) and just over half of the '1873' Insurance Company (*Versicherung Gesellschaft Von 1873*) of Hamburg—which cost the REA nothing beyond a commitment to take full control. Five years later the Corporation made two more moves in the marine field, purchasing another German company, the 'New Fifth' (*Neue Funfte*), and contributing £13,000 to the £25,000 needed to establish the Amsterdam & London Company jointly with local underwriting interests, in order to secure a larger foothold in the prosperous Dutch market. With the help of these companies, and a more active policy of reinsurance, Toulmin was able to take substantial lines—for example, accepting the whole business when any Directors or clients wished it. And he boasted of having effected the largest single policy ever issued in Hamburg: £400,000 on a man-of-war then being built. In addition, the Underwriter expanded the overseas marine agencies of the Corporation from the handful of 1887 to thirty-seven in 1900 (by 1899 they were producing net premiums of £29,313).[1]

In spite of the relative vigour of Toulmin's policy and the general growth of underwriting involved, the Marine Department ended the century without achieving the desired goal of secure and substantial profits. In fact, in June 1900, the Sea Committee, having studied the experience of the previous eleven years, recommended that the agreement with Toulmin should be terminated. Curiously enough, however, although this was accepted by the Court, in October both the Committee and the Court changed their minds in light of Toulmin's agreement to alter his underwriting methods by abandoning reinsurance ('except in the case of excessive risks') and by 'writing a larger account'. In spite of his reprieve, however, the anticipated expansion did not materialize—and therefore it comes as no surprise to learn that Toulmin finally retired late in 1903.

Toulmin's resignation was one more symptom of the continuing problems which had afflicted the management of the Sea Branch for at least thirty years. But problems of this sort cannot continue for a generation without having much wider consequences for the business as a whole. And when Toulmin left the REA the choice of an Underwriter and an underwriting policy produced a bitter and dangerous controversy in the Court itself. The precise basis of this disagreement was not made public— but it was sufficiently serious to range the Sea Committee, led by Sir Nevile Lubbock, against the Governor, Henry F. Tiarks, who had himself been Chairman of the Sea Committee in the 1890s. In fact, according to

---

[1] Between 1879 and 1890 marine agencies (in some cases one firm held the agency at more than one port) were established at Shanghai (1879); Yokohama (1880); Calcutta (1881); Amsterdam, Bordeaux and Smyrna (1887); Adelaide, Bremen, Glasgow, Melbourne, Paris, Sydney and Valparaiso (1888); Buenos Aires and Monte Video (1889); Auckland (N.Z.), Akyab, Antwerp, Bibas, Colombo, Chittagong, Madras, Moulmain, Rangoon, Rio de Janeiro and Zanzibar (1890).

10 16 April 1912

The Times (8 January 1904), it had been 'an open secret for some time past that Mr. Tiarks was strongly opposed to the policy of a section of the Board in regard to the Marine Department of the Company'. The immediate cause of the clash was the question of Toulmin's successor. So extreme was the division of opinion that there was a direct confrontation at the Court itself, with the Governor openly opposing the Sea Committee's recommendation that Augustus Dutton (an REA man who had been in the Sea Department since he first joined the Corporation in 1880) be appointed to the vacancy. But the Court, in spite of the Governor's objections, insisted on accepting the Sea Committee's Report in January 1904. And at this Mr Tiarks resigned—not merely because he had lost the necessary support of the Court but, in his own words, because 'I consider the appointment . . . so detrimental to the true interests of the Corporation that I am quite unable to associate myself with it'. The next week Sir Nevile Lubbock was appointed Governor in his place.

Whatever were the rights and wrongs of Dutton's appointment as Underwriter, his tenure of the office did not last long, presumably because it was not at all successful. In 1907, after a moderate rise in premiums and an even larger increase in losses, he retired at the early age of 45. He was replaced by Herbert T. Hines, who was formerly with the New Zealand Insurance Company. Hines, unlike Dutton, was an established Underwriter, and had to be given a contract with some security: he was appointed for five years at an annual salary of £2,500 (Dutton had been appointed at a salary of £1,500 'during the pleasure of the Court') and profit commission of 5 per cent, with an additional $2\frac{1}{2}$ per cent on profits in excess of £20,000.

Under Hines's regime (he remained Underwriter until 1928) something of a recovery set in. Thus, in the five years 1908–12 average gross premiums were £600,852 (£253,047 net) as against £287,265 (£168,178) in 1901–5— and the underwriting surplus jumped from £35,814 to £56,675 (profits, after deducting expenses, rose from £13,400 to £27,797).

The general trend of steady improvement was punctuated, of course, by short-term crises and exceptional losses. The most spectacular of these came in April 1912 when the White Star liner, the *Titanic*, reputedly the safest ship in the world, sank after hitting an iceberg on her maiden voyage to New York. Of the total loss of £1 million, the REA had retained £76,000—and in reporting on the loss, the Governor admitted that 'it is rather a large sum, but it was rather a large boat, and I think that everyone was led away by its size and by the idea that it was unsinkable. We know better now.'

In overall terms, however, and as far as can be judged from these statistics alone, Hines's management proved successful, and he seems to have brought stability and a moderate prosperity to a Sea Branch which had undergone long-continuing vicissitudes under a succession of other Underwriters. The extent to which Hines's abilities alone would have led to the further development of the Corporation's marine insurance was, however, never known. For his influence was soon submerged in the vast boom brought about by war-time conditions: in 1915 net premiums reached a new record of £854,124 (exceeding, for the first time, the £545,290 of 1814—the last year of the previous great War). By 1916–20 the average premium income was £1,281,597.

NEW DEPARTURES: ACCIDENT UNDERWRITING AND TRUSTEE BUSINESS

While the last decade of the nineteenth century was a major turning-point in the recent history of fire and life underwriting by the REA, it also culminated in an even more radical move towards a modern pattern of insurance. For it was then decided to undertake personal accident insurance (December 1898), employers' liability and fidelity guarantee (1899), and burglary insurance (1900). In fact, it was only apprehension about whether the Charter would allow it, backed by a strongly adverse opinion from legal counsel, which led the Corporation to abandon the idea (put forward by the Sea Committee) of undertaking at least burglary insurance as early as 1890. Had it done so it would have been the first substantial company to enter the field.[1] As it was, the development of a general accident business, and particularly employers' liability, in 1898–1900, was an important, enterprising and even innovating move for the Corporation. This was so not merely because it represented a departure from over 175 years of traditional underwriting but because very few other non-specialist offices had ventured into the accident field by 1899 or 1900. (One of the few to do so was the Guardian, which began employers' liability business in 1897, and the Atlas had undertaken a brief and unsuccessful experiment in the 1880s.) But in 1898 accident business was firmly in the hands of specialist offices like the Ocean, the Employers' Liability and the General Accident; and among other offices only the Sun Life (with premiums of £60,400) the Lancashire & Yorkshire (£46,000), the Lancashire Fire & Life

---

[1] Insurance against the theft of the contents of private houses began at Lloyd's about 1887; and the Mercantile Accident & Guarantee Insurance Company of Glasgow was apparently the first company to issue a burglary policy—in June 1889. See Dinsdale, *Accident Insurance*, pp. 262–6.

(£25,700), and the Rock Life (£10,200) did any substantial accident business. Its early start was to stand the REA in good stead. By 1907, for example, accident premiums amounted to £164,800 and among composite offices its accident business was only exceeded by the London & Lancashire and the Commercial Union—both of which (unlike the Royal Exchange) had grown by amalgamation with very large specialist accident offices.

The important departure point for the REA came with employers' liability insurance, for at the time this was overwhelmingly the most important branch of general accident business. In 1904, for example, it accounted for over £100,000 out of a total of some £117,000 premiums; and in 1907, for some £146,000 out of just under £165,000. The framework for innovation was, of course, provided by the Workman's Compensation Act of 1897, which had created an insurable risk by making employers liable to compensate their workmen for injuries sustained in specified employments. In this, as in other fields of accident business, the Actuary, H. E. Nightingale, appears to have played an initiating rôle within the Corporation. On the other hand, some of the most cogent points in favour of the REA commencing compensation insurance were made by Arthur Wilson Wamsley, then head of the Accident Department of the Credit Assurance and Guarantee Corporation, 'a young and comparatively unknown Company', which was nevertheless issuing policies for £250 per week. In March 1899 Wamsley argued that employers' liability, although new, was perfectly capable of being transacted 'on safe and scientific lines'; that it was a profitable business with good margins; that firms insuring with 'unsubstantial companies' would hasten to place business with 'older and more wealthy institutions' like the REA; and that, quite apart from the existing market, workmen's compensation business was 'certain to increase in importance when the inevitable inclusion of all trades takes place'. Wamsley's arguments proved persuasive. In April 1899 the Court confirmed the recommendation of the Fire and Life Committee that the Corporation transact employers' liability business and appoint Wamsley (then aged 30) as its Superintendent at an annual salary of £350 and 5 per cent commission on net profits. Wamsley—a manager of considerable initiative, force of personality and independence—thus began a long career (he retired in 1934) which was to transform the Corporation's underwriting and ultimately, by leading to the acquisition of two of the most important motor insurance offices, lay the foundation for the modern Royal Exchange Assurance Group.

Once the Corporation had decided to underwrite personal accident and employers' liability risks it was logical that its operations should be extended to embrace fidelity guarantee and burglary business. For one thing, they were attractively profitable; in the case of fidelity business, for example, a survey by the Actuary showed that four (out of the existing five) specialist companies had loss ratios varying between only 29 and 49 per cent over the previous ten years. In addition, however, rounding-out the accident business was the only way to maintain the efficacy of the agency network. As the Actuary argued in 1899, 'all accident companies are prepared to entertain [fidelity guarantee] contracts, and if the Corporation does not follow suit, their agents, who are at present working for employers' liability and personal accident business, will have to take their guarantee business elsewhere, and thus get into touch with other companies to the detriment of the business of the Corporation'. About the same time the REA also adopted pension and disablement insurance (October 1899) and insurance of stockbrokers against loss by inadvertent dealings in forged transfers of stocks and shares (March 1900).

Accommodation for the new Department was quickly found at the Royal Exchange itself, and in a very short time indeed accident business had developed into an important part of the REA organization and a fruitful source of premium income. Until 1904, following the break-up of the 1899 tariff, the Corporation wrote a non-tariff accident business—and did very well, even in the 'reckless scramble for business' which followed that break-up. By 1907 the Department employed thirty-five officials and clerks (and one typist)—compared with thirty in the Sea and twenty in the Life Departments. And in that year accident premiums, which had been a mere £24,124 in 1900, were £164,752. About 90 per cent of this total was accounted for by employers' liability insurance. By 1913, however, employers' liability accounted for merely 50 per cent of the £282,000 accident premium income—third party, including motor, having jumped to second place with just under one-third (£91,000). In 1907 about 10 per cent of accident business came through the foreign agencies which were established in India (1900), Denmark (1901), Belgium (1901), South Africa (1901), California (1902) and Holland (1904), and through the Corporation's one-fifth share in the London-based pool of companies which underwrote risks in the gold mines of Western Australia.

Although premium income kept growing until 1907, the culmination of this first innovating stage of accident business came in 1904. In February of that year the Actuary had reported with great satisfaction that after only four years, at a time when 'many highly responsible companies have shown themselves determined to secure the business at any price', the Corporation's accident business yielded £112,876, had grossed a 7 per cent profit on premiums, and had secured for the REA 'an immense number of new connections . . . leading to the introduction of a considerable amount of other classes of business'. In the same year, 1904, the innovation was institutionalized by giving accident insurance an acknowledged place in the Corporation's departmental and committee structure. First, the various aspects of accident underwriting were united in a new Department, of which Wamsley was appointed Manager, at a salary of £700. As the Treasury Committee pointed out in recommending the change, although the Actuary had devoted considerable effort to accident business, 'the divided responsibility now existing is by no means satisfactory. The Actuary is nominally responsible, but the actual working of the largest part of the business of the branch is in Mr Wamsley's hands, and the latter has no personal access to a Committee of Directors for guidance and advice.' Hence, the first and most important need was to recognize Wamsley's position as a Manager, and support his rôle by giving him an independent Department. The second step was based on the fact that the rapid growth of premiums raised many questions to which the Fire and Life Committee, which had retained general responsibility for accident business, 'can give no proper consideration for lack of time'. Consequently, committee control was transformed to the less senior, but also less busy, Committee of Accounts.

For some time after the middle of 1904 the REA made no attempt to increase the amount of its liability business—in part because of the uncertainty and increased risk provoked by legal decisions increasingly favourable to workmen's claims. Nevertheless in that year the Corporation had joined the Accident Offices' (i.e. the tariff) Association and the fact that rates rose each year between 1901 and 1905 meant that the actual premium *income* also grew, even though the actual risk apparently grew even more.[1] By the autumn and winter of 1906-7 two new and important elements had to be considered. On the one hand, as Wamsley had predicted seven years earlier, the coverage of workmen's compensation legislation was extended, by the Act of 1906 (which came into force in 1907), to embrace *all* trades and employments. As a result, an enormous new market for employers' liability insurance was opened up. The Corporation's Accounts Committee (as the sub-Committee of Court with direct

[1] Examples of workmen's compensation premium rates were:

	Collieries	Builders	Engineers	Textile trades	Wood-working
	s. d.	s. d.	s. d.	s. d.	s. d.
1901	16 9	8 0	6 9	1 9	6 6
1905	26 11	13 11	11 8	3 6	11 0

responsibility) and the Accident Department were naturally eager to take advantage of the situation and expand their operations. On the other hand, however, the Corporation had lost a great deal of money as a result of the San Francisco fire; and this depletion of its reserves, together with the legal uncertainty surrounding liability insurance, led some senior members of the Treasury Committee as well as W. N. Whymper, the Secretary, to propound a policy of extreme caution. In September 1906, for example, Whymper wrote a memorandum pointing out that over the last five years employers' liability premiums of some £435,000 had yielded only 3·6 per cent profit; that unexpired risks could not yet be accurately estimated; that the detailed work involved 'is enormous as compared with other branches of insurance'; and that, because of the appearance of 'a class of professional men whose chief occupation is the taking up of claims for the injured . . . the Corporation is dealing with an entirely different stamp of men to what it was accustomed to in the past and it appears that the business cannot be worked in any other ways'. His conclusion was inevitable: 'While very great credit is due to the Manager and the Department for working up a large business with a youthful and untrained staff, it would appear judicious to go slowly following the traditions of the Corporation, in transacting only the best class of business and remembering that premiums do not necessarily spell profits.'

It so happened that the questions involved were soon confused with fundamental problems of managerial structures and control, for in January 1907 the Governors and the Treasury Committee became so anxious about the policy then being pursued by the Accounts Committee that they asserted the implied responsibility of Treasury Committee to formulate and control 'the general policy of the Corporation'. This produced a new controversy about Committee responsibilities and authorities. The Court thereupon appointed a Special Committee for the Accident Business to meet with the Accounts Committee. The result was an agreement 'that it was not the time to unduly increase the liabilities of the Corporation', and that 'a policy of caution and discrimination should be pursued by eliminating as far as possible the more hazardous risks and by cultivating such classes as the insurance of domestic servants and clerks'.

The Workmen's Compensation Act of 1906 came into effect in the summer of 1907—and the result was an upsurge of proposals, particularly with respect to the newly created liability of employers for domestic servants. It was precisely this sort of business on which the REA had decided to concentrate, and as one element in its new approach the Fire Department issued a prospectus aimed at ordinary householders, inviting proposals to include, in a single policy, insurance against fire, burglary and legal liability to servants. It was a logical innovation in light of both the law and the scope and new aims of the Corporation. In fact, as a consequence of the 1906 Act, there was an 'immense inrush of business' at Head Office in May and June of 1907, temporary help had to be hired, clerks worked 'day and night', and the Court awarded the staff a bonus in recognition of their extra effort.

Admittedly, total liability premiums only increased from £124,000 to £146,000 between 1906 and 1907; but these aggregate figures mask the fact that there was a very large rise in new types of insurance, so that, in the words of the Accident Manager, the nature of risks insured 'has entirely changed and is mainly composed of business of a non-hazardous character'. As much as 40 per cent of the old type of risky business in industrial employments using mechanical power had been relinquished, and replaced by risks of 'a very light character'. In 1907 almost £14,000 premiums were derived from the insurance of domestic servants, £7,500 from that of shops and institutions, and £14,500 from that of warehouses and small trades not using machinery. By 1909 the Corporation had definitely abandoned what had apparently proved a moderately unprofitable 'experiment . . . in writing a considerable industrial business . . . the smaller business is now being written—the large industrial risks not being sought for, and there is a prospect of the Department making a profit'. Indeed, the level of employers' liability premiums of 1907 (£146,000) were not again exceeded before the First World War. (By that time the importance of the Accident Department was indicated by Wamsley's salary, which at £1,500 was the same as the Fire Manager's and only £500 less than the much older Whymper's.)

Contemporaneous with, as well as slightly preceding, the Royal Exchange's accession of relative caution in 1907, there had, in fact, been a great increase in the amount of accident underwriting by fire offices. But, at least in the medium run, the Royal Exchange's new attitude was justified, for in the words of *The Economist* in 1912, 'the companies which were started a few years ago were founded to write one of the most unprofitable forms of insurance ever invented for the sorrow of underwriters'. New (non-tariff) companies were particularly unprofitable; but three out of five leading conservative tariff offices (the London & Lancashire, Railway Passengers, Norwich Union, Sun and Phoenix) had claims and expenses amounting to over 100 per cent, and the other two exceeded 90 per cent.[1]

---

[1] *The Economist*, LXXIV, 403–4 (24 February 1912). The comparable figure for the REA was 91·7 per cent (compared with 92·9 per cent in 1907).

In fact, companies found that they needed to continue accident business for the sake of their connections rather than with any strong hope of good profits. This was certainly the case with the REA. And in 1911 the Governor told the Branch Managers that 'we do not like employers' liability business. We have to do it because we have a feeling that if we refuse customers their employers' liability business we might run the risk of their taking away their fire business to which we attach importance . . . if you take the accident business as a whole you will see that we do not make much out of it. We make perhaps £10,000 out of it.'

Thus, by this time, it was no longer relevant to consider either fire or accident insurance in isolation. In 1898–9 the REA had become the first truly composite insurance office; but by the end of the first decade of this century competitive pressures and amalgamation within the industry meant that virtually every important office was also a composite company. It was no longer a question of whether an office could afford to write accident business, but of whether it could afford *not* to. For policyholders had become accustomed to dealing with one agent and one office for their various insurance needs. And the pressures for diversification were carried and intensified by the rôle of agents, who insisted, for their own sakes, that they be given a full range of insurance to offer potential clients.

Considerations such as these meant that, no matter how sceptical some officials might be, an office like the Royal Exchange was bound to retain a large interest in accident business. More than this, and for the same reasons, it had to round out its offerings. This was illustrated in 1909, when the Corporation launched into another branch of the accident business by acquiring the National Provincial Plate Glass Insurance Company.[1] The National Provincial had been established in 1854—one of the pioneers of a branch of insurance which was then only about two years old (the last vestiges of the glass tax had been repealed in 1845 and of the window tax in 1851). It had been a considerable success, with premium income rising to £45,648 in 1895 and £51,023 in 1905. One of its strong features was that it carried out its own replacements in London and the immediate environs, thus keeping costs down and providing an effective guarantee of speedy service. By 1909 it had an office staff of twenty-eight officials and clerks, and a warehouse employing forty-one skilled hands, eight horses and seven vans.

Until about 1906 or 1907 there had been no real threat to the independence or profitability of the specialist firms in this particular corner of the

[1] Its name was changed to the National Provincial Plate Glass and General Insurance Company in 1912, and to the National Provincial Insurance Company in 1921.

insurance industry. Then, however, the general trend towards an ever more varied composite business brought the large fire and accident offices into the field. And, as they began to transact plate glass insurance the National Provincial realized that it would have to respond, by itself becoming a composite company—if only to hold its existing clients by offering a variety of insurances. In 1909, therefore, led by its enterprising Manager, Wilfred Gale, the company took steps to assume the necessary powers to increase its capital and to offer fire and accident insurance. It was at that point that the REA began seriously to consider acquiring the National Provincial, and with it one of the most vigorous and successful plate glass businesses in the country. By May 1909 the Corporation's Court had agreed to a negotiated price of £61. 2s. 3d. for its 4,105 shares. The purchase was completed in July.

To the REA the direct attractions of commencing plate glass business were undoubtedly considerable. The National Provincial's profits had averaged £13,000 for the previous thirty years, business was rising, and plate glass insurance in general, with a fairly stationary loss ratio of under 50 per cent, was distinctly less hazardous than fire or other branches of accident underwriting. In this context it was also logical that, having decided to launch out into a new area, the Corporation should have concluded that the most effective way to begin was to acquire a substantial, going concern—which had not merely an established agency network and connection, but also a ready-made fund of managerial expertise and an existing office organization. In this way it might avoid some of the problems encountered in the early years of employers' liability insurance when one of the main difficulties, according to the Accident Manager, had been 'the training of the staff, which, with few exceptions, has been entirely recruited from untrained and inexperienced juniors'.

But the direct profits of plate glass insurance were not the only attraction. Indeed, the price paid for the National Provincial shares was based upon the assumption that the existing dividends reflected a 4½ per cent return—not in itself a very munificent profit rate. What was equally, or even more important, was that the new departure enabled the REA to offer a more extensive line of insurance, thereby protecting its existing fire and accident connection from infiltration by the other large offices, then busy acquiring plate glass subsidiaries. In addition, and perhaps even more pertinent, the National Provincial, with over 200 representatives, brought with it an agency connection which could be turned to good account in more than one way. When the Fire Manager, E. B. Hiles, was asked for his opinion, he wrote (26 May 1909) that, reflecting the trend for modern insurance companies to transact all classes of business—fourteen leading fire offices were already underwriting plate glass risks—he strongly supported the proposed acquisition, since, on the one hand, the Corporation might already be losing fire and accident business by not having a complete line, and, on the other, the new agents and clients would provide manifold opportunities for the spread of fire business. In any case, he felt, the National Provincial's agents 'belong to a better class' than any new agents who might be acquired by inspectors in the ordinary course of business: 'The army of inspectors now working for all companies causes the field to be very closely gleaned, and I would value very highly the transfer of a corps of trained agents to this Office.' He concluded as follows: 'To sum up the matter, I consider that if we can acquire some thousands of new agents and their clients, and an old established plate glass business, likely to give profits to the extent required to recoup the Corporation for its outlay, we shall make a very good investment.'

In general, it seems as if the REA *did* make a good investment. Apart from the growth of National Provincial premiums (by 1913 they were about £55,000), the new connections brought in a very useful amount of fire and accident premiums: the National Provincial Head Office, for example, yielded over £2,000 in 1910, and £4,500 in 1913. Admittedly, profits fell in what the Court referred to as 'the unsettled state of the country' immediately before the First World War, when political and labour unrest meant that plate glass windows were not particularly good risks—and after a relatively poor experience in 1911 profits fell further in 1912 'consequent on the losses caused by the Suffragettes', although in 1913 the company had the satisfaction of recovering £1,253. 18s. 3d. from Mr Pethick Lawrence 'for damage done to windows by Suffragettes'. Nevertheless, over the longer run the Corporation had no cause to regret its diversification in the years immediately before the War.[1]

One other aspect of that diversification ought to be mentioned here: in November 1904 the REA became the first British insurance company successfully to offer its services as an executor or trustee.[2] To the *Insurance Observer* this was a 'bold departure': one more example of 'the enterprise displayed by the management of the Corporation . . . since the first attempt

---

[1] Just prior to the War the Corporation also began motor and related third-party insurance on a relatively small scale; in 1911 it undertook machinery insurance (boilers, engines and lifts), which yielded £2,817 premiums in 1913 and led to the employment of engineers for the regular inspections necessarily involved.

[2] The United States had a much longer history of corporate trusteeship. See Thomas F. Anderson (who was later to become Manager of the REA's Trustee and Executor Department), 'Insurance Companies as Executors and Trustees', *JFII*, XII (1909), 357–74.

was made to break away from old traditions and look about everywhere for business'. In fact, as early as 1901, when it had secured a new Act to define its powers and organization, the Corporation had assumed legal power to act as a trustee or executor. But, although it was discussed by the Treasury Committee in March, the suggestion was squashed by the Governor, Henry Tiarks, on the grounds that 'there was no money in it'. However, after Tiarks's resignation, the Committee returned to the subject in the spring of 1904—particularly in light of a Bill then being promoted to appoint a Public Trustee, and another to give trusteeship powers to the Liverpool & London & Globe. Clearly, service as executors and trustees fully conformed with the image of stability, longevity and trustworthiness which insurance companies had taken pains to develop throughout the nineteenth century. And, in this respect, it was entirely fitting that the REA, the epitome of tradition and solidity, should be the pioneer. The prognosis for the new line of business was good. As one (anonymous) eminent authority put it when asked for his advice, 'Success was assured to a strong company starting the business . . . He thought the proposal would be likely to appeal to the wealthy classes as well as to that large section of the respectable middle class known to have an inherent dislike to the legal profession.' Certainly, after a hesitant start, the move proved very popular: in spite of the establishment of the Public Trustees' Office in January 1908 (helped by advice and, ultimately, personnel from the REA) the income from fees rose from £884 in 1909 to £4,107 in 1914; and by the end of 1914 the Corporation managed £16,705,000 in trusts. Even so, no one could pretend that this sort of business was *directly* very profitable: there was a fair amount of work involved, in return for only a moderately small income. Instead, the attractions of the innovation (and the shrewdness of the move lay in foreseeing this) was in the interpenetration of trustee-executor and general insurance business: what the Treasury Committee called 'the successful cultivation of new connections'.

The point about trustee and executor business in this respect was not that it extended the range of services offered to potential and existing policyholders (although, of course, it did that to some extent). Rather, it extended the Corporation's connections by establishing contact with a large number of agents precisely because they were professional men who could be employed by trustees and executors, and who were also in a position to channel insurance business towards the Corporation. The matter was cogently analysed in a report of 1909:

All companies are anxious to (a) secure agents, and (b) tie business; but no one company can offer better advantages than another. A canvasser [i.e. inspector] in seeking an agent is seeking a favour. The agent is the patron. As executors the position is reversed. The company is the patron, and its patronage is towards those professional men who have the control of most fire business—house agents, valuers, solicitors, and land agents. It usually happens that such men are agents for several insurance companies, with no special leaning towards any particular one. The company which can give them business is the most likely to receive business in exchange; and by this means new connections are made and old ones strengthened. These statements are not founded on theory but on actual experience.

Statements such as these give an impression of easy and successful empiricism, and of a Corporation confident in the range of its business and the authority of its position. But it should not be forgotten that the tone was somewhat new at the REA. The innovations which so much extended the variety of business undertaken, like the new efforts which greatly developed the conventional forms of insurance, were a product of a few eventful years at the very end of the nineteenth, and in the opening years of the twentieth, century. The pressures and processes by which these changes had been brought about will be dealt with in the next chapter.

12

The Implications of
Industrial Growth:
competition, control and
amalgamation in insurance
1870-1914

In the relatively short space of the generation before the First World War the Royal Exchange Assurance had undergone radical changes in terms of both the scale and variety of its operations. In the 1880s the respect which its age and solidity attracted was not matched by any admiration for its enterprise or flexibility. But by 1914 it was an important example of the new breed of world-wide composite offices. As has been seen, this transformation had taken place in the context of an industry which was itself undergoing very far-reaching changes. So far we have principally considered the quantitative characteristics of this period of development. In this chapter we turn to its structural aspects: to the pressures and innovations, the changes in organization and control, which both facilitated and were made necessary by sustained growth. In these respects, the history of the Royal Exchange cannot be dissociated from that of other insurance companies. Hence, the following analyses of competitive pressures, of new systems of agency control, and of the problems of large-scale enterprise, will be concerned not only with the Corporation, but also with the insurance industry as a whole.

THE IMPACT OF COMPETITION

To those involved in their management, economic and social institutions rarely seem to stand still. Consequently, if we had to rely solely on contemporary commentators, almost every age would seem one of transition and flux, and each generation would be judged to have experienced a dizzy increase in the pace of its life compared with its more fortunate predecessors. So, in the relatively limited world of insurance in the late nineteenth and early twentieth centuries, men looked around them and asserted, with all the conviction at their command, that times had, indeed, changed; that, in the words of Samuel Pipkin, the General Manager of the Atlas, 'We must move; we must go with the times, we cannot even relatively stand still.' To Pipkin, and others like him, it seemed that 'the curse of the age is greed—the passion of humanity is for gold—the madness of life is in its rush and turmoil'. And the result was that 'each human mind is being sharpened to a hardness and a fineness that will enable it to cut, and cut deeply—even to killing—when it comes into contact with its opponent'.[1]

To some extent, this sort of complaint was becoming a fashion. Nevertheless, the widespread feeling that competition had rapidly and even dangerously intensified throughout the insurance industry—that a moral code of behaviour, as well as premium rates and established connections, were threatened, that attitudes and organization and policies all had to be overhauled in response to a new situation—was much more than an affectation. It was based upon hard and indisputable fact. And, within a traditional office like the REA, it was a feeling that persisted: from the Actuary's apprehension about 'the continued and ever increasing competition to which we are exposed' in 1881, to the view, in 1911, that as far as all types of insurance were concerned, 'the struggle for business is in no way lessened . . . although how it can become fiercer, without peril, it is difficult to say'. By 1910 the Corporation's Newcastle Manager nostalgically looked back on the 1880s as 'the golden days' when 'the "pushful" business-getter was not such an essential element . . . [and] it was more a question of having an efficient administration to deal with the business, which flowed in, than anything else'.

It was, indeed, the mass-marketing elements in the new situation which impressed contemporaries, and alarmed men like Winser, the Royal Exchange Actuary. For one thing, advertising was intensively and very widely used, although the REA Actuary looked upon this new trend with a certain amount of distaste in the early 1860s.[2] At about the same time the Atlas also rejected an intensive advertising programme (partly on the grounds that 'undue or indiscriminate solicitation' produced 'a very inferior kind' of insurance). But by the 1880s, under Pipkin's influence, it ordered a new showcard for display at 700 railway stations, especially 'in new and growing towns'. Meanwhile the Guardian, in order to extend its business, commissioned an 'artistic poster' for display at 2,000 railway stations for five years.[3]

---

[1] Samuel J. Pipkin, 'Some Present-Day Problems of Insurance Business', *PM*, LXVIII, 14 and 15 (6 and 13 April 1907), 261, 278.

[2] Above, pp. 182–3.

[3] Tarn and Byles, *Guardian Assurance*, p. 55.

Yet it was not merely advertising which marked the pushing offices of the new era: premium rates were cut; larger bonuses were promised, and often paid; high-pressure salesmen were employed and amply rewarded; the conditions attaching to life policies were made more liberal and the policies simplified;[1] and the market was saturated with an apparently endless supply of different 'fancy' life insurance schemes (as well as some fire insurance novelties such as guaranteed-value and consequential-loss policies) calculated to appeal to a great variety of disparate social and economic groups. 'We are *traders*,' said the President to the Institute of Actuaries in 1892.[2] In the quest for business growth, life offices greatly extended their fields of operations; and the doubling of insurance per head between 1870 and 1900 was therefore attributed not merely to 'education' and the desire for self-improvement, but also to the competitive eagerness of companies to bring to the attention 'of all classes of the community methods of life assurance adapted to meet every requirement'.[3]

It was significant that this new era of mass marketing coincided with the invasion of the British market by American life offices. For in the United States in the late nineteenth century native insurance companies waged a furious competitive war and perfected a host of high-pressure selling techniques. As a result, when they applied themselves to the British market, American companies acted like an 'electric shock . . . on a body of low vitality'.[4] Although the Equitable Life Assurance of the United States and the New York Life had entered England as early as 1869 and 1870, it was not until the 1880s that their impact (now augmented by another very large office, the Mutual Life of New York) began to be seriously felt. By 1886 the REA Actuary complained that in addition to certain ruthless British offices, 'we have now the American Companies making showy bids for business, but I am at a loss to know how their promises can be fulfilled'. As their influence became increasingly felt, however, the American offices were also admired for their major contribution: the popularizing of life insurance by a multitudinous appeal to different economic groups with a wide variety of policies—particularly those involving an investment element. They appealed 'to the more opulent and speculative classes who did not previously contemplate life assurance as a satisfactory investment, and perhaps by their active propaganda and more attractive forms of life

---

[1] Much of this development took place in the 1880s. It involved the extension of free limits, the payment of the sum assured in the case of suicides, the use of guaranteed surrender values, the expedition of payment on the proof of death, the granting of interim bonuses, etc.

[2] Quoted in *Finance Chronicle and Insurance Circular*, XXII, 435 (15 December 1892), 151.

[3] Morris Fox, 'Varieties of Life Insurance', *JFII*, VIII (1905), 87.

[4] Warner, 'Twenty Years' Changes in Life Assurance', *JFII* (1909), 80.

assurance have caused a greater demand and better appreciation of its advantages and wonderful adaptability to the needs of persons in various stations in life'.[1]

In one sense, when compared with the total amount of life business, the American offices and their new types of insurance policy were relatively insignificant. In the years immediately before the First World War, for example, they accounted for less than 2 per cent of all new sums insured, and for less than £1 million of the £31 million of annual premium income.[2] Admittedly, this was after a decade or so in which they reduced their overseas business (partly because of restrictions in some foreign countries and partly because of scandals in the United States which left them in bad odour). But even around 1900, at the peak of their British influence, the three American Companies could not, quantitatively speaking, have dominated the British market—even though the Mutual Life, the largest of the three, had a premium income of £567,000 (compared with the total British office premiums of almost £22 million).[3] Further, the various experimental policies associated with American thrustfulness were never statistically important: the overwhelming bulk of ordinary life business (some 95 per cent by 1910) continued to be done by conventional whole-life and endowment policies.

Nevertheless, the impact of three powerful and enterprising newcomers could be much more influential than their relative size indicated. In the event, the commercial consequences of American efforts were very considerable. As the REA Secretary put it in 1907 (in the course of a talk at Manchester), 'free trade' in insurance produced 'the greatest good of the greatest number', and 'it was . . . the stimulus of the foreign competitors which stirred our own companies into active life, to their own great benefit and to the advantage of the tens of thousands who have effected policies with the stable and sound companies'.

[1] H. W. Andras, 'Life Assurance Prospects at the opening of the Twentieth Century', *JFII*, IV (1901), 324–5. For a description of the different types of policy and premium-payment scheme, see Fox, 'Varieties of Life Insurance', *JFII* (1905). Fox (p. 88) also had this to say about the American offices: 'Their abnormal activity and ingenuity in furnishing new schemes, developing the investment element particularly so as to make it appeal to the speculative instinct, has had the effect of stimulating their slower moving British cousins in the same direction.'

[2] Andras, *Insurance Guide and Hand Book*, p. 77; Board of Trade Returns (1915). In 1914 the New York Life and the Equitable Life had sums insured in Britain of £5·25 million and £4·3 million respectively. To judge by its premium income (£412,000), the Mutual had just over £7 million of sums insured. Yet these figures are relatively small compared to total sums insured of almost £900 million. (I am most grateful to Mr V. deKanel of the New York Life Insurance Company and to Miss Dorothea L. Havighorst of the Equitable Life Assurance Society of the United States for information about their offices' sums insured.)

[3] *Manchester Guardian*, 1 June 1901. This was exceeded by only six British offices.

The intensification of competition for life business was bound to focus attention on bonus results, for in the last resort it was the financial benefits (whether real or sham) of life insurance which attracted the public—and, by the early years of this century, with-profits policies accounted for some 80 per cent of all sums insured by whole-life and endowment policies. The Royal Exchange Assurance felt this pressure towards larger bonuses particularly keenly, for its bonus distribution limited the policyholders' share of profits to two-thirds, yet by 1892, out of fifty-one proprietary offices, only four distributed such a low proportion, and seven years later there were twenty-four offices distributing 90 per cent. By 1896, even though two or three other offices also distributed only two-thirds of their surplus, special arrangements with regard to share-owning and expenses meant that the Royal Exchange was alone at the bottom of the league: as the Actuary ruefully reported, 'it treats its policyholders with less liberality than any other assurance company'. It was in the 1890s that the rising costs of expansion, the falling rate of interest and intensified competition exposed the weakness of the Corporation's low rate of distribution. As the Actuary pointed out, the character of modern life business made it almost impossible to increase the *margin* of profit, and the only way to increase aggregate profits was by a substantial extension of new business. But to do this the Corporation would have to increase the proportion of surplus distributed as bonus, in order to compete with mutual societies. In 1892 a trade journal had made the same point in cruder but no less effective terms: offices paying too low a bonus rate 'will probably find it imperative to afford more nutriment to the goose that lays the golden eggs!'.[1]

By the end of the 1890s the REA was was very badly placed with regard to bonus payments. In 1899 it became clear that profits were such that if the distribution were kept at two-thirds (at a time when the average proprietary office distributed about 87 per cent of surplus), the actual bonus would have to be reduced to 25s. per cent or even below. The Directors therefore took the unprecedented step of asking the Actuary to write to all branch managers, asking their opinion about the effect on the agency system of such a reduction. The response was a strident and unanimous chorus of disapproval from branch managers, who argued that the result of a lower bonus would be disastrous not merely for the life business but also, through its effect on connections and through the loss of agents, for insurance business as a whole. The Birmingham Manager (Charles D. Butler) sent in a particularly strongly worded protest to the Actuary:

1 *Finance Chronicle and Insurance Circular*, XXII, 435 (15 December 1892), 243.

I should consider it little short of a calamity if the bonus about to be declared fell to 25/- or 20/-%. The competition for life business is becoming more keen every year, and one of the adverse conditions hardest to overcome is a reduced bonus . . . Upon many occasions I have been met with a remark to this effect: 'I have decided to give my proposal to the "Scottish Widows." They give all the surplus back to the insurers, while you only give 2/3rds, keeping 1/3rd for the shareholders.' At the last division of profits in 1895 nearly £84,000 was transferred to the pockets of the shareholders! The public won't stand it. Hitherto our bonus has been a good one, and the attention of the policyholders consequently was not directed to the disposal of the surplus. A drop in the bonus would bring into sharp relief, a fact which the man trying to get business endeavours to keep in the background . . . The lowered bonus . . . [will lead to] strong dissatisfaction amongst agents and insurers, and an increased difficulty in getting new business [while] the other branches of our business are likely to suffer.

The Directors were obviously profoundly impressed with this sort of reaction, for not merely did they decide to recommend the proprietors to agree to an immediate increase in the proportionate division (i.e. for the quinquennium 1896–1900) but they raised it from their original proposal of five-sixths to six-sevenths of surplus. The proposal was accepted by an Extraordinary General Court, 'so as to avoid the necessity of declaring a greatly reduced bonus . . . and . . . disarm the representatives of competing companies in any attempt to draw unfavourable comparisons'. On the other hand, this response must have been partly occasioned by a realization that profits would be even lower than at first predicted. For even with the help of a six-sevenths distribution the bonus for 1896–1900 still fell to 25s.

All this was, of course, an acknowledgement of the dominant climate of opinion—one in which there was 'among the public generally a scarcely controlled impatience for the immediate exhibition of showy bonus results . . . [and] a fallacious vulgar belief in the grandeur and absolute importance of mere big figures'.[1] These were harsh words; but, for good or ill, they reflected the modernization of life insurance, and a trend to which the REA had to conform. Competition obliged offices to 'give the public what it wanted', and fundamental changes in bonus payments, as had been pointed out in the 1880s, were often 'as much forced upon the companies as initiated by them of their own free will'.[2] On the other hand, however, the Corporation was still relatively slow in adapting itself to new realities. And the alteration in bonus policy in 1901 still left the Corporation exposed to considerable competitive pressure: in 1905 all

[1] Quoted in Andras, *Historical Review*, p. 59.
[2] *The Economist*, XLV, 140 (4 February 1888).

except one of twelve leading composite offices declared a bigger bonus than the REA; and in 1910, of fifty-six substantial life offices only four distributed a smaller proportion of their profits to policyholders. Naturally enough, the Actuary was profoundly worried by the implications of this, given the fact that 'nearly every proposal of £1000 upwards is fought for by rival inspectors, armed with particulars of high scales of past bonus . . . The Royal Exchange has increasing difficulty in facing this competition.' He warned that the harmful effects of a low bonus would not be confined to life business. It might also lead to 'the openly expressed discontent of 15,000 policyholders, of whom a considerable section are probably insured in the fire department'. In light of these, and other, arguments, Nightingale made a very strong plea that the policyholder's share of profits be once more increased—to 90 per cent. In spite of this, there was no change in policy before the First World War, although the Directors ultimately bowed to the inevitable, and the bonus was raised to 90 per cent of profits as from the quinquennium commencing in 1916.

Although the question of bonus payments formed the most crucial aspect of the Royal Exchange's competitive posture, its response to the struggle for business was not, of course, confined to action with regard to the life surplus. Thus, albeit gradually, the Corporation was willing to make a varied appeal, with a new range of different sorts of policies, to the insuring (and investing) public. Before the 1890s it had been very cautious on this score. In 1871, for example, the Actuary firmly set his face against any alterations, even of detail, and attacked the new schemes 'so assiduously puffed in some prospectuses', as the desperate devices of managers and actuaries 'driven to their wits' end to attract attention to their various offices'. But after the 1880s, the Royal Exchange, while avoiding the more exotic or hazardous sorts of plans, made reasonably extensive use of this sort of sales device. For example, Nightingale introduced 'Settlement Endowment Policies' immediately on becoming Actuary in 1893, and two years later brought out four new schemes simultaneously.[1] In one sense, of course, such experiments were window-dressing; and Nightingale appreciated this, even though he also realized that they were indispensable. In 1911 he pointed out that 'interviews are usually obtained by the presentation of some assurance novelty. Clients, however, as a rule, do not take it up, but eventually decide on the ordinary Tables.'

[1] *PM*, LIV, 49 (9 December 1893), 850; *PM*, LVI, 31 (3 August 1895). The new schemes were for deferred annuities, investment policies, endowments convertible to pensions or paid-up policies, and a combination of annuity to beneficiaries and the return of half the premiums paid.

In addition to its attempts to increase the bonus division (which the Actuary, in 1908, saw as the principal means of augmenting business with 'the better social classes who carefully study the merits of the various offices') the Royal Exchange also conformed to another recent development by extending its appeal beyond its traditional types of policyholder. In the first decade of this century the Corporation successfully sought an increase in its life business among lower middle-class and even working-class policyholders, and issued 'Thrift Policies', which officially dispensed with medical examinations and appealed to young and relatively low-income clients.[1] In 1909 it also announced a 'special pension and investment scheme' for groups of employees, which also dispensed with the medical examination, and was based upon monthly premiums. By 1912 almost 1,000 'no medical examination' policies had been issued, for an average sum insured of £153.

This new approach played an important part in the general revival of life business which the Actuary (in spite of his anxiety about competitive bonuses) was able to report in surveying the five years 1906–10. Net new sums insured rose from £661,600 in 1908 to over £1 million in 1910. In addition to improvements in agency and branch organization, economic prosperity, special efforts to expedite the issue of policies, and the influence of the new death duties, he attributed this increase to the waiving of medical examinations in special cases, and to 'the special effort recently made to push "thrift" business'. 'Thrift policies,' he wrote,

are usually small and more expensive to work, and arise from a lower social grade than that hitherto canvassed for business. Yet this class of risk is excellent in character, and leads to a rapid extension in the number of policyholders. The latter assure for further sums at later periods when their resources grow. Therefore Thrift and Family Provision Policies form a constantly widening stream of life assurance, which ultimately draws in and brings with it contracts of a much larger size.

It would be absurd to pretend that by 1914 the Royal Exchange Life Department had solved all the problems which had been inherited from the 1860s and 1870s. But there can be no doubt about the change in attitude and practice which had been brought about in the generation after 1885. The need to present a picture of vigorous novelty, the importance of self-advertisement, the vital role of bonus payments combined with the necessity to provide a greater share of profits for policyholders, and the advantages to be derived from a realignment of the social structure of its market—had all been brought home to the Corporation. Each

Above, pp. 256–7.

represented a real advance. And it was, above all, the pressure of a competitive market which had provided the necessary incentives for change —even if it had been a shift in management attitudes which provided the indispensable avenue by which that change began to take effect. In this respect the REA exemplified in microcosm a process which characterized, and radically changed, life insurance as a whole. The struggle for business, the thrust of competitive forces, ultimately extended and diversified the provision of insurance services. In spite of the increased cost of doing business, more people became policyholders, and policyholders secured greater benefits from the availability of insurance and the adjustment of bonus procedures. And the impetus to beneficial change in these directions came from those very forces of competition whose effects on traditional values and personal well-being were so much regretted by some contemporaries.

Compared with the situation in life insurance, competition for fire business in the late nineteenth and early twentieth centuries took somewhat different forms and produced different consequences. In large part this was due to differences inherent in fire underwriting itself: the insurance contract was essentially short-term, the habit of fire insurance was widespread and ingrained, its outcome (even on the average) was unpredictable, and the most important consideration for the policyholder was protection against the contingency for which the policy was taken out, rather than any hope of gain through savings. For these reasons not only was fire underwriting a riskier venture than life insurance but competition was more likely to be concentrated on premium rates. There was, admittedly, a certain amount of variety, whether in the old form of bonus policies and mutual fire offices or through the newer devices of valued and loss-of-profit (consequential loss) policies. And anxious managers attacked both the last two—valued policies for being a 'species of gambling', and consequential loss policies ('evolved by the ingenuity of a few actuaries following the unscientific daring of Lloyd's') for 'giving a man something he never had' and increasing the incentive to arson, carelessness and reckless living,[1] In the event, however, consequential loss policies (which in any case had a long ancestry) became firmly established in the first decade of this century. As a Royal Exchange Branch Manager wrote in 1910, 'Ten years ago that branch was a heresy. Today it is fast developing into a creed. It is a case of demand forcing supply.' In spite of this, however, there is little direct comparison with events in life insurance. The basic fire

[1] Pipkin, 'Insurance Business,' *PM* (1907), p. 260.

insurance contract remained the conventional policy, and the principal selling points related to service and price.

Although competition was potentially fiercer and more concentrated in fire insurance, the Fire Offices' Committee (perhaps for that very reason) exerted a strong countervailing influence throughout the period. In 1864 they had agreed to a rule forbidding members to undertake reinsurance on behalf of non-tariff companies—thus wielding a very powerful weapon against those offices which refused to conform to agreed premiums. And by 1900 they accounted for over 90 per cent of all home business, and for more than 95 per cent of all world-wide business, done by British offices.[1] As far as competition was concerned, the Committee served to abate its intensity and to ensure a 'harmony' of premium rates amongst most of the leading offices. As was only to be expected, therefore, it came under severe criticism as a combination which many viewed as designed to maintain rates at 'monopoly' levels. *The Economist* in 1881, for example, pointed to the then very substantial profits of tariff offices which did not seem to attract fresh capital, or lead to a cut in profits, and accused them of having 'banded themselves together into what is virtually a great trades union, having for its object the restraining of competition and the upholding of rates'.[2]

In spite of their relative success in controlling general premium rates, however, the rôle of the tariff offices cannot be examined solely in terms of a combination making unlimited profit. First, there was always a limit to the strength of the association. We have already seen how the attempt to raise rates excessively after the Tooley Street fire (1861) merely led to the establishment of new companies sufficiently strong to pull rates down again. Second, it fulfilled various functions in addition to the determination of rates: agency commissions, and therefore expenses, were controlled (to the envy of life offices);[3] new or complex risks were investigated and rated; the work of the various Salvage Corps was supervised; the forms and wording of policies were controlled; relations with Parliament, foreign governments and other public bodies were maintained; and a statistical service was provided. Third, the undeniable potential profits of fire

---

[1] Deuchar, 'Tariff Organization', *JFII* (1903), p. lv; *Finance Chronicle*, 15 October and 16 November 1903.

[2] *The Economist*, XXXIX, 532 (30 April 1881). In 1910–20 tariff offices made an underwriting surplus of just over 10 per cent of premiums, compared with about 5 per cent for non-tariff offices (*Policy Holder*, 13 July 1921).

[3] See *The Economist*, LXXIV, 1001 (11 May 1912), which contrasted the life offices' bad record in this regard with that of the FOC: 'Onlookers would say that it is not the tariff which is so wonderful as the loyal faith which the offices have observed to each other all these years, especially on this commission question.'

insurance, irrespective of the efforts of the Fire Offices' Committee, produced a steady pressure on rates and conditions, even though it did not always manifest itself as volatile price fluctuations.

In practice, market forces continued to impose strong pressures on premium rates—either directly or by inducing offices to accept 'rougher risks'. This was said to be the cause of 'the rise, fall and ruin of a large number of fire insurance companies . . . with small experience'.[1] The Royal Exchange, naturally enough, and particularly in its more cautious years, tried to exercise the utmost care in the selection of risks and in resisting the pressure for lower premiums. In 1866, for example, the Treasury Committee expressed satisfaction that the officials had refused bad risks 'rather than follow the example of other offices in unduly lowering the proper rate of premium'. But, even though these were generally profitable years, all was not plain sailing: industry-wide developments could not be completely escaped. By 1881 the Directors were exhorted 'to bring as much business as possible to the Office. The competition is now so great that every exertion is required to maintain the business of the Corporation.' Premium rates were falling, and in 1882 the Directors were warned by the Treasury Committee that 'the constant reduction in the rates of premium will prove a very serious difficulty'.

The competitive situation eased somewhat in the early 1880s, when there were increases in tariff rates and when various foreign offices withdrew from the British market. But this had the result of reducing reinsurance facilities, and by 1885, according to the REA, the trade depression was adversely affecting 'both the volume and the moral character of fire insurance'. Although the Corporation continued to enjoy loss ratios significantly better than the average, its underwriting surplus began to feel the pinch in the 1880s—falling from almost 30 per cent of net premiums in the 1870s to 17 per cent in the 1880s. These developments, of course, provided the appropriate context for the critical changes in the attitudes and policies of the Corporation's Fire Department, which came in the 1880s. Even so, however, as we have seen, it was not external pressure alone which produced the change. Rather, ambition as well as competition was a spur which moved the Corporation into new, and more adventurous, routes.

These twin incentives also took the Corporation into two new arenas of competition: into the business of fire insurance in overseas territories and into the the field of accident underwriting at home. Overseas, although the

[1] Evidence of Percy M. Dove, Manager of the Royal, to the Select Committee on Fire Protection, *PP* (1867), x, *Q*.2530.

market tended to be less susceptible to regulation, the application of tariffs and the huge potential for insurance meant that the REA did not have any particularly severe competitive problems before the First World War. With respect to accident insurance, it is true that in the years immediately around 1900, following the extension of the workmen's compensation law in 1898, there was a fierce struggle for business. Nevertheless, the Royal Exchange had little difficulty in securing business in the opening years of this century, and rates rose steadily after 1901. In 1904 the Corporation joined the informal Accident Offices' Committee—which assumed an official existence as the Accident Offices' Association in 1906. Thenceforth, until the War, the general competitive problems of most accident business (although a motor tariff was not formulated until 1915) did not differ substantially from those of fire insurance. Even so, competition still had a powerful rôle to play, for in accident as in life insurance, the public was in a greater position of strength. By 1910 it seemed that

Schemes regarded as chimerical in the nineteenth century are the commonplaces of the twentieth. For the insurance companies the vox populi is the Vox Dei. The public has only to hint a need for cover for some particular contingency, and its letter-boxes are post-haste crammed with beautiful prospectuses offering full facilities. Dignified insurance companies, heavy with the weight of years, hustle one another in the insurance market place for the nimble half-crown for your domestic servant insurance, or the favour of replacing your broken plate-glass window.[1]

DECENTRALIZATION: AGENTS, INSPECTORS AND BRANCHES

So far the impact of competition has been appraised largely in terms of the price and other characteristics of the actual insurance contract. In fact, however, for both the industry in general and the REA in particular, one of the most critical responses to new market problems and opportunities lay in the adaptation of organization and the application of effort. It was, in fact, the increasingly energetic search for business itself, and the inevitable effect of that search on the agency network of most offices, which created the twentieth-century insurance industry. The reason for this was simple: insurance, if it was to expand, had to be *sold*, and the effective point at which business was done was therefore the contact between agent and policyholder. 'The magic of personal influence', in the words of a President of the Institute of Actuaries, meant that 'the Head Office manufactures the article, but has to look to its middleman to get orders'. Whatever else was important, an effective and vigorous agency network was

[1] *REAM*, III, 4 (July 1910).

indispensable to growth. 'It is not the goodness of the office,' said one MP in 1870, 'but the energy of the agent which secures the largest business.' Of course, this emphasis on marketing had its less attractive side, and some managers were saddened to note the contrast between the 'stately negotiations' and 'strict enquiries' of previous years and the degeneration of legitimate competition, under the influence of 'the smart man', 'into an unseemly scramble for supremacy'. But this sort of intensity was unavoidable if the industry was to grow—no matter how much even a progressive and successful manager might regret the fact that 'we are tumbling over each other all over this little island' in pursuit of increased sales.[1]

As a result of all this, the growth in the number of insurance agents was to some extent an index of both industrial expansion and competition. One estimate for the first fifty years of Victoria's reign held that the number of life agents alone had increased from about 6,000 to 100,000;[2] while the REA, whose growth was by no means exceptional, increased the number of its British and Irish agents from less than 600 at mid-century to about 5,000 in 1900 and over 15,500 in 1912. By 1900 it seemed to the Corporation's Agency Manager that 'the competition for agents is very keen— quite as acute as the contest for life business'.

The sensitive position of the agent in the competitive growth of both life and fire insurance in the late nineteenth century was shown in the increasing pressure on rates of commission. For, in the last resort, it was found that the best incentive to increase sales was a pecuniary one, although there were still men, like the Chancellor of the Exchequer in 1870, who criticized the getting of people to take out life policies 'by a system of puffing, touting, and bribing which is almost unexampled in any other line of business'.[3] Throughout the late nineteenth century commissions and allowances drifted upwards—particularly in life insurance. The Royal Exchange avoided the worst excesses of bidding for the custom of agents; but it could not hold aloof indefinitely. Thus, even though in 1881 the Actuary firmly rejected any increase as 'a dangerous system to which there seems to be no limit when once begun', within five years, confronted by 'offices which rank high in the point of security' paying larger than ever commissions, he was forced to recommend a major adjustment of the Corporation's commission to serve as incentive to agents. In

[1] William Sutton, 'Opening Address', *JIA*, xxviii (January 1890), 177; *Hansard's Parliamentary Debates*, cxcix, col. 732 (23 February 1870); Robert Chapman, 'The Agency System of Insurance Companies', *JFII*, x (1907), 75–6; Pipkin, 'Insurance Business', *PM* (1907), p. 278.

[2] Deuchar, 'Life Assurance Business', *JIA* (1890).

[3] *Hansard's Parliamentary Debates*, cxcix, col. 750 (23 February 1870).

March 1886, therefore, the Fire and Life Committee agreed that in addition to the usual commission of 10 per cent on new and 5 per cent on renewal premiums, agents should be allowed a 'procuration fee' of 10s. 6d. for each £500 of insurance. Generally, however, other companies paid far more substantial amounts. And the situation had got sufficiently out of hand for even such a notorious opponent of business combinations as *The Economist* to advocate an agreement among life offices to stop the competitive bidding, which often produced commissions amounting to 75 or even 100 per cent of the first year's premiums.[1]

In fire insurance, in spite of the efforts of the Fire Offices' Committee, commission still had a disconcerting tendency to rise. Thus the Royal Exchange, which in 1866 had been able to boast that its own rules (as to who should receive how much commission) 'are more stringent than the regulations now proposed as remedies for many evils' by the Fire Offices' Committee, was obliged, in 1881, to increase its commission from 10 per cent, plus the policy fee, to 15 per cent, in order to 'promote an active prosecution of the fire business'. In the early 1890s *The Economist* drew attention to the fact that competition for fire insurance, confronted by fixed premium rates, was taking the form 'of offering bribes to induce intermediaries to take business to one office rather than to another'. The evidence it adduced to show that the agents got more out of the business than the shareholders (for it was a perennial complaint that the only people to benefit from extreme competition were the agent-middlemen), also showed that in fire, as in life, insurance the REA was holding itself somewhat aloof from the competitive bidding on commissions—although its management expenses were exceptionally high, so that the balance of its cost was fully redressed.[2] On the other hand, however, the Corporation was having to pay away greater amounts in commission than in the palmy 1870s, and this trend continued as it fought for business in the 1890s and 1900s. Thus commissions grew from 8·3 per cent of net premiums in 1871–5 to 18·5 per cent in 1911–15. In fact, even in so far as the Fire Offices' Committee rules imposed some restraint upon an overt increase in commission rates, ingenious or unscrupulous offices could get round this inhibition either by establishing local 'Boards of Directors' (which were partly designed to encourage business by offering remuneration to substantial business-getters)[3] or by subsidizing the general expenses of agents.

---

[1] *The Economist*, LVII, 566–7 (22 April 1899).

[2] *The Economist*, LI, 65 (21 January 1893) and 130 (4 February 1893). In 1891 REA commission and management expenses were 12·2 and 21·3 per cent of fire premiums—as against averages of 17·1 and 14·9 per cent for twenty-three leading companies.

[3] See Chapman, 'Agency System', *JFII* (1907), pp. 80–1.

The REA itself established many local Boards in the provinces during the early years of this century. In 1909 the Governor sent a message to fifty local Directors, then attending an official dinner, explaining that their appointment was designed 'to enlist the personal interest, sympathy and energy of local gentlemen of the highest position and influence', since 'in these days of competition no legitimate means of consolidating and extending our business can be left neglected'.

The very great extension of the number of agents also led to important changes in organization. For the concentration on the point-of-sale, together with the need to control the new armies of agents, led inevitably to a rapid decentralization of sales policy and control.

In the first instance, this trend was represented by the appointment of professional, salaried officials—inspectors (also known as 'superintendents' of agents or 'canvassers') whose task it was to supervise and instruct agents, to follow up their contacts and economize on their time, and to press for business in a continuous and systematic way. Inspectors first appeared in their modern rôle about 1850, although as we have already seen, the need to fulfil their functions had been felt well before then: the Atlas, for example, appointed a 'Travelling Agent' from 1826 onwards to visit agents 'with a view to stimulate their exertions in increasing the orders for assurance'. In the second half of the century, intensified competition led to a great extension of this system of agency control. In 1865, for example, the Atlas appointed a salaried Superintendent to visit and exhort its agents, and even though the post soon lapsed, it was permanently re-established in 1881. In 1884 Pipkin, having just assumed control at the Atlas, urged that particular attention be paid to agents in the search for life business, and that 'the agents should be taught by inspectors, superintendents or branch managers how to get business, and should be helped in the getting of it; racy, telling and forcible pamphlets should be supplied, teaching how to answer objections and to meet adverse criticisms and comparisons with other companies'. This was merely one example of an industry-wide movement. By 1907 it was estimated that the fire, life and accident offices employed about 2,000 inspectors.[1]

If the appointment of salaried canvassers, operating either from Head Office or a provincial town, was the first stage in the evolution of new organizational structures, the second was not long in coming. The same sort of consideration that had led to the appointment of inspectors (i.e. the realization that agents needed more continuous oversight and supervision) also resulted in the creation of district and branch offices. These

[1] Pipkin, 'Insurance Business', *PM* (1907), p. 278.

were more suited than distant Head Offices for the tasks of general supervision—besides being needed to relieve some of the pressure of clerical
work which had naturally mounted at Head Offices when inspectors had
been first appointed. Finally, the proliferation of branches and of inspectors
itself produced new problems of control and supervision for the Head
Offices. This, in turn, led to a third stage of structural development in the
late nineteenth-century insurance industry: the appearance of agency
managers. As one commentator put it in 1900:

some of the most progressive offices . . . further developed the principle which
led to the establishment of branch offices, and as the Resident Secretary appeared
above the horizon as soon as the necessity for the development of the agency
system became apparent, so now that bright particular star, the Agency Manager,
has arisen in these latter days of competition to be guide, counsellor, and friend
of Branch Secretaries.[1]

In the early nineteenth century the REA was well aware of the need
which ultimately produced inspectors and branches and agency managers.
But it was not really until the 1860s that the Corporation began to put the
question of agency control on a more systematic footing. In 1871 the
Court appointed a salaried official, John Williams, of Basinghall Street, 'to
canvass for life business' in London at normal agency commission rates,
plus 10s. per cent on the sum assured, with a guaranteed minimum of
£250 annually. However, the burden of supervising and encouraging
agents was carried by Head Office officials until the 1880s (the Secretary,
E. R. Handcock, for example, received *ex gratia* payments for annual
agency visits made in the early 1870s). Yet, conscientious as they undoubtedly were, they were only appropriate in an age when competition was not
felt too keenly. By 1881 the Actuary, in claiming that 'no system of advertising will altogether supply the place of personal exertion', went on:
'I would venture to suggest that what we most require is a constant and
efficient inspection of our agencies, with power to make such changes as
may be expedient in each particular case.' Moreover, he successfully advocated the appointment of 'a really efficient man, well trained in life assurance duties, and also well acquainted with what is going on in the life
assurance world, to act under constant instructions from this Department,
as Superintendent of Town Agencies, and generally to look up business in
and near London'.

In June 1881, therefore, the Corporation appointed Frederick Charles
Dutton at a salary of £250 as its first 'Inspector of Agencies, to procure new
agents, and generally to look up business in the Home District'. Five years

[1] W. M. Potterton, 'Life Agency Work', *JFII*, III (1900), 421–2.

later the Actuary admitted that Dutton had not been satisfactory, but still insisted that two or three such men could be of very great value: 'They should be expected to appoint, *instruct*, and be in *constant communication* with agents. Most of the business obtained by pushing offices, in and around London especially, is I believe procured by this means.' These arguments must have had some effect, for by 1887 we hear of a Mr Fox, 'Life Office Inspector', very actively recruiting agents for the REA. But a much more decisive move came in 1888, when the new Actuary, Gerald H. Ryan, strongly urged that London be divided into six districts, each with an inspector 'to supervise the existing agents, recommend suitable persons for appointment as further agents, and take such other steps as are likely to lead to an increase in life business'. In the event only four such inspectors were appointed in 1888. But an important new departure had occurred. And it was followed by the appointment of inspectors at various provincial branches (e.g. at Bristol in 1890). And in Yorkshire in 1888 it was found necessary to appoint an inspector for the Life Department as well as the existing district inspector, who now concentrated on fire business.

In the 1880s, to a large extent matching the appointment of inspectors, the Royal Exchange also created district and branch offices, thus responding to the necessity of providing a more continuous supervisory and administrative framework for local agents. In fact, important agencies had for a long time many of the characteristics of branches—managing sub-agencies, being responsible for large amounts of premium, and receiving commensurate attention and financial support from Head Office. In the 1860s, for example, the agents at Manchester and Liverpool (the two most important provincial centres) received fairly large subsidies: at Liverpool £100 annually towards offices expenses. This sort of arrangement also enabled the REA, like other companies, to reward its more important agents to a greater extent than was possible at prevailing commission rates. But something more formal, and more amenable to central control, was needed. And in 1881 district offices were opened in Birmingham, Bristol and Manchester. In each case salaried District Managers were appointed (in the first and last instance they were the existing agents) with authority to appoint their own agents—'it being distinctly understood that the Corporation take no risk as to the solvency of such agents'. However, formal branches were not established for a few years longer, although they came reasonably fast when they did: the Court decided to convert Manchester into the first provincial branch in December 1886; in 1887 branches were also opened at Birmingham, Bristol and Liverpool; and Newcastle (1888), Leeds (1889) and Glasgow (1889) soon followed.

These various moves meant that by the 1890s the REA relied on two relatively new types of official, the inspector and the branch manager, both of whom were really products of the climate of insurance enterprise in the second half of the nineteenth century. With the increasing complexity and heightened competition of contemporary insurance, such full-time experts soon came to play a crucial rôle in business-getting. At times, and particularly in the case of inspectors, they bore the competitive heat of the day under trying, and even exhausting, conditions. And it is little wonder that 'a sound constitution' as well as 'a good general education' was suggested as a primary qualification of an inspector.[1] For the insurance business came to be associated with the 'perpetual and unending tramp of emissaries engaged in its service' and to be compared with 'a huge pedlar system: we carry our goods to the people as though we were missionaries with some new gospel'.[2] In this process, inspectors were the leading proselytizers. Indeed, in the last resort they began to take over the basic task of salesmanship from the agents. By 1910 the REA Actuary (who then felt that the Corporation did not have enough inspectors) argued that the intensity of competition for life business meant that it relied more and more on personal canvassing and less and less on the influence of the agent. And the next year, in indicating that the salaries and expenses of inspectors had doubled in ten years, he argued that 'the actual procuration of assurance business, especially life, is drifting more and more into the hands of experts, the agents merely furnishing introductions'.

The framework within which most inspectors operated, and the new funnels for premium income, were, of course, the branch offices. Their managers were important men in the new set-up—and, in the case of the Royal Exchange in the late 1880s, received substantial salaries of £400 or £500, plus profit commission (usually 5 per cent of profits) in the case of fire, and a percentage of sums assured in the case of life insurance. A survey of the Corporation's provincial branches in 1909–10 showed that the seventeen branch offices employed twenty-four inspectors and accounted for a premium income of over £325,000.[3] Nevertheless, the Corporation did not go as far, or as fast, as some companies in the development of branch offices before the First World War. This was a particular handicap for the Life Department. In 1910 the Corporation was not represented in over half of the 300 towns in the United Kingdom with a population of

[1] Potterton, 'Life Agency Work'. *JFII* (1900), p. 423.
[2] Pipkin, 'Insurance Business', *PM* (1907), p. 278.
[3] The largest branches were at Dublin (£59,277 premiums), Manchester (£40,637), Liverpool (£34,719), Birmingham (£33,486), Bristol (£32,007) and Newcastle (£24,297).

1,000 or more. And even though this reflected a relatively small proportion of the total population, the Actuary still felt it was 'of vital necessity' to remedy the defect, in light of the activity of 'other large companies of immense resources and enterprise'. In urging that it had become 'imperative to put on more inspectors at the earliest possible date', he added that 'we can only deplore the fact that more attention was not given to extension 25 or so years ago, when the same results could have been achieved at one-quarter the expense'. This report did, indeed, have a large effect. The Fire and Life Committee agreed to the appointment of more agents in 'outlying districts'; and the employment 'of reliable young inspectors . . . whose duties it will be to select the best agents obtainable, to supervise them at frequent intervals and to cultivate their connections'. As a result, there was a rapid increase in both the number of inspectors and the number of agents (the Corporation's agents increased from about 11,500 in 1910 to 15,500 in 1912).

The search for effective representation was complicated by the fact that the different types of underwriting—fire, life, employers' liability, personal accident, etc.—were increasingly interdependent, and that this was an interdependence of technical specialisms. Specifically, part-time agents were not, and could not really be expected to be, equally well qualified for every aspect of insurance. This particularly applied to the complications of life business, and provided the basis of long-standing complaints by the REA Actuary. In 1866, for example, Winser had claimed that 'some agents who may be very useful in promoting fire business are deficient in those qualities which are necessary to procure life assurance proposals . . . [Some] are ignorant of the very first principles upon which life assurance depends, and consequently unable to cope with shrewder men who represent very inferior offices.' Forty years later a successor, Nightingale, was still arguing that: 'The composite character of the Corporation's business makes it very difficult to put pressure on agents in the interest of the life department without prejudicing the position of the fire business. Moreover, the Corporation's best life agents are sometimes enticed away to other large life companies by the offer of the good existing connection of a deceased agent.' Indeed, by the early twentieth century this was more of a problem because of the proliferation of business within composite companies. And in 1909 the REA Fire Manager emphasized that 'more and more agents are devoting themselves to the transaction of all kinds of insurance business, in consequence, no doubt, of the increasing desire of the public to place all their insurance in one office'.

The fact that agents had become more numerous, their tasks more varied, and the substructures of their supervision and direction (in the shape of inspectors and branch offices) more complex, meant that the various insurance companies had to solve new problems of control and devolution. These might appear in a generalized form and commentators were quick to warn companies not to expect too much too soon from any branch manager: 'Don't tie him up with red tape and expect him to lick creation.'[1] In fact, a good deal of initiative and independence had to be devolved to branch officials—and encouraged through such devices as profit commission. On the other hand, however, and in more particular ways, the branches had to be fitted into a co-ordinated (and, in the last resort, central) plan of action. Indeed, it was envisaged that as new forms of central control (for example agency departments) were fashioned, branch managers might have to assume a somewhat more routine task. The new man, it was felt by some, would be the agency manager:

To him will be entrusted the visions of the Directors in regard to new business, and they will look to him to give them practical effect. To him will fall the duty of formulating the general plan of campaign, and of providing the means to carry it to a successful issue . . . his advent seems to point to a greater homogeneity in the agency work of the office and to a more general uniformity of practice, which will increase the demand on the administrative rather than the initiative ability of the branch manager.[2]

At the Royal Exchange, the need for an Agency Manager to co-ordinate various aspects of the field organization was, in fact, recognized early in this century. The Life Department had appointed R. B. S. Castle as its own Agency Manager in 1896 'to improve the country business'; but in 1903 he was placed in charge of the newly created Agency Department for the Corporation as a whole. In fact, however, the position of the Agency Manager in these early years was somewhat ambiguous. His Department was organizationally part of the Secretary's Office; and, while he had the task of providing general supervision, advice and help in matters relating to agents or branches, he had no responsibility for technical matters concerning insurance or the supervision of the indoor staff of the various branches. Put another way, the branch organization was still the basic charge of the Secretary and, even more important, of the Managers of the various underwriting departments. Thus, where there was reason to be dissatisfied with, say, the fire business at a particular branch, it was the Fire Manager who would take the initiative—as happened at Leeds in 1913 when the joint Fire Managers sent a Head Office man to help increase the Branch's

[1] Potterton, 'Life Agency Work', *JFII* (1900), p. 440.
[2] Potterton, 'Life Agency Work', *JFII* (1900), p. 425.

premium income: 'He will not hold any official appointment at the Branch, but will act as the Fire Managers' representative, and under their direct instruction.'

This situation was perfectly understandable, for the REA was still a highly departmentalized Corporation; there was as yet no General Manager (although a Committee of Management was established in 1911) and the authority and initiative of Departmental Managers was unquestioned. The result, however, was that no *unified* control was effectively established over the growing branches before the inter-war period. Each was subject to pressures (which were not always consistent) from Fire, Life and Accident Managers. This was obviously a difficult position for the Agency Manager —who from time to time expressed his dissatisfaction—and it was widely appreciated that the overlapping of duties might easily give rise to serious friction 'unless the whole situation is treated in a loyal and broad spirit, with a certain amount of give and take'.[1]

Yet whatever the difficulties involved in forging new control structures for the extended system of agencies and branches at the turn of the century, the Corporation remained unwavering in its reliance on an agency system—as distinct from more direct appeals to the insuring public. With the appointment of an Agency Manager, in 1903, there was evidence of 'a genuine desire to draw our agents closer and closer to Head Office: to win their interests and bind them to the Corporation not only by pecuniary but also by personal ties'.[2] One sign of its appreciation of new needs was the *Royal Exchange Assurance Magazine*, first published in January 1903 'to give expression to the bond uniting all those interested in the Corporation', and reflecting the need for a new corporate spirit to unite Head Office and branch employees and agents 'throughout the world'. The *Magazine* was also used to reassure those connected with the Corporation that it shunned any dependence on direct appeals to the public. Rather, it remained what it always had been—an 'Agency Office' the 'first essential of [which] is to support and stand by its agents . . . We know and appreciate the advantages of the system, and we have no intention of avoiding the disadvantages at the expense of our friends.'[3]

THE RISE OF LARGE-SCALE OFFICES

The intensification of competition in the late nineteenth and early twentieth centuries led almost inevitably to an increase in the cost of doing business. Concentrated as the competition was on the extension of branch

[1] Memorandum on Agency Manager, 11 October 1917.
[2] *REAM*, I, 2 (April 1903).
[3] *REAM*, III, 3 (January 1910).

and agency organization, and the expenditure of more effort at the point of sale, it proved impossible to lower proportionate costs. In the case of life insurance, for example, between 1872 and 1888 commissions and management expenses, as a proportion of the premium income of twenty-three offices, rose from 11·68 per cent to 13·83 per cent. And although this percentage then hardly changed between the 1880s and 1912, the fact that the growth of endowment insurance involved a substantial rise in the average premium per £100 insured meant that life business was 'more expensively managed than under the same ratios of expenditure thirty years ago'.[1] There was a comparable increase in the expenses of fire insurance in this period (although it is important to remember that, with the growth of composite offices it was not always possible to distinguish between fire and life and other expenses). In the industry as a whole commissions and management costs rose from some 28 per cent of premiums in 1877-8 to over 34 per cent in 1900, and by 1907 it was apparent that there had been an increase of almost 10 percentage points in the last thirty years as branch management and agency inspection inflated the cost of doing business.[2] The REA also found it more costly to do business: between 1871-5 and 1911-15 commissions rose from 8·3 per cent to 18·5 per cent of net premiums, and management expenses from 14·6 per cent to 19·0 per cent.

This universal rise in the cost of doing business before the First World War was associated with a very substantial increase in the size of individual offices. And it naturally occurred to contemporaries that the increased costs of underwriting might, in fact, be one cause of the appearance of very big insurance companies, seeking to minimize cost increase by securing some economies of scale. In fire insurance, the cost advantages of large-scale operations were not obvious—indeed, there was relatively little variation in the expense ratios of different companies. In 1906, for example, the average expenses ratio of twenty-seven leading fire offices was 34·6 per cent, but seventeen of these had ratios between 33 and 36 per cent. In the case of life insurance, there were other factors than size which might determine expense ratios, and therefore make valid comparisons very difficult.[3] Nevertheless, in contrast to the situation in the fire business, the relative cost of transacting life insurance was in some measure related to

[1] William Sutton, 'Opening Address', *JIA*, XXVIII (January 1890), 173-6; Andras, *Historical Review*, pp. 73-4.

[2] *Finance Chronicle and Insurance Circular*, 15 October and 16 November 1903; Pipkin, 'Insurance Business', *PM* (1907), p. 278.

[3] For example, whether the office was a mutual company not employing agents; the importance of new as against renewal premiums; the extent to which an office transacted other sorts of insurance.

the scale of operations. In the early 1880s, for example, an investigation which ranked ninety-five companies by the size of their premium incomes showed that the proportion of expenses to premiums fell steadily from over one-third for the fourteen offices with incomes below £10,000 to 10·4 per cent for the nine offices with incomes between £200,000 and £250,000. Oddly, however, in the case of the biggest offices, with premium incomes exceeding £250,000, the expense ratio rose again, to 13·3 per cent.[1] A similar conclusion was voiced in a discussion at the Institute of Actuaries in 1889. The apparent anomaly concerning the very largest companies was, however, challenged by a distinguished actuary, T. B. Sprague, who argued that the most recent data, for 1887, showed that the biggest offices were, after all, the cheapest to run: 'It appears to follow that, in life insurance, as in so many other matters, there is an irresistible tendency to consolidation; and that, in life insurance at all events, this tendency is beneficial.'[2] Amalgamation, it was held by the President of the Institute of Actuaries, could provide 'a haven of safety and of good results to the assured, arising out of the economy of expenditure and the concentration of energy upon a condensed field of operation'—although he also warned against the disadvantages of precipitate action: of sacrificing 'the prospects of . . . policyholders to the bewildering dazzle of big figures, wrongly obtained by abnormal expenditure'.[3]

Whatever the rôle of rising costs and the economies of scale, the indisputable fact about the structure of the insurance industry in this period was, indeed, the 'irresistible tendency to consolidation'. Insurance, in every sense, was becoming 'big business'. For not only was its social and economic rôle being enlarged, but both the average size of firms and the relative importance of the very largest companies were increasing. In the case of fire insurance, accurate measurement is difficult because of the absence of comprehensive statistics. But throughout this period fire underwriting was overwhelmingly in the hands of between fifty and sixty companies, and their average premium income rose from just over £160,000 in the late 1870s, to over £500,000 in 1908. Meanwhile, the share of total premiums of the ten largest offices, which had remained at just over 60 per cent for most of the late nineteenth century, shot up to over 70 per cent in the period 1900–15. (Between 1899 and 1904 the share of the nine leading offices rose from 54 to 66 per cent.)[4] We can be more precise in the

[1] *JIA*, XXIII (1882), 362.
[2] *JIA*, XXVIII (October 1889), 136–7, 149–51.
[3] Augustus Hendriks (Actuary of Liverpool and London and Globe), quoted in the *Finance Chronicle and Insurance Circular*, XXII, 435 (15 December 1892), 251
[4] *Finance and Insurance Chronicle*, 2 October 1905.

case of life insurance because of the existence of official statistics. Between 1881 and 1914 the average ordinary premiums of British life offices increased from £116,583 to £308,503, while the share of total premiums earned by the ten largest offices rose from 33 per cent to 43 per cent. Even more spectacularly, the five largest life offices increased their share from 21 per cent to 35 per cent.

The growth of large-scale enterprise was not, of course, confined to insurance: it was a trend which increasingly characterized much of British industry in the generation or so before 1914.[1] To some insurance men it seemed the result of a new business psychology—'the passion for bigness, for big things'—which could be seen not merely in insurance but 'in every other department of life', and which operated 'apart altogether from corresponding profits'.[2] But important as this sort of semi-rational ambition might have been, there was an economic basis for the new developments. At the very minimum it was obvious that, in life insurance, 'nothing attracts the public so much as big figures'.[3] More generally, however, it is clear that market forces—particularly the fears and opportunities of competition—were largely responsible for the emergence of giant new combinations. Constant growth and geographical extension became indispensable means of self-defence. The momentum of expansion had to be maintained; and large offices, especially in so far as they diversified into a composite business and thereby developed mutually strengthening departments, were inevitably in a position of some advantage. In the search for new business, as one journalist pointed out, 'the most potent factor is connection'.[4]

It was for this reason that the most crucial period for the rise of large-scale insurance companies was the first decade of the twentieth century. For it was then, by a process of growth and amalgamation, that modern composite offices made their appearance. Admittedly, the trend towards very large-scale insurance enterprise was already strongly marked in the late nineteenth century, with such offices as the Royal, the Commercial Union, and the Liverpool & London & Globe in fire insurance, and the Scottish Widows', the Standard and the Gresham in life business. But the formation of very large composite offices was essentially the result of a wave of amalgamations after 1900. In that movement the rise of general accident, and particularly employers' liability, business played a vital rôle. Accident business offered opportunities which some older offices, includ-

[1] See P. L. Payne, 'The Emergence of the Large-scale Company in Great Britain, 1870–1914', *Economic History Review*, 2nd series, XX, 3 (December 1967), 519–42.

[2] Pipkin, 'Insurance Business', *PM* (1907), p. 260.

[3] *The Economist*, LVII, 567 (22 April 1899).

[4] *Times Financial, Commercial and Shipping Supplement*, 29 April 1913.

ing the REA, had been quick to seize. Yet the main catalyst for sweeping structural change was the 1906 Act, which extended employers' liability to all workers, including domestic servants, and thereby persuaded both accident and fire companies that the markets for various types of insurance were too intimately related to be separated. On the one hand, the economies of scale, especially in so far as an extended system of agents and branches had become essential, made it logical for individual offices to cater for *all* the main needs of the insuring public. On the other hand, apprehension as well as ambition was at work: offices increasingly found that they could only defend themselves against competition by offering both agents and clients a wider range of services. At the same time, too, the extension of the functions of the broker into non-marine business gave an added and very powerful incentive to offices which could provide varying sorts of cover.[1]

In general, therefore, it could be said that the rise of composite companies was 'probably as much due to a desire to maintain valuable connections as to provide facilities for covering all risks in one office'.[2] This movement was particularly marked in the joining of accident and fire business, for it was in this respect that the importance of 'connection' was most marked: the property-owner who needed to insure against fire also needed to insure against claims from his employees—whether factory hands or domestic servants—and would naturally favour the agent and the company which provided both services. As with the middle-class family, so with the industrialist; as with the new department stores of fashionable London, so with insurance in Edwardian Britain: 'all the shopping could be done under one roof'. And the 'shopping' now included not only accident and fire insurance, but life and even marine insurance as the composite offices acquired marine companies in 'the hope of scooping in new general business through the door of the marine underwriting room', which would become a 'feeding department, managed by the directors with one eye to the fire and accident branches'.[3]

There were various reasons why this process was brought about by amalgamation rather than the steady evolution of individual offices. First, where a company wished to undertake a new line of business it obviously made more sense to acquire a going concern with an established management, agency network and connection. Second, amalgamation was

---

[1] Raynes, *British Insurance*, p. 382.
[2] *The Economist*, LXVI (25 January 1908).
[3] The comparison of the insurance offices and department stores comes from *REAM*, III, 7 (December 1911), 235; the quotation about marine insurance from *The Economist*, LXXVI, 1276–7 (24 May 1913).

the quickest, and often easiest, way to increase the size of operations. Third, the new partner brought in more business of the old type as well as new. And fourth, amalgamation automatically reduced the potential area of competition. In addition, of course, there was the prospect of economies resulting from the avoidance of duplication. In fact, however, amalgamation rarely led to significant cost reduction by the effecting of speedy economies. As the later experience of the Royal Exchange was to show, the nature of the insurance industry—the tenacious loyalty of agents and policy-holders, the sense of corporate momentum and institutional inertia— meant that these economies could only be achieved slowly, because they involved the sinking of corporate identity, the closing of branches, the reduction of staffs, and the like. *The Economist* saw the situation as follows:

> The saving of expenses which must be the ultimate result of an amalgamation is a gradual process. This cannot be otherwise if fair consideration be given to the moral, if not legal, rights of the staff taken over, and it is to the credit of our insurance companies that this side of the question has always been scrupulously kept in view. The immediate advantages are the consolidation of forces for forward movement, the fact that there is one competitor the fewer, the acquire-ment of new connections, and those additional opportunities which do not admit of exact description, but which always come to a business as it grows in magni-tude without loss of financial strength.[1]

Amalgamations had, of course, taken place throughout the nineteenth century. But, although the relatively unstable years of the 1850s and early 1860s had been marked by the absorption of large numbers of small and insecure companies, it was only in the last two decades of the century that a more modern type of amalgamation movement reached significant pro-portions. In the period 1886–1900, for example, an average of nine offices annually amalgamated with others. In the five years 1906–10, however, the average number spurted to thirteen, and in 1910 alone no less than nineteen offices lost their separate identities in this way.[2] Some of these amalgamations involved the joining together of very large fire offices, as when the Atlas acquired the Manchester (1904), the Alliance acquired the Imperial (1902) and the Law Fire and the County Fire (1906), or the Royal

---

[1] *The Economist*, LXIX, 1261 (18 December 1909).

[2] Calculated from lists in the *Insurance Directory and Year Book* (1966–7), pp. 256–72.

Summary details:

Period	Amalgamations	Period	Amalgamations	Period	Amalgamations
1841–5	13	1866–70	46	1891–5	47
1846–50	29	1871–5	22	1896–1900	44
1851–5	39	1876–80	21	1901–5	42
1856–60	92	1881–5	20	1906–10	67
1861–5	60	1886–90	48	1911–15	30

acquired the Lancashire (1901). Symptomatic of the entirely new atmosphere was the absorption of fire offices as old as the industry itself: the Hand-in-Hand and the Union were acquired by the Commercial Union in 1905 and 1908, and the Westminster by the Alliance in 1906. But a more significant element was the amalgamation of fire and accident offices. Thus of the twenty-four largest accident offices in 1899, fifteen were acquired by fire, or fire and life, offices before 1914—eight of them in the brief period 1906–10.[1] Nor did the process of amalgamation stop there: of sixteen specialist marine insurance companies which had existed in 1899, half had been absorbed into composite companies before 1914; and of the twenty-nine relatively substantial proprietary offices doing only ordinary life business in 1899, nine had been acquired by composite offices by 1914 (and sixteen by 1919). To some extent this last development was a consequence of the attraction of life offices for fire companies seeking extended connections throughout the country, and access to the potential fire business of their mortgage and other investments. But the disappearance of specialist proprietary life offices was also the outcome of the struggle for life business itself. In his report on the critical quinquennium 1906–10, the REA Actuary cited various examples of this trend—including the Commercial Union's acquisition of the Hand-in-Hand in 1905 and the Union in 1907, the Alliance's acquisition of the Provident Life in 1906, and the Law Union & Crown's acquisition of the Rock in 1909. As a result of such developments, he predicted that ordinary life business would eventually be controlled by 'influential "composite" companies transacting all classes of business' and by 'a few large mutual offices, who, by maintaining a high rate of bonus in the future, will be enabled to support a separate existence'.

In one respect, of course, the REA had anticipated the most significant feature of this process; for the Corporation was, in fact, a pioneer of composite business. By 1900 it included fire, life, marine and accident departments. To this extent, therefore, it had been both fortunate and forethoughtful. On the other hand, however, although the momentum which had transformed its situation in the 1890s continued (with the help of new accident premiums) to push up its income in the first decade of the twentieth century, the fact remained that its growth was hardly at all characterized by the combinations which other companies used as devices for rapid and dramatic expansion. As we shall see, this was to change in 1917, when the Corporation acquired the Car & General. But in the years before the First World War, and particularly in the period 1906–10, which

[1] Raynes, *British Insurance*, chapter XVIII.

saw the peak of amalgamation activity, the only comparable step taken by the Corporation was the eminently sound and successful, but basically limited, acquisition of the National Provincial Plate Glass Insurance Company in 1909. Up to that time expansion had been secured by the extension of existing business, and even the development of the entirely new Accident Department was started from scratch, rather than by the purchase of going concerns.

In avoiding any extensive participation in the amalgamation boom, the Corporation was expressing satisfaction with and even jealousy of its own traditions. As the staff magazine put it in August 1903, the REA's growing premium income was the result of its own efforts and not of a series of amalgamations. The Corporation was the same as the Corporation of 1720, 'as the full-grown man has the same identity as the infant . . . The Royal Exchange is strong enough to stand alone now as it was in the past.' The Directors and chief officials were, apparently, very reluctant to consider any move which might cloud the Corporation's precise historical identity. Certainly, none of the acquisitions which took place was of serious proportions: full or partial control of four small marine companies was acquired in the 1890s;[1] and two unimportant fire offices, the North Yorkshire Agricultural Fire and the Brewers & General, were purchased in 1896 and 1898. A more significant move came in 1909, when, in order to round out its general accident department the Corporation purchased the National Provincial for some £250,000.

In fact, it was in 1909 that the Royal Exchange was obviously most influenced by the attractions of amalgamation and came nearest to altering its character as a consequence. In addition to purchasing the National Provincial, it made a strong but unsuccessful bid for the London & County Plate Glass Insurance Company, 'a severe competitor' of the National Provincial. Further, it acquired the trust business of the defunct Law Guarantee. But the most dramatic and significant moves came with very serious negotiations between the REA and the London Assurance for an amalgamation of these two ancient and coeval Corporations. This alone showed that the Court and management were not absolutely averse to a change in the REA's independent position and corporate character. The detailed discussions, which seem to have been largely initiated by the Governors of the two Corporations, envisaged an equal alliance which would have been entirely fitting from the historical viewpoint, although not one which would have greatly diversified the Royal Exchange's business— except in the sense of strengthening its overseas position. In the event, the

[1] Above, pp. 259–60.

obstacles to the amalgamation lay almost entirely in the actual financial terms, rather than in any points of principle. In general, Whymper, the Corporation's Secretary, anticipated many advantages from the move: a saving of capital, a long-run economy in reducing overhead costs, a reduction of competition, the ability to retain larger lines in fire underwriting, and 'the prestige of large figures, which undoubtedly has its effect on the public'. More specifically, the Fire Manager felt that, while 'in English business . . . they cannot compare with us', in overseas fire underwriting the London's long experience of almost fifty years had built up a strong and prosperous business which would be of great help to the REA, which 'started almost the last in the race'.

Other than this episode, however, there is little indication that the Corporation was at all tempted to be a serious participant in the pre-1914 amalgamation movement. As a result, it did not attain the spectacular size of the new combinations. (In 1914 the biggest firm, the Commercial Union, had total premiums in excess of £7·5 million, as against the REA's £1·9 million.) Yet it is pertinent to emphasize that, in spite of this, it remained a large-scale composite office, influential as well as old, and with world-wide connections. Further, almost alone of the large composite offices, its growth was based almost entirely on the expansion of its own business rather than the acquisition of other people's.

The fact that the REA differed in degree, rather than in kind, from the very substantial composite offices of the pre-war insurance industry, meant that it shared with them most of the difficulties which were the result of growth and the diversification of underwriting departments. In particular, it encountered the problems of management and control implicit in rapid growth. We have already seen how this affected the structure and administration of agency and branch systems. Comparable problems soon emerged in relation to other areas of corporate organization—in particular, departmental management.

As the Corporation grew, so there arose a tension between the needs, on the one hand, for departmental initiative and self-confidence, and on the other, for some form of central direction and control. The accident business provided an important example of this problem in 1906–7, when the passing of the Workmen's Compensation Act opened a vast new field for insurance companies, and when the ambitions of the Committee of Accounts in this respect had to give way to the more cautious reaction (then also influenced by the depleted reserves following the San Francisco disaster) of the Governors, the Treasury Committee and the Secretary.[1]

[1] See above, pp. 265–6.

In the last resort, it was the central rather than the departmental management which was to determine the development of the Royal Exchange. Yet, in a period of rapid growth, especially growth achieved through, and against the historical background of, strong and relatively independent departments, it was not always easy to assert this crucial principle. In fact, the Corporation only began to wake up to the implications of growth and proliferation in the first decade of this century—and it was admitted in 1909, in the course of negotiations with the London Assurance, 'that efficient management was wanting in the past, and that the greater control now exercised is only beginning to take effect'. By then, however, the need for constant control and co-ordination was beginning to be fully recognized. Business was being extended at home and abroad; new departments were growing rapidly; the Corporation was world-wide in structure, and responsible for a multitude of different types of insurance. The rôle of the Court and its traditional committees was no longer entirely adequate to give a central thrust to, and ensure an effective working in all parts of, the Corporation. More than this, it was also appreciated that the deployment of continuous management functions at the centre would necessitate some more explicit participation by departmental officials in the main deliberation of the Governors and Directors. These twin needs were, of course, being felt in all large and growing insurance offices. In most of them the answer was found in the appointment of a General Manager to serve as a central focus of management and control, and to 'represent' the other officials to the Directors. Indeed, the rise of the modern composite insurance office was functionally related to the birth of the modern General Manager, and there is no example of really successful corporate growth on a large scale and by amalgamation, which was not also characterized by the emergence of a strong, driving individual, possessing and willing to use very great authority. The answer to corporate problems tended to be individual management. At the Royal Exchange, however, the problem was tackled somewhat later, and in a significantly different way.

It was in 1911 that the Court acknowledged its difficulties by asking a special committee to appraise the existing management system in light of 'the increased and increasing operations of the Corporation'. The result was a recommendation 'that some central authority for general management should be created', and that it take the form of a Committee of Management, consisting of the three Governors. The Committee, which would invite Departmental Managers on a regular rota, would be a means 'of concentrating and more effectually supervising the management of the various classes of business conducted by the Corporation'. When the Court of Proprietors accepted these changes, the REA ceased to be 'probably the only insurance company of any importance in the City of London which has no [General] Manager or Management Committee'.

As we shall see, there were some respects in which the appointment of the Committee of Management instead of (or, rather, without) the appointment of a General Manager, was an unsatisfactory solution to prevailing problems.[1] Nevertheless, the move was a clear indication that the Corporation had entered a new era. In particular, it was an explicit acknowledgement that inherited and conventional managerial structures had to be adapted along radical, rather than piecemeal, lines to the demands of large-scale enterprise in the various branches of modern insurance. Slowly, and even painfully, this need had been impressed upon the Royal Exchange. Modernization, building on tradition where appropriate, had necessarily to influence the structure as well as the offerings and operations of the Corporation.

[1] Below, pp. 372-3.

PART D

Capital and Corporation
1800-1914

By the outbreak of the First World War the Royal Exchange Assurance was almost 200 years old. So far, its history in that period, particularly in the nineteenth century, has been treated largely in terms of its under-writing business. Yet no company, and perhaps least of all an insurance company, can be understood solely in terms of its relative success as an enterprise. Its business policy is a projection of its character; all companies have a corporate presence as well as a legal personality. Where the life of the company is prolonged, and where its public image is a critical determi-nant of its success, it is impossible to ignore the factors which, from one generation to another, have shaped its ethos and its social relationships. Moreover, an insurance company's economic functions are not confined to underwriting. Over the long run its wealth, and the savings of its life policyholders, have to be invested in an enormous variety of uses. And this process, too, has reflected a corporate longevity which transcended the lives of any particular generation.

This part of the book is concerned with some of the most important aspects of the corporate character of the REA as they were shaped in the generations before the First World War. As far as its investment function is concerned, as chapter 13 indicates, over the very long run the Corpora-tion was influenced by the same factors, and in the same ways, as other large insurance offices. Nevertheless its own 'style' and outlook had a considerable effect on the timing and medium-term patterns of its invest-ment policies. The character of a corporation is, however, even more direct-ly reflected in its structure and in the lives of its members than in its business policies. The REA's management organization in the nineteenth and early twentieth centuries is examined in chapter 14, and its 'establish-ment' in chapter 15. Each illustrates the extent to which traditional patterns moulded the response of the Corporation to the economic and social forces which were transforming British insurance. At the same time, at a more general level, they exemplify the rôle which historical continuity necessarily plays in the evolution of social relationships within any long-lived institution. Finally, chapter 16 attempts to strike a balance between the business and the social factors—the enterprise and tradition—which interpenetrated the development of the Royal Exchange Assurance in a world in which constant change was becoming a dominant motif.

13

Investment Funds and Capital Markets
1800-1914

This chapter is concerned with the rôle of insurance companies as financial institutions: as channels for savings and sources of investment funds. The main thrust to this rôle naturally came with the growth of life business, and the concomitant and necessary accumulations of huge life funds, in the nineteenth century—although short-term insurances like marine, fire and accident also generated large accumulations, and the companies' paid-up capital was far from negligible. As far as life offices were concerned, their funds (which had been about £28 million in 1837) were estimated at about £50 million in 1856. Thenceforth they continued to rise steeply: by 1877, when the total assets of life offices were about £125 million, they were rightly spoken of as 'one of the largest monetary interests in this Kingdom'.[1] By the end of the century the funds of ordinary life offices had risen to £246 million, and by 1913 to £315 million. In addition, account has to be taken of non-life business (in 1913, for example, the total non-life funds, reserves and paid-up capital of British composite offices exceeded £66 million), and of the increasingly important funds of industrial insurance offices. Altogether, the various assets owned or controlled by British insurance companies on the eve of the First World War exceeded £500 million—equivalent to more than 5 per cent of total national capital.[2]

Although insurance companies were only one of the various types of financial institution to develop in the nineteenth century, their relative size and rapid growth, the absence of great variety in the capital market, and their long-run outlook, gave them a special place in the history of savings and investment. To a very large extent, nineteenth-century savings and investments were private and decentralized and there were relatively

---

[1] Walter Brown, 'Life Branch Work', *JFII*, I (1898), 9. (This paper was originally written in 1877.)

[2] Data for 1856 and 1870: Deuchar, 'Life Assurance Business', *JIA* (1890); for 1913: *JIA*, LVI (March 1925), p. 118. National capital (excluding land, which was, however, represented in insurance assets) is estimated at £9,200 million in 1914 in A. K. Cairncross, *Home and Foreign Investment*, 1870–1913 (1953), p. 4.

few important intermediate organizations between those who saved and those who invested. Some, of course, were evolving: banks, especially joint-stock banks, canalized capital, even though they rarely used it for long-run investment; savings banks, friendly societies and building societies also developed as incentives to the thrift of the growing numbers of lower middle- and even working-class families whose efforts made Victorian Britain a great age of capital accumulation.[1] Even so, life insurance remained the dominant means of stimulating both middle- and working-class savings, and of using those savings for extensive and long-run investment. In the early 1880s the annual increase in their assets was equivalent to about 7 per cent of domestic fixed capital formation. By 1913 ordinary life funds alone (including the ordinary funds of predominantly industrial offices) stood at some £390 million, and were equal to the total funds of all savings banks, friendly societies and building societies.

It should also be emphasized that the investment of their funds has been of critical significance to insurance companies themselves, as well as an influential element in the evolution of the capital market. This is obviously true with respect to life insurance, which is quite explicitly based upon the long-run augmentation of premium income by compound interest, and the profits or surplus of which are dependent in large part on the return from investment. Yet it is also true for other departments—marine, fire and accident. In these cases the very size of the annual premium income, together with the large sums invested as reserves against extraordinary contingencies, generate a steady flow of interest. It is this factor which can, in fact, salvage profit from a year of underwriting loss. Indeed, in the late nineteenth century, offices like the REA or the Atlas expected that interest would cover all or most of their normal dividend payments to shareholders. And in the early twentieth century most leading companies aimed at having reserve funds equal to annual premium incomes and limiting dividends to the amount earned from the investment of those funds.[2] Finally, the business significance of insurance investment was not confined to its use as a direct source of income. In fact, investment decisions were (and are) directly related to the management and profitability of underwriting departments. Thus, loans to individuals were often partly

[1] As early as the mid-nineteenth century deposits in trustee savings banks were about £30 million, the capital of friendly societies was almost £18 million, and building societies had an *annual income* of over £2 million. By 1913 trustee and Post Office savings banks deposits amounted to £256 million, friendly and collecting societies to £64 million, and building societies' assets to £66 million. See Fishlow, 'The Trustee Savings Banks, 1817–1861', *Journal of Economic History* (1961), 39; Hunt, *Business Corporation*, p. 119; Cleary, *Building Society Movement*, pp. 44, 275.

[2] Sir Norman Hill, *et al.*, *War and Insurance* (London, 1927), p. 60.

secured by life policies; while investment in or loans to commercial under-takings or even public authorities were frequently associated with a com-mitment to insure the debtor's property, especially where that property was the security for the loan.

From various angles, therefore, the investment of its constantly accumu-lating funds has always been a vital part of any insurance company's task. Further, that task has grown increasingly complex since the eighteenth century. For the single most important trend in the structure of insurance assets after 1800 was towards the diversification of investment. Writing in 1912 the Actuary of the Prudential contrasted the 'extremely limited' range of investments undertaken by life offices in the 1850s with the situa-tion as he knew it: 'the practice of the present day is to spread investments and to increase the field'.[1] Even so, the restricted variety of investments of the 1850s still represented a notable development away from the heavy dependence on Government securities and, to a much smaller extent, freehold mortgages which characterized the investment policy of life offices in the opening years of the century. By the middle years, in fact, mortgages secured on land and houses had largely replaced the National Debt as favourite outlets for life funds, although significant amounts of capital remained in Government securities and even more had been invested in improvement loans to local authorities, in mortgage and debenture loans to commercial undertakings, in annuities and in loans on life interests and against life policies. However, it was only in the late nineteenth century that substantial variety, and even adventurousness, was introduced: mort-gages fell drastically in importance; colonial and foreign government securities grew in favour; bonds, debentures and even the preferred and ordinary shares of British and foreign joint-stock enterprises became re-spectable items in portfolios.

This diversification was in large part based on the slow evolution of new attitudes and the desire to increase investment income within the bounds of security of capital. But it is also worth remembering that insur-ance companies were themselves dependent on changes in the capital market, which created new investment opportunities. Throughout most of the first half of the century the organized capital market only offered a narrow field for secure investment. For example, other than the public funds, there were at that time very few Stock Exchange securities—and most of these were ruled out by insurance companies as being too risky or speculative. Apart from central and local government loans, therefore, insurance offices relied on investments in which the personal element, or

[1] G. E. May, 'The Investment of Life Assurance Funds', *JIA*, XLVI (April 1912), 139.

at least personal contact between debtors, creditors, and agents, was very marked. This certainly suited the business network created by the offices, linked as they were with a host of agents, brokers and solicitors. Increasingly in the second half of the century, however, not only did insurance companies become more adventurous, but more, and more acceptable, investments and securities were offered as colonial government stocks were marketed and as the evolution of corporations and the Stock Exchange meant that private securities grew in number and trustworthiness as well as fashion.

1800–70: FROM PUBLIC FUNDS TO PRIVATE PROPERTY

Although in the eighteenth century some insurance companies had placed much of their capital in mortgages,[1] in the early nineteenth their assets were dominated by investments in the public funds. The REA, for example, with the exception of a few minor mortgage loans and one very large loan to the Government to help build Regent Street, invested almost exclusively in Government securities. As late as April 1838 they accounted for £1·3 million of its total assets of £1·9 million.[2] Other leading offices had commitments almost as large: the Equitable owned £7·2 million (market price) of Government stock, as against mortgages of just over £800,000, in 1822;[3] and the Atlas had 75 per cent of its total assets of £470,000 in public securities in 1825.

Part of this impressive accumulation was explained by monetary conditions during the Napoleonic Wars, when high interest rates reduced the price of Government stock to bargain levels. Between 1793 and 1805, for example, Three Per Cent Consols were nearly always below 60; and up to 1815 only fluctuated between 55 and 73. In these circumstances insurance companies purchased considerable amounts. Yet the attractiveness of Government stock was too long-lasting to be explained merely by war-time conditions. In fact, the purchase of Government securities had many advantages for insurance companies: they were homogeneous (in 1817 over £680 million of the National Debt of over £800 million was represented by only four stocks); they were extremely 'liquid', in that they could be

[1] Above pp. 74–5.

[2] Differences in procedures (over time and between companies) concerning the valuation of assets make accurate comparison or generalization very difficult. This was most marked for Stock Exchange securities. The REA valued its Government securities at 'cost' (i.e. purchase price) rather than at par or current market price (life valuations, however, used average market prices). In April 1842, to take one example, the Corporation's Bank of England and Government stock had a market value of £1,061,438, an original cost of £861,748, and a par value of £1,011,728. We can, of course, speak about the amounts of ordinary loans, mortgages, debentures and the like (which normally reflected the exact amount of investment) with much more confidence.

[3] Ogborn, *Equitable Assurances*, p. 173.

bought and sold very easily and with little incidental expense; they needed no close oversight; and the interest on them was absolutely guaranteed.

In addition to such investments, on at least one occasion the REA made a very large direct loan to the Government. This happened in 1813, when, under the direction of the architect John Nash, work began on 'New Street', later called Regent Street, to connect Westminster and Regent's Park. The project was the administrative responsibility of the Commissioners of H.M. Woods and Forests. And, as the anticipated cost was exceeded (Nash's estimate had been £384,754 but the final cost, excluding interest on loans, was almost £1·5 million), so they were authorized by Parliament to borrow money on the credit of land revenues. In two instalments, in August 1814 and November 1815, the Royal Exchange lent £300,000 to the Commissioners. The loan was at a 5 per cent rate of interest, which was reduced to 4 per cent in 1822, and repaid soon after.[1] But, in addition to the interest, a clause in the leases granted by the Commissioners obliged tenants to take out fire insurance with the Corporation, and some of these policies were reputed to have lasted well into the twentieth century.

In general however, and with the further and rather special exception of insurance company investment in Government annuities after 1808,[2] most investment with the Government was in ordinary Stock Exchange securities. In spite of their advantages, however, Government securities had two very serious drawbacks: the rate of interest was relatively low once peace-time conditions reduced their yield; and the price at which their value could be realized was unpredictable since it varied inversely with the general rate of interest. Thus, from the mid-1820s, as the price of the funds rose, so their yield fell: the average return on Consols only exceeded 3½ per cent for two years in the period 1828–1914, and for most of the time it was barely above 3 per cent. This, together with the fluctuations in realizable value, was naturally worrying to insurance companies in a period when competition and bonus policies emphasized the importance of investment as a source of profit. It must be remembered, too, that most offices based their premiums on an assumed interest rate of 3 per cent. If the actual yield on investments approximated to that figure, one very important source of surplus would disappear.

Admittedly, the great rise in the capital value of Government stocks

[1] *PP* (1828), pp. 417–18; *PP* (1868–9), xxxv, Pt. ii, 442–3. The Bank of England also lent £300,000 in 1817.
[2] Above, p. 134n. In 1830 the Guardian fearing a re-imposition of the war-time property tax) exchanged £100,000 Consols for a twenty-year annuity: Tarn and Byles, *Guardian Assurance*, p. 85. New Government annuity rates in 1829 were very favourable to investors at very old ages: *PP* (1890–1), XLVIII, 222–3.

since the Napoleonic War had brought considerable profits to offices fortunate enough to have purchased them at low war-time prices. But this gain was once-for-all; and when the Equitable persisted in holding large amounts well into the 1850s, it was criticized by some knowledgeable actuaries for pursuing a policy of 'infatuation'.[1] In 1850 the *Post Magazine* pointed out that the public funds 'barely afford a scale of interest suited to ordinary rates and *extraordinary* bonuses'; and by 1858 it was obvious to nearly all actuaries that, with respect to Government stocks:

the low rate of interest, and the uncertainty of the return of capital when wanted, make them exceedingly unsuitable for the operations of an assurance company, whose pledge is given for a fixed re-payment of capital, and whose profits depend on obtaining more than the rate of interest assumed in its tables. A wise board . . . or actuary would keep no more in them than is absolutely necessary for immediate purposes—would only buy below the average price, and take every fair opportunity of transferring the value to other securities whenever the price ranged considerably above the average.[2]

Further, one of the main arguments in favour of Consols (their liquidity) no longer applied when improved actuarial practice and a steadily growing market for life insurance ensured that the need for cash was predictable and that it could be supplied from a plentiful flow of income. Life funds were accumulated and need not be called upon to pay claims.[3]

Considerations of this sort readily explain the fall from fashion of Government securities. As Table 13.1 indicates, by the late 1830s the REA had begun to reduce its investment in them—and they fell to less than 30 per cent of its assets in 1857. Even this was somewhat high, compared with an office like the London Life (15 per cent) and with the national average, which was later estimated to have been 16 per cent in that year.[4] That this trend was closely associated with the pressures of the competitive market is shown by the fact that the crucial change in the Corporation's investment policy coincided with its adoption of with-profits life insurance in 1841. For it could now no longer ignore the competitive significance of its life surplus or the need to be more active in investment management. In April 1840 Government securities had accounted for some 70 per cent of the Corporation's assets; but within two years they had been reduced to

[1] See C. J. Bunyon, 'A letter to the Members of the Equitable Society' (1859), quoted in Ogborn *Equitable Assurances*, p. 225.

[2] *PM*, XI, 38 (21 September 1850); Samuel Brown, 'On the Investments of the Funds of Assurance Companies', *AM*, VII (April 1858), 244–5.

[3] In 1853 the Manager of the Standard Life pointed out that of his office's annual income of £200,000 more than 50 per cent could be invested: *SCAA*, Q. 938–40.

[4] For the national average: *PM*, LXXV, 654 (15 August 1914). The London Life figure is given in Brown, 'Investments of the Funds of Assurance Companies', *AM* (1858), pp. 253–4.

less than 45 per cent—i.e. from £1·2 million to £860,000. At the same time the Treasury Committee opened a new set of minutes to take account of the more complex decision-making involved in the diversification of investment policy.

TABLE 13.1. *REA pattern of investments, 1838–71*[1]

(£000)	April 1838	April 1843	October 1854	October 1860	April 1871
British Government securities	1,318	631 ⎫	⎫ 557 ⎬	984 ⎫	715
Bank of England stock	103	103 ⎬		⎬	57
Loans to local authorities	201	210 ⎭	526 ⎭	697	796
Mortgages on land and buildings	⎫	⎫	888 ⎫		972
Loans on railway and other debentures and bonds	⎬ 196	⎬ 858	⎬ 391 ⎭	⎬ 780	
Railway debenture stock	—	—	—	100 ⎫	539
Debenture stock	—	—	—	— ⎬	
Loans on life policies	—	—	27	30	46
Loans on life interests	—	—	25	178	9
Annuities purchased	21	18	24	23	10
Loans on stocks	—	—	—	48	—
Loans on reversions	—	—	—	—	76
Indian and colonial securities	—	—	—	96	104
Miscellaneous	—	—	18	186	17
Total investments :	£1,839	£1,819	£2,457	£3,123	£3,342

Of course, the general disadvantages of gilt-edged Stock Exchange securities did not entirely preclude investments in high-quality stock. In 1847, for example, the REA added £25,000 to its long-established holding of Bank of England 7 per cent Stock at a price yielding 3·9 per cent. And in 1858 it subscribed for £100,000 of 4 per cent East India Company loan stock at 97—and immediately sold it on the Stock Exchange at 98. But the most important examples in these respects came in the field of Indian and colonial government securities. In 1853 and 1854, for example, the Corporation purchased £100,000 6 per cent Canadian Bonds for just over 113—i.e. a yield of over 5¼ per cent. It sold half its holdings in 1863, when their price had fallen owing to 'unsettled feelings' in Canada, although five years later it bought £100,000 of 4 per cent Canadian Bonds at 109—this time guaranteed by the UK Government. In the late 1860s the Corporation also bought almost £100,000 of India debenture loan stock. On the other hand, the Corporation had refused to tender for twenty-year debentures of the British West Indies in 1853, even though the 4 per cent interest was guaranteed by Britain, because the effective yield on a similar

[1] Totals do not add because of rounding.

issue in 1852 had been too low: £90,000 had gone to the Economic Life for a return of just under 3¾ per cent on its investments. Nevertheless, as this example illustrates, insurance offices *were* prepared to subscribe to colonial loans (nine offices had tendered for the 1852 loan). And in 1853 the Secretary to the Treasury pointed out that the public loans 'for the improvement of the West Indies, and other parts of the British dominions, had been chiefly taken by insurance offices, and thus those funds which were accumulated for the benefit of private individuals became in the meantime useful instruments of public utility'.[1]

In spite of the beginnings of insurance company investment in what were essentially imperial development loans, this did not redress the dramatic decline in the offices' total holdings of public funds: by 1870–1, even including the 4·8 per cent of colonial securities, they amounted to only some 12 per cent of total assets. British funds alone were barely over 7 per cent.

The overall decline in the popularity of Government securities as an outlet for insurance funds in the middle decades of the century coincided with a sustained increase in the popularity of life insurance and, therefore, in the flow of money needing profitable investment. Between 1837 and 1856, for example, total British life funds rose from some £28 million to £54 million—or, on the average, by over £1 million annually. And in seeking outlets for these funds (and also for the money realized by the sale of Government stock) insurance companies were naturally influenced by the very desire to earn more than about 3½ per cent and to ensure stability of the value of their assets, which had brought Government securities into disfavour with them.

Some of the newly available funds could be invested in personal and individual loans of a sort peculiarly suited to insurance companies. In the 1850s for example, private loans on the security of insurance policies were already very popular, and the REA had an investment of some £50,000 in the late 1860s. By 1871 all life offices had invested over £5 million (almost 5 per cent of total assets) in such loans. Insurance companies also virtually monopolized loans on the security of life interests in estates and trust funds. Such loans, which were also covered by life policies, proved 'a great boon to the tenants of life estates, by substituting the honourable dealings of well known companies for the trickeries and impositions of sharp money lenders'.[2] Throughout the late 1850s the Royal Exchange had

[1] *Hansard's Parliamentary Debates*, 3rd Series, CXXIV, col. 1322 (8 March 1853).
[2] Brown, 'Investments of the Funds of Assurance Companies', *AM* (1858), p. 250; D. Deuchar, 'Investments', *JFII*, I (1898), 325–6.

well over £100,000 lent on the security of life interests, and by 1870 all life offices had loaned some £1·7 million on life interests and reversions. Finally, some offices invested considerable amounts of money in the purchase of private annuities—a practice which commenced during the Napoleonic Wars when the possibility of earning high interest rates on all except Government loans was frustrated by the legal prohibition on charging more than 5 per cent on private loans. Since 'annuities for life of the seller' were legally a form of gambling, they were exempt from the Usury Laws. Insurance companies were therefore attracted to them as alternatives to straight mortgage loans, for they yielded about 8 per cent or more, with a further income to be earned from the insurance policy normally required to cover the life of the borrower.[1] The REA did not participate very extensively in the annuity market: in the 1830s and 1840s it only had about £20,000 invested in this way, although in 1827 it advanced £57,000 on annuities to the Marquis of Chandos, who, as the Duke of Buckingham, was to ruin himself and his estates by financial recklessness. By 1838 the Corporation had invested £35,000 in annuities, including an advance of £8,000 at 10 per cent to Lord Duffus in 1805—which was still producing its annual £800 from the long-lived aristocrat!

On the whole, however, these categories of investment were relatively small as well as highly specialized. A far more important way of increasing and stabilizing investment income was to lend money, to individuals or corporations, which was well secured on real property. And the decline of Government securities in the early years of the century was therefore matched by the rise of mortgages of various sorts. By the late 1850s about two-thirds of all life office investments were in this form.[2] And at the Royal Exchange (which had secured an Act of Parliament, in 1825, to allow it to lend money on the security of estates), while Government securities were being drastically reduced, loans secured on private real property rose from less than £200,000 in April 1838 to £475,000 in April 1842. By October 1850 they stood at some £1 million: almost 50 per cent of all the Corporation's assets.

It was, of course, true that a straightforward mortgage of freehold land or housing offered both much more security of capital value and a somewhat higher rate of interest than Consols. Many an insurance company must have felt like the widow in Anthony Trollope's novel (admittedly written when mortgage rates had fallen somewhat), who had 'every shilling

[1] Dickson, *Sun Insurance Office*, pp. 258–9. (In 1830 the Sun had 28 per cent of its investments in annuities.)
[2] *PM*, LXXV, 654 (15 August 1914).

laid out in a first-class mortgage on land at 4 per cent. That does make one feel so secure! The land can't run away.'[1] Yet this form of loan, whether on land or housing, even though it probably became the single most important investment for insurance companies, was not the only class of asset subsumed in the category of 'mortgages'. In fact, it included any loan secured on property, whether by bond, debenture or legal mortgage, and whether that 'property' was land, buildings, securities, life insurance policies or even income. In October 1854, for example, although the REA had invested £1,374,000 in 'loans on mortgage', only some £888,000 was accounted for by conventional mortgage loans on land and houses. The bonds and debentures of railways, docks, mines, breweries and the like amounted to a further £391,000. Loans on life policies, life interests in property and annuities each accounted for some £25,000. Prior to this date, even the very large loans to local authorities (other than Poor Law Unions) secured on the rates were lumped into the 'mortgage' category. Moreover, even where the reference was quite precisely to the mortgage of land or buildings—and this was by far the most important category, accounting for some 40 per cent and more of life office assets in 1870[2]—it embraced a very wide variety of investments.

There were, however, four principal types of mortgage investment which need emphasis as examples of Victorian economic and social development and of the new rôle of insurance companies in facilitating a sequence of changes critically dependent upon the supply of capital. They were: loans on security of freehold (mostly country) estates; loans to urban developers engaged in the construction of housing, particularly in London; loans to local authorities engaged in physical improvements; and loans to railways and other commercial and industrial firms.

Conventional freehold mortgages presented few if any problems to insurance companies up to the 1850s. Many were no doubt like the REA in preferring a limited number of reasonably large-scale loans; in October 1850 virtually all its mortgages on freehold estates were based on loans to six individuals totalling £200,000; and by the mid-1860s the Earl of Strathmore alone had borrowed £130,000 and the Earl of Charlemont £138,000 from the Corporation. (The average size of the Sun's mortgages was almost £20,000 in the early, and over £30,000 in the later, nineteenth

---

[1] *The Last Chronicle of Barsetshire* (1867), chapter 25.

[2] In addition, loans on local rates and rent charges accounted for 9·3 per cent, debenture and debenture stocks for 9·5 per cent, and loans against policies for 4·8 per cent—and all of these had been lumped together in 'mortgages' by some or most companies in the previous decades.

century.)[1] Clearly, too, the predilection of the companies for reasonably long-term loans made them particularly appropriate agencies for the heavy borrowings to which contemporary landowners resorted for capital improvements to their estates. Between 1846 and 1875, it has been estimated, some £25 million (from all sources) was sunk in agricultural improvements; and in 1853 the Secretary to the Treasury pointed out that since insurance funds were 'of a nature to be invested for a longer period than the funds of banking establishments could ordinarily be, the landed interest had derived the greatest possible facilities in the improvement of their land from the funds accumulated in the hands of these offices'.[2] It was, as the historian of the Sun has pointed out, a case of middle-class savings coming to the aid of the landed interest.[3]

In the 1840s and 1850s Government legislation extended the traditional market for this sort of loan. Up to £4 million of Government loans for drainage and associated agricultural improvements was made available by the Public Money Drainage Acts of 1846 and 1850; and the process of private lending for the same purposes was facilitated by the Private Money Drainage Act of 1849 and the incorporation of various specialist, and privileged, land-improvement companies. Life tenants of settled estates, and other estate-owners, were by this legislation enabled to borrow money in order to drain and improve their lands. Repayment of the loan and interest was by an annuity (usually spread over twenty-five years), which then became a first charge on the estate. The fact that repayment was by an annuity made such a loan particularly suited to a company (since individuals would not normally wish to assume the annual task of re-investing part of their capital). And in the event the specialist land-improvement companies borrowed extensively from insurance offices: according to the Managing Director of one of them, 'we [the Lands Improvement Company] get all our money from insurance companies', effectively selling the rent charges to the offices in batches of £20,000 to £30,000.[4] Apparently, however, the REA did not participate in this business, although it was approached by at least two of the specialist drainage companies (the West of England and South Wales in 1849 and the General Land Drainage and Improvement Company throughout the 1850s) in the hope that it would lend them large amounts of money to

1 Dickson, *Sun Insurance Office*, p. 249.
2 J. H. Clapham, *Economic History of Modern Britain*, II (1932), 271; Hansard's *Parliamentary Debates*, 3rd Series, CXXIV, col. 1322 (8 March 1853).
3 Dickson, *Sun Insurance Office*, p. 250.
4 Select Committee of the House of Lords on the Improvement of Land, *PP* (1873), XVI, Q.899, 900, 931, 932. Compare Q.4031, 4033, 4034.

finance their ventures. This it refused to do, principally because the proffered interest of 4 or $4\frac{1}{2}$ per cent was too low. On the other hand, the Corporation did invest a considerable amount in *direct* loans for drainage purposes.[1]

Considered as insurance investment, mortgages always had a distinct advantage over Government securities in terms of the stability of capital value. Further, for most years in the 1830s and 1840s, when mortgage loans earned 5 per cent, they also enjoyed a distinct advantage in terms of interest—for the yield on Consols then varied between 3 and $3\frac{1}{2}$ per cent. With the exception of 1844 and 1845, when cheap money conditions forced the REA to consider loans at 4 per cent, the Corporation managed to obtain 5 per cent on its mortgages throughout this period. By the early 1850s, however, and particularly in 1852 and 1853, when interest rates reached extraordinarily low levels (Bank Rate was at 2 per cent for nine months) it was lending large amounts on good mortgages at $4\frac{1}{2}$ per cent. Even this was somewhat high: in February 1853 the Corporation's Actuary named eight leading offices which had lent on mortgages as low as $3\frac{1}{2}$ per cent; and 4 per cent was considered a reasonable rate. Apparently, interest rates were depressed because an improvement in the organization of the capital market was attracting investment funds from the general public and trustees into mortgages. More particularly, this improvement was leading to a much closer link between the market for Consols and the market for mortgages: low yields (and therefore high prices) in the former led to a movement of private funds into the latter, with a consequent fall in interest rates. By 1856 a leading actuary claimed that the average difference in their yield was a mere $\frac{1}{2}$ per cent, although even that could make a great difference to the accumulation of a life fund.[2]

These developments naturally had an effect on the willingness of insurance companies to continue to plough money into freehold mortgages. The REA, for example, had increased the proportion of its assets lent on the conventional mortgage of land and housing from some 5 per cent in 1839 to 18 per cent in October 1844 and about a third in the early 1850s. In the late 1850s, however, it ran down this mortgage element in its investments, although there was some revival in the 1860s, as mortgage rates rose, and by 1870 the Corporation's mortgages on land had risen to £747,367 and on houses and other buildings to £201,578—in total, some 27 per cent of assets. See Table 13.2.

[1] By 1878 drainage and improvement companies had lent £8 million to landowners. For the general situation see Clapham, *Economic History of Modern Britain*, II, 271–2; David Spring, *The English Landed Estate in the Nineteenth Century* (1963), chapter V.

[2] Brown, 'Investments of the Funds of Assurance Companies', *AM* (1858), pp. 253–4.

While the REA was accumulating its very large investment in mortgages in the 1840s it was doing more than providing investment funds (or spending money) for rural estate-owners or urban landowners. It was also participating in a striking new development by which a handful of insurance companies helped finance the building activities of various large-scale London housing contractors.

The growth of British cities, and particularly London, in the nineteenth century naturally involved a substantial amount of capital investment in private housing. Traditional builders tended to construct housing to order, using their own, or limited amounts of borrowed, capital. Increasingly, however, estate-owners and building contractors were promoting much more extensive and speculative developments, which built houses ahead of demand and needed a flow of capital much in excess of the entrepreneur's own resources. By the 1850s, according to evidence before a Government commission in 1857, 'the general practice is to build upon a large scale, relying upon a demand for houses when they have been built . . . and raising money upon mortgages as the buildings proceed. Almost the whole of Belgravia and Tyburnia, and countless thousands of villas around London are built upon that principle.'[1] This development was itself dependent on the evolution of new financial arrangements to tap the savings of the general public. A vast amount of capital was, in fact, channelled to builders by solicitors acting on behalf of individual clients. Some of the new joint-stock banks also participated in this novel corner of the capital market. And from the late 1830s or early 1840s, a handful of insurance companies, with a renewed interest in mortgage investment, became important creditors in the field. Nearly all the London business was done by the REA, the London Assurance and the Hand-in-Hand (although about ten others also participated in the period 1840–78).[2]

The REA began its building loans to London estate developers in 1839, with a loan of £49,000 on the security of 'Laing's Estate', of leasehold houses in Clapton and Denmark Hill. This particular investment (very little is known about its details) actually went sour, and the Corporation had to take over the estate some time in 1842 or 1843, invest more money

---

[1] Quoted in J. R. T. Hughes, *Fluctuations in Trade, Industry and Finance, 1850–1860* (1960), p. 226.

[2] For a detailed treatment of these developments see D. A. Reeder, 'Capital Investment in the Western Suburbs of Victorian London' (Ph.D. thesis, Leicester University, 1965). I am most grateful to Dr Reeder for allowing me to use his information. Also see H. J. Dyos, 'The Speculative Builders and Developers of Victorian London', *Victorian Studies*, XI, Supplement (Summer 1968), 641–90. The Hand-in-Hand, which as a mutual company had been closely identified with the building trade, in fact made similar loans to speculative builders in the early years of the eighteenth century: John, 'Insurance Investment', *Economica* (1953), p. 146.

TABLE 13.2. *REA mortgage investments, 1839–70*

	April 1839	Oct. 1844	Oct. 1854	Oct. 1860	Oct. 1870
On land	n.a.	n.a.	£474,251	£212,757	£747,367
On houses	n.a.	n.a.	£413,897	£221,494	£201,578
Total:	c. £100,000	c. £345,000	£888,148	£434,251	£948,945
As proportion of all investments:	5·5%	18·6%	33·4%	13·9%	27·0%

in repairing faulty construction, and manage the estate itself, which it did at a fair return for over sixty years. The Directors nevertheless persevered with such development loans in the 1840s and, quite apart from 'the unfortunate investment' in Laing's Estate, by the summer of 1846 they had invested some £200,000 in loans to three builders (George Wyatt, £135,400; Charles Freake, £40,000; and Matthew Wyatt, £25,000). Small amounts were also lent to another three or four, although the Corporation was careful to concentrate most if its investments on a very small number of builders principally concerned in the construction of high-quality housing in the West End—mostly in the fashionable area of Paddington immediately north of Hyde Park. Loans were generally offered up to 50 per cent, sometimes two-thirds, of the REA Surveyor's valuation of the housing, and extended in instalments either as the houses were actually completed or, more rarely, as work progressed on them. The rate of interest was 5 per cent. Three early examples of this sort of transaction came in December 1840 and January 1841: William Kingdom was to be lent £35,000 on the mortgage of houses then being built in Westbourne Terrace and Hyde Park Gardens; George Wyatt was advanced £10,000 on four 'first-rate houses' in Sussex Square, immediately opposite Hyde Park (estimated value on completion: £20,000); and Charles J. Freake was lent up to £14,000 on seven houses then being built in Eaton Square, to the west of Buckingham Palace Gardens and valued, when completed, at £26,367. In subsequent years Wyatt and Freake extended their loans— Wyatt on houses in Stanhope Street (just east of Regent's Park), and in Sussex Square, Westbourne Street, Bathurst Street and Gloucester Square (all just north of Hyde Park); and Freake on his Eaton Square property. Further, by 1844 the Corporation had advanced £25,000 to Matthew Wyatt on houses in Hyde Park Street, Hyde Park Square, Southwick Street and Gloucester Square.

Throughout the 1840s, therefore, the Corporation was pursuing an investment policy which would perhaps have been considered adventurous to the point of recklessness by a previous generation. Yet the rate of interest was fairly good, fire insurance premiums could be made to benefit on a long-run basis, the loan values were apparently very well secured, and close relations with good customers for loans were established. In the event, however, things did not go smoothly: in August 1846 the Corporation's biggest debtor, George Wyatt, went bankrupt with debts of over £150,000—of which £135,400 (plus £3,229 arrears of interest) was owed to the Corporation. And in spite of all the precautions, including the 50 per cent margin, the security was neither as good nor as saleable as had been hoped. In 1850 the Treasury Committee regretfully reported that the poor prices realized by the sale of houses indicated that there would be a loss of £30,000 (of which £20,000 was arrears of interest). The unpleasantness of this experience apparently proved chastening to the Royal Exchange. Admittedly, it remained loyal to one of its earliest builder-debtors, Charles Freake, increasing its development loans to him to £96,000 by February 1853, and subsequently lending him a further £30,000 on freehold land. But other than this, and a loan of £20,000 in 1852 to James McGill on forty-five houses (selling price: £2,800 each) then being built in Craven Hill Gardens, a 'choice situation' on the 'Paddington Estate', there is little evidence of further development loans of this sort—even though other insurance companies continued them in the 1850s and 1860s.[1]

As we have seen, in 1814 and 1815 the REA had helped finance the construction of one of London's most imposing streets. In the 1840s and 1850s, with its loans to private urban developers, the Corporation made another significant and rather specialized contribution to the construction of London's physical capital. At the same time, however, and together with other insurance companies, it began a much more extensive contribution to the improvement of social capital throughout the country by its participation in loans to local authorities for the varied works of construction which were needed, first, to administer the New Poor Law of 1834, and second (and more importantly) to ameliorate the unsanitary and uncivilized condition of Britain's new and teeming cities.

These loans first became available in the 1830s, when Poor Law Unions began to borrow extensively on the security of the rates, in order to construct workhouses, pauper asylums and other facilities under the New

---

[1] Dr Reeder (pp. 162, 168) shows that the London Assurance invested £89,400 on building loans in 1858–68, and the Hand-in-Hand £105,450 in 1868–78. Earlier, in 1841–2, the London Assurance had invested some £100,000.

Poor Law. In the 1840s and 1850s other authorities also went into the capital market: county magistrates, town councils or improvement commissioners, local boards of health, and burial boards. Town Improvement Commissioners (under special local acts) were empowered to borrow against municipal rates to improve drainage, water supply, and other amenities; local Boards of Health (under the Public Health Act of 1848) could similarly borrow in order to improve public sanitation and burial arrangements. Magistrates and county commissioners also borrowed on the rates in order to build session houses, police stations, houses of correction and lunatic asylums.

Such loans as these had two important advantages for insurance offices. First, being secured by the rates, they had very strong guarantees, particularly where a Central Government agency was involved—as with the Poor Law Board and the General Board of Health. Second, the loans were repayable as annuities over long periods of time: twenty years in the case of Poor Law Unions; thirty years in most other cases. As was the case with drainage loans to rural landowners, this placed the small-scale investor at a disadvantage since part of his capital would have to be constantly reinvested. On the other hand, such loans were 'peculiarly suitable for a corporation or company, whose funds constantly allow of surpluses to be employed in fresh loans, and whose officials are always engaged in seeking after new channels for their application'. As a result of the less keen competition, it was claimed, interest rates were higher than on ordinary mortgages, even though the security was better.[1] There was also an indirect advantage to insurance companies, since local authorities were potential customers for fire insurance policies. When, for example, the REA agreed to lend £25,000 to the Guardians of the West Derby Asylum in June 1849, the Corporation was also promised the fire insurance on the building.

The earliest recorded loan to a Poor Law Union by the REA was in October 1836, when £6,000 was lent to the Guardians at Melton Mowbray. Between then and October 1837 the Corporation lent £212,000 to fifty-two Unions throughout the country. By April 1838 it had £201,551 outstanding in loans to Poor Law Unions, which was more than all its other non-Government investments put together. In the 1840s Poor Law Union loans fell and then rose again, amounting to £179,092 in April 1850. In the same decade, however, there was an increasing amount of lending to other authorities: for example, £10,000 to the Monmouthshire Magistrates to build a House of Correction (1841); £2,500 to the Tunbridge Wells

[1] Brown, 'Investments of the Funds of Assurance Companies', *AM* (1858), p. 248.

Town Improvement Commissioners (1846); £10,400 to the St Marylebone Commissioners for Public Baths and Washhouses (1848); and £50,000 to the Corporation of Manchester (1849). By October 1854 loans to Poor Law Unions had fallen to £128,289 and loans to 'town commissioners' (which apparently included all county and municipal authorities except Poor Law, Health and Burial Boards) had reached £172,975. But even more important in the early 1850s were loans to local Boards of Health, established as a result of the Public Health Act of 1848, with powers to improve cleaning, sewerage, drainage and water supply (the Metropolitan Interment Act of 1850 had facilitated similar borrowing by Burial Boards). By October 1854 the REA had invested £224,347 in such loans. Between October 1854 and October 1860 total loans on the security of local rates increased from some £525,000 to £697,000—Boards of Health rising to £386,000, and Burial Boards coming in at about £29,000.[1]

The rate of interest on loans to public bodies naturally varied somewhat. In 1836 and 1837, £154,600 of the total of £212,000 loans to Poor Law Unions were at 4½ per cent (the balance was at 5 per cent). About 1840, 5 per cent was the prevailing rate, although in 1844 and 1845 low interest rates in general forced some local loans down to 4½ per cent. By 1846, however, the Corporation was once more lending at its anticipated 5 per cent, although its continued insistence on this rate (it initially declined to tender for £500,000 of loans at 4½ per cent invited by the Office of the General Board of Health, in May 1851, for the purposes of the Interment Act) could not be fully maintained in the cheap-money period of 1852 and 1853. Then, among other loans, it lent £6,000 to the Burial Board of Marylebone and £40,000 to the Swansea Board of Health at 4 per cent; and was even underbid on a tender of 4 per cent to help finance a Middlesex County Lunatic Asylum.

In the late 1850s, the Corporation had most of its local loans out at 5 per cent—and was adamant, particularly in light of the great extent of its business, that it wished to maintain that rate. This was so even when the (central) Poor Law Board, with which the REA had a special relationship,

[1]   *REA investments on the security of local rates*

	April 1838	Oct. 1850	Oct. 1854	Oct. 1860
Poor Law Unions	£201,550	£171,774	£128,289	£106,538
Town and county authorities	—	72,875	172,975	175,655
Boards of Health	—	—	224,347	386,351
Burial Boards	—	—	—	28,548
Total:	£201,550	£244,649	£525,611	£697,092
Proportion of total investments:	11·0%	11·6%	21·4%	22·3%

informed the Corporation's Solicitor in 1860 that while Poor Law Unions 'are now borrowing considerable sums which was likely to continue and had no difficulty in getting all they wanted at 4½ per cent, the Board would prefer the money to come from the Royal Exchange if it would lend at that rate'. By the mid-1860s, however, and notably in 1866, the Corporation was having no difficulty in lending money on the rates at 6 per cent, and in October of that year, with £869,000 so invested (and repayments of £40,000 annually) the Treasury Committee 'decided that it was not desirable to add further to the amount now invested in such security and that for the present they would decline any further applications—except in special cases, and then not under six per cent interest'. In 1870 the REA was one of the leading investors in local loans—with £800,000 of assets out of the total for *all* life offices of just over £10 million. And the total insurance loans for these purposes must have been well over 10 per cent of total local authority borrowings (which reached some £93 million in 1874–5).[1]

A more experimental development from the late 1830s was the loan of capital to commercial undertakings. This was made possible not merely by the new life funds but also by the development of the economy which necessitated huge investments in transport and industrial enterprises. What is, in fact, striking is the relative speed with which insurance offices adapted their ideas and practices to take account of the new needs and opportunities inherent in economic growth. As with agricultural and urban improvement, so with railways, docks, shipping, mines and brewing, and the like, although not yet quite so extensively, insurance companies helped channel the flow of capital which shaped the development of Victorian England. It was, of course, too early for insurance funds to be invested in the risky share capital of mid-nineteenth century joint-stock companies. In 1843 investments in railway shares were said to be 'decidedly undesirable and incompatible' with the high character of an insurance company.[2] And as late as 1865 the REA refused to lend £50,000 to the London, Chatham & Dover Railway for six to twelve months on the security of preference shares—even when offered the blandishment of a 40 per cent margin and fire insurances of between £50,000 and £100,000. Although preference and ordinary shares became somewhat more popular in the 1860s (by 1870 they accounted for £3·1 million [2·8 per cent] of British life office assets), for most of the period insurance companies

---

[1] Cairncross, *Home and Foreign Investment*, p. 142.
[2] Evidence of Griffith Davies (Actuary of the Guardian) to the Select Committee on Joint Stock Companies, *PP* (1844), VII, Q.1768.

steadfastly avoided the purchase of non-Government Stock Exchange securities. Yet, where loans could be firmly secured on real property—either through a direct mortgage, or a debenture, or a bond—insurance offices proved surprisingly ready to lend money to commercial enterprises at an early date.

If we take the example of the REA—which was in general one of the most cautious of offices—it had purchased £30,000 of 5 per cent bonds of the London & Birmingham Railway by January 1838. Subsequently, as the Corporation diversified out of Government securities in the early 1840s, it began to lend much more extensively to railways: starting in the spring of 1841 with a loan of £25,000 to the Durham & Sunderland Railway Company (secured by a bond because a mortgage might have made the Corporation liable for leaseholds in the case of the railway's failure), by October 1842 the REA had lent £216,000 (all at 5 per cent) to seven railways—on an assortment of securities including the mortgages of private estates as well as of the railways and their tolls, bonds and debentures. After the first year or so, however, it became more normal to use debentures. Throughout this period, of course, the railways were growing very rapidly indeed: in the United Kingdom mileage open at the end of each year shot up from just under 750 in 1838 to some 1,500 in 1840 and almost 2,000 in 1842. By 1843 the paid-up capital and loans (the latter amounting to about one-third of the total) of UK railways, amounted to £65·6 million.[1]

Even when the Corporation reduced the number of its loans to two, in the face of the collapse of the railway mania in the late 1840s, these two (the Preston & Wyre and the Shropshire Union Railway) maintained the earlier level of the Corporation's financial commitment to railways. The Preston & Wyre owed £38,000 by October 1850. The Shropshire Union had been formed by the United Ellesmere & Chester Canal in 1846, and the REA (which had already lent the Canal Company £15,000 in 1842) extended a loan of £252,543 to facilitate the construction.

Throughout the 1840s the Royal Exchange had about 10 per cent of its investments in loans to railways. By the early 1850s such investments were widely accepted as appropriate for insurance companies;[2] the Government Actuary even told the Select Committee on Assurance Associations in 1853 that his advice to companies had been 'to sell out all their money

---

[1] Mitchell, *British Historical Statistics*, p. 225.
[2] See, for example, Tarn and Byles, *Guardian Assurance*, p. 86; Dickson, *Sun Insurance Office*, p. 262.

in the funds' and invest it in railway debentures and in mortgages.[1] Later in the decade, it has been estimated, debentures (presumably not confined to railways) accounted for about 8 per cent of all life office investment— and railway debentures amounted to 14 per cent of the Rock Life's £2 million of investment in 1856.[2] From the late 1850s the insurance offices also began to purchase the debenture *stock* which railways were beginning to issue: by October 1859 the REA had acquired some £100,000 of such stock.[3]

In October 1869 the REA had £263,595 of investments in railways, and although this represented a proportionate fall from the heady level of 1842 (7·4 as against 12·1 per cent of total investments) it was still a sizeable commitment. Unfortunately, the form of national statistics precludes a similar estimate for all offices, but it is obvious that these investments, together with the loans which helped finance the construction of private housing and public services in the growing urban areas, gave the insurance companies an important rôle in the contemporary capital market: in the mid-nineteenth century nearly half of all British savings went towards the construction of railways and the growth and improvements of towns.[4]

From well before the 1860s the REA was also active in the capital market for other trading companies, even though in aggregate they rarely matched its commitments to railways. By October 1842, for example, it had lent £10,000 to a hotel company; £10,000 on bonds to the Trustees of the Liverpool Docks and £58,000 on debentures to the St Katharine Dock Company; £50,000 to the Royal Mail Steam Packet Company and £20,000 to the Pacific Steam Company. In 1844 and 1845 it lent £90,000, on the security of property mortgages and personal bonds, to two colliery companies; and between 1846 and 1850 lent £100,000 to a brewery company, Felix Calvert & Company, on the mortgage of freehold estates and brewery property—apart from £80,000 to Major-General Calvert, a member of the family, in 1848. By 1871 just under half of the Corporation's £529,280 investment in debentures and debenture stock was accounted for by loans to non-railway companies.

In loans to trading companies, invariably secured on real property, as in loans on urban property, the possibility of fire insurance was an added

[1] *SCAA*, Q.600–1, 608.

[2] *PM*, LXXV, 33 (15 August 1914), 654; Brown, 'Investments of the Funds of Assurance Companies', *AM* (1858), pp. 253–4.

[3] Between 1859 and 1869 UK railway debenture stock and funded debt rose from £5·6 million to £34.5 million: *PP* (1860), LXI, 199; *PP* (1870), LIX, 289.

[4] Cairncross, *Home and Foreign Investment*, p. 2.

attraction—although this did not prevent the Corporation declining to lend the Norfolk Railway Company £50,000 in 1847, or a Leeds locomotive manufactory £25,000 (to whose fire risk of £50,000 the Fire Manager, Edward Bird, pronounced a 'very great repugnance') in 1849. Nor, in these transactions, did the Corporation relax its customary vigilance in matters affecting its good name as well as its security. In 1863, for example, it refused to lend the Metropolitan Railway £200,000 for six months in order to provide the temporary deposit required by Parliament as a preliminary to an application for a Bill to extend the line. The reason was 'that the system is an evasion of the intentions of the legislature, and if, as is quite possible, it should someday be called into question in Parliament, the Corporation would hardly like to have their name mixed up in the matter, as parties in such transactions'. And in 1867 the Treasury Committee brusquely turned down a capital redemption policy in the form of a proposal to participate with the Liverpool & London & Globe in accepting a premium of £712,556 from an American railway company, and contracting to pay £2 million to the railway bondholders after thirty years: 'The railway referred to is not considered a sound speculation, and the proposal is merely a scheme to enable certain speculators to raise money on security of a property of perhaps little or no value.'

Although the REA and other insurance companies were, therefore, still somewhat circumspect in their approach to investment matters in the 1850s and 1860s, the more important point is that their participation in the contemporary capital market was both more extensive and more varied than is usually imagined. As early as the 1840s, in addition to Government securities and loans on conventional freehold mortgages, they were participating extensively in railway development, the financing of dock companies and urban development. By 1870, although a single type of investment, the mortgage, was overwhelmingly the most important category, it included loans for very diverse purposes—ranging from investment and consumption expenditure by the landed aristocracy to the construction of urban and suburban housing and (to a smaller extent) the raising of capital by transport and manufacturing enterprises. In addition to mortgages, however, some 13 per cent of insurance capital was more directly invested in railway and other companies by the ownership of debentures, debenture stocks and preferred and other shares. Almost as much capital was placed at the disposal of local authorities for social improvements. And—through their loans on life policies, life interests, personal security and the like—insurance companies were also significant elements in the lively market for loans to individuals which must have had far-reaching economic and social consequences in Victorian Britain. Altogether, the growth of insurance, particularly life insurance, gave a powerful impulse to the heightened and more effective flow of capital which helped transform the contemporary British economy.

1870–1914: FROM HOME TO FOREIGN INVESTMENT

Between 1870 and 1914 the investments of those insurance companies which transacted life business, whether ordinary or industrial, increased almost fivefold: from some £110 million to over £500 million. Given the fact that British capital, at home and overseas, was slightly more than doubled in the same period,[1] this reflected a considerable growth in their already important rôle as financial intermediaries and channels for investment funds. By the opening of the twentieth century the funds of insurance companies were increasing by more than £10 million annually. No wonder, therefore, that the Secretary of the REA saw them as 'an important item among the capitalists of the world'. From one viewpoint, they attained this position by maintaining the adaptability and pursuing the diversity which had characterized their investment activities between the 1830s and 1860s. In addition, however, the years after 1870 saw fundamental changes in the opportunities and pressures confronting insurance companies: on the one hand, landed property in Britain declined in significance and value, and the return on conventional investments sagged alarmingly in the late nineteenth century; on the other, overseas economic development opened new and broad, but none the less unfamilar, outlets for capital, and the evolution of a formal capital market was accelerated. To those concerned with the investment of insurance funds, times were indeed changing by the 1890s. As one commentator put it in 1891:[2]

Thirty years of the busiest and most changeful century which the world perhaps has known have had their effect, and the changes of the last few years seem the greatest and the most rapid of all. The value of broad acres in England has depreciated; the Three per Cents have lost a twelfth of their sweetness and all of their simplicity; Parliament has repeatedly enlarged the field of investments open to trustees; and the immense demand for and limited supply of securities formerly thought most suitable for insurance companies have had the effect of diminishing to a perilous extent their earning-powers, and has made some of them no longer desirable for our purposes. The keen competition for new pro-

[1] Cairncross, *Home and Foreign Investment*, p. 4.
[2] A. G. Mackenzie, 'On the Practice and Powers of Assurance Companies in regard to the investment of their Life Assurance Funds', *JIA*, xxix (July 1891), 186.

posals in *fin de siècle* insurance has, moreover, led to an increase in working expenses, which, showing as little abatement at present as the thirst of the policy-holder for large bonuses and special advantages, makes it all the more important that a satisfactory rate of interest should be maintained.

Against this sort of background, there were bound to be far-reaching changes in the responses and investment patterns of insurance companies. Three in particular stand out: a sharp fall in the relative significance of mortgages, from about half to less than a quarter of total investments, between 1870 and 1913; an equally spectacular increase in the importance of overseas assets, from about 7 per cent to perhaps 40 per cent and more; and (overlapping with the second) a growth of investment in private bonds, stocks and shares, from some 13 to almost 40 per cent.[1] The main changes in the actual investments, and their proportionate distribution are shown in Tables 13.3 and 13.4.

Throughout the late nineteenth century, and culminating in the 1890s, the most important factor influencing the investment policies of insurance companies was the declining yield of their traditional investments. Although there were some factors peculiar to insurance, this trend was part of a general fall in interest rates: the yield on Consols dropped to a bare 3 per cent between 1881 and 1888, falling even further in the 1890s and standing at a mere 2½ per cent in 1896–8, while in the 1890s the returns from investment in colonial government railway debenture and municipal stock were not very much greater. Evidence for the overall yield of insurance investments comes from the official Board of Trade returns of British offices (and it relates only to the investment of their life funds). It indicates that average yields which were steady at about £4. 10s. od. per cent in the late 1860s and early 1870s, fell somewhat in the later 1870s and sagged to £4. 4s. od. in 1885. They then fell somewhat faster, to £4. os. od. in 1890 and £3. 15s. 4d. in 1900.[2]

---

[1] These, and other measures, are based upon official valuations. The warning given at the beginning of this chapter about the impossibility of accurate measurement because of inconsistencies in procedures relating to the valuation of assets are even more relevant to the late nineteenth century, when the rôle of Stock Exchange securities grew much larger.

[2] The official figures are reasonably trustworthy guides to trends, and rough but adequate indications of magnitudes. However, they should not be too much relied on. The 1870 Act did not enforce consistency of answers to relevant questions, so that companies varied in their treatment of the valuation of assets, income tax, non-invested funds, alterations in the amounts of interest and funds in the course of the year, etc. In addition, yields are derived from annual returns on the assumption that those published in one year refer to company accounts submitted in the previous year and pertinent to the year before *that*. Since this did not always follow, it is not absolutely accurate to sum and average the data—although no better alternative is practicable. Finally, it should be remembered that the yields refer only to life funds and not to *all* investments, which would include some different assets.

TABLE 13.3. *UK life offices pattern of investments (absolute amounts), 1870–1913*[a]

(£ million)	1870	1880	1890	1900	1905	1913
'Mortgages'[b]	51·6	70·9	83·1	85·2	96·9	113·9
Loans to (and securities of) UK local authorities			20·4[c]			31·4
Indian and colonial municipal securities	10·2	19·5	1·7[c]	33·1	44·8	22·7
Foreign municipal securities			0·4[c]			14·7
British Government securities	8·2	5·0	6·4	7·7	9·2	5·3
Indian and colonial government securities	5·3	7·1	12·8	9·3	20·1	19·3
Foreign government securities	1·2	4·4	3·5	10·9	11·7	24·6
Debentures and debenture stocks	10·4	10·6	23·3	52·0	72·3	132·4
Shares and stocks	3·1	7·9	13·1	35·1	42·1	49·1[d]
Loans on life policies	5·3	7·2	9·2	13·2	18·3	29·1
Land, house property, ground rents	4·7	8·1	15·8	29·0	37·3	46·1
Life interests and reversions	1·7	2·7	3·5	7·5	10·0	11·6
Loans on personal security	1·8	1·9	1·3	1·3	2·3	2·4
Total investments:	103·5	145·3	194·8	294·3	365·0	502·6
Agents' balances, cash, outstanding premiums, etc.	6·2	9·8	16·5	19·8	19·4	27·5
Total assets:	109·7	155·1	211·3	311·1	384·4	530·1

[a] Sources: 1870: *JIA*, XLII (July 1908), 314–15; 1880–1913: Board of Trade Returns, 1882, 1892, 1901, 1903, 1914. The returns of individual companies did not invariably refer to the relevant year, although nearly all of them did. The data for 1880–1913 refer to all investments (i.e. whether or not connected with Life Funds) of companies transacting ordinary and/or industrial life insurance. Consequently, the investments of non-life companies are excluded. The figures for 1870 concern companies transacting ordinary life insurance, but since industrial insurance was negligible at that time, this is not a serious ommission.

[b] 'Mortgages' include loans on the security of life interests, reversions or stocks and shares. In 1913 these amounted to just under 20 per cent of 'mortgages' (the balance being loans on the direct security of real property). However, these sorts of loans had only recently enjoyed such a significant popularity. In the late nineteenth century, therefore, the figures for 'mortgages' refer almost entirely to mortgages of real property.

[c] Deduced from data on investments in overseas municipal bonds in Mackenzie, 'Investment of . . . Life Assurance Funds', *JIA*, XXIX (July 1891), 201.

[d] Of which ordinary shares accounted for £18·4 million.

In the case of the Royal Exchange Assurance, figures for quinquennia give a reasonably representative picture of the long-run fall in yields (net of tax). See Table 13.7.

In point of fact, the fall in interest rates was even more serious than is suggested by these figures—which reflect the return on *all* investments, including those made at earlier periods when interest rates were higher.

TABLE 13.4. *UK life offices pattern of investments (proportionate distribution), 1870–1913*[a]

percentages	1870	1880	1890	1900	1905	1913
'Mortgages'[a]	49·8	48·1	42·7	29·0	26·6	22·6
Loans to (and securities of) UK local authorities			10·4[a]			6·2
Indian and colonial municipal securities	9·8	13·4	0·9[a]	11·3	12·3	4·5
Foreign municipal securities			0·2[a]			2·9
British Government securities	7·9	3·4	3·3	2·6	2·5	1·1
Indian and colonial government securities	5·1	4·9	6·6	6·6	5·5	3·8
Foreign government securities	1·2	3·0	1·8	3·7	3·2	4·9
Debentures and debenture stocks	10·0	7·3	12·0	17·7	19·8	26·3
Shares and stocks	3·0	5·4	6·7	11·9	11·5	9·8[a]
Loans on life policies	5·1	5·0	4·7	4·5	5·0	5·8
Land, house property, ground rents	4·5	5·6	8·1	9·9	10·2	9·2
Life interests and reversions	1·6	1·1	1·8	2·6	2·7	2·3
Loans on personal security	1·7	1·3	0·7	0·4	0·6	0·5
Total investments:	103·5m	145·3m	194·8m	294·3m	365·0m	502·6m

[a] Sources and notes as for Table 13.3. Percentages may not add up to 100 because of rounding.

TABLE 13.5. *REA pattern of investments (absolute amounts), 1871–1913*[a]

(£000)	Apr. 1871	Apr. 1880	Apr. 1890	Dec. 1900	Dec. 1913
Mortgages	972·5	1,220·8	1,412·2	991·2	661·4
Loans on life interests, reversions, stocks, etc.	94·3	24·7	108·0	201·5	595·0
Loans to (and securities of) UK local authorities	796·4	611·0	680·3	467·4	207·8
British Government securities	715·3	621·2	386·5	198·6	72·9
Bank of England stock	56·9	57·4	36·1		
Indian and colonial government securities	103·5	181·0	290·2	323·0	134·4
Indian and colonial municipal securities	—	—	—	—	108·5
Foreign government securities	—	—	8·0	282·0	426·9
Foreign municipal securities	—	—	24·0	—	312·3
Debentures, debenture stock, bonds	529·3	831·4	421·0	940·3	1,831·5
Shares and stocks (mostly preferred and guaranteed)	—	190·3	303·9	471·0	586·2
Loans on life policies	46·3	63·2	72·3	104·7	198·4
Purchase of life interests, reversions, annuities	15·7	—	9·5	108·8	209·8
Loans on personal security	3·3	6·2	19·5	—	135·9
Freehold property	8·2	13·7	28·6	238·5	681·9
Total investments:	3,341·6	3,820·7	3,800·4	4,327·0	6,162·7
Total assets:	3,575·0	3,991·1	4,008·6	4,683·9	7,093·1

[a] Source: Board of Trade Returns. In order to make the various categories more comparable with those in Table 13.3, the original groupings have been conflated. Totals may not add because of rounding.

TABLE 13.6. *REA pattern of investments (proportionate distribution), 1871–1913*[a]

percentages	Apr. 1871	Apr. 1880	Apr. 1890	Dec. 1900	Dec. 1913
Mortgages	29·1	32·0	37·2	30·0	10·7
Loans on life interests, reversions, stocks etc.	2·8	0·6	2·8	4·7	9·7
Loans to (and securities of) UK local authorities	23·8	16·0	18·0	10·8	3·4
British Government securities	21·4	16·3	10·2 }	4·6 }	1·2
Bank of England stock	1·7	1·5	·9		
Indian and colonial government securities	3·1	4·7	7·6	7·5	2·2
Indian and colonial municipal securities	—	—	—	—	1·8
Foreign government securities	—	—	0·2	6·5	6·9
Foreign municipal securities	—	—	0·6	—	5·1
Debentures, debenture stock, bonds	15·8	21·8	11·1	21·7	29·7
Shares and stocks (mostly preferred and guaranteed)	—	5·0	8·0	10·9	9·5
Loans on life policies	1·4	1·7	2·0	2·4	3·2
Purchase of life interests, reversions, annuities	·5	—	·2	2·5	3·4
Loans on personal security	·1	·2	·5	—	2·2
Freehold property	·2	·4	·8	5·5	11·1
Total investments (£000):	3,341·6	3,820·7	3,800·4	4,327·0	6,162·7

[a] Source: As Table 13.5. Totals may not add to 100 per cent because of rounding.

TABLE 13.7. *REA yield on life fund, 1871–1915*

	£ s. d.		£ s. d.
1871–5	4 13 3	1891–5	4 2 3
1876–80	4 9 2	1896–1900	3 18 3
1881–5	4 6 9	1901–05	3 16 7
1886–90	4 1 11	1906–10	3 17 1
		1911–15	3 19 1

The *marginal* yield, i.e. the return which could be obtained from the investment of 'new money', was bound to be lower than the average yield in a period of falling interest rates. An estimate made in 1895 suggests that marginal yields might have been more than 10s. per cent less than average yields.[1]

Insurance officials appreciated that very large-scale—even world-wide —developments were responsible for the decline in the return to much

[1] Deuchar, 'Investments', *JFII* (1898), pp. 327–8; compare Mackenzie, 'Investment of . . . Life Assurance Funds', *JIA* (1891), p. 231.

capital investment. In Britain more especially it seemed to them that a stage of economic development had been reached when the supply of funds seeking low-risk investment so far exceeded the demand as to force down interest rates to quite forbidding levels. In the years after 1895, for example, when the return to secure investment was at its lowest, home railway debenture stock, British municipal securities, and Indian and colonial government stock were all producing yields at or below 3 per cent. Nor was this the product of only economic forces: legislation in 1889 and 1893 gave statutory sanction to the investment of trust funds in home and Indian railway debenture and guaranteed stock, and in the stock of municipal corporations; in 1900 similar sanction was given to their investment in the registered and inscribed stock of colonial governments. The resulting flow of investment funds depressed the relevant interest rates even further.[1]

The decline in yields came to an end more or less with the nineteenth century (the low point for the REA was a return of £3. 14s. 4d. per cent in 1902). Nevertheless, its persistence and extent shaped the nature of discussion and decision-making for much of the period; and the new investment policies adopted while it lasted proved equally relevant to the period of rising interest rates, and depreciating security values, which immediately followed. While it lasted the prolonged decline in yields was rightly seen as a major threat to the profitability of life insurance. In the industry as a whole the fall of 7s. 6d. per cent between 1870 and 1888 was equivalent to a reduction of income of £600,000 on the funds of the latter year; while in 1901 the REA Actuary warned his Directors that 'the welfare of the Life Department may really be said to largely depend on the skill of the investing Department in producing the highest rate consistent with safety', and pointed out that a decline of merely 5s. per cent would produce a fall of 3s. 6d. in the Corporation's bonus, while half the entire profits (surplus) of the Life Department were accounted for by the ability to earn 4 per cent rather than the 3 per cent assumed in the premium tables. More than this, the actual rate of interest earned by life companies was getting dangerously near the rates assumed in life calculations, and particularly those used in valuations. As long as low yields lasted—and by the late 1890s many actuaries felt that the possibility of their increasing was 'so improbable that it may practically be left out of consideration in

---

[1] May, 'The Investment of Life Assurance Funds', *JIA* (1912), p. 147. Insurance spokesmen constantly refer to the competition of trustee funds for high-class securities. Where trust deeds were appropriately phrased, trust funds could be invested in the relevant securities even before 1889. If not, then they were confined (before 1889) to British Government and Bank stock, and mortgages of freehold property in England and Wales.

any extended view of the future'[1]—it was vital to re-examine those rates in order to retain a margin of safety. In 1891 the President of the Institute of Actuaries feared that 'the permanent rate of interest had gone down for all time', and advised managers of life offices to 'cut their coat according to their cloth, and reduce the rate at which they valued their liabilities'.[2] In the event, this is exactly what did happen: whereas in 1870 about one in four companies assumed an interest rate of 4 per cent and none assumed less than 3 per cent, by 1908 none exceeded 3½ per cent, and one in four assumed less than 3 per cent.[3]

There was, however, an even more significant response to the fall in yields which was not merely desirable, but necessary. This was to shift investments in an attempt to maintain, or at least restrict the fall in, the rate of interest earned. And it was this response which had the most far-reaching and permanent results for the economic position of British insurance companies. The consequent transformations of attitudes and assumptions were very difficult to achieve; nevertheless the problem of finding suitable investments for rapidly accumulated funds *had* to be solved.

The difficulty of finding suitable investments has become greater. This must be surmounted by increased diligence in search and discrimination in choice. The yield of gold is less than it was, in comparison with the ore which we manipulate. We must improve our machinery. Part of our mine has been worked out. We must sink new shafts and open up new lodes. The offices generally are acting upon such views. The range of investments has become wider, and in the large variety there is more scope for the operations of that law of average upon which our business is so largely founded.[4]

As we shall see, perhaps the most important consequence of this new mood was a great extension of the overseas investments of British offices. However, before discussing the newly important fields of investment sought by insurance companies in this period it is pertinent to note the effect of these trends on two sorts of investment which had dominated insurance company portfolios in the middle decades of the century: mortgages and loans to local authorities.

---

[1] Quoted in May, 'The Investment of Life Assurance Funds', *JIA* (1912), p. 158.

[2] B. Newbatt in discussions of paper by Mackenzie, *JIA* (1891), p. 231.

[3] *The Standard*, 26 November 1910. In contrast to the *fin-de-siècle* gloom about interest rates, it was possible, a mere fourteen years later, to refer to the 'rapid and continual rise in the rate of interest earned by assurance funds, with the result that the principal source of profit exhibits the power of expansion today which is little less than astounding, when viewed in the light of the pessimistic utterances which were wont to fall from the lips of eminent actuaries a few years ago' (*The Economist*, LXXVI, 748 [29 March 1913]).

[4] Mackenzie, 'Investment of . . . Life Assurance Funds', *JIA* (1891), p. 213.

To contemporaries, the most striking result of the changing economic climate of the late nineteenth century was the diminished importance of mortgages on UK property. The sums invested actually increased, but their relative position was transformed from 49·1 per cent of investments in 1870 and 45·5 per cent in 1883 to 25·9 per cent in 1900 and 13·3 per cent in 1913.[1] Admittedly, some of this apparent decline in popularity was illusory, since business firms increasingly borrowed on property by issuing 'mortgage debentures'.[2] But most of it was real. And it came about not merely because of the diminished rate of interest from first-class mortgages, but also because of the agricultural depression and declining land values of the last quarter of the century. 'No security was ever relied on with more implicit faith,' said *The Economist* in 1897, 'and few have lately been more sadly found wanting than English land.'[3] The low returns induced by the mounting flow of *rentier* investment joined with the feeling of unease about the falling rents (25 per cent in the last twenty-five years of the century) and prices of Britain's land, to work a basic change in traditional outlooks—even though money could always be found for some first-class investment secured on freehold property.

At the Royal Exchange the Treasury Committee reported to the Court as early as 1886 that 'the great depreciation in the value of land has occasioned your Committee to review their mortgages'—although, on the whole, they found that the £606,316 involved was soundly invested. Indeed, only three years earlier the Corporation had sold £245,000 of Government securities (at a profit of £37,449) in order to invest the proceeds 'on mortgage of freehold lands of ample value yielding a higher rate of interest'. But this was because it was even then still possible to get occasional mortgages at good rates—and also because mortgages were preferable to low-yielding Government stock, to which the REA had stayed loyal longer than most. Over the longer run the relative importance of the Corporation's freehold mortgages fell inexorably: from almost a third of its investments in 1880 to about 10 per cent in 1913.

Yet even at these levels, as with insurance companies in general, the arguments about the attractiveness of mortgages did not all run one way. As the Secretary of the Corporation pointed out in 1907, mortgages 'often

---

[1] These figures are taken from *JIA*, XLII (July 1908), 314–15, and *JIA*, LVI (March 1925), 118–19. For 1870–1900 the percentages have been adjusted to take account of investments only (not *all* assets). Unlike the table given at the beginning of this section, which concerned all mortgages by all companies, they refer only to UK mortgage investments by companies transacting ordinary business. This, however, makes little difference to the actual proportions.

[2] Andras, *Insurance Guide and Hand Book*, I, 52.

[3] *The Economist*, LV, 839–40 (12 June 1897).

bring grist to the mill . . . in the form of new fire and life connections';
and if there *was* trouble about the payment of interest, then, in contrast to
'the very unpleasant position' of a share- or debenture-holder, who had
to organize a collective effort, 'a mortgagee can use his own energy and
intelligence and frequently restores a property to its former condition'.
Thus it was that the REA in 1894 shared, with the Commercial Union, a
loan of £177,000 at 4 per cent to the Duke of Norfolk on the security of
the Sheffield Markets, and the next year agreed to lend £50,000 to the
Foundling Hospital at the remarkably low rate of 3¼ per cent, on condition
that the mortgaged property was insured with the Corporation's Fire
Department. Thus, too, by the early years of this century the Corporation
found itself owning and running a handful of properties on which
mortgages had been foreclosed. Most of these were reasonably profitable
—like the shops and dwellings in Shaftesbury Avenue on which £34,000
at 4¾ per cent had been lent in 1889, which had 'not retained their
estimated value' by 1895 because 'the Avenue has not achieved the success
anticipated', but which by 1909 were paying 4½ per cent, thus justifying the
original owner's confidence that 'when the Avenue becomes more fully
developed the portion extending from Piccadilly to Cambridge Circus (in
which this Estate is situate) will eventually become a leading and prosperous
thoroughfare'. Others, however, which included one large agricultural
estate and two large blocks of flats in London built by the Corporation
on foreclosed land at a total cost of £152,000, gave continuous difficulty.

In general, therefore, conventional mortgages became less and less
popular among insurance companies in the late nineteenth century. There
was, however, one unconventional and interesting form of loan which enjoyed a brief popularity in the 1890s and which was much favoured by the
REA. This was the mortgage loan on the security of public houses. The
brewing boom in the last decade of the century led to a scramble by
publicans (and breweries) for the strictly limited number of licensed
properties, and this in turn led to a rapid inflation in their cost and a need
to borrow the requisite capital. Paying a tempting rate of 5 per cent, these
mortgages were very attractive in a decade of low and falling yields.
Between 1889 and 1899, therefore, the Royal Exchange, although it
limited its outstanding loans to £150,000, invested a total of £350,000 in
the mortgages of public houses. In spite of their attractiveness, there was
nevertheless one quite doubtful feature of such loans: their security was
not above reproach, since the valuation of licensed properties included a
very generous allowance for 'goodwill' (i.e. the quasi-monopoly position
derived from the artificial shortages of licences). The price of public

houses was generally between £10,000 and £20,000; but in most cases the real property value was a small part of this: 'goodwill' normally accounted for about three-quarters of valuations.

The precarious nature of this sort of security (the value of which could be largely destroyed if the local authorities took away the premise's licence) was obviously appreciated by offices like the REA: in 1895 the Treasury Committee agreed to take out a policy for £150,000 with the Licensed Insurance Company, guaranteeing the value of their mortgages against any loss of licence. By the early years of this century the situation had deteriorated alarmingly: licences were being withdrawn; the brewing boom collapsed; in 1903 the Corporation decided to self-insure licences in face of a doubling of the premium rate by the Licensed Insurance Company; and in 1904 its public-house mortgage loans were said to be 'the only ones that give cause for anxiety, since trade is known to be bad, and the selling value to have fallen to the lowest point'. One house was already taken over; and four premises, accounting for £45,000 of the out-standing loans of £165,000, were being 'carefully watched' and 'trouble is anticipated unless the position of the trade improves'. It did not, and by 1909 the Royal Exchange had lost £7,000 absolutely and found itself in the strange position of owning four foreclosed public houses—two of which were let out to brewers at very low returns (2¼ and 2½ per cent), the remaining two being managed for the Corporation by a Mr Coxen, at even lower returns. By 1912, understandably, it was said of such loans that all 'life assurance companies have ruled them out of their range of invest-ment'.[1] The attempt to seek some relief from the gloom of low-yielding traditional mortgages by lending money on high-cost licensed premises did not, alas, provide much cheer.

The second mainstay of mid-nineteenth century investment, loans to local authorities, also declined in importance in the changing circumstances of later decades, although the decline was more obviously a relative one. Before the 1880s, the excellent security, and the distinctive mode of re-payment, of such loans made them particularly attractive to insurance companies. By the late 1870s they accounted for some £20 million—which was, roughly speaking, 14 per cent of insurance company assets—and a similar proportion of the outstanding debts of all local authorities in England and Wales.[2] Subsequently, however, not only did loans on the security of local rates share in the general fall in interest rates, but local

[1] Andras, *Insurance Guide and Hand Book*, I, 77.
[2] In 1879–80 the outstanding debts of English and Welsh local authorities were £136·9 million (Cairncross, *Home and Foreign Investment*, p. 142).

authorities began to make public issues of bonds and stocks—which attracted more private and individual investors, since they could be held to maturity or traded on the Stock Exchange. The consequent downward pressure on yields was intensified after 1889, when the Trust Investment Act allowed trustees to invest in local authority stock. The yield on such stock was barely over 3 per cent in 1891 and by 1897 their median yield had fallen to less than 3 per cent—a sad contrast with 'the good old days of 5 per cent and upward'.[1] By 1913, although UK local authority investments had grown to £31·4 million, this in fact represented a relative decline (to some 6 per cent of total investments) and was in any case largely accounted for by industrial offices: the ordinary offices in 1913 had merely £10·3 million (about 3 per cent) so invested.[2]

The REA provides an extreme example of this transformation. In 1870 it had been the industry's second largest investor in loans on the rates, holding some £800,000 (or almost 25 per cent) of its investments in this form. By the mid-1880s, however, it was extending loans at a mere 3¾ per cent (e.g. £15,000 to Surrey Magistrates, to build an Industrial School at Woking, in 1886), and by 1901 its loans on the security of the rates together with investments in corporation stocks amounted to merely some £200,000 or just under 5 per cent of its assets. The Secretary, in 1907, could, understandably, look back with envy to the days when such loans, on which the Corporation had never lost a penny, had regularly earned 5 per cent. 'It makes one's mouth water,' he confessed.

The decline in the importance of mortgages and local authority loans obviously marked a new era in insurance investment. To a limited extent life insurance offices could adapt to the new situation by a greater commitment to investments which were particularly apt for their business: loans on life policies, on reversions and on personal security. In the late 1880s, for example, the REA began purchasing, and lending money on, reversions —presumably for the same reason as the Atlas, which took powers to lend on reversions and personal security in 1886 in order 'to bring fire and life business to the office'. Between 1890 and 1914 the Royal Exchange almost trebled its loans on life policies, and increased its loans on life interests, reversions and personal security from negligible amounts to over £600,000. And in 1913 the Scottish Widows' Fund had lent over £2·6 million on the security of its own policies. In spite of all this effort, however, effective

---

[1] Mackenzie, 'Investment of . . . Life Assurance Funds', *JIA* (1891), p. 201; Cairncross, *Home and Foreign Investment*, p. 145. At these rates, local authorities borrowed huge amounts of money: in England and Wales their outstanding debt rose from £234·5 million in 1894–5 to £416·9 million in 1904–5 (Cairncross, *Home and Foreign Investment*, pp. 142–5).

[2] *JIA*, LVI (March 1925), 118–19.

adaptation to an era of lower yields had to be more far reaching; and the net result for insurance companies, far from being a retreat, was, in fact, a broadening of their investment base away from a limited number of conventional assets, and a participation across a wider and more adventurous range, to take advantage of new opportunities.

The search for higher yields meant various things in the context of the late nineteenth century. It meant taking advantage of the prospects of economic development in overseas areas; it meant purchasing Stock Exchange securities, and particularly those of private enterprises, to a much greater extent than before; and, precisely because higher-yielding assets might be riskier than tradition dictated, it meant spreading such investments over as wide a field as possible to reduce the risks of fluctuations. As one actuary put it as early as 1891, 'it being now hardly possible as in former times to obtain investments in which the principal was secure with a reasonable rate of interest, insurance companies must act as private investors would, namely, they must go on the Stock Exchange and not have all their eggs in one basket, but they must be prepared to run risks of fluctuation in value'.[1] Moreover, the new attitude, once assimilated, proved equally appropriate to a radical change of circumstances: with the upturn of interest rates around the turn of the century it was, in fact, intensified. Indeed, precisely because rising interest rates were associated with depreciating security values, it became more than ever important to guard against fluctuations in values by spreading investments. The decline particularly hit gilt-edged stocks. Between 1896 and 1913, for example, Consols fell in price by 37 per cent, railroad debenture stock and preferred stocks by 40 per cent, colonial government stocks by 20 per cent.[2] For this reason, too, therefore, investment policies had to continue to adapt. 'Events of recent years', said one actuary in 1912, 'had taught actuaries that safety and immunity from loss were not to be obtained by simply investing in so-called gilt-edged securities, but rather that a wide field of investment should be adopted by distributing the funds in a large number of varying interests all the world over.'[3] More than this, by the same date the figures seemed to show 'that those offices which have spread their investments the most, and at the same time have gone furthest afield, have suffered the least from depreciation and have also been the ones to obtain the most satisfactory returns'.[4]

[1] A. H. Bailey, in discussion of paper by Mackenzie, *JIA* (1891), p. 229. Compare May, 'The Investment of Life Assurance Funds', *JIA* (1912), p. 135.

[2] *PM*, LXXV, 653, 670 (15 and 22 August 1914).

[3] F. Schooling, commenting on paper by May, in *JIA* (1912), p. 160.

[4] May, 'The Investment of Life Assurance Funds', *JIA* (1912), p. 139.

As we have seen, investment in overseas areas, particularly in India and the colonies, had begun relatively early. By 1870 almost 6 per cent of investments were in overseas government stocks. Nevertheless, what *The Economist* called 'the centrifugal force of declining interest at home'[1] began to push even more substantial amounts of capital overseas in the early 1880s. Nor was this trend solely influenced by the search for higher yields: as British fire insurance extended into the United States and other foreign lands, the need to locate funds abroad and the legal obligation to deposit specified amounts of capital with government agencies, also led to local investment. When the REA began business in San Francisco in 1891, for example, it had to buy and deposit £50,000 of US Registered 4 per cent bonds, and in 1896 it deposited £14,000 of bonds in Argentina. By 1909 it had over £350,000 in American securities deposited with officials or trustees in accordance with local regulations.

For insurance companies as a whole only overseas investments in *public* securities can be measured with any precision (private securities were generally not distinguished with respect to the country of origin). In this respect, Indian and colonial government securities grew from just over £5 million in 1870 to some £17 million in 1895, with a major spurt in the 1880s, when they were paying over 4 per cent.[2] By the early 1890s, however, *their* yields were also declining—to about 3½ per cent or less. In the event, the consequent slack was more than taken up by investment in the provincial and municipal securities of imperial territories. For, even while investment in UK local authorities was becoming less and less re-munerative, the scarcity of capital for local investment overseas attracted, through its higher rates, a significant amount of insurance funds. As early as 1890 Indian and colonial municipal bonds (the yields on which held up much better than that on central government bonds) accounted for £1·7 million of insurance investments. However, most such investments took place in the early years of the century: by 1909 overseas municipal securities amounted to some £25 million out of a total of £413 million assets; and by 1913 this figure had jumped to £37·4 million, or 7·5 per cent of assets—not far short of the £43·9 million in overseas central and provincial government securities. On the eve of war, it was said, 'enormous sums of money at highly remunerative rates' were flowing into such in-vestments—including not only foreign municipal bonds (£14·7 million in 1913) but also those of Canadian towns, which were borrowing in London at rates of up to 5½ per cent.[3] The REA had certainly moved very decisively

---

[1] *The Economist*, LV, 839–40 (12 June 1897).
[2] Mackenzie, 'Investment of . . . Life Assurance Funds', *JIA* (1891), p. 202.
[3] *PM* LXXV, 670, 691 (22 and 29 August 1914).

into this new area of investment. As Table 13.5 shows, in 1890 it had had an entirely negligible investment in overseas municipal securities; by 1913 it had purchased some £420,000 securities in foreign (£312,000) and colonial (£108,000) municipalities.

As with municipal investment, so with the securities of central and provincial governments: by the early twentieth century insurance companies (while not at all neglecting imperial investment opportunities) were becoming much more adventurous about foreign lands. In 1890, when the companies were very suspicious of foreign securities, such holdings had been a mere £3·5 million; by 1900 they were almost £11 million; and in 1913 they reached almost £25 million. (The REA increased its holdings of foreign government securities from £8,000 in 1890 to £282,000 in 1900 and £427,000 in 1913.) In fact, by the first decade or so of this century the combination of economic development, the need to finance war expenditure, greater political stability in South America, and improvements in capital markets, produced a new attitude towards foreign bonds, and 'a large number of attractive loans, which it has been impossible for the keen investor to ignore'.[1]

The rhythm of overseas investments by insurance companies reflected that of British overseas investments in general. A small spurt in the 1870s and early 1880s was followed by relative quiescence in the later 1880s, a moderate growth in the 1890s, and a dramatically intensified boom in the decade before the First World War. By 1913 the holdings of all overseas public securities—Indian, colonial and foreign; central, provincial and municipal—amounted to £81·3 million, or about 16 per cent of total assets.

One other category of overseas investment can also be measured with some certainty. While the attraction of British mortgages was declining, some insurance companies began to explore the more risky, but more profitable, situation in Britain's overseas Empire. The investment of money in mortgages of land in newly developing territories was a logical response to the rapid development of pastoral and grain farming in Australia, New Zealand and Canada. No one could deny that, even at yields of 5½ per cent or more, this sort of investment so far from Head Offices had its drawbacks. 'Again we have the problem of the new risks that await the new method,' said *The Economist*, '—the need for wider knowledge, greater care, more labour than in the past.'[2] This sort of consideration, reflecting as it did the riskiness of overseas mortgages, deterred the REA from making any effective investment in them at this time—although it had £30,000

---

1 Andras, *Insurance Guide and Hand Book*, I, 53. Compare *PM*, LXXV, 670 (22 August 1914).
2 *The Economist*, LV, 839–40 (12 June 1897).

deposits at 4½ per cent in two Australian joint-stock banks in the 1870s ('with the object of influencing marine business') and this money was no doubt used by the banks to help finance their extensive pastoral mortgages. Other companies were, however, less reluctant. Scottish offices pioneered the way in the Australian pastoral boom of the 1880s: by 1888, three of them (the Scottish Widows' Fund, the Scottish Provident Institution and the North British & Mercantile) held overseas mortgages of £3·4 million, or 15 per cent of their assets, out of the total for all insurance companies of £6·3 million. The Scottish Widows' Fund, which had no overseas mortgages in 1880, had invested £1·9 million (out of total assets of £11·1 million) in them by 1890 and £2·4 million (out of £13·1 million) by 1895— although it somewhat reduced this amount in later years. By 1895 all insurance offices had invested £12·6 million in overseas mortgages (as against £70·9 million in British). In the 1890s, however, and particularly in 1898–9, with drought and low prices pricking the pastoral boom in Australia, they encountered new problems in relation to these mortgages. Even so, the situation had improved by the early twentieth century; new outlets for mortgage capital were found with the Canadian boom of the decade or so before the First World War, and by 1913 overseas mortgages, standing at £21·1 million, amounted to 5·5 per cent of the investments of ordinary life offices (4·29 per cent of *all* offices)—as against a mere 13·3 per cent for home mortgages.[1]

Thus, even measured only in terms of the securities of public authorities and mortgage investments, insurance companies had made a very considerable commitment (more than one-fifth of their assets) to overseas areas before the First World War. But such figures are, by themselves, inadequate indications of the new importance of foreign investment–for they ignore the very substantial amounts of capital sunk in railways, public utilities, mines and other private ventures in India, other parts of the Empire, the United States and elsewhere. Unfortunately, the annual summary figures published by the Board of Trade included these in the general categories of debenture, guaranteed, preferred and other stocks and shares. Yet there can be no doubt of the attractiveness of such assets— particularly of the well-secured bonds of overseas railroads. At an early stage Indian railways were especially attractive because of their Government guarantee (in 1876, for example, the Royal Exchange sold £70,000

---

[1] Mackenzie, 'Investment of . . . Life Assurance Funds', *JIA* (1891), p. 199; J. D. Bailey, *A Hundred Years of Pastoral Banking* (1966), pp. 56, 120, 160; *The Economist*, LV, 839–40 (12 June 1897); *JIA*, LVI (March 1925), 118–19. The figures for mortgages in the text refer only to those secured by real property.

of Consols to help pay for its purchase of £100,000 of East India Railway five-year debentures). But their yields, of 4 per cent and more, also fell in the 1890s, with those of other first-class securities—with the additional influence of the Trustee Acts which allowed trustee investments on the stock and debentures of Guaranteed Indian Railways. Hence by the late 1880s and 1890s, insurance companies were buying substantial amounts of American railway securities. Between 1893 and 1896, for example, stimulated in part perhaps by its invasion of the American fire insurance market, the REA increased its holdings of American railway bonds from £81,715 to £285,361—and of Indian Railway securities from £86,197 to £130,091. The Scottish Widows' Fund acquired £1·5 million of American railway gold mortgage bonds in the early 1890s; and the Commercial Union had purchased some £700,000 of American railway securities by 1900. Railways were undoubtedly the single most important category of non-government overseas investments by insurance companies. There was, however, also a considerable investment in the bonds of public utilities—especially in the years before the First World War, when water, gas and electricity undertakings were proving very attractive and offering returns of 5 or 5½ per cent.[1]

Although exact measurements of total overseas investments are not available, a rough idea can be obtained from figures of the REA's investments in overseas governments and railways. These show important trends, particularly considering the relative slowness with which the Corporation undertook overseas business. In 1890 only about 10 per cent of its investments were in such securities—jumping to 14 per cent by 1891, when the Corporation began its main underwriting ventures outside the United Kingdom. Throughout the 1890s, although total investments rose, overseas governments and rails continued to account for some £520,000. But this was obviously judged insufficient by the Actuary, who early in 1901 warned the Directors that the falling yield on life funds made it imperative 'to arrest this downward tendency, either by seeking suitable investments abroad in the same manner as the Scottish Widows' Fund, and some other first-class offices, or by any other method that may commend itself'. (By 1900 the Scottish Widows' Fund held just over £6 million, or some 39 per cent of its total investments, in overseas mortgages, imperial and foreign government securities and American railway gold bonds.) This advice obviously had a powerful effect: by 1909 almost £1·2 million, or over 23 per cent of the REA's total investments, was in such securities. However, even this figure is an underestimate, because it ignores invest-

[1] *PM*, LXXV, 691–2 (22 August 1914).

ment in securities other than those of governments and railways. A memorandum dated June 1907 indicated (with no details) that overseas assets accounted for 35·5 per cent of all assets, and 66·2 per cent of all Stock Exchange securities,[1] while in 1914 the debenture stock of American and other foreign enterprises accounted for some £1·7 million (out of a total of less than £2 million of such stock). In 1913, therefore, when overseas government and local authority securities amounted to almost £1 million, total overseas investment (including an unknown but, presumably, substantial proportion of its almost £500,000 of preferred, guaranteed and ordinary shares) must have represented about 45 per cent of the Corporation's total investments.

With respect to the investments of *all* insurance companies we have to rely on mere guesswork. By 1913 just over 20 per cent of investments were represented by overseas public securities and mortgages. If, as is very likely, the importance of other overseas securities was at least as great for the average company as it was for the REA, then in the years before 1914 British life offices had over 40 per cent of their huge funds in the Empire and foreign lands.

The new commitment to overseas investment was therefore associated with the rise to a new importance of Stock Exchange securities (including those of private business). Indeed, the two were functionally related. First, because the London Stock Exchange handled securities on an international basis: during the pre-war boom in overseas investments, in the three years 1910/11–1912/13, new issues totalled £668 million, of which £537 million represented overseas issues.[2] Second, the same forces that drove insurance companies to invest more and more of their money overseas were also persuading them to invest in Stock Exchange, marketable securities. For all British life offices such investments rose from 25 per cent of their total in 1885 to about 60 per cent in 1913. (The REA paralleled the national trend: its proportion rose from a mere 25 per cent in the late 1860s to over 50 per cent in the late 1890s, and 62 per cent in 1913.) These trends can also

---

[1] The percentages were:

	Stock Exchange	All investments
Great Britain	33·8	64·5
USA	24·9	13·1
Indian and colonial	19·5	10·3
Continent	8·9	5·3
Argentina	4·8	2·5
Rest of world	8·1	4·3
	100·0	100·0

[2] *PM*, LXXV, 670 (22 August 1914).

be seen as the outcome of a greater adventurousness on the part of insurance companies in the search for higher yields. In 1897 *The Economist* commented on the huge increase over the previous decade (more than in any other investment category) of the figures of debentures, shares and stocks:

They show most strikingly . . . the movement of life assurance capital, under the spur of reduced yield, into new paths of employment. [British and American railways and high-class industrial firms] have unquestionably been taken up to a very considerable extent during the present decade by assurance companies . . . Investments which would formerly, on fixed principles, have been set aside without investigation as unsuitable, are now carefully examined, their soundness and possibilities of profit anxiously weighed, by executive bodies which cannot afford to neglect any prudent chance of advantage in a duty which daily becomes more difficult and engrossing, as funds accumulate and 'gilt-edged' securities soar to impossible heights.[1]

It is, admittedly, very difficult to generalize about this trend simply because the official categories ('debentures', 'shares and stocks') embrace such a diversity of assets and, in any case, industrial firms (i.e. excluding railways and utilities) raised only a relatively small amount of money on the Stock Exchange before 1914. But the principal result was clear: insurance companies were responding to the lower yields of mortgage loans and British Government securities by taking a much greater interest in the securities of trading companies. By 1913 debenture stocks and shares accounted for 36 per cent of their assets.[2] Concomitantly, too, as the influence of their huge funds came to be exercized, the companies began to play a much more direct rôle in Stock Exchange transactions by taking the lead in underwriting new issues. The new economic climate of the late nineteenth century had worked a fundamental change in outlook and policy which was to last (and intensify) after the conditions which gave rise to it had faded away.

All companies had come a long way—including the Royal Exchange,

---

[1] *The Economist*, LV, 839–40 (12 June 1897).

[2] *Investments of all British life offices in debentures, stocks and shares* (£ million)

	1870	1880	1890	1900	1913
Debentures	10·4	10·6	23·3	52·0	132·4
Shares and stocks	3·1	7·9	13·1	35·1	49·1
Total:	13·5	18·5	36·4	87·1	181·5
% of total investments:	13·0	12·7	18·7	29·6	36·1

Derived from the Board of Trade Returns. The figures include offices doing industrial and ordinary business. If they had been confined to ordinary offices, the proportion of investments (not, of course, the absolute amounts) would be greater. E.g. in 1913 it was 38·5 per cent.

which in the 1870s had declined to accept the 4½ per cent debenture stock of the Gas, Light & Coke Company, preferring the 4 per cent yield of terminable debentures. Although security was still a dominant criterion of investment policy, insurance companies were now playing a much more active and varied rôle in channelling investment funds into directly productive, non-agricultural enterprises. The cult of the equity was still some way in the future (and its advent was to be postponed by the peculiar investment consequences of war-time conditions in 1914–18).[1] But it is obvious from their new-found commitment to overseas investment, to railways and public utilities, to trading companies and municipalities, that insurance companies were quick to respond to the new pattern of development which characterized the British and world economies in the generation before the First World War. In the course of this response, the companies found a new, vigorous and international rôle for themselves and their funds. And in adapting to the necessities as well as opportunities of late nineteenth-century capital markets, insurance companies had gone a long way towards creating a modern framework for their investment activities—a fitting parallel for the contemporaneous modernization of their underwriting business.

[1] Below, pp. 442–3.

14

Organization
and Management
to 1914

The fact that the Royal Exchange Assurance had been a composite office since 1721 had various implications for its management. Among the most important of these was the opportunity of achieving economies of operation. As John A. Higham, the Corporation's Actuary, argued in 1853, the risks of undertaking all three of sea, fire and life insurance were more than outweighed by 'the diminution of expenses which results from our having one Board of Directors, and one house, and from many other expenses being in common, and divided among three departments'.[1] Nevertheless, it was difficult to take full advantage of the available opportunities without a purposeful and co-ordinated growth of business. And, in the event, the problem of combining an energetic expansion of the Corporation's business with a unified and flexible management of its various affairs was not adequately solved before the First World War.

In fact, a striking feature of the organization of the Corporation in the period was the extent to which it was influenced by the constraints as well as the opportunities of tradition. Institutional arrangements which were already a century old at the end of the Napoleonic Wars naturally brought both advantages and disadvantages to its business: on the one hand continuity, strength and confidence; on the other, a resistance to change and even a complacency about the need for it. The one certain result of this tension between the strengths and weaknesses of tradition was that no transformation would—or could—be sudden. And it was, therefore, by a process of gradual evolution that the REA adapted its management structures to the pressures of change in a maturing economy. Whenever possible, too, the adaptation took place in terms of functions rather than structures. That is, when new tasks were undertaken they were most often fitted into the existing organization, and assumed by traditional officers and established committees. The result was familiarity amid change. The institutional framework of the Corporation was recognizably the same in 1914 as

[1] *SCAA*, Q.2540.

it had been in 1814, even though the character and scope of its underwriting and investment had been transformed.

The Corporation's administrative history is also familiar in another sense. For in adjusting to the new problems of the nineteenth century, the REA became familiar with themes which have characterized its operations, as a large-scale office, ever since. They appeared in various guises: the division of responsibilities between Directors and Managers, the need to adjust the functions and flexibility of committee structures, the importance of ensuring the harmonious interdependence of departments. But essentially, these themes have always reflected the problems of *general* management and co-ordination in a large and diverse insurance company. Indeed, the integration of its different parts is still, as it has been ever since the early nineteenth century, the dominant task of management organization —perennially needing new solutions because its context is perennially changing.

In the nineteenth century, as at other times, the formal structure of the Corporation was composed of two more or less parallel sets of institutions: the Court of Directors and its associated supervisory committees with functional responsibilities (e.g. investment, accounts, marine, fire and life); and the various underwriting and service departments (e.g. marine, fire, life, Secretary's, Cashier's) manned by clerks and administered by officials or (as they have come to be called in this century) the Managers. Since the Court was responsible for formulating policy, any discussion of the Corporation's nineteenth-century organization must start from the Governors and Directors, and move, *via* the various Committees, to the departments and their official heads.

THE COURT AND ITS COMMITTEES

The Charter had stipulated that the Court should be composed of a Governor, a Sub-Governor, a Deputy-Governor (collectively known as the Governors) and twenty-four Directors. And in establishing this hierarchy it had anticipated what was essentially a pyramidical system of government: the Governor was the dominant personality within a framework of traditional authority. The records of the Corporation make it clear that by virtue of his office, seniority and personality a Governor wielded the ultimate executive authority. Controversies at lower levels of management, or high-level decisions relating to underwriting, investment, organization or personnel, would inevitably be considered by him—acting either individually or as Chairman of the crucial Treasury Committee—and on such matters the weight of his opinion was considerable. When, in 1911, it was decided to establish a Committee of Management, the point was made that, by tradition, the Governor was the only recognized 'central authority for General Management'.

There is, of course, nothing surprising in such a situation in an old-established economic and social institution like the REA. More significant than any formal attribution of authority could have been, were the deference produced by prestige and tradition, and the need to repose power and trust in any individual placed at its head. Against this background, the Governor was naturally in a strong position to initiate major changes in organization or policy, to persuade other Directors to reconsider their decisions where necessary, and to commit the Corporation, when speedy decisions had to be taken, in matters of insurance and investments.

The aura of almost unquestioned leadership which inevitably surrounded a Governor naturally implied that he had to be extremely careful to avoid as far as possible any major clash of opinion with other members of the Court. In fact, such a disagreement did occur in 1904 when Henry F. Tiarks was Governor—and led to his resignation. Tiarks had 'strongly dissented' when a unanimous recommendation of the Sea Committee that Augustus Dutton be appointed Underwriter was considered by the Court. Upon being outvoted there, he resigned on the grounds that he could not be a party to a decision which he believed to be detrimental to the Corporation. More pertinent to the present discussion, in a letter to the Secretary, Mr Tiarks put his finger on the crucial point: 'The absence of support on the part of the Directors present after the full statement of my views—abundantly proves that I no longer possess the confidence that must be enjoyed by the Governor for the successful exercise of his function—hence I have no alternative but to resign.'

This event, instructive as it is, was unique in the Corporation's history. Once a man had earned sufficient trust and respect to be elected Governor, he could normally assume that he would retain it. Admittedly, early in the nineteenth century the Court recorded its feeling that no individual filling one of the three Governors' chairs for three years or more 'shall as a matter of *course* be recommended by the Directors for re-election'. But, in fact, time and again, while reminding itself of its original resolution, the Court took pains to ensure the re-election of Governors who wished to continue to serve. There is apparently no instance of a Governor standing down merely because of his having completed the specified period of service—although both Thomas Tooke (1840–52) and Octavius Wigram (1852–70) resigned the Governorship and stayed on as ordinary members of the Court having already served as Directors for forty-eight and fifty-one years respectively.

The Governorship of the Corporation was obviously an onerous and demanding, as well as a powerful, position. Its occupant had to be prepared to make a considerable and continuing commitment of effort, concentration and business skill. Quite apart from the general administration of a large corporation and the oversight of a complex underwriting business, a heavy weight of responsibility was entailed in the management of substantial investment funds. As a result, although seniority was a crucial factor in the election of Governors (of the ten Governors elected between 1812 and 1914, seven had already served on the Court for thirty-three or more years, and the others had an average service of almost eighteen years), the fact remains that business experience and financial acumen continued to characterize the Corporation's Governors. Nor was their experience limited in range. Thus, to take three examples from the middle of the century, Pascoe Grenfell (Governor 1829–38) was deeply concerned with the industries of Anglesey and Cornwall and, as an MP, devoted himself to financial affairs and the problems of the Bank of England; Sir John W. Lubbock (Governor 1838–40) was head of a banking firm; and Thomas Tooke (Governor 1840–52), having started in business life as a Russia merchant, became an expert on economics and monetary matters, a founder (with Ricardo, Malthus and Mill) of the Political Economy Club, and the Chairman of the St Katharine Dock Company.

In these respects, of course, the Governors merely reflected part of the range of concerns and connections of the Court as a whole. As the actual business of underwriting ramified and grew more technical and as the rôle of insurance offices in the capital market developed, so the importance of the twenty-seven members of the Court as links between the Corporation and the commercial and financial world, increased. In the last resort, the contribution of a Director was bound up with his rôle in the world at large —a rôle which might, by its connection with manufacturing or trading firms, generate much fire or marine insurance business; or, through its links with the City, be invaluable in terms of the Corporation's investment business. As in the eighteenth century, this situation led to a very long-lasting connection between the Court and other enterprises. Thus, when the banker Pascoe Grenfell died in 1838 (having been on the Court since 1789), he was replaced on the Court by Riversdale William Grenfell, who in his turn was followed by Charles Seymour Grenfell in 1871—all partners in Pascoe Grenfell & Sons. Similarly, a partner in the firm of Barclay Perkins & Co. has been on the Corporation's Court since 1789. Another very intimate link occurred in connection with the Lubbock family and its banking firm (which acted for the Corporation): Sir John W. Lubbock was elected to the Court in 1798, and to the Governorship in 1838; at Sir John's death, his son (of the same name and also head of the family bank), who was also a prominent mathematician and astronomer, and first Vice-Chancellor of London University, was elected to the Court, on which he served until 1861. *His* son, Sir Nevile Lubbock, was elected to the Court in 1865, and became Governor in 1904—serving until his death in 1914, which ended a family connection of 116 years. Other sorts of tradition were also established. Thus, the Court has always included a Deputy Master of Trinity House—typifying the connection between the Corporation and the world of shipping.

Two disqualifications are worth mentioning here. First, the original Charter of 1720 had stipulated that no one should be a Governor or Director, or hold stock in, both the REA and the London Assurance at the same time. However, these stipulations, which were no longer very relevant to circumstances much changed from the early eighteenth century (when one reaction to the new Corporations had been a fear of monopoly), were repealed by Act of Parliament in 1871. Second, the Corporation's own bye-laws had forbidden any member of the Court to underwrite marine policies in his private capacity. In April 1868, however, this was changed, to allow such underwriting with permission of the Court, since 'in consequence of alterations, of late years, in the system of trade, it has occasioned inconvenience to individuals, without being a real protection of the Corporation'; and three months later the Court, 'believing that the spirit of that Bye-Law was intended to prevent private underwriters becoming Directors of this Board', resolved that any Governor or Director could transact marine insurance business 'in any way they may think proper, save only as private underwriters at Lloyd's. Ten years later the Court even allowed the newly elected Charles Ernest Green to continue underwriting at Lloyd's, being satisfied 'that he will take no active part in underwriting to the detriment of the interests of this Corporation'.

On the whole, therefore, the Corporation's Directors were established businessmen with a stake in other commercial, manufacturing or financial affairs. This, together with their function at the Royal Exchange, generally established a clear line of demarcation between Directors and officers, for the latter naturally tended to be professional insurance men, with long experience in the sole employment of the Corporation.[1]

Indeed, as long as the Managers were simply heads of departments

---

[1] The one exception to the distinction between Directors and officials was the 'Sitting Director'—a member of the Court (normally an ex-Secretary) with special responsibilities for marine underwriting, and some aspects of the fire business. The post lapsed in 1837. See above, pp. 165, 200.

(i.e. until there was a single General Manager) there were powerful reasons for the division between Directors and officials. For the Court was responsible for the supervision of departmental affairs, and it would have been invidious to include among its number the very officials whom it was notionally supervising and even checking. It is, presumably, this factor which explains the timing of the disappearance of the Sitting Director. For the rise of professional departmental management and professional responsibility greatly diminished the importance of his particular rôle. By the 1830s the growth of the Corporation's business, in both size and complexity, created the need for a sharper division of responsibility between, and a greater degree of professional skill in the management of, the Corporation's different departments.

In spite of this last development, the fact remains that membership of the REA Court was not a sinecure. Apart from the stockholding qualification of £1,000 (at prevailing market prices, before it was halved in 1901, this represented an investment of between £2,000 and £4,000 for almost every year in the nineteenth century), which ensured a substantial stake in the affairs of the Corporation, the supervisory duties of the Directors were taken very seriously. Considerable thought was devoted to the membership of Committees, and regular and conscientious attendance was expected. The Court itself met every week on Wednesday at noon, and absentees were fined 10s. (which was divided among those present), while those arriving late or leaving without permission of the Chair, had to contribute 5s. and 2s. 6d. respectively to the Poor Box. Apart from the windfalls from delinquents, members of the Court received regular fees or 'appointments' (by the 1830s these were £300 for Directors and £400 for Governors), which the Proprietors supplemented by equal payments in each of 1856 and 1870 in recognition of 'their able management of the business of the Corporation'.

Although the Court was responsible for the main lines of policy and finance of the Corporation, it had of necessity to delegate the implementation of policy, and even the taking of major initiatives, to a substructure of specialist Committees. And it was by their membership of these that the Directors fulfilled their main responsibilities.

In recognition of their authority, the three Governors were, in fact, *ex-officio* members of all Committees. The other members of the Court—i.e. the Directors—each belonged to one or two specialist Committees. In addition, however, all served in weekly rotation on the *Committee in Waiting*, which met daily, except on Sundays, as a group of three Directors. It was, in effect, the continuing embodiment of the Authority of the Court—

11 Pascoe Grenfell, Governor, 1829–38

supervising the cash books, signing cheques, authorizing payments, retaining custody of and using the Corporation's seal, and 'taking the appearance' and accepting or rejecting proposals for life insurance. Membership was the most continuously demanding of the average Director's duties, and an elaborate system of financial incentives was formulated. In the early part of the century, for example, £5. 10s. 0d., was deducted from a Director's fee for each week's 'Waiting'. Then, on each day, £3. 0s. 0d. (£1. 10s. 0d., on Saturdays) was brought into the Committee Room to be divided among those actually present at the beginning (11.45 a.m.). Thus, if all turned up regularly, a Director would have his deduction exactly reimbursed; if one or more failed to turn up, he or they would be commensurately mulcted, and his collegues benefited.

Apart from the Committee in Waiting, all the Corporation's Committees had specialist functions. The most important, *the Committee of Treasury*, consisted of the three Governors and seven Directors—in practice the most senior. 'The functions of that Committee', it was reported in 1841, 'are of the highest importance: it acts as a council to the Governors.' The Treasury Committee's formal task was 'generally to manage and superintend the revenues and expenditure of the Corporation and to report their proceedings to the Court of Directors'. On a week-to-week basis, of course, its principal function was to manage and superintend the Corporation's investments. But, partly because of the critical significance of its financial responsibilities, and partly because of the presence of the three Governors, it assumed much more general authority and acted very much as an executive committee of the Court, preparing material for, and making recommendations to, that body. For example, it was initially responsible for the scheme for the adoption of the bonus system of life insurance in 1841–2, and for the creation of a separate Accident Department in 1904. It was also concerned with more continuous problems—dealing not only with straightforward monetary matters but also with administrative organization, promotions, the general regulations of the Corporation, major questions of principle, sick leaves and the like. As the Governor claimed in 1907, when there was some controversy in the Court about the desirability of expanding employers' liability business, the intention 'had always been believed to be to make the Treasury Committee responsible for the general policy of the Corporation—and the Departmental Committees for the carrying out of the policy so indicated'. Only in 1912, with the creation of the Committee of Management, did there appear an alternative institutional focus of overall managerial control.[1]

[1] Below, pp. 370–2.

To judge by the criterion of seniority of membership, as well as by apparent function, the next most important body in the early nineteenth century was the *Average Committee*. This had been established in the eighteenth century to settle both losses on the marine branch and losses arising on fire and life policies (the first of these tasks was at that time sufficiently difficult and technical to justify a special payment to members from 1795). In the late 1820s, however, responsibility for the settlement of fire claims was transferred to the new Fire Committee, and the members of the Average Committee, with the addition of the Governors, were formed into a Special Committee for the Sea Business (also known as the *Special Average Committee*), which met monthly and formulated rules 'limiting the power' of Mr Browne, the Sitting Director who managed the Sea Department. But this very close relationship between a supervisory committee and an executive department could not withstand competitive realities: in 1838 increased competition and changing practices in marine underwriting obliged the Directors to delegate much more authority to the Underwriter.

This line of development outlasted the post of Sitting Director, and in 1841 the Average and Special Average Committees were abolished, and replaced by the *Committee for Sea Business*, which was to meet weekly, leaving the initiative 'both in effecting policies, and settling losses, averages and returns' to the Underwriter (the 'Manager of the Sea Business'). On the other hand, the vital character of marine underwriting was acknowledged by the seniority of the Committee and by the provision that once a month it should meet, with a Governor in the Chair, and 'specially enquire into the state of the Sea Business'.

As with the marine business, the other branches of underwriting had their supervisory committees, although they seem to have appeared somewhat late as specialist and continuing bodies. The *Life Committee* and the *Special Fire Committee* were established in the late 1820s, although responsibility for the settlement of life claims was still, somewhat anachronistically, retained by the Average Committee, and the Life Committee only met once a month. In contrast, the Special Fire Committee (which superseded an earlier body, dating from the 1720s, called the 'Committee in Waiting for the Fire Business') was a very busy group. Established in 1825, as a response to the decline in the Corporation's fire underwriting, it was responsible for the overall and detailed supervision of the fire business, appointing agents and settling losses, as well as formulating and overseeing policy. By 1841, owing to the limited amount of business for the Life Committee, it was consolidated with the Life group into the *Fire and Life*

Committee, containing seven Directors, for the joint supervision of both branches. This new Committee also took over the payment of life claims, and with a coherently defined responsibility, it lasted out the century.

Finally, the *Committee of Accounts* was the most junior body—in the sense of containing the most recently appointed Directors. It was a large committee (up to 1841 its maximum membership was 16) and in the eighteenth century it had been charged with the personal examination and checking of the ledgers and journals—which by 1841 'reduced to a mere matter of form, still continues: two members do check the journals and ledgers—receiving 5s. each for a few minutes labour—the Chairman receiving the same sum though never attending'. The position of this Committee seemed 'objectionable' to the reformers of 1841, who therefore recommended the abolition of any special payment and the reduction of the Committee's membership to three (plus, of course, the Governors). It still had general responsibility for examining the books and accounts, but in the main its task was concentrated in the very important area of supervising the Corporation's agents as far as the punctual remittance of accounts and cash balances was concerned—a task which had earlier, between 1816 and 1825, been undertaken by a 'Special Committee of Accounts'.

It is clear from all this that 1841 was a crucial year in the history of the Corporation's committee structure: while the Treasury Committee and the Committee in Waiting continued, the Average Committee had been replaced by a Sea Committee, the Fire and Life Committees had been conflated, and the function of the Committee of Accounts had been narrowed and more sharply defined. Organizationally, these were echoes or precursors of developments which were radically altering the nature of the Corporation's business. In general terms the increased complexity and consequent professionalization of management in each separate branch of the underwriting shaped a new rôle for Committees of Directors—one in which they could not hope to participate fully and in detail in the management of individual departments. This was perhaps most marked as far as marine underwriting was concerned; but it also happened in the field of life insurance and even, in spite of a temporary need for very detailed work by the Special Fire Committee after 1825, in the Fire Branch. More specifically, the early 1840s were a watershed in the development of the Corporation—witnessing the introduction of with-profits policies, the appointment of a Lloyd's man as Underwriter, the effective origins of the Fire Offices' Committee, and a more adventurous investment policy.

It is perhaps not coincidental that these changes in policy and the concomitant changes in organization coincided with changes in the Governorship—first, with the election of Sir John W. Lubbock in 1838, and then, on his death, with the election of Thomas Tooke in November 1840. Tooke in particular seems to have been a vigorous Governor—and the qualities of imagination and systematic thought which characterized his interest and writing in the field of economics and finance, must have proved relevant to his leadership of the REA at this crucial time in its history. Within two months of his assuming the Governorship, he took the Chair of a special Committee to investigate the existing Committees and 'to consider how far the intention of their institution is fulfilled'. It was, in fact, this Committee, led by Tooke, which initiated the various changes in organization already described, and which put forward as one criterion of reorganization, 'that it is essential to the well-being of the Corporation in times of great competition to endeavour to call forth the energies of every member of the Court, by giving him an interest in some one or other of its departments'.

These positive moves to harness and focus the energies of the Directors no doubt reflected some dissatisfaction with the apparent quiescence of earlier years. In re-structuring its Committees along lines more appropriate to contemporary needs, the Court also produced a relatively streamlined organization which, in essence, lasted into the early twentieth century. Under the new system of 1841 there were only four Committees (apart from the Committee in Waiting): Treasury, Sea, Fire and Life, and Accounts. And each of the twenty-four Directors was a member of only one Committee—the Governors, of course, being members of all. It was, in fact, a structure which was made to absorb much more than originally envisaged: for example, when accident business was commenced in the late 1890s it was for some years overseen not, as might have been expected, by a new and specialist committee, but by the Fire and Life Committee in the first instance, and then, when it was more firmly established, by the Accounts Committee.

The only other significant change in committee structure before the First World War came in 1911–12, with the establishment of a Committee of Management. In essence, as will be seen, this move was a response to the continued expansion of old, and the proliferation of new, business. Confronted with the problems inherent in such a growth, and in the need for general oversight and the integrated administration of the various affairs of the Corporation, the necessity of some new move was keenly felt. As a result, in order to establish 'some central authority for General Management', a Committee of Management, composed of the three Governors, was formed in 1911, to oversee 'the general administration of the affairs of the Corporation'.[1] Although this formalized the necessary co-ordinating and high-policy rôle of the three Governors, it did so by giving them a managerial rôle and at the price of postponing for almost another twenty years the appointment of a General Manager—i.e. a senior, full-time official with over-arching responsibilities. Why such an appointment was needed, and why in particular the need became increasingly apparent in the early twentieth century, can, however, only be understood in terms of what was happening to the rôle of Departmental Managers.

THE OFFICIALS AND THEIR DEPARTMENTS

The period leading up to the First World War was marked by the increasing professionalization of the Corporation's insurance management and administrative structure. In only one area did the Directors fully retain their traditional rôle. That was in the management and investment of the Corporation's assets. And this was an area which had always been entirely within the authority and responsibility of the Court—as represented by the Committee of Treasury. Indeed, in the context of other changes, this continuing tradition illustrates the basic distinction which emerged by the late nineteenth century, between the Directors who supervised the Corporation's business and managed its funds, and the officials who were responsible for the management of its underwriting activities.

To knowledgeable contemporaries this difference was vital, and was associated with the increasing technicality of insurance:

Any great interference on the part of the members of such an association, or even of the small body selected from among them to act as directors, will as a rule be of questionable advantage. No doubt the bringing together of men of business having varied knowledge and experience secures a valuable contribution to the aggregate skill that is needed; and their shrewd observations brought to bear on the capacity and character of the experts whom they employ, on the general conduct of the business, and even on some of its details, are of measureless value. Still it remains that between the knowledge of the most able director and that which is possessed by the officers of a fire or life insurance company, there is, or there ought to be, a wide gulf; and, consequently, its success or failure depends more upon its executive officers than in the case of almost any other business.[2]

This distinction was the administrative counterpart of the growth and increasing complexity of the business of insurance, which increasingly

---

[1] See below, pp. 370–3. In recognition of the greatly increased amount of work involved, the fees of the three Governors were increased.

[2] J. M. M'Candlish, 'The Economics of Insurance', *JFII*, XXII (1919), 60–1.

demanded skilled and full-time management and specialized departments. The very forces which produced an urgent demand for 'general management' by the early part of this century also explained the more independent rôle which Departmental Managers could, and had to, play. Thus, if we compare the Corporation's structure in 1915 with what it had been seventy-five years earlier, the contrast is striking. In 1840 there were merely thirty-nine clerks and chief officials in the five main departments (Secretary's, Sea, Fire, Life and Cashier & Accountant's). By the First World War, quite apart from the technical transformation of insurance and the rise of the Corporation's national and world-wide branch system, there were over 400 clerks and chief officials at Head Office, organized into eight departments (the above-mentioned five, together with Accident, Agency and Trustee and Executor). Some of these were further divided into sub-departments: by 1915 the Sea Department embraced separate Underwriters, Sea Claims and Foreign Marine Offices, and the Fire Department included Home, Foreign, Agency and Guarantee Offices.

It is obvious that the resulting increase in specialization of insurance management (which, of course, characterized all insurance companies in the nineteenth century) meant not only new rôles for the Directors, but also a sharpening of the distinctions between the different departmental heads. The same specialization of function which made it almost impossible for members of the Court to assume managerial duties, and which had made the continuance of the office of Sitting Director a dispensable embarrassment, also eliminated the overlapping of duties and the plurality of office-holding which had sometimes occurred in the nineteenth-century management of the Royal Exchange.

This applied, for example, to the Secretary's office and the Marine Department, which were only disassociated when a period of severe competition and the need for heightened thoroughness in marine insurance showed that the confusion of their functions was unsatisfactory.[1] A second, but more accidental (because the result of a particular personality and individual skill) example of the joining of two posts occurred between 1853 and 1860, when John Adams Higham was both Secretary and Actuary. However, the practice of a joint Secretary-Actuary appointment was not continued after Higham's resignation: quite apart from the extraordinary amount of work which must have been involved, it is obvious that the different responsibilities and skills entailed in the respective posts would have made it organizationally disadvantageous, as well as personally very difficult, to continue the experiment.

[1] Above, pp. 202–3.

The Marine Underwriter provided the best (but not the only) example of the need for managerial specialization in the early nineteenth century. Between 1830 and 1843, for example, marine premiums grew more than eightfold, and although in the early part of the century the Underwriter had also undertaken various clerical jobs, by the late 1830s or early 1840s it was acknowledged that the greatly extended scope of marine insurance demanded single-minded concentration—requiring, in the words of the 1843 Committee, 'the unremitting attention required for the due consideration of each individual risk'. In addition, the Sea Office bore witness not merely to the differentiation of the management function in specific areas of business, but also to the differentiation *within* departments which was such an important aspect of organizational change in the nineteenth century. By at least the 1830s there was a distinction between the duties of the Underwriter and the Examiner of Sea Claims (i.e. the adjuster of losses); and in 1888 the two were officially separated into an Underwriter's and a Sea Claims Office, each with its own Manager, although the Underwriter was still, of course, the senior. (The new Manager of the Sea Claims was E. D. Browne, who had joined the Corporation in 1832, and was the son of the former Sitting Director and Marine Underwriter.) In 1901 a Foreign Marine Department was also established—and a Manager appointed between 1911 and 1914.

The Fire Office illustrated the same trends towards specialization and differentiation—as its tasks became greater and more technical, as its relationship with agents and branches became more vital, and as the growth of the tariff association involved it in complicated negotiations and agreements. Thus, its relatively simple division, in the early part of the century, into Town and Country Departments, each with its own superintendent, had given way by the early twentieth century into a quadripartite structure of Home, Foreign, Agency and Guarantee Departments—the whole operating for some years under two Joint Managers, one of whom had special experience and expertise in the foreign field.

The proliferation of the Corporation's business and commitments also involved the development of entirely new functions (as well as the growth of familiar ones) which had to be embraced organizationally. Accident underwriting, which rapidly proved to be a spectacular growth point for the Royal Exchange, was a case in point. When it was begun, in 1899, accident business was made the Actuary's responsibility, and it was not until 1904 that it was associated with its own Department and Manager (A. W. Wamsley). A somewhat different range of problems was presented by the growing need to establish continuous and systematic control over, and direction of, the Corporation's agents. In the 1890s both the Fire and Life Departments had appointed 'Inspectors of Agents', and in 1898 the Life Department appointed its own 'Agency Manager'. But it was not until 1903 that the post of Agency Manager to the Corporation was established; and even then the man appointed (R. B. S. Castle, who had been Agency Manager of the Life Department) was, in fact, attached to the Secretary's Office.[1] And it was still to be some years before the new Department's function could be disentangled from the functions which the separate departments continued, almost jealously, to fulfil.

In the long run, of course, the specialization and strengthening of individual departments raised new issues about general management and the need to co-ordinate and control their operations. But the emergence of strong and relatively independent departments did not bring any particularly severe administrative problems until the end of the period. This was because the size and scope of the Corporation's business did not really reach critical levels until the 1890s or the opening years of this century. For most of the nineteenth century the organization was still sufficiently small to attain co-ordination in informal and personal terms.

Although there was no formal attempt, or institutional innovation, to secure co-ordination at the managerial level in the nineteenth century, there was, of course, one official who was in a special position by virtue of his office. As Secretaries to the Corporation, men like John A. Higham (1854–61), E. R. Handcock (1875–1900) or W. N. Whymper (1900–17) were appointed to fulfil a central function which stood in a quite distinctive relationship to the Governors and the Court, to the committee structure, and even to the other Heads of Departments. In 1838, for example, a special Committee emphasized that the Secretary was the chief and confidential officer of the Corporation, with immediate supervision of the establishment; and that one of the duties of the Heads of Departments was 'to maintain a friendly and confidential communication with the Secretary on all matters relating to the interests of the Corporation'.

Although the Secretary's formal responsibilities marked him out from the general run of Managers, by the late nineteenth century there were various limitations on his assuming the rôle of 'General Manager'. Thus, his responsibilities (for staff, committee co-ordination, correspondence, the affairs of the Court, etc.) meant that his time was already heavily committed. Further, the nature of these duties, and the context which they provided for the Secretary's relationships with the officials responsible for

[1] From 1900 the Secretary's Office also included the Estates Office clerical staff—i.e. the clerks responsible for the management of the mortgaged estates forfeited to the Corporation.

underwriting, to some extent weakened his position *vis-à-vis* the departmental heads. This was particularly so because, given the lines of promotion, the Secretary rarely had any direct experience of work in and administration of an underwriting department.

In spite of these considerations, however, there can be no doubt that, depending on the strength of mind, the appetite for work, and the personality of the individual concerned, a Secretary *could* assert himself in a 'managerial' rôle. From various sorts of evidence it would seem that Handcock and Whymper were to a large extent responsible for the changes in policy and organization which transformed the Corporation in the late nineteenth and early twentieth centuries. And there is a logic about this. For in the absence of a General Manager, the Secretary was the only official in a position to initiate and supervise the relevant policies. More than this, his rôle with respect to the crucial committees, together with the related fact that he was the official channel of communication with, and therefore had the ear of, the Governor, endowed him with the appropriate power and authority.

In Handcock's case, unfortunately, there is little surviving evidence of the ways in which he exercised his authority. But there is little reason to doubt the verdict of a contemporary journal that 'with his appointment began a new era in the affairs of the Corporation', and that he was influential in the creation of branches, the increase of premium, the appointment of new departmental heads, and the creation of a Pension Fund for the staff.[1]

Handcock died in 1900 (at the age of 60, after forty-three years' service) and was succeeded by William N. Whymper, who had been a clerk in the Secretary's Office since 1872. In Whymper's case, surviving records provide considerably more evidence of his active rôle in the general areas of management and policy formulation and execution. It is obvious, for example, that he had a very close relationship with the Governor—and particularly with Sir Nevile Lubbock (Governor from 1904 to 1914). Their letters amply indicate that Whymper was not merely the secretarial channel for the Governor, but his *confidante* and adviser on various far-ranging and important matters of organization, underwriting and investment. In addition, to take merely one example, in the early years of accident writing Whymper played a dominant rôle in determining the organization of the newly formed Accident Department in 1904 and in limiting the expansion of accident underwriting in 1906–7, at a time when the Corporation's resources were strained as a consequence of the San Francisco fire losses.

[1] *The Insurance Index*, VII, 1 (31 January 1891).

More generally, in 1911, the Directors agreed that the Secretary should have the authority to decide any question which was too urgent to wait for one of the daily meetings of the Committee in Waiting. We know, too, from a talk that he gave at the Manchester Insurance Institute, that Whymper had particular responsibility for investments (an Investment Manager was not appointed until the late 1920s), and his talk was full of advice on investment and its problems, including the information that he avoided having a telephone in his office in order to guard against 'the making of hasty decisions on vital matters'. Finally, Whymper was a central figure in various appraisals and negotiations (which in the event came to nothing) for amalgamations with such notable offices as the Sun, the London Assurance and the Atlas in the period around the First World War. Clearly such a man carried a great weight of personal authority in the Corporation. To an office junior (even allowing for the fact that the claim occurred in a humorous article) it seemed that everybody looked on him 'with awe' and that when the junior took letters to him to be signed, 'I simply hold my breath the whole time I am in the room'.[1] To the trade Press in 1908 the fact that the REA was 'one of the most active and progressive insurance companies in existence' seemed largely attributable to his efforts: 'Mr Whymper has a strong individuality and an unusual ability to back it.'[2]

Although Handcock and Whymper, the last two Secretaries before the outbreak of War, were attempting to reshape the structure of management under the influence of new business pressures and needs, the extent to which the result was a large degree of genuine general management should not be exaggerated. Rather, throughout the period up to the 1920s the trends in insurance underwriting and in the Corporation's own structure were concentrating more and more expertise, authority and independence in the hands of the individual Heads of Departments. (It was, of course, this development which bestowed considerable problems of management reorganization on the Corporation in the inter-war years.) It was overwhelmingly in the hands of these men that the prospects of the Royal Exchange resided.

For most of the nineteenth century the men who were recruited for these responsible positions were by and large products of the REA itself. The Corporation's senior officials tended to be recruited from its own clerks. More than this, the continuity of employment meant that most officials had been at the Royal Exchange ever since beginning regular

[1] 'If I were Secretary!' *REAM*, I, 1 (January 1902), 12.
[2] *Insurance Index*, XXIII, 2 (July 1908).

employment (usually between the ages of 16 and 18)—while the tradition of seniority as a principle of promotion meant that frequently the longest-serving clerk was elevated into any vacancy which might occur.

On the other hand, these traditions were not immutable. In the later nineteenth century, no doubt as part of the general response to the need for growth and innovation in a changing insurance world, some senior posts began to be filled by men from outside the Corporation. Admittedly, and for clear-cut reasons, the Secretaries had been and continued to be REA men from the beginning of their career. But in 1841, with the need to revive the Sea Department, Henry Warre was recruited from Lloyd's as Marine Underwriter, and his successor (John Leatherdale, 1864–75) had been recruited at the same time. The next Underwriter,[1] E. F. Gedge (1875–88), had joined the Sea Department in a senior position in 1864; and *his* successor, F. S. Toulmin (1888–1903), came directly to the Underwriter's position from Lloyd's. It was not until Augustus Dutton (1904–7) that the Corporation once more had an Underwriter who started as an assistant clerk (age 18).

The Fire Department experienced a similar, although somewhat later, trend towards the recruitment of men who had made their reputations and learned their basic skills elsewhere. Until 1890 the Superintendents or Managers of the Fire Branch (the former terminology was used until 1855) had all been REA clerks.[2] In that year, however, J. H. Duncan was appointed Manager, having been Assistant Secretary of the London office of the Royal Insurance Company. The point here, however, was that Duncan (like his successor E. B. Hiles, who joined the Corporation as a senior clerk for foreign fire business in the same year) was brought in for particular reasons. He was expected not merely to invigorate the Corporation's fire underwriting (the *Post Magazine*, after his first year, acknowledged signs of 'a very large accession of vitality'),[3] but to do so in the specific and new direction of overseas business. And for this purpose the fact that the REA had relatively limited experience in overseas insurance naturally meant that it had little management resources to call on from its own staff.

The administrative position of the Heads of Department was obviously reflected in their salaries, which, in the nineteenth-century context, were

---

[1] The Underwriter was, in fact, known as the 'Manager of the Sea Office' between 1855 and 1888—at which point his title reverted to 'Underwriter' and a new Sea Claims Department was formed under its own Manager.

[2] Matthew Ward, *c.* 1805–30; Edward Bird, 1830–64; Charles P. Ball, 1865–79; Octavius E. Fooks, 1879–90.

[3] *PM*, LIII, 30 (23 July 1892).

reasonably high. The Underwriter was the best paid of the various officers —as might be expected from the fact that good Underwriters could otherwise hope to earn substantial profits at Lloyd's and that his task was a much more personal one, involving a more direct and explicit connection between the skills of the individual and the profits of the Corporation. Thus it was that, apart from his regular salary of £2,000, Henry Warre received gifts, in recognition of underwriting profits, of more than £62,000 between 1850 and 1867. His successor, Leatherdale, was almost as well treated. By contrast, the Secretary, depending on length of service, earned between £800 and £1,200 for most of the century, although Handcock's salary rose to £1,500 by 1900 and Whymper's to £2,000 by 1917. The growing importance of the Fire Manager was reflected in an improvement to his relative economic position. Edward Bird after seven years as Fire Manager had been earning £600 in 1837, rising to £1,000 in 1865, while J. H. Duncan was appointed at a salary of £1,500 in 1890 and was earning £2,500 ten years later. A similar, although not quite so sharp, improvement took place in the case of the Actuary: Bidder's £400 on appointment in 1838 (rising to £800 in 1848) contrasting with Nightingale's £800 in 1893 (rising to £1,500 in 1900). In 1872 the Court agreed that the salaries of Heads of Departments should be paid free of income tax—following the precedent of clerks' salaries established in 1854.

Men in this position obviously had a special status in the Corporation's affairs. One small but significant aspect of this was the arrangements for meals. For many years a luncheon room was set aside for the exclusive use of the Heads of Departments; then the privilege was extended to the departmental Chief Clerks; but in 1865, since the resulting number was found to be 'inconveniently large', it was decided to confine its future use to Departmental Managers, although all then using the room were to continue to do so. (The annual cost of these lunches to the Corporation was about £600 in the mid-1860s and £700 in the mid-1870s—or just over 2s. 6d. per person per meal.) Such occasions, of course, had an explicit business, as well as a social, function. And when, in 1874, the Governor proposed that the officials might have their lunch somewhat later, since the Directors used the room for lunch first, some Managers protested that they might have to lunch individually out of the office ('finding the prolonged abstinence unfavourable to health') which would impair the utility of communal meals: '[we] would submit that our daily meeting has been of advantage to the service by enabling us to confer on matters of business in which more than one department has been concerned, and to obtain information useful to us in the discharge of our several duties'. Such an argument was perfectly reasonable, and it is therefore not surprising that from 1857 the Directors lunched separately, in the Court Room.

DECISION-MAKING AND ORGANIZATIONAL CHANGE: THE NEED FOR GENERAL MANAGEMENT

The lunch-time separation of Directors and Managers was in one sense a symptom of the line between the Court's concern with matters of high policy and investment, and the officials' professional and technical commitment to insurance underwriting and management. On the other hand, the Directors' responsibilities could be delegated to the Managers when that was a relevant and more efficient thing to do. For example, in the first half of the nineteenth century the daily Committee in Waiting examined and verified the 'Fire Office [i.e. Department] Cash Book'. But in 1858, the Treasury Committee ordered that in future this be done by the Superintendent of the Department, on the grounds that Mr Bird 'from his thorough acquaintance with the books and systems of accounts in use in his department would be able to make a more effective examination than the Committee in Waiting'. (In future the Committee was to verify the Book by Bird's signature.) On the other hand, when management decisions were concerned with problems of far-reaching significance—so that both sets of decision-makers were equally concerned—means were found to harmonize the processes of policy formulation. As with the history of most business enterprises, the form in which events and decisions were recorded does not lend itself to a detailed analysis of the means and discussions by which they were arrived at. But indirect evidence makes it clear that when, for example, there was a substantial overhaul of fire underwriting in the late 1820s, or when the bonus system was introduced into life insurance in 1841-2, the decisions were arrived at and enforced by a combination of the professional skills of the relevant Managers and the authority and commercial expertise of the Directors—although it seems that the Directors were more responsible for taking the initiative in the first case, and the Actuary in the second. As time went on, of course, the rôle of the professional became more than ever important, so that by the late nineteenth century quite significant policy departures—new forms of life policies, larger distribution of bonus, the commencement of accident business, the Pension Fund plan, etc.—were matters in which the relevant Managers played an initiating, even innovating, rôle. Of course, managerial proposals were sometimes turned down—as when the Treasury Committee declined to accept the Actuary's recommendation that the pension scheme of 1890 be a contributory one. Further, divisions of opinion were not always clear cut. In 1907, for example, as we have seen, the Accident Manager and the Committee of Accounts advocated an expansion of liability insurance, while the Secretary and the Treasury Committee successfully opposed it.

The point has already been made, and the argument in the previous paragraph corroborates it, that many of the fundamental changes which took place in the business policy of the REA in the nineteenth century could be accommodated without any fundamental change in its organization. For many aspects of the evolution of insurance implied structural changes of an easy, and easily acceptable, sort—namely, new relationships within the boundaries of existing departments and responsibilities. But the real problem areas for organizational change were naturally to be found far more often on the borderland, and sometimes even the no-man's-land, between existing departments: it was the pressure for changes in policies and attitudes which could not be confined to a single existing organizational unit which was longest and most painful in being satisfied. The main reason for this was, of course, that at the official administrative level, the inherited structure gave a very considerable degree of independence to the individual departments. There was no built-in tendency to active co-operation. In some respects co-ordination could in any case be imposed from above—for example, in the matter of the allocation of general expenses to the individual departments. Thus, in 1869 the Court agreed that the traditional equal division of general expenses between the Sea, Fire and Life Branches should be changed to the extent of charging the Life Department with a fixed sum of £2,000 and transferring the balance of its one-third share to the General Account. And in 1890 the Committee of Treasury successfully recommended to the Court that the Sea and Fire Departments be charged with only 25 per cent each of the general expenses.

Yet there were other problems of growth which could not be so easily resolved, because no institutional arrangements existed for their resolution. Among the most important of these was the question of control on a non-departmental basis as the Corporation extended the geographical scope of its activities through agents and then branches, throughout this country and then abroad. In fact, the confusion and potential inefficiency inherent in such expansion with no clearly defined means of central co-ordination of agents and branches—who were responsible at various levels to the Secretary, the Fire Manager and the Actuary (and later the Accident Manager)—persisted for some time. Each department had its own means of control, but not of course, specialized agents or branches. Indeed, once Head Office had to deal with branches which were really extensions of the

Corporation itself, it was no longer possible to leave matters to the individual underwriting departments. Yet an Agency Manager for the Corporation was not appointed until 1903, and even then continued to work within the Secretary's Office, with no separate Agency Department, for some years.

Important problems of structural innovation and control were also raised by the new departures in underwriting which came in the generation before the First World War. In particular, the introduction of accident insurance was not immediately associated with the development of an appropriate organizational framework. Departmentally, accident insurance was placed under the control of the Actuary until 1904, when it was given independent status under the Accident Manager, A. W. Wamsley. This was done to give Wamsley the advantage of 'personal access to a Committee of Directors for guidance and advice'. At the same time general oversight of accident business was made the responsibility of the Committee of Accounts—principally, it would seem, because that was the Committee with the most spare time! The drawbacks of this somewhat haphazard arrangement became apparent in 1907 when, in the straitened circumstances after the San Francisco fire, the Governors and the Treasury Committee began to press for a policy of caution and moderation with respect to the expansion of accident business—only to be met with a strong protest from the Committee of Accounts, which claimed that it alone had *direct* responsibility for accident insurance. This particular issue was, in fact, resolved by an *ad hoc* Committee formed to confer on the matters of policy with the Committee of Accounts.

This last episode had a much broader significance. For it cast some light on the main sense in which the organization of the REA lagged behind the rapidly emerging needs of modern insurance. And that was with regard to the development of what is now called 'general management'. The growth of the Corporation's business was proceeding in two directions: first, through a substantial extension of older types of underwriting (marine, life and fire premiums almost doubled in the first decade of the twentieth century); second, through the beginning of new types of business (liability, accident, burglary, fidelity guarantee, trustee and executor). This growth, which also implied geographical expansion and the development of new branches, was naturally associated with the emergence of strong, vigorous and independent departments. Paradoxically, however, those departments, precisely because they were independent, posed a mild threat to the continuance of growth. Quite apart from the pressing need to co-ordinate the activities of the various departments, the lack of active and firm central guidance was becoming increasingly obvious. In addition it can be assumed that, as happened at the Commercial Union, the Departmental Heads suffered by not having direct formal access to the Court of Directors or the Treasury Committee. Hence, at the Commercial Union, a General Manager was appointed in 1901, precisely to 'represent' other Managers at Board level.[1]

At the Royal Exchange the inescapable need for organizational change in order to secure the co-ordination of the different departments had become extremely pressing by the opening of the twentieth century. A world-wide and very large-scale composite insurance business could no longer be run on a single departmental basis. In July 1911 the Court appointed a special Committee to consider 'whether in view of the increased and increasing operations of the Corporation the existing system of management is best suited to the requirements of the business and to report to the Court whether any modification or change is in their opinion desirable'. This Committee proceeded to take verbal and written evidence from all the principal officers of the Corporation and in its interim report in August indicated that there was 'a consensus of opinion that the present system is not entirely satisfactory, and your Committee consider that some central authority for General Management should be created'. For this purpose the Committee recommended the appointment of a Committee of Management, consisting of the three Governors, which should meet weekly, at which times different Department Heads should be present— with a regular meeting at least once a month at which all the Heads of Departments should collectively meet the Governors 'to consider any business affecting the Corporation'. In a subsequent report it was also recommended that the daily Committee in Waiting be relieved of most of its detailed work, that it be strengthened by ensuring that one or more of the three Governors should preside and also be present each day between 12.45 and 1.30 p.m., except Saturday, and that all matters for immediate decision should be brought by the Heads of Departments to this Committee —and any question which could not wait for a decision until the next daily Committee should be decided by the Secretary.

These recommendations were informally adopted in Autumn 1911 and when they were considered by the General Court of Proprietors the new Committee was seen as a means 'of concentrating and more effectually supervising the management of the various classes of business conducted by the Corporation'. It was acknowledged that the REA suffered through being 'probably the only insurance company of any importance in the City

[1] Liveing, *A Century of Insurance*, pp. 74–8.

of London which has no [General] Manager or Management Committee'. The idea of a General Manager was rejected on grounds 'of consideration of internal arrangements'—presumably the prospect of difficult relationships if a new and senior official post were created above the existing semi-independent and senior Managers. Instead, the existing and acknowledged rôle of the Governors was regularized and institutionalized.

The policy implications of this step were made clear by the Governor, Sir Nevile Lubbock, in addressing the other members of the Committee and the Heads of Departments at the first meeting on 28 September 1911. He stated:

that the object of the Court in appointing the Governors as a Managing Committee was that they should be kept thoroughly acquainted with all the business carried on by the Corporation. He pointed out that it was not intended that the Committee should interfere with the Heads of Departments in the carrying on of the ordinary business of those Departments, but they wished to be kept informed generally as to what was going on in each Department, and especially to be consulted in regard to any business proposed which was out of the ordinary routine of the various Departments . . . The Governor then stated that two subjects in particular would require the early attention of the Committee, namely, the division of expenses between Departments, and the question of the correspondence both in and out of Head Office. On the latter subject the Actuary was requested to make a report on behalf of all Departments. He further stated that the Committee proposed to go through the records of the existing fire risks, with the view of making themselves generally acquainted with the approximate amount at risk in the various places at home and abroad in which the Corporation does business.

Thenceforth the Committee principally concerned itself with the general oversight of departmental affairs (receiving and considering regular reports from the Heads of Departments), major questions of investments and salaries, and major innovations in procedure and policies.

Organizationally, the establishment of a Management Committee had significant implications for the REA, but it did not mark quite the turning-point which the Court imagined in 1911. The new Committee was in one sense little more than an institutionalization of the Governors' traditional rôle; and, as the Governors themselves appreciated, it was a substitute for the appointment of a General Manager, in terms of his positive function and of providing a focus for managerial representation at the centre. Yet, in retrospect, it seems clear that there *could* be no effective substitute for the sort of explicit appointment that had already greatly influenced the managerial evolution of other insurance companies. To take merely four examples, the Royal of Liverpool owed much of its early success to the appointment of Percy M. Dove (recruited from the Royal Exchange) as Manager in 1845; the Liverpool & London & Globe nominated its Secretary (John M. Dove, Percy's son) as General Manager in 1876; the Atlas, having chosen a powerful new Secretary, Samuel J. Pipkin, in 1884, appointed him as its first General Manager in 1896; and the Commercial Union recognized the new needs of its international business by appointing a General Manager in 1901. Nor was this trend towards a single executive head merely a corporate fashion: it is clear from these and other examples that the drive, unity and purposefulness which were essential for profitable growth could best, and perhaps only, be obtained by a concentration of authority and responsibility. The period around the turn of the century was an 'Age of General Managers' as far as the development of insurance was concerned. It was almost as if the rise of huge new corporate personalities could only be sustained by the efforts of outstanding and powerful individuals. It was this element which was lacking at the Royal Exchange Assurance. Admittedly, its transformation from the late 1880s could be attributed to new and influential Departmental Managers like Gerald H. Ryan, J. H. Duncan and A. W. Wamsley, who broke away from inherited attitudes and pushed the Corporation into advanced modes of business behaviour. But in spite of this, and in spite of the efforts of such influential Secretaries as Whymper and his successor, Percy Frederick Higham Hodge (1917–29), there could be no effective alternative to an explicit decision to create a new, and much more powerful post. Until then, and even taking the Committee of Management into account, the Corporation, compared with most of its leading competitors, lacked a single point of organizational focus and authority. And even though its own, rather special, solution undoubtedly had some strong points, it also had some unsatisfactory features.

The main point in this respect was that the Committee of Management was in itself an anomalous development, precisely because it was charged with a management, as well as an overall policy-making and supervisory, function. Indeed, it reversed a historical trend. For in effect it transferred what should have been direct managerial responsibilities to members of the Court at the end of a long period in which there had been a heightened distinction between policy-making or supervisory and managerial or executive functions. That there was a need to concentrate the oversight of major policies, and that it was appropriate to do so in a Committee of the Governors, were entirely reasonable. But the conjoining with this of the essentially managerial function of co-ordination in a growing institution, rather than the delegation of that function to a professional manager, created almost as many problems as it solved. On the other hand, the fact that the trend towards delegation was apparently abruptly reversed was not so arbitrary a move as it might seem. The function of 'general management' was entirely new in terms of the Corporation's own history and needs. It was obviously very different from older functions like *departmental* management. And it is not surprising, therefore, that its very novelty and significance should have persuaded the Court that it might best be carried out by the Governors, rather than by a salaried official, who might find it very difficult to assert the necessary authority over other officials.

Nevertheless, this was to avoid rather than confront the problems of twentieth-century organization, and there is a sense in which the creation of the Management Committee merely postponed the inevitable (in fact, the first REA General Manager was appointed in 1929). Indeed, the postponement of radical change only aggravated the problem by continuing and enhancing the independent authority of individual departments. Even with the new arrangement, the Governors could not be expected to accumulate the necessary knowledge of detail or continuously devote the necessary amount of time to the tasks of management. There was still, therefore, a gap between the chosen instrument of general management and the departmental officials. And in the last resort this gap could only be closed by the creation of another management level—an innovation which did not detract from the indispensable rôle of the Governors, but which, rather, freed them for the more far-reaching supervisory rôle to which their position and experience were more suited. Organizationally, the appointment of a General Manager was to strengthen both the Governors and the officials in their respective roles. Before that appointment, however, it could not be said that the Corporation had adequately matched its structure to its new tasks.

15

The Establishment
1838-1914

In insurance as in other fields the evolution of the British economy in the nineteenth century had a significant effect on the pattern and character of employment. Conditions of work changed; old skills adapted themselves or disappeared; novel techniques brought new occupations into existence. Such changes were bound to have their effects on the staff at the Royal Exchange Assurance. For example, there was both a substantial increase in employment and a change in the structure of that employment as the Corporation developed new activities and constructed a nation-wide and a world-wide organization. By the early twentieth century the staff were working within a much larger, more competitive and structurally more specialized institution than had been known before 1870. Nevertheless, there were very strong elements of continuity in the conditions of employment and it is significant that in this respect, as in others, the basic characteristics of the Corporation were relatively little affected by the changes in its economic environment and rôle. A career with the REA on the eve of the First World War would certainly have been familiar to the clerks who worked there when Victoria came to the throne.

THE EXPANSION OF NUMBERS AND VARIETIES OF PRESTIGE

The growth of insurance in the nineteenth century was one example of the growth in service industries which accompanied economic development. Between 1841 and 1901, for example, employment in trade, transport, public, professional and similar services rose from about 1·75 million to some 5 million—or from less than a quarter to almost a third of the entire labour force.[1] From the present viewpoint, the most interesting aspect of this trend was the enormous growth in the number of clerks. For the banks and other financial houses, the trading establishments and the railways, the Civil Service and large shops, were dependent on men (and,

[1] Deane and Cole, *British Economic Growth*, p. 142. These figures exclude the 14 per cent of the labour force engaged in domestic or personal service.

somewhat later, women) who had elementary literate and numerate skills.[1] This dependence was the more marked because, compared with manufacturing, service industries offered relatively less scope for the introduction of labour-saving devices; even by the late nineteenth century typing, copying and calculating machines were in their infancies. In the labour force as a whole, therefore, the number of clerks grew from just under 50,000 in 1841 to about 180,000 in 1881. By 1911 there were over 475,000[2] —excluding the 40,000 clerks and officials in banking and the 46,000 in insurance.[3]

The insurance industry obviously provides a good illustration of this reliance on clerical work. For it was dependent on a vast amount of correspondence, of record keeping and record retrieval, of accounting and computing. In 1863, for example, in a period of relative quiescence, and relatively small-scale activity, the REA Fire Department had to process (by hand) some 9,500 fire policies; the Shipping Department was responsible for over 19,000 policies; and the Cashier's and Accountant's Department had to maintain accounts relating to over 500 loans and 550 agencies. And these were merely routine problems. The clerks might also have to brace themselves for such extraordinary events as a change in the premium rates and tables used for the life business—a change which in 1859 led the Atlas Life Department to undertake calculations involving over one million figures and 37,800 individual results—a set of calculations which would have taken one clerk over a year to complete.

There was also another important sense in which the business of the REA was firmly based on the labours of its clerks. For the officials of the Corporation, the Heads and Deputy Managers of specialist departments, themselves tended to rise from the clerical ranks. As new insurance companies were established and other existing offices were enlarged, the Corporation's clerks were recruited for responsible positions elsewhere. But only rarely were 'outsiders' given positions of responsibility within the Corporation. And where this did occur it was usually because of the demand for specific and highly technical skills (as with the Marine Underwriter and the Actuary) or for skills associated with a new activity or department (as happened when overseas fire business was commenced in the early 1890s, or when accident business was commenced a few years later). To this extent, therefore, the distinction between managerial work

---

[1] By 1901 just under 14 per cent of all clerks were women; by 1951 the proportion was almost 60 per cent: David Lockwood, *The Blackcoated Worker* (1958), p. 36.

[2] W. J. Reader, *Professional Men* (1966), p. 211.

[3] *Census of England and Wales, 1911*, vol. x, part I, p. 2.

and clerical responsibilities was not always a sharp one; managers came from the same grades, and the same backgrounds, as their clerks. In this respect the REA was not alone. For example, at Glyn, Mills, Currie & Co., the old City Bank, the senior managerial positions (according to a witness before a Government Commission in 1874) were 'not outside the clerk's posts. They are filled up by promotion from the establishment. We have no classes. We have no line drawn between one set of men and another.'[1]

TABLE 15.1. *REA Head Office staff (by Department), 1840–1913*[a]

Department[b]	1840	1860	1890	1900	1910	1913
Secretary	2	2	3	7	23	29
Cashier and Accountant	12	18	17	25	36	39
Sea	8	11	13	25	35	45
Fire	13	22	26	48	72	86
Life	4	7	6	19	26	31
Accident	—	—	—	12	33	53
Messengers	9	10	11	13	16	18
Typists	—	—	—	—	11	13
Total:	48	70	76	149	252	314

[a] Source: Salary Books.

[b] For the purposes of long-term comparison, the data have been grouped according to a conventional arrangement. In fact, however, a proliferation of functions and departments accompanied the growth of the Corporation after 1890. By the first decade of this century, for example, 'Secretary' includes Trustee and Executor work and an Agency Department; 'Sea' includes separate Sub-Departments for Sea Claims, the Underwriter, and Foreign Marine; and 'Fire' includes Foreign Fire as well as Home Fire.

Table 15.1 indicates the growth of numbers at the REA's Head Office. In the generation after the fire of 1838 there was a gentle expansion of staff, including nine or ten messengers, from about forty-eight to seventy. Subsequently, while the Corporation's business was more or less stable, the number was maintained at about seventy for the next thirty years. Then, quite suddenly, under the influence of the growth in underwriting, the Head Office staff (i.e. excluding staff elsewhere in London and in provincial and overseas branches) virtually doubled in the 1890s: rising from seventy-six to 149. And in the first thirteen years of this century it doubled again. On the eve of the War the Accident Department alone, although only fifteen years old, employed substantially more clerks than the entire Corporation had done in 1840! In this last period, too, there was a minor social revolution: the first typist was employed in 1907; by 1913 there

[1] Evidence of William Newmarch to the Civil Service Inquiry Commission, *PP* (1875), XXIII, Q.4777.

were thirteen typists adding variety and, we may hope, new glamour to the establishment.

The clerks who worked for the Royal Exchange Assurance, whether in its prosperous and stable mid-Victorian years or during the more hectic period of growth after 1890, were by no means average members of a homogeneous clerical labour force. They were near the top of a complex hierarchy in the occupational and social world of nineteenth-century clerks —sharing with the staff of other long-established insurance offices, of the Bank of England and of the better Civil Service Departments, a standard of living, a level of responsibility, and a status, which sharply differentiated them from the mass of clerical employees. In the 1880s and 1890s clerkships with the Royal Exchange or the Bank were considered plum jobs for young men in the City of London.

The Royal Exchange clerk was in no less favoured an economic and social position than his fellow clerk in the Atlas—a post which in the 1860s was reputed to be 'as good as a post in the Bank of England or a Government Office, carrying with it a pension and demanding only short hours'.[1] Both, however, were a world apart from the poor, overworked, underpaid Bob Cratchit of *The Christmas Carol.* And, we may suspect, both were also much better placed than clerks in some less solid and reputable insurance companies. For there were hierarchies even within particular types of activity. Charles Dickens had a keen sense of the varied world of clerks, emphasizing both the abused and deprived position of Newman Noggs, 'clerk and drudge to Ralph Nickleby', and the prosperous, loyal and even pampered status of Tim Linkinwater, who had worked forty-four years for Cheeryble, Brothers, and requested, 'if it wasn't inconvenient, and didn't interfere with business . . . leave to die there'.[2]

Admittedly, superior clerical status might have its drawbacks, especially for adventurous or ambitious young men in a period of slow growth, when the burdens of dull and routine work were not alleviated by the prospect of advancement or by the opportunity of exercising initiative. Referring to the Atlas in the 1860s, for example, Samuel Pipkin, its future General Manager, was honest enough to admit that, 'Oh! it was awful! nearly all above me young—no sign of business development to create chances of promotion . . . The fact is that an insurance junior's life was a very humdrum life.'[3]

[1] Samuel J. Pipkin, 'Fifty Years Reminiscences in the City', *PM*, LXXVII, 52 (23 December 1916), 880.

[2] *Nicholas Nickleby* (first published 1838–9; Oxford University Press, 1950), p. 456.

[2] Pipkin, 'Reminiscences', *PM* (23 December 1916), pp. 880–1.

Pipkin, however, was an exceptionally energetic and able man, who transformed the Atlas when he returned (having left to work for the Commercial Union in 1873) as General Manager in 1884. And, in any case, the attractions of work in offices like the Atlas or the Royal Exchange were not the easy opportunities of spectacular business success. For one thing, success in the world of insurance did not come easily; and for another, even though most managerial posts were filled by clerks who had climbed the entire ladder of promotion, the number of such posts was necessarily limited; most clerks, as in banking, would be 'quite content to jog on in the customary manner'.[1] Instead, it was the decent pay, the good hours, the permanency of tenure, the likelihood of a pension, and the security derived from belonging to a corporate body, which must have attracted most clerks. These characteristics differentiated the 'respectable' insurance clerk very clearly from the mass of the labour force—and, indeed, from the mass of clerks. In the context of the nineteenth century, they were the attributes of the growing but still tiny group of salaried middle class. But viewed in another way, as we shall see, they anticipated for a relatively small and, indeed, privileged group the enconomic and social changes which, in the twentieth century, have transformed the working lives of increasing numbers of people.

INCOMES AND LEISURE

Although the financial rewards of the average REA clerk were not spectacular in comparison with, say, the income of an independent businessman, the fact remains that he was well paid by most contemporary standards. Clerical salaries in the mid-nineteenth century were based on a scale formulated in 1838, when it was decided to abolish the previous system of annual gratuities supplementing ordinary income. Starting at an annual salary of £70 at the age of 18, they rose by regular increments to £150 after twelve years—although there was explicit provision for accelerated promotion, and, of course, for advancement beyond £150 when merited by a clerk's services and abilities.

This basic scale is by no means an accurate guide to the income of clerks at the Royal Exchange around the mid-century, since the Corporation paid their salaries tax-free from 1854 (the Managers had to wait until 1872 for this perquisite) and from time to time they received gratuities in recognition of unusually onerous or exceptionally good work or results. On the other hand, the Directors resisted the encroachment of any regular system of gratuities, or even (in light of the brevity of the normal working day)

[1] Evidence to the Civil Service Inquiry Commission, *PP* (1875), XXIII, Q.4815.

of any payment for moderate overtime work. Indeed, in 1870 such payment was denounced by a Committee as 'a vicious system, inconsistent with the highest interest of the Office'. Five years later the Court again banned overtime payment and awarded, as compensation, gifts amounting to about 15 per cent of each clerk's salary.

As far as incomes were concerned, however, the prospect of accelerated promotion was a more important consideration than either gratuities or overtime. As Gerald H. Ryan, the Actuary, pointed out in 1890, whatever the nature of a fixed salary scale, 'individual merit would be sure to break through the barriers'. In fact, the notional maximum was misleading: nearly every clerk who reached his twelfth year with the REA exceeded the 'norm' of £150. Promotion invariably carried clerks through to more responsibility and higher salaries. Even below the level of really outstanding men like John Higham (who was appointed Actuary at a salary of £500 in his twelfth year with the office), there were those like Augustus Dutton, who was earning £300 after serving eighteen years in the Fire Department, and ultimately became its Assistant Manager, in 1864.

All this, however, was within the existing structure of clerical incomes, and the salary scales remained constant for a generation after 1838. In this respect it must be remembered that prices were not equally stable. When they were falling, of course, the material conditions of the clerical staff must have improved—as happened in the 1840s and for a generation or more after 1874. By contrast, there was a steep increase of about 25 per cent in the cost of living between 1852 and 1856, followed by a slight fall and then relative stability at levels which in the 1860s were still 15 or 20 per cent above those of the 1840s.

As a result, although their temerity is in retrospect somewhat surprising, a large number of clerks petitioned in 1860, in 1865 and in 1872 (when they were joined by some messengers) for some financial aid. In 1860 they had even gone so far as to ask for some 'slight pecuniary participation in the success of the Corporation' to help meet the high cost of 'the necessaries of life'. And in this instance the Court approved of a donation of £20 to each clerk, and £10 to each messenger. In 1865, however, the Treasury Committee refused the request on the grounds that salaries were adequate. And in 1872 the Committee, evidently restless at the presumption of the clerical staff, refused to consider the appeal and reprimanded the petitioners: they (the Committee) strongly 'disapprove of the Clerks memorializing the Governors and Directors and consider it a very objectionable course'.

In spite of this abrupt rejection, however, salary scales were increased later in 1872. (As a result the starting salary became £90.) In future, salaries were to be revised triennially, to coincide with the election of the Governors and Directors. Although there is no record of discussions about the new policy, it was clearly a response to new circumstances which were affecting many firms. In 1875 the Civil Service Inquiry Commission pointed out that there had been a general increase in clerk's salaries as a consequence of the higher prices 'within the last few years'.[1]

In 1891 there was a slight drop in the beginning salary, when a new pension plan was introduced. But the situation in 1890 was broadly representative of the nineteenth century as a whole: starting salaries were £90, making the Royal Exchange Assurance one of the best-paying insurance companies; the average clerk was earning £150 in his mid-20s, and just under £400 at 41; and if he stayed on to 65 he would receive about £600. Rewards were obviously much greater for men of exceptional ability.

It is, of course, impossible to estimate exactly what these figures mean in modern terms. Relative prices have changed too much; a host of new commodities unknown and undreamed of a century ago have made precise cost-of-living comparisons meaningless; expectations and tastes have been transformed; taxes and social services have both mushroomed. If one had to make a very crude guess it would be based on the fact that the cost of a very basic 'basket' of consumables (80 per cent of the value of which is foodstuffs) rose roughly fourfold between the mid-nineteenth and mid-twentieth centuries,[2] and that living costs have probably increased by a further 50 per cent in the last fifteen years or so. This is much too slim a basis—it ignores too many relevant factors—to be interpreted as meaning that a clerk then earning £250 was in the position of a modern recipient of an income of, say, £1,500. But it does give a general idea of the order of magnitude involved. And, when we bear in mind how very much poorer the average person was one hundred years ago, the clerk was by no means badly placed.

Certainly, a nineteenth-century clerk at the REA was in a very favourable position relative to other wage- and salary-earners at the time. He was, of course, able to earn more than the factory worker, bricklayer and coal-miner—whose wages were in the range of £50 to £100 per annum in the mid-century. Whatever the vicissitudes of the cost of living, he could enjoy standards which were indisputably middle class: he earned more than the

[1] *PP* (1875), XXIII, 9.

[2] For a continuous price index for consumables see E. H. Phelps Brown and Sheila V. Hopkins, 'Seven Centuries of the Prices of Consumables, compared with Builders' Wage-Rates', *Economica* (1956).

mass of even skilled artisans; more than elementary schoolteachers; and by the 1890s could anticipate ultimately earning as much as many doctors.[1] In this respect he was similarly placed to clerks in the Bank of England and in other élite City banking houses and insurance offices.[2] Indeed, in 1890 the REA Actuary claimed that the salaries of the clerical staff were 'in excess of those usually paid by insurance companies'. Certainly, a clerk in the Corporation was on the more prosperous side of a line drawn by a contemporary observer in 1871:[3]

£150 and £80 point to two distinct classes of clerks, distinct in their education, business prospects, and various other things, but chiefly in the social usages which custom has made the framework of their daily life. Each sum may be taken as the test of a class. Those in banks, insurance offices and other public companies . . . reside in a fairly genteel neighbourhood, wear good clothes, mix in respectable society . . . At 28 years of age they receive about £150 and hope someday to reach £350 or more.

In addition to the attractions of a regular and reasonable salary, nineteenth-century insurance work had the advantage of hours which were surprisingly short by modern, as well as by contemporary, standards. In 1794 the REA 'hours of attendance' had been fixed at 9 a.m. to 4.15 p.m. But this regulation had quickly been neglected and a convention of commencing at 10 a.m. established. In 1838, therefore, when the Court was reviewing all such arrangements in the aftermath of the fire, a compromise was recommended: 9.45 a.m. to 4.15 p.m. (When the Corporation informed the Sun Fire Office that it intended to open later and close earlier, and that the Phoenix was going to do the same, the Sun promptly followed suit.)

These times were, in fact, quoted by a Committee in 1870 as being 'decidedly shorter than in the Counting House of any commercial firm or banking house' and an extra reason for judging salaries to be 'fair and liberal'. But even so there must have been some laxity; for in 1852 the Corporation was cited as one of those offices (the Globe, the Imperial and the Law Life were among the others) which opened from 10 a.m. to 4 p.m., and thus offered an extra half-hour to the increasing number of clerks who, through the convenience of the railway, found it more pleasant to live outside London.

[1] See F. Musgrove, 'Middle-Class Education and Employment in the Nineteenth Century', *Economic History Review*, 2nd Series, XII, 1 (August 1959), 99–100; Reader, *Professional Men*, p. 200.

[2] See the results of a survey by the Civil Service Inquiry Commission: *PP* (1875), XXIII, Appendix G.

[3] Quoted in Lockwood, *Blackcoated Worker*, p. 27.

Nor was this all; for there were long periods in the nineteenth century when the quiescent approach to business, and its relative stability, produced a leisured atmosphere even within the office. In 1807, for example, five clerks formed themselves into a jocular 'Royal nursery of Genius'—a lively literary and debating society. As their own memoirs record, 'these sons of Parnassus'

had been accustomed to enliven the drudgery of business with an occasional sally of wit; and to step aside from the routine of the Ledger, to discuss the merits of a statesman, or to adjust the claims of the popular writers of ancient or modern times . . . It was the glory of this Society, that they could, after hearing an essay, or a poem, for a short time, return to the business of the office, as the traveller, who steps aside to pluck a flower, resumes his journey with fresh alacrity.

Something like this tradition continued: in the 1850s, to Octavius E. Fooks (one of the senior Fire clerks and later Fire Manager) the temporary absence of his two closest friends, produced boredom rather than busyness, and in a doggerel lament for the loss of jokes and jollity he wrote:

> How slow is the course of the day
> (There's never much speed in its flight)
> But whether they're *here* or *away*,
> Makes the difference of darkness from light.

And as late as the 1880s the West End office had long slack periods in which the clerks were reduced to betting pennies (at odds of 40 to 1) on the chance of a white horse trotting down Pall Mall.

Meanwhile, too, the insurance clerk was sharing in, and anticipating, that expansion of more official leisure which has characterized modern society. As early as 1838, and perhaps before, clerks had been allowed to leave the Royal Exchange on Saturday after the morning's work, if their services were not needed. In 1854, in agreement with other leading offices, the Corporation was closed to the public at 2 p.m. on Saturday. And from 1891 one-third of the clerks, in rotation, were given a complete leave of absence on Saturdays. By the late nineteenth century, too, a regular and generous system of annual leaves had been established: a three-week holiday was the norm in 1881. In addition to these regular occasions, the Corporation was also generous on exceptional occasions. In 1851, for example, clerks were given two days' holiday and the price of two admission tickets to visit the Great Exhibition at Crystal Palace—a gesture which was repeated for the International Exhibition in 1862. The REA was not alone in 1851. Indeed, the lead was taken by the Atlas (with four days' leave). And the *Post Magazine*, in noting this and similar action by other offices, rejoiced that the insurance companies were thereby keeping themselves in the public eye.[1]

MEMBERSHIP OF THE CORPORATION

In terms of income, working hours and leave, therefore, the Royal Exchange Assurance, together with the other leading offices in banking and insurance, must have offered prospects for salaried employment which were difficult to match outside the fields of highly trained professional or managerial work. And to the Directors, as to the historian, the clerk's position, status and responsibilities were those of a member of the educated middle class. Consequently, the Corporation did not view employment as a matter of a mere wage contract. It expected, for example, that the clerks would so organize their lives as to be able to live respectably and without danger of scandal on the salaries which they received. Hence the shock which the Directors experienced at the end of the 1860s when, after the bankruptcy of two members of the staff, it was discovered that a great number of clerks were seriously in debt. A Committee of Inquiry was appointed in 1869—and discovered that 'the . . . ruinous system of borrowing from professional money-lenders' had produced a 'state of demoralization . . . in portions of the Establishment'. The Committee's horror at this 'reckless indebtedness' was hardly lessened by the discovery that some clerks had borrowed from the Corporation in order to pay off professional money-lenders! Of these debtors, no less than eight had to compromise with their creditors.

All this was hardly evidence of the standards of thrift and financial care, nor of the need for independence from external pressure, which the Corporation expected from its employees. Reaffirming that existing salaries were 'fair and liberal', the Committee insisted on the axiom 'that it is absolutely requisite that every clerk in the Establishment must be perfectly free in his pecuniary affairs'. In future, any clerk borrowing from a money-lender was to be liable to instant dismissal. The system of lending the Corporation's money to clerks, except in charitable and other circumstances, was declared to be 'objectionable, and frequently injurious to the clerk'.

It would be wrong either to assume that this level of indebtedness was common (no other similar situation has come to light) or to dismiss the Directors' attitude as unfairly censorious. Indeed, the Directors' attitude was perfectly consistent with their view of the rights as well as the duties and status of REA clerks.

[1] *PM*, XII, 19 (10 May 1851).

The point is, of course, that to deal with the position of clerks and messengers solely in terms of salaries, office hours and recognized holidays is to ignore the fact that the relationships which linked the various members of the Corporation were not only contractual, nor merely commercial. An insurance office of this sort was a 'corporation' in the social as well as the legal sense. On the one hand, it was expected that clerks would not lead scandalous lives, would live respectably on their incomes, would work extra hours when necessary, and would give of their best to the Company all the time. On the other hand, however, such apparent 'paternalism' cut both ways: no one questioned that, in return, and without any formal contract or obligation, the Corporation would foster the clerk's search for security and respectability, help him in the vicissitudes of life, and protect him, when necessary, from the adverse winds of the marketplace and from the impact of personal distress. The same was true, in the appropriate sphere, of the Corporation's messengers—who were from this viewpoint no less members of the Corporation.

It is an oversimplification, but not a serious one, to say that the clerk, and to some extent the messenger, could anticipate that, as long as he was conscientious and honest, the REA would do for him what the modern State, in far less personal ways, is now expected to do for all its citizens. It would guarantee him a secure career with no unemployment. It would help him in sickness and disaster. Besides financial help, the Corporation's doctor's services were freely available to clerks and messengers earning less than £200 annually. Sustaining what could be called a variety of 'welfare capitalism', the Corporation was rare, although not unique. It encouraged an individualism less harsh than that traditionally associated with nineteenth-century industrial relations. Its staff were expected to be responsible, hard-working, provident and self-reliant. But they were not expected to face the world entirely alone; and their individualistic virtues were encouraged and supported by a corporate framework and a willingness to help them withstand misfortunes not of their own creation. They were not left to their own devices to face the often brutal insecurity of economic life in the nineteenth century, when 'the smallest accident in the machinery of a family dependent on labour is frequently sufficient to turn the current of life from one of comparative happiness to irredeemable misery'.[1]

First, then, employment in the Royal Exchange was analogous to, say, entrance into the Civil Service: it more or less guaranteed what Anthony Trollope called 'a respectable maintenance for life'.[2] It was permanent—

---

[1] Quoted in W. L. Burn, *The Age of Equipoise* (1964), p. 96.
[2] *The Three Clerks* (first published 1858; The World's Classics, 1952), p. 12.

or at least as permanent as health allowed. In this respect a clerk in the REA, or in any other solid insurance company, was favourably placed in an age generally marked by business and industrial instability, by periodic massive unemployment among skilled as well as unskilled workers, and by a good deal of insecurity in the working life of even middle-class professional people. To take a representative example: of the thirty-six new clerks who joined the establishment in the 1850s, the 'General Roll of Clerks' records only one as ever being dismissed—albeit a second 'absconded' and a third 'discontinued his attendance', and there may well have been some who voluntarily resigned in circumstances in which they might otherwise have been asked to go. What *is* important is that the concept of retrenchment is unknown to the nineteenth-century history of the Corporation.

The Corporation was, in fact, very reluctant to dismiss anyone at all— and it is significant that Frederic Brassey, the man whose bankruptcy in 1868 had brought to light the money-lending scandal, was quickly reinstated in his position as Assistant (Manager) of the Fire Department at a salary of £400.

On the other hand, although the REA normally offered permanent employment to its clerks, by no means all its clerks stayed with the Corporation throughout their working lives. There was, in fact, more mobility than one might anticipate. Thus, of the 206 new clerks starting work between 1840 and 1899, almost exactly half (105) left before retirement; just over a third (76) retired on pension, and 25 died in service. On the average, those who left before retirement had, in fact, served between eight and twelve years. And this substantiates the view for which there is also other evidence, that, having gained experience, they tended to leave voluntarily to take up other positions.

Another, and most important, indication of the 'welfare' aspects of employment by the REA was the extent to which the Corporation was prepared to spend its own funds in gifts and loans to its staff. In cases of illness or other urgent need, the Governor, together with the Treasury Committee, was empowered to make an outright gift. And this very frequently happened. In February 1814, Mr Crowther, a clerk in the Fire Office, was presented with £10 'in consequence of his indisposition'. In January 1867, E. Cuthbert, a messenger, who had lost three children from scarlet fever and was himself ill, was given £10 and a fortnight's holiday. In September of the same year C. F. Snee, a clerk in the Shipping Office, who had received a loan of £200 in 1879, was given £40 and leave to go to the seaside to recuperate from an illness. These examples could be multiplied many times. Nor was it only the employees who benefited. Throughout the 1860s, for example, Louisa Harding and her invalid sister (daughters of a clerk who retired in 1827 and died in 1834) were given frequent gifts on account of their living 'in very distressed circumstances, obtaining only a very scanty living from a small day school'. And in May 1880 the widow of F. H. Ritherdon (a clerk who had retired on a pension after contracting 'scrivener's palsy') was given £100.

In addition to gifts, the Treasury Committee also lent money without interest, when the need was demonstrated by 'a full and explicit statement of their [i.e. the clerks'] affairs'. Repayments were normally to be spread over not more than ten years. This seems to have been the sort of loan extended to Octavius Fooks, then a junior clerk earning £200, in October 1861. Fooks was able to borrow £120 in recognition of his wife's illness, his large family, and losses on mining shares. And another significant example occurred in November 1864, when an interest-free loan was extended to the widow of the Corporation's Surveyor, to enable her to apprentice her son to a railway engineer. On the other hand, the relatively frequent loans to buy property were made in return for tangible security and normally at the slightly favourable rate of 4 per cent. This was the case with house loans to a clerk, E. H. Britton, in May 1858, and a messenger, J. Smith, in July 1894—each of whom borrowed £150. As one measure of the overall situation, in January 1869 there were outstanding loans of £4,700 to twenty-eight clerks and messengers.

In 1869, however, after the exposure of the excessive indebtedness of clerks, the Surplus and Charity Fund (from which loans and gifts had been made, and which then stood at over £11,000) was closed, and the balance transferred to General Profit and Loss.

The Court also concerned itself with savings, for the Directors considered that thrift as well as respectability were highly desirable attributes for their clerks. And like other City institutions they set about encouraging it. In December 1855, for example, the Governors and Directors expressed the desire 'to encourage the saving of small sums by the clerks and others in the service of the Corporation for their settlement in life, or as a provision for their families'. Henceforth, staff were allowed to deposit money with the Cashier at 5 per cent interest—subject to a maximum annual deposit of £100, and an overall limit of £500. And in February 1860, 'to further encourage provident habits in persons in the service', the limit was raised to £1,000. In 1885, standing at some £8,300, the Deposit Fund represented an average of almost £120 for every member of staff. By 1901 the Fund was over £13,000. Ten years later it reached almost £21,000.

The encouragement of thrift by the use of the growing Deposit Fund for staff savings was, in its way, an important indication of nineteenth-century attitudes and policies. And its most important long-term object was to offer a regular incentive for clerks and others to provide for their old age. The attitudes implicit in this sort of policy were very strong. In 1842, for example, in agreeing to give £60 annually to the widow of the late Cashier, the Court insisted that this was not to be taken as a precedent and that Department Heads should make it known to all the clerks 'that the Court deem it incumbent on every Officer, Clerk and servant of the Corporation to devote a portion of his annual salary towards securing by life assurance such provision for any family that may survive him as may be suitable to their respective stations and not to rely for such provision on the bounty of the Company'.

Earlier in the century the Corporation had, in fact, encouraged the practice of life assurance among its firemen, messengers and doorkeepers by paying premiums on their behalf and then deducting appropriate amounts from their wages. With very few exceptions, where there was real hardship, the Corporation not surprisingly kept to the principle that an employee was responsible for ensuring the welfare of his family after his death. On the other hand, however, it did assume responsibility for ensuring the individual clerk's own welfare after his retirement by making regular provisions for the payment of pensions throughout the nineteenth century.

For most of the century pension arrangements were informal, being decided in individual cases on their merits and entirely within the Court's discretion. This aspect was made clear in the fact that the grants were called 'allowances'. Nevertheless, there are abundant instances of the award of pensions on normal retirement or incapacity. In 1864 a Committee even wondered whether the principle that pensions were only granted where there were no adequate means of support had, in fact, been kept to—certainly, it was claimed, the Court had never refused a proper application.

A survey of the situation showed that between 1820 and 1849 there were twenty-two pensions awarded. The pensioning of messengers was very rare—although it did occur, as with George Parlby, who was granted a weekly allowance of 15s. in 1865, when incapacitated by rheumatism. In the main, however, the pensioners were ex-officers or ex-clerks, and their allowances ranged from 50 per cent to 75 per cent of their salary on the eve of retirement. Indeed, there were at least four instances of retirement on full salary—a gesture which seems to have been reward for long and faithful service. The most spectacular instance was that of Edward Bird, who retired as Superintendent of the Fire Office at Christmas 1865, aged seventy-eight, and after no less than sixty-three years' service. Other examples were James Booth, who retired in June 1822, having been Accountant since 1781 and, presumably, in the service for much longer than that; William Lockhart, who resigned in 1848 (he was then Head of the London Department of the Fire Office) after fifty-two years in the Royal Exchange; and E. D. Browne, Manager of Sea Claims before his retirement in 1890, who had served for fifty-eight years.

The pension arrangements, even granting their informality, were well up to the best contemporary standards in those few institutions which granted them. The Civil Service, for example, paid up to two-thirds of final salary after forty years' service—but the REA Committee of 1864 pointed out that Government salaries, with exceptions in higher departments, were relatively small, so that pensions were often 'quite inadequate to support a man'. The Bank of England in the 1860s was guided by the Government scale, but made 'no kind of promise'; in 1870 its new pension scheme offered two-thirds of salary after forty-five years' service. Finally, the West India Docks, from 1852 onwards, had a contributory scheme, in which the clerk paid half the premium for a policy producing (for example) a pension of £30 for salaries less than £60.

Although the REA arrangements were relatively generous, the clerk could predict neither the size nor even the possibility of a pension. And the lack of certainty with regard to requests for help and actual outlay must have affected the Corporation, too. In 1864 the Revision Committee considered the question of formalizing pensions, but was not prepared to submit a precise scale. On the other hand, it was sceptical about the value of strictly enforcing the 'rule' that pensions should only be paid when there was real need, in case this would hold out 'an inducement to a clerk to be careless in making a provision for himself'. As a rule of thumb it proposed a ceiling of £400 on any allowance and, within that, a limit of two-thirds for fifty years' service. But it rejected the suggestion that clerks contribute a proportion of their salaries, since this 'would take the matter out of the hands of the Court, giving the Clerk the absolute right to the claim; and it would do away with all feeling of an Act of Grace on the part of the Company'.

The Corporation remained quite firm on this last point. But it was not long before the Court committed itself to an acknowledged and regular pension scheme. A non-contributory scheme was adopted in 1880 and came into force on 5 January 1881. The plan was similar to the Bank of

England scheme of the 1870s. The new and official scale commenced at one-sixth of salary after ten years' service, and rose to two-thirds after forty years—although retirement before the age of sixty was possible only in cases of physical or mental incapacity. After sixty-eight it was obligatory unless the Court extended the man's employment. The printed announcement also emphasized that pensions were to be awarded 'during the pleasure of the Court' and could be lower in amount than specified in the scales.

The position of clerks and most officers was thus put on a secure footing from 1881, and effective membership of the Corporation was thereby extended beyond the date of retirement—extended, in fact, for the rest of a man's life. (The Underwriter, Deputy Underwriter and Fire Manager were not in the scheme; and in August 1893, when a new Actuary was appointed, he was also excluded.) But from the Corporation's viewpoint the scheme had two drawbacks: first, the future commitment was unknown; second, there being no special fund, all pensions would be a charge on current revenue in succeeding years. In 1890, therefore, the Actuary drew up a plan for an adequate Pension Fund based 'upon a sound footing'—pointing out that several public companies, including insurance offices, had already started such funds 'in order to relieve the working charges of the future of a heavy burden, and to guarantee to their employees a suitable reward for long and valued service'. On the assumption that the average salary payable at the age of sixty-five was £600, and that the average pension would therefore be £400, Ryan provided an actuarial estimate of contingent pensions. He and the Governor then propounded a plan for establishing a Pension Fund by setting aside over £30,000 from present reserves and augmenting it by annual contributions. As presented to the Treasury Committee, this scheme involved contributions by the staff themselves.

It was obviously in the interests of all concerned to establish such a Fund—but the Treasury Committee did not agree to the proposal made by the Governor and the Actuary that the clerks should contribute. When it finally agreed to set up the Fund, in June 1891, and to credit it with amounts equivalent to 5 per cent of the salaries of existing and 6⅔ per cent of the salaries of future members of the staff, the Committee stated firmly that it had 'decided not to allow the staff to contribute to the proposed Fund as recommended by the Actuary on the grounds that contributions by the staff might give them a legal right to a pension and would take away the free action of the Court of Directors'.

This firmness about basic principles should not be confused with any hard-heartedness. The spirit was more generous than the letter. Quite apart from the fact that there is no recorded instance of a pension being refused, the Treasury Committee itself acknowledged the existence of rights. In 1891, when rejecting the proposal that the Pension Fund should be based on staff contributions it argued, as a supplementary reason, that it would be 'somewhat hard to require old servants of the Company to contribute to the Fund, as under the Pension Rules of 1881 they might reasonably consider they had a moral claim to a pension'.

The Corporation therefore retained and enlarged its status as a paternalistic employer as it entered the period of expansion and organizational change after 1890. With the added security of a Pension Fund (which grew to £47,042 in 1902 and £243,624 in 1923), a firmer commitment to superannuation, and regularity of employment the better ensured by the Corporation's growth, the staff were reasonably well protected against the disadvantages of impersonality and rapid change which might result from the Royal Exchange Assurance's new scale of operations.

ENTRY, QUALIFICATION, PROMOTION

Throughout the nineteenth century, and well into the twentieth, the Royal Exchange Assurance was among the very small number of institutions which offered a secure, respectable and prosperous career to educated youths. And we may assume, therefore, that potential competition for a clerkship with the Corporation was very keen. In fact, however, it remained 'potential', since until the 1930s it was only possible to become a clerk on being personally nominated by a Director. As a result, a clerical position in the Corporation (which in this respect was entirely in line with other institutions) was a privilege in more than one sense. The situation may be compared with Glyn Mills, who were 'overdone with applications' for clerkships and where it was said many applicants would have been glad to enter without a salary.[1]

Patronage was certainly widespread in the City—as was made plain by Sir James Stephens, an ex-Civil Servant, who defended its existence in Government work in the middle of the century: 'Things as they are out of our Public Offices (in Westminster Hall or at the Royal Exchange, for example) would seem to be the model for things as they ought to be within our Public Offices—wit forcing itself upward by its own buoyancy, and mediocrity rescued from depression and wrong by domestic and other alliances.'[2]

[1] Evidence to the Civil Service Inquiry Commission, *PP* (1875), XXIII, Q.4801, Q.4803.
[2] Quoted in Burn, *Age of Equipoise*, p. 142.

At a specific level we know very little about the background of the young men who became REA clerks. Only rarely do we learn such details as that Octavius Fooks, who joined the Fire Office in 1845 and became Manager thirty-four years later, was nominated by his uncle, Sir George Larpent, who was a member of the Court; or that John Higham, the Actuary, who entered the Life Department in 1835, was nominated by Sir John Lubbock, in whose banking house Higham's father, Daniel, had worked since 1811. To judge by the standards of education required, together with the habits and personal contacts which were implicit qualifications, it would have been rare to have employed at that time any other than the sons of professional and commercial middle-class families. It is most likely, for example, that they had a similar background to clerks at the London & Westminster Bank, who, said its Secretary in 1874, 'belong to what I should consider the upper middle classes . . . [the sons of] clergymen, military and medical men and others'.[1]

As with most long-continuing corporations, the Royal Exchange Assurance also had a strongly marked tradition of family employment, which was facilitated by the practice of 'nominating' for clerkships. This was obvious in the eighteenth century, when three members of the Ekins family (Robert, John and Randolph) were successive Cashiers, between 1731 and 1792; or when Samuel Fenning, who was Secretary between 1783 and 1792, was followed in that office by his son, Samuel Fenning Junior, between 1802 and 1840. And throughout the nineteenth century father and son, brother and brother worked side by side.

Sometimes this tendency did not work out happily. Thus William Lockhart, who had a very distinguished career extending over fifty-two years, must have been disappointed in his son Henry, who stayed in the Fire Office merely five years before resigning because of unspecified 'difficulties' and leading 'a very dissipated life' for at least thirty-three years—at the end of which, a cab-driver, he appealed to the REA for some financial help (and got it). But in most instances there was a happier story to tell—as with the Dutton family, for example, represented by Augustus Dutton (serving between 1837 and 1883, and Assistant Fire Manager between 1864 and 1883) and his son, also called Augustus (1880–1907, Underwriter between 1904 and 1907); or John Higham, whose nephew Percy Frederick Higham Hodge entered the Corporation's service in 1885 and became Secretary in 1917. P. F. H. Hodge's son, in his turn, joined the REA soon after the First World War, and went on to become Glass Manager. Again and again the staff records imply family continuity among the

---

[1] Quoted in Lockwood, *Blackcoated Worker*, p. 24.

clerks—and this was only to be expected. The nature of the Corporation, its paternalism and emphasis on personal relations, would naturally encourage this form of social cohesiveness. And there can be no doubt or surprise that applications from the relatives of clerks or ex-clerks were favourably looked on by the Directors when they came to exercise the privilege of appointing new members of staff.

The records of the REA do not make clear precisely what skills were looked for in the candidates for clerkships, other than legible handwriting and a basic numeracy. But it is doubtful if anything beyond a minimum clerical and arithmetical expertise was formally appraised. On the other hand, probationary appointments *were* made, so that clerks had to demonstrate their competence on the job before being given a permanent appointment.

On the whole, the skills needed in insurance did not result from any special and systematic preparatory training. Rather, they were based upon a broad liberal education up to 17 or 18—from which it was helpful to derive a good handwriting and arithmetical training, as well as the more general attributes of a 'well-educated' young man. Detailed knowledge of insurance and its problems, technical and administrative skills, the development of insight and expertise—all these resulted, or were supposed to result, from observation and experience on the job. For most insurance men it was experience above all which counted, and which justified promotion and the wielding of responsibility.

Clearly, then, the qualifications of the overwhelming majority of insurance men in the nineteenth century (apart from prospective actuaries) were based on personal experience and informal on-the-job training. In addition, however, there were the beginnings of professional training with the evolution of local Insurance Institutes, their federation and their assumption of responsibility for education and examination. Admittedly, it took some time before the Institutes became important on a national scale: the first (in Manchester) was founded in 1873; a Federation was established in 1897; the first examinations were held in 1899; London and Liverpool did not establish Institutes until 1907; and a Charter was not obtained until 1912.[1] But a start had been made—even though prior to the First World War it had very little effect on the Head Office of a Corporation like the REA.

In the period under discussion, therefore, clerks at the Royal Exchange (unless they had actuarial ambitions) looked to the Corporation to provide

[1] H. A. L. Cockerell, *Sixty Years of the Chartered Insurance Institute, 1897–1957* (1957), pp. 13–23.

the setting within which informal instruction and prolonged experience would improve their abilities, and prospects, as insurance men. The Corporation was also important in this respect because seniority as well as ability was relevant to promotion. The exact balance between these two elements—or, indeed, the extent to which, for many positions, seniority and extended experience reflected aptitudes—is difficult to define. In 1838 a Court Committee strongly recommended that promotion be based on ability and conduct rather than on relative length of service. On the other hand (and more especially for less responsible positions), it was difficult, and would have been unsatisfactory, to disturb too much the orderly process of salary increments which maintained gradations between clerks. Indeed, given the nature of a corporation and the internal tensions which are likely to incur in it, such an orderly policy is understandable. Yet it was not allowed to impede the advancement of clearly able men or to unduly influence promotion decisions concerning very responsible positions.

As an example of the exceptionally rapid advancement open to a man of great ability in a technical field, we may take the career of John Higham. He began work in the Life Department in 1835 at the age of 15. Obviously possessing mathematical and statistical skills of an extremely high order, he had risen to First Clerk within twelve years; and he was appointed Actuary at the age of merely 27 at a salary of £500. In 1853, still only 33 years old, and with a considerable national reputation, he was appointed Secretary as well, at a salary of £1,000. In these regards, his career should be compared with that of C. J. Riethmuller, an extremely competent man, who became a clerk in the Cashier and Accountant's Office at the same time as Higham joined the Life Department, and was appointed First Clerk to Higham in 1854—at the age of 41. Riethmuller was by no means mediocre: his position was equivalent to that of an Assistant Actuary, and he secured this title in 1873, then being 60 years old.

In the Secretary's office, too, since it was relatively small, there were prospects of speedy promotion—although the fact that a man might become Secretary very young meant that his successor, no matter how able, might have some time to wait. Thus Elias R. Handcock became Secretary in 1875, at the age of 36 and after nineteen years' service (fifteen of which were spent as senior clerk to the previous Secretary). But his successor, the formidable William N. Whymper, who himself became clerk to Handcock at the early age of 21, had to wait until 1900, when he was 44, before a vacancy occurred in the Secretary's chair.

Men like Higham and Handcock were, of course, exceptional. With others, and particularly those in a large department where the ladder of seniority was very long, promotion could be much slower. For example, Octavius E. Fooks became Fire Manager in 1879 after thirty-two years' service. On the other hand the man whom he had succeeded, Charles P. Ball, had become Fire Manager in 1865 at the age of 40 and after merely twenty years' service. It was by no means unknown for clerks to be promoted over their seniors' heads. Thus Charles Ball, the Manager of the Country Department, became Fire Manager in 1865, even though the Manager of the London Department (Augustus Dutton) had six years' seniority. In general, however, promotion was a matter of incremental progress by rules of seniority. And, as a result, those who attained authority were not always the most able.[1]

CONTINUITY AND CHANGE

In most—perhaps in nearly all—important respects, the position of a member of the Corporation's staff at Head Office was virtually the same in the first decade of this century as it had been in the middle of the nineteenth century. He was still reasonably well paid (although the differential between clerical salaries and industrial wages had already begun to narrow), with a secure and middle-class job with relatively very favourable conditions. His security had been heightened by the formalization of his pension rights, and he could still consider himself a continuing member of a Corporation with as much social significance as business implications. As a clerk at the Royal Exchange, he was still a member of a hierarchical as well as closely knit community—one in which social gradations were created and matched by the business and corporate division of labour. Yet his participation in the corporate and business life of the REA gave him, if anything, an enhanced prestige by comparison with clerks in less traditional or aristocratic offices. Indeed, in its first number the staff magazine pointed to the 'spirit of self-effacement' and the affection for the Royal Exchange 'which together form a strong deterrent to our colleagues seeking outside honours'.[2] And he had the comfort of knowing (even in an age when the Corporation's affairs involved a world-wide staff in a highly professionalized industry) that seniority and an early start at Head Office were still the most important factors in his own professional advancement.

On the other hand, however, the structure and operations of the Corporation, like the structure and operations of insurance as a whole, had also been radically changed over the decades before the First World

---

[1] For an appreciation of this after the First World War, see below, p. 459.
[2] *REAM*, I, 1 (January 1903), 2.

War—with distinct consequences for the establishment. Those consequences had three main aspects: first, in terms of the composition of the staff at Head Office; second, as far as concerns the staff outside the Royal Exchange; and third, with respect to the impact of the new environment and problems of insurance by the early nineteenth century.

As we have seen, the dramatic expansion of the REA in the 1890s and 1900s brought with it a substantial growth in the number of staff: a doubling between 1890 and 1900, and another doubling in the next thirteen years. This contrasted with the early nineteenth century not merely because of the absolute numbers involved (less than fifty people manned the Head Office in 1840, as against over 300 by 1913), but because of the *rate* of change. To the typical clerk of the Edwardian Royal Exchange the corporate body of which he was a member must have seemed in a state of perpetual flux. Even so, however, the 'problems' of size should not be exaggerated. For the numbers, even on the eve of the War, were not excessively large—although they provided a dramatic contrast to the 1840s, when the handful of men must have got to know each other extraordinarily well. Regular contact between a high proportion of the staff was still possible, so that mutual knowledge, and the confidence and satisfaction which derive from it, must have been widespread.

In any case, it is important to remember that some of the tensions of expansion must have been absorbed or abated by the structural stratification of the staff: the effective unit of organization was increasingly departmental. And a large part of the growth of these years was, of course, based upon the rise of new units, such as the Accident Department, which was over fifty strong at the outbreak of the War. It is also relevant to note that this sort of development produced, initially, a more heterogeneous establishment; for the older departments, e.g. Fire in particular, continued to consider themselves, and be considered, as prestige elements in the Royal Exchange—a factor which helped 'insulate' their members from some of the more disturbing consequences of rapid growth, and which was itself strengthened by the relative lack of mobility of personnel between the different departments. In the short run, therefore, the accelerated growth of the Corporation induced an unprecedented degree of differentiation between members of the staff. Finally, it should be remembered that organizational lines ran horizontally as well as vertically: in addition to departments, there were managers, assistant managers, clerks and messengers. And in 1906 an entirely new, and no doubt welcome, stratum was added to the Royal Exchange staff: Miss Helen Macmillan was appointed as the Corporation's first typist, at an annual salary of £100.

Miss Macmillan, who was 27, was employed in the Secretary's office and was soon joined by Miss Whitehead. By midsummer 1909 there were no less than eleven typists—although the REA did not employ women as clerks until the staff shortages of the First World War.

From the viewpoint of the Corporation as a whole, however, some of the most critical organizational and staff changes came outside rather than inside Head Office at the Royal Exchange. In particular the extension of business activity from the 1880s onwards led to the establishment of a network of branch and district offices at home and overseas—each employing salaried clerks, inspectors and managers. The first provincial district managers were appointed in November 1881, in Birmingham and Bristol. By 1910 there were seventeen branches outside London. There were in addition various provincial district offices, besides the West End 'branch' (which was considered part of the Head Office) and a branch at Stratford, E., in London. No accurate estimate of the *total* number of employees exists; but it is clear that quite apart from the significant growth of overseas representation, and excluding the vast number of agents (there were over 20,000 British agents in 1919), the new branch offices involved a substantial addition to the total establishment. Thus the number of inspectors alone grew from about twenty-five in 1910 (when the Actuary had urged that it was 'imperative to put on more inspectors at the earliest possible date') to sixty-eight in 1919, while each office naturally had a manager and a clerical staff. In addition, although there was no merging of corporate identity, pre-war acquisitions—notably of the National Provincial Plate Glass Insurance Company in 1909—made further alterations in the composition of the staff.

In one sense, the inherited character of the establishment was insulated from much of this simply because the distinction between Head Office and branch staff was quite strongly maintained until the inter-war period. Only then was there relative mobility between branches and Head Office. Before the First World War the two areas of employment were quite distinct from each other. In another sense, however, the geographical and structural extension of the Corporation's activities created a new situation for all who were involved in its work. For one thing, there was a need for new administrative means of linking the separate parts of the Corporation; and in this respect the appointment of an Agency Manager in 1903 was symptomatic, although the branches continued to operate more or less independently of him. More generally, the need to forge and strengthen continuing links between the staff became increasingly pressing, and could be seen as a matter of morale and communication. It was in this context that it was decided to produce a staff journal. The *Royal Exchange Assurance Magazine* was first published in January 1903 in order 'to give expression to the bond uniting all those interested in the Corporation'; and in its second issue the new magazine (which was sub-edited by St J. G. Ervine, later to attain more renown as a playwright and author) published an exhortation on the need for a new corporate spirit to unite Head Office and branch employees and agents 'throughout the world'. Just over ten years later, in July 1914, it struck the same note: 'The initiation of the REA MAGAZINE was a necessary complement to the scheme of extension on which the Directorate embarked some years ago. Its aim was to consolidate and draw together the world-wide connections of the Corporation which this scheme created; those in Australia with those in Canada, those in the East with those in the West, and all with Head Office.' It is perhaps significant that the Royal Exchange was something of a pioneer in these respects. In its second number, in April 1903, the *Magazine*'s editors wrote that they knew of only two other insurance offices which published journals (the Norwich Union and the Caledonian), and expressed pleasure that the Corporation was 'one of the Companies which has recognized the power which such a magazine can wield'.

The *REA Magazine* (which lasted until 1916) was published in order to counter some of the disadvantages flowing from the 'intense competition for business' which, according to the Actuary in 1910, had 'forced assurance companies to an ever growing decentralisation'. But in terms of the every-day lives of members of the Corporation's staff, it was the competition for business, rather than the decentralization, which had the greater effect. If, in many respects, their business lives and their corporate environment had changed little from those of their early Victorian predecessors, measured by the pace and competitiveness of the insurance industry, the late nineteenth century ushered in a new world for the officials and clerks of the Royal Exchange Assurance. 'For 20 years', wrote the editors of the *Magazine* in 1910, 'the Royal Exchange has been vigorous and awake after perhaps an unduly long period of repose.'

Gone for good were the leisured days of the mid-Victorian years. Admittedly, to later generations, even the period immediately before the First World War was to appear uneventful and cautious. But to the insurance men at the time they demanded far more effort, attention and expertise than their predecessors had known. Much of this new intensity was concentrated at the points where competition was biting most keenly—in the branches and agencies at home and overseas, and in the Accident Department. But in the last resort, all felt the consequences of modernization.

16

Corporate Presence: the Royal Exchange Assurance in the nineteenth century

Measured in terms of capital accumulation, the long-run success of the Royal Exchange was obvious, if not spectacular. On the one hand, it was independent of outside funds for 200 years; on the other, bonus additions augmented its nominal capital and profits were allowed to accumulate to swell its various reserve funds. The nominal stock had stood at £508,329 in 1726; bonus additions to the stock in the hands of investors (some was owned by the Corporation) in 1807 (20 per cent), 1809 (20 per cent), and 1811 (10 per cent), raised the total to £768,263. 17s. 10d., although the £79,044 owned by the Corporation was written off in 1830. The stock then remained at £689,219. 17s. 10d. until 1924, when a further issue of £99,929 was made to acquire the State Assurance Company. Against this, and entirely excluding Life and Annuity Funds, which none the less included *some* elements of profit attributable to the Corporation, its general assets in 1913 exceeded £2·4 million.

In the long run, of course, Royal Exchange stock proved a worthwhile and remunerative investment. One slightly bizarre indication of this came in the early 1880s as a result of various settlements with respect to unclaimed dividends. In December 1883, for example, the Corporation paid out cash and Government securities worth over £2,650 on account of £100 of stock (itself increased to £158. 8s. by stock bonuses) originally owned by Isaac Peixoto, a London merchant of the 1720s, on which dividends and bonuses had gone unclaimed for almost 160 years—since 1725. During that time the yield, in terms of simple interest, had averaged some 15 per cent. However, the chronological pattern of payments on the par value of capital is a more significant measure of the return to the average proprietor—who could not plan so long a future for his investments!

As we have seen, annual dividends, after some long-term fluctuations in the course of the eighteenth century, rose to more than 7 per cent by

1799.[1] Thenceforth, the continued prosperity—even when the fire insurance boom resulted in intensified competition—brought rich rewards to the stockholders. In 1802 they received a 10 per cent bonus (in Government securities); regular dividends of 10 per cent were declared from 1806 to 1825, and were supplemented by 20 per cent stock bonuses in 1807 and 1809, a 10 per cent stock bonus in 1811, a 20 per cent bonus in Government securities in 1812, an extra 5 per cent in 1816, 1818 and 1823, an extra 10 per cent in 1820, the centenary year, and a splendid cash bonus of 100 per cent in 1825.

Thus, dividends held up reasonably well after the Napoleonic Wars, considering the problems which then beset fire insurance. (However, it should be remembered that the Corporation, writing a without-profit business, retained all its life profits.)[2] Nevertheless, after the mid-1820s, dividends sagged as all three branches of insurance, but more particularly life underwriting, came under pressure. Even so, in 1830, when regular dividends were reduced from 8 to 5 per cent, another 100 per cent bonus (this time paid in Consols) was declared. In the 1830s and 1840s, dividends averaged about $8\frac{1}{4}$ per cent. After this, in the calm and prosperous mid-Victorian years annual dividends increased until, between 1861 and 1886, they averaged 20 per cent—with an extra dividend in 1870 to mark not merely the Corporation's third Jubilee but a record fire profit of £42,917. (The officers and clerks also received a gift of £4,000.) In the 1890s the combination of competitive expansion and falling interest rates began to reduce this level of dividend, and by 1914 dividends were 10 per cent.

Long-run movements in the market price of Royal Exchange stock both mitigated these fluctuations in dividends and reduced the average level. Stock rose from a nineteenth-century low of 150 in 1842 (influenced, no doubt, by disastrous fires in Hamburg and Liverpool and the depression of life and marine business) to a high of 441 in 1881. Thenceforth it sagged slowly to about 275 in 1905, before collapsing to less than 200 in the aftermath of San Francisco. Taking the price of stock into account, its actual yield was about 4 per cent in the 1840s; rose to 5 and 6 per cent in the 1860s, 1870s and early 1880s; and then stayed at just over 4 per cent until the First World War.

[1] For dividends in the eighteenth century, see above p. 72.

[2] The 100 per cent cash bonus of 1825 was found as follows:

	£	s.	d.
Life account	325,087	1	3
Fire account	263,973	15	3
Sea account	115,968	1	4
	705,028	17	10

It was, of course, the business of insurance and investment which gave rise to the growth of capital and the vicissitudes of profit over almost two centuries. Nevertheless, while profit-making was of critical importance to the long-run purposes of the REA, its corporate form of organization and its longevity were themselves important social facts.[1] They meant that the Corporation assumed an institutional existence largely independent of (even though influencing) its business purposes.

In terms of the scope of its business and its pattern of organization the Royal Exchange Assurance had attained a new plateau of corporate development in the years immediately before the First World War. In many ways, this was a plateau of modernization. At the same time, however, what the Corporation had become was deeply and unmistakably influenced by what it had been in the past; and even its 'modern' characteristics bore the imprint of its traditional character. The period leading up to 1914 is a good one to use as the terminal date for an appraisal and summary of various general aspects of the Royal Exchange's history. First, because the business history of the Corporation has a unity in the period to 1914. Second, because the War was a turning-point in insurance, as in so much else—and a turning-point which was particularly marked for the REA: thenceforth it was unable to resist (even though it could sometimes retard) the working out of twentieth-century influences on its business and structure. Third, because an understanding of events since 1914 is in part dependent on a knowledge of the historical roots of the Corporation and the Group which have evolved so far away from the pre-1914 world without being able entirely to escape its influence.

It is for this reason that one of the most convenient organizing principles for a general view of the history of the REA is the concept of the corporation: for it is in the nature of corporations to be less mortal than men, and to carry forward, with a momentum of their own, ideas and attitudes which are just as 'real' and certainly as influential as changes in the economic and social environment. The powerful elements of continuity in the history of the Royal Exchange, the extent to which its age influenced its future, were all related to the fact that corporations of its sort, like many other

---

[1] Strictly speaking, the REA did not become a single Corporation in the eyes of the law until 1854—when a private Act formally united the legal entities which had been created in 1720 ('The Royal Exchange Assurance for assurance of ships goods and merchandise at sea'), in 1721 ('The Royal Exchange Assurance of Houses and Goods from Fire') and 1826 ('The Royal Exchange Assurance Loan Company'). But for all practical and most legal purposes it had been a unified body from the outset: the 1721 Charter stipulated that the fire and life Corporation should have the same Governors and Directors as the marine Corporation, while the Loan Company was merely the name given to the two existing bodies when united in the one consolidated Corporation for the purposes of lending upon mortgage security.

social institutions, take on an existence independent of the men who belong to them. More than this, their members come to see themselves in relation to the institution, to envisage as one of their most important functions the maintenance of the corporation and the preservation of its traditions, and to be conscious of its personality and authority as distinct, even, from the men who ostensibly direct it.

'In many ways', wrote the Secretary (P. F. H. Hodge) to Nightingale, the ex-Actuary, in 1928, 'the dear old Corporation is an odd concern. You will remember that about 50 years ago my uncle, old Higham, said that it had muddled on for 150 years and would probably last for another 50. Equally, after 200 years I am inclined to say the same.'[1] Beneath the sentimental phraseology lay an important perception. For the corporate presence transcended not merely the businessmen who composed it, but the business which was, ostensibly, its central purpose. This is not to assert that the REA was unconcerned with enterprise and profit; but it is to claim that its pursuit of the latter and exemplification of the former were shaped by its age, its historical experience and the social framework which it created for its staff. Indeed, one can say more than this. For, just as membership of the Corporation meant much more than an exchange of labour power for a specified annual salary,[2] so the social fact of the Corporation's existence meant that it had developed functions as well as structures, personal satisfactions as well as obligations, which were only very remotely connected with the making of money.

Having said this, however, it is important to emphasize that the 'social' and the 'business' aspects of the Corporation were not in practice independent and non-communicating parts of its existence. The thrust of institutional development may have equipped the REA with structures and attitudes which a set of purely economic incentives might never have produced; but once those structures and attitudes came into their own (certainly by the early nineteenth century, and possibly before), their effects on the business purposes of the Corporation were inevitable and profound. The extent to which the themes of age and tradition, continuity and self-conscious decision-making, have figured in earlier chapters concerned with the insurance business is indirect evidence of this. The Directors and staff of the Royal Exchange in the nineteenth century were aware (at times too much aware) of its long past; their actions and outlooks

---

[1] The occasion for this letter was the Governors' proposal, 'against the advice given them', to award the Underwriter a 'magnificient' pension of £5,000 annually, even though he had been forced to resign as the result of a bad decision.
[2] Above, chapter 15.

were influenced by inherited institutions which they were reluctant to change; they rightly counted membership of the Corporation as a social privilege as well as an economic attraction; they knew the strength of accumulated experience and longevity, as well as the handicaps of precedent and convention; they identified their families, through the generations, as well as themselves with the corporate entity; they were secure because they belonged to something which was older and would last longer than they would, and which provided psychological and social certainty and security. Largely developed under the influence of the vast changes which characterized the economy and society in Victorian Britain, the Royal Exchange Assurance entered the twentieth century with the strengths and weaknesses of a Victorian corporation: strong in its material success, its certainty and confidence, its tradition, its distinctive combination of individualism and collective humanitarianism, its appreciation of competition and security; weak in its reluctance to change, in its overconfidence, in its overdependence on inherited attitudes and inherited structures. Moreover, whatever its strengths and weaknesses, the pre-1914 Corporation was a social fact: its influence was to be felt throughout the inter-war period; its attitudes and ambience were to remain vital determinants of later events; and its reality was to withstand the consequences of the acquisition of other, powerful companies in 1917 and 1928, so that it was not until the 1960s that the Royal Exchange Group began to take shape.

If it is permissible to speak of the Royal Exchange having a corporate personality in the nineteenth century, then, as far as the world at large was concerned, that personality was very much a private, rather than a public, one. The weight of tradition was decisively on the side of privacy and silence, rather than publicity. In this respect, of course, at least for most of the century, the Corporation was no different from many other companies. Business—and particularly a solid and respectable business like insurance —did not divulge facts or opinions about itself, and, in the cause of discretion, even withheld as much detailed information as possible from its own shareholders and Directors. (As late as the early nineteenth century details of profits were not divulged to the Court, and a special 'Committee of Inspection' had to be appointed in 1803 to make the returns and payments of the tax on profits.)[1] This sort of antipathy and secretiveness had an obvious effect on advertising, in contrast to the hectic activity of younger and less inhibited insurance offices. Even under the extreme pressure of

---

[1] The London Assurance Court was not given any detailed statement of accounts until 1828: Drew, *London Assurance*, p. 12.

competition, companies like the Royal Exchange and the Atlas had an aversion to mass advertising, feeling that it was not only beneath their dignity but would have produced an immediate deterioration of their public 'image'. By the same token—at least until towards the end of the century—they preferred the sort of sound and respectable business which it was imagined came from personal reference and direct effort, rather than the unreliable business which (according to the Atlas Chairman in 1866) came from 'undue or indiscriminate solicitation'.

Generally speaking, these habits and attitudes contrasted with those of younger offices, which apart from the need to advertise in order to carve out a niche for themselves, were, in any case, obliged by the various Company Acts under which they had been formed, to publish a minimum of information about the results of their business. Even so, some of them published much more. (On the other hand, a handful of older life offices which were organized on mutual principles did publish data on premium incomes, sums assured and funds.) A good example of publicity by a young office was that of the Royal of Liverpool, established in 1845. As early as 1850 the *Post Magazine* noted that the publication of the Royal's Annual Report, followed by its own commentary, were conjoined as regularly as 'the Queen's Speech on the opening of Parliament, and the debate by which it is invariably followed', and contrasted the Royal's 'full exposition' of its accounts with the practice of offices like the REA, the Sun and the Globe, which were 'not so communicative in respect of their affairs'.[1]

With regard to publicity, an important step forward was taken when the Life Assurance Companies Act of 1870 obliged offices to publish specified data and stimulated many to publish more data than they were legally obliged to do. Yet until the 1870s there was general ignorance of the affairs of many of the most important companies; and even after the Act the situation left a lot to be desired: it was of little use to publish a mass of statistics without an accompanying commentary in the form of a Directors' Report. As the *Post Magazine* emphasized with respect to the Royal Exchange's habit of merely publishing figures, this meant that the materials needed for a comparative analysis were 'out of reach'.[2] The resulting gaps in public knowledge were important for potential and actual policyholders as well as stockholders. As one newspaper pointed out in 1887, in criticizing the REA for publishing nothing more than the basic figures required by the 1870 Act, without any explanation of the data and its fluctuations: 'policyholders are even more interested in the prosperity of

---

[1] *PM*, XI, 35 (31 August 1850); *PM*, XII, 34 (23 August 1851).
[2] *PM*, XXXVI, 28 (10 July 1875).

a "mixed" [i.e. bonus-paying] office than shareholders, and, therefore, we think that special annual reports on business should, in accordance with the modern custom, be attached to the Annual Accounts, and copies either sent to every policyholder, or supplied to those requiring them'.[1]

These considerations might be relevant to all types of insurance; but they were critical in relation to life insurance. As early as 1871 the REA Actuary urged the need for more effective publicity as a means to engender public confidence in the Corporation. Even so, he was mainly thinking of 'a simple statement of figures put in the clearest form, and widely circulated', and 'a wide circulation of the Company's Balance Sheets'. And in arguing that a widespread and public discussion of the accounts 'will be highly advantageous to our interests', Winser was saying no more than the *Post Magazine*, which in 1875 regretted the absence of a Directors' Report, since 'the office would largely benefit by its circulation'.[2]

In spite of these arguments, and until the early twentieth century, the Corporation hardly changed its attitude towards publicity more than it was legally obliged to. As the *Post Magazine* put it in 1885, in complaining that the Corporation did not deign to publish even the amount of its new life business, 'the flood of change which has in recent times swept away so many of the anomalies and incongruities in the official practice of our life assurance institutions has failed to have any effect on the Royal Exchange Assurance, at least as far as the publication of a report with the usual particulars of its operations during the year is concerned'. And even when the Corporation adopted the practice of publishing a Directors' Report, from 1889, it was for some years extremely brief and quantitative, containing merely 'dry business details'.[3] Nevertheless, in this respect as in others, by the first years of the twentieth century the Corporation showed that in spite of its age and tradition, it was capable of adjusting its outlook and behaviour to the demands of modernity. Thus, at the Annual General Court, in June 1906, in the shocked aftermath of the San Francisco disaster the Governor, Sir Nevile Lubbock, departed from the tradition by which only formal resolutions, and occasional questions from Proprietors, were put. Instead, in view of the disaster and 'the very serious loss which the Corporation had consequently sustained', he felt it necessary to make a detailed statement about the fire, its cost to the Corporation, and its implications for future business. The proceedings were reported by a member of the staff of *The Times*, and published by the REA itself. Belatedly, the

---

[1] *The Citizen*, 2 July 1887.
[2] *PM*, xxxvii, 28 (10 July 1875).
[3] *PM*, xlvi, 27 (4 July 1885); *PM*, lv, 28 (14 July 1894).

ancient Corporation was adapting its attitudes towards publicity, bringing them into line with the adaptation of its business outlook and policies. Admittedly, in 1912, a proprietor expressed a sad surprise at the General Court that the Governor had not commented on the loss of the *Titanic* ('I hoped that you were going to make some remarks, but this is a peculiar Corporation and manages its affairs in its own way'). Yet even then the Governor pointed out that the nature and effects of the loss had already been explained to *The Times*. And, in any case, by 1915, under the impact of the War and a new Governor, Vivian Hugh Smith (Governor, 1914–55), the General Court heard an unprecedentedly detailed and frank report on business in 1914.

In spite of the almost obstinate care with which the Corporation kept its affairs private until the very eve of the First World War, there was one general sense in which its corporate personality played a public rôle. For the REA, as a leading City institution, was bound to feel the need to support appropriate public causes.

The most important form which this took was the charitable or ceremonial donation. Between 1803 and 1914, for example, there are records of 364 donations for a total in excess of £28,000. There was an enormous variety in the purposes of this largesse. For example, besides numerous small gifts to individuals in need, it included £10 to help perfect a life-saving machine for use at fires (1819); 50 guineas for a monument to James Watt (1824); £300 'towards the fund for the relief of the distressed working classes in the manufacturing districts' (1842); £50 to 'the committee for promoting the establishment of baths and washhouses for the labouring poor' (1850); £500 to help relieve widows and orphans of the Crimean War (1854); £1,000 to a Committee 'for promoting middle-class education in the City of London' (1866); £200 to help sufferers from the Chicago fire (1871); and £100 to a fund to compensate speculators for not building on the field of the Battle of Waterloo and for erecting a mausoleum for the bones which were constantly being turned up there (1914).

The records make it clear that the Corporation was regularly approached by individuals and organizations in real or pretended need. And in the main, as long as the purpose seemed a legitimate one, the Court was prepared to make a donation. As the above examples imply, the motive was frequently a general altruism. In addition, of course, the Corporation was naturally concerned with its own sphere of interest—as in 1847, when, 'having reference to the extent of the Company's fire and life insurance connection in Ireland', £1,000 was subscribed to the fund 'for relieving the extreme distress in that part of the Empire'; or in 1862, when £500 was donated to help workers in the cotton industry, suffering from the effects of the American Civil War, 'having reference to the extent of the Company's business in the manufacturing district of Lancashire and adjoining counties'.

Although some of these gestures partook of the nature of public relations (and many of them did not), they also shared in the general ethos which went beyond 'pure' business activity. Like the regular loyal Addresses at Royal births, coronations and deaths, they were evidence of an institutional self-consciousness—a sense of continuing corporate existence and personality. Yet even if, as has been argued, the Corporation's history had exemplified powerful elements of continuity in the nineteenth and early twentieth centuries, there were also many vital respects in which it *had* changed a good deal in the generation or so before 1914. It was the same social entity, but operating in, and adapting itself to, a new environment. That adaptation was manifest not merely in attitudes to publicity, but also in the rapid development of its accident business, in the new geographical scope of its general underwriting, in its greater readiness to adopt more adventurous competitive techniques, in the new scope and variety of its investments, and in its general responsiveness to market forces. Admittedly, important areas of its traditional organization were relatively slow to change—for they were the strongest embodiment of corporate continuity. And their failure to change postponed by a generation the fuller adaptation of the REA to the demands of twentieth-century insurance. Nevertheless, new attitudes and practices had made large inroads in the period from the late 1880s onwards. And it is important to re-emphasize how much of this—for the REA, as for the industry as a whole—was due to the powerful forces of competition. Market forces and pressures—whether to secure new business or to defend old accounts, whether to enlarge premium income or to maintain investment yields—were in the last resort the main determinants of business policy, of technical innovation and of changes in organization. And just as the size and structure of British insurance were transformed by growth and change in its market at home and abroad, so the history of individual companies was shaped by the pressures of the market and by market rivalry. Some offices were slower than others in their responses. But adaptation was invariably the prerequisite of any reasonable level of business success. This is not to deny all influence to entrepreneurs or enterprise. But they, too, were in the last resort dependent on the opportunities created by more general economic and social developments, and conditioned by the activities of their competitors.

For the REA this situation created a certain amount of tension between the demands of growth (as expressed in new attitudes and new structures) and the enormously strong tradition reflected in its corporate continuity, and the sense of community which had for so long conditioned the lives of its members. It remained to see how far the Corporation, which in this sense was so much a nineteenth-century institution, could retain its personality intact beyond the gulf of the First World War and into the stressful world of the mid-twentieth century.

PART E

War and Social Change: insurance in the twentieth century

The period since 1914 has been a time of enormous changes in both the extent and the organization of British insurance. Nevertheless, there is a sense in which many of those changes were not as fundamental as they seem, for the foundations of modern insurance in Britain had been effectively laid in the years immediately before the First World War. Thenceforth, much development was, in fact, the logical extension of trends already adumbrated in Edwardian Britain: the continued growth of fire and life insurance with the continued expansion in the country's wealth and income; the rise of accident, and particularly motor, underwriting (which overtook fire business in the 1920s, and was more than twice as large by the 1960s); the international rôle of British insurance; the increasingly important influence of insurance funds in the country's capital markets. There were, of course, genuine departures—some the result of technical change (e.g. the growth of aviation insurance), others the product of innovation and very broad socio-economic developments (e.g. group life insurance and pension schemes). But even some of these can be said to have had roots in the pre-war period. And this is certainly true of the mergers which have continued to produce larger and larger composite companies. Indeed, the merger movement, whose pre-war origins were examined in chapter 12, petered out in the mid-1920s, and the industry's structure remained relatively stable until a renewed consolidation boom in the 1960s attained an unprecedented degree of concentration (in fire and accident business, concentration actually declined between the First World War and the late 1950s).[1]

Of course, this is not to deny that British insurance since 1914 has been characterized by extremely significant developments. For one thing, changes in degree, when carried sufficiently far, can be just as important

1 Below, pp. 438, 531.

as changes in kind. Between 1914 and 1964, for example, the net fire premiums of British offices rose from £29 million to £339 million; accident premiums increased from £17 million to £362 million; and ordinary life premiums from about £30 million to £562 million. These magnitudes implied a fundamental shift in the character of British insurance in the fifty years after the outbreak of the First World War. In addition, however, there have been aspects of insurance—commercial methods and techniques, organization, marketing and control—which have shared with other large-scale enterprises the impact of twentieth-century business change. Certainly the pattern and problems of mid-twentieth century insurance, while in many respects descended from, provide striking contrasts to the patterns and problems of its Edwardian days. And the complexity as well as the extent of the evolution make the historian's task an extremely difficult one: any adequate examination of the British insurance in the twentieth century would itself demand a book-length study. In the last Part of this study, therefore, there will be no attempt to deal systematically with the evolution of the industry as a whole in the period. Rather, only a few of its highlights will be mentioned, and there will be a sharper focus on the recent history of the Royal Exchange Assurance, as one of various possible examples of twentieth-century development.

In the Corporation's case the period after 1914 heightened the problems of scale and organization which had become so pressing in the years immediately before the First World War. In terms of Head Office administration, and links with branches at home and overseas, a large step towards the solution of the inherited problems was taken with the appointment of a General Manager in 1929. On the other hand, however, with respect to both the scale of operations and the structure of control, an entirely new range of problems was opened up with the acquisition of two very important motor insurance companies: the Car & General in 1917 and the Motor Union in 1928. These two, together with the associated companies which they brought with them, and other acquisitions, transformed the situation of the REA from that of a somewhat exceptional unitary enterprise competing against giant composite offices established by merger, to that of a Group of somewhat loosely allied companies with an outstanding interest in the rapidly growing field of motor insurance. On the other hand, the management structures appropriate to this new dimension were not successfully achieved until after the Second World War.

17

Insurance in an Age of Violence
1912-1920

As we have seen, in spite of the long history of insurance in Britain, it was only in the nineteenth century that the underwriting of fire, life and accident risks was firmly and extensively established. Indeed, from one viewpoint, modern corporate insurance was a product of Victorian Britain. As such, it was naturally based upon the relative social and political security which characterized that era, and which was obviously and directly relevant to an industry which sold not ordinary goods or services, but guarantees against extraordinary or remote contingencies. Insurance was, therefore, an industry which might prove peculiarly vulnerable to any widespread breakdown of social harmony or any outbreak of total war. Although the nineteenth century had not been entirely free from strife and unrest, events such as the Napoleonic and Crimean Wars, or the arson which accompanied agricultural rioting, had relatively little impact on life and property within the country, while marine insurance had always been capable of adjusting to war-time problems in an age of sail and cannon. The real test of modern insurance came with the threat of far-reaching destruction associated with the new technology and the great political and social upheavals of the twentieth century.

As far as British society was concerned, premonitions of strife and of the possibility of disintegration came in the insecure years immediately before the First World War, 'when wisps of violence hung in the ... air'[1] and social peace was disturbed by labour unrest, by the increasing militancy of the Suffragettes, and by the intensifying crisis over Home Rule in Ireland. The second and third of these had obvious implications for British insurance companies. Thus, by 1913 and 1914 the earlier problems of plate glass smashing by members of the Women's Social and Political Union,[2] had given way to the apparently more serious threat of arson, and in this case it proved impossible to recover any damages from individuals

---

[1] E. J. Hobsbawm, *Industry and Empire* (1968), p. 163.
[2] Above, p. 270.

while the funds of the WSPU were kept overseas: 'Altogether,' wrote the REA Fire Manager in May 1914, 'the question of incendiarism by the Suffragettes has been one of the most difficult which the companies have had to deal with recently.' (However, a greater danger brought some relief: the outbreak of war in August 1914 brought a halt to the militancy of the Suffragettes.) With respect to Ireland, the strong possibility of civil war must have given pause to more than one insurance office—in spite of the fact that the standard policy form excluded losses from riots and civil war. In December 1913, for example, the REA Governors felt keenly apprehensive on this score and requested that the Dublin Manager should 'preserve our good business, get rid of our less desirable business, [and] add to the existing business only so far as not to increase to any appreciable extent our existing total liability in Ireland'.

Within a year, however, the Corporation had to confront the much more serious threat of an unprecedented World War. To fire offices (which by this time were accustomed to insure against fire and other sorts of damage to property in one comprehensive policy) the War intensified the risk of damage by riot and civil commotion, and also raised the new possibility of damage to property in Britain from enemy action.[1]

The former danger—of riots resulting from the tensions in industrial relations and the xenophobia which were associated with the outbreak of War—was, of course, an extension and aggravation of the pre-war situation, as was the Easter Rebellion in 1916, which did a vast amount of damage in Dublin. In fact, in most circumstances property-owners in Britain could secure some compensation for such damage from their local authorities under the Riot (Damages) Act of 1886. (In Ireland the situation was governed by the Malicious Injuries Acts.) This, however, was a tedious, prolonged and somewhat uncertain process. As a result, there was a demand for private insurance to cover the risk—a demand which the companies soon met, following the pre-war example of some Lloyd's underwriters. This extension of cover was, of course, provided for an extra premium, and was made more palatable to the companies by the fact that in most cases they might recover a large part of the loss from the relevant local authority.[2] In 1915, for example, the REA recovered £2,900 from the Receiver of the Metropolitan Police as a result of damage inflicted in anti-German riots in London. In general, therefore, insurance

---

[1] For these aspects of fire insurance in war-time, see Sydney Preston and Alexander Ernest Sich, 'Fire Insurance During the War', in Sir Norman Hill *et. al.*, *War and Insurance* (1927), pp. 57–97.

[2] The insurers were denied the right of recovery after the Dublin rebellion (Hill, *War and Insurance*, pp. 65–6).

against the risk of civil riot, in spite of the absence of any large body of experience on which to base premium rates, was easily and satisfactorily assimilated to normal procedures. By contrast, the second risk—domestic damage from enemy action—had no precedents at all, and was met by entirely new procedures.

The initial problem in the case of enemy action was the widespread ignorance and therefore apprehension about the extent of the civil damage which might result from a total war of air raids and long-distance bombardment. Hence, although some Lloyd's underwriters accepted such risks up to limited amounts, the main fire offices agreed not to insure against the consequences of bombing. As the REA Fire Manager put it in October 1914, with a foreboding more applicable to the Second than the First World War:

we do not know and cannot guess the extent of a possible loss. Aeroplanes, I believe, travel so quickly that a few of them might drop bombs charged with inflammable materials into more than one congested area, and if the aeroplanes are not speedily disposed of, we might have simultaneous conflagrations at the Docks, the Wood Street district, Oxford Street and Bayswater, and such a state of things is beyond the power of any Fire Brigade, however efficient, to cope with . . . [The funds of fire offices] were never . . . intended to provide for artificial fires over a large area, and, in fact, a general conflagration such as I have hinted at would be more than the fire offices could meet . . . In the case of a foreign enemy we can hardly say what the limit of possible destruction may be.[1]

In addition, in 1915, the National Provincial gave a lead to other plate glass insurance companies by eliminating war risks from its policies. It soon became clear that the widespread anxiety had to be allayed as a matter of public policy. An official Committee of Inquiry, on which the insurance companies and Lloyd's were strongly represented, was therefore established. And its report, dated 9 July 1915, advocating a Government scheme of (voluntary) insurance worked through the insurance companies, was speedily accepted. By its terms, rates varied from 2s. (air-raid damage) and 3s. (air-raid and bombardment) for private houses to 7s. 6d. and 10s. for goods at docks and wharves. Thenceforth, although a handful of companies and underwriters continued to issue policies privately, the bulk of this class of insurance was managed by 'Approved Companies' on behalf of the Government in return for a 10 per cent commission. Throughout the autumn of 1915, for example, the REA staff put in a huge amount of overtime work in order to issue the new policies. Even so, the scheme

---

1 The next day the Fire Manager (on behalf of various policyholders) sought counsel's opinion on the position of lessees with respect to making good bomb damage to leased property.

left out of account those many families in poor areas (which, it so happened, were particularly vulnerable to enemy action), unaccustomed to fire insurance or contact with fire offices. In November 1915, therefore, official arrangements were made for the issue of small-scale insurances, up to £75, through post offices; and in September 1917 free insurance up to £500 was granted to all property-owners.

In the event, of course, actual damage to property fell far short of the initial expectations. Up to November 1918 total premiums were £13·61 million as against losses of only £2·97 million. This was a very low claims ratio indeed and after making the most generous allowance for expenses and the 10 per cent commission (and after halving the original premium rates in February, 1917) the Government made a very substantial profit on its insurance scheme.

On their part, the fire offices' conventional business continued to grow during the War. Indeed, presumably under the influence of inflation, there was a marked acceleration of its growth: between 1914 and 1918 the premium income of British companies (which had increased by about 12 per cent in the previous four years) jumped from £29·9 million to £41·7 million—an increase of just over 40 per cent. The impetus of this expansion was more than maintained in the boom period immediately after the War: the companies' premium income shot up to £49·5 million in 1919 and £58·5 million in 1920.[1] Thenceforth, deflation (wholesale prices fell by about one-third between 1920 and 1921) and prolonged economic difficulties reduced premium incomes, and, apart from the years 1924–8, they did not again exceed the 1920 level until 1943.

Accident business followed a similar path to fire underwriting—relatively little affected by the direct, explicit aspects of the War, it reflected the enhancement of general economic activity in war-time and the drastic increase in prices and activity in the immediate post-war years (see Table 17.1).

On the other hand, life insurance business presents a contrast to fire and accident underwriting in war-time.[2] To the potential policyholder the general insecurity was an initial disincentive to undertake such a long-run commitment, while to the life offices the very high mortality risk among men of military age eroded the actuarial basis of underwriting. As a

---

[1] *Insurance Directory and Year Book, 1934–35*, p. 538. The Board of Trade wholesale price index rose from 100 in 1900 to 117 in 1914, 268 in 1918, and 369 in 1920 (Mitchell, *British Historical Statistics*, p. 476). This, of course, diminishes the significance of the increase of premiums in real terms.

[2] In what follows I have relied on S. G. Warner, 'The Effect on British Life Assurance of the European War (1914–1918)', in Hill, *War and Insurance*, pp. 101–68.

TABLE 17.1. *British offices' accident insurance premiums, 1914–20*[1]

£ million		1914	1918	1920
	Employers' liability	3·7	5·2	8·9
	Personal accident	2·1	2·2	2·7
	Miscellaneous (including motor)	10·9	19·2	33·5
	Total:	16·7	26·6	45·1

result, new ordinary business fell in the first few years of the War—from £59 million (sums insured in the UK) in 1913 to £44 million in 1916. By 1917 an increase to £52 million presumably reflected the consequences of higher prices and incomes, as well as the large popularity of 'War Bond Policies'—i.e. endowment policies in which the sum insured was to be paid in War Bonds purchased by the life office and earmarked for that purpose. In 1918 the upward trend continued (£68 million sums insured); and in 1919 the combination of peace and inflation acted as a spectacular engine of growth: sums insured rocketed to £121 million (between 1918 and 1919 annual premiums for new UK ordinary business rose from £4·1 million to £6·1 million). By 1920 they were £134 million.[2]

Quite apart from new business, however, life offices had the problem (unknown to other branches of insurance operating on annual contracts with the insured) of policies which provided continuing cover. And the fact that it *was* a problem was a measure of the change in social atmosphere and expectations from the settled and secure days of the nineteenth century. For, in the 1880s, in the onrush of confident expansion, the competitive relaxation of conditions had produced 'free and unconditional' policies for civilians—i.e. policies which remained valid even if the insured joined the armed forces, or went to live in an unhealthy climate. Now, in 1914–18, the offices had to continue their liability in the midst of a holocaust whose terrible dimensions exceeded the worst imaginings of actuary or policyholder a mere generation before. And, although there were still policies subject to restrictive conditions, many of them were held by men beyond military age in 1914. In any case, the life offices agreed not to exercise their right to charge an extra premium in such cases, with the result that no civilian policyholder in 1914, who joined the forces,

[1] Source: *Insurance Directory and Year Book*, various issues. The extent of Lloyd's business is unknown.
[2] New business outside the UK displayed a similar pattern: sums insured fell from £8·6 million in 1913 to £4·3 million in 1916; they then rose to £5·4 million in 1918 and £10·3 million in 1919.

was subject to an extra premium.[1] On the other hand, there was the case of policyholders already in the armed forces. Some of these had benefited from a pre-war tendency (again an indication of competition in an age which could hardly envisage the horror of total war) to commute military risks for a moderate annual payment of about 12s. 6d. or 15s. per cent. Many others, however, still had policies with conditions which made it possible to charge extra for extra risks. And in these instances the offices felt it necessary to charge the extra premium allowed for in the case of active service by policyholders who were already members of the Army or Navy. These were set at £5. 5s. per cent for combatants and £3. 3s. for non-combatants, although it soon became tragically clear that these were too low, and by early 1915 the matter was left to individual companies. Renewals in the summer of 1915 were kept at the original extra rates, since these were officially viewed as continuing commitments, and in any case, in the words of the Life Offices' Association, 'it is the general impression that no extra which could be charged in practice would cover the war risk'. On the other hand, war-risk rates for *new* proposals were obviously quite high. Thus, in January 1916 the Royal Exchange Assurance announced a reduction of its terms—but, even so, they were still £7 per cent for non-combatant ranks up to captain; £10 per cent for artillery, engineers and cavalry; and £15 per cent for infantry officers and the Flying Corps.

With respect to ordinary business in war-time, the additional net losses attributable to policies for which extra premiums were charged or held by civilians killed by enemy action have been estimated at about £2·2 million. More serious, were the claims (in excess of peace-time levels) under policies in respect of which an extra premium was *not* charged. Even after allowing for reserves accumulated for these policies, the net extra loss, or 'death strain', in actuarial terms, was about £13·6 million.[2]

The question of marine insurance in war-time contrasted with both fire and life insurance in that its implications (the confidence of shipowners and merchants, and the consequent level of trade to and from Britain) were vital aspects of national policy because of their direct and substantial relationships with the success of the war effort itself. Traditionally, of course, war risks had been regularly covered by marine policies, and the

---

[1] The companies doing industrial business were in a much more delicate position, for they had not generally issued unconditional policies, and could therefore charge all their policyholders an extra premium if they joined the forces. In the event, however, the industrial companies agreed not to exercise this right with respect to any policy issued up to and including 4 August 1914.

[2] Hill, *War and Insurance*, pp. 136–8.

Napoleonic Wars had been successfully fought while Lloyd's and the companies provided effective insurance services. However, by the late nineteenth century it was clear that the past might offer few precedents for an understanding of modern sea warfare. In particular, the torpedo and the submarine brought home to some the possible dangers of indiscriminate hostilities—even though many, including the Admiralty, were ill-prepared for submarine warfare until well into the War.[1] The apprehension felt by marine underwriters was reflected in 1898, when a General Meeting at Lloyd's agreed (by a narrow majority) to exclude war risks from standard marine policies. Thenceforth, such cover was only provided by special agreement—albeit an agreement which was constantly arrived at. The other side of the coin—official apprehension—was based on the extent as well as vulnerability of Britain's overseas trade. Exports and imports had never been greater, nor more important: they were each equal to almost 30 per cent of national income, while as much as 75 per cent of food consumed was imported. The Government had a clear interest in ensuring that this trade was not disrupted, as it most certainly would be in war-time, by any inability of shipowners or traders to secure insurance cover.

In the event, however, in spite of an official inquiry under Austen Chamberlain in 1907 (which wrongly concluded that private enterprise *would* be able to supply adequate marine insurance services in war-time), no Government plans were proposed until the very eve of war in 1913. By that time there was virtually no private insurance of hulls against war risks—instead, temporary insurance in case of war was supplied by mutual clubs of shipowners—while only about 10 per cent of cargoes were covered against war by reluctant underwriters or companies. In this context, in 1913, another official committee recommended that in the event of war the Government should assume 80 per cent of the hull risks covered by the mutual clubs, with rates and conditions set by the Government; and that a State Insurance Office should also provide direct cover for cargoes at a standard premium rate *irrespective of the relative risk of the voyage*, while leaving private underwriters and companies free to insure if they wished. This plan was not, in fact, accepted until the last day or so before the outbreak of War. It came into effect on 5 August 1914.[2]

[1] The propelled torpedo was invented in the 1860s. The submarine had an older lineage, but the first reasonably large modern naval submarine (270 tons displacement) was launched by the French in 1893. A smaller trial model had been launched in 1888.

[2] For the rôle of the State in war-time marine insurance, see Sir Norman Hill, 'State Insurance against War Risks at Sea', in Hill, *War and Insurance*, pp. 11–56; D. E. W. Gibb, *Lloyd's of London*, pp. 220–6.

The hull insurance scheme only lasted until the summer of 1917. By that time the Government had in effect taken over almost the entire mercantile marine, and the system of State control, together with the parlous condition of the war at sea, put an end to the commercial basis of hull insurance—the Government assuming direct responsibility for all war losses. The total underwriting loss on hulls in the first three years of the War was estimated at about £18·5 million—of which the State bore £14·8 million. Nearly all this loss was confined to the period August 1916–August 1917, when the Government kept down premiums in the face of rapidly mounting claims so as to mitigate the growing panic at the losses resulting from Germany's unrestricted submarine warfare.[1] In the case of cargo insurance, the State scheme also operated at a loss (£65 million claims, £5 million expenses, as against £60 million premiums), partly because of the reluctance to raise premium rates as the submarine war intensified after August 1916, and partly because of the bizarre decision to issue Government policies at a standard rate. The inevitable result was that commercial underwriters and offices accepted only good risks, and the Government (which did not refuse proposals) received the bad ones. In fact, as a result, the official Cargo Insurance Office insured only about 27 per cent of the total value of war-time cargoes: the rest, almost £6,000 million, was insured commercially.

Thus, of the four main branches of insurance, war-time measures distorted the marine market most of all. Even so, the distortion worked in favour of commercial underwriting: in general terms these years saw a huge boom in marine underwriting—and, for reasons already explained, private and corporate underwriters were able to cream off the best cargo risks, leaving the worst to the State Office. Aggregate figures are not available, but in the case of the Royal Exchange, for example, net premiums, which had averaged some £253,000 in 1908–12, reached an annual average of £426,000 in 1911–15 and then spurted hugely to average £1,282,000 in 1916–20.[2] The outcome of these figures, which scaled and exceeded the heights of the Napoleonic Wars, a century before, were even more impressive: by 1916–20 the underwriting surplus averaged £428,000, and in the peak year of 1916 it exceeded £500,000.

The Corporation's other business also reflected national trends in these years. In fire insurance, for example, net premiums (which had been some £880,000 in 1913) exceeded £1 million for the first time in 1916, and by

---

[1] Hill, *War and Insurance*, p. 42.

[2] The figures for gross premiums in the respective years were: £601,000, £884,000 and £2,539,000. All figures rounded to nearest £1,000.

the peak year 1920 stood at £1·79 million (over £3 million gross). Profits, taking account of administrative expenses as well as losses and commission, also climbed: from an average of £79,000 in 1910–14 to £181,000 in 1916–20. The increase in the case of life business was by no means so spectacular; on the other hand, in contrast to marine and fire underwriting, it continued into the 1920s. (Life premiums averaged £404,000 in 1911–15, £492,000 in 1916–20, and £695,000 in 1921–5.) Finally, REA accident business, after an initial decline in home premiums, particularly on account of motor business, increased during the War—and even more in 1919 and 1920, when general economic prosperity and the easing of restrictions on petrol supplies greatly increased the demand for insurance. The Corporation's accident premiums, which were mostly accounted for by employers' liability and motor business, grew from £281,000 in 1913 to £442,000 in 1918 and £893,000 in 1920.[1] In addition, however, and quite apart from the steady business success of its plate glass subsidiary, the National Provincial, the REA benefited from the boom in business of the pioneer of specialized motor business, the Car & General. For in 1917 the Corporation acquired this Company—the premium income of which rose from £361,000 in 1913 to £405,000 in 1918 and £890,000 in 1920.[2] In these respects the REA and its subsidiaries reflected the experience of accident offices as a whole, whose business increased most of all in the inflationary years immediately after the War.

In general, therefore, the Royal Exchange Assurance came out of the War a much larger and more successful office than it had been at its outset. In 1916 the Fire and Marine Departments each earned more than £1 million net premiums for the first time in the Corporation's history (£694,000 of the fire premiums came from overseas business) and the profits of all non-life business, £287,000, was also a record.[3] Thenceforth, non-life profits mounted: to £302,000 in 1917 and £457,000 in 1918. In the spring of 1918—influenced by the unprecedented profits, by the acquisition of the Car & General, by the fact that the balance on profit and loss stood at a figure (£726,000) slightly larger than before the San Francisco fire, and by the fact that interest income alone was sufficient to

---

[1] The composition of the Corporation's general accident business was (in £000):

	1913	1918	1920
Employers' liability	141	200	363
Personal accident	29	40	54
Miscellaneous	111	202	476

[2] For the acquisition, see below, pp. 463–4. Approximately 80 per cent of the Car & General's accident premiums were derived from its motor business in these years.

[3] The previous record for profits was £198,000 in 1910. This figure was only approached by the solid mid-Victorian years: £169,000 in 1861 and £166,000 in 1859.

pay dividends—the Governor could respond enthusiastically to a proprietor's congratulations: 'We hope, like you, that the Corporation will go on getting stronger and stronger. I think it is very much alive.' In the first General Court after the War, a year away from the Corporation's Bicentenary, the Governor was able to report a continuation of progress and a further increase in profits: 'I do not believe the Royal Exchange Assurance has ever been in a stronger position than at present.'

The satisfaction expressed by the Governor about the Corporation's wartime experience was also bolstered by a knowledge of the obstacles to normal business which had been overcome. Indeed, one of the most important effects of the War was to impose an enormous strain on the manpower of insurance companies generally—a strain which not only meant that those who did not join the forces had to sustain a vastly increased load of work, but also obliged normally conservative offices like the REA to employ large numbers of women clerks (as distinct from typists) for the first time. The general repercussions of the War in terms of women's economic and social position were therefore aptly reflected in insurance offices. And in insurance, as in other industries, it was a once-for-all change: clerical (although not managerial) tasks ceased to be exclusively male preserves. In 1919 the REA Governor emphasized that the Corporation's business achievements were doubly remarkable in view of staff shortages:

Several times we thought our staff had been depleted until it had reached the irreducible minimum and then we found that the irreducible minimum had to be still further reduced, and this in the face of steady growth in volume of the business handled by every Department. Of course the work never could have been got through had it not been for the loyal services rendered by the ladies who took the place of the men who had gone to war. Business life was in most cases entirely new to them, but the way in which they adapted themselves to new conditions and carried through the large volume of business we are today reviewing is indeed beyond praise. We owe them a deep debt of gratitude.

By February 1918 the Head Office employed 159 lady clerks, of whom all but two were temporary (there were also twenty-two typists). Of the temporary clerks 124 earned £2 or less—and, after some hesitation, it was agreed to increase the salaries of all temporary clerks by five shillings, thus establishing a minimum of £2. Presumably these women and girls came to the REA from varying backgrounds. But some at least continued the tradition of selectivity which had always applied to REA male clerks: some girls came straight from Cheltenham Ladies' College to work for the

Corporation; and in December 1919 the Fire Manager wrote to the College's Principal, saying that one at least had became a permanent clerk, and inquiring 'whether among girls leaving this term or having left previously there is one desirous to earn her own living and preferably reside with parents in London, as we have a vacancy'. Thenceforth, even the REA was unable to return to the pre-war situation.

The men who joined the forces were well treated by the Corporation: all were given leave from the Corporation on full pay, with a guarantee of their jobs on their return at pro-rated increases in their salaries. As the Departmental Managers insisted in November 1918, 'a man is not to suffer for having been away in the War, much less from having joined up at an early date'. In fact, within two days of the outbreak of war sixty members of staff (about 20 per cent of the total) were under orders or on the point of joining a regiment. Altogether, 546 of the Corporation's staff served in the forces during the War—and of these eighty-two (15 per cent) were killed.[1] Those who stayed with the REA found that the combination of increased business, the need to train new clerks and the call of home-based duty could be formidable. As J. L. T. Shephard, then working in the West End Office, later recalled:

I had to draft all fire policies and endorsements, while teaching various females [about] insurance generally. I used to take bundles of policies, perhaps 50 to a 100 at a time to Moor Lane Police Station and examine them before signature, when I got an hour off on an all-night patrol of the Cripplegate area as a City of London Special [Constable]. I think . . . I came up for eight consecutive Sundays to work all day to get the work up to date . . . without interruptions, etc. My writing went to pieces.[2]

And in 1916, when confronted with a twenty-page memorandum from the Law Union about the settlement of an Egyptian loss, the Fire Manager confessed 'that with young ladies keeping our Risk Books for such places as Alexandria, Mexico and Shanghai, together with the supervision of an entirely female staff . . . dealing with policies arising out of daily Zeppelin raids, I have not got a great deal of time left to engage in controversy with the Law Union, assuming any controversy to be necessary'.

Oddly enough, the most lasting effect of the War may well have been on the staff rather than the business of the Royal Exchange Assurance. Admittedly, premium income was given a considerable boost and the Car & General was acquired. Yet these developments were more or less inevitable aspects of general developments, and their implications,

[1] Hill, *War and Insurance*, p. 117.
[2] Letter from J. L. T. Shephard to West End Branch Manager, 7 December 1949.

particularly as regards the adjustment of management organization, were not worked out until some years after 1918. By contrast, as far as the staff was concerned, the War marked a decisive break in continuity. Not only did female clerks invade the *sanctum sanctorum* of the Royal Exchange; but the relative position of the male staff also changed under the impact of inflation and new economic trends. As the Secretary pointed out in 1920, 'in the past, service in the Royal Exchange Assurance was counted among the best in the City of London, ranking with the Bank of England and Rothschilds, but during the last few years the position has not been fully maintained, the scale of pay now ruling being little in advance of that in other first-class offices. It has, of course, in no way kept pace with the present cost of living.' The War, as with other periods of rapid inflation, had, in fact, increased wages (i.e. of manual workers) by more than salaries, so that the income gap between manual workers and clerks had tended to narrow. Certainly the position of the REA clerk had shifted relative to other income recipients as well as to the employees of other insurance offices. By November 1920, in the midst of a wild inflation, it seemed to the Departmental Managers that the Corporation could probably not pay its employees 'such rates of salary as will enable them to live up to the standard they were used to before the War'. Nevertheless, although a watershed *had* been passed, the full consequences of these trends should not be exaggerated: clerical appointment in the REA continued to be most attractive to (and strongly competed for) by middle-class youths—particularly in the late 1920s and the 1930s.

A good deal of attention was, in fact, paid in the immediate post-war period to the adjustment of salaries to the new situation. During the War the general level of clerical salaries had not been increased; instead substantial War bonuses (e.g. 25 per cent in 1917) had been paid. And this practice was continued immediately after the War, for it was an understandable response to rapid inflation, which management felt might be an ephemeral basis for any permanent increase in salaries. In October 1918, for example, a bonus of $33\frac{1}{3}$ per cent was declared with an upper limit of £100, but with special consideration to the circumstances of 'married men with small salaries'. Throughout 1919, however, in the face of rising prices and pressure from staff, who were conscious of the temporary nature of bonuses and of the salary increases in banks and other insurance companies, the Corporation's Managers anxiously debated the question of salaries and bonuses. Ultimately—after considering a profit-sharing scheme which would have paid a 'dividend' on salaries at the same rate as that on stock—in the spring of 1920 salaries were raised to about 30 per cent above their pre-war level, although even this did not fully stop the debate.

Thus it was that the Corporation entered its Bicentennial year conscious of 'the generally unsettled feeling that permeates the country' owing to the effects and aftermath of total war. The anxiety about clerical salaries was only one aspect of the insecurity: at another level the unpredictability of the future provided further evidence. And the composition of the REA staff indicated both the changes which had been brought by the last few (let alone the previous 200) years and the extent to which changes in the scope of its business had made the world its context. In addition to the total Head Office staff of 408, of whom 124 were female clerks, British branch and district offices employed 418 (about one-third of whom were women) and foreign branches 397 clerks. The average salary of permanent male clerks was £356, and of female clerks £179.

In spite of all this, however, the REA came to its two hundredth birth-day with a good deal of justified self-congratulation. Total net premiums in 1920 were £4·3 million—contrasting with less than £500,000 in 1870 and less than £250,000 in 1820. To celebrate the Bicentenary, in addition to various banquets throughout the country, a special bonus dividend of 5 per cent was declared; the members of the Court received an additional year's fees; and in addition to special gifts to the staff amounting to £49,000, the Court adopted a measure calculated to relieve what the Governor, at the Bicentenary Staff Dinner on 29 June 1920, called 'the modern stress of business life': every employee, then and in the future, who had completed thirty years' service was to be given three months' leave and £200 to enable him to take an extended holiday abroad with his wife and family. It was a fitting, paternal conclusion to 200 years of corporate history—and a piquant contrast to the new atmosphere of twentieth-century industrial relations and competitive reality.

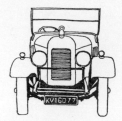

18

British Insurance between the Wars

THE GROWTH OF UNDERWRITING

Between 1918 and 1939 the evolution of British insurance was conditioned, as it had been in the previous two centuries, by economic change and social trends. Yet—as was illustrated in other aspects of British history at the time—these changes and trends did not always pull in the same direction. While economic crisis and political insecurity had adverse consequences for some types of insurance, structural change, long-run growth and new social habits greatly extended the market for other types. The net result was continued expansion—but an expansion in which different sorts of insurance grew at different rates, thus changing (and in some respects radically changing) the basic patterns of British insurance.[1]

Fire insurance remained perhaps the most conventional branch of the industry: not because it was inherently lacking in innovation, but because its function was the most straightforward, the most traditional and the most widely used at the outset of the period. As had been obvious from some time before 1914, the habit of fire insurance had spread so widely in the UK as to be relatively unchangeable. Consequently, the future course of the industry was largely dependent on the growth of insurable values in the UK and the degree to which British offices could penetrate potential markets overseas. In both instances—at home and abroad—the economic vicissitudes of the inter-war period had a distinct dampening effect on the money values involved. As Table 18.1 shows, the spurt in premium incomes during the War was more than maintained in the two post-war years of boom and continued inflation (although the increase in premiums must be seen in the⋅ perspective of a doubling of wholesale prices during the War, and a further increase by about 25 per cent in 1919–20). In 1921, however, there was a sharp fall—associated with the slump which reduced wholesale prices by one-third. Thenceforth, premium incomes recovered and in 1924–8 they exceeded the 1920 level,

---

[1] As with earlier sections of this study, this chapter will be primarily concerned with British insurance companies as distinct from Lloyd's.

TABLE 18.1. *British offices' fire, accident and life business, 1916–40*

(£ million)

Year	Fire (Net premiums)	Accident (Net premiums)			Ordinary life			Industrial life	
		Empl. Liability and Personal Acc.	Motor	Miscellaneous	U.K. Premiums		Sums assured	Premiums	Sums assured
					Total[a]	New			
1916	31·9	5·9	13·1		30·2	2·1	n.a.	19·6	n.a.
1917	36·0	6·5	15·8		30·5	2·8	n.a.	21·0	n.a.
1918	41·7	7·4	19·2		33·8	4·1	n.a.	22·4	n.a.
1919	49·5	8·9	23·7		37·8	6·1	n.a.	25·3	n.a.
1920	58·5	11·6	33·5		41·9	6·6	n.a.	29·3	n.a.
1921	54·2	10·4	36·4		44·1	4·6	n.a.	31·1	n.a.
1922	55·0	8·8	34·0[b]		45·6	4·5	1,144	31·6	n.a.
1923	57·7	8·2	37·5		46·8	4·5	1,182	33·2	693
1924	58·3	8·8	40·8		51·5	4·9	1,209	34·1	716
1925	60·6	9·0	44·5		57·9	4·9	1,291	36·6	751
1926	60·9	9·1	48·7		58·5	4·9	1,353	36·8	832
1927	59·1	9·4	51·7		63·9	5·5	1,398	38·8	870
1928	59·0	9·7	54·3		68·2	5·8	1,439	40·9	903
1929	58·4	9·8	56·3		69·8	5·8	1,492	42·0	920
1930	55·1	9·8	55·8		66·8	6·0	1,591	43·8	953
1931	51·9	9·1	32·5	22·7	65·3	5·7	1,668	45·4	1,006
1932	50·8	8·7	31·8	21·6	67·9	5·5	1,706	46·4	1,035
1933	48·4	8·5	31·3	21·9	71·4	6·0	1,759	47·7	1,051
1934	48·8	9·1	31·9	23·7	71·5	6·7	1,809	50·1	1,089
1935	48·8	9·8	33·3	24·2	74·3	7·3	1,936	51·5	1,123
1936	48·9	10·3	35·3	25·3	77·3	7·7	2,061	53·6	1,176
1937	49·8	11·1	37·4	27·1	80·5	7·9	2,139	55·8	1,216
1938	49·5	11·7	37·9	n.a.	83·9	7·6	n.a.	58·0	1,255
1939	49·6	11·4	36·6	n.a.	84·1	5·7	n.a.	59·8	1,294
1940	51·0	11·4	31·9	n.a.	82·8	4·3	n.a.	62·2	1,313

Source: *Insurance Directory and Year Book*, various issues.

[a] Overseas life premiums were normally well under 10 per cent of UK premiums.

[b] Between 1913 and 1921 'miscellaneous' premiums had to be calculated from the data for individual offices; they may therefore be less accurate than, and are not quite consistent with, data for 1922–40.

although, in light of the continued problems of the British economy it is most likely that the prosperity of the mid- and late-1920s was mainly due to economic growth overseas, and particularly in America (separate data for overseas income are not available, but by all accounts it continued to account for over 50 per cent of all fire premiums).[1] By contrast, the world-

[1] In 1918 and 1928 British fire offices derived premium incomes of £17·4 million and £20·3 million from the United States (although this reflected a relative decline from 42 to 34 per cent of total fire premiums): *PM*, LXX, 46 (15 November 1919), p. 873; *PM*, XC, 20 (18 May 1929), p. 1012.

wide depression of the 1930s reduced British offices' premiums by about 15 per cent: averaging about £60 million in the mid-1920s, they dropped to some £49 million (varying only by £800,000 on either side of this figure) between 1933 and 1939. And it is likely, although again guesswork must replace non-existent data, that this relative stability was the outcome of a rough balance between British and overseas trends. At home, economic recovery—reflected in increases in production, trade and prices —must have increased the demand for fire insurance, even though continued competition kept premium rates down. Overseas, however, and especially in the traditional markets for British insurance, the companies had to contend with continued stagnation, currency instability, heightened competition from indigenous companies, and the intensification of that economic nationalism which was the outcome of world depression and which took the form of greater restrictions and regulation of foreign firms.

On balance, fire insurance had weathered the economic storms of the first part of the twentieth century reasonably well. Standing at £49·5 million in 1938, annual premiums were more than two-thirds above their 1913 level. Even discounting the fact that they had hardly changed since 1933, this still reflected a fairly creditable performance: a compound growth rate of 2 per cent annually over twenty-five years. Yet it also reflected a high tide of relative achievement; no new departures had taken place; and the rate of expansion in 1913–38 contrasted with that of the previous twenty-five years—when premiums had more than doubled, growing at virtually 3 per cent annually. The main and overwhelmingly dominant influences on the spread of fire underwriting had been trends in prices and economic activity—a growth in the size, rather than an extension of the scope, of the market.

In contrast, the most significant insurance development of these years (even though it, too, was obviously affected by economic fluctuation), was largely attributable to changes in social habits and patterns of consumption. This was the spectacular expansion of accident business—primarily and best exemplified in the insurance of motor vehicles, but also illustrated in the substantial increase in insurance against other forms of liability, burglary, household damage, and the like. The global figures for British companies are themselves very impressive: in 1913 'general accident' (i.e. all insurance other than fire, life and marine) accounted for merely some £16 million of premium income; by the eve of the Second World War, it amounted to well over £80 million. From being barely half of fire premium income in 1913, accident income had become the more important by 1927, and by 1939 exceeded fire by some 60 per cent.[1] The relative growth of company fire and accident premiums is illustrated in Figure 18.1.

As Table 18.1 shows, relatively little of this development was based upon the most traditional 'accident' categories—employers' liability and personal accident—even though their doubling from £5·8 million in 1913 to £11·4 million in 1939 was a far from negligible consideration. The really important development came with the growth of motor vehicle insurance.

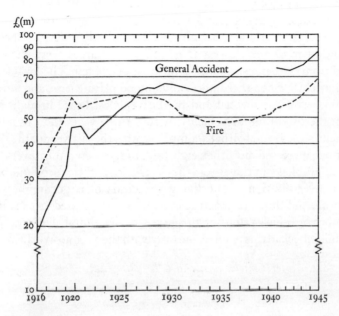

Fig. 18.1: Premium income of British insurance offices, 1916–45

(Source: *Insurance Directory and Year Book*, various issues. (Comparable data for general accident premiums in the late 1930s are not available.)

Until 1931 the data for motor insurance were included in the 'miscellaneous' category; but it is most probable that it accounted for almost half of that category from 1919 or 1920 onwards (by 1931 it was 60 per cent of the total) and that most of the growth in the 1920s was accounted for by motor insurance. Between 1918 and 1928 'miscellaneous accident' premiums increased from £19·2 million to £54·3 million—or by more than 180 per cent.

[1] These figures refer to the income of companies only. However, Lloyd's underwriters were a growing factor in the market: Lloyd's share of total British fire and accident premiums (separate figures are not available) grew from 11·4 per cent in 1928 to 17·3 per cent in 1938. See R. L. Carter, 'Competition in the British Fire and Accident Insurance Market' (unpublished D. Phil. dissertation, University of Sussex, 1968), p. 42, Table VII.

Even though motor and 'miscellaneous' premiums grew by merely one-third in the next decade, this must be set against both the decrease in fire premiums and the adversities of the world economic climate, for accident, no less than fire, insurance was a world-wide business for British companies.

As has already been suggested, the main element in this long-run increase in accident premiums was the expansion of motor vehicle insurance, which probably trebled between 1918 and 1928. In this respect it is significant that the number of motor vehicles in use in the United Kingdom increased in every year between the Wars—even in the depths of the slump. During the First World War it was only after 1916 that there had been a fall in the number of vehicles on the road as resources were increasingly diverted from civilian use and the supply of petrol fell. The low-point was reached in 1918, when there were only 78,000 private cars, and almost the same number of commercial and public vehicles. Peace brought a sharp boom in the use of motor vehicles: within three years their number had more than trebled, and by 1928 (compared with the last year of the War) the number had increased more than eightfold, to 1,333,000. Whatever Britain's economic problems in the 1920s, they were not sufficient to hold back the rise and diversification of the living standards of large numbers of the population. And the same was true even in the 'depressed' 1930s. By 1938 the number of vehicles stood at 2,644,000, having doubled, compared with 1928; and a check to this boom came only with the Second World War:

TABLE 18.2. *Motor vehicles in use in UK, 1914–42*[a]

(Thousands)	Private cars	All vehicles other than agricultural tractors and motor cycles	Motor cycles
1914	132	265	124
1916	142	275	153
1918	78	160	69
1920	187	362	288
1922	319	576	384
1924	482	812	504
1926	696	1,083	646
1928	901	1,333	721
1930	1,075	1,560	733
1932	1,149	1,643	606
1934	1,336	1,874	533
1936	1,675	2,272	510
1938	1,984	2,644	466
1940	1,456	2,042	281
1942	880	1,482	309

[a] Source: Society of Motor Manufacturers and Traders Ltd. Data for 1914, 1916, and 1918 refer to Great Britain only. The number of vehicles refers to registrations at 31 March for the years 1914–20; the highest quarter for the years 1922 and 1924; September for the years 1926–38; and 31 August for the years 1940 and 1942.

This continued increase, amid the economic vicissitudes of the inter-war period, was evidence not merely of structural change in the British economy, which was bolstering new industries even while the older ones stagnated, but of the ascendancy of new living styles—which led to radical changes in the pattern of demand for insurance services. Comparable changes also occurred in other countries where British insurance companies had vital interests. In the United States, for example, the number of motor vehicles registered rose from 1·8 million in 1914 to 26·7 million in 1929. The slump then arrested the pace of growth; but by 1939 the number was 31 million.[1]

Thus, the first and most important influence on the sustained increase in accident business was social change. As more and more people used motor vehicles, so there was a commensurate growth in the need to insure against damage to or loss of the vehicle itself, damage to others' property, or liability for personal injury as a result of an accident. Nor was the increasing use of motor cars the only relevant social change. As they spread, and as the number of accidents inevitably increased, so that the public at large, and with it the courts, became more 'damages-conscious': to the increasing costs of mechanical repairs there was added the increasing cost of any liability for personal injury. The race between premium incomes and the costs of claims in motor vehicle insurance had begun.

As the figures of 'miscellaneous' accident premiums imply, the period of most rapid growth of motor premiums was in the 1920s, when market forces were the determining factors. By the end of the 1920s, however, the frequency and personal costs of road accidents exposed a weakness of the existing system: innocent victims of an accident might suffer personal injuries for which they could secure no compensation unless the motorist was relatively wealthy or had chosen to insure himself against liability claims. Admittedly, it was estimated that 90 per cent or more drivers *were* insured, but accidents involving the rest were sufficiently frequent or sufficiently well publicized to provoke comment and complaint from the public, the Press and the courts. The result was a mounting campaign for compulsory third-party motor insurance (for which there were precedents in Norway, Switzerland, Denmark, and elsewhere);[2] and after a Royal Commission on Transport (1928–9) had considered the question, the Road Traffic Act of 1930, which became operative in 1931, made third-party liability insurance a compulsory obligation on motorists.

The second influence on motor insurance was, therefore, explicitly

1 US Bureau of the Census, *Historical Statistics of the United States* (1960), p. 462.
2 For compulsory insurance, see Dinsdale, *Accident Insurance*, pp. 210–11, 327–9.

legal. The obligation to insure obviously increased the demand for insurance services, even though the companies did not welcome the increase: they suspected that motorists who had to be forced to insure were probably worse risks than those who insured voluntarily. In 1927 the REA Accident Manager told the Governors that 'it would be an extremely bad day for the insurance companies' if there were a compulsory insurance law, 'as to a great extent the present opportunity of selecting the risks would be done away with'. Further, as the Governor told the General Court in 1931: 'Legislation on these lines was not favoured by insurance companies, among other reasons because it is believed that it would lead to an increase in the number of claims, as well as in the amount awarded . . . The provisions of the Road Traffic Act have involved the Corporation in heavy expense and comparatively little new business of a desirable character has so far resulted from its operation.' However, although the profitability of motor insurance *did* apparently decline in the 1930s, it is not certain how much of this was due to the consequences of compulsory insurance and how much to the increased cost of claims.

In any case, as the figures indicate, the growth of premium income slowed down in the second inter-war decade. And in this respect it is likely that the strong influence of compulsory third-party insurance and of the continued increase in motor vehicles (the number doubled in 1928–38) was largely offset by the prolonged troubles of the early 1930s. On the other hand, however, the relative increase in non-motor miscellaneous business, mostly burglary and personal liability, was fairly substantial at the time. Burglary and general household insurance also reflected changes in social habits and the spread of suburbia, while liability business was a crude index of a new socio-legal trend. The latter was, in fact, attributed to the indirect influence of motor vehicle insurance. As the *Statist* put it in 1939: 'Motor insurance has brought in its train a distressing, almost alarming, form of what for the sake of a better name, is known as "damages consciousness". The public are educated to claim for each and every accident or injury arising from whatever cause . . . Encouragement in this attitude is given by both judges and juries. Awards made by Courts for personal injuries contrive to increase in magnitude.'[1] This anxiety was widespread. As the REA General Court was told by the Governor in April of the same year, referring to motor insurance, 'I cannot but feel that the publicity given to the large awards by the Courts is intensifying a claim-consciousness on the part of the public, which, if developed still further, may eventually create a new social problem.'

[1] *Statist*, CXXXIV, 3203 (15 July 1939), Insurance Section, p. 9.

It is, indeed, an interesting reflection on British social habits that, even apart from motor business, personal liability insurance increased so rapidly at a time when premiums for personal accident (i.e. injury to oneself) more or less stagnated. In this respect British habits apparently contrasted strongly with those of other people. One possible reason, adduced by a commentator in 1924, was 'that we have been comparatively free hitherto from the spectacular catastrophes, involving heavy loss of life and limb, that are reported from other countries—notably the United States'. Nevertheless, it was felt to be 'surprising that so many persons whose incomes depend upon their own exertions, and who have heavy responsibilities, should fail to protect themselves against incapacity or even death through accident or disease. It is quite common to find that a prudent man of affairs will cover himself by insurance against practically every other risk of serious loss by unforeseen circumstances, but, when it is a question of spending a few pounds in securing a personal accident policy, he will decline to entertain the proposition.'[1]

In contrast to this relative caution about personal accident insurance, the 'prudent man of affairs' in inter-war Britain continued and intensified his attachment to life insurance in its various forms: between 1916 and 1939, as Table 18.1 shows, ordinary life premiums grew from £30 million to £84 million. Indeed, the growth rates of both premiums and sums assured were higher in the inter-war period than they had been in the more settled and confident years before 1914. Comparing 1886–1913 and 1922–37, the annual growth rate of premium incomes rose from 3·4 to 4·4 per cent, and of sums assured from 2·8 to 4·3 per cent.[2] Over the long run, this acceleration was based on the tendency to insure (or save) an increasing proportion of a growing income. (Between 1921 and 1938 ordinary premiums rose from 1·1 per cent to 2·2 per cent of national income.)[3] In

---

[1] *Statist*, CIV, 2410 (5 July 1924), Insurance Section, p. xxviii. This is not the place to examine 'coupon insurance'—an interesting development of accident insurance which stemmed from the competition for newspaper circulation between the Wars. Various papers (including *The Times* in 1921) came to an arrangement with an insurance company to cover personal accident, or other contingencies, to 'registered readers'. A pioneer of such schemes was the *Daily Mail* which commenced on 1 January 1914 with a private scheme offering payment on death (£1,000), serious injury (£500), or disablement incurred in an accident involving public or private transport. The scheme was initiated after the War, the contingencies extended, and the *Daily Mail* gave the administration of it to the Eagle Star & British Dominion Insurance Company. By the time that this scheme was suspended in 1939 the *Daily Mail* had paid over £2 million in benefits. (I am most grateful to the *Daily Mail* and to its Library, for providing this information).

[2] G. W. Murphy and J. Johnston, 'The Growth of Life Assurance in UK since 1880', *Transactions of the Manchester Statistical Society*, 1956–57, p. 9.

[3] Calculated from national income data in Mitchell, *Abstract of British Historical Statistics*, pp. 367–8, and premium data in Murphy and Johnston, 'The Growth of Life Assurance', *Transactions of the Manchester Statistical Society*, 1956–57, pp. 74–5.

the shorter run there were various other factors which helped account for spurts in, as well as checks to, the progress of life insurance.

As Table 18.1 makes clear, there was a sharp increase in new life business in the last year of the War, and in 1919 and 1920. Initially, a large part of this spurt was based upon the issue of 'War Bond Policies'—short-term endowments payable in War Bonds. Subsequently, however, after the Armistice, there was a renewed demand for more orthodox policies. Much of this came from ex-servicemen—formerly unable to insure their lives at moderate rates while on active service, and now returning to civilian and (many of them) newly married, life. They, and the population at large, also had to face the pressures of inflation: the doubling of prices in war-time had halved the value of life policies. This, and the renewed drive for family security, naturally turned men's minds to this sort of prudence. Between 1917 and 1920 total ordinary premiums increased by more than one-third: from £30·5 million to £41·9 million. To some extent, of course, this brief boom reflected the making-up of a backlog: potential policyholders were compensating for the lull in insurance business in the insecure years 1914–17. Some recession in new business was therefore probably inevitable. To this 'natural' course of events, however, there was added the influence of the slump and deflation of 1921. As a result, new premium income tumbled from £6·6 million in 1920 to £4·6 million in 1921. Nevertheless, long-run trends were upward. Total premiums (i.e. all renewal premiums) naturally kept rising, and in fact doubled between 1920 and 1939. Although a variety of factors were responsible for this continued growth, three in particular deserve emphasis.

First, there was the tendency, already strongly apparent in pre-1914 days, for ordinary life offices to seek business among people with relatively small incomes. This was partly the consequences of the companies' appreciation of the potential market for ordinary assurance among wage-earners who could be induced to insure for small sums on the basis of, say, monthly premiums. But perhaps an even more important influence was the increase in wages and well-being, when compared with pre-war Britain:

In former days [according to the *Statist* a year after the Armistice] the great backbone of life assurance business was found in the support of the middle-classes, men whose income ran from £200 to £2,000 a year. Now its appeal goes forth to every section of the population . . . The great rise in the wages of the manual labourer gives him the means of effecting ordinary life policies instead of confining his contributions to thrift to the much more expensive system of industrial assurance to which the vast majority of his class have hitherto restricted themselves . . . The manual labourer is now in many cases better off than the clerk or the professional man.[1]

And in spite of the unemployment and stagnation which continued in certain industries throughout the inter-war period, there was, in fact, a sufficient prosperity and a sufficiently sustained increase in the real income of large numbers of the employed to buoy up the mass purchase of insurance policies. In the event, industrial insurance continued as strong as ever: premiums rose from £22·4 million in 1918 to £59·8 million in 1939, as the economic position and ingrained habits of working-class families strengthened the traditional outlets for their savings. On the other hand, wage increases and rising standards also created more and more members of the middle class—at least to the extent of enabling them to transfer their demand for life insurance to the ordinary branch.

The second development in the field of life insurance was, in effect, new, although there had been some small anticipations in pre-war Britain.[2] It was the rise of group life and pension plans. As early as December 1918, the *Statist* pointed out that among the 'many . . . directions in which life assurance enterprise may be successfully directed, [one] which is worthy of mention is the group insurance, which has already found great favour in America, and which has lately been put on the British market by one important and enterprising company . . . If this method should find extended favour in this country an extension of life assurance protection is bound to follow . . . to an extent which is scarcely calculable.'[3] Apparently, however, these early group schemes, like the arrangement between the REA and the Musicians' Union in 1921,[4] were largely 'pure' life assurance—that is, usually an annual contract for all employees in one concern, with no medical examination. But by the later 1920s, and again in imitation of American practice, this simple idea was being widely extended to the purchase of a fixed pension (e.g. £1 per annum for each year of service) as well as a death benefit. Private pensions and pension funds, had, of course, existed for some time. What was new was the

---

[1] *Statist*, XCIV, 2181 (13 December 1919), Insurance Section, pp. vi, viii. In the shipbuilding industry between 1914 and 1920 the money wages of unskilled workers trebled—compared with an increase of just over twofold for skilled workers: S. Pollard, *The Development of the British Economy, 1914–50* (1962), p. 86.

[2] Above, p. 280.

[3] *Statist*, XCII, 2129 (14 December 1918), Insurance Section, p. xi. In the excited and optimistic atmosphere of the Peace, the *Statist* was moved to add (after its survey of the various ways in which the demand for life business might grow): 'The whole future of life assurance . . . through the altered conditions of the last few weeks, is crowned and gilded with many shining possibilities.'

[4] Below, p. 451.

formulation and management of specialist schemes by insurance companies with 'an expert staff for investment and administration which mutual funds cannot command'. The movement was seen by the *Statist* as one more example of the fact that

the development of our social conscience is a very significant feature of this generation . . . We have . . . the attention of the reforming element of our business organizations concentrated on the two problems of social amelioration and maximum output. The thoughtful businessman is coming to see that the two things are intimately connected . . . He can satisfy both his social conscience and his business instinct by pensioning off an old employee on an adequate income when bodily strength or mental energy are on the wane . . . Money spent on a sound pension scheme is like the creation of a fund for renewal and improvement of machinery and equipment. It is essential for successful business.[1]

Separate data for 'schemes' business (group life, endowments, pensions, etc.) on a national basis are not available for the pre-war period. But it is significant that the official category of 'other classes' of business, which includes such schemes, grew from 7 per cent of sums assured (ordinary branch) in 1922 to 15 per cent in 1937.[2] Thus even though the period of most rapid development came in the post-war period (by 1955 'schemes' accounted for 40 per cent of all ordinary premium income), a significant start had been made before 1939.

The third powerful influence on life insurance business between the Wars derived from the vagaries of the economic climate. In general terms, of course, the stagnation of large parts of the economy for so many years was bound to act adversely on life insurance prospects. Yet there were strong countervailing forces. The fact that not all sectors of the economy, nor all occupational groups, suffered from stagnation, was one. But another, and perhaps more important, influence was the decline in general interest rates in the 1930s (the yield on Consols had varied between 4·1 and 5·7 per cent in the 1920s; by 1935 it had touched 2·6). While this made the investment function of insurance companies more difficult, it had the result of attracting a greater flow of funds into life insurance policies, which became more attractive to individuals in measure as the return to other investments fell. As the REA Governor put it in 1936: 'A pronounced feature of the last five years has been the rapid rise in the volume

---

[1] *Statist*, CXIV, 2680 (6 July 1929), Insurance Section, p. viii. These pension schemes also nvolved contributions by employees. The insurance companies already managed extensive schemes for the staffs of universities and hospitals based upon the adaptation of conventional deferred annuity and endowment policies.

[2] Murphy and Johnston, 'The Growth of Life Assurance', *Transaction of the Manchester Statistical Society, 1956–57*, p. 22.

of life business transacted in this country. Admirable as this is as a sign of national thrift and economic progress, such increased assurances are also, I think, not unconnected with the recognition by the private individual of the present difficulties of investment. The burden of investment is now thrown upon the insurance companies.' In large part because of the increased attractiveness of insurance as an investment, new premiums rose from £5·5 million in 1932 to £7·9 million in 1937. And even stronger evidence of the rôle of falling yields elsewhere is provided by figures of annuities purchased: purchase money within the UK rose from £4·6 million in 1931 to £13 million in 1932, and averaged some £12·7 million in the period 1932–8.[1]

As far as British insurance companies were concerned those aspects of insurance—fire, accident and life—already touched on, dominated the insurance business in the inter-war period. The companies did, of course, have a fairly substantial marine premium income. But marine insurance was a faithful mirror of the world's economic problems and was generally unprofitable in the years after the First World War. In any case, it was a section of the industry in which Lloyd's was still a very powerful element; and, compared with other sources of premiums, it was in decline: in 1922 a relatively poor year after the war-time boom, British companies earned £21 million in marine premiums, but by 1931–7 their annual average was less than £11 million.[2] In addition to these branches of insurance there were, of course, various novelties—the most important of which was obviously aviation insurance. Data relating to aviation insurance were not distinguished from the general accident figures, so that its quantitative history cannot be traced. Clearly, however, it was of growing significance in a period which saw the birth and growth of commercial aviation.[3] There had, of course, been some activity from the very beginning (the Car & General, for example, was offering aircraft and airship insurance policies at least as early as 1910); but the main composite companies only went into business seriously some years after the First World War. A beginning was made in 1922 when the British Aviation Insurance Group was formed to pool risks by a handful of companies and Lloyd's underwriters. In 1931 the Group was succeeded by a more formal and broadly based enterprise, the British Aviation Insurance Company, in which various leading companies were shareholders; and in 1935 a second office, the Aviation and

[1] *Insurance Directory and Year Book, 1947–48*, p. 335.

[2] For the REA's experience with marine insurance in these years, see below, pp. 446–9.

[3] See Historic Records Working Party of the Insurance Institute of London, *The History of Aviation Insurance* (1967).

General Insurance Company, was established by another group of companies (including the REA).

INDUSTRIAL STRUCTURE AND COMPOSITE BUSINESS

The inter-war period saw relatively few major changes in the structure of the insurance industry—or, rather, the trends towards large-scale composite business which had commenced with amalgamation in the fire and accident fields in the first years of the century came to their culmination in the years immediately after the First World War. Thenceforth, the industry, and its main business groupings, remained relatively stable until the early 1960s, when a new wave of amalgamation occurred. Looked at in terms of the concentration of business, life insurance showed a slight tendency towards greater concentration in the period: the ten largest offices controlling 46·4 per cent of ordinary sums assured in 1913 and 48·5 per cent in 1937. (The top five companies' share rose from 30·1 to 33·4 per cent in the same period.)[1] In fire insurance, on the other hand, the high point of industrial concentration seems to have come before the First World War. Thus, the twelve largest fire offices, which in 1914 had received 81 per cent of premiums earned by British offices (as distinct from Lloyd's underwriters), had declined to 75 per cent in 1928 and 73 per cent in 1938. And there was a slightly greater decline, from 76 to 68 per cent, in the market share of the twelve largest accident companies between 1928 and 1938.[2]

These figures were, nevertheless, still impressive. But perhaps even more significant was the fact that by the inter-war period it was no longer possible to dissociate fire, accident and life insurance business. From the very early years of the century the first and second of these, and to a lesser but still important extent the third, had come to be dominated by the large composite companies and groups.[3] With its culmination in the early 1920s, the full effects of the wave of amalgamations which inaugurated a new era in British insurance, had been felt. If we compare 1899 and 1925, the twenty-four largest accident companies of 1899 had all been brought into composite groups or (in the case of three) formed their own groups by the end of the period; of the twenty-nine proprietary offices specializing in ordinary life business at the beginning, nineteen had been acquired by composite offices by the end; and fully half of the thirty biggest fire offices

[1] Murphy and Johnston, 'The Growth of Life Assurance', *Transactions of the Manchester Statistical Society, 1956–57*, p. 28.
[2] Data for 1914 calculated from *Insurance Directory and Year Book, 1916*; data for 1928 and 1938 from Carter, 'Competition in the British Fire and Accident Insurance Market', p. 39.
[3] Above, pp. 296–9.

in 1899 had become absorbed into or associated with other companies by 1925.[1] In addition, of course, there was a host of lesser acquisitions and amalgamations, while various relatively new motor vehicle insurance companies (which had not even existed in 1899) grew to a large size and were absorbed into composite companies or groups.

The outcome of these developments by the mid-1920s was the formation of a basic network of companies which was to remain familiar until the late 1950s. In constructing that network, the industry's leading enterprises continued to grow: the Commercial Union, for example, acquired the West of Scotland and the British General in the early 1920s; in 1919 the Royal and the Liverpool & London & Globe established a link with each other; the Norwich Union Life and the Norwich Union Fire came together in 1925; and the Prudential ceased to be a purely life office in the 1920s, securing a large income from fire, accident and marine business. The Royal Exchange was relatively distinctive in that its most important acquisitions were largely confined to companies dominated by motor insurance (although these two—the Car & General and the Motor Union—also had other departments and subsidiaries, and the acquisition of the State in 1925 rounded-out the embryonic Group's premium income).[2] Yet the REA had been a reasonably well-balanced composite office from the late nineteenth century.

The fact that the amalgamation movement petered out after the mid-1920s, not to be revived for a generation, presumably reflected, in part at least, the nature of competitive problems in the inter-war period. In general, there seem to have been few strong forces pushing companies and groups towards a closer co-operation than they already enjoyed or felt they needed. Certainly, although competition was maintained among themselves and with Lloyd's, relationships between companies were extremely friendly, and there was in any case a necessary and intricate skein of reinsurance arrangements through treaties and guarantees. These enabled the offices to secure many of the advantages of grouping based on income (if not on economy of expense). Thus it was that the REA Fire Manager could write to the Manager of the North British & Mercantile in 1920, informing him that the Dunlop Rubber Company was building a large tyre factory in Buffalo, and 'as we are interested in the insurances on this side through your good offices, I pass the information on to you for what it is worth, in the hopes that your influence will enable you to secure the business in America'.

[1] Raynes, *British Insurance*, pp. 367–72.
[2] Below, pp. 462–8.

Beyond these considerations, however, and probably most significant, amalgamation petered out in the mid-1920s because, on the one hand, the implications of the new groupings had to be explored and worked out before any new developments were undertaken, and, on the other, some of the main objectives had already been achieved. In this respect, one of the most important points was that there was relatively little immediate and widespread cost-reduction as a result of amalgamation. Insurance companies tenaciously retained their separate identity, and the opportunity of merging branches and eliminating excess or duplicated staff, was hardly ever taken up. Amalgamation rarely involved conflation. Rather, as the companies made clear at the time, the object of acquisition or grouping was frequently the desire or need to extend operations to new types of business, to acquire new management and staff, and to round-out the variety of services offered. Its aim, in other words, was the extension of 'connection'. And, once this was achieved, the process of amalgamation need not continue; instead, growth could be attained by building on what was already possessed. The function of amalgamation was to provide a speedy, large start for expansion. Subsequently, it was possible to expand more 'naturally'.

There was also a second reason for amalgamation which was related to the first, and which could also be satisfied by the degree of amalgamation attained by the mid-1920s. This was the search for stability of profits. It was obvious, for example, that in spite of the potential business unity of the different sorts of insurance, their respective profitabilities were affected by quite different developments. Thus, a large composite company transacting fire, life, motor, empoyers' liability, personal accident, burglary, marine and other business would normally find that fluctuations in the incomes and profits of its various departments did not coincide. And if amalgamation extended the range and/or balance of underwriting business, as it generally tended to do, then it meant that these fluctuations might offset each other. By spreading risks, the composite companies could guard against exceptional losses. And this principle—basic to the whole idea of insurance—could be applied to the location as well as the type of business undertaken. Business could be spread between fire and accident; and, within fire, through a dozen and more countries. Hence one reason for the rise of composite offices operating on a world-wide basis. As the *Statist* pointed out in its review of insurance in 1929, since 'there is no other business where the spread of activities is so wide as that of insurance . . . it is . . . hard to find a single year when economic conditions . . . are wholly unfavourable [to large composite offices] . . . We may not be surprised, therefore, to find that the history of most years in British insurance is one of steady progress, although fluctuations in results may occur in different branches of the business or in geographical areas in which those branches are carried on.'[1]

The rise of very large-scale composite companies transacting all types of fire, accident and life (and, many of them, marine) business, established a trend which was irreversible. Although various important specialist offices continued, especially in life insurance, the market for all sorts of underwriting was henceforth dominated by companies able to offer all sorts of services. The connection between fire and the various branches of accident business was an obvious one. But there was also a strong connection between life and other sorts of business. Noticed in the palmy years before 1914,[2] it was even more apparent in the pressure for business towards the end of, and after, the Great War. In 1918, having pointed out that the composite companies had secured a record level of new business (£20 million sums assured) in 1917, the *Statist* argued that, apart from the industrial offices (and they themselves were to become composites in the 1920s),

the future, so far as development is concerned, lies with the large all-round insurance institutions which enjoy the advantage of an extensive agency organization, and which can assist in the promotion of new life business through subsidies towards initial expenditure granted from other departments or reserves, rather than with the single-line offices. This partly explains the amalgamation movement which continues to be a feature of life assurance history.[3]

In the event, although the competitive force of the composite offices did not reduce specialist offices to unimportance, they became the dominant element in life insurance. In 1938, for example, specialist offices doing ordinary business secured only 26·9 per cent of new life business—as against 45·6 per cent for conventional composite offices and 27·5 per cent for companies transacting industrial as well as ordinary business, the leading examples of which were also, in effect, composite offices.[4]

[1] *Statist*, cxiv, 2680 (6 July 1929), Insurance Section, p. iv.

[2] Above, p. 299.

[3] *Statist*, xcii, 2129 (14 December 1918), Insurance Section, p. x. The *Statist* went on to cite the formation of the Eagle Star & British Dominion in 1917 and its acquisition of the English & Scottish Life in 1918; the Commercial Union's purchase of the Edinburgh Life in 1918; and the Friends' Provident's purchase of the Century in 1918. In each case a purely life office became associated with a composite company.

[4] Data in *The Policy Holder*, 16 February 1956, p. 171.

THE INVESTMENTS OF INSURANCE COMPANIES

The position of insurance companies in the UK capital market in the twentieth century comprises a distinct topic which it would not be appropriate to deal with at any length here.[1] Some of its salient characteristics are, however, worth noting briefly as an indication of the companies' developing rôle in the British economy.

The principal characteristic was also the most obvious one: the accelerated expansion of life business produced an impressive increase in the assets of insurance companies. Ordinary life funds alone grew from less than £400 million in 1913, to some £1,300 million in 1938, while the total assets of all insurance companies rose from just over £500 million to £1,800 million in the same period. In the 1930s they were increasing by about £50 million annually. Important as they had been as channels of savings and sources of investment funds in the late nineteenth century, British insurance companies assumed an increasingly influential rôle in the inter-war years. Perhaps the most notable aspect of this growth was the extent to which the life offices, both ordinary and industrial, attracted the funds of relatively small savers: as the practice of life insurance was extended, the companies served both as an outlet for existing, and an incentive to increased, savings. Comparing the periods 1901–13 and 1924–35, for example, annual 'small' savings grew from £32 million (some 13 per cent of net national accumulation) to £110 million (over half of net investment); and insurance companies were responsible for just over half of the latter figure—that is, for more than 25 per cent of all net accumulation.[2]

Indirectly, of course, this development served to bring the savings of a wider range and a greater number of people to the formal capital market, and particularly to the Stock Exchange. On the other hand, however, some of the trends in insurance investment which had characterized the pre-1914 period were affected by the War and by post-war economic developments. In fact, the War had two important consequences for the general position of insurance companies' investments. First, at a time when the trade balance was under extreme pressure, a large part of their holdings of overseas securities—it has been estimated at some £55 million—was contributed to the various Government schemes to maintain the rate of exchange. In addition to private sales, the companies deposited American

[1] For a recent study of some aspects of this topic, see George Clayton and W. T. Osborn, *Insurance Company Investment* (1965), which also has a useful bibliography.

[2] Pollard, *Development of the British Economy*, pp. 234–5.

and other securities with the Treasury—either for sale on the New York Stock Exchange, in which case the companies were paid the proceeds, or for use as collateral to raise foreign loans, in which case the companies were paid interest on their deposit.[1] The second, and even more far-reaching, consequence of war-time financial problems for insurance investments was based upon the pressure of public finance. The enormous increase in public borrowing (the National Debt grew from under £700 million to near £8,000 million), and the Government's campaign of persuasion and exhortation on behalf of War Loans, produced a marked shift in the composition of insurance companies' assets. In 1913, for example, after decades of disfavour, British Government securities accounted for only about one per cent of over £500 million assets. In 1920, however, they were some 32 per cent of assets of just over £700 million.[2] Thenceforth, even in peace-time, although the proportion of Government securities was reduced (it was some 16 per cent of assets in 1938)[3] it never returned to the negligible level of pre-1914.

Apart from the shifts associated with holdings of British Government securities, and a decline in the importance of mortgages (from just over one-fifth of assets in 1913 to some 10 per cent in the 1920s and 1930s) there were no very dramatic relative changes in the main categories of insurance investments during this period. Even so, the increase in the holdings of ordinary stocks and shares from less than 4 per cent in 1913 to 9 per cent or more (some £150 million) in 1937, reflected a notable change in the relationship between insurance and the finance of industry —as did the relative shift from debentures to preferred shares and the overall increase in the amount invested in debentures, loan stocks and preferred, guaranteed and ordinary stocks and shares: this rose from £181 million to £574 million between 1913 and 1937.[4] Unfortunately, even for this relatively late period, it is not possible to distinguish between home and overseas investment, so that it is impossible to assess the relative importance of insurance companies for *British* industrial and commercial activity.

[1] S. G. Warner, 'The Effect on British Life Assurance of the European War (1914–18)', in Hill, *War and Insurance*, pp. 119–20.

[2] Hill, *War and Insurance*, p. 122. The figures refer to UK companies transacting life business.

[3] Clayton and Osborn, *Insurance Company Investment*, p. 120.

[4] It is difficult to obtain precise and comparable figures for investments: some published data refer to offices transacting life business, others to all companies; some include, while others exclude, industrial life offices. However, the broad trends and amounts are reasonably clear. The data in the text are derived from above, pp. 332–3; Clayton and Osborn, *Insurance Company Investment*, pp. 120–1, 254; 'Insurance Facts and Figures', a mimeographed fact-sheet which the British Insurance Association kindly allowed me to consult.

As large-scale investors, insurance companies could not escape the consequences of general economic fluctuation in this period. Two developments are worth noting for their implication for life business as well as for the profitability of investment. They were the depreciation of securities during the First World War, associated with relatively high interest rates, and the fall in the rate of interest in the 1930s. In the former case, falling values on the Stock Exchange had been experienced for some years before the War, and throughout the period 1899–1913 the companies had had to write down their Stock Exchange investments, by an annual average of some £700,000. In the period 1914–20, however, the average jumped to £3·9 million.[1] Even so, of course, depreciation of investments is not necessarily a permanent loss, although it was one very important factor (war mortality and heavy taxation were others) in the passing of bonuses by so many companies towards the end of, and after, the War. In the event, most of the fall was recouped by increases in security values in the 1920s.

The fall in the rate of interest during the 1930s was, in its way, a more serious phenomenon, since interest income foregone cannot be regained later. Its indirect consequences, in making life insurance more attractive to policyholders, and therefore greatly expanding new life business, have already been mentioned. More directly, and quite ironically, the same force which pulled premiums into life office funds made it more difficult to invest those funds profitably. In the late 1920s the gross yield of life fund investment exceeded 6 per cent (about £5 per cent net of tax) for various offices; whereas by 1938 the gross yield of the funds of twenty-two representative offices had fallen to 4·75 per cent (3·8 per cent net).[2] Once more, as in the 1890s, when the decline in interest rates had been even more alarming, the pressure of falling yields enforced a greater diversification of investment. In the main this went into private Stock Exchange securities: between 1927 and 1937, for example, the proportion of insurance investments accounted for by private securities of this sort rose from 24·5 per cent to 34·4 per cent (British and overseas government securities fell from 43·9 to 34·8 per cent in the same period). In addition, however, insurance companies, accumulating about £1 million every week, extended their direct loans to established companies and began to buy more property as a way of increasing yields.[3]

[1] Hill, *War and Insurance*, pp. 148–9.

[2] William Penman, 'A Brief Survey of Ordinary Life Insurance in Great Britain', *Journal of the American Society of Chartered Life Underwriters*, v, 1 (December 1950), 43–4. I am most grateful to Mr Penman for this reference.

[3] A. T. K. Grant, *A Study of the Capital Market in Britain from 1919–36* (second edition, 1967), pp. 190–1, 239–40.

In the event, however, the investment difficulties of the 1930s were not sufficiently serious to impede the progress of life insurance—or mar the generally good outcome of the inter-war period for British insurance as a whole. Indeed, as had happened in the 1890s, the vicissitudes of the economic climate, by inducing a more vigorous and adventurous search for stability and profits, had perhaps resulted in an overall improvement in the long-run situation. Certainly, the factors influencing investment, as well as those influencing underwriting, were helping to complete the process of modernization for British insurance offices.

19

The Development of the REA between the Wars

Between 1917 and 1928 the position of the Royal Exchange Assurance within the structure of British insurance was radically changed by its acquisition of various other companies—the most important result of which, apart from an overall growth in the Group's total premium income, was to make the Corporation and its subsidiaries a very powerful element in the burgeoning field of motor vehicle insurance. However, before this is considered, it will be as well to examine the pattern of development of the Corporation's own business (as distinct from that of its associated companies).[2] As Table 19.1 shows, while total premium income grew, its composition also experienced some striking changes.

TABLE 19.1. *REA fire, life, marine and accident premiums, 1914–38*

(£000)	Fire	Life	Marine	Accident	Total
1914	856	369	359	262	1,746
1918	1,276	424	1,252	441	3,393
1928	1,744	842	585	1,131	4,302
1938	1,449	1,400	728	1,229	4,806

In general, the Corporation's underwriting experience was satisfactory throughout the inter-war period. The exception to this, however, was its oldest Department—Marine. The First World War, as we have seen, gave an enormous and profitable fillip to marine insurance; and in the palmy years of 1916–20 the REA's *average* net premium income was £1·3 million and its marine underwriting profit £344,000 annually. After the boom year

---

[1] The overseas business of the REA is separately considered in chapter 20. Although it had refused a share in a grouping, in 1930, the REA was also concerned with aviation insurance from 1935, when it invested £23,375 in the Aviation & General Insurance Company—an office formed by a group of leading composite companies. The Corporation's General Manager, MacDonald, became a Deputy Chairman of the new company.

[2] For the distribution of the Group's premium income, see below, p. 468.

of 1920, however, as with other departments, marine business slumped: net premiums fell from over £1 million in 1920 to about £650,000 in 1921.[1] And in the case of marine underwriting, the slump was both deeper and more prolonged. As early as November 1921 Hines, the REA Underwriter, confessed that conditions 'were more involved than he had ever

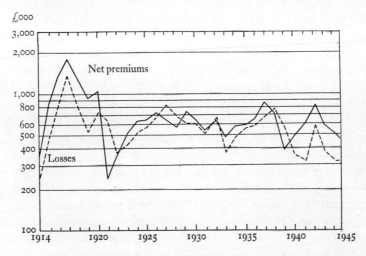

Fig. 19.1: REA marine business, 1914–45

(Source: REA Archives.)

known them to be before, and it was exceedingly difficult to know what course was the right one to pursue. Personally, he favoured *extreme* caution.' Net income in 1921–5 was about 40 per cent of its level in the previous five years, and there was an average annual loss of £127,000. Basically, the boom in insurance during the War and immediate post-war period had attracted large numbers of new underwriters into the business, and fierce competition in the years after 1920 drove down rates. The mid-1920s in particular were full of complaints about the sad condition in marine insurance. Typical of many, was a gloomy report by Hines to the Governors in October 1926: the outlook was 'very depressing' and it was not impossible that the Corporation would lose £250,000 that year alone. By 1928 there were some signs that competition was abating and (in the words of the REA Governor in 1935) 'those who were left were again able to conduct their business on a reasonably profitable basis'. But this state

---

[1] Of this, however, just over £400,000 was disbursed as return on account of previous year's policies.

of affairs did not last long: international economic crisis, and the renewal of underwriting competition in the early 1930s, once more brought heavy losses on the marine account.

The REA was not facing these problems alone. In 1920, for example, it had come to a working arrangement with the Prudential Assurance Company, by which the Corporation managed the Prudential's marine underwriting. And in 1927 the Governor took the lead in organizing a conference of chairmen of marine insurance companies and underwriters, to try to improve the situation in the marine insurance market. Yet the arrangement with the Prudential did not go all that smoothly, as losses mounted in the mid-1920s and the Prudential management became restless (in 1928 the Corporation refused proposals that the Prudential examine the Marine Department's 'statistical management', and that they appoint an Assistant Underwriter). And, although the Governor's initiative led to the establishment of standing Committees of Chairmen and Underwriters respectively, it was not easy to translate personal harmony into an improvement of premium rates and a return of profitability. Moreover, even the harmony was vulnerable to personal mistakes: in 1928 the REA Underwriter accepted a risk in a way which contravened a Treaty of the Institute of London Underwriters, and the error had sufficiently serious consequences, in the context of the Corporation's attempt to improve relationships and the market, to lead to his resignation—albeit at a generous pension of £5,000 annually.

With the appointment of a new Underwriter—Victor Montague Magnus—the way was eventually open for a more systematic approach to the Marine Department's own structure and policy. In April 1930, Hodge, now Assistant General Manager, hinted at the need and opportunity for change in a letter to his old friend, the former Actuary, Nightingale. Having mentioned the payment of £200,000 from Profit and Loss 'to our old friend the Sea, as [its] back years are still costing a lot of money', he went on: 'I think at last, however, there is a very good chance of getting the accounts of the Sea Department brought on to modern lines. If this is done it will have taken over 28 years to carry the work through. However, the idea that the Sea business is something so special and wonderful that ordinary common sense does not apply to it, is pretty well exploded by now, I think.'

There is no precise information on what Hodge had in mind, nor on the immediately subsequent course of events within the Corporation. In May 1931, however, at a meeting of the Special Marine Committee, it was agreed that it would be helpful to both the Corporation and the Underwriter if the position of the Marine Department were investigated 'and a definite policy laid down as to the lines on which the business should be conducted'.

This investigation—which was confined to the work and organization as distinct from the underwriting policy of the Marine Department—was carried out by Price, Waterhouse & Company. In their Report, dated 29 November 1931, the consultants made far-reaching criticisms and proposals with respect to the Department, which was, of course, separately organized and located in Lime Street. Weakness in office control, lack of co-ordination within the Department and with Head Office, a substantial backlog of work, 'a considerable lack of team work', and 'a definite deterioration of morale', were the most serious of their criticisms. As a result, and bearing out Hodge's earlier assertion that the Department was no longer to be considered as being in a special category, there was a drastic shake-up. An administrative manager was installed to supervise the Department, subject only to the Underwriter; various members of the staff were prematurely retired or moved around; economies were immediately effected by a reduction in the establishment. Clearly the Marine Department had lost that effective independence which long years of convention had created. And even though the general economic problems of the 1930s prevented any revival of profits, the office was in a healthier position. In 1938, when Magnus retired, there was an even more significant reorganization. The new Underwriter, N. R. Jenkins, who was recruited from the Sun Insurance Office, was, in fact, made Joint Underwriter with that office, while the Sun's Underwriter, C. C. Turner, was appointed jointly with the REA. Each Company retained its own connections, but henceforth a good deal of business was managed jointly, from the Lime Street office. The Corporation's oldest Department had had to make one more adaptation away from its traditional self-sufficiency. Yet this move, combined with the new blood of joint management, made a significant difference to the Department's business success. Underwriting remained very much a personal, even an idiosyncratic, matter. But the appointment of Jenkins and Turner was a prelude to a more successful and profitable period.

In contrast to marine, the Corporation's life business underwent a fairly substantial increase throughout the period—even though there were no spectacular new developments and it remained only a small part of the total 'market'. Between 1918 and 1939 its annual premium income increased more than threefold, from £465,000 to some £1·5 million, compared with an increase, for British offices as a whole, of about 250 per cent (from £37 million to £92 million). In terms of the securing of fresh business, the annual average of *new* premiums rose from £98,000 in 1921–9 to £150,000 in 1930–9—reflecting new sums assured of £1·9 million and £3·5 million respectively. As Figure 19.2 shows, these averages mask some fluctuation: there was an initial decline from the peak of 1920, when the positive influences of peace and inflation were at their peak. Thenceforth, there was a continued rise, checked only briefly by the onset of the Depression. This increase was intensified by declining interest rates in the 1930s (which made life insurance all the more attractive to policyholders

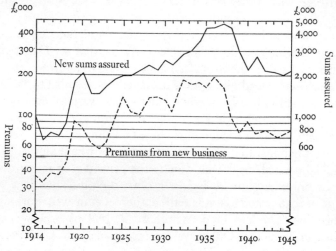

Fig. 19.2: REA new life business, 1914–45
(Source: REA Archives.)

as an investment); and by 1935 the Governor was able to report to the Annual General Court that new life business had doubled in ten years: from £1·86 million sums assured in 1924 to £3·75 million in 1934. By 1937, at £4·65 million, sums assured were much more than twice that of 1920. And between 1931 and 1937 the REA's Life Fund rose from £9·4 million to £13·2 million. Only with the anxieties of 1939–40 did new business decline significantly.

From the viewpoint of its profit potential, the Life Department was of much less direct concern to the Corporation than it had been a generation or so earlier. As Nightingale, the Actuary, pointed out in 1917, 'the life business of the proprietary companies tends to become continually more mutual in character, and the period is rapidly approaching when almost the entire profits will require to be reserved for the policyholders'.

Certainly, in so far as the Corporation distributed 90 per cent of its life surplus to policyholders it could not anticipate a substantial return on its life underwriting. And it was for this reason that the Actuary in 1917 and the Secretary in 1921 each submitted memoranda doubting the wisdom in the latter's words, of the Life Department taking 'a very leading position'. In fact, the annual (proprietors') profits derived from life business increased from £15,000 in 1925-9 to £30,000 in 1935-9—the last compared with over £100,000 from accident and £215,000 from fire business. But, quite apart from the amount of money involved, two other considerations are relevant to any gauging of the importance of life insurance.

First, of all types of underwriting it was the least risky, from the viewpoint of insurance companies, and the one easiest to sell to potential policyholders: given long-run patterns of expenditure and saving, and the tax advantages, life insurance continued to grow at a much faster rate than the national income. As a result, although the rate of profit on life insurance was low, the flow was secure and relatively easy to obtain. This factor was not perhaps fully appreciated at the REA until after the Second World War. Yet, even so, the inter-war performance of the Life Department was still impressive; and the Corporation's willingness to accept a group life contract for the 20,000 members of the Musicians' Union in 1921 (annual premiums were to be £1 for all ages, for a sum assured of £100), and its scheme for the AA staff in 1932, were indications of its willingness to explore new avenues.

The second consideration was, by contrast, fully appreciated at an early date: it was that, with a large composite office, life business might have a value in relation to other sorts of business out of all proportion to its own profitability. The Actuary had made this point in 1917 when warning that there might be little direct profit to be earned from life transactions and that the Corporation should remain content 'with the indirect benefits obtained, i.e. by the fostering of valuable clients of other Departments, and the preservation of agents from the assaults of rival companies seeking fire and other business under the cloak of life assurance'. Indeed, the logic of this sort of argument also implied that in some circumstances it might be justified to transact life business at a loss. In 1916, for example, the REA's Fire and Life Committee, in the face of the competitive decrease in premium rates for non-profit policies, agreed to seek such business at rates which provided no margin at all for expenses (other than commission). This was done precisely to maintain good 'connections', for, as Nightingale argued, since non-profit policies tended to be used to provide for estate duty, or to mitigate income tax liability, they were for large sums and 'frequently upon the lives of men holding important landed estates or running industrial concerns of considerable magnitude. This is exactly the class of persons whom fire and accident offices show a keen desire to cultivate.' After the War, in 1919, when the Actuary advocated an increase in the rates for non-profit policies, his proposal was turned down by the Fire and Life Committee for fear of its adverse effects on agents and on other sorts of business. On the other hand, non-participating policies did not remain unprofitable—and the Corporation encouraged them in the 1920s and early 1930s: by 1935, they accounted for 61 per cent of new business and 42 per cent of all sums assured (by 1940, after the investment motive had influenced policyholders, they had declined somewhat, to 35 per cent of all insurances).

In the event, therefore, life insurance was by no means the negligible factor in the REA's business which some of its officials had anticipated towards the end of the First World War. The general buoyancy of the market, and the relationship between life and non-life business, maintained and extended the Corporation's interest. Indeed, in 1929 the Governor thought it would be as well to envisage the possibility of the REA undertaking industrial life insurance. Nothing came of this particular proposal—in part because the REA, with its existing and successful provision for monthly premiums, was already tapping the market for insurance among people with relatively low incomes. But it was symptomatic of the ambition which could still be a spur to growth.

Unlike its life business, the Corporation's fire insurance premiums did not increase throughout the inter-war period—although in this respect, as in some of their shorter-run trends, they were a reasonably accurate reflection of developments within the industry as a whole. Even so, as far as the Corporation itself was concerned, and excluding the business of its subsidiaries, fire insurance continued to dominate its premium income—although that dominance decreased from its peak in 1920 (when the Corporation's fire premiums reached a level of some £1·8 million, which was not to be exceeded until 1943). By the eve of the Second World War, accident premiums, at £1·2 million, had almost overtaken fire premiums, at £1·4 million.

In the case of fire income, of course, the environment within which the REA operated—that is, the demand for insurance as reflected in the premiums earned by British offices—was relatively stable throughout this period.[1] It was not, therefore, surprising that an office like the REA should

[1] Above, pp. 426–8.

also exemplify relatively little change. (In the 1920s, however, when, as the Fire Manager put it in 1928, some large companies were more concerned with building up a large income even at inadequate rates, than with profits, the REA decided not to 'go out for big figures', preferring a smaller income on good quality business.) As Figure 19.3 shows, from the inflationary high point of 1920 the Corporation's fire premiums declined to £1·37 million in 1924, rose to £1·76 million in 1929, and then fell again, under the influence of depression, averaging just under £1·5 million in the

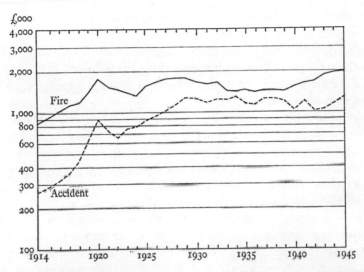

Fig. 19.3: REA fire and accident business, 1914–40. Net premiums

(Source: REA Archives.)

late 1930s. This was a long-run stability which bordered on stagnation: annual premium income, which averaged £1·6 million in 1920–9, fell to £1·5 million in 1930–9. In fact, however, this decline was entirely attributable to overseas business: UK income was more or less constant in the two decades at £428,000 and £426,000, while overseas premiums fell from £1,173,000 to £1,086,000. Moreover in the period 1931–9 home fire premiums actually increased by about 10 per cent, while overseas income fell by almost 20 per cent, reflecting the relative recovery of the British economy compared with many others. The difficulties of the inter-war economy were obviously felt most keenly overseas, and particularly in the United States, which accounted for most of the fall in the REA's overseas fire income: US premiums, which had been £607,000 in 1920, averaged

£495,000 in 1925–9 and £387,000 in 1935–9.[1] And these difficulties had an even greater effect on profits than income: in round figures, the Corporation's annual underwriting profit on fire business in 1921–9 was £120,000, and overseas business accounted for some £90,000 of this figure. By 1931–9, however, although the total annual profit had risen to £140,000, the share of overseas business had fallen considerably—to £66,000. Yet even making allowance for the pressure on profits overseas—a pressure which resulted from mounting competition for conventional business and was to intensify in the post-war world—fire underwriting continued to give a satisfactory return. In the 1930s the Department was able to transfer an annual underwriting profit of just over £140,000 (interest on the funds brought the total up to £185,000) to Profit and Loss. This made it far and away the most profitable department: the accident business, by contrast, earned about £85,000 annually, of which some £45,000 represented earnings on investments.

While the REA's accident business remained less profitable than fire business throughout the inter-war period, it was a significant element in the Corporation's business. However, as Figure 19.3 shows, its growth was concentrated in the 1920s: between 1918 and 1930 accident premiums almost trebled, increasing from £441,000 to £1·28 million. Again, as with fire and life insurance, and helped by an increase in accident premium rates of over 50 per cent in the course of the year, the inflationary boom of 1920 lifted the premium income to a level which was not to be exceeded for some years. In the 1930s, economic vicissitudes restrained premiums, although the REA's accident business which had grown faster than that of the industry as a whole in the 1920s lagged behind it in the 1930s.

As is indicated in Table 19.2, with the exception of employers' liability in the UK, all types of accident insurance shared in the growth which was largely concentrated in the 1920s. Personal accident premiums grew by only a small amount, but there were large proportionate increases in fidelity guarantee; in burglary premiums, no doubt reflecting the increasing habit of domestic insurance in the growing suburbs; and in foreign employers' liability business, exemplifying the trend towards diversification of British overseas insurance interests away from a heavy dependence on conventional fire business. But these together accounted for less than a third of the £700,000 increase in premiums in 1918–28. The balance—almost £500,000—was attributable to third-party (i.e. liability) insurance and motor vehicle policies. Unfortunately, the two were not distinguished in the accounts until 1931; but it is obvious that motor vehicle insurance

[1] For overseas business, see pp. 469–76, 480.

was by far the more important influence—accounting for at least half, and probably much more, of the increased premium income. Here, too, the importance of overseas business was considerable: in the 1930s just over half of the Corporation's accident premiums were earned overseas,[1] and a large part of these must have been derived from motor business. Yet there was also growth at home in this booming area, and by 1930 the REA was deeply involved.

TABLE 19.2. *REA accident business: net premium income, 1918–38*

(£000)	1918	1923	1928	1933	1938
Employers' liability: UK	154	146	146	114	165
Employers' liability: overseas	46	90	136	152	143
Personal accident	40	56	71	111	66
Third party	} 175	} 357	} 652	139	121
Motor				563	585
Burglary	18	34	59	74	88
Fidelity guarantee	9	44	67	58	60
Total:	441	727	1,131	1,210	1,229

Note: Totals may not add because of rounding.

This involvement was only partially measured, however, by the Corporation's own income from motor insurance. For, as already indicated, among its various acquisitions in the period 1917–28 the two which stand out, the Car & General and the Motor Union, were both pioneers in, and heavily committed to, the field of motor insurance.[2] With their help, the Royal Exchange Assurance group of companies accounted for some 25 per cent of all home motor premiums earned by tariff offices in 1929. In 1931, when the parent Corporation earned £521,000 in world-wide premiums, the Car & General and the Motor Union earned £850,000 and £1,426,000 respectively; and four other subsidiaries earned a further £81,000 between them.[3] The Group's total motor premiums (just over £3 million) was almost 10 per cent of the world-wide motor business of all British companies.

As these figures imply, by the late 1920s the balance of premium income in the REA and its affiliated companies had swung decisively in

[1] See, p. 481.
[2] For these acquisitions, see below, pp. 462–8.
[3] The four were: the United British, the State, the British Equitable, and the Local Government Guarantee Society. Between 1929 and 1932, 50 per cent of the capital stock of the United British (which, both before and after these dates, was a subsidiary of the Motor Union) was acquired by the General Reinsurance Corporation of New York.

favour of general accident business: in 1929 the Corporation and its British subsidiaries earned a total of £4·7 million in accident premiums as against £3·2 million fire premiums, £1·3 million life premiums, and £860,000 marine premiums. Although it was to be another generation before the management and organization of these companies were effectively grouped,[1] their motor business can be treated together, if only because of the dominant influence of Arthur Wamsley, the Corporation's Accident Manager, who was largely instrumental in the acquisition of the two most important subsidiaries.

The setting within which the REA group built up its motor premium income was in some ways both precarious and experimental. Many aspects of the motor vehicle insurance business had, of course, been settled in the decade or so of development before 1914. But the War had been a dampening influence, and few companies could have anticipated the combination of premium growth and the problems of cost-inflation and co-operation which beset the companies in the 1920s.

As early as January 1919 the cost of repairs was proving prohibitive, and Wamsley (who, even before the REA's acquisition of the Motor Union, was an influential man in the Accident Offices' Association) attempted, unsuccessfully, to secure an increase in premium rates. The next year, however, the continued price rise and the growing number of accidents enforced a substantial increase in the tariff rates for private vehicles: 20 per cent in January (Wamsley pointed out that this 'would probably just about enable the business to be carried on without loss') and 30 per cent in May. There were further increases in 1921; and, in spite of the brief onset of fierce competition from non-tariff companies and Lloyd's in the winter of 1921–2, Wamsley's confident refusal to lower rates to meet it was justified by the universal decision to raise premiums in February 1922. This, however, was the last major premium adjustment until 1928.

In the 1920s, as far as the insurance of private motor cars was concerned, the principal problem centred on the number of accidents and the difficulty of doing a satisfactory business based upon the ever-increasing numbers of small cars. In practice, claims for damage to inexpensive and low-powered vehicles cost almost as much as those to more expensive ones, even though the premiums on the former were much lower. At the REA, in May 1924, Wamsley informed the Governors 'that the congested state of the streets was leading to many more accidents . . . particularly in connection with the smaller cars, on which there was no margin of profit'. But his hopes for a consequential adjustment of premiums were dis-

[1] Below, pp. 536–41.

appointed, and in October 1926 he was still complaining of the very heavy claims attributable to 'the enormous number of small cars on the road' and the refusal of other companies to increase rates 'presumably owing to their fear of losing this connnection'. In the same year, as the Chairman of the Car & General informed the 1927 Annual General Meeting, about 40 per cent of the vehicles covered by the Company had been damaged at least once!

By the end of the 1920s, however, it was apparent that the raising of the overall level of premium rates was not in itself a solution. The frequency and cost of accidents obliged the companies to think much more seriously about the possibility of adjusting the structure of premium rates in light of the distribution of accidents. And men like Wamsley began to explore the possibility of varying the rates for private cars according to the district in which they were insured. Thus, in 1929 the Accident Offices' Association appointed a special Committee to appraise the problems of rating. It is significant that Wamsley reported this to the Governors as evidence that 'he had won the first round of the battle for the improvement of motor rates'—an indication of his standing in the industry which is corroborated by the fact that in 1929 he was nominated by the Accident Offices' Association as one of its two official spokesmen on compulsory insurance before the Royal Commission on Transport.

Yet it proved extremely difficult to get the sixty members of the Association to agree on the complex problem of district rating, even though business in London and other large cities was patently unprofitable. After intermittent discussions over three years, the AOA's Statistical Committee, in August 1932, produced no less than five alternative schemes with the aim of increasing premiums in bad districts, lowering them elsewhere, and retaining the overall level of income. Even so the members could still not agree, and the situation was taken sufficiently seriously for the Governor of the REA to contemplate the possibility of leaving the Tariff (a step which, he was told by Wamsley, 'would undoubtedly break up the AOA'). In the last resort, however, agreement was inevitable, if only because continuing disagreement was increasingly expensive. And in 1934 the accident offices finally agreed on a scheme which adjusted the rates for private cars according to the accident record of the district. The country was divided into five zones for this purpose; and from 1 January 1935 district rating was added as a fourth factor (value, horsepower and type of use were the others) in the rating of private motor cars.

District rating was an improvement over previous methods of establishing rates, but it was not a panacea for the problems of motor insurance.

The nature of competition and the unpredictability of the cost of claims continued to plague the companies, and to squeeze their profit margins. In 1935, while welcoming the new basis of rating (a step which 'was found to be absolutely necessary from the results of our statistical records'), the Governor told the REA Court of Proprietors that 'it is only with exercise of the utmost care that . . .[motor] business cedes us a profit, and that the margin of such profit is far too small to admit any reduction in rates'. By 1937–9 the Corporation was earning an average underwriting profit of only £10,000 on a premium income of some £575,000. However, the Motor Union and Car & General were somewhat more successful, Their motor insurance underwriting profits in 1938 were £115,000 and £43,000 respectively out of premium incomes of £1·4 million and £1·1 million.

ATTITUDES AND ADAPTATION

There can be little doubt that the First World War was an important dividing line in the history of British insurance. While a previous generation had quite legitimately emphasized the heightened competition and the change in the business environment of the late nineteenth century,[1] the period after 1918 witnessed a striking intensification of these pre-war trends. Institutions, practices and attitudes, which had served well in an earlier environment, now had to be adapted to a keener, more extensive and more complex struggle for business. That adaptation had, in fact, begun before the War, and the groundwork for modern insurance in the industry at large and in venerable offices like the REA had been laid by 1914. Nevertheless, in the Corporation's case, and no doubt in the case of a good number of other offices, the acceleration of competitive developments in the early part of this century was not immediately matched by an acceleration of changes in attitudes and organization. Admittedly, in perhaps the most important respect—the need to extend and diversify its business by amalgamation—the REA took appropriate steps in the decade or so after 1916. In some other areas, however, inherited attitudes and the complacency and traditionalism which came from generations of development, were hindrances to flexible responses and efficient management. This was perhaps most apparent in the years immediately after the War. In 1921, for example, Robert Connew, the newly appointed Assistant Fire Manager (he was to become Fire Manager the next year), undertook a thorough investigation of his Department and reported that he had found 'a very unsatisfactory state of affairs . . . [necessitating a] complete re-

[1] Above, chapter 12.

organization'. Supervision was lacking, work had fallen into arrears, there was little systematic organization, and much of what there was was 'antiquated'. As a result Connew drew up a new system of office routine and took vigorous steps to co-ordinate work more thoroughly. Indicative of the outlook of a future General Manager, he also advocated 'a greater degree of firmness and authority on the part of those who are responsible for the supervision and control of the staff'.[1]

To a large extent, however, the problem was more one of attitude than organization—and in such circumstances, attitudes might be more difficult to change. Thus, in December 1921, when the Departmental Managers were discussing the question of salaries, they had to acknowledge that some of the Corporation's staff, after years of service, were receiving large salaries, but doing unsatisfactory work: 'It was agreed that to a large extent they were the product of the old system of the REA and the only cure would be time. It was also agreed that . . . cases occurred of a man, nominally the Head of a Sub-Department, doing work that any Junior could satisfactorily carry out—still the fault rested largely with the Managers in the past.' The officials then decided that it would be 'contrary to the spirit and practice of the Office' to reduce salaries or to pension off such individuals, although they agreed that their appointments should terminate at 60, no salary increments need be given in future, 'and that, where necessary, their Juniors should definitely be placed over them in the work of the Office'. At the same time the Managers took up the question of the staff's use of the clerks' luncheon room—and were astonished to find that in addition to its use for lunch and tea (and even after some Managers had warned members of their Department), over fifty clerks regularly used it between 10 and 10.45 a.m. This matter, too, was approached with a new seriousness of purpose.

From the early 1920s onwards, therefore, it is possible to trace the emergence of a relatively new outlook within the Corporation, as it was forced to adjust to new circumstances and to dispense with at least some of the attitudes which were proving a hindrance in the setting of twentieth-century insurance. Complacency and even lethargy had sooner or later to give way to a keener spirit of enterprise. Sometimes even the beginnings of this process took some time. Thus, as we have seen, the traditional independence of the Marine Department which had masked an obsolete organization and an almost scandalous inefficiency, was only breached in 1931.[2] Then, however, so far had realism advanced that the remedies

1 For Connew's assumption of the post of General Manager, see below, p. 508.
2 Above, pp. 448-9.

adopted—the early retirement of staff and the demotion of senior clerks —were precisely those which had been shunned in 1921. Even so these developments should not be exaggerated: as with many other aspects of modernization they had to wait for administrative reform, for the rise of an effective General Manager's Office. Only then were the structural prerequisites of attitudinal changes established.[1]

Whatever the problems of adaptation which the inter-war period brought to a Corporation which was already 200 years old, the REA enjoyed a reasonable, if not spectacular, measure of business success. In retrospect, it is apparent that the inter-war period was a time when the Corporation did not take full advantage of the opportunities which its resources and position offered. At the time, however, the attitudes of its staff and the organization of its management were appropriate to the tasks confronting it. Indeed, looked at generally, the Royal Exchange, as with other leading insurance companies, came through the troubled inter-war years remarkably well for a business which was closely identified with so many aspects of the economy at home and overseas. Dividends were regularly declared and rose from 13 per cent of the par value of stock in 1918 to 30 per cent in 1939.[2] Even in the worst years of the slump, in 1931–3, the Governor, speaking at the Annual General Court, was able to express genuine confidence about the condition of insurance business and the position of the REA. No doubt much of this could be attributed to factors mentioned by him in 1932 when commenting on the decline of business and world-wide financial problems: 'the small influences which they have had on our important insurance companies is a tribute to their strength and conservative management'. In addition, however, as was seen earlier, diversity of economic interest—the very factor which, superficially, might seem to make insurance vulnerable to various sorts of economic difficulty—was, in fact, a strength. By spreading their business across a multiplicity of sectors and throughout so many countries, insurance companies had a built-in safeguard against all but the most far-reaching catastrophe. Moreover, the vicissitudes of economic life would normally have more effect on the *level* of their business (that is, on premium incomes), than on its proportionate outcome (that is, on underwriting profit)—although the latter was naturally affected by a reduction of income accompanied by a less than proportionate reduction in expenses; while fire

---

[1] For the administrative structure of the REA between the Wars, see below pp. 504–11.

[2] From 1830 to 1924 the Corporation's capital was £689,219. 17s. 10d. (par value). This was increased to £789,148. 17s. 10d. as a result of a new issue to purchase the State Assurance Company in 1924. In 1927–8, the capital was increased to £946,977. 17s. 10d. as a result of the shares issued to purchase the Motor Union.

insurance claims were influenced by economic depression, as they had been throughout the nineteenth century. (For example, in 1932 the Governor pointed out that 'it really has been an abnormally difficult year for everyone doing business . . . There has been a great reduction in values . . . but there has not been an equivalent reduction in the moral hazard.')

Finally, and perhaps most important, it is as well to remember that insurance companies were financial as well as underwriting institutions and, within the limits set by the capital market and the quality of investment management, could derive profit from the use of their funds as well as from underwriting. At the Royal Exchange, for example, net interest alone (excluding interest earned on the life and annuity funds) was sufficient to cover the cost of dividends in almost every inter-war year. Indeed, in nearly every year of the period underwriting profits posted to Profit and Loss were less than net interest income—which was about £175,000 annually in 1920–9 and £210,000 annually in 1930–8.[1]

Even in the 1930s, when 'cheap money' was a threat to the yield of life funds and when the REA's gross yield on investments dropped from £5. 18s. 6d. per cent in 1931 to £4. 14s. 1d. in 1938, the Governor could still argue that the Corporation was doing gratifyingly well in the face of adversity in the capital market. The fall in interest rates naturally affected the structure of the REA's investments. In the mid-1930s, for example, the Corporation invested an increasing amount in short-dated securities in order both to safeguard against any sudden depreciation of security values and to be well placed if, as was anticipated, interest rates were to rise. Further, as had also happened in the 1890s, lower rates led the REA, along with other offices, even more extensively into the Stock Exchange. In 1922 Stock Exchange securities accounted for 63 per cent of the Life Fund; by 1935 they accounted for 71 per cent. (At the latter date loans and mortgages accounted for 18·7 per cent and property for 10·3 per cent.) On the other hand, in one important respect it was not possible to follow the precedent of the 1890s: in the 1930s the instability of the international economy and the restrictions of economic nationalism restricted British investment overseas—which actually fell. The REA naturally felt this influence. In 1935 the Governor warned the proprietors that 'the

---

[1] As far as underwriting profit was concerned, fire insurance continued to be far and away the most rewarding Department throughout the period, averaging £125,000 in 1918–39, as against less than half that in the case of accident business and a negligible amount from marine insurance. As has been seen, life profits rose from about £15,000 annually in the late 1920s to £30,000 ten years later; annuity profits also increased from £8,000 in the late 1920s to £11,000 in the late 1930s, while trustee and executor business produced about £10,000 in the 1920s and £12,000 in the 1930s.

opportunities of acquiring remunerative investments at home are small, and practically no progress has been made by this country in lending money abroad'. In fact, by 1935, overseas securities, which had accounted for 19 per cent of the Corporation's Life Fund in 1930, had fallen to merely 11 per cent.

More generally, the REA's long-run investment policies paralleled industry-wide trends. Thus, British Government securities, which had been a negligible 1 per cent of total investments in 1913, had shot up under the influence of war-time finance to almost a third in 1920, and were still 14 per cent of investments in 1938. Stocks and shares (other than debentures) had become somewhat more important, amounting to more than 11 per cent of investments in 1938 (as against 9·5 per cent in 1935), and ordinary shares alone amounted to £1·4 million (6·2 per cent of investments). There were also two newly important areas of investment for the REA: Indian and colonial government and local authority securities, which had accounted for merely 4 per cent of investments in 1913, stood at 8 per cent (£1·6 million) in 1938; and the Corporation's new rôle in insurance underwriting was reflected in the fact that almost 10 per cent of its assets was represented by over £2 million of 'holdings in subsidiary companies'. Altogether, the Corporation's assets had grown from just over £7 million in 1913 to £17 million in 1930 and £25 million in 1938. The corresponding figures for actual investments (as distinct from outstanding balances and cash) were £6 million, £15 million, and £23 million. As a leading insurance company, it continued to represent a considerable financial authority.

THE BEGINNINGS OF THE REA GROUP

So far, in discussing the REA's acquisition in this period, only the Car & General and the Motor Union have been emphasized. Yet these two were the high points—as well as the beginning and end—of a process which in less than a dozen years turned the ancient Corporation in a new direction. As we have seen, one of the striking features of the REA in the years before 1914 was its failure, and even unwillingness, to participate in the wave of amalgamations which was transforming the structure of the insurance industry. The reluctance of its Court and officials was partly due to the fact that the Corporation was already undertaking a composite business, and partly due to pride in its own independent and long-run achievement. In addition, however, it was also perhaps based on a misjudgement of twentieth-century insurance trends. Before the First World War the Corporation's Directors and officials might well have imagined that it was possible to maintain the REA's traditional position among British insurance offices with no more radical step than the acquisition of such a specialist office as the National Provincial Plate Glass (1909). If so, they were wrong—and the evidence was all around them, in the extent and complexity of the merger movement.[1] Yet, even so, in 1909 there was a serious attempt to combine with the London Assurance, and the second decade of the century merely drove home a lesson which the first had begun to teach: no company could achieve or maintain a substantial position by relying on 'natural' growth; stature presupposed size and varied departments; and size and varied departments presupposed amalgamation.

The Corporation approached the question of acquiring other offices with a new seriousness during the First World War—no doubt because its financial position was considerably strengthened by its favourable underwriting experience. Voices of caution were still not lacking: for example, in November 1916 the Actuary addressed a confidential memorandum to the Governor expressing anxiety about the possible length and uncertain consequences of the War and urging the 'exercise of the greatest possible caution . . . Though several apparently fine bargains may be offered to the Corporation it is almost certain that better value for our money can be obtained later on, and the quality of our purchases will then be better understood and be more capable of measurement.' Nevertheless, this view did not prevail. Earlier in 1916 renewed negotiations with the London Assurance had almost brought about a merger of the two ancient offices (they had gone sufficiently far for letters to agents and stockholders to be drafted: the merger would have aimed at 'preserving both in wedlock instead of single existence'), but had broken down in September. And the next year the REA purchased the Car & General.

The origins of the Car & General have already been considered.[2] In 1917, largely under the influence of Arthur Wamsley, the REA Accident Manager, the Corporation acquired the Company—which then had a premium income of £413,000, of which £284,000 was derived from motor business. The attraction was clear: the profit potential of a successful accident company, specializing in motor business, with almost 9,000 agents and twenty-eight branches. Even though some initial loss of premium income was anticipated by virtue of the fact that the premium rates of the Car & General (which had been a non-tariff company) would now have to be adjusted to the levels of the Accident Offices' Association,

[1] Above, pp. 293–303.
[2] Above, pp. 234–5.

the Company, as the REA Secretary indicated in a preparatory memorandum, 'appears to possess an exceptional and active organization and to offer possibilities of improvements in profits ... When the War is over, the Corporation should benefit by the acquisition of a Company which has specialized in the class of business [i.e. motor] certain to provide exceptional opportunity for development.' In the spring of 1917, therefore, the REA acquired 105,745 shares of the Car & General for 30s. each. The Corporation found all the necessary money from its own cash reserves, thus avoiding any disturbance of its capital structure. Given the current level of profits, the price was a good one and that part of it paid for the estimated goodwill (£160,000) represented less than seven years' purchase for anticipated profits. More generally, there can be no doubt about the wisdom of the purchase, both in terms of the Car & General's strength, and because it augmented the power of the REA in an important new era of underwriting. Beyond this, too, the purchase was an example of the influence and confidence of the Corporation's Accident Manager, whose success and authority after seventeen years with the REA were now unquestioned. At the Car & General the founder, Frederick Thoresby, retired as Managing Director, compensated by a down-payment of £27,000 and £1,000 annually for five years; Wamsley replaced him; and in 1918 the Car & General's Chairman, Edward Manville (knighted in 1923), was elected to the REA Court of Directors. Peace justified the expectation of development: the Company's premium income jumped from £340,000 in 1917 to £746,000 in 1923 (profits in the latter year were over £90,000). By 1929 its premiums exceeded £1 million—including £785,000 of motor premiums.

A year after the acquisition of the Car & General, in July 1918, the REA also purchased the Local Government Mutual Guarantee Society— a small but successful company, established in 1890 as a specialist in fidelity guarantee insurance for local government officials, which had branched out into other types of insurance from which it derived £48,000 in premiums in 1917. The 'Mutual' was deleted from its name in 1919 and the parent Corporation husbanded its high-quality income: by 1932 premiums were £115,000.

With the end of the War, in the course of the culmination of the industry-wide merger movement, the REA intensified its own efforts to extend the scope of its business by acquisition. In 1919, for example, it was in close negotiation with the Atlas for a merger, and in July the Corporation's Treasury Committee approved the proposal that the REA buy the Atlas by an exchange of shares, 'as it would . . . put out of court the question of the Royal Exchange eventually being taken over by any other company'.

But the negotiations came to nothing: given the implied share prices, the arrangement would have left Atlas shareholders controlling two-thirds of the total stock; and the cash offer which followed was not sufficient to tempt Atlas. Within a few months Wamsley again took a personal initiative in renewing discussions, which had first taken place in 1918, for the acquisition of one of the country's leading accident offices. These came to nothing in 1920, and again in 1921 when Wamsley made a third attempt. Indeed, as late as February 1922, in response to the Governor's question as to whether the Accident Manager wanted the Company, he replied 'that there had never been a shadow of a doubt in his mind of this object—he certainly did'.

In 1918, 1920 and 1921 the REA was very near attaining Wamsley's objective, and the attraction to him of the purchase of this specialist company was obvious. With a premium income of £3 million in 1920, two-thirds of it from overseas business, its acquisition 'would put the REA in possession of the largest and probably the best organized accident business in this country . . . If the Directors can see their way to offer £ for £ in REA stock I am hopeful that I can carry the transaction through.' Yet Wamsley was perhaps excessively sanguine, not only about his prospects of securing the Company, but about its profitability and attractiveness. At each point in time its financial position was found, on close inspection, not to warrant the offer which its Directors felt was necessary, and the REA Directors refused to go along with Wamsley's ambition.[1] In March 1920, when news of a possible merger was leaked to the Press, the value of REA stock tumbled, and an anxious proprietor, echoing similar sentiments expressed in the newspapers, wrote to the Corporation's Secretary requesting a denial of current rumours and arguing that 'it certainly seems incredible that the aristocrat of the Insurance World should take under its wing a dowerless Cinderella'.

With the failure of these negotiations (and the abandonment of a very tentative plan, in 1920, for a tripartite merger of the REA, the Atlas and the Sun), the Corporation's progress towards 'growth-by-merger' abated for about three years. In 1924, however, there was a fresh bout of activity which had more tangible results—the purchase of a relatively small American fire office, the Provident Insurance Company of New York, and the acquisition of the State Assurance Company of Liverpool, established in 1891, a successful, medium-size office, with a premium income of almost £800,000—some £600,000 of it from fire insurance—

---

[1] In 1922 Wamsley admitted 'that what he wanted to get was the organization. He considered the results of the business practically unimportant.'

and a subsidiary, the British Equitable, which was largely concerned with life business. The purchase of the State was an important move. It necessitated the issue of £99,929 of REA stock, thus increasing the Corporation's capital (to £789,148. 17s. 10d.) for the first time since 1830. The cost was just over £1 million, for each of the State's 100,000 shares was exchanged for £1 of REA stock, valued at £5. 8s., and £5. 12s. in cash. The State, a well-organized and profitable company, retained its separate existence: by 1929 its premium income exceeded £900,000.

Finally, three years later the REA completed this phase of its expansion by purchasing the Motor Union Insurance Company, a move which was arranged in December 1927 and completed in January 1928. As with the acquisition of the Car & General in 1917, this was engineered by Wamsley, and directed towards the expansion of the Corporation's concern with accident business in general and motor insurance in particular.

The Motor Union Insurance Company had been established in 1906 as a consequence of the breakdown in the arrangement between the Car & General and the Motor Union (the grouping of local motoring clubs) by which members of the latter secured favourable terms for motor insurance.[1] In its place the Motor Union (containing eighty local clubs and 13,000 members) formed the Motor Union Insurance Company— members of the former being shareholders and policyholders in the latter. In 1911, when the Motor Union amalgamated with the Automobile Association, the joint membership of 35,000 were all eligible for a distinctive policy with the Motor Union Insurance Company, and the special relationship between the AA and the Motor Union Office has continued ever since over the years. On the other hand, the Motor Union lost even the superficial characteristics of a mutual office at a very early stage. It expanded rapidly, and during and immediately after the First World War extended its operation outside the accident field—notably, and ultimately very unprofitably, into marine insurance. By 1926 its (gross) premiums exceeded £2 million—of which £1·3 million was accounted for by motor insurance (£400,000 overseas) and over £600,000 by fire insurance.

In fact, the REA had originally discussed the acquisition of the Motor Union in 1924-5, when negotiations had fallen through because of the complexities of the share-owning arrangements between the Motor Union and its subsidiary, the United British Insurance Company. These were subsequently simplified, however, and in 1927 the way was open for a renewal of discussions. It is obvious that in some respects the acquisition, as negotiated, was a risky venture. First, the underwriting results of the

[1] Above, pp. 235-6.

Motor Union had for some years been unsatisfactory, while even Wamsley, a strong advocate of the purchase, had to admit that it 'had the reputation of being somewhat extravagantly managed'. Second, the price actually paid for its 103,240 shares (£9. 15s., involving the REA in the issue of 157,829 units of its own stock at £6. 10s. each) was clearly somewhat generous: it valued the Motor Union's goodwill at £900,000 and implied a price of fifteen years' purchase of estimated profits.[1] On the other hand, however, Wamsley was adamant about the advantages of its acquisition and that some £25,000 could be saved in management expenses. The Court and officials had long since acknowledged Wamsley's insight and managerial ability in matters affecting accident insurance, and therefore, although (as the Secretary told the ex-Actuary Nightingale in January 1928) the acquisition 'certainly has not been received with the slightest enthusiasm . . . either in the office or out', the purchase went through. Significantly, the Secretary's notes on the discussions leading to the acquisition contain such phrases as 'Banking on A W [amsley] if we buy it' and 'Wamsley to be very closely identified with MU—to touch only high spots [of] C & G and REA'.

In the event, although the Motor Union's underwriting results were handicapped in the short run by bad accounts, particularly in the Fire Department (the REA Fire Manager had characterized the business as 'thoroughly bad') and then by the general economic crisis, Wamsley's confidence was justified. In 1929 a drastic reorganization had reduced Head Office expenses by some £20,000; and by 1933, the marine business having been greatly reduced and the life business absorbed by the REA, the Motor Union made an underwriting profit of £96,000 on a premium income of £1·7 million. In 1938 its underwriting profit was £170,000 on premiums of £1·8 million. In addition, interest income amounted to £69,000 in 1933 and £88,000 in 1938.

The acquisition of the Motor Union was the last significant extension of the Group until the Atlas was acquired in 1959. After 1928, of course, neither the economic climate nor the development of the insurance industry (in which the trend to amalgamation had ceased) encouraged any new attempts at this sort of growth.[2] But in any case the REA had made a significant alteration in its position by the acquisition of the Car & General, the Local Government, the State and the Motor Union in the years 1917–28. While the subsidiaries' premium income was not only slightly larger than that of the parent Corporation, its structure, in terms

---

[1] In addition, the Motor Union's £56,900 investment income promised a return of 5½ per cent on the investment.

[2] Above, pp. 427–32.

of the balance of underwriting, was significantly different. In 1929 the REA itself earned some £4·9 million premiums, as against £5·2 million for its British subsidiaries; and whereas only 26 per cent of the REA's premium income came from accident business, the latter generated almost 70 per cent of its British subsidiaries' income.[1] The Corporation had adapted the extent and structure of its business to some of the pressures of twentieth-century insurance. On the other hand, more time was needed to accommodate its organization and management to those pressures. The administrative implication of having created a powerful new grouping in British insurance still had to be worked out.[2]

[1] *REA Group fire, accident, marine and life premiums, 1929*

(£000)	Fire	Accident	Marine	Life	Total
REA	1,756	1,276	743	1,080	4,855
National Provincial	86	102	—	—	188
Car & General	107	945	34	—	1,086
Local Government Guarantee	59	71	—	—	130
State	686	185	47	—	918
British Equitable	141	34	—	161	336
Motor Union	200	1,788	38	42	2,068
United British	124	304	—	8	436
	3,159	4,705	862	1,291	10,017

[2] For the problems of co-ordinating the management of the Group, see chapter 21.

20

A World-wide Business: the Royal Exchange Assurance overseas

1890-1939

As we have already seen, the re-invigoration of the Royal Exchange Assurance's fire underwriting in the last decade of the nineteenth century was associated with a sharp increase in the scale and extent of its overseas business.[1] And from 1890 onwards the Corporation, as with almost all other insurance companies, became heavily dependent on the premium income and profits of underwriting outside the United Kingdom. In the years around the First World War, as the Fire Manager reminded his colleagues in 1919, when urging them to bring overseas staff into a proposed profit-sharing scheme (in the event the scheme was not introduced), it was the foreign branches 'from whence most of the profit came'. In the period 1916–20, for example, the underwriting profit on overseas fire business averaged some £80,000 annually—as against £15,000 for home fire business. All this was the context for two important themes in the modern history of the REA: on the one hand, its development into a genuinely international business, dependent upon underwriting on a world-wide basis; on the other hand, a tension between the decentralization of initiative demanded by the character of overseas business and the desire for relatively close control which was part of the management heritage of all large insurance companies.

THE GROWTH AND VICISSITUDES OF OVERSEAS BUSINESS

Until the inter-war period the REA's overseas premium income was dominated by fire insurance, and fire premiums were (as they were to continue to be) dominated by overseas business. Thus, as early as 1900, the REA, which in this respect was quite characteristic of British offices in general, derived almost two-thirds of its fire premium income from other countries. And this proportion rose until, in the boom years immediately

[1] Above, pp. 239–43.

after the War, overseas fire income reached a relative peak: in the early 1920s, averaging over £1 million, it accounted for 75 per cent of the Corporation's total fire insurance premiums. Thenceforth, it fell somewhat, although still remaining very high, and after minor fluctuations stood at 70 per cent of a somewhat reduced fire income.

TABLE 20.1. *REA home and overseas fire insurance premiums, 1900–28*

(£000)			
	Home	Overseas	Total
1900	219	259	478
1913	263	621	884
1920	457	1,335	1,792
1928	438	1,306	1,744

Even in the relatively early years of overseas business, while fire underwriting was the main source of premium income, there was a fair amount of marine and accident business, although life insurance was a negligible factor overseas. In the case of marine insurance, in addition to the overseas subsidiaries and agency networks acquired in the late nineteenth century,[1] the REA enlarged its premium income through ordinary branch offices. This was of particular importance with respect to the insurance of the Imperial trade in wool, butter, meat, grainstuffs, etc. In 1908, for example, when it had been decided to replace New Zealand's agency system with a branch office, Ferrers Daniell, then Assistant Secretary, took care to inform the new Manager that the desire of the Corporation's Directors was 'quite as much to build up a satisfactory marine business as to enlarge their operations in the Fire Department'. And, in addition to New Zealand, marine underwriting was of some significance in India (net marine premiums were some £40,000 in 1914), Australia (over £17,000 in 1915) and South Africa (£10,000 in 1914).

Unfortunately, the form in which accounts have survived makes it impossible to measure overseas accident business until the 1930s. There is, however, occasional evidence of its scope. Immediately before the First World War, for example, the Corporation earned net accident premiums of about £49,000 in the USA, £11,000 in Canada, and some £4,000 in South Africa. In North America, motor business seems to have been the most important source of accident income (a fairly large amount of hail underwriting was also done for the prairie farmers of Canada), and in April 1913 the Management Committee placed an upper limit of £40,000

[1] Above, pp. 259–60.

on its US motor business. In addition, the Corporation did a small amount of employers' liability business (some £18,000 premiums) on the Continent and in South Africa and Australia before 1914. Nevertheless, when every possible source of income has been taken into account, all this was no more than the small beginnings of accident business before the First World War. Given an overseas fire income of some £620,000 in 1913, it is unlikely that the REA's accident premiums amounted to as much as 15 per cent of that figure. Nor is this surprising. For, quite apart from the great relative importance of fire insurance for the REA in these years, the general demand for fire underwriting services in overseas areas was still enormously strong—and British offices were still in a relatively very strong position to satisfy it. It was only in the inter-war period, although fire insurance continued to be quantitatively more important, that the scope for overseas accident business grew significantly in relative as well as absolute terms. This was due in part to the inevitable emergence of indigenous insurance companies willing and able to compete for the conventional and widely understood fire business. But it was also due to developments which were also at work in Britain itself—notably the growing use of motor cars, the natural deceleration of the growth in the demand for fire insurance, and the extension of the habit and need for other sorts of business (personal accident, burglary, employers' liability, etc.) with continued economic growth.

As far as the Royal Exchange Assurance was concerned its general involvement in accident, and particularly motor, business in the inter-war years was greatly extended by its acquisition of the two leading specialist motor insurance companies—the Car & General in 1917 and the Motor Union in 1928. The former had largely relied on home business in its formative years; but after its acquisition Wamsley, the REA's Accident Manager, greatly extended its operations overseas. The Motor Union, by contrast, already had an extensive foreign business when it was purchased by the REA: in 1927 its sixty-five overseas agencies and six overseas branch offices brought in about one-third of its £1·5 million motor premium income. In the event, however, and for compelling business and organizational reasons, these subsidiaries, and their overseas branches, tended to retain their separate and distinctive identities.[1] But even apart from the operations of its subsidiaries, the REA itself considerably increased its overseas accident business in the years immediately after 1918 (in the case of American motor business there was a spurt in the war years themselves). Few precise figures have survived, but symptomatic of the

[1] Below, pp. 493–500.

new trend was the increase in Canadian net accident premiums from merely £11,000 in 1914 to £58,000 in 1920 and £60,000 in 1925. By the last date South African accident premiums (which had been less than £4,000 in 1914) had risen to some £45,000; while in West Africa, where hardly any business was done until about 1922, accident premiums exceeded £54,000 in 1927. In 1920 overseas employers' liability insurance brought in some £105,000 of net premiums, and it is likely that as much as one-third of the £429,000 of third party insurance was derived from foreign sources in 1920. By the 1930s overseas accident business regularly exceeded home accident business. As far as its 'bread-and-butter' premium income was concerned, the REA was a world-wide enterprise; with the balance of its premium income quite decisively earned outside the United Kingdom:

TABLE 20.2. *REA home and overseas fire and accident premiums (by source of income), 1931–9*[1]

(£000)		Home	Overseas	Total
1931:	Fire:	419	1,205	1,624
	Accident:	494	624	1,118
	Total:	913	1,829	2,742
1939:	Fire:	457	978	1,436
	Accident:	576	639	1,214
	Total:	1,033	1,617	2,650

The principal geographical features of the REA's overseas business were largely established in the years before the First World War. By 1910 the Corporation had twenty-eight overseas branches, as well as numerous agencies (e.g. the venerable commercial house of Butterfield & Swire in China) dealing directly with Head Office; and it already derived its premium income from, among other countries, Argentina, Australia, Belgium, Canada, China, Denmark, the East Indies, Egypt, France, Germany, Holland, India, Italy, Japan, New Zealand, Russia, South Africa, Spain, the USA, and the West Indies. These provided the main bases for the growth in premium income over the next generation.

In spite of the geographical variety of its insurance business in the early years of the century, the REA, like other companies, was in fact heavily dependent on a limited number of countries overseas—in particular on the United States. As early as 1900, for example, the Corporation derived

[1] A small amount of unplaced business is left out of account.

over one-third of all its fire premiums, and well over half its overseas premiums, from the USA. (In the early years of the century it was decided to limit American business to about one-third of total fire premiums, and this ceiling was explicitly confirmed in 1919.) However, although the United States was, and in this period was to remain, by far the most important source of overseas income, the REA had considerable interests in other countries, too. In 1913, for example, when USA net fire premiums amounted to £328,000, those from western Europe were over £100,000, from Russia £57,000, from Canada £52,000, from India, Burma and Malaya £35,000, and from Australasia some £25,000. (The Russian business was confined to accepting reinsurance handled by a Russian agency, since foreign offices were not allowed to insure directly in Russia.) The War and its immediate consequences had an inevitable effect on the distribution of business. Quite apart from the obvious fact that enemy and enemy-occupied territories were closed to British insurance companies, thus depriving the REA of its reasonably important Belgian business, the Russian Revolution and its aftermath brought to an end what had been an important source of income for the Corporation in the pre-war years— even though as late as 1919 the Corporation (for reasons that are not clear at this distance) was contemplating joining a syndicate to undertake marine and fire business in Russia.

It may well have been that this last move was part of a general strategy of expansion which characterized the Corporation's overseas business in the years immediately after the end of the War. As the world seemed to return to normal, so the REA explored the possibilities of re-entering old or broaching new markets for insurance. Some of these efforts were immediate responses to the ending of hostilities. As far as Belgium was concerned, for example, within a week of the Armistice the Governors discussed the prospects of entry with Major Gordon, aide-de-camp to the King of the Belgians—although a subsequent report by the Corporation's Continental Manager, N. H. Self, dated Christmas Eve 1918 and describing the state of the country as 'inconceivably chaotic', led to the postponement of entry until the summer of 1919. And in Palestine, the Manager of the Egyptian Branch, Everard Stokes, was one of the first two or three businessmen allowed to enter the country by the military authorities after its capture from the Turks: on 4 May 1918 he reached Jaffa sitting on the last truck of a coal train and, smothered as he was with coal dust, 'was held up by a French Algerian soldier who demanded my papers and viewed my begrimed appearance with suspicion'. But a more calculated response to peace came somewhat later, when the REA made systematic efforts to extend its operations. In the autumn of 1919, for example, Head Office received detailed reports on the economic situation and insurance prospects in Greece, Bulgaria, Serbia, West Africa and the South-West Africa Protectorate (formerly German colonial territory), and Brazil. In 1920 the possibilities of commencing business in Roumania and extending it in British East Africa were investigated; and an official of the Fire Department was sent on a prolonged tour of the countries around the Baltic, including Esthonia (where he concluded that 'the time is not ripe for operations there by the Corporation . . . the political situation is complex, financially bad and industrially unsound'). By September 1920, as a result of all this activity, it had been decided to begin business in Finland, Danzig, Roumania, Greece and Serbia; to reorganize the branch structure in the Eastern Mediterranean so as to control business in the Balkans and Asia Minor as well as Palestine, Syria and Egypt; to extend operations in West Africa, where an agency had been established in Lagos in 1919, by sending over a resident inspector; and to appoint agents in the former German territories of East Africa.

The two most important results of this post-war burst of activity were the creation of active new centres of business in West Africa and South-East Europe. The former, after a difficult start (it was almost closed down in 1922 because of disappointing results, but reprieved on the Fire Manager's strong recommendation) was firmly established and by 1927 was producing over £56,000 in net premiums, although this figure declined somewhat in the 1930s. Its creation and growth were tributes to sustained and pioneering efforts by REA men in Lagos, Accra and elsewhere: as late as 1930 the Corporation was the only insurance company with offices on the West Coast and for some time continued to be known locally simply as 'the Insurance Company'. In 1937, in what must have been an innovating move of its sort, the REA established the 'Royal Exchange Assurance West Africa Provident Fund', for the benefit of native clerks. Each clerk contributed 5 per cent of his salary, and the Corporation matched this deposit. Interest at 5 per cent was paid on both amounts, and the whole was payable on death or retirement. Meanwhile, REA business in Greece, Yugoslavia and Hungary also reached significant proportions: in 1930 gross fire premiums were some £40,000 in Hungary and £18,000 in Yugoslavia (net accident premiums were about £4,000 and £3,000 respectively); and in 1935, when the General Manager visited the area, he reported that in 1933 total premium incomes were £37,000 (Hungary), £33,000 (Greece) and £22,000 (Yugoslavia). In each country, as in Egypt, the REA was the best represented of British offices.

In spite of this diversity, however, as had been the case before the War, the Corporation's overseas business was heavily concentrated in a few areas. In 1931, for example, of the £1,280,000 of fire and accident net premiums which were earned by REA overseas branches,[1] the United States accounted for £475,000, Canada for £157,000, Western Europe for some £290,000, and Australasia for £149,000. The concentration was even greater in fire insurance alone: there, North America and Western Europe accounted for some £690,000 of the £845,000 earned by overseas branches (and the £1·2 million total overseas income).

As with other British insurance companies, the Royal Exchange had established the most important aspects of its overseas business well before 1914, at a time when economic and financial stability could be taken for granted as the indispensable basis of international business. It was also the period (as was illustrated after the San Francisco Fire) when the reputation of British insurance companies was supreme—although it remained very high in later years, too: in 1930 the REA's Greek agent was to claim that 'the Greek public does not at all favour insurance companies other than British'. Yet even before 1914 there were various respects in which overseas underwriting was more hazardous than domestic business (in 1910 the REA's Dublin Manager pointed out that overseas fire premium rates were almost three times as high, and in the USA five times as high, as those in the UK).[2] As we have already seen, the rapidity with which underwriting expanded, the relative ignorance of new areas and risks, and the hazardous character of the fast-growing towns of young countries, all made for severe problems.[3] And in 1902 the REA lost a considerable amount of money in South Africa when extensive fires occurred, in the Fire Manager's words, 'before the Corporation was in a position to control effectively the business'; while 'reckless underwriting' by the US Manager greatly enlarged the losses incurred in fires in Baltimore (1904) and San Francisco (1906). In both instances, however, new and more vigorous systems of branch management and risk control were quickly installed. As the Fire Manager reported after an extensive tour of Canada in 1910, exceptional risks (in the Canadian case, the danger derived 'from the large aggregates of damageable goods which are concentrated in relatively small areas') could be met 'by most substantial rates' and careful selection.

To a large extent, therefore British insurance companies found little

[1] A further £440,000 was earned by reinsurance and various arrangements with other companies, £85,000 through foreign agencies, and £20,000 by direct business with Head Office.
[2] *REAM*, III, 3 (January 1910), 106.
[3] Above, pp. 246 ff.

cause for anxiety in the atmosphere or risks of overseas business before 1914. But this situation did not last long, and as it deteriorated, so the problems of overseas business intensified. The War itself did more than introduce an element of short-term instability: it marked a turning-point in Britain's position in the international economy. Thenceforth, as in other industries, although British insurance offices retained an important and vital rôle, their relative strength changed. They were increasingly threatened by the growth of indigenous companies which secured a large share of the straightforward and normally profitable property insurance of private individuals. In addition, the post-war period saw an intensification of economic nationalism, which led to a proliferation and tightening of the regulations and constraints within which the companies were obliged to work in foreign countries. In fact, of course, from the beginning of extensive overseas activity, British offices had had to accommodate themselves to public regulation—notably with respect to the payment of deposits and the publication of accounts. (The REA's entry to Canada in 1910 involved a deposit of $100,00.) Indeed, in 1913 the REA Management Committee, apparently under the influence of the Governor, Sir Nevile Lubbock, expressed the view 'that the deposits in foreign countries had reached an aggregate which it was undesirable to increase', and the next year the Fire Manager told a correspondent that 'as long as the Governor is in office we shall not be able to enter any place which requires a deposit'.

However, in the post-1914 atmosphere in various countries, the problem of regulation and even political hostility became more acute. This could be particularly troublesome in life underwriting: in 1924, for example, Anderson, the REA Actuary, reluctantly confessed his inability to help the Fire Department by undertaking life business in Portugal on the grounds that the laws with regard to keeping all reserves in local currency, together with other problems, meant that 'if there is one place where it is difficult and expensive, and you are harassed in business, it is Lisbon'. But analagous and serious problems also arose in fire and accident insurance—and whether in the form of a threatened boycott of British companies by the Indian Congress Party in 1930–1, or the intermittent threat of nationalization in New Zealand, or the tensions of Australian politics, the REA found itself in a new and much less secure world. In 1936 the Governor spoke to the Annual General Court about the 'fallacy' (that *all* premiums were a 'drain of money') that had led to widespread moves towards national systems of insurance and to a concomitant danger of a major catastrophe in any country confining insurance to its own nationals.

'In return for the small underwriting profit that may be "exported"', he argued, 'there are made available the financial resources of the British offices as a protection for the wealth, the commerce and the industry of any country in which they operate.' Nevertheless, this was not a logic which appealed to governments; and in the same speech the Governor was obliged to complain that 'the conditions imposed upon British companies undertaking accident business by some of our Dominions and also foreign governments are now becoming so onerous that I feel that very little profit can be expected . . . at the present rates of premium charged'. What Lord Bicester in 1939 referred to as 'the struggle for national self-sufficiency' running counter to the free flow of goods and services, was 'bound to have a detrimental effect on the business of insurance'.

Nor was it only the actions of governments or political parties which introduced disturbing notes. The social tensions of the inter-war years also had repercussions for world-wide insurance networks—although, fortunately, few were felt as directly and dangerously as the violent strikes and virtual rebellion which swept over the Rand and dominated Johannesburg in February and March 1922. Every male member of the REA staff there was mustered for active duty, and the Branch Manager sent an excited and vivid account of:

a rebellion and revolution of an appalling kind . . . Needless to say business has been at a standstill and things today, even after the Strike has been declared off, are in a chaotic state. It will take many months before we will return to normal. There has been a great deal of incendiarism, looting, violence and robbery in the outside districts and suburbs but fortunately we were able to keep the villains out of the town proper . . . All this brings me to the point of whether this town is a fit and proper place for our Head Office. Were it not for the fact that we are committed to a long lease and that it would have such a disturbing effect on our business, I would not hesitate to strongly recommend a transfer of control to the Coast.

In general, however, the REA had more cause to worry about less violent forms of labour trouble. The general worsening of industrial relations in the immediate post-war period meant that the service industries confronted the unprecedented problem of trade-union activity. As the Manager of the REA's Egyptian Branch put it in June 1919, when suggesting a bonus of one month's salary for his staff, 'there is a general movement now in Egypt, as indeed in several parts of the World, among the labour [*sic*] class which seems to take an unprecedented extension. Bank, insurance and commercial employees are forming syndicates with a view to protecting their interests and obtaining an increase of salaries and

War bonuses.' Meanwhile, at exactly the same time, the Continental Manager was anxious about the situation in Paris, where a threatened strike of 4,000 insurance clerks finally took place in July (in the event the REA office was not directly affected, although the Manager granted bonuses to all the staff). Five years later, in May 1924, the Royal Exchange received from the Paris syndicate of insurance workers a list of claims for increased salaries and improved conditions of service—including a request for '*la semaine anglaise*', i.e. a working week ending at midday on Saturdays.

Political and social problems of this sort were a powerful new element in the environment of international business. But it is well to remember that they were merely symptomatic of the general economic dislocation of the generation after 1914. Obviously, the world's economic problems had unavoidable and severe repercussions for insurance companies. Chief among these were the violent fluctuations in production, trade and income which had direct effects on the demand for almost all sorts of insurance. 'For the present we have the same story all over the world,' wrote the REA Fire Manager to the New Zealand Branch Manager in the sharp crisis of 1921, 'stagnation of business, depreciation of values and a large number of unexplained fires.' And a decade later, as the collapse of values in primary-producing countries took hold in the slump, the Manager of the REA's Singapore Branch reported that Malaya (relying almost entirely on rubber and tin, which had undergone 'an appalling drop in prices') 'claims the unenviable distinction of having suffered most from the continued world-wide depression. . . . In such times the competition for the reduced amount of insurance business had been most acute.' The resulting lower premium rates and loss of business had reduced the REA's income by 25 per cent between 1930 and 1931. This experience was extreme, but in general the slump of the early 1930s had a severe and chastening effect on overseas insurance business. In the United States, British fire premiums fell from £31·2 million in 1929 to £25·8 million in 1931, the REA shared proportionately in this decline (its US fire premiums fell from £493,000 to £428,000), and in most overseas areas the Corporation's business fell or stagnated. By 1933 overseas fire premiums, which had exceeded £1·3 million in 1929, had fallen to barely £1 million. And they stayed around that level throughout the depressed 1930s.

A related aspect of economic dislocation in the inter-war period, and one which was bound to affect insurance companies operating on a world-wide scale, were the extremes of fluctuations in foreign exchange—which both gave rise to fortuitous losses and gains on revenue and capital accounts, and presented considerable problems with respect to the drawing up of official accounts. As the REA's Departmental Managers agreed in February 1923, the variations in exchange rates at the end of the War and subsequently had made the conventional system of accounting (in terms of fixed exchange rates) 'unworkable and even ridiculous'. And it was tentatively decided to keep all foreign accounts in terms of the relevant currency, only changing them into sterling at the end of the year, and at the rate prevailing on the last day. Even so, there was almost immediate disagreement and within a week the Fire Department had decided to use the rates in force on the date at which the accounts were rendered. A few days later, to the consternation of the Secretary, it emerged that in the past the different departments had used different conventions with regard to exchange rates—a fact which, not surprisingly, 'did not seem right' to Mr Hodge.

Almost ten years later, when the United Kingdom left the Gold Standard (21 September 1931), the shock to inherited ideas and practices was even greater, and at the next General Court, in April 1932, the Governor informed the proprietors that 'the question of foreign exchange was probably the most difficult feature of our business during the past twelve months'. Even after taking into account the increased sterling value of floating assets overseas, the net increase in liabilities resulting from exchange depreciation was £275,000 and an Exchange Reserve Fund of this amount was established. In March of the next year it was decided 'to take the most stringent course' with the accounts and to apply prevailing market rates for all business. On the other hand, in the course of 1933, alterations in the exchange rates, and particularly the depreciation of the dollar, benefited sterling—although the REA Directors, in the Governor's words, 'considered it prudent to adopt a conservative attitude towards the effects of exchange fluctuations upon our underwriting results', and the calculated benefits of the fluctuations were transferred from departmental revenue figures to the Exchange Reserve Account.

Clearly, the troubled early 1930s proved particularly difficult for international insurance companies. Admittedly, by 1935 the British economy was obviously well on the way to recovery, but, as the Governor of the REA pointed out to the General Court, although this was some cause for optimism

as this Corporation grows in strength, so it becomes more largely affected by economic influences outside and beyond Great Britain. In the new world that came into being after the War, many countries have yet to adjust to the strains and stresses imposed by that calamity . . . [Yet] the political and economic position of Europe, the adjustments of international currencies, the great social and industrial experiment now taking place in the United States of America, are probably the greater problems of which we must patiently await a solution, and on which comment today carries us very little further.

In the inter-war period, therefore, the extent of its overseas business was not an unmitigated advantage to the Royal Exchange. Nevertheless, on balance, its presence brought strength, rather than weakness, through the extension of the Corporation's connections and the diversification of its business interests. In one important respect, however, the nature of the market presented special problems which could only be overcome by underwriting on a scale greater than the REA could afford. This was in the United States, where the vast growth of insurance, and insurance offices, made the problems of expense ratios particularly acute: efficient underwriting there increasingly depended on the attainment of a minimum scale of operations which was, in fact, very large. As early as 1932 the REA's Management Committee was forced to discuss the problems of size, when the General Manager reported that, while the Corporation's surplus funds in New York stood at only about $750,000, it was 'of utmost importance' to show a surplus of at least $1 million. The REA was already losing business because its 'connection' viewed its surplus as too small. In the event the Corporation increased its funds in America, but not sufficiently to secure a very large increase in US fire premiums, which, having fallen from £501,000 in 1926 to £332,000 in 1934, had only recovered to £404,000 by 1939. The main point in this respect was that if the Corporation had increased its US business in line with that of the giant American companies, that business would have become a very large proportion of its total income—with a concomitant increase in the risk that a catastrophe might overwhelm it. (San Francisco was still a keen memory.) By 1939, therefore, the REA was on a path which in fact led away from any very active participation in the American market: its business there was so small in relation to many other companies that it was proving difficult to contain costs and maintain profits. In the three years 1937–9 its average underwriting profit in the United States was less than £3,000 on an income of almost £400,000—compared with an underwriting profit of some £85,000 on an income of just under £450,000 in the UK.

OVERSEAS BRANCHES: ORGANIZATION AND CONTROL

The Royal Exchange Assurance derived its overseas business in various ways. The most important method, and the one which gave rise to the most significant problems of management and control, was through the Corporation's own overseas branch offices, which grew in number from twenty-eight in 1910 to thirty-nine in 1934—more than one sub-office being administered by most main branches. These will be the primary concern of this section. But it is important to remember that there were other important channels of overseas premium income. At one remove from the REA were its British subsidiaries—the National Provincial, the Car & General, the State, the Motor Union—which had or developed their own overseas networks, which were not always closely associated with the Corporation's. For example, when it was acquired in 1928, the Motor Union had six fully fledged foreign branches and over sixty agencies. Second, it had from time to time proved convenient for the REA to acquire or establish subsidiaries based in other countries, whether marine insurance companies in major shipping centres (as happened with the Amsterdam & London in 1895 or the so-called Java Companies, a group of four Dutch offices largely concerned with the East India trade, in 1925), or fire insurance companies (e.g. the Provident of New York in 1924). Third, however, the Corporation itself earned a fairly large premium income through a very large number of independent agencies (e.g. those in China and South America), through shared or reinsurance business on a treaty or guarantee basis, and through direct underwriting at Head Office (so-called 'Home Foreign' business). Unfortunately, there are no adequate figures for the inter-war overseas business of subsidiaries, but the structure of the REA's own fire and accident premium income is indicated by the following data:

TABLE2 0.3. *REA overseas fire and accident premiums (by source of income), 1931–9*

(£000)	Fire		Accident	
	1931	1939	1931	1939
Overseas	1,205	978	624	639
Of which:				
Branches	845	679	437	455
Agencies	44	64	41	79
Guarantee	297	224	—	5
Treaty	—	—	146	100
Home Foreign	19	11	—	—

As is implied in this statistical breakdown, the structure of the REA's overseas business did not conform to a single design, but had been fashioned partly by historical circumstances and partly by business need.

Nevertheless, its central element was the Corporation's branch organization. Other things being equal, the branch office system was preferred to
the 'chief agency' system because, as Daniell, the REA Assistant Secretary, pointed out in relation to Australian and New Zealand fire business
in 1908, a successful agent's business was in effect 'personal property'
and could be taken by him 'to the highest bidder or might disappear at his
death'. Moreover, even while it was retained, the Company would be in
the agent's hands, free neither in the selection nor in the extension of its
business. In effect, therefore, the conversion of an agency into a branch
office (which Daniell achieved in New Zealand in 1908, by buying out the
main Australian agent who had formerly controlled that territory) or the
creation of an entirely new Branch (which Hiles, the Joint Fire Manager,
did in Canada in 1910) was equivalent to transposing a microcosm of the
REA to an overseas territory. This was reflected in the creation of local
Boards of Directors, who served to advise on general, but not technical,
matters and to establish links with the local business community which
would generate a helpful flow of premium income: 'the keystone of the
organization of the future' in Australia, wrote Daniell in 1908, 'I have
tried to find in a local Board of Directors'; and in opening a Canadian
Branch in 1910 the Fire Manager's initial opinion that 'I am not aware of
any office which is in a better position [than the REA] to secure desirable
local Directors' was borne out by the appointment of an extremely influential Board headed by Henry Vincent Meredith, General Manager of the
powerful Bank of Montreal.

The branch structure was in itself quite complicated, since individual
branches were not merely responsible for their own small networks of sub-
offices and agents, but had widely varying relationships with associated
agents and subsidiary companies. Thus, it was only in the early 1920s that
the REA's considerable motor insurance business in the United States,
largely managed by the New York firm of Appleton & Cox, was transferred to the care of the American Branch. Earlier, to take another example,
the South African Branch was precluded from underwriting plate glass
risks in the Transvaal because the premium income of the REA's subsidiary, the National Provincial Plate Glass Insurance Company, according
to the Corporation's Plate Glass Manager, was 'absolutely and entirely
under the control' of the firm of Bowins & Brinkworth, who reported
directly to the London Head Office. Indeed, the separateness of the different companies was a vital one. In 1929, for example, the Fire Manager
regretted that expenses could not be lowered by merging the branches of the
various subsidiaries: 'some of the managers held that the business of the

companies was entirely distinct and that it would be jeopardised if their individuality were destroyed'.

Yet even as far as the REA itself was concerned the pattern was neither simple nor static. Some changes were attributable to variations in the rôle of particular agencies and associated firms. But others reflected managerial decisions concerning the scope and responsibilities of individual branches. Thus, while the broad features of most of the Corporation's leading branches—e.g. those in the USA, Canada and South Africa—remained more or less unchanged between the outbreak of the First and Second World Wars, there was considerable innovation in other areas. On the Continent, to take one example, the REA's pre-1914 business was not formally organized into a general branch, although the amount of accident business in Belgium warranted the opening of a Brussels Branch in 1905, and two years later Mr G. Van der Aa (Manager of Blom & Van der Aa, leading REA agents since 1887, and of the Amsterdam & London subsidiary) was nominated 'resident Continental Manager' in Amsterdam. Plans to establish a formal Continental Branch (either in Paris, as the Fire Manager wished, or in London, as the Governor wanted) had to be postponed because of the outbreak of the War. In the course of the War, however, the Paris Office was strengthened by the dispatch of Norman H. Self from London—and by 1917 that Branch was managing the Corporation's fire business throughout France, Spain, Morocco, Gibraltar and the Canary Islands.

In 1919, in the aftermath of the War, it was decided to close the Continental Office in Amsterdam (a decision which had been taken in 1914, but postponed because of the outbreak of war) and establish the Branch in Paris, with Self as Manager, and a territory embracing all the countries in Western Europe, together with the Canary Islands and French North Africa. In 1920, however, there was another major reorganization: the Continental Branch (with Self as 'General Continental Manager') was moved to Dover. Apparently, the immediate reason for this move was the need to avoid the double taxation which would have been involved in maintaining the chief Branch Office in either Paris or Brussels. The 'Continental Branch' managed most of the Corporation's underwriting in thirteen countries from Norway to the Canary Islands and from France to Morocco—although the Paris Office continued in existence, as did the Brussels sub-branch (exclusively concerned with general accident business), the inherited Head Office connections with various agencies, the Amsterdam & London and the various independent companies with which the REA had reinsurance arrangements. By 1931 (earlier figures are not available) the Continental Branch at Dover was handling some £170,000 of fire premiums, while the Paris and Brussels Offices brought in about £115,000 of accident premiums.

The other major post-war reorganization came in the Eastern Mediterranean. Until 1920 the principal office in that area had been that of the Egyptian Branch (established 1912), controlling agencies in various countries. The new branch was, at first, called the Levant Branch, although its name was almost immediately changed to the Eastern Mediterranean Branch. Under it, the Egyptian sub-branch controlled business in Egypt and Sudan; in addition the Levant Branch had oversight of Syria, Palestine, Cyprus, Malta, Constantinople, Smyrna and Roumania. In 1923, however, when the Manager resigned, the Egyptian Branch resumed its independence, with responsibility for Egypt, Sudan, Syria, Palestine, Cyprus and Malta.

The officials who managed such extensive territories were obviously men of influence and authority. And this was particularly true in the period when the delays of long-distance travel made it impossible for Head Office to exercise any very close control of their business policies. Admittedly, the occasional visits from London officials to settle major questions of principle or organization, and to lay down broad guidelines for local action, could be supplemented by frequent correspondence. But this was no substitute for immediate oversight; and in some instances years might pass without a visit (e.g. no Head Office official visited Egypt between 1921 and 1929).

Yet the importance, and distinctiveness, of overseas branch managers was shaped by more than the fact that lines of communication were extended and slow. Overseas territories had varied business characteristics which contrasted sharply with those of the UK, and which could best be understood by men on the spot. Further, the structure of overseas business was such that a small office could control a huge market—and a large income. In contrast to the normal situation in England, branch managers drew business from a comparatively small number of large connections, and were therefore more able to keep in touch with their own business on the basis of personal knowledge. Given this situation—the remoteness, the character of the business, the importance of personal contact in a small community, the need for extensive powers of attorney—overseas branch managers were naturally very influential and independent men, with more authority in their respective spheres than the Corporation's General Manager himself had in the 1930s.

In some circumstances, a Chief Agent assumed many of the characteristics of a branch manager. In 1908, for example, the Chief Agent for Australia and New Zealand, W. A. Walton, had the title of General Manager for Australasia, and received not merely a 25 per cent commission plus a contribution to expenses, but also an annual salary of £2,000. In addition, the new REA Branch Office in New Zealand, which took over Walton's agency business, remained under his general supervision. But, increasingly, the preferred arrangement was a full-time, salaried branch manager, who in these years received a generous profit commission. In the larger branches such men had commensurately more authority as well as duties. They included men like H. Leonard Bell, who took over as General Manager of the Eastern Branch when it was established in 1909, with an area extending from Aden to Singapore; Arthur Barry, who assumed control of the Canadian Branch in 1910 at a salary of £900 plus 10 per cent profit commission, and who after an extraordinarily successful as well as stormy career resigned in 1927 on an annual pension of £2,000;[1] Robert Connew, the future REA General Manager, who was appointed South African Branch Manager in 1911 at the age of 34 and a salary of £1,500 plus 5 per cent profit commission; and Uberto C. Crosby who was appointed to control the REA's American business in 1905 at a salary of £3,000 plus 5 per cent profit commission (rising to 7½ per cent above £10,000 profits) and who retired in 1911 with a present of £750 and a pension of £1,500.

From the standpoint of the Royal Exchange Head Office, therefore, much of the Corporation's business and potential profitability derived from branch offices which were only indirectly controlled by the REA's central Managers. In large part this was both inevitable and desirable, for local conditions could obviously be best understood by men on the spot. Yet there were various aspects of the quasi-independence of overseas branch managers (in particular those in such crucial areas as the United States, Canada, Australasia and South Africa) which could provoke considerable anxiety at Head Office. And, as a result, the years around the First World War, and particularly in the 1920s, were from this viewpoint characterized by a search for more effective means of controlling overseas business.

In the last resort, of course, the Corporation's authority was represented by its power to secure the resignation of an ineffective or incompetent branch manager. But there was a sense in which this power could only be exercised when it was already too late—i.e. when an obvious and serious amount of damage had been done, as in 1904, when the original US

[1] Below, pp. 490–2.

Manager was dismissed for reckless underwriting and highly suspect accounting procedures; or in 1911, when the South African Branch Manager's retirement had to be accelerated because branch management had become 'antiquated and prejudicial to the development of the Corporation's business'.

In fact, before 1914 relatively little continuous effort was made to co-ordinate the activities of individual branches with the outlook and policy of Head Office. Indeed, it was only on rare occasions that senior officials actually visited the more remote areas. This happened, for example, in 1904 when E. B. Hiles, the Fire Manager, travelled to the United States in the aftermath of the Baltimore fire in order to reduce the Corporation's risks; in 1908, when Ferrers Daniell visited Australasia in order to reorganize the REA's business there; in 1910 when Hiles visited Canada, preparatory to the opening of a branch in Montreal; and in 1911, when Daniell visited South Africa in a successful attempt to rescue the Corporation's business there by the appointment of a new manager. But these were very special visits, and it is clear that in the normal course of events men like Hiles and Daniell were too important to be spared from the Royal Exchange for the weeks necessary to visit North America or Australia. Yet it was imperative that the underwriting departments—and particularly the Fire Department, which dominated and was itself dominated by overseas business—should have some better means of control of and access to information than was afforded by ordinary letters and the rare cable, or even by the overwhelming mass of paper (including a copy of every policy issued) which branches were expected to send to London. For a few years in the 1890s the Corporation had had a Foreign Fire Inspector, but between 1899 and 1911 this function, in so far as it was fulfilled at all, had been carried out by senior clerks from the Fire Department (one of them, S. D. Duck, had died in China in 1907 while on a tour of inspection of the Far East). In 1911, however, in partial recognition of the need for systematic oversight, the Fire Department appointed Reginald E. Oldfield as Foreign Fire Inspector at a salary of £250.

Oldfield, who was to become Fire Manager in 1929 and Assistant General Manager in 1933, was then 27, with eight years' service in the REA Fire Department and a degree in Economics. He set off almost immediately on a series of world-wide tours to report on the nature of fire risks accepted and 'the desirability of extending or curtailing business'. Yet at this stage Oldfield was relatively junior and inexperienced, and most of his work was confined to agencies. It is significant that in July 1914, in suggesting that he might visit Australia, the Fire Manager warned him: 'there you would have to go to work very carefully, because you are dealing with a Branch Manager, and I know that they resent visits from travelling inspectors, thinking that they are in some sense acting as spies upon their operations'. This warning reflected a crucial fact about the REA's main overseas branches in these years: they had many of the characteristics of independent businesses—including the fact that their success, when they had been successful, could be largely attributed to the staff on the spot, and particularly the appropriate branch manager, who was able to shape the business with little interference (or help) from Head Office.

By the end of the First World War little had occurred to diminish the prestige, power and independence of the REA's main overseas branch managers. Indeed, if anything they had been enhanced by the war-time interruption of travel and normal communication from Head Office. Yet the problems of control became much more apparent after 1918. In part this was because the acquisition of subsidiaries and the pressing atmosphere of competitive expansion re-emphasized the need for co-ordinated business policies. In addition, however, it derived from the growth of general accident business overseas, which meant that overseas branches became less and less the sole responsibility of the Fire Department. In the event the various Departmental Managers found it increasingly difficult to control the variegated activity of individual branches without far-reaching changes in their own mechanism of consultation and (ultimately) in the structure of the Corporation's management.

As a result, in the immediate post-war years, a new note is discernible in the Corporation's records—one which showed the Departmental Managers much more sensitive to the position of branch officials and more able to influence their actions. In March 1922, for example, the Fire Manager reported to the Governors that he and his colleagues had instituted a closer control of branch expenses since, in the past, 'he feared that foreign Branch Managers had been rather encouraged than otherwise to spend considerable sums in upholding the dignity of the Office, and this had resulted in their considering that the expenses did not really matter'. As a result, Departmental Managers had issued instructions that 'no change in territory or formation of sub-branches should take place without Head Office being first advised and their definite approval obtained'. In fact, the novelty of the post-war situation had been shown two years earlier by the holding of an unprecedented conference of Head Office officials and leading overseas branch managers (from Australia, Brussels, Canada, Egypt, New Zealand, South Africa and the United States). And by the early 1920s the Head Office officials had adapted to the new situation sufficiently far to adopt the new practice of regular, formal meetings at which general policy (particularly towards questions of branch activity) could be discussed, if not always unanimously agreed.[1]

Nevertheless, the new situation imposed pressures for changes in organization as well as attitudes. Managerial control was unsatisfactory until it could be embodied in a single department, or at least a single official. As early as 1921, Wilfred Gale, the Plate Glass Manager, after a tour of Australia and India, made a novel proposal (he was ahead of his time by almost forty years):

I have often thought, and my recent visit has strengthened my opinion, that the Corporation would be wise to consider the appointment of an Overseas Manager at Head Office to control all overseas branches for all Departments. He would, of course, settle all matters after consultation with the various Departmental Managers. Colonial customs and ideas are quite different from the English and such a man as, say, Mr. Locke [the Manager in Australia] would fill such a post excellently, and I think that the appointment would be welcomed overseas.

An even more prescient comment was made by Reginald Oldfield in October 1923, when the Managers discussed the possible need to appoint 'a really good foreign inspector' to establish firmer control of overseas branches. Oldfield (by this time Assistant Fire Manager, but no doubt remembering his own pre-war experiences) pointed out 'that if such an appointment were made it would be necessary for the inspector to rank equally with Head Office officials and be given full power—the man to be sent would really have to be a sort of Assistant General Manager'. Ten years later, it so happened that Oldfield was, in fact, appointed as one of the first two Assistant General Managers, with responsibility for, but not 'full power' over, foreign business. But in 1923 he, too, was ahead of his time—at least in the context of the REA's inherited organization. Although the Governor circulated Gale's 1920 letter, and Oldfield's 1923 proposal was discussed at length, the innovation of unified, as distinct from departmental, control was not introduced until 1960. The departmental influence proved too strong, and in any case, as Wamsley, the Accident Manager (and himself a powerful and jealous departmental official), pointed out in 1923, the best branch managers 'would refuse to be dictated to'.

Both Gale and Oldfield, in indicating the non-departmental nature of the proposed appointment had, in fact, exposed one of the most significant drawbacks of the REA's organization: the lack of a General Manager impeded the co-ordination of departmental activity—and in this particular instance allowed branch managers (who were increasingly in the position

[1] Below, p. 505.

of General Managers, in control of large amounts of premium income in various departments) to 'slip through' their control. In April 1922 the Departmental Managers, at one of their regular meetings, had 'a general discussion . . . as to the attitude of several of the branch managers when visiting this country, and it was stated that some of them apparently thought they could more easily get their own way by appealing to the Governor direct on various points than by submitting them through the Departmental Managers'. On the other hand, in so far as this was a problem of attitudes, it did not always originate overseas. In March 1920, for example, after a trip to India, the Governor pointed out that while in the past he had criticized letters from the Eastern Branch Manager as 'short and not helpful, in reading some of the letters Mr. Bell had received he could not help feeling that the same criticism might be levied against letters sent from the Head Office. He hoped the [Departmental] Managers would always remember the isolated position of the foreign Branch Managers and give them as much information as possible.'

Yet, whether or not the Head Office officials were sympathetic to the position of branch managers, their ability to help and guide them was limited by difficulties of communication and by the organizational structure of the REA itself, which in these years lacked a strong and continuing focus of managerial authority for all overseas business. Consequently, in the inter-war period, much effort and time was wasted by the need to secure inter-departmental co-ordination with respect to the problems of particular branches; and decisive action on the part of the REA naturally tended to be confined to moments of crisis when the problems had grown to such a size that some action was indispensable. More than this, only rarely before the Second World War did senior Head Office officials have a detailed knowledge of overseas business in general, let alone that of a particular branch. As a result it was the more important to allow branch managers a large degree of autonomy. And in the last resort the rôle of Head Office officials was determined by the strength of individual branches—and that strength was largely determined by the abilities and success of particular branch managers. In the nature of the case, most were able as well as independent; and when mistakes occurred it was frequently the result of the wrong choice of man. Thus, when the Manager of an important branch had to be pensioned off in the 1920s, his relative 'failure' should have been seen in the context of his original letter of appointment from the Fire Manager, which reminded him that he had no experience in his new job: 'The defect in your qualifications for the post is quite obvious, and your appointment was made in spite of it.' Nor could he have been heartened by the information that 'coming as you do, a stranger . . . the brokers will think you an easy victim. Your training among orientals should enable you to disarm the least scrupulous broker.'

A significant contrast to this treatment of a relatively unsuccessful branch manager was the example of the Canadian Branch in the 1920s— where the outstanding ability and success of the Manager, Arthur Barry, although it went hand-in-hand with a mode of behaviour which the Head Office officials found most unwelcome, nevertheless effectively prevented them from checking him in any way for many years—and then only by asking for his resignation.

It will be remembered that Barry was the original Branch Manager in Canada. Appointed in 1910 at the age of 37, he was a Canadian with twenty years' experience of fire insurance. After his appointment he built up what the Managers acknowledged (in 1922) was 'a wonderful business' for the REA: fire and accident premiums rose from less than £3,000 in 1910 to £66,000 in 1914 and £167,000 in 1920; and the business was, altogether, very profitable: in the period 1910–26 annual average net premiums were £103,000 and profits to the Corporation (after deducting Barry's 10 per cent) £14,000.[1] And his success was such that in 1920, at the Staff Dinner held to celebrate the Corporation's Bicentenary, the Governor coupled his name (together with those of the Secretary and the Manager of the West End Branch) for special mention in his toast to the REA. Nevertheless, by the early 1920s the Head Office Managers were beginning to get very restless, for Barry's success as well as his personality made him far from solicitous of other people's feelings or of established hierarchies. He continuously failed to reply to Head Office letters, ignored instruction from Departmental Managers, and had an extremely tactless manner of dealing with the Corporation's clients. In 1922 he snubbed the REA Accident Manager by refusing to meet him, when Wamsley visited Canada; and in December of the next year, Connew, after visiting Canada, reported that although Barry was an excellent underwriter with exemplary results, 'his relations with the agents and his methods of conducting business are seriously imperilling the prestige and good name of the Corporation throughout Canada'. The Management Committee took a very serious view of this and other aspects of Barry's behaviour on the grounds that no one should be retained in the REA '—even if they are making money for it —if it is believed that by doing so the reputation of the Corporation will be injured'.

[1] In fact, there was a small loss on accident business. Taking fire underwriting alone, average premiums were £72,000 and average profits £15,000—a very healthy margin.

Yet neither these nor other equally determined discussions changed the situation, or Barry's character. And the problem is worth emphasizing, because, although some of its aspects were distinctive to the Canadian Branch, it illustrated a general difficulty—compounded of relative neglect on the part of Head Office and the obstacles to re-establishing effective control when a strong Manager was also a business success. As one REA official pointed out in 1926, although ruthless in his dealings and much disliked, 'Barry is undoubtedly the smartest Fire Manager in Canada, and . . . an exceedingly clever underwriter'. And in February of the same year the exasperation of the Departmental Managers drove them to submit a strongly worded memorandum to the Governors:

[Mr Barry] has always claimed that having built up the business from the commencement out of nothing, with a minimum of assistance and without any definite instructions, he should not be worried with questions, on detail matters. Under Mr. Hiles' somewhat easy management [i.e. until 1920] few difficulties occurred [but Hiles's resignation and the introduction of accident business and the business of subsidiaries changed the situation] . . . Mr. Barry is the type of Manager who expects to do exactly what he personally likes; comes to England when he likes; goes on trips to the West when he likes; indeed, he is impatient of any control, and here the trouble started . . . Mr. Barry has been clever enough to endeavour to play the Managers off against each other to some extent and has always felt and acted on the assumption that if the Managers were 'troublesome' he could appeal to the Governors.

In itself, however, this recurring difficulty with the departmental officials might not have mattered as long as Barry remained successful. The real problem revolved around the impact of his behaviour on the reputation and morale of the REA in Canada. And after repeated warnings, Barry was summoned to London in October 1927. There, he met the Governors and was reminded that as late as the spring of 1926, when he had been called to London, 'he had been told that it was essential there should be smooth working between the Head Office Managers and himself'. Since no improvement had taken place and 'difficulties were constantly arising', the Governors reluctantly concluded that it was necessary to ask for his resignation—although, in recognition of his enormous contribution to the REA in Canada, he was treated very generously, with a pension of £2,000 annually.

The parting of the ways between the REA and Arthur Barry symbolized the end of an era in the organization of the Corporation's overseas business. For not only did it resolve what had been the most troublesome example of managerial control, but it did so in a way which left no doubt about the authority of Head Office management. Indeed, combined with the pressure of domestic events, the needs of overseas business were largely instrumental in producing the fundamental change in the Corporation's structure which was associated with the appointment of a General Manager in 1929. The new post was, in fact, a product of the twin necessity of resolving inter-departmental conflicts and asserting the overall interests of the Corporation. Each, although more frequently the latter, was amply illustrated in the vicissitudes of insurance abroad. By the late 1920s each was brought home by the expansion of general accident business, which meant that overseas branches could no longer be (if, indeed, they ever had been) effectively managed by the Fire Department. In the event, as with other aspects of control and organization, the full logic of the General Manager's Department was not worked out until after 1945. But even the relatively weak authority of the General Manager in the 1930s, following as it did the practical co-operation between Departmental Managers in overseas affairs in the 1920s, was sufficient to establish a much firmer control and co-ordination of overseas branches. (In later years that control was to become even more effective, as the Group came to rely less on a constant flow of paper and more on systematic statistical reporting and forecasting, together with more frequent personal contact with Head Office officials.) The REA's overseas insurance interests had not expanded spectacularly in the 1930s, when the general influence of world-wide depression was keenly felt. Yet the extended network was strengthened and held together as never before: the structural implications of business expansion had seen to that.

21

Organization and Control
1917-1939

Three related themes stand out in the twentieth-century administrative history of the Royal Exchange Assurance. First, the institution was itself radically changed by the process of amalgamation: the transition from Corporation to Group had inevitable and far-reaching implications for managerial organization and control. Second, the continued growth of business on a nation- and world-wide basis demanded fundamental changes in the inherited relationships between Head Office and branches. Third, and partly deriving from the first two, the respective rôles of departments and general management had to be adapted to the needs of a larger and much more complicated business. Each of these elements can be considered in turn, although in reality they were merely different aspects of the same problem.

THE ORIGINS OF A GROUP

Although the REA had made some small acquisitions before 1914, and had also been tempted by the possibility of a union with the London Assurance in 1909, its business and corporate structures were essentially unchanged before the First World War. In this respect it presented a sharp contrast to most other leading insurance companies, which had grown by extensive merger activity. This was a fact of which pre-war members of the Corporation had been understandably proud; but it was not a situation which could last, as long as the Corporation's management wished to maintain its business position in an age of rapid development. Hence, as has been seen in chapter 19, in 1917 the REA dramatically extended its commitment to motor business by acquiring the Car & General; the next year it purchased the Local Government Guarantee Society and in 1924 the State Assurance Company (together with its subsidiary the British Equitable); and in 1928 it acquired the Motor Union, together with three subsidiaries. The business implications of these moves have already been examined. How did they affect management structures and general organization?

In the event, at least as far as the inter-war period was concerned, the acquisitions had a far greater effect on the scope of business and financial affairs than on administrative organization. Admittedly, ultimate control of their operations rested with the chief officials of the REA. In particular, A. W. Wamsley, the Corporation's Accident Manager, whose energy and ambition had been largely instrumental in the purchase of the Car & General and the Motor Union, and who became Managing Director of both, was effectively responsible for running the companies and regularly reported on their affairs to the REA Committee of Management. Nevertheless, in practice, the organization—both departmental and branch—of the subsidiaries was kept entirely separate from that of the REA itself and no systematic attempt was made to co-ordinate the structure, or in some respects even the business activity, of the Corporation and the other offices. No doubt Wamsley took some care to harmonize the motor business of the REA and its subsidiaries, but he was hardly well placed to ensure co-operation when it came to other branches of underwriting or to general matters of organization and competition.

This situation contrasts strongly with the outcome of the merger movement of more recent years, which has increasingly led to the pooling of business and the integration and streamlining of organization. In the 1920s and 1930s, however, this more literal interpretation of the concept of 'grouping' was much less common.

To take the link with the Car & General as an example, in the early years there appears to have been very little exchange of even vital information. Thus, in 1919 the REA's Agency Manager learned from the Corporation's Hull Branch Manager that the Car & General were about to open a district office at Grimsby—and that the REA's local agent 'appears to have strong objections to not having been advised of this new departure'. Even more seriously, in 1920–1, the Car & General independently appointed agents in Newfoundland and Egypt, only to be informed by the REA Fire Manager that Tariff Association rules prevented both the Corporation and a subsidiary having agents in the same overseas area— with the result that the Car & General could not appoint in Egypt (where the REA already had a branch) and that it had effectively precluded the REA from entering Newfoundland: 'I think this point must have escaped you,' the Fire Manager admonished the Car & General's Secretary, 'otherwise, I am sure that you would have consulted me before going so far as to bar the Royal Exchange opening there.' Nor did the baneful effects of ignorance cut one way: in November 1922 the Governor mentioned to REA officials the case of a Corporation Branch Manager making 'great efforts' to obtain insurance business which it eventually transpired, already belonged to the Car & General! He pointed out that 'this was only an instance and that he knew other cases had occurred on both sides'; and recommended that local branch managers of the two offices should meet monthly and advise their Head Offices of the outcome.

On the other hand, this extreme degree of lack of communication was only characteristic of the initial years of the acquisition. A better flow of information was ultimately established even though it often seemed like communication between independent allies—as in December 1922, when the Accident Manager reported to the REA Management Committee that the Car & General Directors proposed to undertake liability business in the USA. Yet, however good the flow of information, the separateness rather than the identity of the different offices continued to be emphasized. Thus, in the winter of 1922–3, in response to the Governor's suggestion that branch managers of the different companies might meet formally, the REA officials were unanimously of the opinion 'that no good purposes could be served by such a formal meeting', since these branch managers who could easily work together were already meeting, 'while it would be useless to endeavour to force the hands of the others'. Indeed, even the proposal that the branch managers should have a joint dinner on the occasion of the annual conference was received cooly (Car & General Directors claimed that their branch managers 'would feel they were being placed in a somewhat subsidiary position to the managers of the REA [and] . . . that competition between the Companies was really in their joint interest rather than otherwise')—and was only arranged because of the Governor's adamant insistence.

What is, indeed, clear from these early years is that mutual suspicion, as well as ignorance, characterized inter-company relationships. Wamsley frequently had to defend the personnel and quality of business of the Car & General against what he considered to be unfair criticisms from within the REA, and in January 1923 was stung into asserting that although there might be several 'duds' in the Car & General, 'two or three of the men in that Company were better than any in the service of the REA'. And four months later he claimed that the Car & General's fire business had not developed more rapidly in part because of 'the lack of sympathy shown the Car & General men by certain of the REA branch managers'. Indeed, one reason for these initial difficulties was the feeling that the acquisition of the Car & General, and later the Motor Union, was largely the individual work and responsibility of the Accident Manager—so that other departments were somewhat suspicious of the new subsidiaries. This was a particular problem as far as relationships with the Fire Department were concerned, for members of that Department (traditionally considered as the most 'aristocratic' in the REA) were apparently suspicious of both the expansion of accident business and the type and extent of fire business undertaken by the two accident companies. But this factor was essentially a transitory one. More profound, and more reasonable, causes of the absence of real integration lay in the nature of the insurance business itself.

In the last resort, the success of any insurance company lies in the efficiency of its organization (i.e. its ability to minimize operating expenses) and in the extent and quality of its 'connection'. Historically, the latter was the more important element, in the sense that a good connection—a large number of hardworking agents and loyal policyholders—could always generate more profit than a relatively expensive organization could dissipate. Yet such a connection was both intangible and specific: it could be acquired but not necessarily transferred. The goodwill, which was its essence, was directed explicitly towards a particular office (at least as far as UK business was concerned), and could hardly be appropriated by another. It was precisely this factor which made any rapid move towards practical amalgamation so difficult in the case of companies like the REA and the Car & General in the 1920s and 1930s, for the loyalties of employees, agents and policyholders were firmly attached to the name and to the distinct existence of each. It was, of course, for this reason that throughout the inter-war period there was no serious move to amalgamate branches, or even to avoid their duplication in most important towns. And in 1929 (referring to overseas business, although the analysis was almost as true of the domestic market) the Fire Manager pointed out that, although 'the real crux of the fire business was the question of expense' and no real improvement could be expected until the various subsidiaries were merged under one management, nevertheless there was considerable controversy within the REA about this step: 'some of the managers held that the business of the companies was entirely distinct and that it would be jeopardised if their individuality were destroyed'.

Such considerations also explain the gingerly fashion in which the question of managerial control was approached. In May 1922, for example, the Governor asserted that the appropriate REA departments 'should have complete control' of the relevant business of all subsidiaries, but also acknowledged that 'there were certain difficulties in this being carried out immediately'; for their part, the Fire and Accident Managers confessed to ignorance about the business of the National Provincial (acquired thirteen years earlier!). In 1925, when there occurred a vacancy in the

London Branch of the State, although the Deputy-Governor argued strongly in favour of the REA and its subsidiaries being 'looked upon as one [so] that whenever a vacancy occurred . . . the best man should be chosen for the post irrespective of the office to which he happened to belong', this viewpoint was not, in fact, accepted as universally applicable: 'certain difficulties in connection with such an arrangement could not, of course, be overlooked'. Clearly the *allegiance* (and, therefore, the pattern of efficiency) of the staff had not been seriously altered by the acquisition of subsidiaries. The Management Committee's Minutes captured the essence of the situation in discussing management co-operation with the newly acquired State in 1924: 'it was agreed that whatever steps are taken the Liverpool sentiment should be maintained as much as possible'.

There were, of course, aspects of the insurance business where these factors were not important, or where other considerations had to be allowed to outweigh them. In the case of investment policy, for example, co-ordinating control was obviously more desirable, and less harmful to existing loyalties. Hence, in February 1928, soon after the acquisition of the Motor Union, the REA Management Committee concluded that it would be desirable to have an 'Investment Secretary' to oversee the investments of the whole Group (in fact, this post was not officially established until 1933), and that the Accident Manager should tell the Chairman of the Motor Union that, pending the formation of a new Department, the Motor Union Directors should consult the REA before committing any investments.[1] More generally, where some aspect of the business of a subsidiary gave serious cause for concern, the REA was firm in its attitude towards control. This was best exemplified in the case of the Motor Union (which in many respects was, at the time of its acquisition, weaker than the Car & General). Thus, after a thorough investigation, in the summer of 1928, Connew, on behalf of the REA Fire Department, concluded that the Motor Union had too many losing agencies overseas and too much unprofitable foreign treaty business. In light of the fact that the Company had been acquired primarily for its motor business, and that this was the mainstay of its activity, he pressed for the closing of many overseas agencies, the termination of unprofitable foreign treaties, prior consultation with the REA before any new treaties were accepted ('in making this latter recommendation I am actuated solely with the desire to place at the disposal of the Motor Union the knowledge and extensive

---

[1] It is indicative of the character of inter-company links that the official channel of communication should have been the REA's Accident Manager.

experience we possess in regard to this class of business'), and the 'closest supervision' of home branches to ensure the careful selection of risks.[1] Thenceforth, Connew played a strong rôle in the management of the Motor Union's fire business. Similarly, within a few years of the acquisition, the Motor Union Life account was amalgamated with that of the parent Corporation.

Further, with respect to other aspects of insurance underwriting, it is perhaps possible to exaggerate the independence of the Corporation's subsidiaries. For in practice the two most important—the Car & General and the Motor Union—were dominated by Wamsley, until he retired (in 1934). Even so, in acting as Managing Director, Wamsley represented a personal, rather than an institutional and formal, link between the companies. It was, for example, through his own efforts that in 1928 he was 'able to establish a close collaboration between the REA, the Car & General and the Motor Union, which is working well for the joint benefit'. At the same time, he reported, 'I have been able to increase the efficiency of the organization for dealing with motor car claims, by amalgamating the engineering staffs'. But such an organizational innovation was rare in the inter-war years. Rather, co-operation continued to depend on personal and occasional factors. Thus, it was only the fact that a Director, E. R. Debenham, submitted a detailed report on the REA's Birmingham Branch that led, in January 1923, to a discussion, by an *ad hoc* Committee, of the lack of co-ordination between the REA and the Car & General branches in the matter of fire business, and of the possibility of housing the two Birmingham Branches under one roof. (The more extreme proposal that they be combined into one branch for both Companies 'was worth following up but required full consideration'.) More generally, as late as December 1925 the Management Committee acknowledged that 'at the present time no co-ordination exists between the Agency Manager and the agency organizations of the Corporation's subsidiaries', and took the obvious first step of securing his appointment as Consulting Agency Manager to the subsidiaries. Symptomatic of this general situation was a letter, dated February 1930, from the REA's General Manager to the Manager of the Motor Union, which acknowledged a particularly fruitful conference between members of the Group concerning Canadian business, and went on:

While I recognise and appreciate your desire to maintain the individuality of your Company, you will, I feel sure, agree with me that there are many matters

---

[1] In 1926 the Motor Union's gross fire premiums were £609,177—of which foreign business accounted for £467,426.

of importance on which Members of the Group can be helpful to one another without interfering with their own individual liberty of action.

I have in mind such matters as:-

(a) the establishment, or discontinuance, of branches, district offices, or agencies of considerable importance;
(b) the appointment of executive officials or branch managers;
(c) the renewal, or discontinuance, of leases of existing office premises.

Before any decision is taken in future in regard to any of these, or similar, matters of importance, please report the facts to me so that they can be considered in relation to the individual or collective interests of the Companies of our Group.

What is significant about this letter is that it could hardly have been written before the appointment of an REA General Manager (which only came in 1929) and that it still reflected the absence of any continued or systematic co-ordination, let alone integration, of business activity and management. No doubt, under the guidance of the General Manager the Group was brought closer together in the 1930s. But even so, the fact that such a letter could still be written thirteen years after the acquisition of the Car & General, that it anticipated not firm and explicit central policy-making but consultation on specific decisions, and that the possibility of a joint policy (e.g. with regard to the amalgamation of branches) was still very remote, is a powerful comment on the nature of Group co-operation at the time. In 1934 it was agreed that all employees in Group companies with head offices in the UK should benefit from the rule (propounded for REA men to mark the two-hundredth anniversary) that thirty years' service should be rewarded by a three-month holiday. Nevertheless, the corporate entities remained separate and the various departments (including even staff departments) unintegrated. Throughout the period (and in this respect the REA seems to have been little different from other companies),[1] the desire, and perhaps the need, to maintain 'individuality' proved too strong for any countervailing pressure to simplify and rationalize the business organization of the Group as a whole. This was partly attributable to the fact that competition (keen as it seemed to contemporaries) was not yet so fierce and ruthless as to oblige insurance companies to pare down the heavy costs undoubtedly involved in the

---

[1] At least as regards home business. Thus, the Commercial Union, although it managed to pool business and co-ordinate activity in overseas areas in the 1930s, found co-ordination in the United Kingdom somewhat more difficult. For example, in 1931, in spite of achieving the beginnings of local accident claims departments for the Group, the Glasgow Branches of the Commercial Union and some of its subsidiaries moved into a new building, but continued to operate independently. See Liveing, *Century of Insurance*, pp. 198–206.

duplication of business structures. In addition, however, the continuation of independence within the Group was, in fact, a striking indication of the rôle of the corporate personality, of individual loyalty, and of subjective emotions in the business of insurance. And in these respects the REA clearly provided an outstanding example of corporate longevity and of the powerful rôle which tradition played in shaping business policy.

BRANCHES

While the obstacles to the effective control and integration of subsidiary companies proved insuperable in the inter-war years, it was both necessary and possible to improve the organization which linked the REA Head Office with the Corporation's numerous branch and district offices throughout the United Kingdom and overseas. For, whatever the possibility (and even desirability) of maintaining the independence of different companies in the same Group, each of these companies, and particularly the REA itself, had to ensure that, as far as possible, its own activities and policies were unified. Size alone dictated this: by 1919 the Corporation had over 21,000 agents and eighty-two inspectors distributed among twenty-two home branches (four of them in London) and ten district offices. By 1939, although the number of branch and district offices was about the same (and the failure to expand the number of branches was subsequently seen as a weakness of inter-war policy), the number of agents had doubled.

We have already seen, in chapter 12, the extent to which questions of branch organization and control were thrown into sharp relief by the growth in the scale of operations in the decades immediately before the First World War. The continued expansion of business during the War, and the level and complexity of activity in the post-war decade, obliged the Corporation to make further adjustments in the relationships between Head Office and branch offices—even though some problems (e.g. departmental rivalry concerning various aspects of the control) were not tackled until the development of an adequate system of general management in the 1930s, and not satisfactorily resolved until after 1945.

Many of the problems in the early years of this century had revolved around the position of the Agency Manager, who was cast in a somewhat ambiguous rôle with respect to the heads of underwriting departments.[1] Thus, in 1917, when the Committee of Management once more considered his duties, it re-emphasized that he worked under the Secretary, was to provide general help in the extension and supervision of agency and

[1] Above, pp. 292–3.

inspection systems and in the development of new business, but was to do this within limits laid down by departmental heads: 'Technical matters in connection with the various Departments, other than those arising in the course of his duties, and the supervision of the indoor staff and work at branches are outside his province.' Given the Agency Manager's secondary rôle, the other Departmental Managers were naturally placed in a very strong position with respect to branch organization. Historically, the importance of fire business, together with the traditional prestige of the Fire Manager, meant that the latter was *primus inter pares* when it came to influencing individual branches. As far as overseas branches were concerned, this situation continued more or less unchallenged into the inter-war period—for the Corporation's overseas business continued to be heavily (although decreasingly) dependent on fire underwriting. Thus, correspondence with overseas branch managers was the primary concern of the Fire Managers, and the Fire Department appointed an overseas Manager before any other department, or the Corporation itself, had done so. At home, however, where the premium income from other departments, and especially from accident underwriting, was considerable and growing, this conventional arrangement did not go unchallenged. In 1918, for example, in accepting the Governor's proposal (made, significantly, after a private discussion with the Fire Manager) that it might be advisable to appoint assistant branch managers who were 'good Accident men', the Management Committee rejected the implication: it 'did not think that the post of a branch manager should necessarily be restricted to a Fire man'.

In practice, however, the potentially divisive effects of departmentalism on the branch organization of the REA were mitigated by two factors which were of increasing importance in the 1920s: the tendency of the various Departmental Managers to work closely together, and the influence of the Secretary. The former was generally reflected in regular meetings of Departmental Managers, which hammered out agreed policies towards branch organization. And it was specifically exemplified, to take one example, in the crucial task of appointing inspectors. Thus, after the foundation of the Agency Department (1903) the old practice of selecting branch inspectors on a departmental basis was abandoned. Instead, through the co-ordinating influence of the Agency Manager, who was primarily responsible for appointments, inspectors were appointed to cover all types of business (a procedure which policyholders and agents clearly preferred). And when the practice was reviewed in 1919 the Agency Manager claimed that not only had 'every other company . . . since instituted a similar system, but if the old policy of employing an inspector to represent a single department were reverted to it would prove impracticable'. With this verdict the various Managers agreed—even though the Fire Manager, Ferrers Daniell, had some qualms that inspectors had a natural inclination 'to follow lines of least resistance' and might therefore neglect fire business, which was relatively hard to obtain.

The Secretary's rôle was a much more personal one, and in the 1920s owed much to the warmth and wisdom of Percy F. H. Hodge (1917–29), who was obviously an exemplary holder of a sensitive office. His surviving letters well illustrate the frank and friendly paternalism with which he conducted correspondence with branch managers—who looked upon him as a confidant and personal adviser. In 1920, for example, one man who found it difficult to maintain what he felt to be the necessary social position of an REA branch manager on an annual salary of £695 was advised by Hodge not to press his claim for more; admittedly, times were hard, wrote the Secretary, 'All the same, if I was to endeavour to keep abreast with the principal officers in the other big insurance companies, the Directors would have to increase my present remuneration four or five times over —a course which, unfortunately, they show no immediate anxiety to take.'

In the last resort, however, the Secretary could only deal with individual and personal (rather than general business) problems. And it was therefore left to others to co-ordinate Head Office relationships with the branches. The heightened need for closer links was felt during the War. In 1917, for example, it was decided that every branch should be visited by a Director at least once a year, and that branch managers were to visit Head Office at least twice a year for consultations with their 'visiting Directors' and with officials. And in December 1918 the Management Committee took the logical step of deciding to organize regular annual conferences of Home Branch Managers and officials—the first conference taking place in the spring of 1919. It was significant that the Governor's suggestion for such a conference was based upon the example of the Car & General, which had held annual meetings from well before its acquisition by the REA, although at that time 'they practically resolved themselves into a lecture given by Mr. Thoresby to the branch managers', whereas under Wamsley's influence they had become much more genuinely conferences. From 1919 onwards the REA conferences, together with the formal reports of Directors on their visits to individual branches, provided regular opportunities for integrating Head Office and branch policies. Even so, the older tradition of departmentalism adjusted only with reluctance: in 1924 the Governor had to insist that the Branch Manager's Conferences should continue to be held annually (the Departmental Managers had suggested biannual meetings) and the Head Office officials expressed the hope that they should have personal appointments only with those branch managers who were resident far from London—e.g. Ireland in and north of Newcastle.

In fact, it was only the personality and purposefulness of the man at the centre which could mould a unified and coherent policy for the Corporation and its branches. Until the end of the War one problem had been that the REA's Agency Department was supervised by its original Manager, R. B. S. Castle: and Castle, whatever his undoubted merits as the Corporation's pioneer of agency co-ordination, suffered from the inescapable disadvantage of working from a subordinate position with respect to the Managers of the underwriting departments. Appreciating this and realizing that he could not expect promotion at Head Office, Castle accepted the Managership of the Liverpool Branch Office in 1919 —thus opening the way for a different, and stronger, appointment as Agency Manager. His successor was Alexander MacDonald—a man whose calibre was to earn him promotion to Secretary in 1930 and General Manager in 1931.

Although little direct evidence survives, it seems that MacDonald relatively quickly asserted the authority which was potentially inherent in his office. In 1921 his Department was given separate and equal status with the others, with the significant domestic result that he was given the privilege of using the Managers' Lunch Room. But even before then he had exerted his influence. In 1920, for example, he produced a comprehensive analysis of all the Corporation's branch and district offices, which concluded by emphasizing the critical rôle of inspectors, the need to keep them much better informed about agents' business, and the necessity of providing them with effective transport. On this last point, MacDonald expressed dissatisfaction with the motor cycles then in common use, and recommended that inspectors be provided with good 'run-abouts'; 'pending the appearance of a cheap English car, I recommend the purchase of Ford cars'. But his most urgent plea was for the appointment of *more* inspectors, in spite of 'the bugbear of expense'. Even though they would not all pay their way at once, he argued, the intensified competition and the fact that in the industry as a whole a large number of indoor staff 'in consequence of their Army training, conceived a distaste for office work and have been placed in the field by several companies', made such appointments necessary if the REA was to hold its own. The new Agency Manager then appended a variety of suggestions for improved methods of business-getting—including better communications between departments, the routing of inquiries through the Agency Manager's office, the payment of all claims through the relevant inspectors, co-ordination of advertising by the Agency Department, and the collection of overdue premiums by inspectors under the supervision of the Agency Department. The significant and unprecedented feature of these proposals was that they not only involved changes in departmental procedures (and therefore exemplified a new sphere of discussion for the Agency Manager), but were also explicitly based upon a new rôle for the Agency Department, which thereby became a continuing focus of information and a centre of initiative.

In the last resort, however, the extent and influence of these changes should not be exaggerated. The authority and influence of the Agency Manager were not such as to override those of the individual underwriting departments—or even of the powerful managers who controlled the individual branches. All that he could do was to try to persuade various people to work more closely together. And, indeed, the problems of co-ordination went much deeper than questions of relative authority. For the REA had not inherited official positions or formal structures which, at the managerial level, would make manifest the general interests of the Corporation, as against the particular interests of departments or branches. As long as its business was neither very extensive nor very complicated, and as long as one underwriting department was clearly dominant, this did not greatly matter. By the inter-war years, however, circumstances had changed sufficiently for the drawbacks to become obvious. In the last resort, the only possible answer was to follow the path already trodden by almost every other major company, and appoint a General Manager to exercise an overall, and integrating, administrative authority. Even when this was done, at the end of the 1920s, it by no means solved the problems of co-ordination. But it at least provided the bases of such a solution.

THE EMERGENCE OF GENERAL MANAGEMENT

As has already been implied, the organizational problems surrounding the relationship between the REA and its subsidiaries, and between Head Office and branches, were partly generated by the Corporation's failure to follow the example of other companies in appointing a General Manager before the First World War. Instead, the obvious need for some new administrative focus had led to the formation of a Management Committee in 1911.[1] But this Committee, which consisted of the three

[1] Above, pp. 370–2.

Governors, although adequate for many aspects of long-term policy-making, was an unsatisfactory instrument for co-ordinating the Corporation's varied activities and departments precisely because it was removed from the tasks of daily management and administration. As a result, and in spite of the active co-operation of the different Managers, the Corporation was handicapped by the unchecked existence of strong and quasi-independent departments throughout the 1920s. And a generation later there were many members of the Corporation who could look back to this period, around the First World War, as one in which the rigidity of departmental division was sharpened by the aristocratic *hauteur* and exclusiveness of the Fire Department—virtually a corporation within the Corporation—which exemplified the tardiness with which the REA had adjusted its organization to the new demands of insurance business in the early twentieth century.

In practice, of course, it was impossible to run the REA without a more explicit provision for departmental co-ordination than was made by the rather high-level Management Committee. Consequently, as we have already seen, from at least the immediate post-war years the Managers of the various departments met together with the Secretary, to discuss matters of mutual interest—in particular, questions concerning the staff and branch organization. In 1922 it was decided to formalize these meetings, and they were arranged on a fixed day every fortnight. In some respects, these official meetings, together with the daily discussions over lunch, filled part of the gap caused by the absence of a General Manager. For example, it was from such meetings in 1923 that there came a proposal to establish a central stationery and printing department (each department had previously dealt with its own supplies), in order to co-ordinate and supervise procedures. More generally, the meetings of officials also gave them the opportunity of bringing into line any Departmental Manager who strayed into unco-operative independence—as happened in 1923 when the Marine Underwriter, Hines, 'said that he could not see that there was much use in his attending' the annual conference of branch managers, 'as he really had nothing to say' to them, and was immediately admonished by the Agency Manager, who pointed out that his refusal to write marine risks (e.g. on china clay at Plymouth) frequently lost the Corporation business in other departments and that the branch managers deserved some explanation.

In spite of all this, however, the fact remained that 'departmentalism' imposed a barrier to really effective co-ordination and to the decisive pursuit of the Corporation's general interest. Indeed, the regular meetings of Managers, precisely because they were an independent forum for discussions between equal and powerful individuals, provided an alternative focus of departmentalism which strengthened the Managers by setting them apart from other committees and giving them a collective vested interest in resisting any encroachment on their authority. Hence the reluctance with which the underwriting Managers accepted equality of status for the Agency Manager in 1922—a reluctance exemplified by the explicit proviso that their supremacy in 'technical' matters should be maintained. Hence, too, in the same year, their complaint that some overseas branch managers when visiting London 'thought they could more easily get their own way by appealing to the Governor direct on various points than by submitting them through the Departmental Managers'. (They requested the Secretary to consult the Governor on this issue.)

But perhaps the most significant example of managerial pride in these post-war years came in 1922 and 1923 as a consequence of the earlier decision to increase the participation of Directors in general management by organizing regular visits and reports on individual branches. In November 1922 E. R. Debenham, a member of the Court, submitted a private and confidential report on expenses to the Governor, based in part on figures which the Governor had instructed the Managers to provide. The Governor circulated the memorandum and recommended the establishment of a Committee of Directors to consider it. Its details have not survived, although it is clear that it recommended changes in accounting procedures which the Departmental Managers were reluctant to accept. But the main point of principle involved was clear enough: in the frank words of the minutes of the Departmental Committee, 'the Managers expressed considerable annoyance that Mr. Debenham had made this report without consultation with them and the matter was discussed at some length. It was eventually decided to ask the Governor to meet the Managers and discuss the whole question of expenses with them before appointing the proposed Committee.' After some months of negotiation the Committee was, in fact, appointed in April 1923, although the Governor was careful to point out to the Court that conditions at the REA 'differed materially from those existing in Mr. Debenham's business', and Hines, the Marine Underwriter, brought the crux of the problem into the open by emphasizing 'that he considered the implied suggestion that the Managers could not look after their own business was a very unfortunate one'. Admittedly, the fact that the whole question of the amount and (departmental) distribution of expenses had been brought into the open did at least have the beneficial effect of stimulating the Managers to discuss

12   Lord Bicester, Governor, 1914–55

the need to reduce costs—and, incidentally, to discover that they needed much more statistical information about branches than they possessed. Yet the controversy also illuminated an attitude which inevitably hampered strong central action: in June 1923, in deciding that it was necessary to reconsider the existing allocation of joint expenses between departments, the Managers also agreed that the matter should *not* be raised at the special Committee of Directors, and then fell in with the Secretary's proposal that if the problem was to be 'satisfactorily' dealt with, 'it would be as well that the matter should not continually be mentioned at the Management Committee [i.e. by individual Managers to the three Governors], as it had been in the past, as this was likely to cause the subject to be taken up at the Directors' Committee'.

Now, the Departmental Managers may well have been right in their implied view that such questions as the control and allocation of expenses were in the first instance matters for management rather than the Court. But there can be no doubt that the issues raised by Debenham (who in January 1923 was also strongly advocating greater co-ordination between the REA and the Car & General in Birmingham)[1] *did* need a single focus of attention—and that, given the vacuum left by the absence of a General Manager, it was inevitable that institutional and even personal relations would come under considerable strain.

In the 1920s those strains were in part alleviated by the personality and influence of the Secretary, Percy F. H. Hodge, who was inescapably pulled into a peace-making and leadership rôle, and of such a senior official as H. E. Nightingale, the Actuary (1893–1922), whose enforced absences because of illness, according to Hodge, deprived the Managers' Lunch Table of a calming influence. 'When you are away', he wrote in 1922, 'things never run as smoothly as when you are here. I do not mean that we have been having "rows", but little incidents seem to occur more frequently.' But Nightingale retired in the same year, and Hodge himself—increasingly overworked, and with neither formal managerial authority nor any direct experience of an underwriting department—could not adequately play the rôle of General Manager. Indeed, by 1928, when he was 59 and somewhat ill, Hodge's own work load was such that it became necessary to appoint a Joint Secretary. This was E. A. de M. Rudolf, than aged 42 and a man whose strength and determination were generally considered as complementary to Hodge's gentleness and tolerance.

In the last resort, however, the problem of ensuring that the Corporation's general interests should take precedence over those of individual

[1] Above, p. 498.

departments could not be solved, or even adequately tackled, by moderate reform. Rather, it became increasingly obvious that the REA would be obliged to reorganize its management hierarchy so as to introduce a General Manager. There was, in fact, no other way of ensuring that the multifarious and interlocking problems of the twentieth-century Corporation were adequately tackled. And in September 1929, no doubt heavily influenced by the acquisition of the Motor Union in 1928, which had added one more dimension to the complexity of corporate management, the Court took the final plunge and appointed Robert Connew as its first General Manager.

Connew—'a strong man' of 'powerful character'[1]—was admirably suited to the demands of the new post. He had extensive experience of overseas business—first as Calcutta Branch Manager for the Imperial Fire Office, next as South Africa Manager for the Alliance, and finally as REA Branch Manager in South Africa from 1911 to 1921. Brought back to London in 1921, he had become Fire Manager the next year, and throughout the 1920s asserted what was clearly a powerful personality to maintain the influence of his Department and earn respect for himself. His surviving letters and memoranda show him as a formidably efficient and dedicated personality, lacking the warmth and human sympathies which characterized the Corporation's Secretary, but able to command willing co-operation as well as eager respect. He was a powerful advocate of strong managerial control, whether within a department (as in 1921, when he exposed a sorry state of affairs in the Fire Department)[2] or in the Group as a whole (as in 1929, before becoming General Manager, when he argued that the only effective way of lowering costs was to merge all subsidiaries under one management and organization).[3] By all accounts Connew was the right man for the new job, and it says much for the changes which time and experience had brought to the REA that in seeking its first General Manager the Corporation should have turned to someone who not only had extensive overseas experience but who was (by traditional standards) a relative 'newcomer' to the Corporation as well as its Head Office.

Unfortunately, however, he was given little opportunity of wielding the new authority which his promotion brought. For in March 1931, after less than twenty months in office, Connew died, at the age of 55. There can be little doubt that his premature death seriously retarded what looked like being the REA's accelerated progress towards really effective managerial reorganization. For Connew's successor was Alexander MacDonald

---

[1] *The Policy Holder*, 14 August 1929, p. 1407.
[2] Above, pp. 458–9.
[3] Above, p. 496.

(Agency Manager, 1919–27; General Manager in Canada, 1928–30; and Joint Secretary 1930–1), and MacDonald, although by no means timid, could not match Connew's self-confident forcefulness or his wide-ranging command of detail. MacDonald was also handicapped by his relative lack of experience in any underwriting department—a drawback which, in contrast with Connew's position, placed him at a disadvantage in dealing with Departmental Managers. Hence, although the assertion of the new, supra-departmental influence of the General Manager continued throughout the 1930s, it seems most probable that, had Connew lived, his particular brand of vigorous self-confidence and expertise would have secured more positive results in terms of both integration and business achievement.

Nevertheless, the fact remains that from 1929 the REA *did* at last have a central and individual point of general management and was therefore able to begin to remedy the various defects which its absence had induced in the first generation of the twentieth century. What is striking, for example, is the extent to which the Committee of Management now tended to be given firm leads by proposals from the General Manager—who also regularly attended the Court and the Treasury Committees, as well as the Departmental Committee in rotation. Far more business relating to underwriting and organization was considered in the context of positive recommendation from Connew and then MacDonald. As a result, the General Manager became not merely the spokesman for the various Managers (representing their interests, both as a group and as individuals at the Court, Management and Treasury Committees) but also the initiator and controller of major aspects of corporate policy. From innumerable instances of the sort of centralizing function which was unknown in the 1920s, we may take the following: in February 1933 the Governors in the Committee of Management considered an official demand to increase the deposit in Hungary and 'decided to leave the matter in his [the General Manager's] hands'; the next year they accepted without question his recommendations for various new appointments in Head Office Departments; in 1935 they agreed to his proposals for mechanizing the Corporation's accounting at a cost of £10,000; and in 1936 approved of his suggestions regarding new salary scales at Head Office and in UK branch offices. Clearly, a novel influence was at work in the REA's decision-making process (however familiar it might have been in that of other companies): there was a single centre of policy formulation and a new, individual focus of administrative authority and responsibility.

As all this shows, the modern rôle of the General Manager's Department began to take shape in the 1930s. Throughout this period the Secretary's

Office was made its adjunct. While Connew was General Manager, the Joint Secretaries worked under his guidance; and when Hodge retired in 1930 he was replaced by MacDonald because the forceful Connew needed to strengthen his Department. ('I propose to do so', he wrote in terms characteristic of the man and his position, 'by appointing you Joint Secretary . . . and this has been agreed to by the Governors.') In 1933, however, when Rudolf retired as 'Manager' and Secretary, MacDonald added the Secretaryship to his General Managership. By that time, however, it was obvious that the pressure of work and the demands of new administrative structures necessitated a further strengthening of the General Manager's Department. From June 1933, therefore, two new posts of Assistant General Manager were created, and filled by A. E. Phelps (who had been a most successful branch manager, first at the Law Courts and then in the West End Branch) and R. E. Oldfield (the Fire Manager). In addition, A. A. G. Ashton was appointed Investment Secretary to assume immediate and specialized control of a task which had been and remained the responsibility of the General Manager.

Thus, by the early 1930s, the REA was very much in the hands of a new management team—a change which was brought about partly because of the implications of managerial reorganization, but principally because of the vicissitudes of personal careers. One by one the men who had guided the Corporation in the 1920s gave way to a new generation: Hines, the Marine Underwriter, retired in 1928; Hodge retired in 1931; Connew died in 1931; Rudolf retired in 1933; and Wamsley retired in 1934. In most instances their successors at the REA had similar backgrounds and training. In one case, however, that of A. E. Phelps (Manager from 1931 and Assistant General Manager from 1933), there was a significant departure— for Mr Phelps was the first Manager to be promoted from branch work, which was in some ways more competitive and more demanding than work at Head Office.

Helped by new influences such as these, as well as by new structures, general management was an increasingly important force in the 1930s. The traditional authority and independence of Departments was slowly eroded; central services (e.g. the purchase of stationery, cleaning, heating and lighting) were streamlined and their costs reduced; the General Manager's Department began to play a dominant part in the crucial task of appointing branch managers and departmental officials; and there was the beginning of an emphasis on the need to reconcile the interests of different Departments and to appraise particular branches or accounts or areas by an examination of their *overall* performance.

But if this was the beginning of a process, its end did not come until well after the Second World War. Indeed, as already mentioned, by modern standards the General Manager's authority was circumscribed in the 1930s. This was to some extent the case with respect to Home branches and Departments; but it was particularly so with respect to subsidiary companies and to the REA's overseas business. In the latter case problems of communication and the lack of any sustained overseas experience by MacDonald left a good deal of independence with the individual branches, and hardly disturbed their conventional links with individual Head Office Departments.

Whatever the exact achievements of the REA's General Manager in the 1930s, the events of the inter-war period re-emphasized the significance of professional management and administration. Yet it should not be forgotten that the basic structure of the Corporation remained unchanged. Final authority continued to rest with the Court and the Governors—and, in particular, with the Committee of Management, which had been created in 1911 precisely in order to provide a single focus of the Corporation's general interest. The fact that so many of the problems of co-ordination and control had to be answered at the level of professional managers should not be allowed to obscure the fact that the members of the Court continued to play a powerful rôle in the history of the REA.

This was especially true of the Governor himself throughout the period. Vivian Hugh Smith, who was elevated to the Peerage as Lord Bicester in 1938, combined considerable prestige in the REA and in the City (he was Chairman of Morgan Grenfell) with an exceptionally long tenure of office. He was Governor of the REA from 1914 to 1955, and this, in itself, enhanced the authority that he was able to exercise. His presence over four decades, together with his dedication to the Corporation, introduced a continuity which no management structure could have done. Lord Bicester, according to one of his officials, 'saw himself as the embodiment of the REA', and, as a result, his involvement in major policy decisions and the overall direction of the Corporation was the more intimate. The self-conscious community ethos which continued to characterize the Corporation found a continuing expression in the Governor's paternalistic rôle as head of the society which was the REA. And individual managers, over all these years, were successful in measure as they earned his trust and confidence. On balance, there can be little doubt about Lord Bicester's influence or its longevity. Yet even so, in the last resort, it could not be a substitute for a more vigorous and powerful concentration of management authority. And for that, the Corporation had to wait until the post-war years.

22

The Royal Exchange Assurance since 1939

Since the outbreak of War in 1939 the world has undergone economic and social changes of a type and extent which were bound to affect insurance companies in radical, if not always entirely new, ways. Internationally, quite apart from the hazards and uncertainties involved in the War itself, the last generation has witnessed extraordinarily far-reaching changes in political and economic systems; and these have been of the most direct relevance to businesses engaged in the provision of services on a world-wide basis. Related to this, the rise of independent states in the formerly dependent territories of Africa and Asia, and the translation of nationalism into economic terms, have brought new pressures to bear on expatriate businesses such as insurance offices. On the other hand, both at home and abroad sustained economic development (as well as sustained inflation) has enormously increased the demand for insurance services—because of the growth in the value of capital, stocks and domestic possessions needing to be insured against fire; because of the striking and prolonged boom in motor car ownership; and because of trends in personal income and se-curity-consciousness which have made individual and group life insurance schemes even more attractive. Beyond these developments, which were in some respects no more than the acceleration of long-run trends, the more dramatic aspects of technical and economic innovation—the jet airplane, the nuclear power station—have presented insurance companies with problems of risk and capacity which, while reminiscent of the situation at earlier states of industrialization, were in their most important aspects completely new.

British insurance companies naturally responded to these changes, and to the associated shifts in competitive pressures, costs and profits, in dif-ferent ways. Nevertheless, by the 1960s (although it had taken a decade or more to manifest itself) the dominant trend was clear. Large as the principal offices were immediately after the War, they had to grow even larger if they were to operate at economical cost levels and to encompass the variety and amount of insurance necessary to provide an adequate service. After a generation's lag, therefore, the merger movement recommenced, and since 1959 the giant composite offices have become even bigger. Yet the 1960s has not been merely a decade of heightened industrial concentration. In addition, and to an unprecedented extent, that concentration has been accompanied by genuine organizational change. The search for lower costs and more effective business-gathering has led to a more purposeful grouping of the activities of affiliated companies and to a combination of the devolution of some Head Office functions to regional offices and the central provision of new services, such as those of the computer, as well as more traditional ones.

All these pressures and structural changes were reflected, albeit to varying extents, in the Royal Exchange Assurance. Its community and its business were comparably affected by the Second World War; the pattern of its income shifted in response to post-war economic and social trends at home and abroad; it had to adapt its outlook and structure to cater for new insurance needs; and, perhaps most significant of all in the long run, the same pressures which had induced a renewed merger movement in the industry at large led, at the Royal Exchange, first to the acquisition of the Atlas Assurance Company (in 1959) and a genuine grouping of the activities of the REA and its various subsidiaries, and then to a merger with the Guardian Assurance Company (in 1968), which, unlike previous acquisitions, brought about a decisive transformation of the REA's corporate status. The importance of this move was, indeed, a measure of the significance of recent events in the insurance industry. For the Royal Exchange they marked the completion of an epoch in which the Corporation had relied upon its own resources of growth. Henceforth, with the opening of a new phase in its history, the bases and patterns of development were bound to be different in many fundamental ways from what they had been in the past.

WAR, 1939–45

In June 1939 members of the Royal Exchange Assurance had ceremoniously opened the East Molesey Sports Ground, acquired and constructed by the Corporation in the last two years of peace. Three months later the sports facilities were closed at the outbreak of hostilities with Germany. And the abrupt closing was symbolic of the fact that in many ways, as far as insurance offices in general were concerned, the drama of the Second World War was felt perhaps more keenly at the personal and community level than at the level of business endeavour. With respect to much underwriting activity, the need to economize on scarce human resources, and to satisfy basic needs of the public with the least bother, led to the acceptance of nation-wide agreements and schemes which diminished competition and introduced much routine into the operations of insurance companies. The war-time lives of their employees, on the other hand, were characterized by anything but routine. By 1943, for example, 465 (some 55 per cent) of the 839 male staff members employed by the REA in the United Kingdom in 1939 had joined the armed services. (A fairly large number of the 346 female employees had also gone into some form of war service.) The posts vacated were filled by women and older men and in some ways the labour shortage seems to have been less acute than during the First World War. Yet there remained the problem of the critical shortage of trained personnel for key positions and, as happened twenty-five years earlier, the inevitable result was that those who remained had to work at an extremely high pitch of intensity. In addition to this factor, the war-time staff had to put up with a considerable amount of physical inconvenience unknown in the calmer domestic circumstances of the First World War.

Most of this inconvenience was caused by the realization that London was bound to be a major target for air attacks. Knowing this, at the time of the Munich Crisis in September 1938 the Committee of Management was laying plans for the safety of the staff and the protection of the Corporation's records in the event of war. And in April of 1939 the Committee arranged for the vaults of the Royal Exchange to be protected against bomb blast and poison gas by the installation of girders, bulkheads, facilities for routine office work, and an emergency ventilation system. For many Departments, however, evacuation was obviously the best answer to the risk of air-raids. Indeed, even before the outbreak of hostilities the Corporation had acquired Chesterton Lodge, in Oxfordshire, as a possible site for part of its operations. When War broke out the Overseas and Trustee and Executor Departments were already there; in September 1939 the Home Fire and Accident Departments were moved to East Molesey, where the sports facilities were turned to more commercial use; and the Life and Mechanization Departments went to Welwyn Garden City in August 1939. While some of the staff set up home in, or were recruited from, the new localities, others began the strange routine of being resident near their work during week-days and returning home only at the week-ends. Meanwhile, the General Manager's and Secretary's Departments, together with the Investment Section, stayed at Head Office—where, too, the Court continued to meet throughout the War, its traditional routine varied only by the absence of many of its members on war service and the presence of waitresses rather than waiters at its weekly lunch.

13   The REA Accident Department evacuated to East Molesey

14 Bomb damage, 11 January 1941 *H. S. Merritt*

Although the War was costly in terms of the lives of those REA men in the forces (fifty-two were killed) and involved considerable change in the pattern of everyday life of those who remained with the Corporation, there was, in fact, little direct disturbance to the REA and its staff by virtue of enemy action. The nearest the building itself came to being damaged was on the night of 11 January 1941, when a bomb hit Bank Underground Station, killing eighty people sheltering there.

If the War introduced sweeping changes into the lives of the men and women who worked for the Royal Exchange Assurance, it also changed the Corporation's business—albeit not always in equally dramatic ways. Admittedly, as with all businesses operating on a genuinely international scale, the REA found that its network of activity was seriously disturbed by the world-wide spread of hostilities and the extent of enemy occupation. Important branch offices—in Paris and Singapore, for example—obviously had to be closed down: others had their activities seriously impaired; and communication was slow and difficult. Yet the actual amount of overseas business increased. Thus, comparing 1944 and 1939, although there was a slight decline in foreign accident income (largely attributable to the world-wide shortage of petrol and new motor cars which curtailed the demand for motor insurance), the REA's overseas fire premiums grew in a heartening fashion: from some £980,000 to almost £1·25 million. Much of this increase came from North America: US fire insurance premiums, which were barely £400,000 in 1939, had risen to £550,000 by 1944 under the influence of war-time boom conditions. But the increase in fire business in other parts of the world (from £578,000 to some £700,000) was in its way an even more important achievement in the face of world-wide insecurity. And in the depths of the War, in April 1943, the Governor was able to report to the Annual General Court that the Corporation's 'excellent' fire business was holding its own extremely well overseas.

As far as marine and home insurance were concerned, the problems of war risks were alleviated by the systematic, if belated, efforts of the Government. As early as 1937, appreciating the enormous destructive potential of modern warfare, the offices belonging to the British Insurance Association had agreed to exclude all non-life war risks on land from their policies. And a mere month before the outbreak of War, on 4 August 1939, Parliament filled part of the gap by passing the War Risks Insurance Act, which applied to stocks of commodities in the UK and to ships and their cargoes. With respect to the former, the Board of Trade was given a monopoly of insurance against war risks although, as a matter of convenience and efficiency, the fire offices were employed as its agents. With respect to marine insurance, the Board of Trade opened a War Risks Insurance Office. However, in contrast to the First World War, steps were taken to prevent the insurance companies creaming the market and leaving bad risks to the State:[1] on voyages to and from the United Kingdom, the companies agreed not to quote rates which were less than those of the Government (although they were allowed to quote whatever rates they liked on voyages between countries overseas). In December 1939 the Government agreed to pay compensation for war damage to private property at the conclusion of hostilities. And in 1941 the main outlines of the Government's provision for insurance were completed by the War Damage Act, which provided for the insurance of buildings, business plant and equipment, and private chattels—compulsory in the case of buildings, voluntary in the case of all other risks. Once again, the insurance companies were to act as agents. Altogether they issued 18 million policies and collected £300 million in premiums on behalf of the Government under the war-damage insurance schemes. (As far as goods in its own possession were concerned, the Government agreed to insure them with the companies and Lloyd's by a pooling arrangement with predetermined quotas.)

As with the other insurance companies, the REA naturally participated in those various arrangements, notably as an agent for the Board of Trade for the war-risk commodity insurance scheme and for the insurance of the contents of business premises and private dwellings. In addition, the Corporation provided members of the local Technical Committees, established to improve methods of fire prevention; of the Committees created to help the Ministry of Food salvage food and animal feedstuffs; and of the Board of Trade Committees which helped settle claims under the War Risks Insurance Act of 1939.

As far as its conventional home business was concerned, there was one area in which the War had a substantial and direct effect on the REA. As private cars were taken off the road because of the non-availability of petrol supplies, so its motor insurance premiums shrank. The decline was mitigated by the fact that car-owners continued to insure their (garaged) vehicles against fire and theft, by the retention of a good share of the insurance of commercial road transport, and by the increase in the number of public-service vehicles—notably of the National Fire Service and Civil Defence. In spite of this, however, REA motor premiums fell from £575,000 in 1939 to £430,000 in 1944 (they stood at £382,000 in 1943), while the combined accident income of the Car & General and the Motor Union fell from some £3·1 million in 1938 to £2·2 million in 1944. On the

---

[1] Above, pp. 419–20.

other hand, increased business in the other branches of accident underwriting (notably employer's liability, which, under the influence of war-
time full employment rose from an income of £155,000 in 1939 to £229,000
in 1944), almost made up for this decrease. The Corporation's general
accident premiums fell by only 4 per cent between 1939 and 1944.

The Corporation's marine insurance, although it derived considerable
benefit in terms of *profitable* income, did not experience anything like the
remunerative expansion of the 1914–18 War—in part, perhaps, because
the official arrangements were less favourable to the private companies.
Even so, however, strengthened by the reorganization of the Marine
Department which had taken place in 1938, the Corporation's net premium
income increased from just under £400,000 in 1939 to £813,000 in 1942,
before falling back to some £514,000 in 1944. Although these levels were
generally lower than those obtaining in the 1930s, the important contrast
was in the level of the underwriting surplus, which had been negligible or
negative in the years immediately before the War, but averaged some
£208,000 in the years 1940–4.

The REA's life business, by contrast, was relatively quiescent throughout this period. New sums assured, for example, fell consistently below
the level of 1939 (£2,965,000) as war-time insecurity, together with the
inter-company agreement to cease canvassing for business, reduced the
effective demand for life insurance. (The overall level of new sums assured
within the UK by British offices stagnated during the War: it fell from
£288 million in 1938 and £170 million in 1939 to £110 million in 1940, and
had only recovered to £150 million in 1944.) In common with other leading
companies, the REA included the risk of death by enemy action within the
UK at the normal premium rate for approved civilian lives.

The Corporation's home fire insurance business was consistently
favourable during the War. Rising prices and levels of economic activity
helped increase premiums, from some £460,000 in 1939 to £700,000 in
1944. Meanwhile, with war risks excluded, low loss ratios substantially increased profits: even after expenses had been taken into account, the surplus on home business rose from about £90,000 annually in the late 1930s
to an average of £172,000 in 1941–4.

In terms of its overall underwriting, therefore, the REA had come
through the War, not merely unscathed but with its business and financial
position considerably strengthened. Between 1938 and 1944, for example,
the Corporation's aggregate premium income rose from £4·8 million to
£5·1 million—and, as has been seen, war-time underwriting tended to be
distinctly more remunerative than that of the 1930s. At the same time, the

activities of its subsidiaries were also more profitable. In their case, it is true, aggregate income fell slightly: from £4,954,000 in 1938 to £4,839,000 in 1944. But this was largely a reflection of the dependence of the Car & General and the Motor Union on motor insurance (the State and the British Equitable, by contrast, increased their aggregate premium income from £907,000 to £1,386,000). And even in the case of these two companies the outlook was far from discouraging. At the General Court in April 1943, for example, the Governor pointed out that the Car & General and the Motor Union, after years of husbanding their resources and ploughing back profits, were now paying large dividends to the parent Corporation: in 1942 their combined premium income had been over £3 million, and their underwriting profit in excess of £300,000.

As had happened a generation earlier, the War affected not only the underwriting business of insurance companies but also (and from some viewpoints to a greater extent) their investment pattern. In particular, the structure of capital markets and the pressures of national finance provoked an enormous flow of funds into British Government securities: as a proportion of British insurance companies' assets they rose from some 21 per cent in 1937 to 36 per cent in 1946 (given the increase in assets, this reflected a growth from some £370 million to £1,010 million).[1] The REA, which in 1939 had had just under 14 per cent of its Life Fund invested in British Government securities, had increased this to 38 per cent by 1946: at the 1943 General Court the Governor pointed out that all 'new money' since the outbreak of War had, in fact, gone into British Government loans. One important consequence of this trend was that it accentuated the fall in investment yields which had already been a marked feature of the 1930s. For war finance between 1939 and 1945 was based upon 'cheap money': Government loans were not issued above 3 per cent, and sometimes at lower interest rates. As a result, the gross yield of the REA's Life Funds, which had already fallen from £4. 16s. per cent in 1937 to £4. 12s. 3d. in 1939, tumbled even further, to £4. 4s. 8d. in 1942 and £4. 2s. 6d. in 1944. These figures were not yet a serious threat to life offices, although, by reducing surpluses and bonuses, they diminished the attractiveness of with-profits policies. Partly, no doubt, because it was assumed that they were associated with the War and that the War would not last for ever, they did not give grounds for the sort of anxieties which had been provoked by declining yields in the 1890s. Nevertheless, they provided one more reason for looking forward to the end of hostilities and for anticipating, as the Governor did when addressing the Annual General Court in

[1] Clayton and Osborn, *Insurance Company Investment*, p. 254.

April 1944, that the Corporation's freedom of action as a financial institution would be restored with the longed-for peace.

BUSINESS TRENDS IN THE POST-WAR WORLD

In the years immediately after the War, although it was some time before the financial environment returned to normal, the Royal Exchange Assurance was certainly able to continue and enhance the expansion of its underwriting business.

The most spectacular aspect of post-war revival in underwriting trends was, of course, the motor insurance branch, since this had been the department most constrained by war-time shortages and was the most immediately affected by the renewed vigour of economic growth and the advent of relative prosperity: the number of vehicles (other than motor cycles and agricultural tractors) on the roads in the UK jumped from 1·4 million in 1944 to 3·4 million in 1950, and 12·6 million in 1968. For British offices as a whole motor premiums, for home and overseas business, rose from £34 million in 1945 to £155 million in 1953, and reached £391 million in 1963. In the same years the motor premium income of the REA Group increased from £2·8 million to £10·2 million and £23·8 million— although the last figure includes £3·8 million earned by the Atlas and its associated companies, which had been acquired in 1959. Initially, until the motor car industry was able to increase the supply of vehicles sufficiently to meet the voracious domestic demand, the perennial problem of motor insurance—the pressure of rising repair costs—was exacerbated by the relatively large number of old (not to say ancient) cars on the road, the consequent greater vulnerability to costly damage and the difficulty and expense of obtaining spare parts. On the other hand, the severe problem of road accidents did not abate even when new cars came on to the road: by the early 1950s some 5,000 people were killed and 200,000 injured annually in traffic accidents in the UK. The frequency and costs of accidents were constant threats to the profitability of motor insurance. As a result, although motor business continued to grow at a spectacular rate (from 1959 its premium income exceeded that of fire business), it was a class of underwriting which gave constant cause for anxiety.

Quite apart from the very rapid growth of motor insurance, general-accident business in the post-war years went from strength to strength. Even in the case of employers' liability insurance, which was at first severely curtailed by the National Insurance (Industrial Injuries) Act of 1946, which from 1948 eliminated the employer's statutory liability, there was a subsequent boom as employers learned, and were taught, to insure against their remaining common-law liability. In the case of the REA, for example (figures for its subsidiaries are not available), employers' liability income from UK business, which had fallen from £283,000 in 1947 to £126,000 in 1949, had risen to £345,000 by 1957. (Employers' liability business overseas also rose after the War: from £208,000 in 1946 to £709,000 in 1958.) More generally, other types of accident insurance— personal accident and travel, burglary, public liability, fidelity guarantee —had all benefited from the full employment, economic growth, inflation and security-consciousness of the post-war world. Between 1948 and 1958, for example, the non-motor accident business of all British offices, having almost doubled in the four years after 1944, doubled again—from just under £100 million to some £210 million. The REA shared in this expansion: non-motor accident premium between 1944 and 1958 rose from some £1·5 million to over £5 million. Much of this business has been based upon the spread of an existing form of insurance until it is adopted by large numbers of individuals—e.g. personal accident or travel insurance

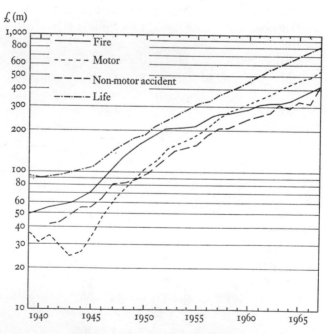

Fig. 22.1: British offices: net premium income, 1939–67

(Sources: *Insurance Directory and Year Book*, various issues; *Post Magazine*, various issues; Life Offices Association.)

or public liability. In part, however, it has also been a response to new areas of insurance, as with the world-wide application of Contractors' All Risks policies to vast undertakings such as the erection of dams and nuclear power stations—where the contracts are reckoned in terms of millions of pounds, and can only be covered by being spread around the insurance market.

The fire insurance business of the REA was affected by the same forces of economic growth and inflation which had shaped the expansion of general accident business. Indeed, given the growth in popularity of householders' comprehensive policies (handled by the Fire Department) much of what was accounted for as fire business was, in fact, insurance against non-fire risks such as frost, storms, flooding and the like. In 1954, for example, claims paid under householders' comprehensive policies as a result of damage by burst pipes, storms and flooding exceeded those resulting from fire damage under the same policies. Overall, the Fire Department's income grew in a most satisfactory way: between 1944 and 1963 the REA's income rose from some £1·2 million to £7·5 million—while the figures for the original Group as a whole were £2·7 million and £11·1 million (the Atlas Companies brought in a further £5·9 million at the

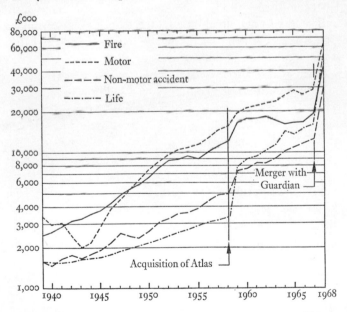

Fig. 22.2: REA Group: net premium income, 1939–68

(Source: REA Archives.)

latter date). These figures compare with an increase in fire premiums from some £65·1 million to £314·6 million for all British offices in the period 1944–63. By the early 1960s, however, it was obvious that two relatively new trends were affecting the security of fire underwriting as far as the offices were concerned.[1]

One has already been mentioned: the growing popularity of insurance against the direct and indirect consequences of storms, frost, floods and other natural disasters. Insurance against 'weather perils', although it had existed—largely as 'accommodation business'—in the inter-war period, was properly established only in the post-1945 years. In the event, in part, perhaps, because of the increased rôle of insurance (and therefore the need to gather statistics), but also because the British climate was at times unusually severe, there has seemed to be almost unprecedented damage in the post-war years. In August 1952, for example, a cloudburst following prolonged rain in North Devon produced a flood disaster which cost thirty-three lives and some £500,000 in property damage—which the insurance companies treated as storm or tempest damage. (In the immediate post-war period cover against flooding was frequently excluded from policies.) In 1953 the great sea floods on the East Coast killed over 300 people and caused between £30 million and £50 million of damage, although the offices refused liability if flood was an excluded peril. Occasional tornadoes and whirlwinds hit parts of Britain throughout the 1950s. Frost and storms early in 1956 did about £5 million of damage. (The REA found that frost-damage claims exceeded fire claims under householders' comprehensive policies.) In 1960 extensive flooding caused millions of pounds of damage in the West Country and South Wales—and in the same year, in response to public demand and official pressure, insurers agreed to make flood cover more freely available. The winters of 1961–2 and 1962–3 were especially severe, with frost, gales and snowstorms. In 1962–3 claims of some £20 million were paid by virtue of the effects of the coldest winter since 1740 and the heaviest snowfall for 150 years. In general, as the REA Home Fire Manager warned, having virtually overcome the hazard of a massive conflagration by new procedures and limits, the offices faced an almost equivalent danger in the case of storm, tempest and flood, as in 1953, 1960, 1962 and 1963: 'It takes a lot of premium to make up for such losses.'[2]

The second new trend in fire underwriting, which manifested itself

---

[1] For some aspects of post-war development, see two articles by A. R. Doublet (Home Fire Manager of the REA Group until his retirement in 1968): 'Storm, tempest and flood', *JCII*, LXIII (1966), 17–30; 'Current trends in the fire department', *JCII*, LXIV (1967), 17–26.

[2] Doublet 'Storm, tempest and flood', *JCII* (1966), p. 29.

abruptly at the end of the 1950s, was a substantial increase in the annual value of property destroyed by fire in the UK. Thus, whereas 'fire wastage' had varied between £24 million and £28 million for several years before 1959, in that year it rose to £44 million (the previous record was just under £28 million in 1955)—and by the mid-1960s was averaging £77 million. (By the late 1960s it had touched £100 million.) There is no satisfactory explanation for the abruptness of this increase. But, in looking at the problem in a long-term context, it is clear that various factors were responsible for the rise, in addition to the obvious influence of sustained inflation. An increase in the amount of arson, and an apparent increase in carelessness by employees and householders (smokers and children playing with matches are notorious causes of fires) no doubt reflected important but obscure changes in social outlook and social behaviour. In addition, however, there were more prosaic causes involved in the nature of industrial development: the increased use of electrical equipment in business and private premises; the more extensive use of cardboard and plastic in packing and the proliferation of new industrial materials; greater sophistication of industrial processes involving the concentration of complicated and valuable equipment and the handling and transport of expensive products; and, of particular importance, a rapid growth of 'un-divided risks' in the form of giant factories and warehouses in which the demands of modern industrial and handling techniques necessitated huge, 'open-plan' production lines and floor areas. These last allowed fire to sweep through extensive areas unhampered by traditional dividing walls or fire breaks. Again and again in the late 1950s and early 1960s the REA Governor warned of the dangers inherent in such large concentrations of machines and stocks—moved by the knowledge that a small number of very large fires was responsible for much fire damage (three fires caused 20 per cent of the wastage in 1959, and in 1965 less than 1 per cent of all fires accounted for over 60 per cent of losses in the UK). As we shall see, coming as they did after a period of downward pressure on premium rates, these developments severely aggravated the situation with respect to the profitability of fire underwriting.[1]

The oldest form of insurance, marine underwriting, has in the post-war years continued along its own distinctive path. Still an important aspect of the business of the REA and other leading composite groups, marine business has shared in the economic growth of the last generation. Between 1945 and 1963 the premium income of British companies rose from £23 million to £95 million, while the REA's premiums grew from

[1] Below, p. 530.

£450,000 to £1·2 million (£1·0 million to £3·1 million in the case of the Group as a whole).[1] As an adjunct to marine insurance in the sense that it provided cover for hulls and cargo, aviation insurance was rapidly becoming an important section of the market. The REA had been connected with other companies as a shareholder in the Aviation & General Insurance Company since 1935. After the War, however, it became increasingly clear that the growth of civil aviation had created an entirely new outlook for this form of underwriting. In 1946 the Governor had emphasized its business prospects in the first post-war General Court, although for some years the Corporation confined its commitment to the insurance of passengers. In 1959, however, the decision was taken to have a direct stake in every aspect of the aviation market, and a new Department was opened in 1960 under the management of Mr C. F. R. Ward, formerly an underwriter at Lloyd's. The subsequent growth and profitability of aviation business fully justified the decision.

While accident, fire and marine underwriting each provided an index of post-war prosperity, the growth of life business is perhaps the best example of the response of insurance to the advent of relative affluence and inflation. This was reflected in the renewed tendency for the public to save an increasing proportion of rising incomes by taking out life policies: between 1946 and 1960, for example, ordinary life premiums as a percentage of total personal income in the UK rose from 1·54 (it had been 2·02 in 1938) to 2·52.[2] Given this boom, in the eight years after the War ordinary premium income grew at the spectacular rate of 10·4 per cent, compared with 4·4 per cent in the inter-war period and 3·4 per cent in the years before 1914.[3] And the high rate continued: between 1953 and 1967 the annual growth rate of ordinary premiums was some 9·7 per cent. Sums assured by ordinary policies grew from £2,590 million in 1945 to £12,867 million in 1962 and £16,100 million in 1966. In the first five years of the 1960s alone the annual level of new sums assured more than doubled. Moreover, these figures refer merely to business *excluding* pension and life schemes—whereas the sustained post-war boom in British life insurance has been based not only on a very substantial growth of individual policies but also on a spectacular increase in pension and group plans. Between 1951 and 1955, for example, 'schemes business' rose from less than one-third to two-fifths of total premiums, while by 1965, although

---

[1] Lloyd's marine premiums grew from £25 million to £89 million in the same period.

[2] Clayton and Osborn, *Insurance Company Investment*, p. 255. *Total* life premiums (i.e. including industrial assurance) rose from 2·72 per cent to 3·45 per cent.

[3] Murphy and Johnston, 'The Growth of Life Assurance', *Transactions of the Manchester Statistical Society, 1956–57*, p. 9.

the percentage had only increased slightly, the number of UK policy-holders stood at 5 million and the annual premium income at £317 million.[1]

At the REA the distinctive characteristics of life underwriting were well appreciated. Quite apart from the post-war changes in the level and distribution of income, and the increase in prices, which were natural stimulants to this form of thrift, the income-tax advantages were a powerful lever to increased sales (and one which grew even more powerful with the steep rise in income-tax rates). In line with modern trends the REA has devoted special attention to the family-income benefits and decreasing temporary or term assurances, which have been particularly stimulated by the income-tax situation, and by the reduction in premiums following the continuous fall in mortality at younger and middle ages. Lower premiums and an increased awareness of the value of inexpensive life cover led to a vast increase in non-profit term assurances: at the REA they grew from a negligible amount in 1948 to over one-third of total sums assured in 1963. Associated with this development has been an increasing emphasis on group pension business and the self-employed pension business (which was given very considerable tax advantages by financial legislation in 1956). In general throughout the post-war period it has been obvious that no other form of insurance was quite as easy to sell to potential policy-holders as life insurance. Between 1945 and 1967 the REA's life premium income rose from £1·5 million to £5·5 million; and its sums assured from £44·9 million to £236·8 million. By the 1960s, of course, the Atlas has also to be taken into account: between 1958 and 1967 its life premiums rose from £2·4 million to £5·5 million and its sums assured from £75·2 million to £231·2 million.[2] These achievements, associated as they were with increasingly profitable investment conditions in the later part of the period,[3] brought good profits to proprietors and policyholders alike. Thus, the proprietors' 10 per cent share of life profits realized £500,000 for the REA for the triennium 1964–6 (it had been as low as £91,000 in 1946–8), and £469,000 for the Atlas in 1965–7. Bonus rates also rose: the REA's bonus, for example, increased from 20s. in 1945 to 42s. in 1954 and 65s. in 1966.

In general, by the late 1950s and 1960s the higher bonuses derived from

---

[1] Murphy and Johnston, 'The Growth of Life Assurance', *Transactions of the Manchester Statistical Society, 1956–57*, p. 25; Life Offices' Association, *Life Assurance in the United Kingdom* (1967), p. 12.

[2] The British Equitable also transacted life business until 1948. By 1967 sums assured by outstanding policies had declined to £2 million.

[3] Below, pp. 526–8.

the new profitability of investment activity meant that policyholders as well as offices were concentrating on the investment aspects of life insurance, particularly in the context of the rising prices of equities. Indeed, by the late 1960s a small but growing number of offices were experimenting with life policies whose value was explicitly linked to that of equities, through unit trust funds. This was an obvious response to the manifest pressures of rising prices, a booming stock market and new consumer attitudes. In addition, however, it was stimulated by the mechanism of competitive innovation, for the decade of the 1960s had seen a spectacular increase in the unit trust movement, and the unit trusts themselves had begun, most successfully, to innovate by the issue of life policies linked to their units in schemes for regular savings. Some of the established life offices had responded first by associating themselves with similar schemes, and then by combining the equity element with traditional endowment policies. At the end of the decade it was not yet clear how far this new fashion would carry the life industry as a whole (many offices, including the REA,[1] had not yet joined), or whether it would be justified by trends in the value of equity capital. But it had already demonstrated two important lessons: first, that life policyholders and companies alike had become dominantly concerned with investment in the context of apparent long-run inflation; second, that the forces of competition and emulation were still strong enough to give a new shape and direction to the industry. And, novel as their manifestation was, they were lessons which were logical continuations of the previous 200 years of life insurance history.

When we turn to the post-war investment activities of insurance companies we find that they exemplified a pattern which was in many ways inverse to that illustrated by their underwriting activity. In the immediate post-war years, for example, when underwriting business was booming, the continuation of low interest rates combined with the insecurities of the capital market to keep the return on investment (measured either in terms of yield or appreciating values) very low. From the late 1950s, however, when competitive pressure was producing severe problems in underwriting, yields and the value of ordinary shares both rose. In the case of the REA Life Fund, for example, the yield, which had averaged £4. 4s. 7d. in 1941–5 dropped to £4. 3s. 11d. in 1946–50 and had only risen to £5. 0s. 11d. in 1951–5. Yet by the late 1950s it was £6. 1s. 11d., while in 1961–5 it stood at £7. 1s. 1d. At the same time (although the increase in interest rates was associated with a decline in the price of Government

---

[1] The Guardian, however, had begun to issue 'Guardhill Trust Units' in association with life insurance protection.

securities) the value of ordinary shares rose much more sharply from the late 1950s: in 1952 their average price was no higher than it had been in 1945 (although there had been some increase in the intermediate years); between 1953 and 1960, however, share values increased almost threefold, and more than doubled again in the next eight years.

Associated with these trends—as also with the trends in general prices —has been an acceleration of the evolution of the insurance companies' own investment portfolios towards holding more ordinary shares and property (although conventional types of mortgage loans also increased in the 1950s). Initially, the war-time structure of investment persisted: British Government securities were some 40 per cent of total British companies' assets in 1946 (the figure had been just over 20 per cent in the late 1930s) and had only dropped to 32 per cent by 1951. Ten years later, however, the percentage had fallen to about 18, while ordinary shares, which had averaged less than 10 per cent of total assets in the late 1940s, rose in importance (particularly in the late 1950s) until, by the early 1960s, they accounted for about 22 per cent of all investments. Meanwhile, real property and similar investments, which had averaged barely 5 per cent of investments in the late 1940s, had risen to just over 8 per cent in the late 1950s and 10 per cent in the early 1960s.[1]

The revival of a more adventurous investment policy by insurance companies in the late 1950s and 1960s was obviously related to an improvement in investment conditions and to an appreciation of the long-term character of inflation. The policy was exemplified in an unprecedented increase in the proportion of assets with market values liable to fairly large fluctuations and in a more active approach to investment. This was demonstrated not merely by the growth of direct equity investment, but by the proliferation of links with property developers in the late 1950s. At that time the insurance companies lent huge amounts of money for development (in return for a fixed-interest income and a share of equity capital in the property companies) or purchased property subject to development and leased it back to the developers.[2] The partnerships were unusual as well as profitable combinations of financial sobriety and entrepreneurial verve, although at times some aspects of them were frowned upon by the Treasury, which was anxious to see investment funds directed into what they regarded as more productive uses.

---

[1] Clayton and Osborn, *Insurance Company Investment*, p. 254; British Insurance Association, *Insurance Facts and Figures*. Also see *Report of Committee on the working of the Monetary System*, 1959, Command 827, paragraphs 235–51.

[2] Clayton and Osborn, *Insurance Company Investment*, pp. 179–82.

The Royal Exchange Group reflected the broad pattern of changes in investments which were exemplified by the industry as a whole. Between 1946 and 1968, for example, when its total investments grew from some £16 million to £68 million, the proportion accounted for by British Government securities fell from 41 per cent to 8 per cent. In the same period ordinary shares rose from 6 per cent to 35 per cent (or from barely £1 million to £23·5 million). On the other hand, the Group did not participate as extensively as other companies in the boom in property investment. Even so, it did begin to make some extensive purchases in the late 1950s, and by 1968 had almost 5 per cent of its investments in free-hold property. As part of the new policy, the Group began to build new office blocks at home and overseas, which could be used for its own business purposes as well as to generate rental incomes. In the 1960s it provided custom-built accommodation for its main area offices in the UK as well as its overseas operations in Australia, New Zealand, West Africa and elsewhere.

As with policyholders investments in with-profits contracts, so with the insurance companies' own investments: recent trends are an extension and intensification of familiar historical factors. In particular, the changes in structure and outlook which have characterized the distribution of insurance assets reflected a heightening of the offices' traditionally important rôle in capital markets. The total (life and non-life) investments of British companies, which were some £1,750 million before the Second World War and £2,500 million at its end, exceeded £5,000 million by the late 1950s and £11,000 million ten years later. More or less doubling every decade, the funds of British offices were of critical significance: by the early 1960s they were disposing of over £600 million of 'new money' annually.

COMPETITION AND MERGERS

In the immediate post-war years the Royal Exchange Assurance, together with other British insurance offices, encountered relatively few problems in its underwriting business. Motor insurance, as has been mentioned, ran into some difficulties because of the shortage of new cars and spare parts, and its long history of the rising costs of claims continued. And in 1947 the Fire Department made a small loss—the first since the San Francisco fire in 1906. Yet in general, business boomed and profits held up well as the British and world-wide demand for insurance grew in the years of peace. Symptomatic of the new confidence was the increase in the Corporation's dividend in 1946 (the first time in eleven years that it *had* been raised) from 30 per cent to 32½ per cent. In the inter-war years, as the proprietors were told at the Annual General Court in May 1946, the business had been consolidated by 'the prosaic process of ploughing back the profits'. Some of the harvest could now be reaped, And in that first year of peace, although the American experience was unhappy, the Corporation's own fire premiums exceeded £2 million for the first time, its accident income exceeded £1·5 million, and the Car & General and Motor and Union each earned premiums in excess of £2 million. Two years later, the Corporation's Fire and Accident Departments each made profits of some £230,000—on premium incomes of £2.9 million and £2 million, respectively—while, as the Governor pointed out with some satisfaction, the Group as a whole was over £600,000 richer as a result of business in 1948. In 1949 fire premiums had leaped to £3.5 million and profits to £480,000; Group income had risen by about 10 per cent in the year, to £16·75 million; and, as the proprietors heard the next spring, it was in general a record year for the Group, marked not merely by high income and good profits but by a complete readjustment of the Group's international position: 'we have largely re-established our overseas business on a pre-war basis'. By 1950 Group accident premiums alone exceeded £10 million—a level which, in 1945, had not been reached by the fire, accident and marine branches combined. The Group's departmental profits were almost £1·7 million.

Addressing the Annual General Court in May 1952 (and, incidentally, drawing attention to a record profit of £847,000 on the Group's fire premium income of £8·3 million), the Governor argued that the period 1946–51 had witnessed the 'economic rehabilitation' of much of the world, and that the general deflationary and restrictive measures which had recently characterized the economic policies of various countries might mark the end of an era and presage a slower rate of premium growth. He was certainly right on the latter point. Whereas, between 1946 and 1951, the aggregate fire and motor premium incomes of all British offices increased by 133 per cent (from £133 million to £310 million), the rate of increase dropped to 48 per cent in 1951–6 and 40 per cent in 1956–61. The comparable rates of growth for the REA Group were 107, 53 and 34 respectively. Admittedly, even these rates of growth were reasonably high by long-run standards, but they represented, as Lord Bicester had predicted, a sharp break with the immediate post-war experience.

While the principal reason for this relative check to the pace of expansion lay outside the insurance industry, in the combination of the ending of the immediate post-war recovery phase and the economic problems of the early 1950s, it was accompanied by a change in the marketing situation.

Although the REA found the early 1950s reasonably profitable (the Group's fire underwriting surplus averaged about 10 per cent annually between 1951 and 1956, dropping to just over 4 per cent in 1957–9), such business as there was came under increasing pressure from competitors— a pressure which was enhanced by the activities of brokers as well as companies. By the end of the 1950s the REA Home Fire Manager, surveying the industry as a whole, could look back on a decade in which heightened competition had lowered the average premium rate and widened the scope of cover, with the result (especially given continued inflation) that underwriting profits had dwindled from some 10 per cent to less than 2 per cent. In the five years 1961–5 the REA made an *average* loss of £142,000 on its fire business at home and overseas, compared with an average profit of £612,000 ten years earlier. In 1962 British companies as a whole made an underwriting loss on their fire business. These events in fire insurance are especially important because that branch of the industry had traditionally been a solid and profitable field of underwriting. In addition, however, the profitability of motor underwriting also fell, although national premium incomes grew threefold in the 1950s, as against fire premiums' increase of less than 80 per cent. Between 1956 and 1960, for example, motor underwriting made losses in three years and averaged only just over 1 per cent profit on premium income in the remaining two. Nor were these problems at all confined to the UK market for insurance. Consistently bad results in North America, from which so much of British premium income was derived, were to have a profound effect on the organization as well as profitability of the large British composite offices. And these trends continued into the next decade: data for the ten leading composite offices in 1962–6 show that they made a loss each year on their aggregate fire and accident business. And even though the balance of profitability was redressed by income from investments, it has been estimated that the rate of profit, measured against estimated capital employed, fell from over 20 per cent in the early 1950s to about 7 per cent in 1961–6.[1]

Two organizational aspects of the new situation of the 1950s and early 1960s can be emphasized here. The first was itself a factor in the intensification of competition: the profitability of insurance both attracted new companies, and, continuing a pre-war trend, led to more active competition from non-tariff companies and Lloyd's underwriters. Indicative of the

---

[1] Doublet, 'Fire insurance: past and present developments', *JCII*, LVII (1960), 100; Doublet, 'Current trends', *JCII*, LXIV (1967), 20–1; Raynes, *British Insurance*, pp. 384–7; Carter, 'Competition in the British Fire and Accident Insurance Market', pp. 42, 211–12, 386–7.

'new' competition was the fact that from 1958 to 1967 some fifty-nine British and sixty foreign insurance companies were formed to transact fire and/or general insurance business in Great Britain—although these included a number of cut-price, unsound and in some cases fraudulent motor insurance companies, the collapse of which in the mid-1960s (eleven companies were compulsorily wound up in 1966–7) helped erode public confidence in new companies. But the shift of custom away from tariff companies was, perhaps, the more significant fact. In 1948, for example, tariff companies controlled 65·3 per cent of combined fire and accident premiums; by 1963 their share had declined to 58·5 per cent.[1] When the tariff companies raised their premium rates for most industrial and commercial fire risks in 1963–5, however, Lloyd's and the non-tariff companies followed suit. In addition (and in response to continued under-insurance in the face of inflation) a *pro rata* average for all fire insurances other than private house insurance and churches was introduced in July 1967.

The second element in the new situation was in large part a response to the revival of intensive competition in fire and accident business. From the late 1950s onwards, the merger movement, which had been in abeyance since the 1920s, was renewed. In the years 1956–67, for example, as a consequence of thirteen mergers, twenty-two leading British companies coalesced into nine groups. And there can be little doubt about the connection between this accelerated concentration and the struggle for business—although in addition to following the conventional approach of merging in the search for an extended 'connection', the large composite groups now, effectively for the first time, sought the economies of scale made possible by mergers and inherent in the possibility of integrating staffs at Head Offices and branches. As a result of this merger boom, the trend towards diffusion, exemplified since the late 1920s, was reversed from the late 1950s: considering the world-wide business of all British companies (i.e. excluding Lloyd's underwriting), the twelve largest groups accounted for 70 per cent of fire premiums in 1956, 86 per cent in 1963 and 87 per cent in 1968; in the same years the shares of the twelve largest groups in British companies' accident business were 70 per cent, 80 per cent and 89 per cent. By 1968 the *three* largest groups controlled over half of all corporate fire and accident business.[2]

[1] Carter, 'Competition in the British Fire and Accident Insurance Market', pp. 321, 333.

[2] Carter, 'Competition in the British Fire and Accident Insurance Market', pp. 39–40, 212–13. In 1928 the twelve largest companies had controlled about 75 per cent and the three largest 37 per cent of corporate fire and accident business. See the list of acquisitions between 1953 and 1969 in *PM*, cxxx, 10 (6 March 1969), 435.

In contrast to its rather belated participation in the merger movement which spanned the First World War, the Royal Exchange Assurance was involved in the new developments of the late 1950s from a relatively early stage. It did so, however, after a period in which the industry as a whole had expanded faster than the Group: for in spite of the substantial increase in its premium income, the Group's share of total British offices' fire and accident premiums declined slightly, from 4·6 per cent in 1948 to 4·1 per cent in 1958. In the latter year the Corporation made an important structural adjustment to one of the severest problems of the British companies—operations in North America. It agreed with the Atlas and the Sun to place their US business under a single manager, in order on the one hand to reduce operating expenses and, on the other, to achieve a more significant degree of bargaining power *vis-à-vis* the independent and powerful American agents. But this tackled only one aspect of the problem and in 1959, preceded only by the Guardian (which had acquired two relatively small companies in 1956 and 1957) and the giant Commercial Union (which acquired the North British & Mercantile in April 1959),[1] the REA helped initiate the wave of mergers by acquiring the Atlas Assurance Company.

The Atlas was also, by most standards, an ancient company. Founded in 1808, in the midst of the Napoleonic War boom in fire and life insurance,[2] it had enjoyed a long career of sustained if not spectacular growth—in the course of which, too, it had acquired other offices (notably the Manchester Assurance Company, purchased and fully absorbed in 1904, and the Essex & Suffolk Equitable Insurance Society, in 1911). By 1928 it ranked ninth in point of fire income and twelfth in point of combined fire and accident incomes among British companies. Thirty years later its combined fire and accident income stood at just over £12 million compared with the REA Group's £30·6 million, while its life business was about 20 per cent larger than the REA's:

TABLE 22.1. *REA and Atlas fire, accident, marine and life premiums, 1958*

(£000)	Fire	Accident	Marine	Life	Total
Existing REA Group	10,204	20,396	4,993	3,381	38,974
Atlas and Essex & Suffolk	7,602	4,791	791	4,131	17,315

[1] The need to strengthen their American business, which accounted for 45 per cent of the combined non-life premium incomes of the two Companies, was a dominant motive in this merger: Raynes, *British Insurance*, p. 387.

[2] Above, pp. 111, 122, 133.

The REA acquired the Atlas by an exchange of £2 of its stock for three Atlas shares, each of the latter having a nominal value of 10s. The total new issue was £3,666,667 of REA stock, with a market value of some £15 million. The Corporation's authorized capital was increased to £16 million.

While the Atlas brought considerable strength to the REA's Life Department (this was especially true of group life and pensions business, which the Atlas had developed much further than the REA), it also provided the basis for a firm rounding-out of the Group's fire and accident underwriting—particularly overseas, where the Atlas had been well established since the vigorous policies of Samuel J. Pipkin in the 1880s. Of course, even before the merger, in 1958, the REA and the Atlas, together with the Sun, had agreed to a policy of close co-operation in North America. And there was, in fact, a strong historical logic to the merger: quite apart from the good relationships which had subsisted between the two Offices ever since the early nineteenth century, it will be remembered that there had been at least one previous attempt to merge—in the summer of 1919—which had gone very far before foundering on an amicable disagreement as to the terms.[1] In August 1919, Vivian Smith, the REA Governor, had expressed what was obviously genuine regret on personal as well as business grounds: 'I think the associated companies would have made a splendid business', he wrote to the Atlas Chairman. Yet his term of office as Governor was so long (he retired in the Autumn of 1955) that it was only by four years that he missed presiding over the successful acquisition of the Atlas forty years later.

The acquisition of the Atlas, even more than the earlier acquisitions of the Car & General, the State and the Motor Union, marked a decisive turning-point in the modern history of the REA. For it brought into sharp relief questions of the scale and organization of business activities which were characteristic of the twentieth-century insurance industry, and which the Corporation was now obliged to confront in a more decisive manner than ever before.

First, the merger showed a new appreciation of the need to grow more rapidly than had been the case in the recent past, and to attain, as quickly as possible, a size which more accurately reflected the strategic and competitive realities of the mid-twentieth century. Indeed, although the possibility of obtaining new economies of scale and integrated operations was undoubtedly a factor in the merger, perhaps equally important at the time was the need to make some defensive move away from the relatively small

[1] Above, pp. 464–5.

size which might have made either Office vulnerable to unwelcome acquisition as well as competition. In any case, as a result of the purchase, the reconstituted REA Group rose in the 'league table' of composite offices: by 1963, with an aggregate fire and accident income of over £53 million, it ranked fifth among British company groupings. In the event, however, this was only a first step. Other offices had also merged and in 1963 the REA, although fifth, was overshadowed by the first four groups (the Royal, the Commercial Union, the General Accident and the Northern & Employers), which had an average fire and accident income of some £125 million. By 1967, so rapid had been the continued growth of the biggest groups that the gap between the REA (the fire and accident income of which had risen to £63 million) and the Royal (£276 million), the General Accident (£150 million), the Commercial Union (£148 million) and the Northern & Employers (£120 million) had widened—while the Sun Alliance Group, having acquired the REA's sister company, the London, in 1965, now had a fire and accident income of £101 million.[1]

For the REA Group, however, the problem of size was not only a matter of its scale relative to other groups. In addition, and in most respects even more important, there was the question of whether its scale was sufficient to enable it to take full advantage of the potentialities of the world-wide market for insurance. By the end of the 1950s there was clearly some doubt on this score. But even before then it became apparent that the Corporation's long struggle to remain a force in the United States was an unequal one. Indeed, as has been seen, the critical problem of the American market was already apparent in the 1930s: its enormous size, and the indispensable strategic advantage of large-scale operations meant that unless an office was huge (and sometimes even then) it ran the constant risk of being left with too much bad business and of incurring excessive expenses relative to premium income.[2] Throughout most of the post-war period this has been brought home to the REA by steady underwriting losses in the United States—although hope, joined with aspirations and even considerations of prestige, kept the Corporation in that hazardous market. There were, in any case, important investment advantages in maintaining the American business link. By the early 1960s, however, it was clear that some drastic change was needed. Even with the Atlas and Sun-Alliance pool, insurance operations were altogether too limited in America. In 1962, therefore, it was decided to withdraw the REA from the US market for non-marine insurance (though the Atlas continued on a strictly limited

---

[1] *The Economist*, 13 July 1968, xiv.
[2] Above, p. 480.

basis, under the management of an American firm: Chubb & Son, Inc.). The withdrawal took place the next year, and in 1965 the Governor reported to the General Court that in 1964, the first full year of the new arrangements, group premiums had fallen by almost £4 million as a result of the move, although the loss had been more than made good from other sources.

The American market was *sui generis*. Nevertheless, the problems of the scale of operations were more general and more continuous than this. And the fact that even after the acquisition of the Atlas the gap between the REA and other groups widened in the mid-1960s was responsible for another, and major, structural adjustment of its position at the end of the decade. In March 1968, implicitly acknowledging the new environment of very large-scale activity, it was agreed to merge on equal terms with the Guardian Assurance Company, forming for that purpose a new Company, the 'Guardian Royal Exchange'. On the basis of 1968 figures, the resulting enterprise had a fire and accident income of some £148 million. And as if to re-emphasize the new necessities, in the same month (March 1968) a merger between the Commercial Union and the Northern & Employers was announced, giving a new Group with a fire and accident income of some £267 million.[1] On the very eve of its 250th birthday the REA had made what will in all likelihood prove a fundamental step away from a corporate independence which was no longer appropriate to the competitive world of modern insurance.

The second respect in which the acquisition of the Atlas in 1959 (and even more the merger with the Guardian a decade later) reflected a distinctively new trend in the history of the REA was in its implications for the organization of the Corporation and the Group. For, in sharp contrast to earlier acquisitions, the purchase of the Atlas was immediately followed by a vigorous and systematic campaign to integrate and group the structures and activities of all the companies associated with the REA. As was happening with other large British offices, this was a symptom of the new urgency with which costs and competitive efficiency now had to be

[1] As a result of these structural changes, the principal composite groups, on the basis of 1968 fire and accident premium incomes, were:

	£million
Royal	336
Commercial Union/Northern & Employers	304
General Accident	171
Guardian Royal Exchange	148
Sun Alliance and London	110
Eagle Star	65
Phoenix	64

(*Policy Holder*, vol. 87, no. 38, 19 September 1969)

approached. The independence and lack of co-ordination which had been satisfactory and even comfortable in the inter-war years, could no longer suffice.[1] In order to appreciate the implications of this change of direction, however, it will be necessary to consider the general problem of management in the context of post-war history since 1945.

MANAGEMENT STRUCTURES AND GROUPING

Before the Second World War, although the Royal Exchange Assurance had had a General Manager since 1929, there had been relatively little change in the traditional autonomy of individual Departments within the Corporation.[2] Yet until the Corporation's own management structure was better unified, it was idle to imagine that even the prerequisites for a genuine grouping of administration and operations existed. The obstacles to true general management were formidable. In fact, they were to some extent a function of the tardiness of the creation of the post of General Manager itself, for the longer it had been postponed the more firmly entrenched had become the individual Departments, and the collective interest of Departmental Managers in their own authority. The events of the 1930s did, at least, have some influence in these respects. But it was not until the years after 1945 that there was accelerated change in the REA's management structure towards effective interdepartmental authority.

The War itself, by disturbing inherited relationships and attitudes, no doubt had a rôle to play in this trend—as did the post-war realization that times had changed in many respects, not least in the sense that corporate success now depended on rapid and integrated growth. But a more personal factor, the importance of which was a logical concomitant of the position and potential of general managership, was the appointment of a new General Manager, Mr A. E. Phelps, in 1946. Mr Phelps (who had joined Head Office in 1931 after a successful period as Branch Manager in the West End) was, by all accounts, an archetype of the modern General Manager. Discounting Robert Connew's brief tenure of office, he gave the Corporation its first taste of that drive for co-ordination and control which has been the ideal rationale of the twentieth-century 'GM' in all insurance companies. The assertion of central control which is associated with Mr Phelps's career (he retired in 1953) was exemplified at home and abroad, since he not only secured far-reaching changes in the relationships of the various Head Office Departments with his own, but began the series of extended trips to overseas branches (in his instance made the more impor-

[1] Above, pp. 493–500.
[2] Above, pp. 504–11.

15   The REA Office at Amsterdam

16　REA, Lagos

17 South Wales Area Office

tant by virtue of the war-time gap in any visits from Head Office to most overseas branches) which have now become an accepted and routine part of a General Manager's function. Deeply committed to the Corporation, with a widespread reputation for generosity as well as tough-mindedness, Mr Phelps derived particular and necessary support in his difficult task of asserting a modern version of general management, from the complete confidence of the Governor, Lord Bicester, who clearly appreciated that, with respect to underwriting and insurance matters, the time had come for professionalism at the centre.

As a consequence, there was genuine progress towards central management in the late 1940s and early 1950s. Nevertheless, the level of achievement in terms of structural innovation should not be exaggerated. For one thing, the REA was in large part making up lost ground: the concept of general management which Mr Phelps asserted had been familiar to other large composite companies for many years—indeed, since before 1929. For another, the changes of these years, no matter how much they strengthened the position of the REA General Manager, did so within a relatively unchanging institutional framework: the REA Group was still only a loose collection of quasi-independent companies, each with its own branches and sub-structures. As far as the separate companies were concerned the undoubted authority represented by Mr Phelps was not embodied in a new set of management institutions; the inherited pattern of companies and departments and branches remained intact while he was General Manager and during most of the tenure of office of his successor, H. A. Walters (1954–60). If, therefore, these years had created the managerial prerequisites of institutional change, it still remained for that change to be achieved in terms of the effective integration of the REA Group's structure and activities. Indeed, even with respect to such an apparently straightforward matter as the sharing of fire underwriting risks, before 1951 each member of the Group dealt independently with its acceptances and reinsurances—with the result that the smaller companies were limited in the amount of business they could accept. In 1951, however, reinsurances were centralized on a Group basis: any constituent company could now make use of the resources of the Group as a whole in connection with acceptances.

When it came, the fundamental move towards the grouping of administrative operations was associated with two developments which have already been touched on: first, the sharp intensification of competition in the second half of the 1950s; second, the acquisition of the Atlas, a move which was related to the new competition and which increased the

Group's fire and accident business by 40 per cent. Each of these developments focused attention on the urgent need to secure economies and also to take advantage of the opportunities of closer co-ordination which had been relatively neglected ever since the acquisition of the Car & General over forty years before.

In fact, the new policy had its origins before the Atlas was purchased. By 1958, for example, the staff training programme which had been introduced for the outdoor officials at the parent Corporation only, had been extended not merely to clerical and potential overseas staff, but to employees of the REA's subsidiaries. And in May 1959, the Governor, Lord Kindersley, emphasized to the General Court that the process of grouping and integration was going forward: 'More remains to be done in this field before we can be satisfied that we are using our resources to the best advantage, and further substantial progress may be expected in 1959, but it is not a task which can be unduly hurried if we are to preserve the goodwill which all members of the Group have built up over many years.' By the summer of 1960, with the Atlas now part of the Group, Lord Kindersley reported various changes in personnel which exemplified the new spirit: the executive was strengthened by the appointment of Mr H. R. Roberts as Deputy General Manager and of three Assistant General Managers (Mr W. H. Carter, Mr R. W. Peattie and Mr C. A. S. Cooper); the Home Accident Manager of the Atlas, Mr W. A. T. Harper, was also appointed Home Accident Manager of the REA; and, perhaps most significant because most overdue, the post of Overseas Manager was created (and filled by Mr H. C. Brett, formerly Overseas Fire Manager) to act for all branches of insurance and for the Group as a whole 'with a view to co-ordinating our activities abroad'. The importance of the last move, of course, lay precisely in the fact that for more than two generations the various underwriting Departments and for more than one generation the various companies, had not been obliged to pursue a consistent policy overseas in the context of the Group's interest as a whole. Although the system had not always worked badly, it was too likely to lead to either fragmentation of central control and lack of responsibility overseas or to inconsistency in Head Office decision-making. As the Governor pointed out, the fact that overseas branches were larger, and not particularly locked into an existing organization, meant that the benefits of the merger, in terms of grouping, would be felt there earlier: by the end of 1960 all the principal overseas territories would have been visited by senior Head Office officials and 'integration of a substantial kind' would have been achieved in North America, Australia, New Zealand, India and Pakistan.

At home, however, because of 'the closely knit structure of existing organizations', progress would inevitably be slower; but even here co-operation was taking place and plans were far advanced to pool Group facilities for fire surveying and the handling of claims. Nine Group claims bureaux were established in various cities in 1960. And it was significant that the new moves towards effective grouping were associated with a strengthening of general management which augmented the number and authority of senior officials with interdepartmental functions.

From 1960 onwards there was extremely rapid progress towards the integration of home as well as overseas business—progress which was clearly influenced by the appointment of Mr H. R. Roberts as General Manager.[1] Under his active leadership, in 1961 and 1962 Group Investment, Mechanization and Home Fire Departments were established; the integration of most overseas branch activity was completed; home motor and other accident business were divided, and the division reflected in the creation of a Group Home Motor Department (based on the Motor Union's operation and managed by a Motor Union man, Mr S. F. Langford) and a Group Home Accident Department (based at the Royal Exchange under Mr W. A. T. Harper, an Atlas man); and a Group Staff Department was established, under Mr R. A. Stallard, a former Atlas Assistant Manager, 'to streamline and standardize conditions of service' for the 10,000 staff employed by the Group in twenty-five countries. Up to that date salary structures and conditions of service had varied from company to company within the Group.[2]

One incidental but striking aspect of these various moves was the extent to which Head Office appointments were made on a 'Group basis' and without that regard for the seniority and precedence of 'REA men' which in earlier years had mirrored the *de facto* independence of the various associated companies. And in 1963, when Mr M. A. Wilkinson, originally an official of the Atlas, was appointed as Assistant General Manager of the Royal Exchange Assurance (for it should be borne in mind that the various constituent companies retained their separate *legal* identities) it was significant not merely in this respect but also because in 1966 Mr Wilkinson was to become General Manager of the REA Group. Subsequently, in 1968, he was appointed Managing Director—the first manager in the modern period to be elected to the Court of Directors.

[1] Mr Roberts had spent the early part of his career in the REA's Indian and South African branches, returning to Head Office in 1950 as 'Assistant Manager'.

[2] The acquisition of the Atlas and the Essex & Suffolk (which had a Staff Council) also stimulated fresh thought about the position of employees in the existing Group, and soon led to the formation of an REA Staff Association.

Given its main aims, grouping was not only a matter of reorganizing Head Office Departments and personnel. As had happened overseas, it was also necessary to co-ordinate the activities of branches in the UK. At home, however, this was a more difficult and therefore slower process: the UK branch organizations of individual companies were strongly rooted, the loyalties of policyholders and agents were more firmly tied to companies, and there were different accounting systems in use. Moreover, the fact that the areas covered by individual company branches often varied greatly from each other meant that any grouping would involve a vast amount of reorganization of territory. Nevertheless, it was a task which had to be done, and in the event the REA combined this grouping with a fundamental reorganization of its group branch structure: the branch offices were relieved of the work of issuing policies, maintaining detailed records and receiving payments. Instead, they concentrated on maintaining and expanding business, while what was formerly 'inside work' at the branches was transferred to a limited number of area offices, each with a Group Area Manager, which contained specialist staff and equipment for the control of branch offices. On the other hand, what was, from the viewpoint of branches, a measure of centralization, to secure economies of specialization and scale, was also, from the viewpoint of Head Office, a measure of decentralization: many of its responsibilities and personnel were shifted to the areas, which thereby assumed major control functions—and to that extent eliminated the duplication traditionally involved in the checking of work at Head Office which had already been checked in the field.

These moves began in 1963, and in June of that year the Governor, in his address to the General Court, emphasized their twofold aim: to strengthen the Group's selling organization and to increase the economy and efficiency of administrative structures. The first three area organizations had been formed (Solent, East Anglia and East Midlands) and were about to commence operations. Three Group Agency Managers had been appointed to oversee the whole plan. The scheme went ahead rapidly, and was associated with the standardization and streamlining of procedures and accounting practices throughout the Group (a task undertaken by the newly established Organization and Methods Department working in conjunction with a Group Systems Committee and the Mechanization Department). By June 1966 the Governor was able to report 'that the major part of the task of re-grouping and reorganizing the whole of our branch structure has now been completed by the establishment of eighteen area headquarters'. Economies had already been achieved, and more were looked for as the new system got into gear and more advanced statistical

18   Lord Kindersley, Governor, 1955–70

and accounting techniques were adopted. And the next year Lord Kinder-sley could inform the Court that costs had been cut and methods improved, and that from 1 January 1967 a new mechanized accountancy system linked to the Group's computers had become fully operative for all companies. (The Group had acquired its first computer—a De La Rue Bull 300—in 1961.)

By the mid-1960s, therefore, after barely half a decade of hectic activity, the REA Group of companies had undergone a very substantial reorganiza-tion, leading to a genuine grouping of activity and control. This, in turn, emphasized the need to adapt management structures and forms of business control to the pressing demands of large-scale operations in an increasingly competitive environment. The provision and processing of information, marketing and the overhaul of staff-management functions came under much closer scrutiny. Nor were the important consequences of grouping confined to business organization: the social activity of the staffs—which, until the 1960s, had been organized into separate clubs for sport, drama, motor rallying and the like—also came together. In an odd but significant way the Group's victory in the insurance offices' competitions for rugby and association football in 1966 was symptomatic as well as symbolic of the added strength which a grouping of hitherto separate activities could bring!

In the overhaul of structures and attitudes which characterized the early 1960s, the rôle and responsibility of top management were obviously crucial. And in this respect the close relationship between the Court and the officials was an important attribute of the organization. Compared with their predecessors, the Court in general, and Lord Kindersley in particu-lar, assumed a much more direct, and in many ways less purely formal, concern with major issues of policy. As the world of insurance changed— as financial and political considerations became more pressing than ever before—so the importance of the senior members of the Court, men with wide-ranging experience and ties, was re-emphasized. And the traditional rôle of the Treasury Committee, developed in the eighteenth century for similar purposes, was reaffirmed in a more modern setting. Yet even in matters of underwriting and administrative organization it was essential to secure close and continuous co-operation between members of the Court and the officials. This was especially true of the Governor and the General Manager. And it was only with the help of Lord Kindersley's detailed grasp of the business, based not only upon experience at the Royal Exchange but also on thousands of miles of international travel to overseas branches, that the effective foundation for far-reaching reorganization were constructed.

By the mid-1960s the REA was, in fact, inherently stronger and more efficient, more alert and responsive, than it had been for some time past. Ironically, however, these large improvements came at a time when the environment of enterprise was itself being transformed at an accelerated rate. As a result, the strengthening of the REA's competitive position which the grouping of the early 1960s brought was not in itself sufficient to withstand the market pressures towards a further sharp increase in the size of the Group. And the merger of the REA and the Guardian was indicative of the new epoch which had arrived for the insurance industry in general and the REA in particular. For it was envisaged from the outset (in 1968) as a genuine merging of activities: a coalescing of two organizations into a single, new Group. In the past the principal motives for mergers and acquisitions could generally be satisfied without a radical change in organization. Certainly, the appreciation that grouping was desirable or necessary followed (and sometimes followed belatedly) the actual acquisition. Now, however, organizational change was itself one of the principal motives in the merger movement: competitive strength could no longer be based upon corporate independence or administrative stability. A new epoch had opened and, of necessity, had begun to exert its powerful influence on the Royal Exchange Assurance.

Conclusion

Enterprise and Tradition

The special features of a long-lived corporation are bound to have a profound historical tenacity: the very forces which make for survival cannot easily be replaced. This is particularly true of insurance companies. For the nature of the services they offer and the strong, personal elements in their relationships with agents and policyholders, provide a particular justification for the maintainance of a distinctive corporate personality. As a result, amalgamations and mergers in insurance have rarely resulted in the rapid absorption of corporate identities. Even in the 1960s, when the rate of concentration accelerated and the economic pressures towards the closer grouping of operations were unprecedentedly strong, the inherited web of relationships and attitudes which characterized insurance offices proved strikingly durable in the face of large-scale organizational change. Although the pressures have been much more difficult to withstand in the last decade or so, and will perhaps be impossible to withstand in the next, there are, in fact, still very few examples of a complete break in the social history of an insurance company.

In 1968, after virtually 250 years of corporate autonomy—an autonomy which had effectively survived the acquisition of other large companies in the twentieth century—the Royal Exchange Assurance merged with the Guardian Assurance Company. This break in the organizational history of the REA, although not immediately decisive in terms of the continuity of its corporate presence, was by far the most important structural change in its long history. And while it is unlikely that the merger, in creating a new enterprise, will completely submerge its two main constituents, it is likely to produce very far-reaching changes. Its occurence therefore provides an appropriate point from which to survey some general historical aspects of the relationship between continuity and convention on the one hand, and enterprise and business achievement on the other. First, however, it is necessary to examine the extent to which the REA's corporate presence has changed in the recent past. By the First World War, as was

seen in chapter 16, the Corporation exemplified many of the habits and
structures and outlooks which had helped fashion its identity in the early
nineteenth century. How far has it changed in this respect in the half
century which has passed since 1918?

Superficially, twentieth-century corporate change, as measured in
terms of business organization, has been very far-reaching indeed. Even
before the merger with the Guardian, the Corporation had become the
Group, a single focus of general management had been developed, and a
new administrative structure had been articulated. In fact, however, important as all this was, most of the really significant developments took
place in the very recent past. For example, it was only after the acquisition
of the Atlas in 1959 that there was an active and successful attempt to
group the operations and organizations of the REA and its subsidiary
companies. Before then—for example, as late as the 1930s, when the
combined income of its subsidiaries rivalled its own—the REA remained an
independent unit, continuing on its own way and only forging very loose
links with such offices as the Car & General or the Motor Union. Similarly, although a General Manager was appointed in 1929, this was in
itself somewhat late and it took almost another generation before the presence of general management ensured the effective and continuing co-
ordination of the various Departments.

This tardiness of structural evolution can be attributed in part to influences which were and are common to the insurance industry in general. For
there are costs as well as benefits involved in any drastic reorganization.
Familiarity and stability have their advantages in business as well as social
settings—and especially in insurance. In addition, however, the Royal
Exchange was perhaps exceptional in the extent to which it exemplified the
influence of tradition and the momentum of historical continuity. It was
among the last to change some aspects of its structure, because it had been
among the first to adopt them. And the inherited strength of its corporate
identity is an explanation, if not always a justification, of why it took so
long to coalesce its organization with that of other members of the Group.

Yet a discussion of tradition in terms of formal organization, although
directly relevant to the analysis of business success, omits some of the
most important considerations in any business history. Formal organization, while responsive to external pressures, is also a reflection of the
resilience of inherited relationships and of the pattern of business and
social attitudes which characterize a firm. In the case of the Royal Exchange
Assurance, the diffused influence of tradition, which was so pervasive in
the years before 1914, endured, albeit with a lesser intensity, into subse-

quent decades. The attitude towards the Corporation's departmental structure, the relative slowness with which the principle of effective general management was adopted, the respect which was shown towards established procedures and intra-company relationships—all demonstrated the longevity of conventional elements within the REA. In addition, other aspects of nineteenth-century traditions also survived into the different world which emerged after the First World War.

Employment in the Royal Exchange, for example, was still an attractive and prestigious prospect for young men. Indeed, given the continuing favourable pay and conditions on the one hand, and the vicissitudes of the country's economic life on the other, the relative attractions (at least in the context of middle-class employment) may have been as great in the 1920s and 1930s as they had been two or three generations earlier. Certainly, a young man of 16 or 17, commencing clerical work in the mid-1920s at an annual salary of £80 and, after a probationary year, joining the permanent staff at £120, was better off than most of his contemporaries with comparable qualifications—besides receiving a salary increase which, in proportionate terms, has never been exceeded since! And it was symptomatic of the scarcity as well as the prestige of such jobs, that until the early 1930s, they were still obtainable only on the nomination of a member of the Court of Directors. Moreover, the factors which in the nineteenth century had made a job at the REA as much a social position as a contractual relationship were still very much in evidence (even if the Corporation was no longer such a rare example of this variety of welfare capitalism). A strengthened and extended pension scheme, generous arrangements for leaves, security of tenure, automatic salary increments, financial help and loans when in need, the distinction of working for an ancient Corporation with a Royal Charter—all exemplified the corporate identity and the sense of corporate membership which, in some sense, transmuted employment into a social privilege. And old traditions were embodied in new forms: as has happened over the last half-century since the then Governor, Vivian H. Smith, gave a donation to Christ's Hospital in 1921, enabling the Corporation to exercise the right of nomination to the School—a right which has been used to help the sons of employees where they were in need. The Corporation continued to involve, but at the same time transcend, much of the lives of those who composed it at any one time.

These aspects of corporate life in the twentieth century, which were closest to the everyday concerns of the REA's employees, also found parallels in the more general rôle of tradition within the Corporation. This was exemplified in management attitudes, in the rôle of the Court, in the internal hierarchy of official positions, and in the tendency to avoid abrupt innovation. In 1939, once more on the eve of an enormous social and economic upheaval, the REA presented almost as many similarities as it did contrasts to itself in earlier generations. Yet tradition is not influenced by tradition alone: it is not invariably isolated from its environment. The changes in institutions and attitudes initiated by the social and economic pressures of the inter-war world were enormously accelerated by the Second World War and its aftermath. In these respects the last generation has achieved what earlier periods of intensified competition and change had failed to achieve. Admittedly, it was not until the late 1950s and 1960s that the new attitudes began to take effect: before then there was little adequate grouping and the separateness of the companies was reflected, for example, in the differences in conditions of employment. (The attractions of employment by the REA were distinctive to the Corporation rather than its subsidiaries.) Nevertheless, in the last fifteen years or so the grouping of the REA companies has been pushed forward in terms of attitudes as well as formal structures; the basic management structure has been overhauled and modernized; drastic policies, such as the withdrawal from the US market, have been pursued in spite of the implied break with tradition and prestige; innovation in methods and outlook have begun to transform the Corporation's reality as well as its image. Finally, the ultimate break with tradition came when the REA abandoned its separate and distinct identity in order to merge—at least in terms of formal organization—with another company.

In many ways, no doubt, all this proved advantageous to the Corporation. Nevertheless, it is as well to re-emphasize that in the context of the insurance industry the fact that the organization, internal relationships and business attitudes of a particular company are strongly influenced by traditional factors is not in itself always a business disadvantage. Tradition is not necessarily the enemy of enterprise. Admittedly, it may well be associated with inflexibility, excessive conservatism, and a preference for seniority and the familiar, rather than business talent and innovation. On the other hand, considerable strengths and potential may lie in the solidity and confidence which are also associated with a genuine business tradition, in the fact that institutions and assumptions have stood the test of time, in the relationship between age and stability and public appeal, and in the support which these factors give to the morale of employees. There can be little doubt that the developments of the period since the Second World War have, on balance, brought far more strength than weakness to the REA. Yet some valuable things have also been lost—not least that sense of corporate identity and participation which was a bond as well as a tradition (and also had its economic costs) in an earlier age.[1]

Over the long history of the Royal Exchange Assurance the necessary changes which have taken place in procedures or organization—the adoption of with-profits policies in 1841, the expansion overseas in the 1890s, the creation of the post of General Manager in 1929, the grouping of activities from 1959 onwards—have tended to be far more the result of external pressures than of 'spontaneous' innovation. To a considerable extent this was because the stability of inherited attitudes and institutions tended to inhibit innovatory enterprise. The very 'corporateness' of the REA, at a time when many other enterprises were more susceptible to the influence of individual personalities, made it difficult to accept change where that change involved the disruption of existing assumptions and structures. On the other hand, the business advantages of 'corporateness' —stability, loyalty, accumulated wealth, reputation—mitigated the effects of conservatism and made it easier for the Corporation to accept and absorb the inevitable when it happened. Beyond this, too, there were certain sorts of innovation which involved little or no disruptions of existing activities, and these (sometimes among the most drastic) could be relatively easily absorbed by the REA. Notable examples in this respect were the pioneering development of general accident and trustee and executor business in the period 1899–1904, and the acquisition of such large specialized motor insurance companies as the Car & General and the Motor Union in 1917 and 1928. What these experiences showed was that it was easier to add something entirely new to an existing set of arrangements than to change those arrangements: innovation by an extension into motor or employers' liability insurance was easier than innovation by, say, a dramatic new sales campaign for life insurance. In addition, however, such innovations were associated with a particular individual—A. W. Wamsley—who joined the Corporation to create an Accident Department and then, by dint of commercial success and force of personality, was principally responsible for the acquisition of the two accident companies. It is in any case significant that it was some time before these drastic innovations were allowed to have any far-reaching effect on the Corporation's basic structure. On the one hand, the organization of the Accident Department was accommodated into the existing departmental pattern with little regard for the administrative implications of large-scale composite business. On the other, the Car & General and the Motor Union remained very much separate companies until the 1950s and 1960s: they

[1] Above, chapter 16.

were added to, rather than integrated with, the activities of the REA itself.

None of this is to deny that large corporations can be enterprising and innovatory. But the characteristics of a traditional, historic Corporation were such as to resist all but the most powerful incentives to radical change. By the mid-twentieth century these incentives were considerable enough, and new attitudes had been developed sufficiently far, to set in train a series of changes which transformed the REA and the Group of which it was the most senior member. By that time, too, the individual element which had historically been so important in the development of enterprises was becoming less so: the complex and large-scale activities of modern insurance companies locate the entrepreneurial function more firmly than ever before with groups of men within the enterprise. Imaginative administration and complicated planning cannot be the sole responsibility of an individual. And in this sense the feeling for the corporate group and the links between individuals which have traditionally characterized an office like the REA are not irrelevant qualities in the second half of the twentieth century—even though the facts of continuing growth and constant change will make their maintenance and application the more difficult.

A final point worth emphasizing in relation to the respective rôles of enterprise and tradition in business development concerns the mechanisms of long-run growth in the insurance industry as a whole. Looking at the nineteenth century, for example, there is a sense in which the traditionalism of an office like the REA—a traditionalism which was only changed in response to market forces and competition—differed in degree but not in kind from the enterprise of many other companies which took initiatives with respect to competitive techniques or administrative structures. For the process of industrial expansion and change was, in fact, based upon pressure and response, competition and emulation. Where innovations were 'spontaneous' there was in any case room for only one pioneer: the rest were all, in varying degrees, followers. But in the main industrial progress did not result from the independent and isolated occurrence of innovation; instead, the pressure for change came again and again from the market for insurance services and from the mutual interactions of the competitive process. With few exceptions, even the most enterprising of companies needed the incentives which only the changing configuration of markets and the continuing struggle for business could bring. And the difference between these offices and the unenterprising was far more a difference in the degree of responsiveness to economic pressure than in 'spontaneity' or 'inventiveness'. This was so, for example, with respect to the introduction of with-profits policies and the rise of endowment policies in nineteenth-century life insurance; the large changes in the pattern of investments in the last 150 years; the expansion of overseas business; the nineteenth-century development of branches and agents; the twentieth-century growth of composite business and its associated merger boom; the evolution of motor insurance over the last seventy years; and the recent trend towards equity-linked life insurance. The dynamic influence of policyholders' demands has always been a critical factor. In this process the difference between enterprise and tradition or conservatism relates principally to the speed of response to changing demands and situations. Innovation for its own sake, or a volatility of response to apparently changing conditions, have their own dangers of which insurance companies, given their economic function and social rôle, ought to be fully aware. On the other hand, slowness of response can be too uniform for comfort. Yet for the fashionable and the traditional alike, as for the varying degrees and dimensions of enterprise, experience is a remarkably efficient instructor.

With respect to the Royal Exchange Assurance, the lessons of experience were most rapidly assimilated in the years after 1945. They indicated that the future lay with large-scale, fully integrated, composite Groups. And, in response to a rapidly developing situation, the Corporation moved towards managerial and administrative reforms of a far-reaching sort in the 1960s. The change was inevitable and, in terms of its ultimate outcome, desirable. Yet, precisely because it involved not merely a merging of the Corporation's single identity with that of another company, but also constant structural adjustments which were integral aspects of that change, some individuality as well as a certain commercial vulnerability was likely to be lost. After some 250 years, it was unlikely that the REA would disappear entirely, or that it would cease to have some special characteristics. And the institutional resources which its history had created were bound to be potential strengths for its future development. But equally, many of the specific attributes which a quarter of a thousand years had shaped, were bound to be transmuted in the forcing house of the second half of the twentieth century.

A Note on Sources

I. THE ROYAL EXCHANGE ASSURANCE

A business historian cannot be better than his sources, and some of the most glaring gaps in this history are attributable to the fire which destroyed the Royal Exchange in 1838 and to the intermittent disposal of the Corporation's records since then. On the other hand, many valuable records have survived. In addition to the published reports and accounts, and a great deal of miscellaneous and unlisted material, retained in folders and single-volume collections, the following were of particular use:

> *Orders of Courts and Committees*, 1753–1832
> *Minute books of the Annual General Court of Proprietors*, 1838–
> *Minute books of the Court of Directors*, 1838–
> '*Rough Treasury Minutes*': *Agenda books of the Committee of Treasury*, 1840– (These provided invaluable information on investment and other policies in the nineteenth century)
> *Special Report Books*, 1838–
> '*Domesday Book*' (a compilation of annual statistics from 1720 which was started by John A. Higham in the 1870s and has been brought down to the 1960s)
> *Minute books of the (Special) Fire Committee*, 1825–1933
> *Fire Registers* (Those for the eighteenth and early nineteenth centuries are deposited at the Guildhall Library)
> *Agenda books of the Committee of Management*, 1911–39
> *Early Records*, vols 1–12 (a miscellaneous and important collection of minutes, memoranda and reports, relating to the eighteenth and nineteenth centuries)
> *Minute books of Fire and Life Committee*, 1838–1922 (Refers only to life business)
> *Cashier's Order Books*, 1813–48
> *Fire Manager's Letter Books*, 1913–22
> *Fire Manager's Special Reports*, 1895–1941
> *Secretary's Special Report Book*, 1908–31
> *Secretary's Confidential Books*, 1915–24
> *Secretary's Private Letter Books*, 1917–30

'*Secretary REA*' (a collection of miscellaneous records and reports, 1890–1941)
'*Extracts from Court Minutes, 1838–1938*' (a collection of miscellaneous records and reports)
Manuscript balances and accounts, 1734–65, 1768–80
Manuscript lists of assets, 1838–97
Salary Books, 1837–
The Royal Exchange Assurance Magazine, 1903–16

Information about the REA was also derived from documents and books in other archives and libraries. This particularly applies to the years of its origin when, in addition to documents in the Treasury's records in the Public Record Office and occasional information in contemporary newspapers and in [A. Boyer's] *The Political State of Great Britain*, volume xx (for specific references see footnotes in chapters 1 and 2), an abundance of material was made available in the *Special Report* from the Commons Select Committee on insurance and other subscriptions in 1720 (British Museum, 357. b. 3/30: for full title, see list of abbreviations at front of this book); in the *House of Commons Journals*, volume xix; in various pamphlets in the British Museum (357. b. 3); in a list of subscribers to the original Mercers Hall scheme (British Museum, 8225. a. 38: '*Mercers Hall: A List of Names*') and in J. Castaing's *The Course of the Exchange*.

The following more modern publications were also of considerable use for these years: J. Carswell, *The South Sea Bubble* (1961); P. G. M. Dickson, *The Financial Revolution in England: A Study in the Development of Public Credit, 1688–1756* (1967); P. G. M. Dickson, *The Sun Insurance Office, 1710–1960* (1960); J. H. Plumb, *Sir Robert Walpole*, volume I (1956); F. B. Relton, *An Account of the Fire Insurance Companies* (1893); W. R. Scott, *The Constitution and Finance of English, Scottish and Irish Joint-Stock Companies to 1720*, 3 volumes (1910–12); and W. N. Whymper, *The Royal Exchange Assurance: An Historical Sketch* (1896).

Once it was firmly established, the Royal Exchange Assurance was never again quite so dramatically in the public eye as it had been in 1718–21. As a result there is much less abundant published information and comment for later periods. Apart from occasional references in the standard works on the history of insurance (see below, section 3), the two most useful sources were the *Post Magazine*, which published information and comment on all leading companies from the mid-nineteenth century onwards, and the statistical *Returns* published by the Board of Trade from 1872 onwards.

2. ASSOCIATED COMPANIES

Little detailed work was done on the records of the REA's subsidiaries, although the Minutes of their main committees, and in the case of the Atlas a well-ordered set of nineteenth-century reports and memoranda, are preserved at Head Office. The nineteenth-century Atlas records were used to extend the picture of contemporaneous insurance. A typescript history of the Car & General by St John Nixon, preserved at the REA, also proved very useful.

3. THE INSURANCE INDUSTRY

Although there is a relative abundance of published source material, insurance has never attracted the attention of professional historians to the extent that its economic and social significance undoubtedly warrants. The number of recent studies, particularly of broad aspects of the industry's history, is therefore extremely limited. (For a more detailed listing, see the bibliography in section 4.)

The best general survey is H. E. Raynes's *A History of British Insurance* (second edition, 1964), a substantial and informative survey by an insurance man, which stands out in terms of its scholarship and its concern with broad themes as well as specialist detail. The history of Lloyd's is told in C. Wright and C. E. Fayle, *A History of Lloyd's* (1928); D. E. W. Gibb, *Lloyd's of London* (1957); and F. Martin, *History of Lloyd's and Marine Insurance* (1876). Industrial assurance has been badly neglected in spite of its links with working-class history: the only survey is Dermot Morrah's somewhat lightweight and one-sided *A History of Industrial Life Assurance* (1955). An extremely specialized *History of Accident Insurance in Great Britain* (1954) by W. A. Dinsdale provides a good deal of (alas non-statistical) factual information, but too little analysis. And there is a vast amount of detail in Cornelius Walford's idiosyncratic but indispensable *Insurance Cyclopaedia: being a Dictionary . . . a Biographical Summary . . . a Bibliographical Repertory . . . an Historical Treasury . . . and [an] . . . Account of the Rise and Progress of Insurance*, six volumes (1871–8), which reached the letter 'H' before its author ran out of publishing support. (His notes for much of the unfinished sections are deposited in the Library of the Chartered Insurance Institute.) Walford also wrote two general historical surveys of some interest: 'History of Life Assurance in the United Kingdom', the *Assurance Magazine*, XXVI (1886–7); and 'Fires and Fire Insurance Considered under their Historical, Financial, Statistical and National Aspects', *Journal of the Statistical Society*, XI (1877). F. B. Relton's *An Account of the Fire In-*

surance Companies (1893) is full of detail about the early history of the Sun and other offices. There is a useful collection of studies of the effect of the 1914–18 War on insurance in Sir Norman Hill (ed.), *War and Insurance* (1927). Reinsurance has been dealt with, although by no means comprehensively, in C. E. Golding, *A History of Reinsurance with Sidelights on Insurance* (second edition, 1931). The Historic Records Working Party of the Insurance Institute of London has produced a dozen or so brief histories of various technical aspects of insurance, ranging from aviation insurance to weather insurance, and the development of mercantile fire insurance in London (see listing in section 4). From the technical viewpoint it is also worth consulting P. R. Cox and R. H. Storr-Best, *Surplus in British Life Assurance: Actuarial Control over its Emergence and Distribution during 200 years* (1962). Finally, the general professional aspects of the industry are dealt with by H. A. L. Cockerell in *Sixty Years of the Chartered Insurance Institute, 1897–1957* (1957), R. C. Simmonds, *The Institute of Actuaries, 1848–1948* (1948), and A. R. Davidson, *The History of the Faculty of Actuaries in Scotland, 1856–1956* (1956).

Some of the best work on insurance history has been done in relation to the history of particular companies—although even here the number of significant studies (out of numerous commemorative volumes) is very limited. One of the best is P. G. M. Dickson's scholarly history of *The Sun Insurance Office, 1710–1960* (1960), which is also very useful for the history of fire insurance up to the first years of the twentieth century. Equally important for an understanding of the problem of modern life insurance, especially in its formative years in the late eighteenth and early nineteenth centuries, is M. E. Ogborn's *Equitable Assurances: The Story of Life Assurance in the Experience of the Equitable Life Assurance Society, 1762–1962* (1962). A less penetrating study of a large composite office, although it provides some insights into modern organizational problems, is Edward Liveing's *A Century of Insurance: The Commercial Union Assurance Group, 1861–1961* (1961). A recent work provides considerable information about the development of a large-scale composite and industrial insurance office: R. G. Garnett, *A Century of Co-operative Insurance: The Co-operative Insurance Society 1867–1967: A Business History* (1968). Two specialized offices are admirably dealt with in books by W. H. Chaloner: *Vulcan: The History of One Hundred Years of Engineering and Insurance, 1859–1959* (1959) and *National Boiler, 1864–1964: A Century of Progress in Industrial Safety* (1964). Bernard Drew has written two company histories which are interesting, if discursive: *The London Assurance: A Second Chronicle* (1949) and '*The Fire Office*': *being the history of the Essex and Suffolk Equitable Insurance Society Limited, 1802–1952* (1952). And Professor A. H. John has made excellent use of the London Assurance's records in his study of 'The London Assurance Company and the Marine Insurance Market of the Eighteenth Century', *Economica* (May 1958). Well above the average of anniversary studies is Aubrey Noakes's *The County Fire Office, 1807–1957* (1957).

It is difficult to secure adequate and unambiguous historical statistics of insurance—especially for the nineteenth century and earlier. Since 1870 in the case of life, since 1909 in the case of fire and general accident, and since 1931 in the case of motor insurance, reasonably detailed figures of premiums, losses, expenses, assets and sums assured by life policies have been reported by companies to the Board of Trade and published in its annual *Returns*. Admirable summaries for most of the twentieth century can be found in various issues of the *Insurance Directory and Year Book*, formerly known by what is now its sub-title: the *Post Magazine Almanack*. The British Insurance Association also now regularly publishes a fact sheet. And modern life insurance data have been subjected to extensive statistical analysis in G. W. Murphy and J. Johnston, 'The Growth of Life Assurance in UK since 1880', *Transactions of the Manchester Statistical Society, 1956–57*. The period before the 1870s, however, is much less well served. Data on sums insured in the UK by fire policies for the period 1782–1868 were published at various times and the official figures have been reprinted in B. R. Mitchell and Phyllis Deane, *Abstract of British Historical Statistics* (1962), p. 461. Later figures for sums insured against fire in London can be found in K. Maywald, 'Fire Insurance and the Capital Coefficient in Great Britain, 1866–1952', *Economic History Review*, second series, IX, 1 (August 1956), and some important statistical facts are embedded in Cornelius Walford's 'Fires and Fire Insurance', *Journal of the Statistical Society*, XL (1877). Various estimates of the growth of life insurance between 1837 and 1887 are reprinted and discussed in D. Deuchar, 'The Progress of Life Assurance Business in the United Kingdom during the last Fifty Years' (1888)—the principal parts of which were published in the *Journal of the Institute of Actuaries*, XXVIII (1890), and the full version in the *Transactions of the Actuarial Society of Edinburgh*, II, 5. Deuchar was concerned with premiums, sums insured and accumulated funds, as well as the number of offices. This last is also dealt with in statistics compiled by S. Brown and reprinted in his evidence to the Select Committee on Assurance Associations: *Parliamentary Papers*, 1852–3, XXI, Q.1683.

Contemporaneous and historical material is to be found in the fairly voluminous pamphlet literature of the nineteenth century: for example, in F. M. Eden, *On the Policy and Expediency of Granting Insurance Charters* (1806); Francis E. Baily, *An Account of the Several Life-Assurance Companies Established in London, containing a view of their respective Merits and Advantages* (second edition, 1811); Charles Babbage, *A Comparative View of the Various Institutions for the Assurance of Lives* (1826); F. G. Smith, *Practical Remarks on the Present State of Fire Insurance Business* (1832); Robert Christie, *A Letter to the Right Honourable Joseph W. Henley Esq., M.P., President of the Board of Trade* (1852); and W. D. S. Pateman, *Life Assurance: its schemes, its difficulties and its abuses* (1852). Parliamentary records yield much information. See, for example, the *Special Report* of 1720 (British Museum, 357. b. 3/30); the *Report* of the Select Committee on Marine Insurance of 1810 (*Parliamentary Papers*, 1810, IV); and the *Report* of the Select Committee on Assurance Associations (*Parliamentary Papers*, 1852-3, XXI). But the best, and so far largely untapped, contemporary sources of information and analysis are the insurance journals—notably, the *Post Magazine and Insurance Monitor*, published continuously since 1840; the *Assurance Magazine*, later rechristened the *Journal of the Institute of Actuaries*, and published since 1850; and the *Journal of the Federation of Insurance Institutes of Great Britain and Ireland*, later rechristened the *Journal of the Chartered Insurance Institute*, published since 1898.

Very little systematic work has been done on the history of investment by British insurance companies. Exceptions are: A. H. John, 'Insurance Investment in the 18th Century', *Economica* (May 1953); and George Clayton and W. J. Osborn, *Insurance Company Investment: Principles and Policy* (1965). In addition, various of the company histories mention the topic in passing. But for basic analyses of nineteenth-century trends it is necessary to go back to contemporary journals: S. Brown, 'On the Investment of the Funds of Assurance Companies', *Assurance Magazine*, VII (April 1858); A. H. Bailey, 'On the Principles on which the Funds of Life Assurance Societies should be invested', *Assurance Magazine*, X (1861); A. G. Mackenzie, 'On the Practice and Powers of Assurance Companies in regard to the Investment of their Life Assurance Funds', *Journal of the Institute of Actuaries*, XXIX (July 1891); D. Deuchar, 'Investments', *Journal of the Federation of Insurance Institutes*, I (1898); G. E. May, 'The Investment of Life Assurance Funds', *Journal of the Institute of Actuaries*, XLVI (April 1912).

Original material for the history of individual insurance companies is often well preserved in their archives. In addition, the Guildhall Library

has a good collection of Minute books and other records for various offices
—including the Hand-in-Hand, the Sun, the London Assurance, the
Globe and the Indemnity Marine.

4. BIBLIOGRAPHY OF PRINTED MATERIALS

The following list has a twofold aim: to provide a useful bibliography of
insurance history and to list all the works used in the present study which
are directly or indirectly relevant to the history of insurance. It does *not*
purport to be comprehensive or even adequate in terms of systematic
coverage of all the main aspects of British insurance over the last 250
years. The abbreviations of journal titles are the same as in the text:

> *AM* : *Assurance Magazine*
> *JCII* : *Journal of the Chartered Insurance Institute*
> *JFII* : *Journal of the Federation of Insurance Institutes*
> *JIA* : *Journal of the Institute of Actuaries*
> *PM* : *Post Magazine and Insurance Monitor*

These journals repay intensive study by anyone interested in the history
of insurance: they still contain a mine of untapped information. Other
sources of statistical information on an annual basis are the *Returns* of
insurance data published by the Board of Trade since 1872 and the
Insurance Directory and Year Book (formerly the *Post Magazine Almanack*).

Aislabie, John, *Mr. Aislabie's Second Speech on his defence in the House of Lords,*
　　on Thursday, July 20, 1721: British Museum 517.k.16/30.
Anderson, T. F., 'Insurance Companies as Executors and Trustees', *JCII*, XII
　　(1909).
Andras, H. W. (ed.), *Historical Review of Life Assurance in Great Britain and Ire-*
　　land : A Supplement to the Insurance Guide and Hand Book (fifth edition, 1912).
—(ed.), *The Insurance Guide and Hand Book*, two volumes (fifth edition, 1912).
—'Life Assurance Prospects at the opening of the Twentieth Century', *JFII*,
　　IV (1901).
Anon., *A New-Year's Gift for the Directors, with some account of their plot against*
　　the two assurances (1721): Guildhall Library.
—*Consideration on, and answers to, the reasons presented to the Honourable the*
　　House of Commons against the passing of a Bill brought in by the Royal
　　Exchange Company for the granting, purchasing, or selling annuities upon, or
　　for lives (1793).
—*Employers' Liability Assurance Corporation Jubilee* (1930).
—*Hints to the Agents and Friends of Assurance Offices by the Spirits of Robert*
　　Christie Esq., F.I.A.!! Manager of the Scottish Equitable Assurance Company,
　　and William Newmarch Esq., Secretary to the Globe Insurance Company
　　(1852): British Museum 8227.c.6.

Anon., 'History and Principles of Life Assurance', *Edinburgh Review*, XLV (1826–7).
—*North British and Mercantile Centenary 1809–1909* (Edinburgh, 1909).
—*Phoenix Family Story* (1949).
—*Princes Street, Edinburgh : The Life Association of Scotland, 1838–1938* (1938).
—*Reasons humbly offered by the Societies of the Mines Royal &c. who insure ships and merchandise, with the security of a deposited joint-stock* (1720): British Museum 357.b.3/86.
—*Reasons humbly offered by the Sadlers Hall Society for their Establishment to insure Houses and Goods from Fire throughout England, with the Security of a Deposited Joint Stock* (1720): British Museum 357.b.3/101.
—*Remarks on a Letter by Robert Christie, Esq., F.I.A. Manager of the Scottish Equitable Life Assurance Society on one of the Registered Companies under the Joint-Stock Act* (1852).
Babbage, Charles, *A Comparative View of the Various Institutions for the Assurance of Lives* (1826).
Bailey, A. H., 'On the Principles on which the Funds of Life Assurance Societies should be invested', *AM*, X (1861).
Baily, Francis E., *An Account of the Several Life-Assurance Companies Established in London, containing a view of their respective Merits and Advantages* (second edition, 1811).
Banks, J. A., *Prosperity and Parenthood, A Study of Family Planning among the Victorian Middle Classes* (London, 1954).
Barnard, R. W., *A Century of service : the story of the Prudential 1848–1948* (1948).
[Barrow, John,] 'Babbage on Life Assurance Societies', *Quarterly Review*, XXXV (1827).
Beaumont, John A., *Observations, Cautionary and Recommendatory, on Life Assurance* (1841).
Besant, Arthur Digby, *Our Centenary : being the history of the Clerical, Medical & General Life Assurance Society* (1924).
Best, Alfred M. Company, *Best's Special Report upon the San Francisco Losses and Settlements* (New York, 1907).
Bignold, Robert, *Five generations of the Bignold family 1761–1947, and their connection with the Norwich Union* (1948).
Blackstock, William Witt, *The historical literature of sea and fire insurance in Great Britain, 1547–1810. A conspectus and bibliography* (1910).
Blackstone, G. V., *A History of the British Fire Service* (1957).
Blake, Robert, *Esto Perpetua : The Norwich Union Life Insurance Society, 1808–1958* (1958).
Blayney, Frederick, *A Practical Treatise on Life Assurance* (1837).
—*Life Assurance Societies Considered as to their Comparative Merits* (1848).
Board of Trade, *Report by Mr. Malcolm and Mr. Hamilton, Assistant Secretaries to the Board of Trade, upon the Accounts and Statements submitted to the Board of Trade, under the Life Assurance Companies Act, 1870 : Appendix to Board of Trade Returns, 1874.*

Boyer, A., *The Political State of Great Britain*: for 1720–21.

Brown, Samuel, *Defects in the Practice of Life Assurance and Suggestions for a Remedy* (1848).

—'On the Investment of the Funds of Assurance Companies', *AM*, VII (1858).

—*Is the Present Competition in Life Assurance Companies advantageous . . . ?* (1853).

—'On the Sufficiency of the Existing Companies for the Business of Life Assurance', *AM*, IV (1854).

—'On the Progress of Fire Insurance in Great Britain, as compared with other Countries', *AM*, VII (1858).

Brown, Walter, 'Life Branch Work', *JFII*, I (1898).

Bulan, Alwin E., *Footprints of Assurance* (1953).

Burn, W. L., *The Age of Equipoise* (1964).

Cairncross, A. K., *Home and Foreign Investment, 1870–1913* (1953).

Carswell, J., *The South Sea Bubble* (1961).

Carter, R. L., 'Competition in the British Fire and Accident Insurance Market' (D.Phil. dissertation, University of Sussex, 1968).

Castaing, J., *The Course of the Exchange*: for 1719–21.

Catchpole, W. L. and Elverston, E., *BIA Fifty, 1917–1967: Fifty Years of the British Insurance Association* (1967).

[Chadwick, Edwin,] 'Life Assurances', *Westminster Review*, XIX (1828).

Chaloner, W. H., *National Boiler, 1864–1964: A Century of Progress in Industrial Safety* (1964).

—*Vulcan: The History of One Hundred Years of Engineering and Insurance, 1859–1959* (1959).

Chapman, R., 'Insurance Field Work: Its Light and Shadows', *JCII*, VI (1903).

Chapman, Robert, 'The Agency System of Insurance Companies', *JFII*, x (1907).

Christie, Robert, *A Letter to the Right Honourable Joseph W. Henley Esq., M.P., President of the Board of Trade, Regarding Life Assurance Institutions, with Abstracts of all the Accounts Registered by London Life Assurance Companies* (1852): British Museum 8226.c.82(9).

Civil Service Inquiry Commission: Report & Evidence: Parliamentary Papers, 1875, XXIII.

Clapham, J. H., *Economic History of Modern Britain*, three volumes (1930–8).

—*The Bank of England: A History*, two volumes (1944).

Clayton, G., 'The Role of British Life Insurance Companies in the Capital Market', *Economic Journal* (1951).

Clayton, George and Osborn, W. J., *Insurance Company Investment: Principles and Policy* (1965).

Cleary, E. J., *The Building Society Movement* (1965).

Cockerell, H. A. L., *Sixty Years of the Chartered Insurance Institute, 1897–1957* (1957).

Colvin, Alexander, *Actuarial Figments Exploded. A Letter to the Right Hon. J. W.*

Henley, M.P. President of the Board of Trade, in Defence of the Life Assurance Offices Registered under 7 & 8 Vic., cap. 110 (1852): British Museum 8227.c.3.

Committee on the working of the Monetary System: Report (1959): Cmnd 827.

Coode, G., *Taxes Paid on Insurance against Loss by Fire: Revised Report: Parliamentary Papers*, 1863, XXVI.

Cooke, C. A., *Corporation, Trust and Company* (1950).

Cox, Jonathon, *How to Make a Fortune* (1857).

Cox, P. R. and Storr-Best, R. H., *Surplus in British Life Assurance: Actuarial Control over its Emergence and Distribution during 200 years* (1962).

Danson, J. T., *Our Next War, in its Commercial Aspect with some account of the Premiums paid at Lloyd's from 1805 to 1816* (1894).

—*Underwriting in England, France and America during the last three Years* (Paris, 1883).

—*The Underwriting of 1872* (1873).

Davidson, A. R., *The History of the Faculty of Actuaries in Scotland, 1856–1956* (1956).

Davies, E. A., *An Account of the Formation and Early Years of the Westminster Fire Office* (1952).

Davies, K. G., 'Joint-Stock Investment in the Later Seventeenth Century', *Economic History Review*, second series, IV (1952).

Deane, Phyllis and Cole, W. A., *British Economic Growth, 1688–1959* (1962).

Dent, Alan (ed.), *Bernard Shaw and Mrs. Patrick Campbell: Their Correspondence* (1952).

de Morgan, Augustus, *An Essay on Probabilities, and on their Application to Life Contingencies and Insurance Offices* (1838).

Deuchar, D., 'Investments', *JFII*, I (1898).

—'The Progress of Life Assurance Business in the United Kingdom during the last Fifty Years', *JIA*, XXVIII (1890) (Principal parts: full version in *Transactions of the Actuarial Society of Edinburgh*, II, 5).

—'The Necessity for a Tariff Organization in connection with Fire Insurance Business', *JFII*, VI (1903).

Dickens, Charles, *Dombey and Son* (1846–8).

—*Nicholas Nickleby* (1838–9).

—*The Life and Adventures of Martin Chuzzlewit* (1843).

Dickson, P. G. M., *The Financial Revolution in England: A Study in the Development of Public Credit, 1688–1756* (1967).

—*The Sun Insurance Office, 1710–1960* (1960).

Dinsdale, W. A., *History of Accident Insurance in Great Britain* (1954).

Doublet, A. R., 'Current trends in the fire department', *JCII*, LXIV (1967).

—'Fire insurance: past and present developments', *JCII*, LVII (1960).

—'Storm, tempest and flood', *JCII*, LXIII (1966).

—'The Abolition of the Fire Insurance Duty—1896', *PM*, CXIV, 40 (3 October 1953).

Drew, Bernard, '*The Fire Office*': *being the history of the Essex and Suffolk Equitable Insurance Society Limited, 1802–1952* (1952).

—*The London Assurance: A Second Chronicle* (1949).

DuBois, A. B., *The English Business Company after the Bubble Act, 1720–1800* (1938).

Dyer Simpson, J., *1936: Our Centenary Year* (Liverpool & London & Globe Insurance Co. Ltd) (1936).

Dyos, H. J., 'The Speculative Builders and Developers of Victorian London', *Victorian Studies*, XI, Supplement (Summer 1968).

Eden, F. M., *On the Policy and Expediency of Granting Insurance Charters* (1806).

Fishlow, Albert, 'The Trustee Savings Banks, 1817–1861', *Journal of Economic History*, XXI (1961).

Fothergill, Charles George, 'On the causes of Fires in London during the last twenty-four years, from 1833–1856 inclusive', *AM*, VII (1857).

Fox, Morris, 'Varieties of Life Insurance', *JFII*, VIII (1905).

Francis, E. V., *The History of the London and Lancashire Insurance Co. Ltd.* (1962).

Francis, John, *Annals, Anecdotes, and Legends: A Chronicle of Life Assurance* (1853).

Garnett, R. G., *A Century of Co-operative Insurance: The Co-operative Insurance Society 1867–1967: A Business History* (1968).

Gaskell, Mrs, *Mary Barton* (1848).

Gayer, A. D., Rostow, W. W. and Schwartz, A. J., *The Growth and Fluctuation of the British Economy, 1790–1850*, two volumes (1953).

Gibb, D. E. W., *Lloyd's of London* (1957).

Gilbert, Bentley B., *The Evolution of National Insurance in Great Britain* (1966).

Giuseppi, John, *The Bank of England: A History from its Foundation in 1694* (1966).

Golding, C. E., *A History of Reinsurance with Sidelights on Insurance* (second edition, 1931).

—'The Development of Fire Reinsurance in the United Kingdom', *JCII*, XXV (1922).

Gosden, P. H. J. H., *The Friendly Societies in England, 1815–1875* (1961).

Grant, A. T. K., *A Study of the Capital Market in Britain from 1919–1936* (second edition, 1967).

Hannam, W., *A Gift to the Uninsured: 30 short replies to 30 common objections* (1857).

Higham, C. D., *Notes on the Actuaries' Club* (1929).

Hill, Sir Norman (ed.), *War and Insurance* (1927).

Hillman, W. E., *Illustrations of the Theory and Practice of Insurance* (1847).

Hobsbawm, Eric and Rudé, George, *Captain Swing* (1969).

Hobsbawm, E. J., *Industry and Empire* (1968).

Hughes, J. R. T., *Fluctuations in Trade, Industry and Finance: 1850–1860* (1960).

Hunt, B. C., *The Development of the Business Corporation in England, 1800–1867* (1936).

Hutchinson, John, *A Popular View of Life Assurance* (1846).
Insurance Institute of London, Advanced Study Group, *The History and Development of the Home Private Car Comprehensive Motor Policy* (1949).
—*The Historical Approach to Public Liability Insurance* (1948).
Insurance Institute of London, Historic Records Committee, *Development of Mercantile Fire Insurance in the City of London* (1962).
—*History of Family Income Policies* (1962).
—*Institute Cargo Clauses* (1964).
—*Institute Time Clauses—Hulls* (1963).
—*Shipping & Insurance Sketches, 1867* (1967).
—*The History of Aviation Insurance* (1967).
—*The History of Children's Deferred Assurances* (1963).
—*The History of Fidelity Guarantee* (n.d.).
—*The History of Life Assurance Underwriting* (1967).
—*The Work of the Insurance Companies in Combating and Preventing Fire* (1966).
James, James H., *A Treatise on Life and Fire Insurance* (1851).
—*Modern Assurance Societies Vindicated* (n.d., 1853?).
John, A. H., 'Insurance Investment in the 18th Century', *Economica* (May 1953).
—'The London Assurance Company and the Marine Insurance Market of the Eighteenth Century', *Economica* (May 1953).
Jones, David, *On the Value of Annuities and Reversionary Payments*, two volumes (1843).
Lee, Grace Lawless, *The Story of the Bosanquets* (1966).
Leigh-Bennett, E. P., *On this evidence: a study in 1936 of the Legal & General Assurance since its formation in 1836* (1936).
Levien, J. W., *Atlas at War* (1946).
Liveing, Edward, *A Century of Insurance: The Commercial Union Assurance Group, 1861–1961* (1961).
Lockwood, David, *The Blackcoated Worker* (1958).
Loudon, J., 'The Ethics of Efficiency', *JFII*, IX (1906).
M'Candlish, J. M., 'The Economics of Insurance', *JCII*, XXII (1919).
Mackenzie, A. G., 'On the Practice and Powers of Assurance Companies in regard to the investment of their Life Assurance Funds', *JIA*, XXIX (July 1891).
Mackenzie, Robert Kirkwood, 'San Francisco: The Earthquake and Conflagration of the 18th April 1906', *JFII*, X (1907).
Magens, Nicholas, *An Essay on Insurances* (1755).
Marryatt, Joseph, *The Substance of a Speech Delivered in the House of Commons on the 20th February, 1810, upon . . . Marine Insurances* (1824).
Martin, F., *History of Lloyd's and Marine Insurance in Great Britain* (1876).
Mason, A. E. W., *The Royal Exchange: A Note on the Occasion of the Bicentenary of the Royal Exchange Assurance* (1920).
Maxwell, Sir Herbert, *Annals of the Scottish Widows' Fund Life Assurance Society During One Hundred Years, 1815–1914* (1914).

May, G. E., 'The Investment of Life Assurance Funds', *JIA*, XLVI (April 1912).
Maywald, K., 'Fire Insurance and the Capital Coefficient in Great Britain, 1866–1952', *Economic History Review*, second series, IX, 1 (August 1956).
Menzies, Robert H., *Life Assurance Viewed as a Profitable Investment* (1853).
Mercers Hall: A List of the Names of Subscribers for Raising the Sum of One Million Sterling, as a Fund for Insuring Ships and Merchandize at Sea; Which subscription was begun the 12th of August 1717 and completed the 16th January 1717/18: British Museum, 8225.a.38.
Miller, Thomas H., *A Practical Introduction to Life and Fire Insurance* (1841).
Millerson, Geoffrey, *The Qualifying Associations* (1964).
Mitchell, B. R., with Deane, Phyllis, *Abstract of British Historical Statistics* (1962).
Morgan, William, *The Doctrine of Annuities and Assurance on Lives and Survivorships* (1779).
Morrah, Dermot, *A History of Industrial Life Assurance* (1955).
Murphy, G. W. and Johnston, J., 'The Growth of Life Assurance in the U.K since 1880', *Transactions of the Manchester Statistical Society, 1956–57*.
Musgrove, F., 'Middle-Class Education and Employment in the Nineteenth Century', *Economic History Review*, second series, XII, 1 (August 1959).
Neison, Francis G., *Reply to Mr. Christie's attack on the Law Property Assurance Society* (1852): British Museum 8227.c.66(1).
Noakes, Aubrey, *The County Fire Office, 1807–1957* (1957).
Ogborn, M. E., *Equitable Assurances: The Story of Life Assurance in the Experience of the Equitable Life Assurance Society, 1762–1962* (1962).
Ostler, J., 'Cost Price of Fire Insurance', *JFII*, III (1900).
Park, James A., *A System of the Law of Marine Insurance* (1786).
Pateman, W. D. S., *Life Assurance: its schemes, its difficulties and its abuses* (1852).
Payne, P. L., 'The Emergence of the Large-scale Company in Great Britain, 1870–1914', *Economic History Review*, second series, XX, 3 (December 1967).
Penman, William, 'A Brief Survey of Ordinary Life Insurance in Great Britain', *Journal of the American Society of Chartered Life Underwriters*, V, 1 (December 1950).
Perkin, H. J., 'Middle-Class Education and Employment in the Nineteenth Century: A Critical Note', *Economic History Review*, second series, XIV, 1 (August 1961).
—*The Origins of Modern English Society, 1780–1880* (1969).
Phelps Brown, E. H. and Hopkins, Sheila V., 'Seven Centuries of the Prices of Consumables, compared with Builders' Wage-Rates', *Economica* (1956).
Pipkin, Samuel J., 'Fifty Years Reminiscences in the City', *PM*, LXXVII, 52 (23 December 1916).
—'Some Present-Day Problems of Insurance Business', *PM*, LXVIII, 14 and 15 (6 and 13 April 1907).
Plumb, J. H., *Sir Robert Walpole*, vol. 1 (1956).
Pollard, S., *The Development of the British Economy, 1914–50* (1962).
Potterton, W. M., 'Life Agency Work', *JFII*, III (1900).
Price, Richard, *Observations on the Expectations of Lives* (1769).

—*Observations on Reversionary Payments* (1771).

Raynes, H. E., *A History of British Insurance* (second edition, 1964).

—'The place of ordinary stocks in investments of life funds', *JIA* (1929).

Reader, W. J., *Professional Men* (1966).

Reed, Albert, S., *The San Francisco Conflagration of April 1906 : Special Report to the National Board of Fire Underwriters' Committee of Twenty* (New York, 1906).

Reeder, D. A., 'Capital Investment in the Western Suburbs of Victorian London' (Ph.D. thesis, Leicester University, 1965).

Rees, G. L. and Horrigan, W., 'The Disposition of Life Office Investments, 1929–1945', *The Manchester School*, May 1959.

Relton, Francis Boyer, *An Account of the Fire Insurance Companies, Associations, Institutions, Projects and Schemes Established and Projected in Great Britain and Ireland during the 17th and 18th Centuries including the Sun Fire Office : also of Charles Povey, the Projector of that Office, his Writings and Schemes* (1893).

Ridley, Percy E., 'The Tooley Street Fire, 22nd June, 1861', *JCII*, xxxv (1932).

Robinson, Sir Harry Perry, *The Employers' Liability Assurance Co. Ltd., 1880–1930* (1930).

Rudé, George, 'English Rural and Urban Disturbances on the Eve of the First Reform Bill, 1830–1831', *Past and Present*, number 37 (July 1967).

Ryan, G. H., 'Valuation and Distribution of profits in U.K., 1876–1900', *JIA*, xxxviii (1900).

T.S., *A Letter to a Member of Parliament by a Merchant* (1720): British Museum 256.b.3/62.

Schooling, Sir William, *Alliance: 1824–1924* (1924).

Scott, W. R., *The Constitution and Finance of English, Scottish and Irish Joint-Stock Companies to 1720*, 3 volumes (1910–12).

Scratchley, Arthur, *Observations on Life Assurance Societies and Savings Banks* (1851).

Select Committee of the House of Lords on the Improvement of Land : Report & Evidence : Parliamentary Papers, 1873, xvi.

Select Committee on Assurance Associations : Report & Evidence : Parliamentary Papers, 1852–3, xxi.

Select Committee on Fire Protection : Report & Evidence : Parliamentary Papers, 1867, x.

Select Committee on Fires in the Metropolis : Report & Evidence : Parliamentary Papers, 1862, ix.

Select Committee on Friendly Societies : Report & Evidence : Parliamentary Papers, 1852, v.

Select Committee on Joint-Stock Companies : Report & Evidence : Parliamentary Papers, 1844, vii.

Select Committee on Marine Insurance : Report & Evidence : Parliamentary Papers, 1810, iv.

Select Committee on the Savings of the Middle and Working Classes : Report & Evidence : Parliamentary Papers, 1850, xix.

Shepherd, A. F., *Links with the Past : A Brief Chronicle of the Public Service of a Notable Institution* (history of the Eagle & British Dominions Insurance Company) (1917).

Simmonds, R. C., *The Institute of Actuaries, 1848–1948* (1948).

Smith, F. G., *Practical Remarks on the Present State of Fire Insurance Business : The Evils of Competition pointed out, with Hints for Improvement* (1832).

Soper, George I., *On the Life Assurance Offices, their National and Social Advantages, their Principles and Practice* (1846).

Spring, David, *The English Landed Estate in the Nineteenth Century* (1963).

Strousberg, B. H., *Conspiracy Detected : in a letter to the Right Hon. J. W. Henley Esq., M.P., President of the Board of Trade, in Refutation of Certain Statements published by Robert Christie, Esq., and others on the subject of Life Assurance* (1852): British Museum 8227.c.66(8).

—*Judgement Before Trial* (1853).

Sturrock, John, jnr., *The Principles and Practice of Life Assurance* (1846).

Sutton, William, 'Opening Address', *JIA*, xxviii (January 1890).

Swiney, William, *Letter to the Right Hon. B. Disraeli, M.P., Chancellor of the Exchequer* (1852): British Museum 8227. c. 7: title page missing.

Tarn, A. W. and Byles, C. E., *A Record of the Guardian Assurance Company Limited, 1821–1921* (1921).

Tarn, A. W., 'Assets of Life Offices in the Colonies', *JIA*, xxxiv (1896).

Thackeray, W. M., *The History of Samuel Tidmarsh and the Great Hoggarty Diamond* (1841).

Thomason, H. A., 'Origin and Growth of Endowment Assurance Business', *JIA*, xxxiv (1896).

Thomson, W. T., *The Present Position of the Life Assurance Interests of Great Britain : a letter to Mr. Henley* (1852).

Trollope, Anthony, *The Last Chronicle of Barsetshire* (1867).

—*The Three Clerks* (1858).

US Bureau of the Census, *Historical Statistics of the United States* (1960).

Walford, Cornelius, 'Fires and Fire Insurance Considered under their Historical, Financial, Statistical and National Aspects', *Journal of the Statistical Society*, xl (1877).

—'History of Life Assurance in the United Kingdom', *JIA*, xxv and xxvi (1886–7).

—*Insurance Cyclopaedia : being a Dictionary . . . A Biographical Summary . . . a Bibliographical Repertory . . . an Historical Treasury . . . and an . . . Account of the Rise and Progress of Insurance*, six volumes (1871–8).

Warner, S. G., 'Twenty years' Changes in Life Assurance', *JFII*, xii (1909).

Whymper, W. N., *The Royal Exchange Assurance : An Historical Sketch* (1896).

Wilson, Charles, *England's Apprenticeship, 1603–1763* (1965).

Withers, Hartley, *Pioneers of British Life Assurance* (1951).

Wright, C., and Fayle, C. E., *A History of Lloyd's* (1928).

Yeo, Alfred, W., *Atlas Reminiscent* (1908).

Young, T. E., 'Ethics of Insurance', *JCII*, i (1898).

Index

Aberdeen, REA supports fire brigade, 164

Aberdeen, Earl of, 141

Accident insurance: growth of, 209, 224–37, 411, 417, 427–33, 519–21; and development of composite business, 296–8, 438. *Also see* Boiler, Burglary, Employers' liability, Fidelity guarantee, Hail, Motor vehicle, Personal accident, and Plate glass insurance; Royal Exchange Assurance

Accident Offices' Association, 227n, 230, 237, 264, 265, 284, 456, 457, 463–4

Accidental Death Insurance Company, 227, 232

Accidental Insurance Company, 227–8

Accra, 474

Actuarial techniques and mortality tables, 54–6, 58–9, 64–6, 115, 131–2, 254n

Actuaries: importance of, 146; professional role of REA actuaries, 176. *Also see* Actuarial techniques, Atlas Assurance Company, Institute of Actuaries, Royal Exchange Assurance

Adelaide: REA marine agency, 260n

Aden, 485

Advertising: first advertisement by REA, 95; as new competitive device, 134–5, 182, 274; attitude towards, of REA, 152, 173, 179, 182–3, 403

Aegis Life Assurance Company, 126, 152

Agassiz, A.D.L. (REA Director), 78, 80

Agassiz, Lewis (REA Director), 78

Agassiz family, and REA, 76n

Agents: REA agencies, 51, 83, 98–100, 153–4, 170, 179–84, 252–4, 269–70; and competition for business, 134–6, 284–7; and rise of composite business, 269–70, 291, 297; and inspectors and branches, 287–93. *Also see* Commission

Agricultural insurance; relative importance in 1830s and 1840s, 110; and arson in 1830, 160

Air raids: and insurance, 415–16, 423; and protection of REA, 514

Aislabie, John, 34

Akyab, REA marine agency, 260n

Albert Life Assurance Society, 142, 182

Albion Fire & Life Insurance Company, 134n, 168

Albion Flour Mill, destroyed by fire, 89–90

Alexandria, 423

Alliance British & Foreign Fire & Life Insurance Company, 128, 162, 198, 199n, 298–9, 508

Alresford, REA agency, 99

Amalgamations: *see* Mergers

Amicable Contributors for Insuring from Loss by Fire: *see* Hand-in-Hand

Amicable Society for a Perpetual Assurance Office, 9–10, 53, 54, 56, 110

Amsterdam: marine insurance at, 15; REA marine agency, 260n; REA general agency, 483

Amsterdam and London Insurance Company, 260, 481, 483

Anderson, Sir J.W. (Director of REA), 80

Anderson, Thomas F. (Manager REA Trustee and Executor Department, later Actuary), 270n, 476

Andover, REA fire engine at, 163

Andras, H.W., 111n, 134n, 218n, 220n, 223n, 224n, 236n, 276n, 278n, 294n, 337n, 339n, 343n

André family, and REA, 76n

Anglesey, 352

'Anglo-Bengalee Disinterested Loan and Life Assurance Company', 138

Annuities: 55, 60n, 118n, 437; sale by REA, 66–7, 257–8; sale by Government, 134n, 313n; purchase by REA and other insurance companies, 313n, 315, 317

Annuity Act (1777), 60n, 118n

Ansell, Charles (Atlas Actuary), 133

Antwerp, REA marine agency, 260n

Appleton & Cox, 482

Architects and Builders Fire and Life Insurance Company, 115

Argentina, and REA business and investments, 243n, 342, 346n, 472

Arkwright, Richard, insures with REA, 90

Armstrong & Whitworth, Sir W. G., Ltd, 234n, 235

Arson, 158–60, 167, 413–15, 523

Ashton, A.G. (REA Investment Secretary), 510

Asia Minor, and REA business, 474

Asquith, H.H., 229

Charter and begins business as REA, 32–3, 47; financial insecurity in first months, 34–44; debt to Government remitted, 42–3; extends powers to fire and life insurance, 37–9, 41, 48–51; acquires Sadlers' Hall Society, 48–9; organization, capital and stock-ownership, 12–13, 17, 18, 20, 36, 37, 39–41, 44–6, 68–72; composition of Court and links with City of London, 75–80; clerical staff, pay and conditions, 70–1; fire brigade, 95–8

Business to 1870: growth in eighteenth century, 56, 58, 61–8, 81; adopts new basis for life business, 55, 64–6; secures power to deal in annuities, 66–7; 105; profitability, dividends and investments in eighteenth century, 72–5; fire business in eighteenth century, 81–95; agents and agency organization, 51, 98–100, 152–4, 170, 173, 179–85; overseas business, 105, 155–7; fire business to 1870, 110, 126, chapter 7 *passim*; and Hamburg fire (1842), 156–7, 246; and Tooley Street fire (1861), 246; and early tariff association, 160–3; fire brigade and London Fire Engine Establishment, 151, 163–6; and fire marks, 50, 167; life business, 62, 63–6, 136, chapter 8 *passim*; introduces with-profits policies, 168–73, 178–9, 355, 367, 547; reaction to competition in life business, 168–74, 178–85; endowment policies, 173; prestige of REA life business and Actuaries, 174–6; life business in Ireland, 177–8; marine business, 61–2, 186–91, 199–206; loses exclusive marine privileges, 191–9; relative importance of REA, 122, 124, 147; and advertising, 152, 172–3, 179–81, 182–3

Business, 1870–1914: growth of fire business, 238–46, 283–4; overseas business, 214, 241–51, 264, 283–4, 301; organization and control of overseas business, 481–7; in USA, 242–3, 246–51, 470–3; and Baltimore Fire (1904), 475, 486; and San Francisco earthquake and fire, 246–51, 266, 399, 404–5, 475; acquires fire insurance companies, 300; growth of life business, 238–9, 251–8, 279–81; reaction to competition in life business, 252–7, 274–81; increase in bonus division, 255, 277–9; increase in endowment policies, 255–6; extends social range of policyholders, 256–7, 280; annuity business, 257–8; marine business,

238–9, 258–62; acquires marine insurance companies, 259–60; and *Titanic* loss, 261, 405; begins accident business, 105, 232, 262–4, 283–4; growth of accident business, 262–70; employers' liability, 262–8; fidelity guarantee, 264; burglary, 262–4; motor, 264; plate glass and acquisition of National Provincial, 268–70, 300; boiler, 270n; damage by Suffragettes, 270, 414; trustee and executor, 270–2; conservatism and enterprise, 238–41, 244–5, 251–4, 270–2, 283–4, 300, 349–50, 400–3, 406–7; agents and agency organization, 252–3, 269–70, 271–2, 285–93; inspectors, 255, 271, 288–91, 396, 500, 503; establishment of branch organization, 241, 244, 255, 289, 292, 396; branch managers, 277–8, 289; and merger movement, 299–301, 462–3; attempted mergers with London Assurance (1909, 1916), 300–1, 364, 463; relative importance of REA, 214–15, 245, 301

Business since 1914: growth of fire business, 413–16, 420–1, 446, 452–4, 468n, 470–5, 515, 517, 521–3, 528–36; marine business, 420, 446–9, 468n, 470, 517, 523–4; life business, 418, 421, 436–7, 446, 449–52, 468n, 517, 524–6; group life and pension business, 451, 525; accident and motor business, 421, 446, 453, 454–8, 468n, 470–2, 481, 516–17, 519–21, 528–36; aviation business, 446n, 524; overseas business, 454–5, 469–81, 515; in USA, 480–2, 495, 515, 530, 533, 534–5; attempted merger with London Assurance (1916), 463; acquisition of Car & General (1917), 234, 237, 299, 412, 421, 423, 439, 455–6, 462–8, 471–2, 533, 547; acquisition of Local Government Mutual Guarantee (1918), 464; attempted mergers with Sun and Atlas (1919–20), 364–5; acquisition of Provident Insurance Company of New York (1924), 465; acquisition of State Assurance Company (1924), 398, 439, 465–6; acquisition of Motor Union Insurance Company (1928), 237, 412, 439, 455–6, 462, 466–8, 471–2, 508, 533, 547; inter-war economic problems, 447–8, 450, 453, 478–80; experience in First World War, 418, 420–4; experience in Second World War, 513–19; business and profitability since 1939, 520–36; withdraws from USA, 534, 546; acquisition of Atlas Assurance Company (1959), 467, 532–4,

580 *Index*

538, 544; merger with Guardian Assurance Company (1968), 513, 535, 542; agency system, inspectors and branch organization, 500–4; relative importance of Group, 531–5; traditional elements, 458–9, 496–7, 499–500, 543–9

Investments, capital and profits: capital, investments and profitability in eighteenth century, 45–6, 71–5; profitability in nineteenth and twentieth centuries, 245–6, 398–9, 421–2, 454, 460, 461, 530; investments, 1800–1914, chapter 13 *passim*; investment in Government securities, 311–12; loan to help build Regent Street, 311, 313; investment in mortgages, 317–26, 337–8; loans to local authorities, 318, 323–6, 340; investment in urban development, 321–3; investment in railways, 326–30; overseas investment, 342–6; investment in stocks and shares, 346–8; yields on investments in nineteenth century, 320, 325–6, 334–5, 345; capital and dividends since 1800, 398–9, 460–1, 466, 533; investments and yields in twentieth century, 461–2, 518–19, 526–8

Organization, staff and corporate 'personality': organization and staff in eighteenth century, 44–5, 68–71; control of home and overseas branches, 241, 244, 480–92, 500–4; branch managers' meetings, 495, 502–3; problems of organization and management since 1800, 266–7, 292–3, 301–3 chapters 14 and 21 *passim*; role of Governor, 44, 350–3, 511, 541; problems of general management and appointment of General Manager, 293, 302–3, 358–9, 368–73, 492, 504–11, 536–42; officials and departmental structure, 359–70, 373, 375–6, 395, 458–9; professionalization of management, 353–4, 359–62; problems of departmental rivalry, 501–2; 505–8; problems in formation of REA Group, 412, 462–8, 493–500; effective integration of REA Group in 1950s and 1960s, 536–42, 544, 546, 549; messengers, 51, 376, 379, 384, 385, 386, 387; clerical staff condition of work and pay since 1800, chapter 15 *passim*, 422–4, 514–15, 545; Staff Association, 539n; employment of typists, 376–7, 595–6, 422–3; clerical salaries and leisure, 378–84; paternalism, 383–7; recruitment and promotion of staff, 379, 390–4; pensions and Pension Fund, 363,

387–90, 545; and publicity, 402–5; charitable bequests, 405–6; Bicentenary celebrations, 425, 499; *Royal Exchange Assurance Magazine*, 293, 397; Corporate 'personality', continuity and tradition, 300, 307–8, 349–50, 382, 400–2, 458–60, 496–7, 499–500, 511, 543–9

Royal Exchange Assurance for assurance of ships goods and merchandise at sea, 400n

Royal Exchange Assurance of Houses and Goods from Fire, 50, 400n

Royal Exchange Assurance Loan Company, 400n

Royal Exchange Assurance Magazine, 293, 397

Royal Insurance Company; foundation (1845) and early success, 124, 155, 176, 182, 214–15, 242, 245, 247n, 297; managerial links with REA, 176, 242, 365; appoints General Manager, 372; publicity and advertising 182, 403; acquisitions, mergers and relative size, 296, 298–9, 439, 534, 535n

Royal Lustring Company, 36

Royal Mail Steam Packet Company, 328

Rudé, George, 160n

Rudolf, Edward Arthur de M. (REA Secretary), 507, 510

Russia, REA business in, 243n, 472, 473

Russia Company, 76, 78

Russia merchants, 76

Russian Revolution, 473

Ryan, Gerald Hemington (REA Actuary), 253–4, 289, 372, 379, 389

Sadlers' Hall Society (fire insurance), 26, 41, 46, 47, 48–9

St Catherine's, 88

St Katherine Docks, fire insurance premium rates, 128, 162

St Katherine Dock Company, 328, 352

St Marylebone Commissioners for Public Baths, 325

Salaries of REA officials and clerks, 203, 204–5, 259, 261, 265, 267, 366, 378–81, 424–5

Saltpetre as fire risk, 158

Salvage Corps, 282

San Francisco: REA and other British agencies and Branches, 214, 243; earthquake and fire, 246–51, 266, 342, 363, 475, 528

Santiago, 214

Savings, 310, 442; through life insurance policies, 66, 133, 115–17, 221–2, 256–7, 275–7, 280, 437, 524–6

Savings banks, 113, 117, 310

Schooling, F., 341n